D1527063

New Contexts for Eighteenth-Century British Fiction

New Contexts for Eighteenth-Century British Fiction

"Hearts Resolved and Hands Prepared": Essays in Honor of Jerry C. Beasley

Edited by Christopher D. Johnson

UNIVERSITY OF DELAWARE PRESS
Newark

Published by University of Delaware Press
Co-published with The Rowman & Littlefield Publishing Group, Inc.
4501 Forbes Boulevard, Suite 200, Lanham, Maryland 20706
www.rlpgbooks.com

Estover Road, Plymouth PL6 7PY, United Kingdom

British Library Cataloguing in Publication Information Available

Library of Congress Cataloging-in-Publication Data
New contexts for eighteenth-century British fiction : "hearts resolved and hands
prepared" : essays in honor of Jerry C. Beasley / edited by Christopher D. Johnson.
   p. cm.
   Includes bibliographical references and index.
   ISBN 978-1-61149-040-4 (cloth : alk. paper) — ISBN 978-1-61149-041-1
(electronic)
   1. English fiction—18th century—History and criticism. 2. Literature and
society—Great Britain—History—18th century. 3. Politics and literature—Great
Britain—History—18th century. 4. Literature and history—Great Britain—
History—18th century. 5. Beasley, Jerry C. I. Beasley, Jerry C. II. Johnson,
Christopher D., 1964–
   PR853.N49 2011
   823'.509355—dc22   2010051504

Printed in the United States of America

Contents

v

Introduction

Christopher D. Johnson

Inventas—vitam excoluere per artes.
They polish life by useful arts.

> Virgil, *Aeneid*, 6.663, Quoted by Samuel Johnson
> in *The Rambler*, No. 67, Tuesday, 26 June 1753

New Contexts for Eighteenth-Century British Fiction: "Hearts Resolved and Hands Prepared" is a collection of thirteen essays honoring Professor Jerry C. Beasley, who retired from the University of Delaware in 2005 after thirty-six years of service. The subtitle is taken from Tobias Smollett's poem, "Ode to Leven-Water," a pastoral tribute to Scotland, which first appeared in *The Expedition of Humphry Clinker*.[1] As it is positioned in the novel, the poem has a distinctly janiform quality. Evoking memories of a time when the speaker "envied not the happiest swain," it recalls the carefree joys of youth, yet it also captures the curiosity of the novel's principal character, Matthew Bramble, as he anticipates his journey toward the Scottish Highlands. In this way, the poem seems especially fitting for a festschrift, which, like all good celebrations, looks to both the past and future.

The essays collected here, written by friends, collaborators, and former students, reflect the scholarly interests that defined Jerry's career, but they do more than pay homage to a judicious editor and insightful critic. They also point to new directions of inquiry and remind us that discovery is not an ending, but a commencement. Several of the essays suggest new directions in biographical writing. Others enrich our understanding of eighteenth-century fiction by examining works that have for too long been inaccessible and overlooked. Still others use political pamphlets, material artifacts, and what modern readers might call urban legends to place familiar

1

novels in new contexts. Finally, there are essays that demonstrate the vital importance of bibliographic study and remind us of how much work is still to be done.

For some of the contributors, the essays may prove to be unexpectedly nostalgic. When we began our graduate careers in the 1980s and 1990s, Delaware's English department was distinguished by its emphasis on primary research, especially textual work, the sometimes grubby business of recovering lost documents, filling in historical gaps, and preparing critical editions and bibliographies. This focus permeated every aspect of the program. While our peers at other universities were reading Terry Eagleton's *Literary Theory: An Introduction* in their methods of research courses, George Miller assigned us Richard Altick's *The Art of Literary Research* and Philip Gaskell's *New Introduction to Bibliography*.[2] By the end of our first semester, we had all spent many weeks in the special collections room of Morris Library, painstakingly transcribing and annotating our first editing projects. A few years later, many of us were still haunting rare book rooms as we completed dissertations based on archival findings.

This approach, however demanding, was both exciting and liberating, especially for those of us who as undergraduates had been trained by weary practitioners of New Criticism. Although gifted and dedicated teachers, many of these scholars had become disenchanted. The texts of their canon had given up their essential meanings, and the new directions of literary theory seemed to mark the end of their discipline. As younger scholars argued for the inclusion of works that resisted formalist interpretation and others used the ideas of Jacques Derrida and Paul DeMan to question the very possibility of meaning, some of our former professors saw themselves as the last practitioners of a dying art. A few of us had been discouraged from attending graduate school, not only because of the bleak job market but also because, for our undergraduate mentors, the best days for English departments were in the past. At Delaware, though, we quickly discovered that we could be more than caretakers of an exhausted discipline intent on devouring itself in a deconstructive frenzy. We could, instead, be contributors to a growing and vibrant field of study.

The department, we quickly discovered, was full of impressive scholars engaged in important projects. J. A. Leo Lemay, the distinguished colonial American scholar, had recently published three books and was drafting the first volumes of his magnificent Franklin biography.[3] Hershel Parker, contributor to the Newberry edition of the *Works of Herman Melville* and author of the pugnacious *Flawed Texts and Verbal Icons*, was writing his own groundbreaking biography of Melville.[4] Thomas O. Calhoun had written an important book on Henry Vaughan and was preparing the definitive edition of Abraham Cowley's poetry.[5] Robert Hogan, who had produced many books and a number of editions, was collecting and editing the poetry of both Thomas Sheridan and Patrick Delany.[6] Jay Halio was deciphering the complicated textual history of *King Lear*.[7] Hans-Peter Breuer had recently published a volume of Samuel Butler's notebooks.[8] Charles Robinson, the department's graduate director, had published *Mary Shelley: Collected Tales and Stories*. He had also recovered a cache of Hazlitt correspondence and was piecing together his exhaustive study of the composition of Mary Shelley's *Frankenstein*, work that would eventually lead to bragging rights for producing the most definitive edition of that famous novel and a well-deserved spot on the cover of *The Chronicle of Higher Education*.[9]

There was also, of course, Jerry C. Beasley. In addition to his excellent monograph, *The Novels of the 1740s*, Jerry had published two important bibliographical studies, *A Check List of Prose Fiction Published in England, 1740–1749*, and *English Fiction, 1660–1800: A Guide to Information Sources*, which cataloged hundreds of titles, many by women authors whose role in the history of the novel was still largely unrecognized.[10] More recently, Jerry had become the general editor for the magisterial University of Georgia Press *Works of Tobias Smollett*, a project that has served as a model of responsible editorial policy and careful, thorough scholarship since the publication of Jerry's inaugural edition of *Ferdinand Count Fathom* in 1988.[11]

Some of us had met Jerry while still undergraduates when he interviewed us during campus visits. As our first months in Newark passed, we discovered that those interviews had played important roles in our choice of Delaware. Jerry, we recalled, carefully reviewed the program, answered our questions patiently, and listened attentively as we clumsily discussed our interests and expectations. He was a warm, genuine person, entirely without pretense, and his enthusiasm and good humor were contagious. We had also heard some rumors. One suggested that Jerry was an accomplished musician who, along with Tom Calhoun, wrote raucous songs and played in a group called "The Elderly Brothers." Another claimed that, following a tradition begun by the former chair Zack Bowen, Jerry organized a yearly "Songfest," a no-holds-barred night of debauchery in which faculty members and graduate students sang viciously about each other and the occasional dean or provost. Those rumors ended up being true.

No one, of course, was better prepared to help us become scholars than Jerry, who seemed to be an expert in every aspect of the discipline. Readers of *Tobias Smollett, Novelist* know that Jerry is a skilled explicator who finds deep resonance and compelling complexity in Smollett's prose. In his classes, he insisted that we engage the novels closely, reading passages aloud, feeling the texture and rhythm of the works to discover their beauty. He also contributed to the new directions of literary criticism, as was made especially clear in 1987 with the publication of his daring issue of *Studies of the Novel*, which focused much-needed attention on eighteenth-century women's fiction.[12] In his courses, he provided a rich assortment of both major and minor texts, and he emphasized the importance of many as-yet-unedited works. Long before ECCO, he introduced us to little-known writers (Penelope Aubin, Delarivière Manley, Mary Davys, Charlotte Lennox), many of whom he had written about within *The Dictionary of Literary Biography*.

As he taught us the history of the novel, he helped us see paths for our future careers, and he gave us the skills to travel those paths. He made sure, for example, that we understood the critical tradition. We read Alan D. McKillop and Ian Watt, as well as the pioneering works of Jerry's friends Martin C. Battestin, J. Paul Hunter, and John Richetti. We also wrestled with less traditional approaches. *The New Eighteenth Century* was, indeed, new in the late 1980s, and Jerry's graduate students were expected to learn it, along with the works of Nancy K. Armstrong, Jane Spencer, and Janet Todd.[13] Perhaps most importantly, Jerry pushed us to be better researchers and clearer writers. It seemed we were forever preparing annotated bibliographies, and he insisted on thoroughness and accuracy. He encouraged us to experiment with theoretical approaches, but he never let us hide behind jargon or critical cliché. He pushed us toward more sophisticated and nuanced readings, but he insisted on precise sentences. His responses to our work were always generous, encouraging, and reassuring, even as they were challenging and directive.

For several years while I was a research assistant (and occasional backup guitarist for "The Elderly Brothers"), Jerry and I shared an office in the basement of Memorial Hall, long before that building's magnificent renovation in the 1990s. It was little wonder the department wanted him to serve as chair. He was a wonderful boss. There was much work to do as he prepared book reviews for *The Eighteenth Century: A Current Bibliography* and completed the first volumes of the Smollett edition, yet the pace was relaxed. There were deadlines, but never crises; excitement, but never tension. When reviews arrived, I typed them into the computer, printed them on a noisy dot-matrix printer, and left them for Jerry to edit. He carefully improved the texts, culling out unnecessary words, strengthening weak sentences, and clarifying ambiguous phrasing. Without compromising the reviewer's evaluation, Jerry made certain that each work would be useful for future readers. With the Smollett edition, he was even more attentive. Recognizing that the texts would serve as standard editions for generations of scholars, he made sure everything was right, all the citations current, all the annotations clear and helpful. We spent dozens of hours generating and refining indices, knowing that readers would depend on them. Through his patient, gentle example, I came to understand that scholarship was not about recognition, job interviews, and tenure. It was about producing something of enduring value, something that would serve as both a finished product and a reliable starting point.

The essays collected here embody that same spirit. There is a strong emphasis on primary research, and many of the essays represent the culmination of years of archival work. Following Charlie Robinson's warm and funny tribute to his friend, the collection offers three essays that address biographical concerns. O M Brack Jr., textual editor for *The Works of Tobias Smollett*, discusses some of the challenges facing Smollett's next biographer. The most complete biography of Smollett is still Lewis M. Knapp's 1949 *Tobias Smollett: Doctor of Men and Manners*.[14] Although an important resource, Knapp's work is out-of-date and at times misleading. Brack notes that future biographers need to understand Smollett in terms of eighteenth-century book culture and discover how Smollett would have understood himself as writer, not only of the novels that modern readers privilege but also of the journalistic and historical texts that tend to be dismissed as "hack" work. Only through such an understanding, Brack argues, can we "illuminate Smollett's life, not only as an author, but as a man."

Using life-writing theory, Paula R. Backscheider examines the work of Elizabeth Singer Rowe and discovers that the author created a rewarding lifestyle centered around her self-fashioned identity as a writer. Readers inclined to view Rowe only as a didactic writer may be surprised by Backscheider's insightful readings of Rowe's contributions to the *Athenian Mercury* and the poet's "unusual power to draw men into writing about her physical body." More importantly, Backscheider demonstrates that Rowe's writing provided a space in which she could understand herself as an author and as an autonomous woman. Through Backscheider's analysis, we discover that Rowe's fiction, especially *Friendship in Death* and *Letters Moral and Entertaining*, should be read not only for its religious content but also for its secular themes, which align it with later works, including Sarah Scott's *Millenium Hall*.

Alexander Pettit, who has recently completed a volume of Richardson's early works for *The Cambridge Edition of the Works of Samuel Richardson* and who has replaced Jerry as the general editor of *The Works of Tobias Smollett*, considers three of Richardson's works from the 1730s: *The Infidel Convicted, The Apprentice's Vade Mecum*, and *A Seasonable Examination of the Pleas and Pretensions of the Proprietors of, and Subscribers to, the Playhouses*.[15] Pettit discusses these pamphlets within the context of contemporary polemical writings, most notably the Caleb D'Anvers contributions to *The Craftsman*. If the Rowe that emerges from Backscheider's examination is refreshingly unexpected for her courage and independence, the Richardson found by Pettit confirms our worst suspicions. More of an opportunistic partisan than a thoughtful writer, Richardson, we learn, freely recycled his own prose in ways that appeared to give greater authority to his ideas. Often exploiting public fear, he sacrificed logic and accuracy for sensationalism and profit.

The next four essays provide valuable readings of novels, several of which could not have been taught a generation ago. Robert A. Erickson discusses John Cleland's *Memoirs of a Woman of Pleasure*, arguing that the novel provides a "secular neo-libertine 'gospel.'" Erickson supports his claim by positioning Cleland's fiction within the contexts of *Paradise Lost*, the cultural history of the "Family of Love" phenomenon, and the New Testament. Jerry's former student Susan K. Howard examines Charlotte Lennox's transatlantic novel, *Euphemia*, which includes an account of a transcultural adoption. Howard argues that Lennox's work shares thematic characteristics with other narratives, both fictional and nonfictional, in which white adoptees benefit from time spent as members of aboriginal families. Although such opportunities for "cross-cultural contact and enrichment were lost" as nineteenth-century American culture defined itself in opposition to Native Americans, Lennox's novel captures a more tolerant moment when "the imaginative integration of differing cultures" was possible. Howard's essay is the first to cite her recently published edition of *Euphemia*, which will make Lennox's important novel available to modern readers.

Marta Kvande and Melissa Mowry, also former students, explore the sometimes hidden political content of early eighteenth-century women's fiction. Continuing the focus of a collection she recently edited with Diane Boyd, Kvande discovers that Jane Barker's *Exilius* "creates space for women's voices" in which passive suffering becomes a sign not only of moral virtue, but also Jacobite allegiance. Though far more subtle than a work such as Manley's *The New Atalantis*, Barker's novel promotes a political agenda, even as it appears to be little more than imaginative fiction.[16] Like Kvande, Mowry addresses issues of public and private identity. Building on the argument Jerry offered in his groundbreaking article, "Portraits of a Monster: Robert Walpole and Early English Prose Fiction," Mowry suggests that Eliza Haywood was a "political writer long before she published *The Adventures of Eovaai*" in 1736 and that her rejection of tyranny, as revealed in *Love in Excess*, rejects Lockean constructions of individualism, which she believed were ultimately corrosive to social order.[17] Mary Anne Schofield, one of Jerry's first doctoral students at the University of Delaware, provides a lively, far-reaching review of Eliza Haywood scholarship. Schofield shows how the myth of the "two Haywoods" (the salacious author of *Love in Excess* and the more restrained author of *The History of Miss Betsy Thoughtless*) has persisted from the late eighteenth century to the present. Only recently have scholars begun to dismantle this overly restrictive understanding of the prolific and ingenious Haywood.

The collection's final essays return to Smollett. Drawing upon a wide range of primary sources, including popular poems and songs as well as artifacts from material culture, Rivka Swenson discusses *Roderick Random* within the cultural narrative of "Scottish exile, diaspora, and depopulation" and demonstrates that Smollett separates Scottish narrative from Jacobitism. In the end, Roderick achieves a stable Scottish identity, but it is not defined in opposition to Hanoverian England, as is made clear when Roderick plans to return to England as an established Scottish property owner rather than a refugee. My essay also looks at *Roderick Random*, but for a different purpose. Hoping to position Smollett's novel within the cultural conditions that sparked the Mary Toft hoax in 1726 and Hogarth's satirical treatment of the hoax in 1762, I consider the role of the imagination in Smollett's work. Although the essay owes debts to the works of Dennis Todd, Geoffrey Sill, and others, the greatest debt is to Jerry's discussion of Smollett's narrative structure and spatial form in *Tobias Smollett, Novelist*.

Leslie A. Chilton, who has edited three volumes of *The Works of Tobias Smollett*, provides a useful illustration of the kind of work advocated by Brack at the beginning of the volume.[18] Placing two of Smollett's early pamphlets within the cut-throat world of eighteenth-century medical literature, Chilton explores Smollett's use of the picaresque, which the author viewed not as a model to be rigidly followed but rather as a device, "much like a surgical instrument to pick up and then lay down when the job was done." James E. May's comprehensive study of the authoritative editions of Smollett's *Continuation of the Complete History* brings the collection full circle. Brack argues convincingly that Smollett scholars need to pay careful attention to all of Smollett's writings, including his collaborations and works of nonfiction. Through his detailed analysis and bibliographic descriptions, May provides essential tools to do exactly that. From May's exhaustive account of this complicated serial publication, careful readers will discover many teasing glimpses of Smollett's life as writer.

As I type these words, I see a picture taken in 1989 of Jerry, Tom Calhoun, and me standing on a platform playing guitars before a packed audience in the old University of Delaware field house. It was a beautiful spring morning, and we were part of a baccalaureate celebration. Tom had written several songs for the graduates, including a hilarious reworking of the Everly Brothers' hit "Wake Up, Little Susie." The picture brings back fond memories of good days in Newark when generous scholars—Don Mell, Charlie Robinson, George Miller, Philip Flynn, Leo Lemay, Tom Calhoun, Michael Rewa, Elaine Safer, Barbara Gates, Bruce Finney, and others— helped prepare me for what has become a rewarding career. My greatest gratitude, though, belongs to Jerry Beasley, who first taught me to read eighteenth-century fiction, introduced me to the challenges and rewards of our profession, and put up with me as I wrote a dissertation. Like many of the contributors to this volume, my career has been shaped by Jerry's thoughtful and generous guidance, just as my critical perspective has been shaped by his extraordinarily keen scholarship.

There are other debts that must also be acknowledged as well. The contributors to this volume produced exceptional essays, and they have been patient and helpful as I have tried my hand at editing. Fred Carter and Richard Chapman, president and provost of Francis Marion University, provided me with a sabbatical during the fall semester of 2008, and Jon Tuttle was good enough to serve as interim chair during my absence. In addition to the normal responsibilities that accompany that office, Jon held the department together as the General Assembly imposed the largest cuts to higher education in the state's history. My colleagues at FMU, especially Lorraine de Montluzin, Mark Blackwell, David Cowles, Beckie Flannagan, Meredith Love, and Jo Angela Edwins, have read my work in progress and helped me understand how this volume needed to be put together. Lorna Clymer has provided friendship, support, and guidance throughout this project. Benzena O. Shells provided life-saving technical assistance as the manuscript reached completion. My wife Christine and our children, Benjamin, Daniel, and Maggie, have listened uncomplainingly, as they always do, whenever I become obsessed with a writing project.

Final thanks must go to Don Mell, director of the University of Delaware Press. For more than twenty years, Don has been a friend and mentor. He has encouraged and assisted me in this project from the beginning, and without his good assistance, it would never have been started, let alone completed.

NOTES

1. *The Expedition of Humphry Clinker*, ed. Thomas R. Preston, *The Works of Tobias Smollett* (Athens: University of Georgia Press, 1990), 241–42.

2. Terry Eagleton, *Literary Theory: An Introduction* (Oxford: Basil Blackwell, 1983); Richard D. Altick, and John J. Fenstermaker. *The Art of Literary Research* (New York: Norton, 1981); Philip Gaskell, *A New Introduction to Bibliography* (Oxford: Oxford University Press, 1972).

3. Benjamin Franklin, *Benjamin Franklin's Autobiography: An Authoritative Text, Backgrounds, Criticism*, ed. J. A. Leo Lemay and P. M. Zall (New York: W. W. Norton, 1986); J. A. Leo Lemay, *The Canon of Benjamin Franklin, 1722–1776: New Attributions and Reconsiderations* (Newark: University of Delaware Press, 1986); *"New England's Annoyances": America's First Folk Song* (Newark: University of Delaware Press, 1985).

4. Hershel Parker, *Flawed Texts and Verbal Icons: Literary Authority in American Fiction* (Evanston, IL: Northwestern University Press, 1984); *Herman Melville: A Biography, Volume 1: 1819–1851* (Baltimore, MD: Johns Hopkins University Press, 1996); *Herman Melville: A Biography: Volume II, 1851–1891* (Baltimore, MD: Johns Hopkins University Press, 2002).

5. Thomas O. Calhoun, *Henry Vaughan: The Achievement of Silex Scintillans* (Newark: University of Delaware Press; 1981); Abraham Cowley, *The Collected Works of Abraham Cowley, I: Poetical Blossomes, The Puritans Lecture, The Puritan and the Papist, The Civil War*, ed. Thomas O. Calhoun, Laurence Heyworth, Allan Pritchard, and Ernest W. Sullivan II (Newark: University of Delaware Press, 1989); *The Collected*

Works of Abraham Cowley: Volume 2: Poems (1656), Part 1: The Mistress, ed. Thomas O. Calhoun, Laurence Heyworth, J. Robert King, and Ernest W. Sullivan II (Newark: University of Delaware Press, 1993).

6. Thomas Sheridan, *The Poems of Thomas Sheridan*, ed. Robert Hogan (Newark: University of Delaware Press, 1994); Patrick Delany, *The Poems of Patrick Delany: Comprising Also Poems about Him By Jonathan Swift, Thomas Sheridan, and Other Friends and Enemies*, ed. Robert Hogan and Donald C. Mell (Newark: University of Delaware Press, 2006).

7. Jay Halio, *The First Quarto of King Lear* (Cambridge: Cambridge University Press, 1994); William Shakespeare, *The Tragedy of King Lear*, ed. Jay Halio (Cambridge: Cambridge University Press, 2005).

8. Samuel Butler, *The Note-Books of Samuel Butler, I: 1874–1883*, ed. Hans-Peter Breuer (Lanham, MD: University Presses of America, 1984).

9. Mary Shelley, *Mary Shelley: Collected Tales and Stories*, ed. Charles E. Robinson (Baltimore: Johns Hopkins University Press, 1976); Charles E. Robinson, "William Hazlitt to His Publishers, Friends, and Creditors: Twenty-Seven New Holograph Letters," *Keats-Shelley Review* 2 (1987): 1–47; *The Frankenstein Notebooks: A Facsimile Edition of Mary Shelley's Novel, 1816–17*, two vols. (New York: Garland Publishing, Inc., 1996). See also Jennifer Howard, "The Birth of Frankenstein," *Chronicle of Higher Education*, November 7, 2008, B12.

10. Jerry C. Beasley, *The Novels of the 1740s* (Athens: University of Georgia Press, 1982); *A Check List of Prose Fiction Published in England, 1740–1749* (Charlottesville: University of Virginia Press, 1972); *English Fiction, 1660–1800: A Guide to Information Sources* (Detroit: Gale, 1978).

11. Tobias Smollett, *The Adventures of Ferdinand Count Fathom*, ed. Jerry C. Beasley, *The Works of Tobias Smollett* (Athens: University of Georgia Press, 1988).

12. *Studies in the Novel* 19 (1987).

13. *The New Eighteenth Century: Theory, Politics, English Literature*, ed. Felicity Nussbaum and Laura Brown (New York: Methuen, 1987).

14. Lewis M. Knapp, *Tobias Smollett, Doctor of Men and Manners* (Princeton, NJ: Princeton University Press, 1949).

15. Samuel Richardson, *Early Works*, ed. Alexander Pettit, *The Cambridge Edition of the Works of Samuel Richardson* (Cambridge: Cambridge University Press, forthcoming).

16. *Everyday Revolutions: Eighteenth-Century Women Transforming Public and Private*, ed. Diane E. Boyd and Marta Kvande (Newark: University of Delaware Press, 2008).

17. Jerry C. Beasley, "Portraits of a Monster: Robert Walpole and Early English Prose Fiction," *Eighteenth-Century Studies* 14 (1981): 406–31.

18. Tobias Smollett, *Poems, Plays, and The Briton/Tobias Smollett*, ed. O M Brack Jr., Leslie A. Chilton, and Byron Gassman, *The Works of Tobias Smollett* (Athens: University of Georgia Press, 1993); *The Devil upon Crutches by Alain René le Sage, Translated by Tobias Smollett*, ed. O M Brack Jr. and Leslie A. Chilton, *The Works of Tobias Smollett* (Athens: University of Georgia Press, 2005); *The Adventures of Gil Blas de Santillane, Translated by Tobias Smollett*, ed. O M Brack Jr. and Leslie A. Chilton, *The Works of Tobias Smollett* (Athens: University of Georgia Press, 2011).

1

The "Super" Jerry C. Beasley

Charles E. Robinson

Two simple points dominate this essay: I (and we) very much miss Jerry C. Beasley at the University of Delaware; and I am honored to be one of the many friends he made as he journeyed from Nashville, Tennessee, to Traverse City, Michigan—with his longest gig in Newark, Delaware.

In each of these three cities, Jerry combined his interests in both the academic and the artistic. In Nashville, during his undergraduate studies at Peabody College of Vanderbilt University (1959–1963), Jerry supported himself by his musical talents, with some expectations that he might break out of secondary school teaching and become a famous rock & roll singer. What Nashville and the schools and the airwaves at radio station WLAC lost, we eventually gained after Jerry earned an MA at the University of Kansas and a PhD at Northwestern University and took his first tenure-track job at the University of Delaware in 1969, little thinking that he would find a venue where he could combine his musical and scholarly and teaching talents in such a seamless and productive and selfless way for more than thirty years.

Not too many years after Jerry arrived at the University of Delaware, the legendary Zack Bowen arrived to chair the English department. That three-hundred-pound, tennis-shoed, cigar smoking, exaggerating, and funny ex-used-car salesman did many creative things for the department, one of which was to throw his weight in support of the English department's annual songfest.[1]

By 1977 Jerry had joined with another Delaware professor, Tom Calhoun, to form the duo of "The Elderly Brothers," Jerry the lead singer on acoustic guitar delighting everyone with rock & roll songs and parodies and witty performances. As you would expect from "good people" such as Jerry and Tom, "The Elderly Brothers" often volunteered to do free and benefit concerts. Not long after Tom's unexpected death in 1994, Jerry formed a larger and even more popular band called "Jerry and the Juveniles," even once (and only once!) letting me sing backup to his version of Ritchie Valens's "Oh Donna" at a DuPont Country Club dance ("letting me" is a euphemism for my walking up to the stage, uninvited, chanting the refrain of "Oh Donna"). A night with Jerry was filled with the heartbreak of the 1950s and 1960s: "Heartbreak Hotel," "Runaround Sue," "Sincerely," "Teen Angel," "Wake Up, Little Susie," and "When I'm 64" (no longer in Jerry's repertoire). Those privileged to attend the EC/ASECS Conference at the University of Delaware in 1995 will remember Jerry's "Do Wah Diddy" that burlesqued *Clarissa*, Samuel Johnson, and James Boswell.

Harmony was that which marked Jerry's tenor and tenure at Delaware, as evidenced in the recitative of the halting conversations he and I had every semester as I planned the graduate course program from 1981 through 1993 (except for the semester when Jerry kindly volunteered to replace me when I was on sabbatical): CER: "Jerry, I am planning the schedule—can you teach a course in . . ." JB: "Charlie, whatever needs to be taught." CER: "Is afternoon or eveni . . ." JB: "Whenever." CER: "Do you prefer Mondays or Tuesd . . ." JB: "Whatever day helps you the most." CER: "Thanks." And all of this negotiated as we passed each other in the hall in less than ten seconds—now, that's a team player!

That was Jerry—always willing to help out—putting the needs of the graduate program and the Department of English and the University of Delaware before his own personal needs or preferences. That selfless service manifested itself shortly after Jerry joined the University of Delaware in 1969 (by which time I had been at Delaware four full years)—and that service was his hallmark through the year 2005, when he (with more sense than I have) retired (and now, six years later, I still labor in these same fields—but am able to claim that I have enjoyed his friendship for forty years).

In 1971, at the end of his second year at the University of Delaware, Jerry was elected to the department's Executive Committee, on which he served as an elected or ex officio member almost every year until his full retirement in 2005. Also, in 1971, he was a member of the search committee for the next chair, Charles Bohner, who was to be succeeded by Zack Bowen, under whom both Jerry (as associate chair) and I (as director of graduate studies) served for a number of years. Indeed, our paths crossed more directly when, in 1985–1986, Jerry volunteered to serve as acting director of graduate studies in English when I was on sabbatical leave. He did not have to help me out, but there was never any hesitation when I asked him to replace me during that leave. Even more revealing of his nature was his service as acting chair of the Department of English for two and a half years after Zack left us for Miami. Those who have been acting chairs know that such positions can be thankless and burdensome—but Jerry selflessly served the department with his usual concern for graduate students, staff, and faculty (including part-time faculty whom Jerry treated as equals). There were no second-class citizens in the department run by Jerry. That is why we elected him official chair of the Department of English from 1999 through 2004. Shortly after the labors of that chairmanship, Jerry and his beloved Fleda retired to Traverse City, Michigan, where I am not surprised to learn that he has volunteered his time and efforts in the local theater, book festival, and library. This is the same Jerry who would visit retired faculty in local nursing homes here in Delaware—and the same Jerry who would be the first to congratulate other faculty for winning awards or gaining distinctions that, in some cases, should have gone to him!

Jerry was indeed distinguished in both his scholarship and his teaching—both of which revealed the same kind of service for others. If he undertook a book or an article, it would not be a self-serving or opaque work of scholarship; its purpose was to be "useful" for other readers, who would benefit from Jerry's research. Consider, for example, his first book, *A Check List of Prose Fiction Published in England, 1740–1749*.[2] Those 338 entries, accessible by an index, proved invaluable for the pre-computer-database world of scholarship—this "mere" listing could direct the scholarship of others interested in fictional patterns, in publishers, in prices, in locations for rare copies of rare titles. As you might expect, Jerry in his "Introduction" profusely praised the staff of the Newberry, Penn, Yale, and Harvard libraries. As you also might expect, there are copies of this valuable book in three hundred university and college libraries—and in the hands of many individual eighteenth-century scholars. At this writing, only three copies show up in Addall.com, their cost of $70–$175 suggesting their value. And only recently I had an e-mail from a scholar at Monash University who indicated he "regularly" used this book in his research.

James L. Harner gives Jerry good marks in his *Literary Research Guide: An Annotated Listing of Reference Sources in English Literary Studies*, noting that "Beasley's checklist is complemented by his analysis of narrative forms in *Novels of the 1740s*," which Jerry published ten years later with the University of Georgia Press in 1982.[3] Nearly eight hundred copies of this important critical work are recorded in WorldCat, and it is labeled, again as we would suspect, as "useful" and "valuable" and "provocative" and "ambitious" and "professional" by reviewers in *RES, YES, MP, JEGP, AN&Q, EC*, and *TLS*. And in the acknowledgments, Beasley thanks for their assistance the likes of Mayo and Battestin and Mell and Park and Richetti, names familiar to those who respect the details of eighteenth-century scholarship.

In between the two books named above came a 1978 book that once again proved "useful"—Jerry's judicious and generous guide through the maze of eighteenth-century scholarship (WorldCat records copies at seven hundred libraries). This Gale publication, *English Fiction, 1660–1800: A Guide to Information Sources*, when coupled with two other Gale guides (Donald C. Mell's *English Poetry, 1660–1800*; and Donald H. Reiman's *English Romantic Poetry, 1800–1835*, Reiman later moving to Delaware in the 1990s) testify to the bibliographical and editing strengths of the faculty of the University of Delaware, which over the years has been peopled by such editors as Irving Ribner, Jay Halio, Lois Potter, Leo Lemay, and Hershel Parker.[4]

And it should come as no surprise that Jerry became a scrupulous editor who brought reliable texts to various audiences. He was one of the editors for an important Garland facsimile reprint series in the mid-1970s, *The Novel in England, 1770–1775*. More important was his involvement with the University of Georgia Press *Works of Tobias Smollett*, for which he was general editor for a number of years. Many times I saw him reading typescript or proofs of these volumes, and he was personally responsible for the introduction and notes to *The Adventures of Ferdinand Count Fathom*. Before that edition, he and Robert Hogan edited *The Plays of Frances Sheridan*; afterward came his edition of Eliza Haywood's *The Injur'd Husband* and *Lasselia*.[5] Jerry's acknowledgments in these volumes demonstrate to all who pause to read them that a good editor has many debts, and WorldCat reveals that each of these editions is available in four hundred to five hundred libraries, where many students and scholars will themselves become indebted to Jerry.

Neither I nor Jerry will know the many yet to be influenced by his scholarship—but we both know those University of Delaware PhDs whose dissertations he directed. Five of them here acknowledge their debts to Jerry by contributing essays to this volume: Susan Kubica Howard, Christopher D. Johnson, Marta Kvande, Melissa Margaret Mowry, and Mary Anne Schofield. Jerry directed their dissertations, as he did those by Barbara G. Betz, Marilyn D. Button, William A. Davis, Phillip A. Everson, John T. Farrell, Robert P. Fletcher, Bradley P. Howard, James R. Keegan, Donna L. Lubot, Amy R. Moreno, Renate Muendel, Marie Regina O'Brien, Julie O'Leary, Linda R. Payne, Charles Reilly, and Gregory M. Weight. Many of these dissertations involved editing projects, nearly all of these "Jerry" students have entered the world of higher education, and most of that number are enjoying the life of tenure-track positions. All have distinguished themselves and, in so doing, distinguished Jerry, their mentor. Jerry's imprint is also on MA theses by Aileen Douglas, John Michael Phelan, and Heidi A. Pierce; and, as second reader on other dissertations and theses, he improved the professional writing of many University of Delaware students.

Jerry guided his students through the writings of Austen, Beckford, Dickens, Sarah Fielding, Hardy, Haywood, Lennox, Sarah Scott, Sheridan (Frances and Thomas), Smollett, Trollope—and even James Wright. And such words as "domestic" and "empowerment" and "gender" and "oriental" punctuate the titles of his students' dissertations. Equally illuminating are the words that appear in the acknowledgments of these dissertations: Jerry is thanked numerous times for his "patience," "assistance," "advice," "encouragement," "astute commentary," "thoughtful direction," "proofreading"—and, most significantly, "friendship."

I have left many things out of these reflections on Jerry Beasley, not mentioning his many articles or reviews or lectures—or his teaching awards and his high marks in teaching evaluations each semester. But such mentions would merely reinforce what we all know to be true of Jerry: he was "all of a piece." And I will grace him (and myself) by suppressing three of the four limericks that I composed for the party that marked his retirement from chairing the Department of English; however, one of these limericks (with my attempt to sing one more time in Jerry's presence), which suggests my respect for the man who guided us through some challenging years in the department, does demand to be quoted:

(Inspired by one of the songs from *Jesus Christ, Superstar*)

> Although it is not very fair
> To Webber and Rice, the pair:
> "HEY, JB, JB,
> You're alright by me!
> JB, JB, Superchair!!"

NOTES

1. For a sense of Zack's presence as department chair, see his hilarious and insightful "Narratives, Tricksterism, Hyperbole, Self-Image(s), and Schizophrenia: The Joys of Chairing an English Department," *ADE Bulletin* 118 (1997): 5–9.

2. Jerry C. Beasley, *A Check List of Prose Fiction Published in England, 1740–1749* (Charlottesville: University of Virginia Press, 1972).

3. James L. Harner, *Literary Research Guide: An Annotated Listing of Reference Sources in English Literary Studies*, fourth ed. (New York: Modern Language Association, 2002), 272–73; Jerry C. Beasley, *The Novels of the 1740s* (Athens: University of Georgia Press, 1982).

4. Jerry C. Beasley, *English Fiction, 1660–1800: A Guide to Information Sources* (Detroit: Gale, 1978); Donald C. Mell, *English Poetry, 1660–1800* (Detroit: Gale, 1982); Donald H. Reiman, *English Romantic Poetry, 1800–1835* (Detroit: Gale, 1979).

5. Tobias Smollett, *The Adventures of Ferdinand Count Fathom*, ed. Jerry C. Beasley, and O M Brack Jr., *The Works of Tobias Smollett* (Athens: University of Georgia Press, 1988); Frances Sheridan, *The Plays of Frances Sheridan*, ed. Jerry C. Beasley and Robert Hogan (Newark: University of Delaware Press, 1984); Eliza Haywood, *The Injur'd Husband* and *Lasselia*, ed. Jerry C. Beasley, *Eighteenth-Century Novels by Women* (Lexington: University Press of Kentucky, 1999).

2

Tobias Smollett: The Life of an Author

O M Brack Jr.

Over the twenty-five years of his writing career, Tobias Smollett commented frequently on living the life of an author, particularly the life of a professional author who was forced to make a living with his pen. Given the fact that he is remembered today because he was an author, especially of novels, it is surprising that his biographers have not examined what it was like for an expatriate Scot living in England, writing, not in Scottish, but in English, attempting to make a living with his pen, in the mid-eighteenth century. Lewis M. Knapp's *Tobias Smollett: Doctor of Men and Manners*, published almost sixty years ago and still the standard biography, devotes little space to the enormous canon of Smollett's miscellaneous writings, and even for the novels the reader is given the few facts Knapp was able to discover about the composition, publication, and reception, with emphasis on the last. Knapp's failure to understand such basic bibliographical concepts as the difference between an edition and an issue and his lack of understanding of how booksellers advertised their wares in the newspapers, for example, have filled the accounts of Smollett's publications in his biography, his edition of *Letters*, and his entry for Smollett in the *New Bibliography of English Literature* with misinformation and bibliographical ghosts. Jeremy Lewis, a professional writer of some standing himself, gives several useful insights into the life of the author in his recent biography, but he chooses to write about only two of the five novels and a handful of other works that happen to interest him. To put it differently, the biography is an extended personal essay, long on

Lewis and short on Smollett. What is needed is a new biography of Smollett, one that captures what it was like for Smollett to live the life of an author in mid-eighteenth-century London. An excellent model is to be found in James G. Basker's *Tobias Smollett, Critic and Journalist*. Although limited primarily to Smollett's work for his two periodicals, the *Critical Review* and the *British Magazine*, Basker demonstrates how a thorough knowledge of the conditions of authorship—relations with booksellers, publishers, printers, editorial assistants, and the reading public—can provide additional information on Smollett's life.[1] This essay considers some of the problems facing a biographer of Smollett and offers suggestions on how knowledge of the complete canon of Smollett's writings in the context of the history of the book can illuminate Smollett's life not only as an author but as a man.

The first problem facing the biographer is what Paul-Gabriel Boucé named "inverted autobiography."[2] Smollett's reputation, as Boucé and others have shown, has been seriously damaged by biographers and critics identifying Smollett with his literary creations. The fact that many of Smollett's strongest statements about the life of an author in the mid-eighteenth century are in his works of fiction creates difficulties for the biographer that cannot be ignored. Yet Smollett insisted that his novels should not be read as autobiographies. Concerning *The Adventures of Roderick Random*, for example, Smollett writes that he is a "little mortified" that persons have taken "umbrage at many passages of the work, on the Supposition that I myself am the Hero of the Book, and they, of consequence, concerned in the History."[3] Such identifications persisted, and in Smollett's "Apologue," first introduced in the fourth edition of *Roderick Random* in 1755, he reminds readers to *"seek not to appropriate to thyself that which equally belongs to five hundred people."* And he insisted in his letter of May 8, 1763, to Richard Smith in New Jersey that "the only Similitude between the Circumstances of my own Fortune and those I have attributed to Roderick Random consists of my being born of a reputable Family in Scotland, in my being bred a Surgeon, and having served as a Surgeon's mate on board a man of war during the Expedition to Cartagena. The low Situations in which I exhibited Roderick I never experienced in my own Person." Like all authors, Smollett puts himself in his works, but where is his biographer to draw the line between fiction and fact? How much is "fact" in any meaningful sense of the word? Is Smollett simply recording his sentiments about facts of which even he was not totally aware? As tempting as it might be for the biographer to avoid the problem of "inverted autobiography" by simply ignoring statements about authorship made in the fiction, doing so would eliminate much valuable evidence. The biographer of Smollett must weigh all of the surviving evidence carefully.

The second problem for a future biographer is that of evaluating Smollett's statements about the conditions of authorship in his letters and nonfictional writings. At first glance, this problem seems more easily resolved than the problem of how to use fiction as evidence. A closer examination, however, demonstrates how difficult letters and nonfictional writing are to evaluate, as separating what Smollett means from what he says takes subtle critical analysis. It has been remarked that the style of his letters resembles that of his novels. As Kenneth Simpson observes, "Smollett's mastery of English and his residence in London from an early age led to his being habitually designated an English novelist." But there is also clear evidence of a "Scottish literary tradition," represented by the "fondness for the mingling of contraries, the fluctuation between the real and the surreal whereby the bizarre penetrates the patina of normality. . . . An acute sense of physicality, and above all physical incongruity that approximates to the absurd or grotesque, often represented by means of animal analogies." The "true origin," Simpson adds, quoting Kurt Witting, "is in a tradition characterized by 'a grotesque exaggeration, a reckless irreverence, an eldritch imaginative propensity.'"[4]

A letter to John Harvie of December 10, 1759, provides an example of this "Scottish literary tradition": "If I go on writing as I have proceeded for some years, my hand will be paralytic, and my brain dried to a snuff. I would not wish my greatest enemy a greater curse than the occupation of an author, in which capacity I have toiled myself into an habitual asthma, and been baited like a bear by all the hounds of Grub-street." In this instance, the level of "grotesque exaggeration" seems relatively clear. But the level of exaggeration, if in fact there is any, is often not clear, as, for example, when Smollett writes to Samuel Richardson on October 12, 1760: "Other tradesman can acquire wealth by employing a number of good hands under their immediate direction, but an author of genius and reputation must, it seems, be a journeyman for life, and be obliged to subsist by the labor of his own hands." Is Smollett writing in this Scottish literary tradition, so prominent in his novels, or is his comment to be taken at face value? At this time, in his fortieth year, Smollett was at, or near, the height of his fame, at least during his own lifetime, having published three novels, two translations of works by Le Sage, a translation of *Don Quixote*, and his *Complete History of England*, as well as having begun writing *A Continuation of the Complete History of England* and initiated the *Critical Review* and the *British Magazine*. The complaint to Richardson, voiced here, has been heard before, and the refrain will be repeated, with some modulation, to the end of his life.

Samuel Johnson, considered by many to be the prototype for the professional author of the eighteenth century, had this to say about the life of an author in *Adventurer* 138 (March 2, 1754) more than a year before the publication of his great *Dictionary of the English Language* (1755), which was to bring him fame, if not fortune, in his forty-sixth year:

If we apply to authors themselves for an account of their state, it will appear very little to deserve envy; for they have in all ages been addicted to complaint.

The neglect of learning, the ingratitude of the present age, and the absurd preference by which ignorance and dulness often obtain favor and rewards, have been from age to age topics of invective; and few have left their names to posterity, without some appeal to future candour from the perverseness and malice of their own times.

I have, nevertheless, been often inclined to doubt, whether authors, however querulous, are in reality more miserable than their fellow mortals, The present life is to all a state of infelicity; every man, like an author, believes himself to merit more than he obtains, and solaces the present with the prospect of the future: others, indeed, suffer those disappointments in silence, of which the writer complains, to shew how well he has learned the art of lamentation.[5]

The question for the biographer of Smollett is this: How much allowance should be made for the lamentations? To what extent do Smollett's frequent complaints truly reflect his perceptions of the life as an author?

Not unexpectedly, authors' complaints focus heavily on their booksellers/publishers. Samuel Johnson, at least the older, more familiar figure in James Boswell's *Life of Samuel Johnson, LL.D.* (1791), often takes the side of booksellers, calling them "generous, liberal-minded men."[6] Smollett, however, goes on in his October 12, 1760, letter to Richardson to call some booksellers "a set of contemptible reptiles who have enriched themselves by works which have scarce afforded their authors the necessaries of life." Not only authors but also booksellers and printers require the necessaries of life, resulting in a certain amount of inevitable conflict. It is also worth noting that the fact that complaints of authors about booksellers far outnumber those of booksellers complaining about authors should not lead to siding with authors; after all, it is authors who have the pen in their hand.[7] There is another reason why most of what we know about writers, Smollett included, and their relationships with their booksellers and printers are written to the authors' advantage. The biographies, editions of writings, editions of letters, and often the author bibliographies are written, edited, and compiled by those interested in the authors' writings. Not only are the author/publisher relationships likely to be distorted because of sympathy toward the distress of the author but also out of ignorance of the way the book trade worked in the eighteenth century.

In his essay "What is the History of the Book?" Robert Darnton observes, "the basic condition of authorship remains obscure for most periods of history." Darnton then raises questions about patronage, the nature of a literary career, and an author's relationships with publishers, printers, booksellers, and reviewers. "Until these questions are answered," Darnton asserts, "we will not have a full understanding of the transmission of texts."[8] All of these questions cannot be answered in the space of an essay, but they suggest an outline for how Smollett's career might be reconsidered. First, the new biography of Smollett needs to focus on Smollett's life as an author.

What did he really think about living the life of an author? How seriously can we take his statements in fiction and nonfiction alike? Just what was Smollett's own relationship with the book trades? Second, Smollett's life needs to be examined in the context of other authors, great and small, and their relationships to the book trade during the mid-eighteenth century.

The surviving evidence indicates that Smollett called himself an author, occasionally, a writer.[9] Since his lifetime, he has most often been referred to as a novelist, usually English novelist—a much more limited term than author—and one that suggests a number of problematic assumptions, including that being Scottish and writing in English is the same thing as being English and that the only writings a critic needs to be concerned with are the novels. To counter this limited view, a biographer needs to consider Smollett as a professional author, although this term has the danger of being so broadly defined that its inclusiveness makes it of little use.

When the term "professional author" first came into use is uncertain, but it figures in James Ralph's *The Case of Authors by Profession or Trade* (1758), as does the term "Journeyman-Author."[10] Johnson's *Dictionary* is not much help, as it defines "Professional" as "Relating to a particular calling or profession," and "Profession" as "Calling; vocation; known employment."[11] The *OED*, however, defines "Professional" as "of a person or persons: that engages in a specified occupation or activity for money, or as a means of earning a living, rather than as a pastime. Contrasted with *amateur*." Thus far, the definition sounds neutral, but the *OED* adds, "Sometimes applied disparagingly to a person who makes a trade or profession of something usually associated with higher motives." The first illustrative quotation in this sense is dated 1606, although no mention is made of an author. In the case of "journeyman," Johnson defines it simply as "a hired workman; a workman hired by the day." The *OED* is again more helpful: "one who, having served his apprenticeship to a handicraft or trade, is qualified to work at it for days' wages; a mechanic who has served his apprenticeship or learned a trade or handicraft, and works at it not on his own account but as the servant or employee of another; a qualified mechanic or artisan who works for another. Distinguished on one side from *apprentice*, on the other from *master*." In a figurative sense, the *OED* adds, "(chiefly depreciatory): a. One who is not a 'master' of his trade or business. b. One who drudges for another; a hireling, one hired to do work for another." The first illustrative quotation is dated 1548, although again an author is not mentioned. These definitions suggest that when one of these terms is encountered, it is necessary to distinguish if it is merely descriptive or has a sting of sarcasm in its tail.

Calling someone a professional author does have the advantage of dividing writers into two classes: those who make a living with their pen and those who write for pleasure and fame. Professional authors find it necessary to take on projects, large and small, that divert them from what they, or we, consider their major works. For authors writing in English in the eighteenth century, these additional writings are frequently labeled "hack-work." "Hack" is from "hackney," literally someone for hire, but also suggesting prostitution, with all its implications of meanness, servility, commonness, and staleness. Less often, at least in the case of Smollett, they are labeled "Grubstreet" productions, a term defined succinctly in Johnson's *Dictionary*: "GRUBSTREET: Originally the name of a street in Moorfields in London, much inhabited by writers of small histories, dictionaries, and temporary poems; whence any mean production is called *grubstreet*."[12]

In the mid-eighteenth century, the pretense was still in full force that a gentleman wrote at his leisure and without concern for remuneration and that those who had to write to make money to live could not, therefore, by definition be gentlemen but were rather "hackney-writers."[13] That this division is overly simplistic requires no comment: any reader can think of good and bad writings by gentlemen and good and bad writings by authors who make their living by their pen. Of the authors who expect to be paid for their writings, only a very small number manage to live by writing only belles lettres—poems, plays, short stories, novels, and essays.

A critical document in the confusion between gentleman authors and hackney writers can be traced directly to Smollett. In his "Proposals for Publishing Monthly the Progress or Annals of Literature and the Liberals Arts" announcing the *Critical Review*, which appeared in the *Public Advertiser* December 19, 1755, and was repeated December 24 and 30, he writes:

> The Work will not be patched up by obscure Hackney Writers, accidentally enlisted in the Service of an undistinguishing Bookseller, but executed by a Set of Gentlemen whose Characters and Capacities have been universally approved and acknowledged by the Public: Gentlemen, who have long observed with Indignation the Productions of Genius and Dullness; Wit and Impertinence; Learning and Ignorance, confounded in the Chaos of Publication; applauded without Taste, and condemned without Distinction; and who have seen the noble Art of Criticism reduced to a contemptible Manufacture subservient to the most sordid views of Avarice and Interest, and carried on by wretched Hirelings, without Candor, Spirit, or Circumspection.[14]

Smollett's enemies, who had been handled roughly in the early numbers of the *Critical Review*, were quick to seize on his distinction between gentlemen and hackney writers and use it as a point of attack. In *The Occasional Critic* (1757), for example, John Shebbeare begins his assault on Smollett by quoting the sentence from the "Proposals" that reads, "The Work will not be patched up by obscure Hackney Writers . . . but executed by a Set of Gentlemen," and then observing, "Hath he not been a Compiler and Translator by the Yard at *hackney* Pay; did he not for Hire write the Treatise on Midwifery. . . . What is a Man then less than a *Hackney*-Writer, on whom every Bookseller may mount, as he may a Horse at a Livery-stable, by paying so much aside."[15]

That authors in the eighteenth century hurled the epithet "hack" or "hackney writer" at each other is not surprising, but it is surprising that modern scholars continue to use it as a term of critical judgment. In *A Study in Smollett, Chiefly "Peregrine Pickle"* (1925), Howard Swazey Buck states that Smollett's method for revising the first edition of *The Adventures of Peregrine Pickle* (1751) for the second edition (1758) "was probably fairly characteristic of his regular hack methods." Buck then explains, "In hackwork expediency is the watch word. In the revision of *Peregrine*, nine parts are expedience and one part literary art."[16] What were Smollett's "regular hack methods"? Buck does not say. Knowing what "expediency" means is no help ("suitability to the circumstances or conditions of the case") and "expedient" ("conducive to advantage in general, or to definite purpose; fit, proper, suitable to the circumstances of the case") (*OED*). What are the circumstances of the case? The booksellers, who owned the copy, wished to publish a second edition and, presumably, paid Smollett to revise it. For a variety of reasons, Smollett wanted to eliminate some of the satirical attacks in the first edition, which he later considered to be in poor taste. Simultaneously, he made extensive stylistic revisions of the kind he made earlier in *The Adventures of Roderick Random* and *The Adventures of Gil Blas*. Of the thousands of changes between the first and second editions, which variants are "expediency" and which "literary art"? Are the revisions "hack" work simply because Smollett may have been paid to make them?

Smollett's *Complete History of England* (1757–1758), written near the height of his creative powers, has not fared well with critics. In the *Cambridge History of English Literature*, for example, William Hunt observes, "History was written as hackwork" by an author of "eminent genius." Although Smollett's *History* "favors the Tory side and is written in a robust and unaffected style," Hunt asserts that Smollett "should not be considered as a historian."[17] Johnson defines "History" as "A narration of events and facts delivered with dignity" (sense 1) or as "Narrations; relation" (sense 2). The *OED* is more helpful in its definition of "Historian": "A writer or author of a history; esp. one who produces a work of history in the higher sense, as distinguished from the simple annalist or chronicler of events, or the mere compiler of a historical narrative." Is Hunt suggesting that Smollett is a "mere compiler of a historical narrative" as opposed to being the author of "philosophical" history like David Hume? If so, why is Smollett's history "hackwork"? If Smollett was simply an "annalist" or "chronicler" or "compiler," then why all the fuss about his writing a "Tory" history? Both Smollett and Hume wrote histories for the booksellers, and both were paid. On several grounds it is possible to argue that Hume's history is better. Although it never achieved great popularity, it certainly has survived the test of time. Smollett's history is a well-written, fast-paced narrative that was popular for decades after Smollett's death but has now faded. Payment for writing does not appear to be the issue here. Is popular history then "hack-work"? Perhaps it is time to abandon the term as a relic of the eighteenth century, recognizing that it is more an expletive than a useful descriptive or critical term.[18] If most of Smollett's writings can have "hack" attached to them, then they are unimportant to literary critics, who need to read only the major novels, as Jeremy Lewis did for his biography.

As Samuel Johnson remarks in the Preface to his edition of the *Dramatick Works of William Shakespeare* (1765), "Every man's performance, to be rightly estimated, must be compared with the state of the age in which he lived, and with his own particular opportunities."[19] As Johnson understood, there is a limit to how much anyone can learn and understand about a distant century, and the historian and biographer must be careful not to assume they know more than they do. But the term "hack" is a reminder about how important it is to understand a critical or satirical term in its historical context. To attempt to use "hack" seriously as a twentieth- or twenty-first-century critical term, as has frequently been done in the case of Smollett, is to cut off a biographer from many of Smollett's writings that provide an understanding of him as an author and a man. To show how a better understanding of historical context, especially a knowledge of the history of the book, might provide a more thorough understanding of Smollett's life, we should turn to a few of his writings.

Smollett's early works, particularly *The Regicide*, reveal much of his understanding about authorship. Smollett had been apprenticed to a surgeon in Glasgow but seems to have had an early ambition to make his mark as an author. Word must have gone out to the provinces that the way to make it as a writer in London was with a verse tragedy, as Samuel Johnson, John Home, William Julius Mickle, and undoubtedly many others, arrived in London with a tragedy in hand, expecting that it would be brought to the stage and bring them fame and fortune. If patronage was dead and an author could live only on his own by writing, the message had not reached Scotland. Smollett spent much time, and created a great deal of frustration for himself, trying to find a patron for his tragedy. His resentment for the failure to have *The Regicide* staged is tied to his belief that the system had not worked as it should have. He felt that either the potential patrons had not played their proper roles or that they were frustrated by ignorant theater managers. Unable to discern the lack of merit in his tragedy and unable to make the patronage system work on his behalf, he then—and only *then*—turned to the public. To Alexander Carlyle, on February 14, 1749, he wrote, "despairing of seeing my old Performance represented, I have at last taken the advice of my Friends, and opened a Subscription for publishing it, which in all appearance will answer my warmest Expectation." In February

1749 William Strahan printed two thousand proposals and about May 12 a subscription edition appeared but without a list of subscribers, suggesting that this form of patronage had also failed, although in the preface Smollett thanked the public for the "uncommon encouragement . . . received in the publication of the play." The subscription edition was followed six weeks later by a trade edition.[20] Even making some allowance for changes in taste, *The Regicide* is not good drama. It is a play written by a young man who had read classical drama, even some Racine and Corneille perhaps, but who knew little of the theater. Tragedies were not in fashion and, for that matter, neither were main pieces. In the decades following the Stage Licensing Act of 1737 (10 Geo. II c. 28), the two licensed theaters, Drury Lane and Covent Garden, averaged less than two new main pieces a year.[21] Variety was introduced by reworking old pieces and by minor entertainments at the end of the day's performance—farces, pantomimes, dances, and so on. It exceeds belief to think that Smollett, living in London, and having a keen interest in the theater, did not know this. He appears to have ignored it, choosing instead to nurse his resentment.

The details surrounding Smollett's difficulties with bringing *The Regicide* to the stage are familiar to anyone who has read Knapp's *Life*. Knapp, however, simply repeats the findings of Buck's 1927 *Study in Smollett*, the most egregious example in Smollett studies of Boucé's "inverted autobiography." At first glance, Buck's autobiographical reading of the "Preface" to *The Regicide* against the Melopoyn chapters in *Roderick Random* and the discussion of the English stage in *Peregrine Pickle* seem persuasive. But it is here that the biographer of Smollett, attempting to establish what Smollett really thought about his life as an author, encounters serious difficulties. Buck assumes the "Preface" is the factual account, and since the characters and events in the two novels more or less conform to these "facts," he treats the fiction as fact. If the "facts" of the "Preface" sound like the accounts in the fiction, does not this suggest a problem? Is it possible that what Buck assumes are three factual documents might just as easily be three fictional documents? If that was the case, of course, the three documents might be dismissed as evidence, but the case is much more complex. After nearly ten years of trying to bring *The Regicide* to the stage, Smollett must have felt frustration, resentment, and anger, all of which seem to boil up in the "Preface." But this same style and tone are also to be found in letters written on matters of considerably less importance and may, as in the letters quoted at the opening of this essay, represent no more than a bow by Smollett to his Scottish literary tradition. The aggrieved author, in other words, may be in part a persona, like the later splenetic traveler in *Travels through France and Italy*. Even if these issues are resolved, there are additional questions that may prove vexing for the biographer. Since in the three accounts the characters are given fictional names, has a fictional name been assigned to the correct real person? What about the chronology? Little information is provided by Buck and, consequently, Knapp on the history of the theater during the decade Smollett was trying to bring his tragedy on stage. Was Smollett treated differently from other young would-be playwrights?[22] Was Smollett treated as badly as he wishes his readers to believe?

It is important to return briefly to the publication of *The Regicide*. Why was a bookseller willing to invest in producing two issues of a tragedy that never reached the stage? If Smollett underwrote the printing himself, his doing so might explain his financial difficulties at the time, but then he was frequently in financial difficulties. If he did not receive patronage in the form of financial support, he must have received encouragement, at the least. Subscriptions are sold to patrons, friends, and those who, for a variety of reasons, wish to be seen as supporting such a project. Even though the lack of a published subscription list suggests that the scheme failed, Smollett, as indicated in the letter quoted above, was optimistic that it would succeed. All of the issues surrounding the attempt to bring *The Regicide* to the stage and its publication require careful reexamination by a future biographer in the historical context of theatrical history, patronage, printing, subscription publication, book selling, and distribution.

However badly Smollett may have been treated or not treated by patrons, theater managers, and booksellers, he was not sufficiently discouraged to give up hope of bringing something on the stage. After failing to reach the stage with his tragedy, Smollett tried his hand at comedy, with *The Absent Man*. It also failed to reach the stage and has disappeared.[23] He also spent time on the libretto for "Alceste," a masque with music by Georg Frederick Handel, which for some reason was never performed, although he may have received £100, half the payment he was to receive for his work.[24] Either he was very foolish or very tenacious, as it was only in 1757 that Smollett was finally to make it to the stage briefly with *The Reprisal*, a topical farce attacking the French, when anti-French feelings were running high in the early years of the Seven Years' War. Clearly, the chances of making it to the stage were slim, as Smollett had to accept at some point, so why the persistence? Perhaps, as an author always in need of money, Smollett was determined to succeed, as he knew the stakes were high. The stage was the quickest way to fame, and the money was excellent. For nine performances and the sale of the copy of *Irene* in 1748–1749, for example, Samuel Johnson received nearly £300, a sum it would have taken him more than three years to earn working for Edward Cave and the *Gentleman's Magazine*.[25]

The concern with *The Regicide* and the possible evidence *Roderick Random* might offer have overshadowed what is most useful: the view these works provide of the life of an author in the mid-eighteenth century. In chapters 62 and 63, near the conclusion of Smollett's first novel, *Roderick Random*, the hero does go to prison, where he meets a tragic poet, Mr. Melopoyn.

Undoubtedly, the passage was suggested by Smollett's recent experiences with *The Regicide*, but a strict autobiographical interpretation is implausible. Melopoyn, for example, suffers a great deal more than there is reason to believe that Smollett ever did. Perhaps the chapters are best interpreted as the worst-case scenario for a failed tragedy writer. In any case, Melopoyn travels to London at the age of eighteen with a tragedy in his pocket, hoping to gain "a large share of fame as well as fortune."[26] When his finances become insufficient because of the delay in having his tragedy brought upon the stage, he decides to "write something in the poetical way . . . for a pretty sum of ready money" (383). By this, he hopes to establish his character, procure friends, and make his tragedy "appear next season to the best advantage, by being supported by interest and reputation" (383). Melopoyn continues, "Having heard what friends Mr. Pope acquired by his pastorals," he turns to composing eclogues, only to be told that if he intended to profit by his talents, he must write something "satirical or luscious" (383). Scorning to "prostitute" his pen in this manner, he is told by another bookseller that he should write "a piece of secret history, thrown into a series of letters, or a volume of adventures, such as those of Robinson Crusoe, and Colonel Jack, or a collection of conundrums, wherewith to entertain the plantations" (383). Unable to perform in this manner, he offers himself as a translator and, finally, to printers of halfpenny ballads and sensational tracts.

Eager to establish his character, procure friends, and make his tragedy appear to best advantage, Smollett turned to poetry. After the report in London of the defeat of the rebels at Culloden April 16, 1746, Smollett composed the "Tears of Scotland." It was set to music by James Oswald and had a popular reception. Although he wrote more lyrics for Oswald, he also wrote satire, verse satires heavily indebted to the late work of Pope. Smollett may have hoped that poetry would do for him what it had done for Pope, but he was to be disappointed once again. *Advice*, published in September 1746, and its sequel, *Reproof*, published in January 1747, were slightly revised and published together in 1748. At the time of the sale of John Osborn's copies on November 14, 1751, 566 copies of the poems remained, and they were not reprinted until 1777, when they appeared as part of a collected edition of the poems and plays. It is curious that Smollett did not turn to writing for the periodical press earlier than he did. Perhaps, like Melopoyn, he desired not to write for a journal "calculated to foment divisions in the commonwealth" (383). Unlike Melopoyn, Smollett did not write anything "luscious," such as secret histories, conundrums, or halfpenny ballads. As Boucé points out, Melopoyn should "not be viewed as the autobiographical representation of Smollett the young thwarted playwright." He is, instead, "a fictive *doppelgänger*, stemming from Smollett's gnawing artistic frustration, but no factually faithful specular image."[27]

Although the Melopoyn chapters cannot be given a strict autobiographical reading, the larger picture provides valuable insights into the state of authorship in the mid-eighteenth century. Smollett, like other professional authors, had to write in a variety of genres on a variety of topics to earn a living. Smollett's biographer needs to examine statements like those in *Roderick Random* carefully testing them against Smollett's career as an author and the careers of other professional authors to establish the truth, to the extent it can be known, of what it was like to be a professional author in the mid-eighteenth century.

In 1748 Smollett turned to translation and the novel almost simultaneously. He may not have awakened to find himself famous, but *Roderick Random* was a best seller by the standards of the time. Dr. John Moore, Smollett's friend and biographer, tells us that by "Roderick Random Smollett acquired much more reputation than money."[28] The printing ledgers of William Strahan provide information on the printing of the first ten editions of the novel, but it is not known how much Smollett received for the copy, which may have been as little as thirty guineas. At this stage of Smollett's career, a reasonable comparison might be made between him and Edward Kimber, who received thirty guineas for *The Life and Adventures of Joe Thompson* in 1750. Like *Roderick Random*, Kimber's novel was two volumes in duodecimo and was popular enough to have gone through six editions by 1783. In 1755 Kimber received almost an identical sum for his *The Life and Adventures of James Ramble*.[29] If this seems low, browsing through the William Upcott papers in the British Library show authors receiving as little as ten guineas for copy.[30]

In any case, Smollett may not have made much money, or enough money, from *Roderick Random*, for in the same year he translated Alain René Le Sage's *L'Histoire de Gil Blas de Santillane* (1715–1735) in four duodecimo volumes, and it was published October 13, 1748. The following February 14, he wrote to Alexander Carlyle, "Gil Blas was actually translated by me, tho' it was a Bookseller's Job, done in a hurry, I did not chose to put my name to it; however, of three thousand copies that were printed, scarce 400 remain unsold." Of course, his name never appeared on the title page of any edition of *Roderick Random* during his lifetime either, but Smollett expected his name to be known, and the second edition of *Gil Blas*, published February 28, 1750, carried on its title page: "A NEW TRANSLATION, by | The Author of RODERICK RANDOM." This translation, still considered the best English translation, had seven editions in Smollett's lifetime and numerous editions since. How much Smollett may have received for the translation is unknown. The going rate for translation at mid-century was a half guinea to a guinea a sheet; however, some translators were paid more and some less. Charlotte Lennox, for example, was paid £1-5-0 per sheet for translating 69½ sheets of *Memoirs for the History of Madame de Maintenon* for a total of £86-17-6.[31] With the success of *Roderick Random*, Smollett may have been paid at a higher rate. At a guinea a sheet, he would have earned about sixty guineas. Should we suppose the success of *Roderick Random* and his earnings from translating *Gil Blas* did not provide Smollett with financial security since he turned to translating Le Sage's *Le Diable boiteux* and Cervantes's *Don Quixote?* At the same time, he was soliciting subscriptions in order to publish *The Regicide.* By 1750 he was also at work on his second novel, *The Adventures of Peregrine Pickle,* published February 25, 1751. All of these details suggest that the financial arrangements for Smollett's publications require further examination by a future biographer.

    After Smollett's failure to establish a practice as a surgeon, the tepid reception of his poems, and the failure of *The Regicide* to reach the stage, the popularity of *Roderick Random* and *Gil Blas* seems to have lifted his spirits and boosted his confidence. So confident was he that his second novel would be a best seller that he entertained the notion of keeping the entire copy himself and had the novel entered in the Register at Stationers' Hall three days before the announced date of publication. Within days Smollett changed his mind and sold the copy to William Strahan, who may have been the printer of the first edition, although no record survives. The size of the first edition of *Peregrine Pickle,* then, is not known, but since the first edition of *Roderick Random* was two thousand copies, it may have been as many as three thousand copies. In any case, a second edition of one thousand copies was not published until March 4, 1758, seven years after the first. In the "Advertisement" to the second edition, Smollett claims that "certain booksellers and others" used all of their "art and industry" to "stifle" the novel "in the birth."[32] Thomas Birch, in a letter of October 14, 1752, to Philip Yorke, Earl of Harwicke, says that "the ill success of his *Peregrine Pickle* . . . ruined his reputation among the booksellers, against which he breathes immortal revenge." Is Smollett blaming the booksellers for something that was his fault, or is there something more here? A biographer of Smollett needs to explain, for example, why booksellers would wish to "stifle" a novel, especially if they had invested money in it. On the basis of Smollett's popularity with *Roderick Random* and *Gil Blas,* was *Peregrine Pickle* printed in a large edition and then failed to find a readership? Did he eliminate the attack on Henry Fielding found in the first edition because Fielding was dead and eliminate the attack on David Garrick because Garrick had produced *The Reprisal?* Perhaps the reasons are more complicated. How can the numerous other revisions in the novel be explained? Might they not provide some clues as to why the first edition failed? If Smollett lost bargaining power with the booksellers, what were the consequences? In 1753, he sold the copy of *The Adventures of Ferdinand Count Fathom* to some booksellers. Perhaps there was no specific quarrel with a bookseller or booksellers, although any bookseller who read, or heard about, chapters 101 and 102 on the "College of Authors" in *Peregrine Pickle* in which

booksellers are described as having "from time immemorial, taken all opportunities to oppress and enslave their authors; not only by limiting men
of genius to the wages of as journeyman taylor, without even allowing them
one sabbath in the week, but also in taking such advantages of their necessities, as were inconsistent with justice and humanity" might be forgiven for
feeling attacked and insulted.[33]

Nevertheless, to put the money paid Smollett by booksellers in perspective, at £400 for the copy of *Peregrine Pickle*, Smollett would have received
about £7-10-0 per sheet.[34] For his third novel, published February 15, 1753,
Smollett received £120 for the copy or about £5 per sheet. At the very end
of his career, Smollett received £210 for *The Expedition of Humphry Clinker*
or about six guineas per sheet.[35] With the failure of *Ferdinand Count Fathom*,
for which a second edition did not appear until 1771, Smollett was forced
to accept the fact that he could not make a living as a novelist. He was to
write only one other novel between 1753 and the publication of his mas-
terpiece in 1771, *The Adventures of Sir Launcelot Greaves*, published serially
in the *British Magazine* during 1760–1761 in the attempt to attract readers
to a new magazine.

Typically, authors became involved in large projects that would provide a
sustained income over a number of years while they completed other works
for which the pay was less certain. Such a project for Smollett was the modern
part of the *Universal History*. Little is now remembered of the *Universal History*,
and even the most ardent scholar has few, if any, occasions to consult it, but
as Guido Abbatista has shown, it was a "work long wished for by the learned
of all nations," nothing less than the history of the world. The work was
translated several times into French and Italian, as well as into German, and
it is drawn upon for numerous articles in the *Encyclopédie*.[36] This monumental
work was not undertaken by an academy but by a conger of booksellers. The
Ancient Part began appearing in numbers in May 1730, eventually reaching
seven folio volumes by November 1744. The *Modern Part*, with which Smollett was concerned, was announced as early as 1747 but did not start appearing until January 1759. Publication took six years to complete and filled
sixteen folio volumes or forty-four octavo volumes. Smollett shared editorial
duties with John Campbell, and through editorial supervision, which meant
a great deal of rewriting or personal compilation, he seems to have been responsible for nearly a third of the modern part—1,370 folio pages.[37] A letter
of April 4, 1759, provides a window on the editorial process:

I have just received from your [Samuel Richardson's] house eight printed
sheets of the Modern History . . . which I suppose have been written by Mr.
Shirley; but I protest I know not what to do with them. Pray, Sir, are those
proof sheets to be corrected for the press, or are they already printed off? There
is an intimation in the margin of the last page that Mr. Shirley goes no farther,
and that you have been at a stand for several months. But this defect I cannot

remedy until I have completed the chasm upon which I am at work; and now I talk of that chasm, I cannot help repeating my complaint that Dr. Campbell should have left the task to me of filling a chasm of fifteen or sixteen sheets, with the description of a country which all the art of man cannot spin out to half that number.

The biographer must examine not only Smollett's contributions to the *Universal History* but also the impact his work on that monumental project had on his life and career. For example, although the editorial work provided Smollett with a steady income, it was a grinding task that was made increasingly difficult by his poor health and one that left him little time or energy for other writing. In the October 12, 1760, letter to Samuel Richardson, quoted in part above, Smollett's frustration with the project is evident. He asserts, "I can always employ my time to much greater advantage than I could possibly reap from the completion of this work, and am now fully resolved to have no new engagements with the proprietors in any volume of abridgement. At least I shall never tie up my hands in such a manner as to render myself a slave for life to a work which I should never live to accomplish." Despite his strong resolution to the contrary, he carried the forty-four octavo volumes of the *Modern Part* with him when he went to France and Italy for his health in 1763–1765 and again when he left England for the last time in autumn 1768. He did not live to see the extensive revisions he made for a new edition of the *Universal History*, which appeared in sixty volumes in 1779–1784.

With the *Complete History of England* (four volumes, 1757–1758) and *A Continuation of the Complete History* (four volumes, 1760–1761, volume 5, 1765), Smollett, in fact, became a historian and even he, in his almost continuous state of frustration, did not call it a "bookseller's job." In a letter to William Huggins on July 2, 1758, Smollett maintained that "in writing the History of England, I can safely say I had no other view in the Execution . . . than historical Truth, which I have displayed on all occasions to the best of my Knowledge without Fear or affection. . . . I look upon the Historian who espouses a Faction, who strains Incidents or willfully suppresses any Circumstances of Importance that may tend to the Information of the Reader, as the worst of Prostitutes. I pique myself on being the only Historian of this Country who has had Honesty, Temper and Courage enough to be wholly impartial and disinterested. . . . When I said Impartial I ought to have excepted the Infirmities of human Nature in which I own myself involved." Shortly after the printing of the first quarto edition of the *Complete History*, the booksellers announced an octavo edition in 110 six-penny numbers. According to Smollett's own testimony, he spent "the best part of a year revising, correcting, and improving" the work.[38] The first number appeared February 25, 1758, and by September 28 more than ten thousand copies were being sold weekly. By February 1762 fifteen thousand copies

of the *Complete History* had been sold and by November 1763 more than
sixteen thousand copies. If these figures sound like a promotional stunt by
the booksellers who owned copy, it is worth noting that the bankruptcy
proceedings for James Rivington and James Fletcher in 1760 show that
thirteen thousand copies of the second edition had been printed. Smollett
received three guineas a sheet for writing the history—£1048-19-0—and an
additional £500 for revising the work. Robert Anderson, one of Smollett's
early biographers, reports that Smollett cleared £2,000 from his history,
and this may be correct, although it is important to remember that assistants and supplies had to be paid for with this money.[39]

At this point in his career, Smollett was a virtual mill for projects. In
1755 he had an ambitious scheme for establishing an Academy of Letters,
something along the lines of the French Academy. For some reason the
academy never materialized, but the *Critical Review or Annals of Literature*,
which made its first appearance February 1, 1756, was "a small branch" of
this "extensive plan." As mentioned earlier, "Four gentlemen of approved
abilities" conducted the *Critical Review*, but in the early years Smollett
seems to have done most of the work. For the first eleven numbers, for
example, he reviewed sixty-seven books. In the beginning of 1760, he
began editing a new monthly periodical, *The British Magazine, or Monthly
Repository for Gentlemen and Ladies*. Smollett not only contributed a chapter
a month for two years of *Sir Launcelot Greaves*, and some poetry, but according to an advertisement in July 20, 1761, in Benjamin Collins, *Salisbury
Journal*, he also was the author of the following "standing articles": "The
Introduction to the Study of Belles Lettres," "The History of France," "The
History of Canada," and "The Peerage of England," besides a "variety of occasional ones." No wonder he described himself as "tied down to the stake
of periodical publications."[40] Also, from May 1762 until February 1763,
he wrote thirty-eight numbers of *The Briton* in an unsuccessful attempt to
defend Lord Bute's ministry. Although he was paid some unknown amount
for writing the numbers, he did not receive the pension or consulship for
which he had hoped.[41]

In 1769 Smollett published his prose satire, *The History and Adventures
of an Atom*.[42] He also contributed "A small part of the Translation of Voltaire's Works, including all the notes historical and critical," for thirty-five
volumes.[43] He made other translations, *Les aventures de Télémaque* from the
French of François de Salignac de la Mothe-Fénelon, for which he received
£70; he edited three volumes of William Smellie's *Midwifery*; he edited Alexander Drummond's *Travels through different Cities of Germany, Italy, Greece,
and Several Parts of Asia, as far as the Banks of the Euphrates* (1754), for which
he received one hundred guineas; and compiled a seven-volume *Compendium of Authentic and Entertaining Voyage* (1756), for which he contributed
to the fifth volume his "An Account of the Expedition Against Carthagena,"

and received about £155. Finally, he also compiled the eight-volume *The Present State of All Nations* (1768–1769).[44]

All of this work was completed in a career of less than twenty-five years. His health never seems to have been good, but by his early forties it was bad. As Smollett himself described it in the *Travels through France and Italy* (1766), "one year ago, the patient underwent a sudden transition from an active to a sedentary life of hard study and application, by which the fibres were gradually relaxed; and in consequence of reading and writing in a stooping posture, his breast became affected."[45] Dr. Gentili, who first visited Smollett at his little estate, *Il Giardino*, on the side of Monte Nero, near Leghorn, Italy, on September 14, 1771, wrote in his diary after Smollett's death on September 17, 1771, "He died asthmatic and consumptive without trying to help himself. . . . A man of matured talent enduring the blows of human life, but almost misanthropic."[46] He was fifty.

In many ways Smollett is typical of other professional authors, although, understandably, he did not think so. He shared with Johnson and Henry Fielding the inability to manage his money. In addition to the funds for his writings, he received at intervals remittances from a "moderate Estate" in Jamaica, yet his letters are filled with pleas for loans.[47] Like other professional authors, he had to be involved in projects, often large ones, in order to earn a living, and these took time away from his major works or at least the writing he would rather have been doing. Individual authors had individual relationships with individual booksellers. Booksellers had to judge the market and assign work to authors that fit their abilities. To make bad choices was to risk bankruptcy, a not uncommon phenomenon among booksellers in the period.[48] Smollett edited three volumes of William Smellie's *Midwifery* because he was a physician; he translated large amounts from the French because he could do it quickly and well; his ability to write fast-paced narrative made him an able historian; his abilities as an editor overlapped with those as a translator in the edition of Voltaire's works; his abilities as an editor and a historian overlapped in the *Universal History*, and so on. Like James Boswell, many scholars have failed to grasp the psychology of the author who earns his living by his pen and can achieve satisfaction and a sense of personal integrity by performing an assigned task well. "I was somewhat disappointed," Boswell writes, "in finding that the edition of the English Poets, for which he was to write Prefaces and Lives, was not an undertaking directed by him: but that he is to furnish a Preface and a Life to any poet the booksellers pleased. I asked him if he could do this to any dunce's works, if they should ask him. JOHNSON. 'Yes, Sir, and *say* he was a dunce.'"[49] Unlike Johnson, Smollett seems always to have been reluctant to accept the role of professional author, although there appears to be nothing to which he did not give his best effort, even when he knew the work would be anonymous, and there is certainly nothing he wrote he needed to be ashamed of and nothing that cannot be read with profit by a twenty-first-century reader. Why then this reluctance to accept the role of professional author?

It is time for Smollett's life to be examined anew, but his next biographer must drop the prejudices and the accompanying vocabulary of the eighteenth century and recognize that Smollett cannot be fully understood without an examination of the entire canon of his writings. Understanding Smollett as an author in the mid-eighteenth century by examining the context the history of the book provides is a good place to start. It is not an easy task. The chance of discovering a new cache of external evidence is small, and the biographer is left with interpreting and reinterpreting the information already available. An attempt to understand what Smollett meant by what he wrote in both his fiction and nonfiction will require subtlety and tact. Nevertheless, much evidence for Smollett's views of the life of an author awaits critical examination, not only in the editorial comments Smollett makes in the early numbers of the *Critical Review*, for example, but also in his anonymous reviews where he has much to say directly and indirectly about the state of authorship in the mid-eighteenth century.[50] Large projects, such as the *Universal History*, need to be examined, not just to discover what writings Smollett may have contributed but also to understand his editorial role. *The Complete History* and *A Continuation of the Complete History* also need to be carefully examined, not just for Smollett's technique as a historian but also for his observations on authors and their milieu. Behind the posturing and the rhetoric, just what was Smollett's life as an author, and what was his relationship to various members of the book trade and to his readers? Until a biographer can answer the questions raised by this essay, old prejudices will be perpetuated, and Tobias Smollett, the Scottish author of some of the best novels in English, will continue to be misunderstood, his life and career shrouded in an undeserved obscurity.

NOTES

1. James G. Basker, *Tobias Smollett, Critic and Journalist* (Newark: University of Delaware Press, 1988). Another model is an excellent biography written by a professional author, John Wain. See *Samuel Johnson, A Biography* (New York: Viking, 1975). A considerable body of evidence on Smollett's life as an author and on the history of the book has surfaced since the publication of Lewis M. Knapp's *Tobias Smollett: Doctor of Men and Manners* (Princeton, NJ: Princeton University Press, 1949). Some of this information has been published in various volumes of the University of Georgia Press edition of *The Works of Tobias Smollett*. O M Brack Jr. and James E. May are collaborating on a bibliography of Smollett's works, which will contain additional evidence. See also Jeremy Lewis, *Tobias Smollett* (London: Jonathan Cape, 2003). For background on authorship and the book trades, see, for

example, Pat Rogers, *Grub Street: Studies in a Subculture* (London: Methuen, 1972); Brean S. Hammond, *Professional Imaginative Writing in England, 1670–1740, "Hackney for Bread"* (Oxford: Clarendon Press, 1997); Richard B. Sher, *The Enlightenment and the Book: Scottish Authors and their Publishers in Eighteenth Century Great Britain, Ireland, and America* (Chicago: University of Chicago Press, 2006); James Raven, *The Business of Books: Booksellers and the English Book Trade, 1450–1850* (New Haven, CT: Yale University Press, 2007).

2. Paul-Gabriel Boucé, *The Novels of Tobias Smollett*, translated by Antonia White in collaboration with the author (New York: Longman, 1976), viii, and chap. 2: "Autobiography and the Novels," 40–67. See also *Tobias Smollett, Scotland's First Novelist*, ed. O M Brack Jr. (Newark: University of Delaware Press, 2007), 15–16, 35–36; and John Skinner, "*Roderick Random* and the Fiction of Autobiography," *A/B: Autobiographical Studies* 9 (1994): 98–114.

3. Tobias Smollett to Alexander Carlyle, June 7, 1748. All references to Smollett's letters are from *The Letters of Tobias Smollett*, ed. Lewis M. Knapp (Oxford: Clarendon Press, 1970) and are cited by date.

4. Kenneth Simpson, "Tobias George Smollett," in *Oxford Dictionary of National Biography*, 407. See also Simpson's *The Protean Scot: The Crisis of Identity in Eighteenth-Century Scottish Literature* (Aberdeen: Aberdeen University Press, 1988), 14–40; and Kurt Witting, *The Scottish Tradition in Literature* (Edinburgh: Oliver and Boyd, 1958), 71. For the resemblance of the style of Smollett's letters to that of his novels, see Philip Stevick, "Stylistic Energy in Early Smollett," *Studies in Philology* 64 (1967): 718–19. Jerry C. Beasley gives an excellent account of Smollett as a Scottish novelist in *Tobias Smollett, Novelist* (Athens: University of Georgia Press, 1998), especially 3, 6–9, 223. See also Beasley's "Tobias Smollett: The Scot in England," *Studies in Scottish Literature* 29 (1996): 14–28.

5. Samuel Johnson, *The Idler and The Adventurer*, ed. W. J. Bate, John M. Bullitt, and L. F. Powell, *The Yale Edition of the Works of Samuel Johnson*, vol. 2 (New Haven, CT: Yale University Press, 1963), 493.

6. James Boswell, *The Life of Samuel Johnson, LL.D.*, ed. G. B. Hill, revised and enlarged by L. F. Powell, six vols. (Oxford: Clarendon Press, 1934–1950; vols. 5–6 [second ed.], 1964), 1:104.

7. The ability to understand author/publisher relationships is further complicated by the fact that a writer's correspondence is likely to be kept—although in the case of Smollett little enough has survived—and the publisher and printer correspondence is jettisoned as an out-of-date business archive. James E. Tierney has edited the correspondence of Robert Dodsley, perhaps the best known bookseller of the eighteenth century. *The Correspondence of Robert Dodsley, 1733–64* (Cambridge: Cambridge University Press, 1988) contains only 393 letters to and from Dodsley, of which eighty-nine are written to, and six from, only one author, William Shenstone. For Benjamin Collins, who ran an extensive business in Salisbury (which included printing, book selling, dealing in patent medicines, and banking), only a few letters have been located. Since he had numerous business arrangements with the London book trade, including owning shares in books and periodicals, including Smollett's *Expedition of Humphry Clinker*, hundreds of letters must have been written over a half century. A portion of Collins's business records survived until the end of the nineteenth century but cannot now be located. See C. Y. Ferdinand, *Benjamin*

Collins and the Provincial Newspaper Trade in the Eighteenth Century (Oxford: Clarendon, 1997); and Charles Welsh, *A Bookseller of the Last Century* (London: Griffin,
Farran, Okeden, & Welsh, 1885). Even when records have survived, as in the case of
William Bowyer and William Strahan, they tell us more about the authors and the
popularity of their works than about the day-to-day running of a printing business.

8. Robert Darnton, "What is the History of the Book?"(1982) reprinted in *The
Book History Reader*, ed. David Finkelstein and Alistair McCleary (London: Rout-
ledge, 2002), 12, 18. For a good recent discussion of the nature of authorship, see
Sher, *Enlightenment and the Book*, chaps. 2 and 3.

9. See, for example, Smollett's letters to Alexander Carlyle, June 7, 1748; William Huggins, February 17, 1758; John Harvie, December 10, 1759; John Moore,
August 19, 1762; Richard Smith, May 8, 1763; William Hunter, February 24, 1767;
and David Hume, August 31, 1768.

10. James Ralph, *The Case of Authors by Profession or Trade, stated with regard to
booksellers, the stage, and the public* (London: R. Griffiths, 1758), 24.

11. References to Samuel Johnson's *Dictionary of the English Language* are from
the first edition of 1755.

12. In *Fifty Years' Recollection of an Old Bookseller* (Cork: Printed for the Author,
1835), William West draws a distinction between a "hackney writer," a "*garretter*,"
and "grub-street" writer. He considers the "hackney writer" a higher order than
the other two. In this category he includes Smollett, Johnson, and Goldsmith. See
especially 68–71. See also, Rogers, *Grub Street*. Patrick Crutwell, editor of Johnson's
Selected Writings (Harmondsworth: Penguin, 1982), placed all of his writings before
The Vanity of Human Wishes (1749) under the heading "Grub Street Journalist." This
is to make the term "Grub Street" meaningless.

13. In the William Upcott papers in the British Library is a letter from Mr.
C. A. Vasely, who might be taken as an example of the gentleman author. He wrote
to John Nourse on July 16, 1757: "Sir, I think that you may now pay the hundred
guineas to Mr. Woodhouse for his labor as Amanuenses in regard to British Customs, which will be in full consideration of the Copy-right . . . as to my own labor
& skill in the Work I do freely present you with the whole; Wishing you great profit
& hoping to my self some reputation" (BL Add. MS 38728 f. 253). Mr. Vasely appears to have gained no reputation. According to the *English Short Title Catalogue*,
J. Nourse published *The British Customs: Containing and Historical and Practical
Account of Each Branch of that Revenue. . . .* By Henry Saxby, of the Customhouse,
London in 1757 and *A Survey of British Customs. . . .* By Samuel Baldwin, of the
Custom-House, London in 1770.

14. Quoted in Basker, *Tobias Smollett, Critic and Journalist*, 31–32. Unknown to
Smollett, Samuel Johnson and some members of the book trade were planning
another "literary annals"—*The Literary Magazine*. An advertisement of December
25, 1755, announcing the publication in the *Public Advertiser*, in which Johnson
may have had a hand, makes sarcastic allusions to Smollett's proposals: "This work
will be carried on by Gentleman who write for their Amusement, and whose Circumstances and Situation in Life are such as to render them entirely independent of
Booksellers, from whom they have nothing to hope or fear." See Basker, 33–34; and
Donald D. Eddy, *Samuel Johnson, Book Reviewer in the Literary Magazine: or, Universal
Review, 1756–1758* (New York: Garland, 1979), 1–5.

15. John Shebbeare, *The Occasional Critic; or, the Decrees of the Scottish Tribunal in the Critical Review Rejudged* (London, 1757), 3, 4. See also Shebbeare's *An Appendix to the Occasional Critic: in which the Remarks on that Performance in the Critical and Monthly Reviews are Examined* (London, 1757), 9.

16. Howard Swazey Buck, *A Study in Smollett, Chiefly "Peregrine Pickle"* (New Haven, CT: Yale University Press, 1925), 18. This book is unreliable; nothing should be taken from it without verification.

17. William Hunt, *Cambridge History of English Literature*, vol. 10: "The Age of Johnson" (Cambridge: Cambridge University Press, 1939), 331–32. The other author with whom Smollett is being compared is Oliver Goldsmith.

18. Leigh Hunt and William Hazlitt, to take two examples from the nineteenth century, wrote much that would now be called journalism but seem to have escaped being labeled hacks, as have Ernest Hemingway and Anthony Burgess, to pick two among many twentieth-century examples.

19. Samuel Johnson, *Johnson on Shakespeare*, ed. Arthur Sherbo, *The Yale Edition of the Works of Samuel Johnson*, vol. 7 (New Haven, CT: Yale University Press, 1968), 81.

20. Tobias Smollett, *Poems, Plays, and "The Briton,"* introduction and annotations Byron Gassman with text ed. O M Brack Jr., *The Works of Tobias Smollett* (Athens: University of Georgia Press, 1993), 71–76, 572–75.

21. See George Winchester Stone Jr. and George M. Karl, *David Garrick: A Critical Biography* (Carbondale: Southern Illinois University Press, 1979), 160; and "The Making of the Repertory," in *The Theater World, 1660–1800*, ed. Robert D. Hume (Carbondale: Southern Illinois University Press, 1980), 181–209.

22. See, for example, Kalmia A. Burns, *David Garrick Director* (Pittsburgh, PA: Pittsburgh University Press, 1961), 13–17.

23. Smollett may be alluding satirically to his experiences with the "The Absent Man" when he speaks of the "North Britain" who "had, in the beginning of the season, presented a comedy to the manager of a certain Theater, who, after it had lain six weeks in his hands, returned it to the author, affirming their was neither sense nor English in the performance." See *The Adventures of Peregrine Pickle*, ed. James L. Clifford (Oxford: Oxford University Press, 1964), 643.

24. See *Poems, Plays, and "The Briton,"* 76–77, 572; and Smollett's letters to Alexander Carlyle, February 14, 1748/1749, and October 1, 1749.

25. See *The Poems of Samuel Johnson*, ed. David Nichol Smith and Edward L. McAdam, rev. J. D. Fleeman, second ed. (Oxford: Clarendon Press, 1974), 276.

26. Tobias Smollett, *The Adventures of Roderick Random*, ed. Paul Gabriel Boucé (Oxford: Oxford University Press, 1999), 380. References are to this edition.

27. Ibid., xi.

28. John Moore, *The Works of Tobias Smollett, M.D., with Memoirs of his Life*, eight vols. (London, 1797), 1:cxxi. In addition to whatever copy money Smollett received, he was probably paid for revising the second, third, and fourth editions of the novel since, for example, he was paid to revise *The Devil upon Crutches* and *The Complete History of England*. See Alain René Le Sage, *The Devil upon Crutches, translated Tobias Smollett*, ed. O M Brack Jr. and Leslie A. Chilton, *The Works of Tobias Smollett* (Athens: University of Georgia Press, 2005), 236–37, and James E. May, "The Authoritative Editions of Smollett's *Complete History of England*," in *Tobias Smollett, Scotland's First Novelist*, 240.

29. S. A. Kimber, "The Relation of a Late Expedition to St. Augustine with Biographical Notes on Isaac and Edward Kimber," *Papers of the Bibliographical Society of America* 28 (1934): 81–96; F. G. Black, "Edward Kimber: Anonymous Novelist of the Mid-Eighteenth Century," *Harvard Studies and Notes in Philology and Literature* 17 (1935): 27–42; Jeffrie Herrie, "Edward Kimber," *Oxford Dictionary of National Biography*; BL Add. MS 38728 f. 125.

30. In fact, on January 14, 1764, a Mrs. A. Woodfin reported that she received from Thomas Lowndes "the Sum of Five Guineas which with other Five Guineas which I am hereafter to receive in Books at the accustomed Bookseller Price. I acknowledge to be a full consideration for the Novel by me wrote & called *Mariane Middleton*" (BL Add. MS 38728 f. 212). Frances Burney received twenty guineas from Lowndes for *Evelina.* See Joyce Hemlow, *The History of Fanny Burney* (Oxford: Clarendon, 1958), 87–88. See also Harry Ransom, "The Rewards of Authorship in the Eighteenth Century," *Texas University Studies in English* 18 (1938), 47–66.

31. BL Add. MS 38730 f. 126.

32. Tobias Smollett, *Peregrine Pickle*, second ed. (London, 1758), 1.iii.

33. Ibid., 4.99.

34. See Albert Smith, "The Printing and Publication of Smollett's *Peregrine Pickle*," *Library*, fifth series, 26 (1971): 39–52; and "*The Adventures of Peregrine Pickle*, 1758 and 1765," *Library*, fifth series, 28 (1973): 62–64. For more detail see Smith's unpublished doctoral dissertation, *The Printing and Publication of Early Editions of the Novels of Tobias George Smollett, with Descriptive Bibliographies* (University of London, 1975), especially 146–258. See also O M Brack Jr., "Toward a Critical Edition of Smollett's *Peregrine Pickle*," *Studies in the Novel* 7 (1975): 361–75; and "*Peregrine Pickle* Revisited," *Studies in the Novel* 27 (1995): 260–72.

35. Tobias Smollett. *The Expedition of Humphry Clinker*, Introduction and annotations Thomas R. Preston with text ed. O M Brack Jr., *The Works of Tobias Smollett* (Athens: University of Georgia Press, 1990), 441–43. The figures are approximate. *Roderick Random* has approximately three hundred words per page (1:2), *Peregrine Pickle* 285 words (1:2), *Ferdinand Count Fathom* 285 words (1:3), and *Humphry Clinker* 240 (1:2).

36. Guido Abbatista, "The Business of Paternoster Row: Towards a Publishing History of the *Universal History* (1736–65)," *Publishing History* 17 (1985): 5–50.

37. See Louis L. Martz, "Tobias Smollett and the *Universal History*," *Modern Language Notes* 56 (1941): 1–14; and *The Later Career of Tobias Smollett* (New Haven, CT: Yale University Press, 1942), 7–8.

38. See Smollett's letter to Richard Smith, 8 May 1763.

39. See James E. May, "The Authoritative Editions of Smollett's *Complete History of England*," in *Tobias Smollett, Scotland's First Novelist*, 240–305; and Patricia Hernlund, "Three Bankruptcies in the London Book Trade, 1746–61: Rivington, Knapton, and Osborn," in *Writers, Books, Trade*, ed. O M Brack Jr. (New York: AMS Press, 1994), 77–96.

40. A unique copy of the weekly *Salisbury Journal* is in the Beinecke Rare Book and Manuscript Library, Yale University. See also *Letters*, 96.

41. See *Poems, Plays, and "The Briton,"* 233–34.

42. See Tobias Smollett. *The History and Adventures of an Atom*, Introduction and annotations Robert Adams Day with text ed. O M Brack Jr., *The Works of Tobias Smollett* (Athens: University of Georgia Press, 1989), xlix–lxiv, 325–26.

43. *Letters*, 113.
44. Ibid., 113; See also Martz, *Later Career*, 104–80.
45. Tobias Smollett, *Travels through France and Italy*, ed. Frank Felsenstein (Oxford and New York: Oxford University Press, 1977), 93.
46. Knapp, *Tobias Smollett*, 298.
47. See, for example, *Letters*, 112. Several years ago I carefully combed through John Orbell and Alison Turton, *British Banking: A Guide to the Historical Records* (Burlington, VT: Ashgate, 2001) and wrote to all the relevant archivists in search of any financial records of Smollett that might have survived. None were located. I am grateful to the following archivists: Pamela Hunter, C. Hoare & Co.; Isobel Lang, Coutts & Co.; Jane Waller, ING Bank N.V.; Nicholas Webb, Barclays Group Archives; Miriam Yamin, The Royal Bank of Scotland Group.
48. See Hernlund, "Three Bankruptcies," 78–122.
49. Boswell, *Life*, 3:137.
50. See, for example, the opening paragraph of Smollett's review of Richard Rolt's *A New and Accurate Account of South America*:

The *British* learning of this age is grown into contempt among other nations, by whom it was formerly revered; and nothing has contributed to this disgrace, so much as the inundation of mean performances, undertaken for the emolument of booksellers, who cannot distinguish authors of merit, or if they could, have not sense and spirit to reward them; according to their genius and capacity. Without considering the infinite pains and perseverance it must cost a writer to form and digest a proper plan of history; compile materials; compare different accounts; collate authorities; compose and polish the stile, and complete the execution of the work; he furnishes him with a few books, bargains with him for two or three guineas a sheet; binds him with articles to finish so many volumes in so many months, in a crouded page and evanescent letter, that he may have stuff enough for his money; insists upon having copy within the first week after he begins to peruse his materials; orders the press to be set a going, and expects to cast off a certain number of sheets weekly, warm from the mint, without correction, revisal, or even deliberation. Nay, the miserable author must perform his daily task, in spite of cramp, colick, vapours, or vertigo; in spite of head-ach, heart-ach, and *Minerva'*ss frowns; otherwise he will lose his character and livelihood, like a Taylor who disappoints his customer in a birth-day suit—What can be expected from a wretched author under such terrors and restraints, but a raw, crude, hasty, superficial production, without substance, order, symmetry or connection, like the imperfect rudiments of nature in abortion; or those unfinished creatures engendered from the mud of the *Nile*, which the old philosophy fabled as the effect of equivocal generation [*Critical Review* 1 (March 1756): 97–106].

3

Elizabeth Singer Rowe: Lifestyle as Legacy

Paula R. Backscheider

In this essay, I intend to argue that Elizabeth Singer Rowe created a satisfy-ing lifestyle, one that supported an identity as a writer, and that both the lifestyle and authorial identity were influential in fiction, poetry, and the lives of women.[1] Rowe is beginning to attract new critical attention, and I hope to add a dimension to recent critical work that explicates her place as a poet, writer of prose fiction, devotional writer, or "tactical" player in the evolving publishing economies.[2] In contrast to these studies, which focus on a single genre or practice, mine attempts to bring her life, her writing, and her legacy together. Her significance, I believe, has been underesti-mated in literary and women's studies. In order to make the case for her unusual, groundbreaking, and influential creation of an identity for herself as a writer, I will work partly within the methodologies of life-writing theo-rists, an admittedly experimental approach.

"Life writing" is a comfortable, somewhat baggy term to describe all kinds of biographical and autobiographical discourses. Nancy K. Miller observes that "the rubric remains open to new departures as critics and scholars respond to the proliferation of self-narration and self-portraiture in both popular and high culture modes."[3] In fact, life writing creates a category protected from the inherited genre demands of "autobiography" and "biography." It was a popular term in the seventeenth and eighteenth centuries and included all kinds of autologous texts, some *belles lettres*, such as travel narratives, and others unstructured and highly experimental, such as Charlotte Charke's *Narrative of the Life of Mrs. Charlotte Charke* (1755). In the last twenty years, feminists have begun to theorize life writing, and they often describe it as documents of many kinds written out of a life or lives. Life writing may cover a considerable part of a person's life, coherent segments of it, or be about ways of living and material culture. As Marlene Kadar observes, until quite recently the writing and study of life writing were most often concerned with the subjects' *bios*, "life, way of living; their *aute*, authority and originality; or their *graphia* (signs) or hermeneutics."[4] After a period when life-writing theorists concentrated on the constructed self or what Ulric Neisser identified as the "conceptual self" (the self posited as category),[5] attention has moved to investigating the self and self-experience as, especially, in dynamic relationships to constructing forces and as a changing, not evolving, process.

In fact, this current shift in attention is moving toward what Augustine described as his goal, to express "what I am inside myself, beyond the possible reach of . . . eyes and ears and minds."[6] As James Olney explains in his important, highly reflective book, Augustine was "attempting to make his mind present to itself so that he may make it present also to his readers."[7] Olney conceptualizes an especially arresting extension of life-writing study. He concludes his book with an argument that Samuel Beckett was intensely aware of and influenced by his "predecessors," the canonical autobiography writers Augustine and Jean-Jacques Rousseau, and yet he created a new kind of life writing, partly because he was writing "in a time he felt was inimical to form."[8] The body of work Beckett left in a variety of forms and fragmentary revelations and accounts and the fact that he wrote about the self rather than the life, Olney argues, is the autobiographical form for our time, one he calls "periautography."[9] In one of her most recent publications, Sidonie Smith emphasizes that the boundary between biography and autobiography is "permeable," and the "history of an autobiographical subject is the history of recitations of the [performative] self."[10] For her and other theorists, the unity of the subject exists in constructed expressions that are more nuanced and socially responsive than has been previously recognized.

My experience treating eighteenth-century women's poetry as life writing in the *British Women Poets of the Long Eighteenth Century: An Anthology* led to recognition of how many ways life writing was being carried out and how applicable the work of Olney and Smith are for women's literary writing. This life writing was, indeed, highly fragmentary, but much of it might more accurately be called "episodic," as women wrote, for instance, annually on such topics as their birthdays or Charles I's execution. Importantly, many of these poems were about the self, and, although they vividly described ways of living and might refer to specific events in their lives, the emphases were on the experience and the experiencing self, the mind's reactions, and movement over time. Poetry offers a wealth of performative positions in which women can try on subject positions and identities. As Eliza Haywood's writing demonstrates, early novelistic fiction also encouraged the creation of individual, authoritative, performative positions such as Haywood's "great arbitress of passion."[11] In a time when the lives and actions of players inflected interpretation of their stage roles, the relationship between actual performer and performance was richer, more complex, and more blended than it is now. Where Rowe chose to locate herself as subject and how she gestured toward herself are telling sites for investigation. As Susan Stanford Friedman says, "Not recognizing themselves in the reflections of cultural representation, women develop a dual consciousness—the self as culturally defined and the self as different from cultural prescription."[12]

This description could apply to many Nonconformists as well as women. Theorists note that oppressed or dominated peoples "often particularize a dialectic between these two generalized subject-positions, between the subject as acted upon and produced by social discourse and the subject as acting to change social discourse and, therefore, its own subject-position."[13] Philosophers, linguists, historians, and literary scholars agree that the long eighteenth century was the critical period of the development of concepts of self.[14] John Locke famously wrote, "Every one is to himself that which he calls *Self*," and Keith Thomas points out the considerable "growth of a larger vocabulary for self-description."[15] For a number of quite obvious reasons, expressions of awareness of a self separate from and sometimes in conflict with the self produced by social discourse and identified with a role or occupation are much more common in the writings of men.[16] There is no question that Nonconformists' awareness of the contrast between their socially imposed subject position and their interior life that affirmed their individuality and their "true identity" was well developed and often expressed even among the lower orders.[17] Rowe's father had been imprisoned for his religion, and nearly half a century of prison writings by John Milton, John Bunyan, Richard Baxter, and others inscribed just this divide. As Milton wrote in *Paradise Lost*, "The mind is its own place" (1:254). Rowe, as a woman and a Nonconformist, created identities from non-dominant positions. The importance of her work is increased by the fact that expressions of the individual self are rarer among women.

Rowe also grew up in and inherited a strong belief in the responsibility to witness. The latter is a complicated concept, for it draws together the religious, the political, and the social. As literary historians such as N. H. Keeble have demonstrated, Nonconformists saw writing as a public service with moralistic and educative purposes.[18] More than permission to write, they had an obligation to do so, and we are slowly recognizing the high percentage of writers with this background. Rowe was one of them, and, as she aged, she staked out themes, imagery, and narrative strategies that became more outward directed, more exemplary and even didactic, and, I shall argue, attempted to assure their endurance. Leaving no traditional autobiographical writings, she, like Samuel Beckett in our time, used a variety of forms to record not the chronological sequence of her life but the emergence and development of her sense of self. In so doing, Rowe created an identity for herself as a writer within the particular cultural milieu in which she lived. Here, too, the Nonconformist tradition provides context as seventeenth-century men left large numbers of diaries, autobiographical papers, and personally revealing meditations. Reading Oliver Heywood's texts led Keeble to call him "the author of his own life, its historian and interpreter."[19] Fragmentary, episodic, and cropping up in literary texts, these writings can be compared to Rowe's lifelong project.

Although obscured by her reputation as an overly pious, one-note writer, the life writing in Rowe's texts is rich and leads to a repositioning of Rowe within her own time. Rowe published her first poem, *Habbakkuk*, in John Dunton's *Athenian Mercury* in October 1693, when she was nineteen. She had kept a notebook of poems (now lost) while she was at boarding school and corresponded with Dunton as early as 1691.[20] His periodical held considerable interest for her and provided an important venue for her early life writing. Married into one of the brilliantly educated, heroic Nonconformist families,[21] he included a wide variety of material, only some of it alignable with Dissent. His paper excerpted and translated fiction such as *The Religious Slave and his Adventures*, which reminds readers of Penelope Aubin's later texts.[22] "Novels" such as Charles Gildon's *Post Boy Robb'd of his Mail* were routinely advertised in it, and in the winter of 1691–1692 it began publishing original poetry (including Jonathan Swift's *An Ode to the Athenian Society*), and then "Poetical Mercuries," entire issues devoted to questions and responses in verse. The paper included answers to a broad assortment of questions. It discussed medicine, courtship, marriage, gender, science, religion, and love, and Rowe's texts sometimes reflect her agreement with opinions in the answers.

From the beginning, Dunton worked to draw in women readers and contributors. The cover of the second volume began to advertise: "Resolving all the most Nice and Curious Questions proposed by the Ingenious of *Either* Sex" (emphasis mine), and the October 1, 1692, issue promises, "The Ladies Questions will be Answered next Tuesday, and after that once every Fortnight, 'till we have Answer'd the many ingenious Questions lately sent us by the Fair Sex."[23] This rather odd combination of compliment ("ingenious" and respectful attention) and condescension ("Fair Sex") characterized his tone, but as revolutionary as his paper was, certainly his attention to women was even more so. Dunton reveals himself to be an astute critic and gives steady attention to poetry. His unusual attention to women comes through in statements such as this observation, which appeared in the answer to a question about the best poem and best poet ever to exist: "*Sappho* has an Inimitable softness which melts the Soul at the very hearing the sound of her words in those few precious Fragments she has left us; nor did ever any come so near her since as Mrs *Behn*."[24] The *Athenian Mercury*, then, provided Rowe an ideal environment to begin to define herself as a writer and defender of Dissenting ideology.

Both *King William Passing the Boyn* and *Habbakuk* are strongly, even zealously ideological. Dissenters had greeted William and Mary with joy and optimism and identified with the ideals of the Glorious Revolution throughout the eighteenth century. These early poems by Rowe are histori-cally significant. First, they are examples of women's participation in public affairs. Although largely unnoticed until now, women wrote an unbroken stream of political poetry, and poets such as Anna Laetitia Barbauld and Carolina Nairne devoted significant portions of their career to ideological poetry writing.[25] These two early poems of Rowe's and a poetic question discussed below that she posed should be set beside poems such as Dan-iel Defoe's *The True-Born Englishman*, contextualized as such, and used to explicate the temper and propagandistic efforts of the time. Second, *Hab-bakuk's* publication in a periodical set an empowering example for women, and periodical publication became a major venue for women.[26] Third, the beginning of Rowe's distinctive poetic style is emerging in these poems. Her religion and the experience as a persecuted minority gave emblematic significance to warfare and confidence in her readers' ability to penetrate emblem, typology, and allegory.[27] She consistently wove together a sense of eternal time and purpose with quite particular events. She used the language of inspired religious poetry (*"Oh were the potent inspiration less!/ I might find words its Raptures to express"*), but she also employed concrete descriptions of the master strategy and bloody battle of the Boyne. The alternation of enthusiastic, sometimes extravagant language with specific, economical description is characteristic of her work, and the two registers became more smoothly and artfully integrated.

Fourth, these poems show knowledge of respected poetic genres, of current preferences, and original adaptation of both. *Upon King William's Passing the Boyn* is a classical elegy, the public form traditionally devoted to war and love, and *Habbakuk*, in addition to its topical appeal expressing the sentiments of Dunton's readership, was in the faddishly popular Pindaric ode form. The companion poem, "To the Compiler of the Pindarick now recited," effused, "How *vast* a *Genius sparke*s in each Line!/ How *Noble* all! how *Loyal*! how *Di-vine*!" Rowe was complimented, then, on her patriotism as well as her poetic skill, which Dunton did note to be "somewhat uncorrect." To his regret, with a few exceptions, most of the poetry the *Athenian Mercury* published was dog-gerel. An offering from a "Platonick Gentleman" begins,

Since Love hath kindled in our Eyes
A chast and holy Fire,
It were a Sin if thou or I
Shou'd let this Flame expire.
(May 10, 1692)

Dunton even labeled some issues "The Doggerel Mercury," and having a new source of quality poetry clearly pleased him. He began to publish religious and patriotic poems as often as poetic questions and answers. For example, *To the most Illustrious Prince Lewis of Baden, On his Happy Arrival in England* appeared in the January 23, 1694, issue and *A Paraphrase of David's Elegy on Saul and Jonathan* on February 13, 1694. Dunton asked Rowe for more poetry, popularized her as "the Pindarick lady," and devoted one issue of his paper to her poetry. The quality of the poetry Rowe would submit over the next two years helped establish periodicals as important popularizers and taste-setters of poetry, and Rowe's example made such publication acceptable for women.

To create an identity as a writer, a person must create a lifestyle to make writing possible and believe she has the right to do it. Beginning in 1693, Rowe began to move toward defining herself in these terms. After publishing in the October 1693 issue, she did not publish again until May 1694, although she submitted revealing questions of considerable interest to her. One began, "I was once Reprov'd by a Minister for Wearing of Pearl," and an early portrait of her shows her wearing pearls and a low-cut dress with a lacy stand-up collar.[28] More to the point, in the same issue, she asks, "What Books of Poetry wou'd you Advise one that's Young, and extremly delights in it, to read, both Divine and other?"[29] Such lines of inquiry had been present from the paper's beginning, as questions such as the following indicate: "Whether it be proper for Women to be Learned?" (May 23, 1691). Dunton had fostered an environment of trust and commonality from the beginning of the paper, and, although some questioners and contributors had identities, the community provided cover by being stronger than the individuality of any single questioner. Rowe's submissions, then, drew upon her Nonconformist background to enable an exploration of her identity and possibilities as a woman and as a woman writer.

After the seven-month absence, her poems flowed into print beginning with two questions written in verse. The first indicates continuity with her earlier Williamite poems:

'Twas nobly thought, and worthy—still!
So I resolv' t' employ my Loyal Quill.
Virtue, and our unequall'd *Heroes* praise!
What *Theams* more glorious can exalt my Lays?
William! A Name my Lines grow proud to hear!
A Prince as Great, and wondrous Good, as e're

> The sacred Burden of a Crown did wear.
> Resolve me, then, *Athenians*, what are those,
> (Can there be any such?) You call his Foes?
> His Foes, curst word, and why they'd pierce his Breast,
> Ungrateful Vipers! where they warmly rest?
> (May 29, 1694)

The June 5 issue carried another question in verse and offered a rather daring submission, her paraphrase of Canticle 5, verses 6–16. In this dream experience, the maiden dreams her beloved knocks on the door, but, when she opens it, he is gone. An extravagant description of his beauty is punctuated by the question of why her beloved is superior to other loved ones asked by the "Daughters of Jerusalem." The Athenians uncharacteristically printed this poem without comment or reaction, although their inclusion of John Lloyd's *Shir ha shirim, or, The Song of Songs being a paraphrase . . . in a pindarick poem* (1682) as recommended reading to her on October 24, 1693, provides a kind of context.

Almost exactly a year later, on June 18, 1695, the *Mercury* printed *To one that perswades me to leave the Muses* and four more of her poems, filling the entire issue with her work. In this important poem, she confidently asserts her identity as a writer and gives a clear signal of her professional dedication:

> Forego the *charming Muses!* No, in spight
> Of your ill-natur'd Prophecy I'le write,
> And for the future *paint* my thoughts at large.

In lines strikingly similar to lines in Alexander Pope's much later poems, lines that came to be the most commonly used permission statements in women's poetry,[30] she writes,

> I waste no Paper at the *Hundreds* charge;
> I rob no *Neighbouring Geese* of Quills, nor slink
> For a collection to the Church for ink:
> Besides my *Muse* is the most gentle thing
> That ever yet made an attempt to *sing*:
> I call no Lady *Punk*, nor Gallants *Fops*.
> (June 18, 1695, p. 1)

She admits, "Yet I'm so scurvily inclin'd to Rhiming,/ That undesign'd my thoughts *burst out a chiming.*" As I argue in *Eighteenth-Century Women Poets and Their Poetry*, permission is a major consideration in women's poetry, and this poem is full of the permission statements that later women used and is important for that reason. She writes, "And let the world think me *inspir'd, or mad,/* I'le surely write whilst paper's to be had." Katherine Philips had used variants more easily identified with the satiric *Difficile est non saturam non scribere*,[31] and other women before Rowe had employed highly imaginative forms. For instance, Galesia in Jane Barker's *Love Intrigues* (1713) writes a pledge to be a poet on an ash tree: "Methinks these Shades, strange Thoughts suggest/ Which beat my Head, and cool my Breast;/ And mind me of a Laurel Crest."[32] Anne Finch's *The Appology* (c. 1706–1709) portrays poetry as a harmless propensity and pleasure and includes a jokey passage in which she compares her writing to other women's frailties: "Lamia to the manly Bumper flys" while the poet "heats her brain" by writing poetry.[33] As for Rowe, the setting inspires and reinforces the dedication to poetry, and being a poet is determined by the Muses, her fate, or destiny. Later poets claim a vocation in the manner Rowe did. In *The Power of Destiny*, Mary Whateley writes that even were she a man her "strong Propensity" to "write in Rhyme" would have determined that she would be a poet: "In short, whatever my Employ had been,/ It soon had yielded to this darling *Sin*."[34]

More importantly, *To one that perswades me* calls attention to Rowe more insistently than her other poems. She refers to her experience at boarding school, mentions enjoying "Novels" and Sedley's and Dryden's plays, says she is "veh'mently in love,"[35] and for the first time describes the setting and lifestyle that allow her to write:

> All that a Poet loves I have in view,
> *Delightsome Hills, refreshing Shades,*
>   *and pleasant Valleys too,*
> Fair spreading Valleys cloath'd with lasting green,
> And Sunny Banks with gilded *streams between,*
> *Gay as Elisium,* in a Lovers Dream,
> Or *Flora's* Mansion, seated by a stream,
> Where free from sullen cares I live at ease,
> Indulge my Muse, and wishes, as I please,
> Exempt from all that looks like want or strife,
> *I smoothly glide along the Plains of Life,*
> Thus Fate conspires, and what can I do to't?

She concludes, "And welcome all the *inspiring* tender things;/ That please my *genius*, suit my make and years." In this declaration of independence, Rowe blends idiomatic, direct language ("*Old Puss* [her boarding school teacher] shall damn no more") with descriptions and ideas that display the pastoral bent that she develops and increasingly relies on in her poetry and prose.

Rowe's 1693–1704 poetry includes many poems and passages about courtship, love, and marriage, and she was making the most important decision eighteenth-century women ever made: whom to marry. The themes evident in her personal life reinforce the seriousness with which she regarded shaping her lifestyle and reveal aspects of her temperament that have been overlooked but strongly color her writing. The men who courted

Elizabeth Singer and in whom she had various kinds of interest were not dull, plodding, steady sorts. She frustrated and even exasperated Dunton and Matthew Prior, although it must be said that both were demanding and exasperating men. As Kathryn King has described, Dunton behaved extravagantly and published flamboyant accounts of their relationship with threats to publish the five hundred letters they had allegedly exchanged.[36] Matthew Prior seemed set on testing her acceptance of him by refusing to conform to her demands on his behavior. He insulted her religion and sent her his obscene reworking of the Baucus and Philemon myth, *The Ladle* (1703), then nudged her to comment on it. Both men found she was "exquisite at giving one uneasiness so far off" and occasionally expressed anger.[37] Both men were volatile in other circumstances. Other suitors, Isaac Watts and the American Benjamin Colman, also found her willful and independent and were known for holding their own. Thomas Rowe had "natural warmth in his temper of which he had not always a perfect command."[38]

Unlike the others, however, Rowe was the son and grandson of Nonconformist clergymen and a dedicated, impressive scholar who had been educated at the University of Leiden (the English universities were not open to Dissenters). He was a poet and translator and, when he died of consumption in 1715 at age twenty-eight, was working on a series of lives of classical heroes who had opposed tyranny as Nonconformists believed they were. Elizabeth Rowe's poetry about love and him is strikingly sensual, and his poems in *Miscellaneous Works* seem to address Rowe as Tibullus's Delia. His translation of Tibullus *Book 1. Elegy 3* and *An Ode. To Delia* are included in her *Miscellaneous Works*.[39] In *An Epistle to a Friend, Written in the Spring 1710* (the year they were married), he writes, "Tell her how I waste away/. . ./ Waste in woes the tedious night,/. . ./ That brings not *Delia* to my sight" (2:267), and in the Tibullus translation: "Nor *Delia*'s here, whose presence could create/ Health and new life, each raging pain abate,/ And reconcile my soul to all the ills of fate" (2:248).

The poetry that Prior published in 1703 may be a remarkable record of his hopes and frustrations with her, one that metaphorically and allegorically expresses experiences mirrored in Dunton's and Colman's correspondence with her.[40] *The Ladle* includes a realistic vignette of marriage:

> The honest Farmer and his Wife,
> To Years declin'd from Prime of Life,
> Had struggl'd with the Marriage Noose;
> As almost ev'ry Couple does:
> Sometimes, My Plague! sometimes, My Darling!
> Kissing to Day, to Morrow snarling;
> Jointly submitting to endure
> That Evil, which admits no Cure.
> (lines 79–85)

In Ovid's *Metamorphoses*, Jupiter grants the old couple who had been his gracious hosts a wish, and they ask to die together. In Prior's version, the couple is granted three wishes, and the wife blurts out, "A Ladle for our Silver Dish/ Is what I want, is what I Wish." The husband is enraged at the wasting of the valuable wish, and says, "I Wish the Ladle in your A—." That his aggravation brings about violence and then the loss of all three wishes might be symbolic. Running through the correspondence of Rowe's suitors are two alternating tones: practical, grounded statements and fanciful, platonic posturing. Although published lovers' letters shared this characteristic, Rowe seems to have demanded more of the latter than most actual correspondents—or somehow called it out of rather different men. In *The Ladle*'s mythological account—which concludes with the outburst of anger that must be repaired—the practical lines about marriage ("My Plague!" . . . "My Darling!") seem of a piece with the apparently hardheaded Colman's slotting of his relationship with Rowe.[41]

Rowe also seems to have drawn men into writing unusually specifically about her physical body. Prior complained of not yet having the opportunity of "saluting" (kissing) her, and Colman described her as "comely in body, lowly in dress."[42] Her marriage to Thomas was described as a "frenzy of love,"[43] and Dunton went further than any of them by publishing this description: "Her MOUTH is little and pretty, her LIPS of a charming Red. . . . As to her NECK and BREASTS, they are the best size that ever you saw, and of a dazling Whiteness, as well as her ARMS and HANDS: As to her BODY 'tis small and of a curious (meaning 'beautifully wrought') Shape, and is supported with handsome LEGGS, as I do believe (for I never saw 'em)."[44] She was also drawn to men who enjoyed poetry and drew poetry out of them. A biographer describes her as falling "hotly in love" with Isaac Watts upon reading his *Horae Lyricae*,[45] and reading their hymns side-by-side as the years pass reveals reciprocal influence. Most of the men addressed poems to her, and all associated poetry with her, which suggests the success of her efforts to define herself as a woman writer. Colman, for instance, upon request wrote of Rowe and her father's estate: "Such Eden's streams, and Banks, and tow'ring Groves:/ Such Eve her self, and such her Muse and loves."[46]

These years of courtship were the years during which she gained a reputation as a writer, first as Dunton's Pindarick Lady and then as "Philomela," the heavenly singer of Frome, both begun as fanciful projections onto her that pleased her. She drew each man into her world: each came to her rural retreat, visited her father's estate or the Thynne's gardens and gracious home, and then was expected to write of a pastoral retreat. Each experienced her unusual romantic spirit, active imagination, idealism, and religious seriousness as she transformed tumultuous and potentially volatile relationships into the sort of idealized courtship found throughout her later life writings. Equally important, while she was casting her suitors as poets and pastoral figures, in her 1694–1704 poetry she began to reveal simultaneously that she thought of herself as a poet.

By 1704, Rowe may have been the most respected English woman poet of all time; she was certainly a phenomenon of interest. Eight of her poems were published in Jacob Tonson's prestigious and profitable *Poetical Miscellanies: The Fifth Part* (1704), and she was the headliner on the title page of the first edition of *Divine Hymns and Poems on Several Occasions. By Philomela and Several other ingenious Persons*, which prints thirty-five of her poems.[47] *The Vision*, the poem that Rowe selected to open the collection of poems she left for publication, was first published in Tonson's *Miscellany*. It has been read as a statement of her commitments as a poet, a giving up of themes other than religious. Contextualizing it with her 1694–1704 poems, however, suggests that it is also experimental, a trying on of voices and poetic stances. In the same *Miscellany*, Rowe published two paraphrases of parts of Torquato Tasso's *Jerusalem Delivered*, including the section on Armida's Garden; pastorals, including *An Imitation of a Pastoral of Mrs. Killegrew's*; and a coterie poem, *In Praise of Memory; Inscrib'd to the Honourable the Lady Worsely*. As in the *Athenian Mercury* and the 1696 collected poems, she displays a range of styles, influences, and original work.[48] *The Vision*, however, like *To one that perswades me*, is important life writing. It expresses dissatisfaction with the quality of her previously written religious poetry, and an accurate way to interpret the poem may be that it introduces to the public one of the most engaged and creative religious poets in English literary history. A few of the other poems in this collection include extended life-writing passages. *On the Creation*, a narrative poem filled with vivid imagery, for example, links her "aspiring Muse" to her themes.[49]

In *The Vision*, the setting and the state of mind that was anticipated in *To one that perswades me* is more fully realized and beautifully described. She rehearses the subjects of her poetry:

> 'Twas here, within this happy place retir'd,
> Harmonious pleasures all my soul inspir'd;
> I take my lyre, and try each tuneful string,
> Now war, now love, and beauty's force would sing:
> To heav'nly subjects now, in serious lays,
> I strive my faint, unskilful voice to raise:
> But as I unresolv'd and doubtful lay,
> My cares in easy slumbers glide away;
> Nor with such grateful sleep, such soothing rest,
> And dreams like this I e'er before was bless'd;
> . . . .
> The place was all with heav'nly light o'er-flown,
> And glorious with immortal splendor shone;
> When! lo a bright ethereal youth drew near,
> . . . .

Angelic his address, his tuneful voice
Inspir'd a thousand elevating joys:
When thus the wond'rous youth his silence broke,
And with an accent all celestial spoke.

To heav'n, nor longer pause, devote thy songs,
To heav'n the muse's sacred art belongs;
Let his unbounded glory be thy theme,
Who fills th' eternal regions with his fame;
And when death's fatal sleep shall close thine eyes,
In triumph we'll attend thee to the skies;
We'll crown thee there with everlasting bays,
And teach thee all our celebrated lays.
This spoke, the shining vision upward flies,
And darts as lightning thro' the cleaving skies.[50]

The poem begins with a leisurely retreat into a peaceful bower, the kind of setting so beautifully created by Anne Finch, who had become part of Rowe's circle at Longleat, the country estate of the Weymouth family.[51] With phrases such as "sacred contemplation" and "lofty arches," the verse anticipates the conclusion with its harmony among setting, poetry, and Heaven. In the next verse, the inspired poet takes the traditional lyre and then names the subjects of her earlier poems. Yet unsatisfied—"faint, unskilful voice," "unresolv'd and doubtful"—the poet falls asleep. The calm verses give way to the second set of verses, the appearance of the vision and his address to her. "To heav'n, nor longer pause, devote thy songs," the vision says, and his speech gives her the great subject of her verse but also brings her into the highest rank of poets. She will be crowned with "everlasting bays," and the angels will, in turn, teach her their "lays." This poem is an unusual example of the then-popular poems that describe the poetic kinds and identify the ones most congenial to the author as Finch's *The Critic and the Writer of Fables* does. Without hesitation or apology, she identifies herself as a poet, transforms the classical topos into a Christian one, and describes the embrace of her vocation. The poem's subtle move to place the poet among the angels rather than among the poets on Parnassus or in the Elysium Fields, as progress and circuit of Apollo poems do, is the kind of little-noticed, confident, self-assertion that should be read as an imaginative adaptation of a familiar poetic form and as life-writing inscribing her authorial identity.[52]

ROWE'S LEGACY

To one that perswades me to leave the Muses begins with a description of a beautiful natural setting with these lines:

> Since Heaven to me has a *Retreat assign'd*,
> That would inspire a less *harmonious* mind.
> All that a Poet loves I have in view

The Vision opens with a similar setting, this time with understated religious imagery such as "lofty arches" formed by tree branches, and affirms, "Harmonious pleasures all my soul inspir'd;/ I take my lyre." For the rest of her life, Rowe creates such spaces and develops revisionary uses for them. These spaces are recurring imaginative situations that can be identified as life writing. This natural space becomes a place for creativity, inspiration, contemplation, consolation, and intimate friendship. As it will for poets extending through the Romantic period, it becomes associated with inspired poetry that brings humankind, the natural world, and metaphysics together. Her texts, then, are the space in which she creates an identity as a writer and the lifestyle that supported it, one that she then influentially propagated. These texts almost invisibly left her major legacy.[53]

The most original and influential use of this space came to be a secular one and is prominent in a number of tales in *Friendship in Death* (1728) and *Letters Moral and Entertaining* (1728–1733). In them, women (and occasionally men) find secluded, beautiful outdoor retreats. Their stories are often formulaic, familiar to all readers of English prose fiction written in the first decades of the eighteenth century, but Rowe adds several elements that will, in their turn, come to be a code if not a formula in eighteenth-century fiction. Women find peace of mind and acceptance of their circumstances in these secluded natural settings. Another person, usually a male suitor-to-be but sometimes a woman, comes into the setting. The heroine "auditions" this person, and, if he or she proves to be entirely in harmony with her lifestyle and principles, an ideal union results. Melinda, for instance, loses all of her money, disguises herself as a servant, and eventually becomes the financially secure companion to the sea captain's wife who has employed her.[54] In another story, Bellamour enters a cottage he finds, not bothering to knock since he assumes no "persons of distinction" live there. He walks all the way upstairs where he opens a door and finds a mother reading to two beautiful daughters, who are wearing white and embroidering flowers on white silk.[55] The house is a magic kingdom filled with cultural articles, such as a harpsichord, globes and folios of maps, fine furniture, and books, including opera music books. The accomplished women in their cultured setting prefigure, of course, the community that Sarah Scott creates in *Millenium Hall* (1762). In this story, however, the sisters and their mother audition and test Bellamour and Alphonso, another suitor, and happy marriages result.

One of the most detailed stories, one with a rare religious element, is the story of Rosalinda, told over several letters, as most of these are. Rosalinda runs away from the father who would marry her to a "Papist" and becomes an upper servant.[56] This disguised, persecuted heroine trades her brocades, jewels, and "fine China on an Indian cabinet" for "flowers in her bosom" and helps her mistress arrange "a set of Delft dishes on a free-stone chimney-piece" (2:12–13). The mistress treats Rosalinda like a sister as they chat and decorate the house, and her only work is with her needle in "some verdant retreat" (3:128). She encounters a "gentle youth" in an "Arcadian" setting reading _Pastor Fido_: "you would believe him some poetical form: he is so elegant, so beautiful" (2:8). This tale, like most of hers, is remarkably specific about material objects and economics. This "prince" is from a noble family, one "remarkable for heroes and beauties," but his extravagant ancestors have reduced the estate to a mere two to three hundred pounds a year (2:8).

Fiction of the first half of the century usually depicted ideal love with sexual attraction as well as intellectual and temperamental harmony, and Rowe builds this element in dramatically. She reverses a signature scene in amatory fiction by having Rosalinda come upon "the lovely youth reclined on a mossy bank, lost in downy sleep" in a fragrant honeysuckle bower (2:11). She gazes on Lucius for a while and then slips away. In six letters, Rowe stages encounters in which the lovers become acquainted, and Rosalinda's agency is developed. Then he inherits an additional £6,000. Once married, Rosalinda continues to drift around the gardens, ornamenting the estate as it provides a beautiful setting for her. She describes herself as "charm'd with the wonders of the poetical world" (3:134) and enjoys books and elevated conversation. Rosalinda, the rightful heir to £8,000, hears that her father is pleased with her noble marriage and hopes for reconciliation. This is, of course, an early example of inheritance repair,[57] and Rowe is also one of the first writers to repair fortunes with commercial gain from the Empire.

Rowe's narratives of women who withdraw from society, often in disguise, contrast to the survival narratives written by Aubin and Haywood in more than their happy endings. In fictions such as Haywood's _The British Recluse_ (1722) and _The Rash Resolve_ (1723), the women can seem like exiles beaten from the field, and the endings, as with _The Rash Resolve_ in which the mother surrenders the child she has carefully reared to his father and conveniently dies, are unsatisfactory. In contrast, Rowe creates the beautiful life and depicts the virtuous life; yet virtue is not the sole requirement for happiness. Moreover, her heroines differ widely in their propensities, temperaments, and preferences and are self-aware about these characteristics. Lavinia in Part 2, letter 4, is one of the women who retires to the country to avoid the temptation of an improper passion. The style of the letter indicates her lively temper, her ability to laugh at herself, and, most of all, her delight in the city and its fashionable abundance. Her element is in the world of the Duke's shapely legs with clocks on his stockings and his gilded wainscots, not her ancestral home, "a Gothick heap" with bow rather than Venetian windows. She writes self-consciously about not being happy but hoping to acclimate herself and find her "delicacy" worn off. Reading the religious musings of characters as ideological, while correct, is incomplete. Amintor's coming to terms with the death of his wife is nuanced rather than an example of a flattened ideology. In the final six-letter sequence in Part 3, Laura, Charlotte, and Philocles are all somewhat developed and change over the course of their encounters. Charlotte, for example, comes to take initiative and display agency.

Rather than following their lovers, Rowe's women take the initiative in retiring and are discovered by men worthy of them. They establish relationships and a sociopolitical order that contrast markedly to those they have left and that their friends describe in their letters. The number of women who escape repressive situations, situations that threaten their selfhood and moral aspirations, through disguise is striking. Rowe's heroines are determined, daring, and resourceful. When these women are placed beside the heroines of other tales in which women go into solitary retreat, their dedication to autonomy and preservation of a lifestyle—interior and social— make clear that the theme of independence is more central in Rowe's work than in fiction by other women immediately preceding her. In the 1720s, the fraction of novels had risen to 0.51 percent of published books,[58] and, as Rowe's writing, especially *The History of Joseph*, indicates, Rowe knew this fiction. In a time when women writers were using the conclusions of prose fictions to demonstrate the implications of social practices and to emphasize that there were no satisfactory solutions to numerous situations, Rowe dramatizes the struggle for peace of mind and moves fiction in a new, obviously welcome direction. In fact, her fictions appeared in the time of the lowest output of prose fiction, a fact I interpret to indicate that the plots, themes, and devices of the 1720s had burned out.[59]

Rowe seems to be refining rather than challenging women's abilities and roles. Her women characters are happiest and most themselves when they live in a private sphere narrative. If the roles and activities of these couples are strongly gendered and traditional, the relationships are not. The women are alike in virtue, intelligence, discrimination, mutual interests, and respect, but they control the pace of the courtship and make the final determination of the outcome, including, if there is marriage, the couple's activities. In later volumes of the letters, Rowe begins to develop theories of charity, and the characters are shown in relation to more people of various ages and classes, as Rosalinda and Lucius are in their benevolence and, more strikingly, in their conversations with, for instance, a poor minister's daughter.

While the earlier novelists expose the ramifications of the existing sex-gender system for women, Rowe shows characters fighting to attain peace of mind and managing to carve out an autonomous existence within repressive situations. This struggle becomes the central plotline for later novelists such as Mary Collyer and Elizabeth Griffith.[60] Rowe introduces "liberty" into fiction by domesticating the term that was a current site of hegemonic struggle. Characters in plays were demanding "dear liberty," and women poets such as Sarah Fyge Egerton and even Anne Finch were railing against "custom," which restricted their freedom to use discretionary time productively (Egerton, for instance, mentions the liberty to think philosophically).[61] Octavia Walsh compared her longing for solitary time in a natural retreat to slaves' for life and liberty: "In this Retreat permit me now to seek/ For my own self, from whom I long have stray'd."[62] Rowe thus joins a major cultural debate, and what personal liberty should mean is negotiated with husbands and public opinion. Sometimes Rowe's women succeed by dropping down the social scale, either by retiring to the country or by disguising themselves as upper servants. Sometimes, as later heroines do, with great effort they scale down their desires and, in consequence, their image of happiness, as Frances Burney's Cecilia does. Rosalinda describes the ideal she has accepted:

> Just as the bounds of this luxuriant retreat stands an antient oak; the extended boughs are a shelter from the mid-day sun, which perhaps your Ladyship would endure, rather than screen your beauty in such a rustick shade: *Elysian* groves and myrtle bowers are better suited to the delicacy of your imagination; but I am now reconciled to nature in its greatest negligence, and seated in this venerable recess, find virtue and liberty the principal springs of human happiness. My hours are here at my own disposal, nor am I obliged to devote them to ceremony and vain amusements. I find myself under no necessity . . . to do a thousand unreasonable things for fear of being singular and out of the mode. (3:129)

"Liberty," "virtue," and a beautiful natural setting make perfect happiness—as does "I am now reconciled." This utopian state, hard won and different from what the young woman imagined, is attained by many later novel heroines. Characters found this life in the wilds of Canada, by an abusive husband's bedside, and on a garden bench in the moments free from domestic care. This life was glorified in novels such as Sarah Scott's *Millenium Hall*, and domestic scenes came to feature accomplished women forming female-only families in aesthetic settings like Rowe's little society in the cottage.

Because of her representation of reading, of appreciation of poetry and music, and of the aestheticism of the garden settings—highly cultivated or "wild"—Rowe's fictions were powerful, concentrated carriers of the polite moralism or gentility movement. Lawrence Klein identifies 1660–1730 as the period during which "'politeness' rose to prominence in English discourse," and, because of who she was, Rowe's fictions appearing when they did gave impetus to the establishment of these values. Concerned with civility, "reasonableness," moderation, proper behavior, the "art of pleasing in company," "refined sociability," and "grasp of form," these texts and hers propagated, institutionalized, and established as normative the values inherent in the *Tatler, Spectator,* and especially Shaftesbury's *Characteristicks of Men, Manners, Opinions* (1711).[63] Through the conduct of Rowe's protagonists and through the identification of an imagined audience with admirable characters, Rowe introduced a model that became ubiquitous in the novels by women for most of the rest of the century. In addition to her firm moral principles, she had a highly developed taste for pleasure, what Lawrence Klein has called "capacities and interests concerned with the 'ornamental' aspects of life, such as taste, style, fashion, and politeness."[64] Jerry Beasley pointed out that she and Aubin were "conscious innovators." He notes that by "licensing the author's invention to play freely over its subject" writers like Rowe "confirmed new possibilities of form, range, and seriousness in contemporary novelistic fiction."[65] Beasley and John Richetti, among the pioneers of close reading of early women's fiction, opened doors with their suggestive observations, but later critics have ignored opportunities to integrate Rowe in their studies of themes, narrative strategies, and trends.

Rowe's self, especially her interior life and its harmony with natural settings, became increasingly prominent subjects in her writing in the 1690s. This writerly self developed in her middle years when she circulated her poems widely in manuscript, a practice we now regard as a kind of publication. Her friends encouraged her, read her work, and thought of her as a writer. In 1728, when she was fifty-four, she published *Friendship in Death* and began a period demonstrating both seasoned professionalism and an affirmation of herself as a writer. The three volumes of *Letters Moral and Entertaining* and the original and expanded *History of Joseph* appeared; Edmund Curll capitalized on the moment with a new edition of her poetry, *Philomela*, and it is divided into the subjects of her poetry, including "Poems Sacred to Love and Friendship." Her knowledgeable, experimental approach to prose fiction and poetry is everywhere evident. For example, half of the *Devout Soliloquies* are blank verse and half are heroic couplets; both kinds have varied stanza patterns. *The History of Joseph* draws richly upon the fiction of her time and is one of the most creative long narrative biblical tales of the century.[66] Indeed, she may have intended it to be an epic in the family with Milton's and his classical antecedents, as is suggested by its construction and allegorical development.

At the time of her death she was collecting and arranging (and occasionally slightly revising) her poetry. She gave the bulk of her work to her in-law relatives Theophilus Rowe and Henry Grove and the manuscript that became *Devout Exercises for the Heart in Meditation and Soliloquy* (1738) to Isaac Watts to publish. The only other woman poet of the century to do this kind of careful preparation for immortality was Anna Seward, well known for her strong self-perception as a critic, poet, and literary force and for her aggressive participation in critical controversies. Both women show consideration of the advantages (such as reputation and market appeal) and of the likelihood of publication in their choices, as Seward chose Sir Walter Scott for her poetry and Archibald Constable, publisher and founder of the *Edinburgh Review*, for her letters.

Rowe left as her legacy the example of an active, charitable, virtuous *life as a woman writer*. She was among the most-read writers of the century as demonstrated by a comparison among the sales of the combined *Robinson Crusoe* and *Farther Adventures* by Defoe (the customary way they were sold), Samuel Richardson's *Clarissa* (1748–1749), and her collected prose fictions. In the 1740s, there were three editions of *RC/FA* and six of Rowe's; in the 1750s, four of *RC/FA*, five of *Clarissa*, and nine of hers, and in the 1760s four of *RC/FA*, three of *Clarissa*, and an astonishing fourteen of hers. By 1825, there had been at least eighty-eight editions of *Friendship in Death*, seventy-nine including *Letters Moral and Entertaining*, and at least 111 of *Devout Exercises of the Heart*. Visitors, including many of the bluestockings, traveled to Longleat and read the Countess of Hertford's collection of her poems and letters.[67] Part of the *Memoirs* of her life that had prefaced the *Miscellaneous Works* was serialized in *The Gentleman's Magazine*, and the editor introduced it by saying they are sure it will be of interest because they *"daily* receive Encomiums" on the occasion of her death.[68] Her poetry and prose fiction were enormously influential both in content and form. Dozens of books like Elizabeth Harrison's *Miscellanies on Moral and Religious Subjects* (1756) were recognized as written under her influence.[69] Indeed, I found no examples of the phrase "Moral and Entertaining" in titles before hers, but beginning in 1740 there was a marked increase in fictions with it in the title. Early examples suggest the breadth of its popularity: *Conversations Moral and Entertaining, between an English gentleman and A Knight of Malta* (1740) and *Novellas españolas: Or moral and entertaining novels translated from the Spanish* (1746). Ann Murry's *Mentoria: or, the Young Ladies Instructor, in Familiar Conversations on Moral and Entertaining Subjects*, first published in 1778, enjoyed eight more editions in ten years.

With Richardson's *Pamela* (1740), Rowe's fictions look forward to and helped inspire many mid-century novels by women that define and illustrate a new, "accomplished" woman whose private and social conduct is a civilizing model that aims to become normative. More significantly for women, she shifted attention from victimhood to the kingdom of the mind. Beasley argues that for Rowe and Penelope Aubin the imagination became "a potential source of moral and emotional truth, proving by their example that prose fiction, acknowledged as such, might be as reliable a record of human life . . . as the most conspicuously authenticated biographies . . . many of which were themselves surreptitious fictions."[70] The life Rowe constructed and lived and the ability of her characters to imagine and actualize a similar lifestyle valorized the power of the mind. By the end of the century, many women had interiorized Rowe's conception. Anne Hunter, for instance, begins a poem, "Dear tranquil shades, where freedom reigns,/ Where calm content has fix'd her seat." She continues with verses on solitary reading and on a friend, whose presence is "most welcome to my peaceful vale."[71] We have not yet begun to identify the degree and specifics of her influence as a writer and as a woman asserting her identity as a writer.

NOTES

1. Among these focused studies are Norma Clarke, "Soft Passions and Darling Themes from Elizabeth Singer Rowe (1674–1737) to Elizabeth Carter (1717–1806)," *Women's Writing* 7 (2000): 353–71; Sarah Prescott, "Elizabeth Singer Rowe: Politics, Passion, and Piety" in *Women and Poetry, 1660–1750*, ed. Sarah Prescott and David E. Shuttleton (Houndmills, Basingstoke: Palgrave Macmillan, 2003), 71–78; Sharon Achinson, "'Pleasure by Description': Elizabeth Singer Rowe's Enlightened Milton" in *Milton and the Grounds of Contention*, ed. Mark Kelly, Michael Lieb, and John Shawcross (Pittsburgh, PA: Duquesne University Press, 2003), 64–87; and Kathryn King, "Elizabeth Singer Rowe's Tactical Use of Print and Manuscript" in *Women's Writing and the Circulation of Ideas*, ed. George Justice and Nathan Tinker (Cambridge: Cambridge University Press, 2002), 158–81. One of the few recent studies to address Rowe's fiction is Sarah Prescott's "The Debt to Pleasure: Eliza Haywood's Love in Excess and Women's Fiction of the 1720s," *Women's Writing* 7 (2000): 427–45.

2. This essay is adapted from my in-progress book, *Revising the History of the Novel*. Many of these arguments are worked out in detail in it. I would like to thank my research assistant, Elizabeth Kent, for her contributions to these projects.

3. Nancy K. Miller, "The Entangled Self: Genre Bondage in the Age of the Memoir," *PMLA* 122 (2007): 545. Thomas Mayer and Daniel Woolf agree that the term allows consideration of "a much broader range of forms than even an elastic meaning of biography can easily stretch around." See *The Rhetorics of Life-Writing in Early Modern Europe*, ed. Mayer and Woolf (Ann Arbor: University of Michigan Press, 1995), 26n 1. Carolyn Barros and Johanna Smith note that the term "draws in and validates variant forms of first-person narratives." See *Life-Writings by British Women, 1660–1815*, ed. Barros and Smith (Boston: Northeastern University Press, 2000), 21.

4. Marlene Kadar, "Whose Life Is It Anyway?" in *Essays on Life Writing*, ed. Marlene Kadar (Toronto: University of Toronto Press, 1992), 4. She is paraphrasing one of Sidonie Smith's insights from *A Poetics of Women's Autobiography: Marginality and the Fictions of Self-Representation* (Bloomington: Indiana University Press, 1987).

5. Ulric Neisser, "Five Kinds of Self-Knowledge," *Philosophical Psychology* 1 (1988): 35–59. Among those categories are race, ethnicity, class, and gender. Paul

John Eakin summarizes some of the research on the conceptual self and argues, "Much of the most interesting work in autobiography studies in the last ten years has . . . been devoted to the conceptual self, exploring the 'vast background of cultural presuppositions' that informs it." See *How Our Lives Become Stories: Making Selves* (Ithaca, NY: Cornell University Press, 1999), 35.

6. *The Confessions of St. Augustine*, trans. Rex Warner (New York: Mentor, 1963), Bk. 10, chap. 2, p. 212; qtd. in James Olney, *Memory and Narrative: The Weave of Life-Writing* (Chicago: University of Chicago Press, 1998), 116.

7. Olney, *Memory and Narrative*, 17.

8. Ibid., 422.

9. Olney notes that the term "periautography" refers to the assignment to write intellectual memoirs that resulted in *The Autobiography of Giambattista Vico* (Pt. 1, 1725; Pt. 2, 1731). See *Memory and Narrative*, xv, 16–17, 417–22.

10. Sidonie Smith and Julia Watson, "Fifty-two Genres of Life Narrative," *Reading Autobiography: A Guide for Interpreting Life Narratives* (Minneapolis: University of Minnesota Press, 2001), 197; and Smith, "Performativity, Autobiographical Practice, Resistance," *Auto/biography Studies* 10 (1995): 21.

11. This epithet was one of James Sterling's exuberant descriptions in *To Mrs. Eliza Haywood on Her Writings*, one of the prefatory poems in the 1725 edition of her *Secret Histories, Novels and Poems*.

12. Susan Stanford Friedman, "Women's Autobiographical Selves: Theory and Practice" in *The Private Self*, ed. Shari Benstock (Chapel Hill: University of North Carolina Press, 1988), 39.

13. Summarized by Shirley Neuman, "Autobiography: From Different Poetics to a Poetics of Differences" in *Essays on Life Writing*, ed. Kadar, 223.

14. Keith Thomas points out that "In early modern times, this sense of individuality becomes more visible" and "the idea that everyone had a distinctive 'inner' self, held in check by the demands of living with other people, was widely expressed." See *The Ends of Life: Roads to Fulfillment in Early Modern England* (Oxford: Oxford University Press, 2009), respectively 38 and 40, and see 37–43, 107, and 188–89. See also Galen Strawson, *Selves: An Essay in Revisionary Metaphysics* (Oxford: Oxford University Press, 2009).

15. *Essay concerning Human Understanding* (1690), fifth ed. (London, 1706), 2:27, 223; and Thomas, *Ends of Life*, 40. See also Dror Wahrman, *Making of the Modern Self: Identity and Culture in Eighteenth-Century England* (New Haven, CT: Yale University Press, 2004) and David Wootton, "The Language of Self: The Birth of Self-Consciousness," appendix to "Unhappy Voltaire, or 'I Shall Never Get Over it as Long as I Live,'" *History Workshop Journal* 50 (Autumn 2000): 148, 152.

16. These expressions by women have been primarily located in diaries and letters. See James Daybell, *Women Letter-Writers in Tudor England* (Oxford: Oxford University Press, 2006).

17. See N. H. Keeble's discussion of "liberation into self-hood" among Nonconformists in *The Literary Culture of Nonconformity in Later Seventeenth-Century England* (Athens: University of Georgia Press, 1987), 196–205; "true identity," 204. Evidence could be multiplied endlessly; for example, in 1662, Richard Baxter preached a series of sermons titled "The Mischiefs of Self-Ignorance," and linguists have docu-

mented that many of our words including "self" were coined in such texts. Tellingly, many of Keith Thomas's examples are from the writings of Nonconformists.

18. Keeble, *Literary Culture*, especially 135–50.

19. Ibid., 208.

20. Henry Grove and Theophilus Rowe, "The Life of Mrs. Elizabeth Rowe" in *The Miscellaneous Works in Prose and Verse of Mrs. Elizabeth Rowe*, two vols. (London, 1739), 1:li. *The Athenian Mercury* mentions Singer's poem, *King William Passing the Boyn* in the December 1, 1691, issue. Dunton published it when he collected her poetry into a volume in 1696.

21. Dunton's wife Elizabeth was the daughter of Samuel Annesley who had been educated at Oxford, received an honorary doctorate from Oxford through the influence of the Earl of Pembroke, preached before the House of Commons, and, after becoming a Nonconformist in 1662, developed the largest Dissenting meetinghouse in London in spite of relentless persecution. See Paula Backscheider, *Daniel Defoe: His Life* (Baltimore, MD: Johns Hopkins University Press, 1989), 7–9.

22. *The Supplement to the First Volume of the Athenian Gazette; containing the Transactions and Experiments of the Forreign Virtuoso's* (London, 1691), 5–8.

23. Volume one of the paper, then called *The Athenian Gazette*, read simply, "Proposed by the Ingenious," (from March 17 to May 30, 1691). This statement appeared on many single issues in the first year. The collected papers in volume two also have *Gazette* on the cover, although individual issues have been the *Athenian Mercury* for weeks.

24. *Athenian Mercury*, July 11, 1691, p. 1. In the January 12, 1691/1692, issue, Sappho and Behn are compared. Behn was strongly royalist, and Dunton's praise for her is remarkable in that strongly partisan time.

25. See my "Hanging On and Hanging In: Women's Struggle to Participate in Public Sphere Debate" in *Everyday Revolutions*, ed. Diane Boyd and Marta Kvande (Newark: University of Delaware Press, 2008), 30–66.

26. Among the poets for whom it was especially important are Jane Brereton and even Elizabeth Carter. Mary Robinson rose to being the poetry editor for the *Morning Post*.

27. Keeble, *Literary Culture*, 146–47.

28. A remarkable number of eighteenth-century women poets left a portrait of themselves as young women in which they were dressed rather fancifully and arranged their hair in abundant ringlets and also had a portrait of themselves as mature women in the "poet costume"—a sober, draped outfit with hair in a bun or under a cap.

29. *The Athenian Mercury* 12 (October 24, 1693), 1–2.

30. See *Epistle to Dr Arbuthnot* (1735) in *Imitations of Horace*, ed. John Butt, *The Poems of Alexander Pope*, vol. 4 (London: Methuen & Co.; New Haven, CT: Yale University Press, 1961), lines 129–30; and *The Dunciad, with notes variorum* in *The Dunciad*, ed. James Sutherland, *The Poems of Alexander Pope*, vol. 3 (London: Methuen & Co.; New Haven, CT: Yale University Press, 1963), lines 190–93. Pope also styles his a "gentle Muse" in similar lines; see *Epistle to Mr Jervas* and *Epistle to Dr Arbuthnot*. Pope knew her poetry well; he published Rowe's *On the Death of Mr. Thomas Rowe* in his second edition of *Eloisa to Abelard* in 1720.

31. Cf., *Lucasia* ("but pity does engage/ My Pen to rescue the declining Age") and *To the Honoured Lady E.G.* ("To write with more success than I can live,/ To cure the Age") in *Poems* (London, 1667), respectively 34 and 61.

32. Jane Barker, *Love Intrigues* in *Popular Fiction by Women, 1660–1730*, ed. Paula Backscheider and John Richetti (Oxford: Clarendon, 1996), 88.

33. *The Poems of Anne Countess of Winchilsea*, ed. Myra Reynolds (Chicago: University of Chicago Press, 1903), 13.

34. Mary Whateley, *The Power of Destiny, Original Poems on Several Occasions* (London, 1764), 13–16. See also Jane Brereton's *Epistle to Mrs. Anne Griffiths, Poems on Several Occasions* (London, 1744), 33–35. After the publication of Pope's poetry, his lines, especially from *Epistle to Dr. Arbuthnot*, became a common source of women's permission to write statements.

35. If this is a factual statement, Benjamin Colman is the most likely referent.

36. These accounts are scattered throughout Dunton's publications, most notably *The Athenian Spy* (1704), *The Life and Errors of John Dunton, Citizen of London* (1705), and *Athenianism: or, the New Projects of Mr. John Dunton* (1710). *The Double Courtship* is a sixty-one-page description in *Athenianism*. See Kathryn King's excellent account, "Elizabeth Singer Rowe's Tactical use of Print and Manuscript," in *Women's Writing and the Circulation of Ideas: Manuscript Publication in England, 1550–1800*, ed. George L. Justice and Nathan Tinker (Cambridge: Cambridge University Press), 161–66. King calls *The Double Courtship* "alternately hilarious and sinister," 165.

37. See especially Prior's letter of November 16, 1703, excerpted in H. Bunker Wright, "Matthew Prior and Elizabeth Singer," *Philological Quarterly*, 24 (1945): 75–76. The quotation is from Prior's letter, 76. Shortly after Dunton's wife died in May 1697, he hurried to see Rowe, was summarily dismissed, and married hastily and badly.

38. Considering the source, Theophilus Rowe's biography, Thomas Rowe must have had more than ordinary temper. See "The Life of Mrs. Elizabeth Rowe," lxxii.

39. Interestingly, given Elizabeth's many writings about death, Tibullus often seems haunted by death, and it is in Elegy 1.3 that he writes, "Death with your greedy hands, Death, black Death, hold off!/ Hold off, black Death, I beg; my mother is far away;/ she cannot gather my burned bones to her grieving breast." And on the century's enjoyment of Tibullus, see Paula Backscheider, *Eighteenth-Century Women Poets and Their Poetry: Inventing Agency, Inventing Genre* (Baltimore, MD: Johns Hopkins University Press, 2005), 279–86; quotation from 280.

40. The poems are conveniently grouped by year in the standard edition, *The Literary Works of Matthew Prior*, ed. H. Bunker Wright and Monroe K. Spears, two vols. (Oxford: Clarendon, 1959), 1:196–214. Compare, for instance, *To a Lady: She refusing to continue a Dispute with me, and leaving me in the Argument* (1:200–202) with surviving correspondence. See Wright, "Matthew Prior and Elizabeth Singer," 71–82.

41. See Matthew Prior, *The Ladle*, in *The Literary Works of Matthew Prior*, 1: 202–7. Adaptations of this poem were common; both Jonathan Swift and Lady Mary Montagu wrote witty variations. See also Clayton Chapman, "Benjamin Colman and Philomela," *New England Quarterly* 42 (1969): 214–31.

42. Wright, "Matthew Prior and Elizabeth Singer," 79, and Chapman, "Colman and Philomela," 219, respectively.

43. Thomas Wright, *Isaac Watts and Contemporary Hymn Writers* (London; Farncombe & Sons, 1914), 104. See his somewhat fervid account of Rowe's courtship and marriage, 72–77, 101–4.

44. Dunton, "The Double Courtship," 3.

45. Thomas Wright, *Isaac Watts and Contemporary Hymn Writers*, 73.

46. Quoted in Chapman, "Benjamin Colman and Philomela," 219.

47. The publication history of this collection is somewhat confusing. The second edition changes the title slightly and the order of the names: *A Collection of Divine Hymns and Poems on Several Occasions by the Earl of Roscommon, John Dryden, Mr. Dennis, Mr. Norris, Mrs. Kath. Phillips, Mrs. Singer and others.* The first collection was printed by R. Janeway for R. Burrough, both known for religious publications, and the next added the prestigious John Baker to the "printed for" list. The 1709 oddly returns to "Philomela," and the 1719 returns to Mrs. Singer. This time it is printed for W. Taylor, publisher of *Robinson Crusoe.*

48. In 1696, he collected her poems and published *Poems on Several Occasions. Written by Philomela.* These early poems reveal a woman who knew traditional and popular poetic forms, who wrote on a wide variety of subjects including friendship, politics, public figures, various kinds of love, and philosophy, and was already ambitiously experimenting with form. In addition to Pindaric odes, there were verse epistles (Horatian and Ovidian), pastorals (monologue and dialogue), fables, eulogies, songs, and elegies. She was conversant with the poetry of women as well as men, as poems influenced by Katherine Philips and a poem published later, *An Imitation of a Pastoral of Mrs. Killigrew's,* indicate. Some poems employ techniques associated with Crashaw, Herbert (a poet vigorously defended and recommended by the *Athenian Mercury*), and Matthew Prior, and, like so many poets of her generation, she tried verse with Milton's *Il Penseroso* and *L'Allegro* in mind. *To Madam S— at Court* is a lighthearted cavalier lyric.

49. *Poetical Miscellanies: The Fifth Part . . . By the most eminent hands* (London, 1704), 379.

50. The changes from the 1704 to the version in the 1739 are minor, and, because capitalization and punctuation have been somewhat modernized, I have reprinted the latter. The only significant variant is the change of the line "His lovely Brows Immortal Lawrel bind" to "Wreaths of immortal palm his temples bind," a Christian rather than a Greek wreath. See *Miscellaneous Works,* vol. 1, 1–3.

51. Rowe's father was an acquaintance of Henry Thynne, and he became Elizabeth's French and Italian tutor. She and his daughter Frances, later Countess of Hertford, became close friends in spite of the twenty-five-year difference in ages. See Sarah Prescott's summary, *Women, Authorship and Literary Culture* (Houndmills: Palgrave Macmillan, 2003), 174–82.

52. A large number of poets in the long eighteenth-century wrote these popular poems. In the circuit of Apollo poems, Apollo came to earth, searched for excellent poets, and crowned the best; the progress poems traced a history of poetry, sometimes beginning with the Greeks and sometimes with English poets. Both were important to canon formation.

53. In the interest of brevity, I will not trace the development and uses through the religious poetry of Rowe's middle years.

54. This device occurs in slightly earlier fiction; examples are Eliza Haywood's *Rash Resolve* and Arthur Blackamore, *Luck at Last*, both 1723. Similar parallels could be identified for Rowe's other prose fictions.

55. The story of Melinda is in Rowe, *Letters Moral and Entertaining* collected with *Friendship in Death*, ed. Josephine Grider, two vols. (New York: Garland, 1972), 2:76–84, and of Bellamour and the sisters, 1:131–38 and 2:68–72; quotations, 1:132. All references to Rowe's *Letters Moral and Entertaining* are to this edition.

56. The story of Rosalinda is in *Letters Moral and Entertaining* 2:1–18 and 3:126–42. In addition to contextualizing Rowe's work with women's prose fiction, she should also be considered in relation to Nonconformist writing. Defoe, for instance, has the story of a woman who discovers she is married to a Papist as Part II of *Religious Courtship* (1722); it could have served as a warning to Rosalinda.

57. I am pointing out the later apparatus for what Michael McKeon discussed as "patriline repair" in *The Origins of the English Novel, 1600–1740* (Baltimore, MD: Johns Hopkins University Press, 1987), 132–33.

58. Paula Backscheider, "The Novel's Gendered Space" in *Revising Women: Eighteenth-Century "Women's Fiction" and Social Engagement*, ed. Backscheider (Baltimore, MD: Johns Hopkins University Press, 2000), 6.

59. Cheryl Turner lists forty-nine novels published by women in the 1720s and only seven in the 1730s (she does not include Rowe's *Letters*); William McBurney's *Check List of English Prose Fiction 1700–1739* (Cambridge, MA: Harvard University Press, 1960) shows a similar precipitous drop. See Turner, *Living by the Pen* (London: Routledge, 1994), 212–13.

60. For somewhat different reasons, Beasley cites Rowe's influence on Richardsonian and post-Richardsonian fiction. See *Novels of the 1740s* (Athens: University of Georgia Press, 1982), 174–78.

61. See *The Emulation* and also lines 1–8, 33–35, of *The Liberty* (both 1703).

62. Octavia Walsh, "On Solitude" (1734), in *British Women Poets of the Long Eighteenth Century: An Anthology*, ed. Paula Backscheider and Catherine Ingrassia (Baltimore, MD: Johns Hopkins University Press, 2009), 339.

63. Discussions of this movement are numerous; see Lawrence Klein, "Shaftesbury and the Progress of Politeness," *Eighteenth Century Studies* 18 (1984–1985): 186–214, and "Politeness for Plebes" in *The Consumption of Culture, 1600–1800*, ed. Ann Bermingham and John Brewer (London: Routledge, 1995), 63–82, and John Brewer, "'The most polite age and the most vicious': Attitudes towards culture as a commodity, 1660–1800" in *The Consumption of Culture*, 341–45. Helen Sard Hughes reports that Rowe enjoyed Shaftesbury's *Characteristics of Men, Manners, Opinions, Times* and Berkeley's *Minute Philosopher*. See "Thomson and the Countess of Hertford," *Modern Philology* 25 (1928): 445.

64. Klein, "Politeness for Plebes," 364.

65. Beasley, *Novels of the 1740s*, 165, 166 respectively.

66. This poem should be contextualized with Milton's *Samson Agonistes*, Cowley's *Davideis*, Prior's *Solomon*, Elizabeth Hands's *Death of Amnon* (1789), and Yearsley's *On Jephthah's Vow*.

67. Melanie Bigold, "Elizabeth Rowe's Fictional and Familiar Letters: Exemplarity, Enthusiasm, and the Production of Posthumous Meaning," *British Journal for Eighteenth-Century Studies* 29 (2006): 3. Bigold notes that Rowe's letter writing "was

a fundamentally formative literary activity that reinforced her sense of a literary vocation in the republic of letters," 2.

68. Emphasis mine. *Gentleman's Magazine* 9 (1739): 261.

69. See Samuel Johnson's review of this book in *The Literary Magazine* 1 (September 15, 1756–October 15, 1756), 282–88.

70. Beasley, *Novels of the 1740s*, 166.

71. Anne Hunter, *Ode to Conduit Vale, Blackheath* in *British Women Poets of the Long Eighteenth Century*, 357.

4

The Headwaters of Ooziness
(Richardson the Polemicist)

Alexander Pettit

James L. W. West III, editor of F. Scott Fitzgerald and Theodore Dreiser and biographer of William Styron, has recently declared scholarly editing "an exercise in *biography*." While acknowledging the importance of "variant tables, diagrams, and lists of emendations," West maintains that what editors really do is "construct in their minds a conception of the author's creative personality that will undergird all that they, as editors, wish to do to the texts."[1]

West's observation helped inspire my work as editor of Samuel Richardson's early publications, most pertinently his polemical pamphlets.[2] I was intrigued to discover that the "creative personality" created or exhumed during the process belonged to a very nasty man whose nastiness is of a very familiar sort in the early years of the twenty-first century. I began my initial research shortly after George W. Bush's victory in the hugely controversial 2000 presidential election; I completed the task almost eight years later, as a very different sort of citizen prepared to assume the presidency, having flourished in spite of a noxious campaign in which his patriotism, his religion, and his integrity were shrilly and often maliciously called into question. To my ears, the rhetoric of the American right, circa 2008, sounded distinctly Richardsonian, and Richardson seemed prescient of those qualities that one might least like to find flourishing 250 years after the author's death. This confluence made my work both more troubling and more interesting than it might otherwise have been.

Immersion in this author at this time has made me appreciate Coleridge's brief biography of Richardson. Like Coleridge, I "greatly, very greatly, admire" Richardson on the basis of his novels (particularly *Clarissa*),[3] or at least I usually experience only intermittent difficulty enduring the author's self-congratulatory Puritanism in works that offer much by way of compensation. Coleridge famously qualified his praise, however, and no one has identified Richardson's toxicity with greater skill than he. The Richardson that Coleridge was "vexed" to admire was a sickroom-smelling über-moralist saddled with a mind "so very vile . . . so oozy, hypocritical, praise-mad, canting, envious, [and] concupiscent."[4] Richardson has disgusted countless readers less eloquent than Coleridge, of course, but academics, at least, have perhaps been willing to overlook Richardson's oozier side because the author has helped focus important debates about class and gender. Now that these discussions have, in effect, become institutionalized, it may be that we no longer require this service. Absent this contribution, Coleridge's Richardson becomes easier to discern.

Not the least remarkable feature of Coleridge's appraisal is that Coleridge almost certainly wrote it in ignorance of the works that would best have supported it. Cantingness, specifically, and vileness and ooziness more generally, declare themselves with impressive force in works that Coleridge presumably did not read and, in any case, would not have associated with Richardson: *The Infidel Convicted* (1731), freshly attributed to Richardson; *The Apprentice's Vade Mecum* (1735), known as Richardson's since 1943 but recently demonstrated to be a pastiche of original and borrowed prose; and *A Seasonable Examination of the Pleas and Pretensions of the Proprietors of, and Subscribers to, Play-Houses* (1735), since 1954 recognized as Richardson's and as beholden to *The Apprentice's Vade Mecum* for some of its content.[5] If editing a text is shaping a life, then reporting on a life shaped by editing would seem to fall within the purview of an editor's responsibility. In the opinion of this editor, the Richardson who emerges, hostile to both new ideas and simple pleasures, is far more oozy than admirable.

The most pertinent feature of Richardson's polemical efforts is their interconnectedness. Extensive sections of *The Infidel Convicted*—incorporating precedent bits from Addison's *Evidences of the Christian Religion* (1721)— appeared in the third part of *The Apprentice's Vade Mecum*. The first part of *The Apprentice's Vade Mecum*, in turn, provided much of the anti-theater screed for the *Seasonable Examination*. Alan Dugald McKillop and John A. Dussinger have variously noted these borrowings; from Keith Maslen, we know that Richardson printed all three pamphlets.[6]

These overlays have biographical and generic implications. Richardson's tendency to restate a small set of prejudices in a variety of contexts suggests a nearer congruency of author and utterance than obtains in the comparatively sophisticated polemics with which the period abounds. Richardson often seems to have been playing a game without realizing that it *was* a game. His interest remained fixed on forms of social control, not on modes of discourse; and the performativity intrinsic to the liveliest sort of polemic was alien to him. Witless and unrelentingly sincere, Richardson mounted a triadic assault on the pitfalls that he saw yawning before unformed youngsters. He battled on two overlapping fronts: irreligion (*The Infidel Convicted* and *The Apprentice's Vade Mecum*) and its supposed agent, the stage (*The Apprentice's Vade Mecum* and the *Seasonable Examination*). The movement of his pamphlets is toward greater specificity and prescriptiveness: the bigoted and largely preceptual deductions from scripture and patristic history of *The Infidel Convicted* are honed and reapplied in *The Apprentice's Vade Mecum*, then advanced in support of a specific piece of anti-theater legislation in the *Seasonable Examination*.

Although modern readers are quick to recognize the imprecise relationship between writer and voice in satire, we are slower to impute this complexity to polemical writing. This is understandable, given that satirists such as Pope and Swift reward study in ways that Henry St. John, Viscount Bolingbroke, and John, Lord Hervey do not. But the genres are not discrete. Pope, for example, is often incidentally a polemicist, and Swift is often avowedly one. Our lack of interest in the generic particulars of polemic, however, have impeded recognition of Richardson's shortcomings as a polemicist, specifically his unconventional lack of ambition with respect to performativity—or pretense, or vocalization, or the careful deployment of character or personae.

Polemic in the period characteristically attempts some degree of vocal complexity. For example, the *Craftsman*, the most successful newspaper associated with the opposition to Sir Robert Walpole, purported to be the work of one "Caleb D'Anvers," a mellow gent "in the cool Evening of Life, when our Passions are more easily governed."[7] Yet the three principals who collectively inhabited that pseudonym—Bolingbroke, William Pulteney, and Nicholas Amhurst—were all hearty and sub-fifty in 1731 (Amhurst was only thirty), and no one has seriously suggested that any of these men was dispassionate. By way of counterpoint to this contractive, unitary persona, Bolingbroke, solo, would pretend to polyvocality in *Remarks on the History of England* (1730–1731) and *A Dissertation upon Parties* (1733–1734), both originally published in the *Craftsman* and both purporting to be transcriptions by one Humphrey Oldcastle of the "minutes" of a disinterested "Company, which often meets, rather to live than to drink together."[8] Even the title of the paper engaged the playful conventions of the genre: the "craftsman" was the "crafty" Walpole, the paper's target, not its eidolon or its voice. The contributors to the *Craftsman* knew that sophisticated polemic, like sophisticated satire, required a protean sense of identity, the better to convey the modulations of authority that keep readers off-balance and interested.

These affectations describe generic practices, not biographies or, necessarily, beliefs. It is an open question how much the contributors to the *Craftsman* actually cared about the material they produced, ideologically speaking.

Bolingbroke's insincerity is legendary; Pulteney jilted the opposition upon the receipt of a peerage in 1742; and Amhurst, widely regarded as opportunistic, was rumored to have offered his services to Walpole prior to having sold them to Bolingbroke and Pulteney.[9] The paper's principals were notably uninterested in the travails of those who facilitated the circulation of their ideas. When the paper's first printer, Richard Francklin, was jailed in 1730 for printing the fifth and sixth installments of the *Remarks on the History of England*, Bolingbroke was content to plow ahead with the offending series, even as Amhurst favored caution and Francklin, released after one week, prepared for trial.[10] Seven years later, Francklin's successor Henry Haines was jailed for printing the *Craftsman* for July 2, 1737. His abandonment by Amhurst, Pulteney, and Francklin prompted the outrageously acerbic *Treachery, Baseness, and Cruelty Display'd to the Full; in the Hardships and Sufferings of Mr. Henry Haines, Late Printer of The Country Journal, or, Craftsman* (1740), in which Haines blistered the paper's principals for their "Perfidy *and* Baseness" in hanging him out to dry.[11] The "liberty" that Caleb D'Anvers trumpeted in number after number was evidently of the theoretical sort.

Unlike the corporate Caleb, Richardson eschewed the use of personae, favoring, insofar as anonymous publication allows, a direct and uncomplicated mode of address. His rota of topics was as narrow as Bolingbroke's but seems narrower still due to the vocal or characterological uniformity with which he presents it. The loss of vocal agility is compensated for by a gain in sincerity, or what we might imagine as credible, if rhetorically straitening, passion. Richardson the polemicist seems to be writing "as" Richardson, transferring whole passages from text to text and context to context as he does so.

The Infidel Convicted, which bears the date 1731 on its title page, was first advertised in the *Daily Journal* for December 7, 1730. In the advertisement as on the title page, the work promises a "Brief DEFENCE of the CHRISTIAN REVELATION," while promoting a paternalistic or pedagogical angle of a sort that would characterize Richardson throughout his career as a writer: he "address'd" the work "to the serious Consideration of the British Youth in general, and in particular of such of the Young Gentlemen of the Inns of Court, as are tainted with Atheistical or Deistical Principles, but are not wholly given up to a Reprobate Mind."[12] As Dussinger has demonstrated, the compilation draws heavily on works by Sherlock, Locke, Addison, and others.[13] Dussinger notes that the subtitle of *The Infidel Convicted* corresponds to Richardson's address in *The Apprentice's Vade Mecum* to "young working-class men who might be 'infected' by the same disease of deism and scepticism."[14] The importing of material on regulating the behavior of youth from *The Infidel Convicted* into *The Apprentice's Vade Mecum* (and from that work into the *Seasonable Examination*) would ensure the continuance of Richardson's high-minded inoculative program.

Dussinger recognizes that the similar modes of address are only the most outward instance of textual bequeathal. A whopping 3,424 words from *The Infidel Convicted* would reappear in *The Apprentice's Vade Mecum*; again, material already dragged from Addison into Richardson's first pamphlet would be dragged into his second one, there to complement disparate entries from an olio of intolerance titled *The Scholar's Manual* (1733) and to squat sourly alongside happier if also revenant passages from Locke's *Reasonableness of Christianity* (1695).[15] The professedly cumulative nature of *The Infidel Convicted* (and *The Scholar's Manual*) represents a large class of pamphlets in the period, the intent of which is to present the author or compiler as one of many writers pressing precisely the same point. As the subtitle of *The Infidel Convicted* suggests ("Corroborated by Unanswerable ARGUMENTS from Mr. LOCKE"), some authorities had particular cachet at such times, none more than Locke, Christian scripture excepted. Because polemic is—or, in skilled hands, pretends to be—doggedly literalistic and hostile to the nuances of the sources that it adduces in support of its own blunt agenda, works like *The Infidel Convicted* and *The Scholar's Manual* operate in part by presenting flattening and otherwise distortive recontextualizations of the sources upon which they draw. Unlike his more artistic contemporaries, Richardson presents these recontextualizations through his own voice and without a hint of irony.

Richardson's initial target in *The Infidel Convicted* is the anti-miraculist Thomas Woolston (d. 1733), author of *Moderator between an Infidel and an Apostate* (1725); the six *Discourses on the Miracles of our Saviour* (1727–1729); and the two-part *Mr. Woolston's Defence of His Discourses on the Miracles of Our Saviour* (1729–1730). This "Scoffer" (*IC*, 10) had been imprisoned several times in the late 1720s and early 1730s and seems to have been released from custody, although not allowed to reside outside of the Mint, roughly five months before the publication of *The Infidel Convicted*.[16] The pamphlet is part of a clangorous exchange about and by Woolston during the years 1729 and 1730, and Richardson's own contribution may reasonably be seen as an argument against allowing Woolston the sorts of civil liberties that smugger citizens had by 1730 come to take for granted. Woolston would die in the Mint, his ongoing persecution no doubt bolstered by the climate of bigotry into which he had been released and to which Richardson had contributed.

Woolston's argument throughout the *Discourses* and the *Defence* was that scripture read literally offered more silliness than substance. Read metaphorically, Woolston asserted, scripture took on considerable resonance and directive power, and for this reason he would continue to define himself as a Christian, in spite of the literalist harangue that his writing inspired. Into the fray jumped Richardson, trailing clouds of Addison and scripture. Richardson's question-begging retort is thin, and as such no service to, most notably, Locke: we know, Richardson asserts, that the miracles reported by the four Evangelists were empirical phenomena—not "*allegorical* and *mystical*" ones (*IC* 12)—because the Evangelists say as much, and their authority is unimpeachable. Richardson tacks on a coda in which he claims that skeptics like Woolston stand condemned proleptically as the latter-day "Scoffers" that St. Peter had safely if sneeringly envisioned in his second epistle.[17]

More disturbing still is the transparency with which Richardson moves from arguing for the validity of exegetical literalism (to reject Christ's miracles is to reject the "*whole Canon; the Old,* as well as the *New Testament*" [*IC,* 13]) to arguing for its rectitude and utility as a means of social control. The bulkiest section that Richardson would transport from *The Infidel Convicted* into *The Apprentice's Vade Mecum* concerns the regulative power of Christianity, particularly with respect to those lower than Richardson on the social scale. Richardson introduces this section by noticing "*Two* shocking *Letters* from a *Deist* to his *Friend,* lately published": an alarmist pamphlet, printed by Richardson, entitled *Two Letters from a Deist to His Friend, Concerning the Truth and Propagation of Deism, in Opposition to Christianity* (1730).[18] Dussinger notes that Nicholas Stevens wrote the letters in question and that the clergyman and poet Samuel Wesley (the elder) provided the commentary.[19] In both *The Infidel Convicted* and *The Apprentice's Vade Mecum,* Richardson draws on Wesley's cautionary Preface: "[The letters] were written by one who was then a member of the University of *Oxford,* but since expell'd; and found in the escrutore of his unhappy friend, who sent himself out of this world by his own hands, to learn the truth of a future state."[20] Wesley's design in compiling and commenting on the letters—and possibly Richardson's design in printing them—was to provide a circussy glimpse into the mind of the "real" Deist, in fact a young scholar whose studies in divinity had caused him to question the wisdom of his teachers. "The following Letters," the barker barks, "indeed pull off the mask, and present a very unusual spectacle, a *Deist* speaking his real sentiments, which are as contrary to his pretentions, as light to darkness."[21] The spectacle pretends to humanitarian status when Wesley says of the comments that he has appended to Stevens's private letters, "God grant they may be instrumental towards keeping men from that place of torment, which is ordain'd for hypocrites and unbelievers."[22] Eagerly endorsing the pretense of a pietist as confident and inflexible as himself, Richardson would claim that Wesley had "sufficiently expose[d] the *iniquitous Design*" of deists (*IC,* 22; *AVM,* 69).

Wesley had done no such thing. Instead, he posited a causal relationship between two phenomena that were not demonstrably correlative. A disturbed youngster of twenty or twenty-one had corresponded with a contemporary whose studies had raised in him concerns about "the self-interested designs of tyrannical Priests" and whose lucubrations were unequal to the task of reconciling a good God and "the dismal apprehensions of eternal damnation." This young recipient had subsequently killed himself.[23] Richardson, enthusiast for fallacy that he was, must have been rendered nearly rapturous by Wesley's grotesque deployment of *post hoc ergo propter hoc.*

Richardson would also have appreciated Wesley's interest in social control. He frames his pamphlet as an attempt to enforce orthodoxy and docility among the *"Multitude"* (*IC*, 22, 23); the *"ungovernable Many"* (*IC*, 23); and the *"Generality* of Mankind" (*IC*, 23). Remarking on the Templars at the Inns of Court, whom he regards as the most threatened subset of "British *Youth in general,"* he finds that *"many of* [them] *have taken a very deep Taint of this Infection of Infidelity"* and that *"many of* [them] *affect servilely to repeat . . . the senseless Buffoonery and lewd Scoffs of the most virulent Apostate that has appear'd since the Time of the Emperor* Julian" (*IC*, iii)—invoking, historically, the anti-Christian emperor Flavius Claudius Julianus (AD 331–63) and, hysterically, Julian's alleged progeny, indigent Tom Woolston of the Mint. Wesley opts for demographic breadth and Richardson for specificity, but the authors share the sense of threat essential to the genre in which they write, however unselfconsciously. When Richardson nods at *"the principal Leaders of the present Apostacy"* (*IC*, i), we recognize the familiar gambit whereby alarmists seek to threaten their readers with images of fecund threat and to rally them to beat it back—thereby incidentally implying that the "threat" is not so threatening as all that. Note the comparative honesty of Pope, whose instances of superpopulous threat in *The Dunciad* and elsewhere are refreshingly immune to amendment.

As always in such instances (Pope's work now included), anarchy is the underlying fear. "Can there by any Assurance," asks Richardson of those who question the literal veracity of scripture, "that Persons so *professedly* abandon'd to their *sensual Appetites,* will be with-held by the *Laws of Society,* much less by a Sense of *Moral Duty,* which they themselves, under the Dominion of their *partial Passions,* are to be the *Judges* of?" (*IC*, 22; *AVM*, 70). Behind the bluster and the familiar drooling linkage of skepticism and sexuality lies an important question about social regulation that, framed less contentiously, had concerned Hobbes and many other bona fide intellectuals. But Richardson does not intend a simple interrogative. By casting the question rhetorically, he tries to render his argument axiomatic: given Woolston, thus anarchy, to skip a step or two. The social controls that Hobbes found necessitated by the fallenness of all humankind, Richardson would apply selectively or, as a logician might have it, relativistically, to those who did not worship as he did. In this way, his ideological confreres are today's Jerry Falwell and James Dobson, not his near contemporaries Hobbes and Harrington.

One might like to suppose that Richardson could have recognized the shoddiness of Wesley's pamphlet (and of Leake's contemporaneous regurgitation). The pretenses of polemic, however, are not sophisticated, nor are they really meant to persuade. Rather, they inflame or, as we say today, "energize a base." Richardson, part of the base at issue, lacked the discrimination necessary to make this simple judgment: in Wesley's work, he saw truth, not affect or stance or even a platform for positions on Church sanctity in which the author had a vested interest. This does not mean that Richardson erred in reading Wesley as sincere. Rather, it means that he erred in not recognizing Wesley (or himself) as operating in a generic medium that is not fundamentally "about" sincerity and that is, as such, an inadequate channel for the dispensation of prescriptive morality.

The exercise in flabby logic that Richardson praises in *The Infidel Convicted* resonates throughout the third part of *The Apprentice's Vade Mecum*, becoming for Richardson an opportunity for practical extrapolation. In both pamphlets, he trades heavily in the sort of prescriptive argument that Wesley had advanced in his account of the suicidal student; but in *The Apprentice's Vade Mecum*, Richardson shifts his attention from the Templars—a rhetorical convenience in *The Infidel Convicted*—to the young apprentices with whom he, as a printer, was intimately familiar and about whose welfare he seems genuinely to have cared.[24] These are the youngsters whom he will safeguard against the perniciousness of such as Stevens and Woolston, who personified to him, as they did to Wesley, the easy tumble from credulousness to skepticism to immorality and the attendant cost to social stability. It is not surprising that in *The Apprentice's Vade Mecum*, Richardson offers his only positive comment on a contemporary play: George Lillo's dreary *London Merchant* (1731), the plot of which follows just this trajectory.[25]

The design of *The Apprentice's Vade Mecum* ensures that Richardson's oozy intolerance will take on the prescriptive tenor for which it yearns in *The Infidel Convicted*. Advertised intermittently during the fall of 1734 and probably published late that year, *The Apprentice's Vade Mecum* comprises three parts, the first two devoted to the training, obligations, and appropriate behaviors of apprentices. The third part, Richardson notes, has been added "*at the Request of a judicious Friend*" (AVM, x), a gambit that he would reuse in *Pamela* (1740) and *Letters Written to and for Particular Friends* (1741). It may be that Richardson here intended William Webster, bigot, clergyman, and editor of the astringent *Weekly Miscellany*, which Richardson printed.[26] Webster may have served a similar function in *Pamela*, the first edition of which included a letter that he may have written, praising Richardson's manuscript and recommending its publication.[27] The possibility that the "*judicious Friend*" of *The Apprentice's Vade Mecum* was Richardson himself, however, is arguably enhanced by the fact that Richardson draws so heavily on his own work from *The Infidel Convicted* in the third section of *The Apprentice's Vade Mecum* and, less confidently still, from Richardson's disquieting laxity with respect to distinguishing real people from his own imaginative creations, most creepily in his commentary on his novels.[28]

If Richardson's *"Friend"* were of the intrapersonal or imaginary sort (or a flesh-and-blood buddy doing Richardson's bidding), then we find in the preface to *The Apprentice's Vade Mecum* a preview of the bifurcation that Richardson would employ in the work's third section. Richardson acknowledges that he is reproducing material from *The Infidel Convicted*, but he credits his own work to *"another Author."*[29] That is, Richardson uses himself in *The Apprentice's Vade Mecum* for much the same purpose as he had employed Locke and others in *The Infidel Convicted*. The accretive effect of the argument registers differently when we recognize Richardson as the author and compiler of the precedent pamphlet. The author's ego comes to the forefront, and, as a consequence of the diminution of the pool of authorities, so does the thinness of the claims that Richardson advances. Repetition thus correlates positively to clangorousness (and ooziness) and negatively to ethos, at least for modern readers aware of the pamphlets' common authorship.

But repetition is not stasis. Pasted into *The Apprentice's Vade Mecum*, the dull controversialist cant of *The Infidel Convicted* takes on a new contextual vigor. The pedagogical pretenses of the earlier work, compromised by the abstractness intrinsic to theological dispute, become clearer in the later one, moored as it is in the practical, quotidian concerns of readers who presumably cared little about the likes of Locke and (in his controversialist mode) Addison.

Richardson presents himself as a reluctant party to the decision to append a third and more abstract section to his guidebook. *"We could not but comply with the Desire"* of the *"Friend"* who recommended the addendum, he avers, recording his own initial inclination to consider only *"Morality,"* rather than religion more broadly, which *"Province,"* Richardson says, he had hoped to *"leave . . . to better Pens"* (x). Richardson posits salubrious morality, but not orthodox religion, as something like a corollary of his two more plainly prescriptive sections. He had indulged, he says, *"the Vanity to hope, that any one who duly attended to the Rules we presumed to lay down, could not make a bad Man, or even an indifferent Member of Society"* (x).

Richardson's initial design was perhaps preferable to the expanded format on which he settled. The assertion that the sustained practice of good behavior habituated youth to a morally dignified life is far from irresponsible; and a cover-to-cover emphasis on deeds and their consequences would have given the pamphlet a cohesiveness that, as Richardson seems to have realized, it ultimately lacked. The *vade mecum* genre is designedly a practical one; and, as we shall see in a moment, Richardson himself apparently declined to believe that ready access to the arcana of theological controversy stood in any immediate way to serve his targeted audience.

So what is the controversialist material *doing* in the pamphlet? Biblio-graphically speaking, bulking it up. At no cost or inconvenience other than that which attends newly setting up type, Richardson was able to import a substantial body of text from other volumes that he had printed. But surely Richardson could have written up a section of milk-and-water morality on short order, without violence to his initial design. Given all this, it seems reasonable to suppose that Richardson persuaded himself or was persuaded that ramping up the final section from "morality" to "religion" served a valid instructional purpose, analogous to the pamphlet's earlier sections on behavior to masters, fellow servants, and so forth. And this purpose seems to have been to register alarm, promote bigotry and racism, and frighten a youthful readership into compliance with the socialized dictates of an extreme sort of Protestantism that was not as widely respected as Richardson liked to pretend.[30] Richardson's design, that is, is not "practical" at all, but in the context of a "practical" manual comes to seem so: as one must avoid taverns, play-houses, and "eye-servants," so must one avoid the company of those who do not share Richardson's doctrinal biases.[31] The abstractions of *The Infidel Convicted* in this way become prescriptive, but—as Richardson seems to have realized when he abandoned his emphasis on "morality"—not quite, or not yet, pertinent. Richardson acknowledges that the section will "be of Use to fortify the Mind of the young Man as he advance[s] to riper Years and Understanding in the Belief and Practice of the Christian Religion" (56), rather than providing guidance in the here and now. Richardson is wriggling. His caveat suggests that he recognized, for example, the limited appeal of the facile retromingent assault on Julian the Apostate and other early opponents of Christianity (see *IC*, 51; *AVM*, 78) to even the period's most precocious working-class tweens and teens, toiling wearily toward their "riper years." Youth, not ripeness, however, describes the intended readers of the pamphlet; and presumably Richardson did not really believe that a dose of patristic polemic administered to an adolescent apprentice could linger long enough to inoculate a mature tradesman. Richardson intended incidentally to give his young readers a heads-up about the snares of heterodoxy that awaited them but principally and more immediately to render them wary of the sort of tolerance that distinguishes the most generous minds of any period.

    The third section begins with an instance of the "horde" trope beloved of polemicists and satirists. "The present Age," Richardson writes, "is so lamentably overrun with Atheism, Deism, and Infidelity, that it is matter of no small Concern, that it should be necessary to caution a young Man on this Head" (55). Is it not distressing, he asks, that

> after upwards of 1700 Years, in which Christianity has triumphed over all its Enemies, converting Principalities and Powers from Paganism to the Light of the Gospel, we should now have our most Holy Religion to defend? And this

not from the successful Invasions of the open and profess'd Enemies of our Faith, which have often overturn'd States and chang'd Religions; but from an upstart Race of Libertines, that have risen up among our selves; and who, under the Notion of Freedom of Thought and Liberty, have run into all manner of Licentiousness. (55–56)

The enemy is within, teeming, muscular, and determined. How weary Richardson's words must have sounded to an intellectually catholic reader in 1743, had such a one have happened upon the text.

Richardson wraps up his defense of the literally miraculous in *The Apprentice's Vade Mecum* by proposing fresh strategies whereby sober youths might avoid Christians who fall into Hawthorne's category of "[i]ndividuals of wiser faith . . . who kn[o]w that Heaven promotes its purposes without aiming at the stage-effect of what is called miraculous interposition."[32] The residual hostility to Woolston, who had died in January 1733, is unseemly, but for the true believer threat survives its local manifestations. Speaking of habitués of "Clubs and Societies" who "propagate Infidelity," Richardson enjoins, "[l]et the Young Man . . . avoid such Company, as the Bane of his future Peace and Welfare" (84). The anti-miraculist is thus on the same footing as the "lewd Women" against whose company Richardson had warned in the first section—somewhat more reasonably to a modern secularist, given the comparative tangibility and inconvenience of diseases biochemically and metaphorically transmitted.[33]

The clap that Richardson's "infidel" transmits is not "infidelity." Worse, apparently, it is "*Doubt*, or *Uncertainty*," specifically "*Religious Doubts . . . of all others the most affecting*," because if the doubter errs, "how dreadful will be the Mistake!"[34] Thus might Pascal have spoken were he witless and of hidebound intellect; thus might not the greater-still Herbert (or Donne, or Johnson) have spoken, he who recognized doubt as the occasion for renewed faith and the application of humility to one's own self, even as he stood, heart and mind vibrant, before the great mystery of God. Ironically, an ideology that insisted on the phenomenological veracity of the most outlandish events reported in scripture sought as well to strip religion of its most compelling feature: the environmental mystery that reminds us of the limitations of our minds and thus of the necessity of our souls. More compelling than miracles that we may choose to interpret literally are those that we can barely intuit, most obviously the presence of divinity itself. One cannot wish the Reformation out of the historical record; but one can observe that Richardson's literalistic Protestant zealotry trades in an acceptance of the preposterous and a rejection of the incomprehensible that is only rarely compatible with mature intellectual inquiry and mature artistic expression. Is this a source of the "sickroom" feeling that disturbed Coleridge? It is, in any case, the quality that informs my own sense of the crabbed "creative personality" of the author whose dingier works I have prepared for republication.

The roughly ten pages transported from *The Apprentice's Vade Mecum* into the *Seasonable Examination* are of a different sort, topically, as one would expect from the occasion of the later pamphlet: the introduction in the House on April 3, 1735, and the committing one week later of "A Bill for Restraining the Number of Houses for Playing of Interludes, and for the better Regulating Common Players of Interludes," nicknamed Barnard's Bill after its author, Sir John Barnard. The Bill was prompted by continuing concerns about the "immorality, violence and the decay of neighborhoods that had provoked antitheatrical sentiments in the late 1720s," when Thomas Odell had opened his Goodman's Fields theater without proper letters patent.[35] A more proximate cause was the reappearance in February 1735 of a mysterious notice from 1733 announcing an abortive or spurious proposal for a new non-patent theater in St. Martins le Grand.[36] The *Seasonable Examination* was published April 28, 1735, in an attempt to shore up support for Barnard's Bill, which would, in fact, tank a mere two days later.[37]

Insofar as it considered plays themselves rather than the urban sordor that their staging occasioned, Barnard's Bill is a vestige of Collierite anxieties about the linguistic and thematic degradation of the English stage, rather than an anticipation of Walpolite concerns about the political dangers of drama that would inform the successful Stage Licensing Act of 1737. One of the Bill's three provisions, for example, prohibited performances of "any Tragedies, Comedies, Plays, Operas, or other Entertainments of the Stage . . . containing any prophane, obscene or scurrilous Passage, or any Passage offensive to Piety or good Manners."[38] Richardson found this much to his liking, as Collier would have done.[39] But Richardson's principal reason for gushing (oozing?) over Barnard's Bill derives from a matter that Collier, writing before the loosening of the patent system and the concomitant expansion of theaters, had no reason to address: the proposed expansion of theaters into mercantile districts. The concern had surfaced several years earlier, upon the opening of Goodman's Fields. At that time, Robert D. Hume notes, the theater's "city neighbours were protesting vigorously at the intrusion of such an enticement to vice and debauchery into a sober business district."[40] Barnard's Bill attempted the difficult task of turning back the clock, in this case by reinstating the patent system that Odell had flouted. As Vincent J. Liesenfeld observes, the bill recognized "three distinct patents . . . and name[d] the individuals in whom they were currently vested."[41] In this way the bill sought the renewed centralization of power among a few patentees and incidentally the acing out of newer entrepreneurs who would expand the theater beyond the precincts that the patentees controlled.

This is right in Richardson's wheelhouse. Arguing a point that the House would soon reject, Richardson defended "the Prerogative of the Crown," which, prior to the opening of the non-patent theaters, "had always . . .

been allow'd to have an indisputable Right to license the Persons who pretended to act or perform Interludes, Plays, or other Entertainments of the Stage"; furthermore, the new entrepreneurs stood "in Defiance of the City-Magistracy, [in order] to avoid whose Cognizance and Controul" theaters were now "to be set up just without the Limits of the City" (*SEPP*, 4). Richardson grounds his call for geographical restriction in an umbrous body of work. "[A]ll our modern Plays," he writes, "and most of our ancient ones too, are calculated for Persons in Upper Life; and . . . the good Instructions, if any, they inculcate, lie much above the common Case" (*SEPP*, 17; *AVM*, 10). His inability or disinclination to name, much less to discuss, an example draws on the familiar "unidentified—thus really scary—threat" motif that he had already imported from *The Infidel Convicted* into *The Apprentice's Vade Mecum* and that continues to characterize particularly craven forms of scare-mongering in the current century. In this respect, Richardson differs from the learned, if admittedly cranky, Collier, who had objected to the representation of the upper classes in plays staged for an undefined audience and had condemned contemporary drama for what he took to be its failure to live up to earlier and more instructive models.[42] Richardson had no interest in dramatic history and regarded the instructive capability of drama as circumscribed by the boundaries of class and, thus, geography that separated himself and his targeted audience from the vague, debauched upper class with which he would continue to fumble in *Pamela*, as Fielding and other anti-Pamelists uncharitably if accurately implied.[43]

Most of the material that Richardson moved from *The Apprentice's Vade Mecum* into the *Seasonable Examination* constituted at its initial appearance a defense of boilerplate language from the apprentice's indenture of retainer against "*haunt*[*ing*] *Taverns or Play-houses*."[44] In the earlier work, Richardson had warned young apprentices of the dangers of relaxation or pleasure. To this end, he had enumerated six principal arguments against the frequenting of playhouses by apprentices: "Because Plays are calculated for Persons in upper Life"; "Because of the Expence of Time and Money"; "Because of the Resort of lewd Women"; "Because Trade and Men of Business are the Objects of Ridicule in most Plays"; "Because of the shameful Depravity of the *British* Stage"; and "Because of the Danger of the Mind's being too much ingag'd and diverted from Business by these Representations"—that is, because of the danger, slangily, of having fun (*AVM*, 10–14). These points recur, abridged, in the *Seasonable Examination* (17–18). Richardson was quick to recognize that Barnard's Bill offered an opportunity to repackage his earlier (already repackaged) work. In the *Weekly Miscellany* for April 26, 1735, for example, *The Apprentice's Vade Mecum* is advertised as containing "*some occasional Remarks on Playhouses, and particularly on that in Goodman's-fields*"; previous advertisements had not noticed the pamphlet's interest in the stage.

Like *The Apprentice's Vade Mecum* (and like *The Infidel Convicted*), the *Seasonable Examination* is a pastiche. When the condensed sextet of objections to the theater appeared in the *Seasonable Examination*, Richardson would credit "a little Treatise, that perhaps has done some Good as to the Case in Hand" (16)—*The Apprentice's Vade Mecum*. Richardson uses the "little Treatise" to rebut the usual welter of menacing voices, here present in the form of long passages from the petitions against the bill that had been received on April 10. Other themes from *The Apprentice's Vade Mecum* appear in paraphrase, without credit.[45]

Once more, Richardson bolsters his authority by invoking his own work. Once more, the polemics at issue register differently depending on whether or not the reader is onto Richardson's trick. Readers outside of Richardson's immediate circle (in these admittedly pre-circular days for Richardson) may have been snookered by the "little Treatise" cited in the *Seasonable Examination*, but readers today need not be. And the "trick" is not innocuous, given the centrality to polemic of accretive and polyvocal argument, the putative distillation of broad collective outrage. It would be inaccurate to regard Richardson as unique or even unusual in employing gimmickry of this sort, but for all that, our "biography" of Richardson must shift a bit when we recognize that the only concordant voice that Richardson advances in the *Seasonable Examination* is his own. This allows us to regard Richardson as isolated, rhetorically, and shouting without much support for an ultimately unworkable piece of legislation.

Richardson's commitment to the suppression of the stage ended with the collapse of Barnard's Bill. He seems to have had nothing to say about the Licensing Act. This makes sense, given the specificity of his interest in protecting working-class youth and his belief that the theater was a playground for folks higher-browed and edgier than himself and his presumed charges. Richardson's involvement in the discussion was circumscribed by his desire to keep the theaters out of mercantile neighborhoods and to keep mercantile workers out of the theaters. As the vagueness of his strictures against "all our modern Plays" suggests, his interest was in social control, not literary criticism or even literature, to use the term more broadly than he would have done. Collier, by comparison, is a model of scholarly engagement.

Granted, the final version of the Licensing Act did include a clause limiting the location of theaters, possibly inserted by Barnard himself.[46] But the main thrust of the Act was elsewhere, specifically on the prepublication examination of playscripts; it may be that this slid the matter as it were rheostatically from the moral to the partisan and pragmatically political zone and, as such, alienated the unaffiliated moralizer Richardson. Like Barnard, Richardson was interested in limiting the access of the population to putatively immoral plays; unlike Walpole, he was not interested in censorship per se. Richardson may even have been irritated with Walpole for his attempts to insinuate into Barnard's Bill a clause, authorizing censorship, that seems to have ensured the Bill's failure.[47] The original provision of the Licensing Act—that any actor, manager, prompter, or other theater personnel lacking the authority granted by "Letters Patent" would be "deemed to be a Rogue and a Vagabond"—might not have interested Richardson that much, either.[48] Richardson's antipathy for the theater endured but in a residual sense, evident when Pamela opines, anachronistically, that "the Stage, by proper Regulations, might be made a profitable Amusement."[49] Otherwise, Richardson seems to have lost interest in the topic.

Richardson's own commentary on his early polemics is dismissive and exculpatory. In a 1753 letter to his Dutch translator Johannes Stinstra, he acknowledged his editorship of Sir Roger L'Estrange's *Aesop's Fables* (1692; 1739) and his authorship of *Letters Written to and for Particular Friends*. Richardson dismisses these works as "not worthy of [Stinstra's] Notice."[50] He repeats this judgment with respect to a "few other little Things of the Pamphlet-kind I have written," while noting that he had composed these unidentified works "with a good intention."[51] Barring the discovery of more "little Things," it is safe to say that Richardson intended the three works on which I have focused in this essay. Richardson's fondness for specious self-deprecation should discourage us from taking his dismissiveness too seriously, the more so as the nod at "good intention" pulls his statement in a different direction altogether: in Richardson's weirdly flat polemics, intention is everything.

The three works that I have discussed may represent Richardson more clearly than polemic usually represents its author. If they do, then Richardson's was indeed a mind "so very vile . . . [and] oozy." I suppose we will always honor *Pamela* because it is provocative, *Clarissa* because it is provocative and irritatingly magnificent, and *Sir Charles Grandison* because, irritatingly, it is there. But by reading these novels alongside Richardson's earlier works, we may be able to recognize in their author a sustained habit of small-mindedness that, while it may merit our interest, need never warrant our approval. At the very least, perhaps we may begin more self-consciously to isolate and reject the "vileness" of a writer who relentlessly played to the worst tendencies of a good people, puffed up all the while with a phony moral exceptionalism that the most tolerant novelist of the eighteenth century lampooned, pitch-perfectly, as "vartue."[52]

NOTES

1. James L. W. West III, "The Scholarly Editor as Biographer," in *Textual Studies and the Common Reader: Essays on Editing Novels and Novelists*, ed. Alexander Pettit (Athens: University of Georgia Press, 2000), 81.

2. My volume of Richardson's early works is forthcoming in *The Cambridge Edition of the Works of Samuel Richardson*, ed. Thomas Keymer et al. (Cambridge: Cambridge University Press).

3. *Coleridge's Notebooks: A Selection*, ed. Seamus Perry (Oxford and New York: Oxford University Press, 2002), 82. Coleridge notes that "it has cost & still costs my philosophy some exertion not to be vexed" by his admiration for Richardson.

4. Ibid, 82. See also Coleridge's comparison of Fielding and Richardson: "To take [Fielding] up after Richardson, is like emerging from a sick-room heated by stoves, into an open lawn, on a breezy day in May," from *Specimens of the Table Talk of Samuel Taylor Coleridge*, ed. Carl Woodring (Princeton, NJ: Princeton University Press, 1990), 295.

5. For the attribution of *The Infidel Convicted*, see John A. Dussinger, "'Stealing in the great doctrines of Christianity': Samuel Richardson as Journalist," *Eighteenth-Century Fiction* 15 (2003): 451–506; for *The Apprentice's Vade Mecum*, see Alan D. McKillop, "Richardson's Advice to an Apprentice," *Journal of English and Germanic Philology* 42 (1943): 40–54, and, for the constituent sources, Dussinger, "Fabrications from Samuel Richardson's Press," *Papers of the Bibliographical Society of America* 100 (2006): 259–79; for the *Seasonable Examination*, see McKillop, "Richardson's Early Writings—Another Pamphlet," *Journal of English and Germanic Philology* 53 (1954): 72–75. References to these works use the abbreviations *IC*, *AVM*, and *SEPP*.

6. See McKillop, "Richardson's Early Writings"; Dussinger, "Stealing," 459–60; and Dussinger, "Fabrications," 263–64. See also Keith Maslen, *Samuel Richardson of London, Printer* (Dunedin: University of Otago, 2002), nos. 397 (*IC*), 616 (*AVM*), 751 (*SEPP*).

7. *Craftsman*, December 4, 1731.

8. *Craftsman*, June 13, 1730.

9. Having failed to form a ministry after Walpole's fall in 1742, Pulteney accepted the earldom of Bath, thereby sacrificing his last claim to credibility. For Amhurst's unsavory reputation, see Simon Varey's essay, "*The Craftsman* 1726–1752: An Historical & Critical Account," in his edition of William Arnall's *The Case of Opposition Stated* (Lewisburg, PA.: Bucknell University Press, 2003), 120.

10. See *Craftsman*, August 15 and 29, 1730. See also Alexander Pettit, *Illusory Consensus: Bolingbroke and the Polemical Response to Walpole, 1730–1737* (Newark: University of Delaware Press, 1997), 37, 65–71, where I endorse the possibility that Bolingbroke's rashness resulted from certainty that Francklin was not in serious legal jeopardy. That argument is perhaps overly generous to Bolingbroke.

11. Henry Haines, *Treachery, Baseness, and Cruelty* (London, 1740), iv. Haines does not identify Pulteney by name; Bolingbroke left England, and the *Craftsman*, in 1735. Amhurst replied to Haines in the *Craftsman* for October 18, 1740. Francklin was again arrested in 1731, this time for printing *Craftsman* for January 2, 1731. On that occasion, a pamphleteer mocked Bolingbroke: "this Hero . . . fights behind little *Franklyn*, and lets him take all the Blows." See *The Craftsman's Doctrine and Practice of the Liberty of the Press Explained to the Meanest Capacity* (London: 1732), 55.

12. Richardson printed the *Daily Journal*. See Maslen, *Samuel Richardson of London*, 300.

13. Dussinger, "Fabrications," 274–75.

14. Dussinger, "Stealing," 460.

15. See Dussinger, "Fabrications," 261–64; for the word count, see 263 n. 9. The material common to *IC* and *AVM* was written by Richardson, excepting two sections from Addison (*Evidences*, 10–12 and, paraphrased, 21–23; *IC*, 50–54; *AVM*, 77–82). *The Scholar's Manual* was compiled by John Leake.

16. The second part of *Mr. Woolston's Defence* was first advertised in the *Daily Journal* for May 28, 1730; on June 18, 1730, the *Grub-Street Journal* noted that "Mr. Woolston is now closely confined in the King's Bench Prison"; the paper added, wittily, that "*Mr.* Woolston *himself owns this to be* literally *true*." For biographical data, see *Oxford Dictionary of National Biography*, s.v. "Woolston, Thomas," by William H. Trapnell (http://www.oxforddnb.com/view/article/29963/).

17. *IC*, 14; see 2 Peter 3:3: "Knowing this first, that there shall come in the last days scoffers, walking after their own lusts" (KJV).

18. *IC*, 22; *AVM*, 69. Dussinger establishes Richardson as the printer of *Two Letters*; see "Fabrications," 273.

19. Dussinger, "Fabrications," 273. Dussinger cites the *ESTC*.

20. *Two Letters*, v; cf. *IC*, 22, *AVM*, 69. Dussinger follows V. H. H. Green's account of the suicide of Robert Jennens and the discovery of Stevens's letters in his desk. The absence of Jennens from the newspapers may suggest that the account is bogus. Stevens fared well, more impressively if he indeed "fled the country" after Jennens's death. See "Fabrications," 273, 274 n. 29. The *London Evening-Post* for August 14, 1731, states that "the Rev. Mr. Nicholas Stevens, M.A. and formerly fellow at Trinity College in Oxford (Son of Henry Stevens, Esq, Serjeant at Law) took the Degree of Doctor in Physick the 25th of July last, with great Applause and Honour." This matches the sketch of Stevens reproduced below, note 23; neither source mentions an expulsion, "former fellow" presumably indicating Stevens's postgraduate status. The death that Dussinger (i.e., Green) imputes to Jennens seems athletic: "[he] committed suicide by cutting his throat and leaping from a window in the Middle Temple at the Inns of Court"; see "Fabrications," 273.

21. *Two Letters*, iv–v.

22. Ibid., vi.

23. Jennens "matr[iculated] 15 Oct., 1722, aged 15"; Stevens, son of Henry Stevens of London, "matr[iculated] 17 Dec., 1720, aged 16"; see Joseph Foster, *Alumni Oxoniensis: The Members of the University of Oxford, 1715–1886* (1891), s.v., "Jennens, Robert" and s.v. "Stevens, Nicholas." The quotations are from *Two Letters*, 2, 17–18. Stevens does not doubt the existence of God. Rather, his observation that "the moral world [is] . . . a very bungling piece of workmanship" prompts him to conclude "that as surely as God is a wise Being, so sure it is that this world has respect to something else," 5.

24. *AVM* originated in a letter from Richardson to his nephew, upon the latter's entrance into apprenticeship; see "An Unpublished Letter; from Mr Samuel Richardson, to His Nephew, Thomas Richardson," *Imperial Review* (1804), 609–16. William M. Sale notes that Richardson "accepted the responsibility for the moral guidance of his apprentices and felt that he stood in the relation both of parent and of master to them." Although Richardson asked exceptionally high premiums, "at all periods" of his career as a printer, "he was prepared to accept boys whose fathers were unable to pay any premium"; this practice, however, was not uncommon. See *Samuel Richardson: Master Printer* (Ithaca, NY: Cornell University Press, 1950), 17, 19.

25. "I could be content to compound with the young City Gentry, that they should go to this Play once a Year, if they would condition, not to desire to go oftner, till another Play of an equally good Moral and Design were acted on the Stage," *AVM*, 16.

26. Maslen, *Samuel Richardson of London*, 300; Richardson printed three books by Webster; see Maslen, nos. 869–71.

27. In their edition of Richardson's novel, Thomas Keymer and Alice Wakely assert that Webster "probably" wrote the letter; see *Pamela*, ed. Keymer and Wakely (Oxford: Oxford University Press, 2001), 526 n. The letter appears on pages 7–10 of that edition.

28. See, most impressively, *Samuel Richardson's Published Commentary on "Clarissa,"* ed. Florian Stuber et al., three vols. (London: Pickering & Chatto, 1998).

29. *AVM*, 69. See also above, n. 15.

30. For racism, see Richardson on the "Absurdities of divers Nations": "many *Indians* . . . worship the Devil," 66. Cf., for instance, Pope, sympathetically, on the "poor Indian" in *An Essay on Man* (1733–1734), 1.99–112; Johnson on the imagined liberation of "Indians" from colonial rule in *Idler* 81 (November 3, 1759); and Fielding's Parson Adams on the superiority of "a virtuous and good *Turk*, or Heathen" to "a vicious and wicked Christian" in *Joseph Andrews*, ed. Martin C. Battestin (Middleton: Wesleyan University Press, 1967), 82.

31. The dual injunction against patronizing taverns and playhouses is codified in the indenture of retainer by which apprentices were bound; Richardson defends it in *AVM*, 7–9, 9–14. For "*Eye-Servant[s]*"—domestics who work only when their employers are watching them—see *AVM*, 27.

32. Nathaniel Hawthorne, *The Scarlet Letter*, ed. William Charvat et al. (Columbus: Ohio State University Press, 1962), 121.

33. See *AVM*, 10; Richardson is warning young men against frequenting the theater. The passage is reproduced in *SEPP*, 17–18.

34. *AVM*, 84. See also Leake, *The Scholar's Manual*, on Deists: "all they say amounts to no more than a *Doubt*. And they expect no other Assurance when they die. So that the utmost of their Hopes is to die in this *Doubt*. And what a dismal Condition it is to die in a Doubt, where the Hazard on the other Side is eternal Misery! It is being in Hell, before they go thither," 20. Richardson reproduces the passage, uncredited, in *AVM*, 68–69.

35. Vincent J. Liesenfeld, *The Licensing Act of 1737* (Madison: University of Wisconsin Press, 1984), 24; for Odell, see Liesenfeld, 15–16.

36. Ibid, 27.

37. Ibid, 53.

38. "A Bill for Restraining the Number of Houses for Playing of Interludes" (London: 1735), in Liesenfeld, *Licensing Act*, 164.

39. See *SEPP*, 12–13, on "the shameful Depravity of the *British* Stage"; cf. Collier, "The Profaneness of the Stage," in *A Short View of the Immorality, and Profaneness of the English Stage* (London: 1698), 56–96.

40. Robert Hume, *Henry Fielding and the London Theatre, 1728–1737* (Oxford: Clarendon Press, 1988), 40.

41. Liesenfeld, *Licensing Act*, 33.

42. See Collier, *Short View*, 141–46, and *A Defence of the Short View of the Immorality and Profaneness of the English Stage* (London: 1699), 21–23.

43. Fielding's critique of Pamela's (and "Booby's") ersatz gentility is codified in *Shamela* (1741). See also John Kelly, whose *Pamela's Conduct in High Life* (1741), as Keymer and Wakely point out, "made a virtue of its respect for etiquette that Pamela had flouted, or that Richardson had simply got wrong," xxvi–xxvii. Keymer and Peter Sabor flesh out this argument in *"Pamela" in the Marketplace* (Cambridge: Cambridge University Press, 2005), 75–80.

44. See above, note 31.

45. See *AVM*, on the seductive "dazling Scene" of the theater (11; cf. *SEPP*, 19); the "incompatib[ility]" of an apprentice's hours and the times of performance (15; cf. *SEPP*, 16); the "infamous Troop of wretched Strollers, who by our very Laws are deemed Vagabonds" (17; cf. *SEPP*, 6); the degraded subjects of contemporary drama (17–18; cf. *SEPP*, 16); and the seediness of neighborhoods in which theaters operated (10, 18–19; cf. *SEPP*, 16–17).

46. See Liesenfeld, *Licensing Act*, 139–40.

47. Ibid., 49–52.

48. "The Licensing Act" (1737), in Liesenfeld, *Licensing Act*, 191. The provision harkens back to early modern legislative attempts to declare actors vagrants (for examples, see Liesenfeld, 161–62) rather than to the recent Barnard's Bill. Richardson had, however, invoked old vagrancy laws in *AVM* and *SEPP*; see above, n. 45.

49. Richardson, *Pamela*, vol. 4 (1742), 81. See also a dyad of letters between a son threatening to *"turn Player"* and his horrified father, who offers assistance should his son settle on "any other Employment" in Richardson's *Letters Written to and for Particular Friends* (London, 1741), 59–61.

50. Richardson to Stinstra, June 2, 1753, in *Selected Letters of Samuel Richardson*, ed. John Carroll (Oxford: Clarendon Press, 1964), 233.

51. Ibid., 234.

5

Cleland's Gospel of "Extasy"

Robert A. Erickson

In one of the earliest discussions of the representation of Nature in John Cleland's *Memoirs of a Woman of Pleasure*, Roy Porter called attention to how certain writers of the English Enlightenment, such as Locke and Shaftesbury, argued that Nature was essentially good and that proper behavior should seek to realize the life-affirming potentialities of human nature rather than to deny, reform, extirpate, or conquer them. The senses were considered essential to human nature, and the purpose of life was the pursuit of happiness and pleasure: "If Nature was good, then desire, far from being sinful, became desirable. And the sexual instincts were undoubtedly natural desires. . . . The body became the seat of sensation, of consciousness; within the Condillacian tradition, touch became the prime sense."[1] This view of psychological morality, Porter argued, informs Cleland's novel: "throughout this work, the 'principle of pleasure' was presumed to be the *primum mobile* of human action. . . . Of the pleasures, sex was reckoned to be supreme and natural. Fanny [Hill] was 'guided by nature only,'" and Fanny is "a woman of pleasure."[2] In this essay, I want to extend the sort of investigation begun by Porter and suggest that Cleland's *Memoirs* of Fanny Hill constitutes a secular neo-libertine "gospel" of sexual ecstasy concerned with expressing a new "Truth" about human sexual relations, permeated with religious allusions that have largely gone undiscussed.[3] More specifically, I argue that the novel testifies to the deification of the phallus as the most important component of life itself. In making this argument, I look particularly at Cleland's subtle intertextual adaptation of three important religious discourses: the representation of Nature and sexuality in Milton's *Paradise Lost*, the religious cultural phenomenon of the sixteenth and seventeenth centuries known as "The Family of Love," and the Gospels of the New Testament.

THE NEW GOLDEN AGE

The *Memoirs* was published in two parts, Volume 1 in November of 1748
and Volume 2 in February of 1749. The second part focuses on the "public" Fanny Hill and recounts her initiation into a utopian community of
prostitutes led by Mrs. Cole, whose household is supported by a group of
wealthy upper-class libertines, young but "veteran voluptuaries" who style
themselves "the restorers of the golden age, and its simplicity of pleasure,
before their innocence became so unjustly branded with the names of
guilt and shame."[4] The golden age Cleland most likely had in mind was
that mythic period in earliest times when human beings lived lives of ease
and pleasure, far removed from toil, pain, and sin, and the version of the
golden age he probably had most vividly in mind was that of Ovid in the
opening of the *Metamorphoses*. Yet Cleland's fictional libertine utopia of
sexual pleasure also recalls Milton's *Paradise Lost*, itself the culmination of
golden-age garden utopias, where "Nature," personified as a bounteous,
fecund, playful and innocent female imaginative artist, becomes an ally of
God, and where "bliss" become Milton's recurring term for sexual pleasure.

Mrs. Cole functions as the successor to the greasy Mrs. Brown of "Volume I" and these two governesses, or bawds, are contrasting versions of the
Mother Midnight figure I have discussed in her various forms (as midwife,
bawd, and fate figure) as she appears in a variety of eighteenth-century
novels, including those by Defoe, Richardson, and Sterne.[5] After giving a
much more conventional depiction of the realities and dangers of early
eighteenth-century prostitution in his account of Mrs. Brown's luring of
Fanny in the first part (Volume I) of the *Memoirs*, Cleland carefully removes
almost all the negative or sordid aspects of prostitution in his portrayal of
Mrs. Cole and her "little family of love" (93). This contrasting of the two
houses of convenience further reinforces the utopian and almost idealized
nature of the community of male and female sexual partners in the second
part. Mrs. Brown's house is not particularly elegant, but Mrs. Cole's establishment has a "drawing room, the floor of which was overspread with a
Turkey-carpet, and all its furniture voluptuously adapted to every demand
of the most study'd luxury" (111). This drawing room, replete with signs of
ease and sumptuousness, becomes the center of the action for an orgiastic
saturnalia of "country dancing" (a common mid-eighteenth-century term
for sexual intercourse) in which Fanny is initiated into Mrs. Cole's family.

Cleland's "restorers" of the golden age seem to represent an idealized
version of the libertine world of Charles II's Restoration, and Fanny's one
love is named Charles. Though he is not a member of Mrs. Cole's secret
institution of libertines, he comes to represent, in virtually god-like fashion,
Cleland's celebration of the power of the phallus. The emphasis in Cleland's version of the golden age paradise is on "liberty," "simplicity," "in-

nocence," and "naked truth," and here the reader finds important parallels between the *Memoirs* and *Paradise Lost*. Milton, too, emphasizes simplicity and naked innocence, as well as "freedom" of the will, with Adam and Eve "Authors to themselves in all" (3.122).[6] Like Milton's Paradise before the Fall, "Then was not guilty shame, dishonest shame / Of Nature's works, honor dishonorable, / Sin-bred, how have ye troubl'd all mankind / With shows . . . of seeming pure, / And banisht from man's life his happiest life, / Simplicity and spotless innocence. / So pass'd they naked on" (4.313–19). With the angel Raphael present, Eve at table "Minister'd naked . . . in those hearts / Love unlibidinous reign'd, nor jealousy / Was understood, the injured Lover's Hell" (5.443–49). Fanny, like Moll Flanders, proudly recalls her natural beauty as "a ruddy, healthy, firm-flesh'd country-maid: and . . . that nature had done enough for me, to set me above owning the least favour to art . . . there was no dress like an undress" (96).

THE FAMILY OF LOVE

Cleland's vocabulary, especially his use of the phrase "little family of love" (93) to describe Mrs. Cole's community of prostitutes, suggests the influence of more than Ovid's paganism and Milton's Christianity. "The House, Service, Community, or Family of Love"—it went by several titles but the latter was its chief appellation—was a heretical religious movement founded in the 1540s by the Dutch visionary Hendrick Niclaes, a prosperous merchant. Niclaes, like his later German counterpart, Jakob Boehme, was a prolific writer, and he had the benefit of a printer in Cologne and a bilingual translator in England.[7] Between 1573 and 1575, eighteen of his works, originally written in the mid-sixteenth century, appeared in English translation, and several communities of the original Family of Love were established on English soil. Niclaes' works were reprinted in the 1640s, and Cleland may well have read some of them. Milton himself refers several times to the "Familists" in his prose works, comparing them without disapproval to the primitive Christians in *The Reason of Church Government* (1642).[8] By the end of the seventeenth century, "Familism" had virtually died out in England, but by the mid-eighteenth century the "family of love" was a byword for religious libertinism.

Drawing upon Alastair Hamilton's useful account, we may describe Niclaes' doctrine as follows: before the Fall, man, or Adam, had enjoyed unity with God, but Adam turned his attention on himself and sought the knowledge of Good and Evil.[9] God then created a new man in his image, Jesus Christ, whose death on the Cross established a new union between God and man. Man again turned aside from God in a second Fall, "a veil had descended between God and humans," the teachings of Christ were abused, Scripture was misinterpreted, and the ceremonies and sacraments of the Church were observed out of superstition.[10] A small group of enlightened souls, however, continued true commemoration of these rituals. Apparently influenced by the medieval doctrine of the three ages of the Trinity (the Old Testament age of the Father, the New Testament age of Christ, and the contemporary age of the Spirit), Niclaes proclaimed that in this, the last age of time, God had sent another "new man" to enlighten the world and to prepare for the New Age. This *Homo Novus* was none other than Niclaes himself, who always signed his prophetic name with his initials, H. N.: God "wrought a great and wonderfull Woorke upon Earth, out of his holie heaven, and raised-upp Mee HN."[11]

The new church he founded was the Family of Love. It welcomed all believers, including Jews and Moslems, but this was God's last call: anyone who failed to heed it would be damned. Like Milton in *De Doctrina Christiana*, the new religion emphasized the authority of the Spirit over the Scriptures and, like the Anabaptists, emphasized adult baptism in obedience to the "Service of Love." The writings attributed to the English Family of Love also stressed, with conspicuous regularity, as Christopher Marsh has shown, the repeated phrase, "it is very true." This peculiar emphasis on the all-encompassing "truth" of Familist doctrine is also seen in two of Niclaes' most important works and is repeated in several key places within Cleland's novel.[12]

Niclaes' writings are characterized by a high degree of ambiguity and even self-contradiction, and this ambiguity made them vulnerable to all sorts of interpretive possibilities by his enemies. The term "House of Love," for example, implied a brothel, and the frequent and multivalent use of the word "love" in his writings blurred distinctions between erotic and religious love. In androcentric language that carried undertones of erotic arousal, especially in the recurrence of the word "upright," Niclaes declared that the process of adult baptism or spiritual regeneration was one in which man became "godded": "God the Father . . . manneth himself according to the inward man . . . godded or made conformable in a good-willing Spirit to the upright Righteousness with Him . . . we . . . bear or carry, as men of God, His holy Name . . . in all love."[13] This spiritually "godded" man enjoyed life in a new paradisal state, a "Land of Peace," or a city of "God's Understanding," what Marsh calls "a mystical Utopia," one that could be reached, apparently, in this life.[14] Niclaes' murky allegorical language further opened him up to the scandalous inference that in this new paradise, nudism and polygamy were the order of the day: "as they are eueryone, spiritual Children of God and Christ, and are not couered with any Foreskinne of the sinfull Flesh . . . therefore do they likewyse, with their spirituall Members, walke naked and uncouered both before God and before one-another. . . . [they] do not vow or bind themselues in the Matrymony of Men, nor yet suffer themselues to be bounde therein: but are like the Angells in Heauen."[15] Niclaes also seems to affirm communal ownership of property and the liberty of the unrestricted gaze: "There is noman that clameth any thing to be his Owne. But all whatsoeuer is theare, is free and is theare left free, in his vpright Foorme. Theare is also noman denyed to vue anything in Freedom, of all what is profitable and needfull for him. For they stande all in the Equitee, as one in the Loue."[16]

Although these assertions are often qualified, Niclaes' enemies, and even some of his followers, fastened on the "freedom" of the elite male and "elder" membership of this church enjoying common property that included the sexual favors of one's neighbor's wife. In the eponymous comedy attributed to Thomas Middleton, the "Family of Love's" central activity, as Marsh points out is, not surprisingly, "extra-marital group sex."[17] The central motif of Familist adultery became a staple in the popular mind. Marsh further notes that the beliefs of such radical sects "were frequently perceived, at least in literary comment, as being inextricably linked to sexually licentious lifestyles." In a work of circa 1641, for example, the Family of Love's members were said to believe "that a man may gaine salvation by shewing himselfe loving, especially to his neighbours wife."[18] In the so-called Surrey Confession of 1561, two alienated members of the Family exposed their former fellows by asserting that the sect affirmed that "Christ is come forth in their fleshe, even as he came forth of the virgin Mary," believed that "all things are ruled by nature, and not directed by God," enjoyed compulsory adultery within the group in obedience to a world before Adam's fall, denied the Trinity and the conventional Christian belief in heaven and hell, and believed no one under thirty should be baptized.[19] Furthermore, "when anyone was received into the congregation he pledged that all his goods would be held in common amongst the rest of the brethren and was welcomed with . . . a ritual kiss of admission."[20]

Before focusing on the text of the *Memoirs*, let us take a brief look at the utopic parallels between the original English version of the Family of Love and Cleland's version. These include the notion that all things are ruled by Nature, the emphasis on public conformity and secret liberty, the language of androcentric dominance and control of the community of believers, the ritual adherence to a "naked truth" held in common, the ritual kiss of admission, the emphasis (whether figurative or literal) on "walking naked and uncovered both before God and one-another" in the secret "service of love," and the sharing of common property. These parallels suggest that Cleland is not making a simple passing allusion to a common byword for religious license when Fanny refers to her "little family of love."

Another important element shared among The Family of Love, *Paradise Lost*, and the *Memoirs*, is angelhood. Niclaes' new "spiritual Children of God and Christ" are not bound in matrimony but move freely "like the Angells in Heauen."[21] When Fanny first sees Charles, her lover-to-be, she asks her reader to imagine "a fair stripling," "his hair in disordered curls," a face with "all the roseate bloom of youth, and all the manly graces" (34–35). This description is based on Milton's picture of Satan in his disguise of the "stripling Cherub" who deceives the archangel Uriel: "Not of the prime, yet such as in his face / Youth smil'd Celestial, and to every Limb / Suitable grace diffus'd . . . Under a Coronet his flowing hair / In curls on either cheek play'd" (3.636–41). Fanny will go on to refer to "this angelic youth" as her "new guardian angel" (38) and "the idol of her senses" (48).[22]

In Mrs. Cole's establishment Fanny "found everything breath[ed] an air of decency, modesty, and order," and she soon finds that "this little family of love" also includes a strong, if again idealized, economic component: "the members found so sensibly their account in a rare alliance of pleasure with interest . . . they had been effectually brought to sacrifice all jealousy, or competition of charms, to a common interest; and consider'd me as a partner, that was bringing no despicable stock of goods [i.e., her body as a commodity] into the trade of the house" (93). As in Milton's Paradise, there is no "jealousy" or "injured lover's hell" in Cleland's libertine utopia, but, as in Niclaes' Family of Love, there is also a potent fiscal incentive for good behavior.

It was typical of eighteenth-century libertine prose fiction, as Peter Wagner and others have shown, to use the language of religion for purposes of burlesque, parody, and satire.[23] Certainly this is part of Cleland's project in the *Memoirs*, and the novel is undoubtedly an exuberant work of comic prose fiction, but clearly there is more than parody and burlesque at work here. The *Memoirs*, whatever else they may be, ultimately celebrate an alternative religion of sexuality, one shaped by both Niclaes and Milton, centered on the power of the phallus, which replaces the early modern sectarian emphasis on the Spirit as the primary source of pleasure, of "extasy." Incorporating features of the most well known, yet least understood, religious movements of revolutionary England, Cleland creates a sexual utopia in which the phallus is the source of salvation for both women and men.

GOSPEL AND LAW

The *Memoirs* of Fanny Hill depict a fictional male fantasy of Ovidian "natural religion" not far removed from what Cleland's biographer refers to as his subject's "belief in 'natural religion' [as] symptomatic of a desire to reform but not destroy an established institution."[24] In his life, Cleland expressed clear affinities with Deism and the notion that all religions have certain fundamental beliefs in common. In a letter to his publisher, Ralph Griffiths, he asserted, "I can safely say without the least offence intended to the Christian one, that all religions seem purely local, and all of them . . . ultimately center in the adoration of Gods, which must be right, however erroneous their different modes of worship may be."[25] The stress on "local" and "natural" gods suggests physicality and "place," and the stress on universal "adoration" suggests an innate religious instinct. This totalizing view of religious experience is analogous to Cleland's lifelong pursuit of a universal language, partially actualized in his slender monograph or "Sketch," *The Way to Things By Words* (1766). In this work, Cleland announces his discovery of the roots of Greek words in the Celtic language, and asserts, "The words we at present make use of, and understand only by common agreement, assume a new air and life in the understanding, when you trace them to their radicals, where you find every word strongly stamped with nature; full of energy, meaning, character, painting, and Poetry. . . . Here I subjoin a few words, in familiar use, which may serve to prove, that words are not merely arbitrary signs, but are, in their original formation, big with meaning, emphatic, and picturesque."[26] One could hardly find a more accurate description of the language of *Fanny Hill*. In this work, Cleland—joyfully and creatively—is concerned not so much with sex as with inventing a new, "radical," and primordial language for sexual experience and relationship. And the *Memoirs'* embedded story of the power and reign of the phallus, coupled with the gospel of ecstasy, contains religious resonances that may go well beyond the scope of Cleland's authorial intentions.

Although the term "Gospel" has become almost synonymous with the four narratives that begin the New Testament, a gospel narrative is the recounting and celebration of a new god, and a gospel can be anything proclaimed as the absolute truth or, more loosely, any doctrine or rule widely or fervently maintained.[27] A gospel is a religious handbook, and the stress on something new, instructive, compelling, and entertaining also links "gospel" with the early "novel." The *Memoirs* combines these elements in a narrative celebration of the phallus as if it were a new god,[28] and the chief celebrants are Fanny and her three friends in Mrs. Cole's "house of convenience," Emily, Harriet, and Louisa. In the first part of her narrative, Fanny tells the story of how she was brought to London by Esther Davis, initiated into the pleasures of sex by the bisexual prostitute Phoebe Ayers in Mrs. Brown's house, introduced to the power of the phallus in voyeuristic scenes with Mrs. Brown and with the young prostitute Polly and her Italian lover. With the advent of nineteen-year-old Charles into her life, Fanny comes to the full realization of the importance of the phallus and the pleasure it brings to her, a culminating pleasure that becomes her virtual reason for being. Toward the end of the first letter, as we have seen, she can define her own "natural philosophy" in terms of this primary principle or "instinct" of sexual pleasure (80). The *Memoirs*, then, is a testament of the power of the Phallus, and the two parts constitute a first and a second testament. In this way, the novel belongs to that kind of bipartite fiction in which the second part is not only a continuation of the first but also expands, comments on, and, in some sense, redeems it. Taking fiction in its broadest sense as a dialogic prose narrative that tells the story of imagined characters and events which may or may not have an origin in historical fact, we might take as examples of this special bipartite fiction such remarkably different texts as the Christian Bible, with its Old and New Testaments, *Don Quixote*, *Oroonoko*, and *Robinson Crusoe*, among many others.[29]

Considering the *Memoirs* then as a bipartite fiction with gospel ramifications, the first testament of the novel focuses on the private Fanny, her initiation into the world of sexual pleasure, and the paramount importance of the phallic "idol" or god in her personal world. This world is ruled by the phallus, and the first testament of the *Memoirs* spells out what might be called the Law of the Phallus in Cleland's unique fictional revival of the early modern naturalistic religion of male libertinism.[30] This law might be stated as follows: the Phallus is the source of sexual pleasure for women and men, and this ultimate pleasure is the "extasy" of orgasm.[31] Some form of the word "extasy" is used at least twelve times in the novel as a synonym for orgasm. The first testament establishes the power of the Phallus in Fanny's world, and the second testament spreads the gospel of ecstasy in the public sphere of eighteenth-century London. This second part of the *Memoirs* focuses on the public Fanny as a kind of sexual missionary, as she herself puts it, "passing thus from a private devotee of pleasure, into a public one, to become a more general good" (92),[32] and besides recounting her initiation into a utopian community of prostitutes, contains a variety of adventures with several men (including her secret witnessing of two men having intercourse), and a series of four "passion" narratives celebrating the theophanic possession and redemption of women by the Phallus, culminating in the restoration to her of Charles, the primary Phallic god in Fanny's life.[33]

TRUTH, THE "SISTERHOOD," AND WOMAN-MAKING

On the first page of her memoirs Fanny declares that she will write the "loose part" of her life with the same liberty that she led it: "Truth! stark naked truth, is the word" (1). At the beginning, in the middle, and at the very end of her story, Fanny Hill invokes, as the model for her peculiarly candid form of discourse, the icon of truth as a naked woman. In examining the sexual and religious discourse of the *Memoirs*, I will consider Fanny as the manifestation of "Truth" in relation to the theme of "woman-making" and the Phallus in these three important moments of her narrative.

The trope of naked truth usually took two conventional forms, either as truth standing on a hill and surveying the scene below or truth lying hidden at the bottom of a well.[34] Cleland, the lifelong philologist, plays multiply upon this trope of naked truth in the name of his heroine, Frances Hill. "Frances" is derived from Old French *franc*, meaning free, frank, open, candid.[35] A "Frank" was a freeman, and a "franc" is still a monetary unit. The Old High German *franco* signified a spear or javelin. This cluster of connotations helps suggest Fanny's uniquely independent role ("a hill not to be commanded") in the commercial world of prostitution and her relation to the virile member. "Fanny" recalls the name of the prostitute/bawd Fanny Cock in Hogarth's *Marriage a la Mode* (a generic version of "spear in the hill"), and the surname Hill alludes to the *mons veneris* not only as the "center" (80) of sexual attention in the novel but also as a place of prospect for Fanny's retrospective narration and embodiment of the truth of sex.[36] For Fanny, the vagina is the most important part of the female body, and her name defines her essence, her personal vision of "the sovereign good of human nature," and the entire dynamic of the novel. She will tell how she "emerg'd at length, to the enjoyment of every blessing in the power of love, health, and fortune to bestow" (1). Fanny Hill herself is Cleland's version of the natural "Truth" of sex.

The trope of naked truth appears again near the beginning of the second volume of the *Memoirs* when Fanny, standing before her male judges "in all the truth of nature" (121), undergoes her initiation into Mrs. Cole's "little family of love."[37] Mrs. Cole, as the "governess" of this small "domestic flock," and as a surrogate mother to Fanny, whom she sees as the daughter she had lost, wins "intire possession" of her (92). Fanny's first sight of the community organized and run by this new "mother" and matriarch is one of "decency, modesty, and order" as she encounters three young women, "demurely employ'd on millinery work" in a shop that she soon discovers is a front for the brothel. These extraordinarily beautiful and dexterous eighteen- to nineteen-year-olds—blonde Emily and Harriet, dark-haired Louisa—design, sew, and sell women's hats.[38] They serve as Cleland's revised libertine version of the Greek fates, the most ancient divine trinity, only they are sewing the fates of the women who come within their purview. Throughout the novel, Cleland, possibly imitating Milton in *Paradise Lost*, skillfully interweaves allusions to classical and Christian mythology to fashion his unique male libertine alternative gospel of ecstasy. These young libertines are intent on creating their own pornotopia, a "secret institution" (94) that functions as a kind of mystery cult with a "sisterhood" (94) attended by sympathetic male collaborators. Mrs. Cole as the governess of this institution preaches "edifying . . . lessons" to her girls on "the doctrine of passive obedience and non-resistance to all those arbitrary tastes of [libertine] pleasure" (96), and she is a high matriarch always under the control of a young libertine patriarchy.[39]

One of the chief rituals of this revived libertine cult is the initiation of new members, and "the ceremony of [Fanny's] reception into the sisterhood" takes place that very night. As a prelude to this culminating ceremony, each of the three young fates is asked to "entertain the company with that critical period of her personal history, in which she first exchanged the maiden state for womanhood" (96). These three "little histories" (111), recounted by Emily, Harriet, and Louisa (each name a subordinate feminine version of male names that suggest aristocratic rule), constitute a kind of synoptic gospel celebrating the immanent, mysterious, and overpowering dominion of the Phallus over womankind, and the preliminary delineation of the male process of what may be called "woman-making," a motif alluded to in Volume I by Fanny's tutor Phoebe, a name that recalls Diana, the goddess of chastity, but also the Phoebe of Romans 16. 1–2, whom Paul commends to his new congregation as a "servant of the church . . . that ye receive her in the Lord, as becometh saints, and that ye assist her in whatsoever business she hath need of you: for she hath been a succourer of many, and of myself also."[40] Fanny's story is the fourth and culminating gospel of ecstasy.

THE GOSPEL OF EMILY AND VIRGIN SACRIFICE

Her blue eyes "streaming with inexpressible sweetness," the fair Emily (from the feminine form of Aemilius), tells how she ran away from home after her barbarous parents beat her for breaking their china bowl, "the pride and idol of their hearts" (97). She is overtaken on the road to London by a "sturdy country lad . . . a perfect plough-boy" (97). In this chthonic myth, she goes to bed with him in all innocence in an inn and, in the mutual warmth of their bodies on a bitter night, takes fire from his touching "that part of me, where the sense of feeling is so exquisitely critical" (98). In this version of woman-making, the lad soon "made [her] feel the proud distinction of his sex from mine," and she cannot help asking him, "what that was for?" (98). The indefinite "that" (the most general pronominal form) for the phallus, even more vague than "that part" of her, is the only term in this narrative for the Phallic god that is referred to everywhere else in the novel only by epithets.[41]

The Phallic god is introduced in mutual warmth, a rising force almost independent of the "innocent" young people subject to its "new" power, and Emily notes that its "omnipotent thrust murther'd at once my maidenhead, and almost me: I now lay a bleeding witness of the necessity impos'd on our sex, to gather the first honey off the thorns" (99).[42] Emily is a virgin martyr in the natural libertine religion of sexual ecstasy. In this first gospel of the "omnipotent" Phallic god, to which Fanny is also an eyewitness, the thorn is the phallus, and women gather the honey. The libertine doctrine of the necessary sacrifice of virgin vaginal blood goes a long way toward explaining the almost obsessively violent and repetitious descriptions of the loss of virginity recurring in the novel, and especially of Fanny's defloration by Charles in part 1. The doctrine is echoed by Robert Lovelace in Richardson's *Clarissa*, when in his first letter in that epistolary novel, he tells his friend Belford that in response to his being jilted by a woman of quality, he will have his revenge "upon as many of the sex as shall come into my power. I believe . . . I have already sacrificed a hecatomb to my Nemesis in pursuance of this vow."[43]

The defloration passage begins with another invocation of truth. After finding that his "engine of love-assaults" is too large to penetrate her "darling treasure," and that her "virgin-flower was yet uncrop'd," Fanny tells him "that he was the first man that ever serv'd me so: truth is powerful, and it is not always that we do not believe what we eagerly wish" (40).[44] The autonomous fury of the Phallic god controls even Charles, its instrument, in the ecstasy of male orgasm.[45]

The theme of violent virgin blood sacrifice has its male parallel in the Bible. In the book of Hebrews, "the word of God" is represented as more sharp and powerful than any two-edged sword, "piercing even to the dividing asunder of soul and spirit, and of the joints and marrow, and is a discerner of the thoughts and intents of the heart . . . but all things are naked and opened unto the eyes of him with whom we have to do" (Hebrews 4:12–13).[46] This striking example of the action of the "word of God" tears apart not only soul and spirit but, like a material object, separates the joints from the bones, and renders all the parts naked and open as in an anatomical operation. Christ is represented as a new kind of high priest, pure and "without spot" (Revelation 9:14),[47] a successor to Moses, who "took the blood of calves and goats . . . and sprinkled both the book, and all the people, Saying, This is the blood of the testament which God hath enjoined unto you. Moreover, he sprinkled with blood both the tabernacle, and all the vessels of the ministry" (Hebrews 9:19–21). But Christ entered into the holy place "not by the blood of goats and calves, but by his own blood . . . having obtained eternal redemption for us" (Revelation 9:12). The word "blood" is used twelve times in chapter 9. As the doctrine of the blood sacrifice of the Son of God on a Cross produces the new life of the resurrection, so by implication the doctrine of the bloody pain of female virgin sacrifice by the Phallus, an instrument of impalement, leads to "inexpressible" pleasure and a new kind of resurrection of the female body. The passive, innocent, tender young women of these narratives, including the young Fanny Hill herself, are the female counterparts of the meek and compassionate Christ of the Gospels who becomes the ironic "King of the Jews," and the eventual monarch of the "kingdom of God." But the exaltation achieved by these female sacrificial victims does not reach the status of royalty. The "rifler of her virgin-sweets" becomes for Emily "everything to me now" (99).

It is only after her own violent initiation into the power of the Phallus that Fanny offers her loving description of its appearance in "the angelic youth"

(45), the sleeping Charles. In the biblical Gospels, the motif of food and feasting recurs in a variety of forms and situations, culminating in the shock of Jesus saying to his disciples (many of whom "walked no more with him" after hearing it), "Except ye eat the flesh of the Son of man, and drink his blood, ye have no life in you" (John 6.53, 66). The shock value of Cleland's narrative lies mostly in the descriptions of the heroine's (and other women's) pain in defloration, but Fanny, too, emphasizes, more than once, the plea-sures of sexual/visual consumption: "nor could I refuse myself a pleasure that sollicited me so irresistibly, as this fair occasion of feasting my sight with all those treasures of youthful beauty I had enjoy'd." Like Venus in the opening of Lucretius's *De rerum natura* hovering over the passive Mars, Fanny describes her relationship with Charles: "I hung over him enamour'd indeed! And devour'd all his naked charms with only two eyes, when I could have wish'd them at least a hundred, for the fuller enjoyment of the gaze" (44).

THE GOSPEL OF HARRIET

Harriet's story is again prefaced by the narrator's ritual account of the girl's extraordinary beauty, and again her name (the feminine of Henry, connoting female rule), is indicative of her superior status among the "fair sex." In an image that recalls the elevated prospect of "Truth," she views from her perch in an ancient manorial summer house overlooking, through a window, a river in which a youth is swimming, and here she ventures first to cast her eyes "on an object so terrible and alarming to [her] virgin modesty as a naked man" (101). Harriet's brightly illuminated outdoor view of the swimming youth is framed by an old "casement" window, as she is presented with the "novel sight" of the "whitest skin imaginable," and the sun playing upon it makes it "perfectly beamy," like the radiance of an angelic figure of luminous power, "water born," unconfined by mortal limitations.[48] The white skin and "fine polished limbs" recall the appearance and texture of the phallus in the first part, and the undulating "bush" of fine black hair on his head gives way to the "black mossy tuft; out of which appear'd to emerge a round, softish, limber, white something that play'd every way, with every the least motion or whirling eddy" (101–2). That part "captivates" her attention. Again, as in the first half of the novel, the female voyeuristic gaze is stressed, but now the vision is more fluid, phenomenological, and insinuating, kindling "the fire of nature, that . . . began to break out, and make me feel my sex for the first time" (102), a more indirect and impressionable form of woman-making than in Emily's account, beginning with the first numinous appearance of the image of the phallus. When the youth disappears and she thinks he may have drowned, she runs down to the canal in a "madness" of fear, swoons, and is wakened by "a sense of pain that pierced me to the vitals" (103). Again, as with Emily, her innocence is ravished unawares in "streams of blood." She is the victim of rape, but "how quick is the shift of passions from one extreme to another!" (103). She then tells how the youth had learned the trick of holding his breath and appearing to come back to life, and how he raised her from her trance ("I felt, no more than the dead" [103]) by his triumph over her virginity. She concludes her passion narrative with praise for "the instrument of the mischief, which was now . . . resuming its capacity to renew it" and forgiveness ("I felt it a point of my own happiness to forgive him" [104]) for the ravisher whom she now "passionately lov'd" (105). This gospel account again stresses, but far more mysteriously than the first, the indefinable capacity of the Phallic god ("a white something") to rise from wavering softness and instability to overpowering triumph, virtually a libertine narrative version of the Pauline paradox of strength emerging from weakness.

THE GOSPEL OF LOUISA

Louisa's dark-haired beauty, in contrast to that of the two striking blonde women, is "exquisitely touching" (106), and this narrative of a beautiful young woman born of an illicit union between a journeyman cabinetmaker and his master's maid again emphasizes, more than the other two, the lowly origins of these willing female sacrifices to the Phallic god.[49] Transferring gently away from the female gaze upon the male, the initial emphasis in this narrative is on the sense of touch and female masturbation as a path toward self-knowledge as Louisa moves resolutely toward "a kind of title to womanhood" (106), a self-induced process of woman-making that can be completed only by the intervention of the Phallus. In this version of the trope, Cleland begins to incorporate subtle verbal echoes of New Testament passages, beginning with the young woman's recognition (recalling St. Paul's "when I became a man, I put away childish things" [1 Corinthinans 13:11]) that her "new sensations . . . demolish'd at once all my girlish play-things and amusements: nature now pointed me strongly to more solid diversions" (106–7). Nature in Cleland's gospel is still the handmaid of the Phallic god, only here sexual pleasure, driven by "instinct," is Nature's "favourite passion" (100). As was the case with Emily and Harriet, Louisa lives in a state of virgin innocence and ignorance, but she is much more given to self-introspection than they are, and only she suffers, in her solitude, "furious excitations of desire . . . expecting the long'd-for relief . . . burning and fretting" (107). She cuts herself off from society and withdraws further into her sexual obsession: "Man alone, I almost instinctively knew . . . was possess'd of the only very remedy that could reduce this rebellious disorder" (107). One day she withdraws into the bedchamber, unlaces her stays, throws herself on the bed, and gives herself up to "the old insipid shifts of self-viewing, self-touching, self-enjoying, *in fine* to all the means of *self-knowledge* I could devise, in search of the pleasure that fled before me, and tantalized me with that unknown something that was out of my reach; thus all only served to enflame myself, and to provoke violently my desires, whilst the one thing needful to their satisfaction was not at hand" (108).[50] In the Gospel of Luke, Jesus visits the home of Mary and Martha. Mary sits at his feet and hears his word, but Martha is busy with the chores of hospitality and asks Jesus to command her sister to help her. "And Jesus answered and said unto her, Martha, Martha, thou art careful and troubled about many things: But one thing is needful: and Mary hath chosen that good part, which shall not be taken away from her" (Luke 10:41–42). The double stress on Martha's name emphasizes Jesus' love for her and the seriousness of his injunction. In Cleland's version, Louisa, the counterpart of the contemplative Mary, awakes (as did Harriet) to find a man with her (though not inside her), a young and perfectly handsome man who seemed to her "no other than a pitying angel, dropt out of the clouds" (109). Besides recalling Miltonic and Familist angels, this one is reminiscent of the "angel of the Lord" who "descended from heaven," rolled back the stone from the tomb, sat upon it, and spoke to the two Marys after Jesus's resurrection from the tomb: "He is risen . . . Come see the place where the Lord lay" (Matthew 28.2–6). In a remarkable shift to the present tense, Louisa then says, "He is now lain down by me" (109). She describes his immediate application to her "center," and finally the apotheosis of her long-frustrated gaze, the conjoined motif of touching, and the multiple pun on the biblical word "part" (recalling Fanny's admiration of "that capital part of man" [26]), all combine to form a virtual theophany of rapture, with hints of a sexual Eucharistic feast, terminated by the blood sacrifice: "I met with too much good will, I felt with too great a rapture of pleasure the first insertion of it, to heed much the pain that follow'd: I thought nothing too dear to pay for this the richest treat of the senses; so that, split up, torn, bleeding, mangled, I was still superiourly pleas'd, and hugg'd the author of all this delicious ruin" (110).

THE GOSPEL OF FANNY

The fourth gospel in the *Memoirs* is reserved for Fanny herself in the final pages of the novel. Her reuniting with Charles, a new Charles who has lost his fortune on the Irish seas and "had now the world to begin again" (180), recalls Milton's Adam who has "seen one world begin and end" (12.6); Adam takes the hand of Eve, at the end of the poem, as "The world was all before them" (12.646). Fanny, now a kind of second Eve, one who sacrifices Vice to Virtue in her "tail-piece of morality," makes her final appeal to truth: "but let truth dare to hold it [Vice] up in its most alluring light: then mark! how spurious, how low of taste, how comparatively inferior its joys are to those which Virtue gives sanction to, and whose sentiments are not above making even a sauce for the senses, but a sauce of the highest relish!" (187).[51] Echoes of food and the new Eucharistic feast recur all through Fanny's final descriptions of love-making with Charles.[52]

The new Charles is also elevated into a new realm of virtuous action with royal and even godly allusions to the Restoration of Charles II as Fanny "forgives" her "supreme idol" in a torrent of interjections: "Say you are still mine,—that you still love me . . . I forgive you— forgive my hard fortune in favour of this restoration" (178). As Harriet forgives her rapist in her gospel, so Fanny forgives her lover and deflowerer in hers. The Charles of the second testament redeems the unfaithful Charles of the first. "That favourite piece of manhood" draws out her deepest feelings. "Nothing can be dearer to the touch," she says, as she finds herself "re-inflamed under the pressure of that peculiar scepter-member, which commands us all" (183). This idealized young Charles the Second is far removed from the satire of "scepter" poems, as Fanny is "now in touch at once with the instrument of pleasure, and the great-seal of love."[53] In an echo of I Peter 3.7, she seems to relish her subordinate role as the royal and godlike Phallus pours "such an ocean of intoxicating bliss on a weak vessel, all too narrow to contain it," that she is lost in "an abyss of joy" (183). In recalling her "extatic distraction" of that sublime moment, the narrator (like Louisa) switches into the present tense: "I see! I feel! The delicious velvet tip!—he enters might and main with—oh!—my pen drops from me here in the extasy now present to my faithful memory!" (183). In a final exercise of literary "woman-making," Cleland now engineers a pornographic reassertion of the power of the male phallus even over his brilliant recreation of the female writer in the retrospective Fanny, who "had now totally taken in love's true arrow from the point up to the feather" (184). As the "love-fire" (a term favored by the heterodox Lutheran visionary, Jakob Boehme) blazes in every pore and vein of her body, Fanny feels "a system incarnate of joy all over" (184). She is the female incarnation of joy, wrought by the Phallic god and his "blissful touch," a deification of the primal sense of touch centering now in this final gospel not in the vagina, "the favourite center of sense" (80), but in the heart, or rather in a fusion of the vagina and the heart in a new center of sense. As they resume the tumultuous motions of genital intercourse after a pause to "relish on this intimatest point of re-union," Fanny expands on the gradual interpenetration of their voices and bodies in a vision that culminates in her closest approximation to the experience of spiritual ecstatic union with the divine, except that here the god is the phallic Charles:

> as our joys grew too mighty for utterance, the organs of our voice, voluptuously intermixing, became organs of the touch: And, oh, that touch, how

delicious! How poignantly luscious!—And now! Now! I felt! To the heart of me, I felt the prodigious keen edge, with which love, presiding over this act, points the pleasure . . . .Thus happy then, by the heart, happy by the senses, it was beyond all power, even of thought, to form the conception of a greater delight . . . . *Charles* . . . penetrated me so profoundly, touch'd me so vitally, took me so much out of my own possession, whilst he seem'd himself so much in mine, that in a delicious enthusiasm I imagin'd such a transfusion of heart and spirit, as that coaliting, and making one body and soul with him, I was him, and he, me (184).[54]

This language echoes that of the Gospel of John, where Jesus says to the Jews, "the Father is in me, and I in him" (10.38), and in the culminating prayer on his relationship with the Father, before the Passion narrative begins, Jesus prays that those who believe in him "all may be one; as thou, Father, art in me, and I in thee, that they also may be one in us . . . .I in them, and thou in me, that they may be made perfect in one" (17.21–23).

Charles performs, in this ecstatic union with his beloved, a final superhuman feat, which if not a miracle is the closest thing to one in a gospel which celebrates Nature in all her sexual vivacity and power of transport, as well as her finite mortality. Just before her final appeal to "truth" as "Virtue," Fanny concludes her narrative of the truth of sex with an account of how Charles achieves a kind of resurrection of the Phallus with three successive erections and ejaculations without withdrawing from her: "for *Charles*, true to nature's laws, in one breath expiring, and ejaculating, languish'd not long in the dissolving trance . . . we play'd over again the same opera. . . . But still there was no end of his vigour . . . he was proceeding then amazingly to push it to a third triumph, still without uncasing . . . I obtain'd at length a short suspension of arms, but not before he had exultingly satisfy'd me that he gave out standing" (185).

Leo Steinberg, in his meticulously researched *The Sexuality of Christ in Renaissance Art and In Modern Oblivion*, perhaps best known for its commentary on the *ostentatio genitalium* in a multitude of paintings of the infant Christ, also finds a series of sixteenth-century paintings (with titles and inscriptions like "Ecce Homo," *Christ as Victor over Sin and Death, Man of Sorrows*), representing the Risen Christ with an erect phallus, his loins draped. These paintings of the Risen Christ may also have some connection with the doctrine of "Christ come forth in the flesh" in the sexualized religious cults of sixteenth- and seventeenth-century northern Europe, like the Family of Love. Though he concludes that such images remain "deeply shocking," Steinberg argues that these painters "may have attempted a metaphor of the mortified-vivified flesh . . . if, in the exegetic tradition, [the organ of generation's] circumcision on the eighth day prefigures the Resurrection, the final putting away of corruption; then what is that organ's status in the risen body? . . . would not the truth of the

Anastasis [literally, the 'again standing,' the Resurrection], the resuscitation, be proved by its erection? Would not this be the body's best show of power?"[55] Reflecting on this final example of "the truth of sex," given by a historian of religious art, I suggest something similar may be happening in Cleland's naturalistic and pagan gospel of "extasy," leading to the triumphant power of the repeatedly erected Phallic god, exemplified in Charles, Fanny's "supreme idol" (178).

NOTES

1. Roy Porter, "Mixed Feelings: the Enlightenment and Sexuality in Eighteenth-Century Britain," in *Sexuality in Eighteenth-Century Britain*, ed. Paul-Gabriel Boucé (Manchester: Manchester University Press, 1982), 4–5.

2. Ibid., 5.

3. I discuss eighteenth-century libertinism in *Mother Midnight: Birth, Sex, and Fate in Eighteenth-Century Fiction: Defoe, Richardson, and Sterne* (New York: AMS Press, 1986), especially in chap. 25: "Lovelace, Ovid, and 'the Sex.'" This discussion of Lovelace as libertine and "natural philosopher" of women and sex is relevant to Cleland's depiction of libertinism in the *Memoirs*.

4. John Cleland, *Memoirs of a Woman of Pleasure*, ed. Peter Sabor (Oxford and New York: Oxford University Press, 1985), 92–95. References are to this edition.

5. See *Mother Midnight*, especially the Introduction, for the roles of the midwife-bawd.

6. Fanny makes a point of noting that before participating in the orgiastic ball to which she is invited at her initiation into the "secret institution," "I was perfectly at my liberty to refuse the party, which being in its nature one of pleasure, suppos'd an exclusion of all force, or constraint," 113, recalling Adam's admonition to Eve after the Fall: "force upon free Will hath here no place," 9.1174. One of the veteran voluptuaries soon leads Louisa "'nothing loth'" to the public couch for their sexual performance, an allusion to *Paradise Lost* 9.1079 set off with quotation marks by the author himself and pointed out long ago by Michael Wilding in *"Paradise Lost* and *Fanny Hill," Milton Quarterly* 5 (1971): 14–15. References to Milton's work are from John Milton, *The Complete Poems and Major Prose*, ed. Merritt Y. Hughes (New York: Macmillan Publishing Co., 1957).

7. Twenty-three of his works survive in English translation. See Janet E. Halley, "Heresy, Orthodoxy, and the Politics of Religious Discourse," *Representations* 15 (1986): 98–120.

8. See *The Reason of Church Government*: "But my hope is that the people of England will not suffer themselves to be juggled thus out of their faith and religion by a mist of names cast before their eyes, but will search wisely by the scriptures and look quite through this fraudulent aspersion of a disgraceful name [such as Puritans and Brownists] into the things themselves: knowing that the primitive Christians in their times were accounted such as are now called Familists and Adamites, or worse," 659.

9. See Alastair Hamilton, *The Family of Love* (Cambridge: James Clarke, 1981).

10. Christopher Marsh, *The Family of Love in English Society, 1550–1630* (Cambridge: Cambridge University Press, 1994), 24.

11. Quoted in Marsh, *Family of Love*, 24.

12. Ibid., 55–56.

13. Hamilton, *Family of Love*, 35.

14. Marsh, *Family of Love*, 24.

15. Hamilton, *Family of Love*, 37. Cf. Henry More in *An Explanation of the Grand Mystery of Godliness* (London 1660): Niclaes is "a Pimp or second *Sardanapalus*" (the Assyrian monarch who lived in great luxury) who encourages orgies "by lusty animadversions against Shamefacedness and Modesty in men and women." More further alleges that once sectarians reach the "state of full Perfection . . . they cannot sin, do what they will," and "hold that there is no Difference of Good or Evil, and that Sin is but a Conceit [except] to those that know not their own Liberty," More is cited by James G. Turner in *One Flesh: Paradisal Marriage and Sexual Relations in the Age of Milton* (Oxford: Clarendon Press, 1987), 85, 85n79.

16. Quoted in Hamilton, *Family of Love*, 10.

17. Marsh, *Family of Love*, 205.

18. Ibid., 237–38.

19. See Hamilton, *Family of Love*, 118, and Marsh, *Family of Love*, 66.

20. Hamilton, *Family of Love*, 117, 119.

21. Marsh, *Family of Love*, 24.

22. Charles is referred to as Fanny's "idol" (usually defined as the image of a god used as an object or *instrument* of worship) at least four other times in the narrative: "idol of my fond virgin heart," 37, "idol of my soul," 55, her eyes' "supreme idol," 178, and "my idoliz'd youth," 182. The word "idol" reinforces Cleland's sense of the pagan nature of the neo-libertine gospel of sexual ecstasy.

23. See Peter Wagner, *Eros Revived: Erotica of the Enlightenment in England and America* (London: Secker and Warburg, 1988), chapter 2. See also his edition of the novel, *Fanny Hill: Memoirs of a Woman of Pleasure* (New York: Viking Penguin, 1985), 228n48. Compare *Mother Midnight*, 147, 279n47.

24. William H. Epstein, *John Cleland: Images of a Life* (New York: Columbia University Press, 1974), 140.

25. Quoted in Epstein, *Images of a Life*, 140.

26. John Cleland, *The Way to Things By Words* (Menston, UK: The Scholar Press, 1968), 23–24.

27. The literal Old English meaning of *godspel* as a good story or good news became, with the shortening of the *o*, the Middle English *godspell* as the story of a god. See the etymological accounts of "gospel" in the OED.

28. Compare Nicholas Venette, in a work Cleland almost certainly had read: "It is observable, that the Ancients ranked the *Virile Member* among the number of their Gods . . . to intimate [its] Empire and Dominion . . . .'tis the Father of human Kind . . . .The Law of the *Old Testament* orders the Womans Hand to be cut off, that should scornfully or injuriously have handled those Parts," *The Pleasures of Conjugal love Explain'd: In an Essay concerning Human Generation* . . . . (London, c. 1730), 1. From 1700 on this work went through numerous editions in the eighteenth century. The best account of phallic culture in ancient Greece is Eva Keuls's *The Reign of the Phallus: Sexual Politics in Ancient Athens* (Berkeley: University of California Press,

1985). Compare also Robert Markley's brief comments on the phallus in the *Memoirs* as "the 'secret' of masculine, patriarchal authority" and "the phallus as godhead" and "symbol of masculine power" in "Language, Power, and Sexuality in Cleland's *Fanny Hill*," *PQ* 63 (1984): 347.

29. The two parts of the fiction may or may not be clearly labeled. *Oroonoko*, in the brief compass of its novella form, has an African and an American part; the original *Robinson Crusoe* (the island narrative, published 1719) has two parts demarcated by Crusoe's discovery of the footprint in the exact middle of the narrative. I discuss the two parts of *Oroonoko* in chapter four of *The Language of the Heart, 1600–1750* (Philadelphia: University of Pennsylvania Press, 1997), and the two parts of the original *Robinson Crusoe* in "Starting Over with Robinson Crusoe," *Studies in the Literary Imagination* 15 (1982): 51–73, reprinted in part in *Major Literary Characters: Robinson Crusoe*, ed. Harold Bloom (New York: Chelsea House, 1995), 35–45.

30. Cleland's possible connection to the Scottish secret society, the Most Ancient and Puissant Order of the Beggar's Benison and Merryland, via a possible early version of *Fanny Hill* and Cleland's distant relative Robert Cleland, is discussed by Epstein, *John Cleland: Images of a Life*, 69–71. However tenuous this connection, there is no doubt that Cleland's recuperation of male libertinism in the novel has affinities with other actual male societies like the Hell-Fire Club and others in the eighteenth century.

31. This "law" is far more literal and material than that which has come to be associated with Jacques Lacan, especially his sense of the symbolic nature of the phallus in "The Signification of the Phallus" in *Écrits: A Selection*, trans. Alan Sheridan (New York and London: W. W. Norton, 1977). In terms of its function in this novel, I define "phallus" as the erect male organ, and "Phallus" as the erect male organ in its godlike symbolic role.

32. Roy Porter discusses how the "spreading sexual joy was equated with the maximising of public happiness" in utilitarian habits of Enlightenment thought. See "Mixed Feelings: The Enlightenment and Sexuality," in *Sexuality in Eighteenth-Century Britain*, ed. Paul-Gabriel Boucé (Manchester: Manchester University Press, 1982), 5.

33. David Weed correctly, in my view, sees all the deviations from heterosexual genital intercourse in the novel, all the "possibilities of female masturbation, lesbianism, heterosexual anal sex, and sodomy" as practices that are "incomplete and misdirected, dead ends, wrong turns on the sexual highway," and that Charles "becomes the standard by which all other men are judged." See "Fitting Fanny: Cleland's *Memoirs* and the Politics of Male Pleasure," *Novel: A Forum on Fiction* 31 (1997): 11, 17.

34. A third trope, that of Truth dismembered and reassembled, is given its most memorable formulation in Milton's *Areopagitica* : "Truth indeed came into the world with her divine Master, and was a perfect shape," but "a wicked race of deceivers . . . took the virgin Truth, hewed her lovely form into a thousand pieces, and scattered them to the four winds," 741–42. Milton's allusion in this passage to the Osiris myth also recalls Isis' reassembly of her husband's body parts *sans* penis. The trope of Truth at the bottom of a well was so well worn by the early eighteenth century that Swift included it in his "Tritical Essay on the Faculties of the Mind" (1707), a succession of academic clichés.

35. The name of the older, experienced, and remarkably candid female instructor in sex to the sixteen-year-old Katy in *The School of Venus* (1660) is also named Frances, and the name is abbreviated "Frank," giving her an insouciant bisexual air.

36. See Douglas Brookes-Davies, "The mythology of Love: Venerean (and related) iconography in Pope, Fielding, Cleland and Sterne" in *Sexuality in Eighteenth-Century Britain*, ed. Paul-Gabriel Boucé (Manchester: Manchester University Press, 1982), 184–85. The OED gives "fanny" as a reference to the female buttocks and pudendum as an American usage only, but this seems too restrictive; cf. Pope's "Lord Fanny," as well as Bacon's essay "Of Truth" for Fanny's surname. The phrase "truth of sex" comes of course from Michel Foucault's commentary on the transformation of sex into discourse in *The History of Sexuality: Volume I: An Introduction* (New York: Random House, 1990), parts 2 and 3.

37. In her first self-description in the novel, Fanny says she had all the points of beauty universally requisite to "our sovereign judges the men," 14.

38. See also the allusion to the "little milliner" in the famous "screen scene" of Sheridan's *The School for Scandal* (1777; IV.iii) and milliners becoming virtual types for easy sexual conquest, like the depiction of female servants in Richardson's fiction.

39. Mrs. Cole as preacher is a specific allusion to the two incendiary sermons preached in 1709 by Henry Sacheverell, perhaps the most flamboyant and reckless of High Church polemicists, on the necessity of "non-resistance" and "passive obedience" to King and Church in all circumstances. See John Arbuthnot, *The History of John Bull*, ed. Alan W. Bower and Robert A. Erickson (Oxford: Clarendon Press, 1976), l–li, 153. This allusion (not noted in the Sabor and Wagner editions of the *Memoirs*), and the ones to personal female "little histories," 111, discussed below suggest that Cleland was familiar with the John Bull pamphlets of 1712 (probably via Pope's version of *The History of John Bull* in the many editions of the Pope-Swift *Miscellanies in Prose and Verse*, 1727–1742) and scandalous political allegorical novels of the period, such as Delariviére Manley's *The New Atalantis*. See the introduction to *The History of John Bull* for a further discussion of the "little history" genre, especially lxxvi–lxxix. William Cleland, John Cleland's father, was a close acquaintance of Pope and Arbuthnot; see Epstein, *Images of a Life*, 16–20. The word "edifying" is used eight times in the Pauline epistles.

40. All biblical quotations are from the Authorized King James Version of 1611 (AV).

41. It has become a commonplace in the criticism of this novel that Cleland carefully eschews vulgar terms for the phallus and the vagina, but a chief reason for these ingenious euphemisms was to avoid prosecution for obscenity. See Epstein's account of the "legal pitfalls" connected with the publication of the *Memoirs* in *Images of a Life*, 74–83.

42. "'It is dear-bought Honey that is licked off a thorn' . . . 1721: Spoken of the ill Effect of unlawful Pleasures." See Morris P. Tilley, *A Dictionary of the Proverbs in England in the Sixteenth and Seventeenth Centuries* (Ann Arbor: University of Michigan Press, 1950), 316.

43. Samuel Richardson, *Clarissa: or, The History of a Young Lady*, ed. Angus Ross (New York: Penguin Books, 1985; 2004), 143. This is one of many "libertine" links between the two novels.

44. Again, compare Milton on the dismemberment of the "virgin Truth" in *Areopagitica*, 742. Fanny, a figure of "Truth," seems to be saying that violence to the female is a necessary part of the truth of heterosexual intercourse.

45. The *locus classicus* for the phallus (and the womb) as raging animals within the human body "maddened with the sting of lust" and beyond rational control is Plato's *Timaeus* (91bcd), quoted in *Mother Midnight*, 263n46. See also the quotation from the French physician, Pierre Dionis, on how "the Yard grows furious and seeks to be satisfy'd: the Animal has no more command of itself, and Man very often forgets and loses the Exercise of his Reason," *A General Treatise of Midwifery*, (1719), quoted in *Mother Midnight*, 222.

46. Compare Louisa, "pleas'd to the heart" as the phallus "search'd her senses with its sweet excess," 164–65. In this novel, the Phallus takes the place of the "heart-searching" God of the Old Testament, the *kardiognostes*. See *The Language of the Heart*, 47, 220.

47. "Pure and without spot" was taken to mean that Christ was chaste, and not "defiled with women." See Revelation 14:4.

48. The conventional poetic trope of angels in heaven having their long hair "laved" by water or other liquid appears in Milton's "Lycidas": "Where other groves, and other streams along, / With *Nectar* pure his oozy Locks he laves," ll. 174–75. Cleland's water scene and his diction ("dewy," "whitest skin," "wantoning," "melted" and other expressions) recall the scene in *The Faerie Queene* when Sir Guyon notices and then gazes at the "Two naked Damzelles" bathing in a pool, II.xii.63–68.

49. Despite her lowly origins, Louisa's name (from medieval Latin *Ludovicus*) also recalls (French) royalty and romance heroism.

50. Compare Mary Wollstonecraft: "This regard for reputation . . . took its rise from a cause that I have already deplored as the grand source of female depravity, the impossibility of regaining respectability by a return to virtue, though men preserve theirs during the indulgence of vice. It was natural for women then to endeavour to preserve what once lost—was lost for ever, till this care swallowing up every other care, reputation for chastity, became the one thing needful to the sex." See *A Vindication of the Rights of Woman*, ed. Carol Poston, second ed. (New York: Norton, 1988), 133; and Charles Dickens's title for the first chapter of *Hard Times* (1854).

51. This passage seems to be a parody of Delariviére Manley's theory of the "little history" genre (referred to earlier) in which she asserts that "Historical Novels," "these little pieces which have banished Romances," should be used for moral purposes: "The chief end of History is to instruct and inspire into men the love of virtue and abhorrence of vice by the examples proposed to them: therefor the conclusion of a story ought to have some tract of morality which may engage virtue." See Arbuthnot, *The History of John Bull*, lxxvii–lxxviii.

52. Cleland was not the first to link the Eucharist with sex: Rochester alludes to venereal disease in his poignant plea to "ye powers above": "Is it just that with Love cruel Death should conspire, / And our tarses be burnt by our hearts taking fire? / There's an end of communion, if humble believers / Must be damned in the cup like unworthy receivers." *John Wilmot, Earl of Rochester: The Complete Works*, ed. Frank H. Ellis (New York: Penguin Books, 1994), 35. References are to this edition.

53. In Rochester's "On King Charles" we learn that the king's "sceptre and his prick are of a length," 30; the Lord Chancellor of Great Britain is the keeper of the "Great Seal" with which official papers are stamped.

54. Compare Martin Buber: "Ecstasy is originally an entering into God, *enthusiasmos*, being filled with the god. Forms of this notion are the eating of the god; inhalation of the divine fire-breath; loving union with the god . . . being rebegotten, reborn through the god; ascent of the soul to the god, into the god. The Apostle Paul does not know whether his soul was in the body or outside the body." See *Ecstatic Confessions*, ed. Paul Mendes-Flohr; trans. Esther Cameron (San Francisco: Harper and Row, 1985), 4.

55. Steinberg, *The Sexuality of Christ in Renaissance Art and In Modern Oblivion*, second ed. (Chicago: The University of Chicago Press, 1996), 86–89.

6

Transcultural Adoption in the Eighteenth-Century Transatlantic Novel: Questioning National Identities in Charlotte Lennox's *Euphemia*

Susan K. Howard

Many eighteenth-century transatlantic novels, novels by European writers set at least partially in North America, include scenes in which aboriginal and Euro-American cultures meet.[1] In some of these novels, the aboriginal culture is used to critique aspects of the Euro-American or European culture.[2] Voltaire's *L'Ingenu* (1767), for instance, presents a titular Huron hero who is far superior to the religious fanaticism exhibited by the French; Frances Brooke's *History of Emily Montagu* (1769) records the epistolary interchange between British visitors to Quebec and their friends in London about the noble aboriginals of Canada; and in *Letters from an American Farmer* (1782), Crèvecoeur's Farmer James plans to ask the aboriginals to adopt him and his family so that they might escape the corruption of Euro-American society in the throes of revolutionary fervor and learn to live closer to the land within a simple and enlightened society. Some of these novels, including Tobias Smollett's *Humphry Clinker* (1771) and Susanna Rowson's *Reuben and Rachel* (1798), incorporate the popular form of the captivity narrative to suggest ways in which the aboriginal societies they chronicle counter the stereotyped version of the savage aboriginal in contemporary captivity narratives. In Rowson's novel, for instance, siblings William and Rachel Dudley are captured by Narragansetts, but the aboriginals' actions are mitigated by a narrator who conjectures that their "lands had been invaded by strangers, and . . . [they] perhaps had suffered from the cruelty of the invaders."[3] Sold to an eastern tribe, the children are adopted and are so loved by their aboriginal family that the chief, their adoptive father, cannot bring himself to return them to their birth family. In Smollett's novel, the narrative of the captivity of the Scottish Lismahago, who lived happily with his Miami captors until the tribe decided to sell him back to the English, suggests that those whom England regularly marginalized at this time could enjoy a greater sense of belonging among people whose society was generally viewed as uncivilized and primitive.[4]

In a similar vein, British novelist Charlotte Lennox's 1790 novel, *Euphemia*, like her first novel, *Harriot Stuart* (1750), is partially set in colonial New York and also includes a captivity narrative of sorts. Where the emphasis in *Harriot Stuart* is on the capture of the white woman by members of the Mohawk tribe, with its attendant fear and violence, the captivity narrative in *Euphemia*, as in *Reuben and Rachel*, emphasizes the aftermath of the capture and includes glimpses into the life that Euphemia's young son, Edward Neville, leads among the Hurons, particularly with his adoptive mother, and with the Jesuits in Canada. In both novels, Lennox, like Rowson and Smollett, uses the genre of the captivity narrative against its often propagandistic purposes—its ability to establish race as a category of difference and justification for inhumanity—as a means of helping her primarily British audience to consider issues of gendered, cultural, and national identities in a constructive and progressive way. In Lennox's first novel, the lead Mohawk who steals Harriot from the garden outside the British fort at Albany turns out to be Harriot's spurned white lover, Belmein, in disguise. In *Euphemia*, while Lennox's discussion of Edward's time with his adoptive family is sparse, it still shows clearly that within his adoptive family, Edward was loved and nurtured. The compassion and concern his adoptive mother felt for him even on her deathbed is sincere and heartfelt. Equally important, Edward's easy acceptance of his Huron mother is, as Christopher Flynn has written, an example of the "blurring of racial categories" Smollett had shown with his Scottish characters and Lennox had shown earlier in *Harriot Stuart* through her treatment of the Dutch.[5] In this respect, Lennox's aim in including a captivity narrative is not to show the "failure of adoption to effect permanent changes in British character," as Joe Snader contends is the case for the eighteenth-century British novelists who include captivity narratives in their works, nor to communicate "anxiety about American transculturation," as he also contends.[6] Rather, *Euphemia*'s rendering of the captivity narrative with its emphasis on the transcultural adoption of a white child by an aboriginal mother suggests that Lennox's aim, common to much transatlantic literature of the period, is to reveal what can be gained by both parties in such a cultural exchange, and indeed that the only viable post-revolutionary American identity is one that embraces such an exchange.

The emphasis developed in these late eighteenth-century transatlantic texts on the positive aspects of aboriginal life, experienced intimately by Euro-

Americans adopted into various tribes, is a striking departure from the emphasis developed in most captivity narratives written between the seventeenth and nineteenth centuries in America, which generally chose to dwell on the violence and cruelty of the capture itself as well as the subsequent struggle on the part of the Euro-American captive to endure abuses at the hands of her aboriginal persecutors, rejecting any temptation to assimilate or convert until she could be rescued or escape. The majority of captivity narratives were motivated by the desire to paint the aboriginal in a negative light in order to make the taking of their lands less morally repugnant, or, as in the case of Mary Rowlandson's *Narrative of the Captivity and Restoration of Mrs. Mary Rowlandson* (1682), to establish the continued purity of the captive and the ultimate beneficence of Providence. Rowlandson's narrative was so popular both in America and Britain during the eighteenth century that it was never out of print. Peter Williamson's captivity narrative, published originally in 1758 in York, England, went through many editions, and with each new edition, the depiction of the aboriginals' atrocities grew more heightened.[7] Even Mary Jemison's story, in the hands of James Seaver, her early nineteenth-century editor, emphasized graphically the brutal capture of Jemison and her family, rather than the lifetime she lived contentedly among the Senecas.[8] Indeed, even with such an orientation, Jemison's story caused many readers to view her as un-American.[9] In short, there are few depictions within captivity narratives of those Euro-Americans who, once captured, were adopted into native tribes and lived out their lives with their adoptive families, many of them choosing to remain with their adoptive kin even when offered the chance of return to their birth families or cultures. Instead their stories appear embedded in late-eighteenth-century transatlantic fictions. It has been suggested that the dearth of nonfiction accounts can be explained by both the lack of literacy among these transculturated individuals and their lack of interest in or opportunity to tell their more positive stories of life among the aboriginal peoples. "Having embraced Indian culture as their own," Kathryn Derounian-Stodola and James Levernier note, "many of these captives probably had little, if any, desire to communicate with white audiences."[10] And while there are few depictions of such families in prose, there are even fewer visual representations of such transracial adoptive families, which suggests that there was unease among Euro-Americans, and especially British Americans or the British in America over this phenomenon. Both James Axtell and Gary Ebersole quote contemporary sources that note this phenomenon with a mixture of curiosity, wonder, and concern. For instance, Cadwallader Colden, in his *History of the Five Indian Nations of Canada* (1727), notes that neither the French who had been taken captive by the Iroquois nor the English captives were willing to leave the tribes they now belonged to, and Colden wonders at this given the "liberty and . . . plenty" the inhabitants of New York enjoyed.[11] Benjamin Franklin, in a letter to Peter Collinson, Crèvecoeur, in *Letters from an*

American Farmer, and Robert Bage, in *Hermsprong* (1796), all make the same observation, in the same spirit of wonder.[12] Others, however, like Mary Jemison's biographer, James Seaver, note that few aboriginals taken in by white families chose to remain with them, while many white adoptees remained with their aboriginal families. Ebersole writes, "This situation was a source of great consternation for many Euro-Americans, since it ran counter to most of their theological presuppositions as well as to the assumption that theirs was an undeniably superior (and infinitely desirable) civilization."[13] In addition, Keitel notes, such a phenomenon suggests the "possibility of accommodation between two diverse cultures."[14] Lennox's use of the captivity narrative in particular and her depiction of the aboriginals and aboriginal adoption of whites—certainly more positive than most contemporary records—clearly argues that the formation of a national identity for Americans circa 1790 requires a recognition of the need to respect the autonomy and individuality of all peoples as they join to make a nation.

After all, such a choice on the part of these "white Indians" who decided to remain with their aboriginal adoptive families called into question not only the justified removal of the aboriginal from his tribal range but also the long-held belief in Britain that families created by biological bonds were best because they ensured a pure ancestral line and an unsullied path to inheritance.[15] Adoption legislation was not passed in Britain until 1926, though the British did practice informal adoption, usually of male children among extended kin, often as a means of ensuring the continuance of the estate. Other children were "put out" into domestic service, indentured, or apprenticed. Still other orphaned or homeless children without extended family were placed in almshouses before the middle of the eighteenth century when London opened its first foundling hospital.[16] Adoption in America was formalized earlier than in Britain—in 1851, in Massachusetts—and prior to that date, colonial children, like those in England, could be placed in apprenticeships for extended periods of time, almost becoming members of their masters' households.[17] Along with the almshouse, there were also private agencies in several colonial cities for the care of orphaned children.[18] Especially among the New York Dutch, adoption of non-relative children by families concerned for their welfare did occur, and often the legal system was used to ensure that the adopted child could inherit.[19] Carp goes so far as to state that "colonial America showed little preference for the primacy of biological kinship" in its adoption practices.[20] Indeed, according to Presser, by the middle of the nineteenth century in America the custom of taking children in to educate and nurture was "widely practiced . . . and had come to be referred to as adoption."[21]

In sum, informal adoption in the eighteenth century was practiced in both England and America. Such adoptions may have benefited the child brought into a family, though their primary focus, especially in Britain, was on the needs of the family or the estate rather than on the child. Carp makes the point, as do others, that in both America and England, though obviously more so in England, the "legal opposition to adoption stemmed from a desire to protect the property rights of blood relatives in cases of inheritance," as well as the existence of other child welfare mechanisms that made "adoption for social welfare purposes unnecessary" in the eyes of society.[22]

Of those informal adoptions that did occur, probably few were instances of transcultural adoption among families in the British, French, or Dutch communities, and even fewer were transracial adoptions, where aboriginal or African children were fostered by Euro-Americans[23]; however, many aboriginal peoples of North America readily adopted members of other tribes taken in battle or those in need of a community to which they could belong, as well as Euro-American captives taken to replace native family members killed in battle or by disease or accident, or Euro-Americans seeking "asylum" with them. Their main goal in adopting seems to have been the continuance of the tribe.[24] Of those aboriginal peoples who practiced adoption, the Iroquois, whom Lennox writes about, were at the forefront.[25] Indeed, Francis Jennings notes that the Senecas, who belonged to the Iroquois Confederacy, adopted "whole villages of Hurons after the breakup of the Huron Nation under Iroquois attack."[26] Similarly, Calloway sees the Iroquois as the "true assimilationists of early America" because they took in other aboriginal peoples under the Great Tree of Peace as refugees, an act Father Lafitau, an early Jesuit ethnographer of the Iroquois, deemed "a gentle conduct . . . [which is] excellent policy."[27] "Adoption," Calloway writes, "became such a vital means of replenishing the losses occasioned by constant warfare that adoptees came to outnumber pure-blooded Iroquois."[28] Their adoption practices suggest they had no interest in cultural or racial purity; once one was adopted by the Iroquois, one became Iroquois.[29] "By a legal fiction embodied in the right [*sic*] of adoption," Hodge writes, "the blood of the alien may be figuratively changed into one of the strains of the Iroquoian blood, and thus citizenship may be conferred on a person of alien lineage."[30] Holm asserts that "total assimilation was the ultimate goal of adoptions" among the Iroquois.[31] Individual, familial, and national identities under such a system were flexible, responsive to circumstances and determined by actions, not blood. As Perdue notes of the Iroquois, "Kinship terms were not merely quaint metaphors; they were essential for the conduct of human affairs."[32] Certainly, there is documented evidence from Euro-American adoptees during the seventeenth through nineteenth centuries that suggests that the bonds within aboriginal transracial adoptive families were so strong that there was no distinction made between adopted and biological children, even to the point that adopted members of the tribe could become chiefs.[33] Rowson acknowledges this phenomenon in *Reuben and Rachel* when William's adoptive father, Okooganoo, proclaims that William is "the son of my choice" and makes him sachem of the tribe.[34] Similarly, Caswell shares the true story of the Old White Chief, who at four was taken from his mother and adopted by a Seneca woman of whom he says, "from that hour I believe she loved me as a mother . . . [and I] returned her the affection of a son."[35] In addition, Caswell quotes from a monument in the "old Indian burying ground, four miles from Buffalo, NY, a tribute to the Indian race" and the Euro-American captives adopted by the tribes: "'The adoption was not a mere form. Real affection, and in fact all that the heart prizes and longs after in relationships, was bestowed upon them.'"[36] Rev. John Williams, in his captivity narrative, *The Redeemed Captive of Zion* (1704), laments that the Mohawks who had captured his daughter Eunice "would as soon part with their hearts as my child."[37] As Axtell notes, these adoptees found "that the color of their skin was unimportant; only their talent and their inclination of heart mattered."[38] Clearly, among these tribes, a more fluid and expansive notion of family, one not limited by biology, existed.

Historians suggest neither aboriginals nor Euro-Americans initially saw race in colonial America as a distinctive marker of difference. Following Enlightenment philosophies of Locke and Rousseau, which had proposed that all people were born equal and had, therefore, the "same potential for improvement," early English colonists saw race as a product of the climate and believed that "all that separated the Indians from the Anglo-Americans . . . were cultural differences."[39] As late as 1797, Jefferson was advocating intermarriage between aboriginals and Americans as a civilizing force, but his seems to have been a minority voice at this point in the history of America since, as the colonial period wore on and aboriginal lands became more sought after, aboriginals came to be seen as inferior, their race viewed as a limiting factor.[40] Joanna Brooks suggests that

> the concept of "Indianness" was an Euro-American invention imposed upon people of color of various . . . indiginous American ethnic affiliations to advance the economic and political dominance of whites. . . . Indigenous Americans were racialized as "Indians" in colonial policies that legitimated their enslavement and extermination, and the appropriation of their traditional territories.[41]

This situation only worsened after the revolution when the necessity to determine a national identity required a concomitant silencing of anyone who did not fit into the narrow definition of "American"; indeed, "whiteness was stipulated as a requirement for citizenship in the Naturalization Law of 1790."[42]

In addition to challenging assumptions about racial and cultural boundaries, the matrilineal family structures that created these kinship bonds among the Iroquois in particular also challenged the patriarchal family structures in place in Britain and British America during the eighteenth century as well as English common law, which clearly held that it was the father who had rights to his children; indeed, the mother "had no rights under the common law," as Lennox well knew since the conflicts she and her husband experienced were often over his ability to exert influence on his children and her lack of legal recourse.[43] But among aboriginal peoples in North America, in the case of both the Mohawk and Huron tribes Lennox writes about, women possessed power. While women clearly labored in aboriginal societies—in the fields as well as the longhouse—their influence within their society was substantial and overt, unlike many of the Euro-American women who were seen as too frail for wilderness life.[44] Indeed, it was they who chose those whom the tribe would adopt. Jennings writes that if a woman had lost her husband or son, "she had an unchallengeable individual right to 'adopt' a prisoner in his place."[45] It was women who oversaw the important requickening ceremony that welcomed people into their lineage.[46] In addition, a child in such a culture received his or her lineage from her/his mother; hence, there were no illegitimate children among aboriginal cultures that held a matrilineal social structure.[47] Probably most foreign to an English patriarchal society is the fact that, as Fenton notes, among the Iroquois, the "rights of property, of both husband and wife, were continued distinct during the existence of the marriage relation; the wife holding and controlling her own, the same as her husband, and in case of separation, taking it with her."[48] It is no wonder that the British in particular, among whom the rights and responsibilities of women were far fewer than their male counterparts, would feel threatened by matrilineal aboriginal societies in which women were viewed as "providers and peacemakers."[49]

Lennox, who had lived for a time in colonial New York in the 1740s, where her father served at various forts as a military officer, and who had probably seen the gathering of the Iroquois Confederacy for its triennial meeting with the governor of New York, which she describes vividly in *Harriot Stuart*, chooses to explore the idea of adoption of Euro-Americans by aboriginal peoples in a way that does not deny the grief Euphemia feels for the loss of her son, but which balances this with her feeling of gratitude toward the Huron mother who adopted and cared for Edward. In addition, the narrative of Edward's captivity sends the reader back to an examination of the roles patriarchy and imperialism played in his being taken by the Hurons. It was, in fact, Mr. Neville's negligence, his showing off Britain's colonial possessions to a British tourist, that led to his son's wandering off and being lost in the woods in the first place.[50] Equally important, through the narration of the Nevilles' servant William, who is taken along with Edward by the Hurons and also adopted into that tribe, Lennox allows for the trauma of separation both William and Edward experience, but unlike the authors of many captivity narratives, she does not dwell on the violence of capture.[51]

This is consistent with what Snader notes about the use of captivity narratives by eighteenth-century British novelists in order to "raise . . . an initial
fear and excitement before concentrating more substantially on displacing
these emotions."[52] While Edward returns to his mother, and eventually to
England, the novel suggests he has been marked by his transracial and transcultural experience, as has his mother. Through his adoption experiences,
he is no longer simply the child of a British imperialist—his father, like
Lennox's, having come to America as a military officer, charged to defend
the forts at Albany and Schenectady against aboriginal and French forces in
the British fight to gain dominion over the continent. Rather, Edward's is a
hybrid identity that reflects his British heritage as well as his ties to the aboriginal peoples and to the French Jesuits who have harbored him for many
years.[53] This is not to say that Edward has fully assimilated the Huron culture. Like many Euro-American captives/adoptees, he does not succumb to
the influence of the educational techniques used by the aboriginal peoples
on captives to encourage them to forget their English or French identity and
assume an aboriginal one, primarily because he is with that tribe for such a
short time.[54] As Temma Berg notes, Edward never loses the sense that he is
the white, Protestant child of Euphemia Neville, and Ebersole agrees that Edward "retains essentially English values."[55] Yet the relationship he has with
his Huron adoptive mother and his Jesuit adoptive father nurture him until
he can return to his biological mother, and they leave a mark on him, making him the young man he is in the end. Pointing out the "critical role . . .
Indian women played in facilitating the identity transformation," Ebersole
suggests that this appears "almost exclusively in nineteenth-century narratives," but *Euphemia* certainly depicts the softening influence of the aboriginal woman on the young Euro-American male adoptee that we also see in
Caswell's story of Old White Chief.[56] Indeed, as Wyss notes, "such a mixed
identity is closer to a native definition of race, traditionally seen as far more
cultural than biological," though she suggests that these hybrid identities go
even beyond aboriginal ideas, thus "destabilizing both Euro-American and
traditional Native American assumptions about racial identity."[57]

   Edward appears to his mother, on his return after nine years away, in
Mohawk dress, having journeyed from Montreal, where William had found
him among the Jesuits, down to the country around Albany. He is wearing these clothes because he was given them by two Mohawk fur traders,
"sensible, honest fellows, of some consequence in their tribes," who had
been hired by the fort doctor to help Edward and William escape, not from
native aggression but from a tyrannical British military officer at the fort at
Oswego.[58] Like many who returned to Euro-American society after living
among the aboriginal peoples—Peter Williamson, for instance—Edward is
not readily recognizable as the child he was when separated from his birth
family and is "taken for an Indian," as Williamson was.[59] Euphemia and her

female companions know him by a birthmark in the shape of a bow and arrow, which his nurse suggests was inspired by his mother's imagination having been captured by a group of aboriginal men in the woods soon after her arrival in America and while she was pregnant with Edward. From the moment of his return, Edward, who has lost his English and only speaks French, is viewed with curiosity and referred to by people in America and then in England as "the handsome Huron" or "our handsome Indian," even as "our dear Huron" (386, 393). Such epithets emphasize Edward's hybrid identity, one tied in the eyes of others not to the Mohawks in whose clothes he appears, nor to the French Jesuits among whom he was educated in the Catholic faith and French language, but rather directly with the Huron tribe who adopted him.[60]

While Edward is not one of those "white Indians" who were captured, adopted by a tribe, and happily integrated into the tribal community, his time among the Hurons has marked him in a spectacular way. His return to his birth family occurs just as they are leaving America to return to England. Mr. Neville has finished his military career, and so he and his family are no longer involved directly in the colonial program. The fact that Edward continues to be referred to as a Huron, even jokingly, after his return to the home country, may simply imply the contemporary British yen for importing and exploiting the spectacle of the aboriginal, but especially given Lennox's previous novelistic treatment of that figure in *Harriot Stuart*, it also suggests her sense that such transcultural and transracial experiences as Edward's ought not to be left behind but will inform one's sense of self and will, as a result, expand the concept of family, community, even nation. These conceptions have been broadened by the recognition of the legitimacy of his hybridity.

Certainly, Euphemia is forced through Edward's situation to embrace colonial America's diverse cultures. This has an important consequence for her and her children, since it allows her to question patriarchal authority. When this occurs, says Bowers, the "maternal becomes a crucial (though frequently denied) site on which battles over agency and authority . . . [are] fought."[61] Perhaps as an acknowledgment of what she owes his adoptive Huron mother, who chose and protected Edward, along with her own maternal concern for her children, Euphemia is empowered to question her husband's irresponsibly dangerous parenting and, once she has received an inheritance given solely to her, she is able to act to take her children's education out of his hands. I link this action on her part to the example set for her by the Hurons' matrilineal culture. By the end of *Euphemia*, the patriarchal family concept is severely constrained, as is the sense of the nuclear family's superiority. These joint developments support Flanders's observation that in many eighteenth-century novels, "supportive relationships outside the conjugal family compensate somewhat for the ineffectiveness of family structures."[62] Certainly, in *Euphemia*, the idea of family has expanded, as it is clear that Euphemia's former governess, now companion, Mrs. Benson will remain with her; that the boy Euphemia fostered on the ship over to America has become a "brother" to Edward; and that Euphemia and her family will be reunited with her friend and correspondent Maria Harley and her family in a happy community (386). In Lennox's novel, as in some aboriginal societies, transracial/transcultural adoption allows for what Sara Dorow sees as a more "expansive embrace of nation and family," specifically an embrace of less traditional bonds of kinship and the diminishment of the paternal role. This inclusivity has implications for issues of national identity in pre- as well as post-revolutionary America.[63]

I do not think Lennox ever got over her American experience, and I think it impelled her throughout her life, certainly in her marriage and in her literary career, to question the status quo that included racial, ethnic, and gender inequalities, the authority of the husband over his wife, and his sole possession under the law of their children (which in both Mr. Neville's and in Alexander Lennox's cases have near-tragic consequences), as well as the inequalities of the literary marketplace, where female writers needed the patronage of male writers in order to succeed. In this respect, she strikes me as a daughter of America but also as a more critically attuned and objective representative of the British imperial state.[64] British America, as the French philosopher Raynal pointed out in his 1770 history of North America, had not created a sense of itself as one people.[65] If the new country is to be better than its parent, it needs to recognize the many peoples in it and integrate them. Aside from the autobiographical currency of Lennox's choice of New York as a setting for *Euphemia*, she may also have been aware of the fact that the middle colonies—New York, Pennsylvania, New Jersey—were the most socially diverse and complex colonies, home to Dutch, British, German, Scotch-Irish, Africans, and aboriginal tribes, and yet, as Henretta notes, "these colonies never degenerated into plural societies ruled only by naked force."[66] These states were known for their heterogeneity, their greater degree of ethnic and racial tolerance, and their ability to deal with differences politically, through the legislature. In this regard, they were very similar to the Iroquois Confederacy, with its emphasis on peace, union, democracy, and respect for all voices. It is for these qualities, including their capacity to welcome diverse peoples into their society through adoption, that Benjamin Franklin, in plans for a colonial union expressed first during the 1750s, acknowledged some debt to the Iroquois.[67]

For Lennox, national identity should not rest on the extermination of another culture or race.[68] Indeed, aboriginal adoption of white Euro-Americans can be seen as having the potential to disrupt the colonial impulse by exposing future colonizers—and future citizens—to the allure of the aboriginal culture enough to enable appreciation of that culture and understanding of the benefits of transracial, transcultural adoption. It might be helpful here to consider Sir Henry Maine's theory in *Ancient Law* (1861) that

> the early patriarchal civilizations would not have been able to grow out of their "swaddling clothes" without the custom of adoption . . . without the fiction of adoption, primitive tribes could not have absorbed each other, or could not have combined except on terms of absolute superiority on one side and absolute subjection on the other.[69]

Perhaps Massachusetts was the first state to pass adoption statutes because its lawmakers had learned from those aboriginal peoples who had lived in the northeastern portion of colonial America—from the Iroquois in particular—the value of adoption as a democratizing force and the need to legislate it, more intimately and immediately than Britain would, despite the message Lennox was trying to communicate to her British audience within her fiction.[70]

The dearth of pictorial representation of transracial families in pre-revolutionary America does not mean these families did not exist—they did. But perhaps they weren't deemed worthy of representation, or they were viewed as dangerous, or as too much of an anomaly to provoke much interest; however, one very powerful image of such families is captured in Benjamin West's *Henry Bouquet Receiving English Captives from Native Americans*, which illustrates the trauma experienced by the aboriginals and their adoptive children as they were returned to their birth families at the end of the French and Indian War in 1764 in Ohio. William Smith, a historian who chronicled the expedition, wrote of the aboriginals

> who delivered up their beloved captives with the utmost reluctance; shed torrents of tears over them, recommending them to the care and protection of the commanding officer. Their regard to them continued all the time they remained in camp. They visited them from day to day; and brought them what corn, skins, horses and other matters, they had bestowed on them, while in their families; accompanied with . . . all the marks of the most tender affection.[71]

And he described how many of the captives resisted a return to white society and how some of them were bound so that they might not run back to their adoptive families. Of them, Smith wrote, "It is no wonder that [they] considered their new state in the light of a captivity, and parted from the savages with tears."[72]

As Ebersole points out, and Smith's chronicle makes powerfully clear, the large number of "white Indians" relative to the small number of aboriginals adopted by and remaining with Euro-American families suggests that "cultural assimilation was largely a one-way process," and was, therefore, a concern among some in Euro-American society.[73] Despite this, these adoptive families, which contained both Euro-Americans and aboriginal peoples, may be seen as success stories of a kind. Select aboriginal cultures achieved what Barbara Melosh calls "the possibility of kinship across groups separated by national and ethnic particularism and . . . riven by long histories of discrimination, oppression, and conflict."[74] For those Euro-Americans captured by aboriginals and adopted into tribal life who did choose to return to their biological families and Euro-American culture, the culturally acceptable action was to forget the intimate time spent within another culture and with those of another race. Subsequent narratives depicting the captivity/adoptive experience were often used to witness to that erasure. What is interesting about Lennox's *Euphemia* in particular, and other transatlantic novels of the late eighteenth century, such as Rowson's *Reuben and Rachel*, is that this is not so. Time has not been erased but has positively left its mark.[75] For Lennox and other transatlantic writers, the crossing of cultural borders in fiction, the imaginative integration of differing cultures, may, like Bizzell's formulation of American jeremiads, "spur people to action and imagine . . . that a better civil state can be achieved," both within America and between America and Europe.[76] As Haberlein notes, "the course Indian-white relations was to take in the new American republic was still relatively open at the time of the revolution"; the boundaries between these two worlds was "permeable."[77] Transatlantic novelists, including Lennox, recognized this, and suggested in their works that readers had a choice: to "other" the aboriginal or explore a "middle ground" where both cultures could coexist. The works of the bicultural writer William Apess, of the 1820s and 1830s, are a sad footnote to Lennox's *Euphemia* and other eighteenth-century transatlantic novels in that they reveal that America chose the first course, and, as a result, aboriginals also began to see themselves as a distinctive culture, incapable of blending with Americans of European heritage, and opportunities for cross-cultural contact and enrichment were lost.[78]

NOTES

1. I wish to thank the following for their help in researching this essay: Leslie Lewis and Kate Joranson, reference librarians at Duquesne's Gumberg Library, and research assistants Lee Ann Glowzenski and Justin Kishbaugh. Many thanks also to Jessica Jost-Costanzo for help copyediting the essay, and to Christopher Johnson for asking me to contribute to the volume: it was a pleasure. This essay is dedicated to Jerry Beasley, who introduced me to Charlotte Lennox—many, many thanks.

2. This would not have been anything new for English audiences who had read with interest the articles in the *Spectator* and the *Tatler* in 1710, which introduced them to the four Iroquois kings who were visiting London and whom these periodicals painted as noble savages in order to critique British society. See Troy Bickham, "'A Conviction of the Reality of Things': Material Culture, North American Indians and Empire in Eighteenth-Century Britain," *Eighteenth-Century Studies* 39.1 (2005):

29; and Eric Hinderaker, "The 'Four Indian Kings' and the Imaginative Construction of the First British Empire," *William and Mary Quarterly*, third series, 53.3 (1996): 504–5.

3. Susanna Rowson, *Reuben and Rachel; or, Tales of Old Times*, two vols. (Boston: Manning and Loring, 1798), 1:142.

4. This trend of viewing the aboriginal as noble savage is in stark contrast with depictions of the aboriginal in novels by such early American writers as Charles Brockden Brown and Ann Eliza Bleecker. Neither Brown's *Edgar Huntly* (1799) nor Bleecker's *History of Maria Kittle* (1793) concedes that the aboriginal is anything other than the stereotypical savage.

5. Christopher Flynn, *Americans in British Literature, 1770–1832: A Breed Apart* (Aldershot: Ashgate, 2008), 95.

6. Joe Snader, *Caught Between Worlds: British Captivity Narratives in Fact and Fiction* (Lexington: University Press of Kentucky, 2000), 173–75.

7. Mary Rowlandson, *A True History of the Captivity and Restoration of Mrs. Mary Rowlandson* (London, 1682). Peter Williamson, *French and Indian Cruelty* (York, 1758). See John Sekora, "Red, White, and Black: Indian Captives, Colonial Printers, and the Early African-American Narrative," in *A Mixed Race: Ethnicity in Early America*, ed. Frank Shuffleton (Oxford: Oxford University Press, 1993), 96.

8. Hillary Wyss notes that, in this respect, the "form of the captivity narrative imposed by Seaver . . . is inadequate to contain Jemison's story." See "Captivity and Conversion: William Apess, Mary Jemison, and Narratives of Racial Identity," *American Indian Quarterly* 23.3/4 (1999): 69. See also Susan Walsh, "'With Them Was My Home': Native American Autobiography and *A Narrative of the Life of Mrs. Mary Jemison*," *American Literature* 64.1 (1992): 49–70.

9. Evelyne Keitel, "Captivity Narratives and the Powers of Horror: Eunice Williams and Mary Jemison, Captives Unredeemed," *1650–1850: Ideas, Aesthetics, and Inquiries in the Early Modern Era* 5 (2000): 278.

10. Kathryn Derounian-Stodola and James Levernier, *The Indian Captivity Narrative, 1550–1900* (New York: Twayne, 1993), 73.

11. Cadwallader Colden, *Five Indian Nations* (New York, 1727), qtd. in James Axtell, "The White Indians of Colonial America," *The William and Mary Quarterly*, third series, 32.1 (1975): 57.

12. May 9, 1753, pub. in Leonard W. Labaree et al., ed., *The Papers of Benjamin Franklin*, thirty-six vols. (New Haven, CT: Yale University Press, 1961), 4:481–82. J. Hector St. John dè Crèvecoeur, *Letters from an American Farmer*, ed. Albert E. Stone (New York: Penguin, 1981). Robert Bage, *Hermsprong*, ed. Pamela Perkins (Peterborough, Ontario: Broadview Press, 2002).

13. Gary Ebersole, *Captured by Texts: Puritan to Postmodern Images of Indian Captivity* (Charlottesville: University Press of Virginia, 1995), 191.

14. Keitel, "Captivity Narratives and the Power of Horror," 296.

15. See Stephen Presser, "The Historical Background of the American Law of Adoption," *Journal of Family Law* 11 (1971): 448; Yasuhide Kawashima, "Adoption in Early America," *Journal of Family Law* 20 (1981–1982): 682–83.

16. See John Demos, *A Little Commonwealth: Family Life in Plymouth Colony* (Oxford: Oxford University Press, 1970), 73; Presser, "Historical Background," 454; and Kawashima, "Adoption in Early America," 680–81.

17. The motivating factor for Massachusetts' adoption statute was to "secure to adopted children a proper share in the estate of adopting parents who died without benefit of a will." See Presser, "Historical Background," 465. See also Burton Sokoloff, "Antecedents of American Adoption," *The Future of Children* 3.1 (1993): 17–18; Kawashima, "Adoption in Early America," 681; *The Praeger Handbook of Adoption*, ed. Kathy Stolley and Vern Bullough, two vols. (Westport, CT: Praeger, 2006), 1:1.

18. See Presser, "Historical Background," 473. As Stolley notes, the first orphan asylum in America was formed in 1800 by Hannah Stillman in Boston, an indicator that women's domestic roles could be enlarged to address the public needs of a city. See *Praeger Handbook*, 1:3.

19. Kawashima notes that "adoption was practiced more extensively in New York and it usually occurred in families with Dutch names." See "Adoption in Early America," 688–89; Carp adds Puritan Massachusetts to Dutch New York on this count and also notes the existence in colonial America of "testamentary adoption," by which childless couples used their wills to provide "for relative children or those children who'd been put out to them." See E. Wayne Carp, *Family Matters: Secrecy and Disclosure in the History of Adoption* (Cambridge, MA: Harvard University Press, 1998), 6–7.

20. Carp, *Family Matters*, 5.

21. Ibid., 459.

22. Carp, *Family Matters*, 5–6. See also Presser, "Historical Background," 448, 453; Jamil Zainaldin, "Emergence of a Modern American Family Law: Child Custody, Adoption, and the Courts, 1796–1851," *Northwestern University Law Review* 79.6 (1979): 1045.

23. William Apess, for instance, was born to the Pequot tribe, rescued from an abusive situation with his grandmother and subsequently lived and worked in white families from youth, but he was not "adopted" by any of the white families who took him in. Most captured aboriginal children were used as servants in North America or sold as slaves to British families in the West Indies. See Mary Rowlandson, *The Sovereignty and Goodness of God*, ed. Neal Salisbury (Boston: Bedford, 1997), 141–44.

24. Because the aboriginal peoples were not concerned with inheritance or titles to land, adoption was a more welcome practice among them. It must be noted, however, that not all aboriginal tribes took Euro-Americans captive in order to adopt them. Some did so out of vengeance for loved ones lost in war, or to ransom captives, or to stem the tide of white expansion into aboriginal territories, and for political purposes. See Keitel, "Captivity Narratives and the Power of Horror," 276; however, the Iroquois "mourning war" called forth by the matrons of the clan was specifically meant to replace dead kin with new captives, and grief with joy and social balance. See Todd Holm, "American Indian Warfare: The Cycles of Conflict and the Militarization of Native America," in *A Companion to American Indian History*, ed. Philip Deloria and Neal Salisbury (Oxford: Blackwell, 2002), 157; Pauline Turner Strong, "Transforming Outsiders: Captivity, Adoption, and Slavery Reconsidered," in *A Companion to American Indian History*, 344; Jose Brandao, *"Your fyre shall burn no more": Iroquois Policy toward New France and Its Native Allies to 1701* (Lincoln: University of Nebraska Press, 1997), 44; Jay Vest, "An Odyssey among the Iroquois: A History of Tutelo Relations in New York," *American Indian Quarterly* 29.1/2 (2005): 142.

25. Many writers of captivity narratives, fictional and nonfictional, do not specify the tribal identity of the aboriginals they depict. Lennox's specificity may simply be autobiographical—it was the Iroquois of whom she would have known most as a girl living in Albany—but her use of this particular tribal confederacy allows her to strengthen her argument in interesting ways, both because of the tribe's adoption practices, outlined above, and also because of the qualities attributed to the Iroquois: their orientation toward peace and union; their perseverance in the face of adversity from outside, especially through the use of adoption; and their matrilineal structure. See Daniel Richter, *The Ordeal of the Longhouse: The Peoples of the Iroquois League in the Era of European Colonization* (Chapel Hill: University of North Carolina Press, 1992), 7; Paul Radin, *The Story of the American Indian* (New York: Liveright Pub., 1944), 273–89.

26. Francis Jennings, *The Invasion of America: Indians, Colonialism, and the Cant of Conquest* (New York: W. W. Norton, 1975), 151–52.

27. Colin Calloway, *The American Revolution in Indian Country: Crisis and Diversity in Native American Communities* (Cambridge: Cambridge University Press, 1995), 124. Rev. Joseph Lafitau, *Customs of the American Indians Compared with the Customs of Primitive Tribes*, ed. William Fenton and Elizabeth Moore (Toronto: The Champlain Society, 1977), 172.

28. Colin Calloway, "An Uncertain Destiny: Indian Captivities on the Upper Connecticut River," *Journal of American Studies* 17 (1983): 189–210; qtd. in Derounian-Stodola and Levernier, *Indian Captivity Narrative, 1550–1900*, 5. For more on Iroquois adoption, see also William Engelbrecht, "Iroquois Adoption," in *The Praeger Handbook of Adoption*, 1:355; Damiel K. Richter, "War and Culture: The Iriquois Experience," *William and Mary Quarterly*, third series, 40.4 (1983): 541; Brandao, *Iroquois Policy*, 44; Lafitau, *Customs of the American Indians*, 341–44; Kathleen DuVal, *The Native Ground: Indians and Colonists in the Heart of the Continent* (Philadelphia: University of Pennsylvania Press, 2006), 243; William Beauchamp, "Civil, Religious and Mourning Councils and Ceremonies of Adoption of the New York Indians," *Archeology* 123 (1907): 341–411; Keitel, "Captivity Narratives and the Power of Horror"; and June Namias, *White Captives: Gender and Ethnicity on the American Frontier* (Chapel Hill: University of North Carolina Press, 1993).

29. Aboriginal peoples did not have a Western idea of nation "nor did race play much of a role in their thinking." See Cheryl Walker, *Indian Nation: Native American Literature and Nineteenth-Century Nationalisms* (Durham, NC: Duke University Press, 1997), 4.

30. Frederick Hodge, ed., *Handbook of American Indians North of Mexico* (Washington, DC: Government Printing Office, 1907), 617.

31. Tom Holm, "American Indian Warfare," in *A Companion to American Indian History*, 157.

32. Theda Perdue, "Cherokee Relations with the Iroquois," in *Beyond the Covenant Chain*, ed. Daniel Richter and James Merrell (University Park: Pennsylvania State University Press, 2003), 141.

33. Derounian-Stodola and Levernier, *Indian Captivity Narrative, 1550–1900*, 81; Axtell, "White Indians," 81.

34. Rowson, *Reuben and Rachel*, 1:159.

35. Harriet Caswell, *Our Life among the Iroquois Indians* (1892; Lincoln: University of Nebraska Press, 2007), 53–54.

36. Ibid., 54.

37. Quoted in Pauline Turner Strong, *Captive Selves, Captivating Others: The Politics and Poetics of Colonial American Captivity Narratives* (Boulder, CO: Westview Press, 1999), 136.

38. Axtell, "White Indians," 81.

39. Brian Dippie, *The Vanishing American: White Attitudes and U. S. Indian Policy* (Middletown, CT: Wesleyan University Press, 1982), 4. Elise Lemire, *"Miscegenation": Making Race in America* (Philadelphia: University of Pennsylvania Press, 2002), 47.

40. Lemire, *"Miscegenation,"* 37; Joanna Brooks, *American Lazarus: Religion and the Rise of African-American and Native American Literatures* (Oxford and New York: Oxford University Press, 2003), 4.

41. Joanna Brooks, "Working Definitions: Race, Ethnic Studies, and Early American Literature," *Early American Literature* 41.2 (2006): 315–16.

42. Brooks, *American Lazarus*, 1.

43. Grace Abbott, *The Child and the State*, two vols. (Chicago: University of Chicago Press, 1938), 1:6. Abbott notes that "under the old Persian, Egyptian, Greek, Gallic, and Roman law, [and thus under English Common Law, which was based on Roman Law], the father had absolute power over his children," 1:3.

44. Dawn Lander, "Eve Among the Indians," in *The Authority of Experience: Essays in Feminist Criticism*, ed. Arlyn Diamond and Lee Edwards (Amherst: University of Massachusetts Press, 1977), 201. A distinctive feature of aboriginal households was that women "were more active and visible than English women in maintaining their families." See Ann Marie Plane, *Colonial Intimacies: Indian Marriage in Early New England* (Ithaca, NY: Cornell University Press, 2000), 99.

45. Jennings, *Invasion of America*, 152; Namias, *White Captives*, 4; Richter, *Ordeal of the Longhouse*, 35.

46. Richter, *Ordeal of the Longhouse*, 36.

47. Engelbrecht, "Iroquois Adoption," 8.

48. Fenton and Moore, *Customs of the American Indians*, 326.

49. Dean Snow, *The Iroquois* (London: Blackwell, 1994), 129.

50. See Christopher Castiglia, *Bound and Determined: Captivity, Culture-Crossing, and White Womanhood from Mary Rowlandson to Patty Hearst* (Chicago: University of Chicago Press, 1996), 149. It may be significant that Lennox chooses Hurons as Edward's and William's captors/adoptors, as this tribe in particular was much feared among colonists. See Gordon Sayre, *Les Sauvages Americains: Representations of Native Americans in French and English Colonial Literature* (Chapel Hill: University of North Carolina Press, 1997), 262.

51. Edward and William are not taken in a raid. If they had been, the Hurons would have been more likely to have taken them for ransom, as aboriginal tribes in Canada usually did, whereas the aboriginals in New England raided in order to bring back adoptees. See Axtell, "White Indians," 61.

52. Snader, *Caught Between Worlds*, 172.

53. The Jesuits of Canada saw a need to restructure aboriginal society, which was often communal and matrilineal, as a patriarchal hierarchy. See Richard Drinnon, *White Savage: The Case of John Dunn Hunter* (New York: Schocken Books, 1972), 22. Jesuits and Iroquois wanted to assimilate one another; both failed to do so. See Mat-

thew Dennis, *Cultivating a Landscape of Peace* (Ithaca, NY: Cornell University Press, 1993), 213. For the British in America, the contamination of French Catholicism was as feared as aboriginal cruelty. Indeed, in the late seventeenth-century captivity narrative of Hannah Swarton, Williams's early eighteenth-century narrative, as well as the mid-century narratives of Robert Eastburn and John Gyles, the true hardship is not the initial difficulty of the march with the aboriginals who capture them but the struggle to withstand the Jesuits' or Christianized aboriginals' efforts to convert them to Catholicism. See Sayre, *Les Sauvages*, 263; Strong, *Captive Selves*, 123.

54. See Axtell, "White Indians," 81.

55. Temma Berg, "Getting the Mother's Story Right: Charlotte Lennox and the New World," *Papers on Language & Literature* 32.4 (1996): 391; Gary Ebersole, *Captured by Texts: Puritan to Postmodern Images of Indian Captivity* (Charlottesville: University Press of Virginia, 1995), 321.

56. Ebersole, *Captured by Texts*, 211.

57. Wyss, "Captivity and Conversion," 65.

58. Charlotte Lennox, *Euphemia*, ed. Susan Kubica Howard (Petersborough, Ontario: Broadview Press, 2008), 383. References are to this edition.

59. Richard Vanderbeets, "The Indian Captivity Narrative as Ritual," *American Literature* 43.4 (1972): 561; see also Axtell, "White Indians," 64.

60. Axtell quotes several contemporary sources, including Peter Kalm, who "find it difficult to distinguish European captives from their captors, 'except by their color, which is somewhat whiter than that of the Indians.'" See "White Indians," 64.

61. Toni Bowers, *The Politics of Motherhood: British Writing and Culture, 1680–1760* (Cambridge: Cambridge University Press, 1996), 141.

62. W. Austin Flanders, *Structures of Experience: History, Society, and Personal Life in the Eighteenth-Century British Novel* (Columbia: University of South Carolina Press, 1984), 159.

63. Sara Dorow, *Transnational Adoption* (New York: New York University Press, 2006). In this respect, Lennox's use of the captivity narrative reveals not the "fragility of family" Ebersole suggests, but the strength of new family structures, and unlike captivity narratives that were written by men, it emphasizes the significance of women in society. See Ebersole, *Captured by Texts*, 195.

64. Indeed she uses the travel narrative, as other writers did, to critique British and British American society at times, rather than to voice a "straightforwardly nationalistic" perspective. See Katherine Turner, *British Travel Writers in Europe, 1750–1800: Authorship, Gender, and Identity* (Aldershot: Ashgate, 2001), 10.

65. Abbé Gillaume Thomas François Raynal, *A Philosophical and Political History of the British Settlements and Trade in North America*, trans. J. Justamond (Edinburgh, 1779). The process of nation building, the creation of an American identity, had begun in the 1740s with the interaction among the Europeans, aboriginals, and Africans in North America. See Mary Geiter and W. A. Speck, "Anticipating America: American Mentality before the Revolution," in *Britain and America: Studies in Comparative History, 1760–1970* (New Haven, CT: Yale University Press, 1997).

66. James Henretta, *The Evolution of American Society, 1700–1815: An Interdisciplinary Analysis* (Lexington, MA: D.C. Heath and Co., 1973), 115.

67. Carl Van Doren, *Benjamin Franklin* (New York: Viking, 1938), 209.

68. Brooks, *American Lazarus*, 1.

69. Quoted in Presser, "Historical Background," 445.

70. Like Brooke's and Imlay's novels, Lennox's American novels were marketed to London audiences. See Julie Ellison, "There and Back: Transatlantic Novels and Anglo-American Careers," in *The Past as Prologue*, ed. Carla H. Hay and Syndy M. Conger (New York: AMS Press, 1995), 321.

71. Quoted in Strong, *Captive Selves*, 191.

72. Quoted in Ibid. See also Benjamin Franklin's and Cadwallader Colden's descriptions of the reluctance of some Euro-American adoptees to return to their birth families in Strong, *Captive Selves*, 191–92.

73. Ebersole, *Captured by Texts*, 191.

74. Barbara Melosh, *Strangers and Kin: The American Way of Adoption* (Cambridge, MA: Harvard University Press, 2002), 166.

75. Rowson is concerned in *Reuben and Rachel* to "establish a Euro-American political identity" that does not deny the aboriginal. Like Lennox, Rowson lived both in England and America, and therefore had "mastered two social dialects, the British and the Euro-American." Like Lennox, she, too, "inverts, reverses, and undoes Rowlandson's racism," using instead the Enlightenment trope of the noble savage to establish the value of the aboriginal culture. See Carroll Smith-Rosenburg, "Subject Female: Authorizing American Identity," *American Literary History* 5.3 (1993): 497. The "experience of crossing cultural boundaries . . . is not inherently disabling" to a person, but indeed, "people who venture become more complicated psychologically." See James Clifton, ed., *Being and Becoming Indian: Biographical Studies of North American Frontiers* (Prospect Heights, IL: Waveland Press, 1993), 29.

76. Patricia Bizzell, "The 'Mixedblood' Rhetoric of William Apess," in *American Indian Rhetorics of Survivance*, ed. Ernest Stromberg (Pittsburgh, PA: University of Pittsburgh Press, 2006), 36. Late eighteenth-century British writers were "seeking a way to rewrite a connection between England and her former colonies," but such efforts failed due to the physical distance between the two countries. See Christopher Flynn, *Americans in British Literature* (Aldershot: Ashgate, 2008), 5.

77. Mark Haberlein, "Contesting the 'Middle Ground': Indian-White Relations in the Early American Republic," in *The Construction and Contestation of American Cultures and Identities in the Early National Period*, ed. Udo Hebel (Heidelberg: Universitatsverlag, 1999), 1.

78. See Haberlein, "Contesting the 'Middle Ground,'" 16; Scott Stevens, "William Apess's Historical Self," *Northwest Review* 35.3 (1997): 73.

7

Jane Barker's *Exilius*: Politics, Women, Narration, and the Public

Marta Kvande

Jane Barker has lately been getting her turn in the critical spotlight. She has garnered attention as a poet, a novelist, and a Jacobite, and she has recently been the subject of an important book.[1] Of her fiction, the two "patch-work" novels—*A Patchwork Screen for the Ladies* (1723) and *The Lining of the Patchwork Screen* (1726), both consisting of stories patched together—have received the greatest part of this attention as the most formally interesting, the most autobiographical, and the most relevant to considerations of female authorship. But her novel *Exilius: or, the Banish'd Roman* (1715) has a good deal to tell us about understandings of genre and narration, about notions of the public sphere, about the practice of political discourse, and about con-ceptions of authorship in the late seventeenth and early eighteenth centuries. Not surprisingly, these threads all intertwine in Barker's novel. The narrative form of *Exilius* engenders and instantiates a specific kind of public which, in turn, creates space for women's voices and for suppressed political voices.

Form may be one of the reasons *Exilius* has not received much attention. It has most often been classified as a heroic romance of the kind written by Madame de Scudéry, and while scholars of British literature pay lip service to that genre's connections to the early novel, we tend neither to read nor write about heroic romances.[2] Barker's patchwork novels, by contrast, have been considered formally interesting because they are patchwork—collections of stories, or framed-novelles, in Josephine Donovan's terminology.[3] *Exilius*, we should note, shares some important features with this form as well as with heroic romances. Its semihistorical characters, its Roman and Egyptian settings, its focus on love, didacticism, and grand heroic deeds all link it to the romance tradition, but its structure—a series of narratives told by many different speakers—places it within the framed-novelle tradition. Of course, these two genres share many characteristics and might even be said to over-lap in their concerns: both are more or less female-centered, and both tend to place women at the center of the plot and action and at the center of the concept of the public. In the romance, women (and the love they inspire) are central to public events like wars and negotiations, as in Madeleine de Scudéry's *Clélie*, which revises Livy's *History of Rome* to place women at the center of the founding of the Roman Republic.[4] And in the framed-novelle, as Josephine Donovan argues, women writers (beginning with Christine de Pisan and Marguerite de Navarre) adapted the form to focus on stories about women told by women and "to articulate a women's standpoint."[5] Further-more, as Donovan shows, the framed-novelle has "its roots in oral culture and in a gift economy," both of which offered greater roles for women.[6] Because framed-novelles most often represent their tales as told orally, they become part of an exchange between the speakers. As Donovan suggests, oral storytelling of this kind is itself a kind of gift economy.[7] And because most framed-novelles were produced as manuscripts, they also function within a model of literary publication much closer to gift exchange than to the marketplace. As Margaret Ezell has shown, "the manuscript text operates as a medium of social exchange, often between the sexes, neither private nor public in the conventional sense of the terms, and a site at which women could and did comment on public issues concerning social and political matters."[8] Barker was an active participant in such a manuscript circle (largely composed of students at St. John's College, Cambridge), and *Exilius* was most likely circulated in manuscript (possibly as early as the 1680s) before its eventual print publication.[9] Leigh Eicke points out that such manuscript circulation "became the method of choice" for proscribed groups and that the "ritual" of gift-giving associated with manuscript circulation "would have appealed to Jacobites" as a means of fortifying the community and as a link to an "older aristocratic culture."[10] The framed-novelle structure of this novel thus offers an image of the kind of community in which it was produced.

Because this kind of community constitutes a very different kind of public than the bourgeois public sphere, it also allows for differing kinds of politi-cal discourse—in this case, Jacobite discourse. Whereas the bourgeois public sphere (described by Jürgen Habermas as developing at this time) requires "abstract universality" from participants, other kinds of publics allow for and even depend on markers of identity to construct a space for discourse.[11] Julie Choi has suggested a connection between the notion of the bourgeois public sphere and the development of authoritative third-person voice in the novel.[12] Barker's novel, however, suggests that such a development required the erasure or concealment of an earlier tradition in which publics or narrative voices could be authorized by markers of political and social identity. The narrators of Barker's novels all authorize themselves by displaying their passive suffering and endurance. This stance fits not only the royalist idea of obedience due to the monarch but also a more specifically Jacobite posture of endurance until the hoped-for restoration of the Stuarts. As a narrative stance, passive suffering allows each narrator to claim a generalized moral virtue, which might be read by the uninitiated as without political content. But to the knowing reader, it also allows these narrators to claim a specifically political virtue—faithfulness to the rightful king. The moral stance is, in fact, a political stance. Each narrator's willingness to suffer patiently marks her (and sometimes him) as a loyal subject who endures for the sake of the Stuart monarch, a subject whose primary identification is, therefore, political. These narrators, then, have a particular kind of authority, not only the authority of a political subject but also the authority of a special political community. As Jacobites, they speak a kind of secret language intended not only to communicate to other Jacobites but also to signify their membership in that community. By using Jacobite ideas in their stories, they show themselves to belong to a select group and, therefore, by a circular, self-authorizing logic, to possess the authority of that group. Their use of Jacobite tropes and ideas thus further authorizes them as knowing members of a secret political community, a counterpublic dependent on particular political markers.

In addition to the idea of passive endurance, the recurring themes of exile and marriage in *Exilius* point to the text's Jacobite allegiance. The novel's preface identifies the work's main themes as *"Heroick Love"* and *"Marriage,"* statements that seem straightforward enough. [13] The preface can certainly be read as a simple statement of the moral value of love in marriage and as allying the novel with the heroic romance tradition. But its language and tone suggest another layer of meaning. Barker describes her novel as old-fashioned, as espousing values no longer holding sway in the world: *"Heroick Love of late . . . has been as it were rallied out of Practice . . . whilst Interest and loose Gallantry have been set up in its Place, and monopolized all its Business and Effects"* (A2). Such nostalgia hints at the Jacobite sense that they were the keepers of old ideals that the modern world had rejected. And if, as Lois Potter has suggested, the term "heroick" became "virtually synonymous with Cavalier" during the Restoration, Barker could very well have been drawing on this association to link her novel with Stuart loyalism.[14] Furthermore, the decline of heroic love is not the result of a simple shift in attitudes but a kind of usurpation; other ideas and behaviors have been "set up in its Place" (A2). Barker goes on to suggest that because heroic love is closely tied to *"Virtue and Honour"* (A2v), this usurpation has led to widespread moral laxity: *"How far this has been an Inlet to that Deluge of Libertinism which has overflow'd the Age, the many unhappy Marriages, and unkind Separations may inform us"* (A2–A2v). With the wrong values in place, nothing goes as it should, and people do not behave according to moral standards. The suggestion of usurpation in this passage has obvious Jacobite implications. Less obviously, the moral charges carry Jacobite meaning as well. Paul Kléber Monod notes that Jacobite political writing consistently called attention to "the moral disintegration of government and society under an illegal usurpation."[15] Barker's argument in her preface follows this pattern: the moral collapse she describes comes in the form of libertinism and bad marriages. The fact that these moral problems affect marriages is yet another clue, since for Barker and other Jacobites "marriage [served] . . . as an image of wished-for political legitimacy."[16] Indeed, the "unhappy Marriages" could be seen as a covert way to hint at dissatisfaction with the ruler, and the "unkind Separations" could be taken to refer to the rightful king's exile. Putting these pieces together, we can see Barker's coherently Jacobite argument: the values associated with the rightful ruler have been displaced, and because no one has maintained the right kind of faithfulness, moral anarchy rules. The mention of vows as problematic further establishes a connection to the political situation. "*Those who enter the holy State of Matrimony through the Gate of Perjury, by vowing everlasting Love where their Affections scarce surmount Indifference*" parallel those who too readily swore allegiance to the new rulers—an oath that could only be seen by Jacobites as perjured, since it contradicted the loyalty already owed to the Stuart kings (A2v). The preface thus provides a number of clues to the novel's political positioning—clues which can pass as innocuous when taken at face value but can also be read for their coded meaning by the initiated. Barker's politicization of marriage thus helps to build a counterpublic, a public defined by its specifically Jacobite politics.

The kind of coding Barker uses to indicate political value seems different than the coding used by writers like Aphra Behn and Delarivière Manley. Behn and Manley's tropes—such as the claim that the text is a translation, the use of displaced settings and invented names—were widely recognized and serve to announce their political intent to a broad audience; moreover, this displacement helped make it possible to claim that the authors were disinterested rather than advocating for a specific group. In contrast, Barker's tropes seem intended to make her political intent clear only to a select group. The obvious explanation for this difference is the relative levels of danger attendant on the kinds of political messages the writers conveyed. Although Manley was arrested for libel, her Tory polemic fit within the developing party system. The risks she and Behn ran were, therefore, less than that of Barker, whose Jacobite writings could have been prosecuted for treason. Barker's need for a greater degree of secrecy thus leads to a less apparently public code and narrative stance. In turn, this allows her narrators to appear more innocuous and more abstractly universal (in the Habermasian sense). In other words, her narrators do not seem to have specific markers of particular social or political identity. Because they may not appear to be advancing the agenda of a particular group, they can, therefore, more easily meet the criteria needed for entry into the public sphere.[17] But this appearance of universality is a fiction. Barker's novel speaks from a Jacobite point of view. Even to those who do not recognize the text as specifically Jacobite, the novel clearly propounds ideas and values that subtly argue against the Whiggish values that were coming to dominate politics and the marketplace. The apparent disavowal of particular identity allows for the covert assertion of that identity.

This is not to say, of course, that the novel's moral message is a ruse. Rather, while the novel can be read simply for that moral message, the moral message itself carries a political value.[18] Within the novel, each narrator emphasizes his or her resignation, obedience, and passive endurance (usually during some kind of exile or other suffering) as a way of subtly identifying his or her political allegiance and good faith. These subtly politicized narrators, in turn, help alert readers to the novel's political points. Clelia, the first of the novel's narrators, faces a conflict that reappears repeatedly in the linked stories: the conflict between love and duty. After consulting an oracle about the propriety of her love for Marcellus, she initially concludes that "a young Lady ought to interpret [the oracle's] meaning according to the dictates of filial Obedience, and to have no other Will but that of her Parents" (I: 9). Filial obedience can easily be assimilated to the idea of political obedience, especially under the divine right, patriarchalist paradigm of kingship held by Jacobites. Clelia appears to transgress quite flagrantly, in spite of her resolutions, by writing to Marcellus after her parents have forbidden the marriage. She is careful and emphatic, however, in castigating herself for this disobedience, saying, "I can never forgive my self, therefore wonder not if my Friends remain disobliged" (I: 11). Her moralizing reasserts the values she violated. She even takes the behavior of her uncle, whose son Asiaticus has been lost, as a model: "his Wisdom, Patience, and Resignation under his Sufferings, have been such Lectures to me as I hope I never shall forget" (I: 12). Her uncle's situation—the loss of someone dearly loved—is a rough parallel to her own, and both can be seen as variations of the "lost lover" trope common in Jacobite writing.[19] In this context, the resignation displayed by the uncle and wished for by Clelia becomes the patience and endurance needed by the Jacobite faithful as they await the restoration of the Stuart line. It is Clelia's commentary on her narrative—the moments when she makes readers aware of her presence as narrator—that provide the clue to its political meaning.

Clarinthia, who suffers far more shocking trials during her story, displays just the kind of patient endurance for which Clelia wishes. Even though her father, Turpius, sequesters her in order to further his plan to make her marry his illegitimate son, she submits to her confinement, saying, "I too

well knew my Duty to him and Heaven" to disobey by writing to anyone
without her father's permission (I: 26). Unlike Clelia, Clarinthia is able
to maintain her obedience despite her awareness that there is something
wrong with the situation. When Turpius himself begins to take a sexual
interest in his daughter, even to the point of attempting to rape her, her
filial duty is tested even further.[20] She is fortunately rescued from the rape
by a stranger who kills her masked assailant. Her gratitude for this rescue is
stifled, however, when the mask is removed and she realizes that it is her
father who has been killed. She is loath to accept any further help from
the stranger, "his Hands still wreeking with my Father's Blood; (for wicked
as he was he was still my Father)" (I: 32). Clearly, the duty of obedience
is not to be set aside, even in the case of such obvious evil as incestuous
rape. Nothing, according to Clarinthia, can nullify the obligation she owes
him, and she cannot be grateful to his murderer, no matter what she has
been saved from. Although this position may appear extreme, it accords
with the Jacobite idea of passive obedience, which is due even to a king
who "violated all the laws and behaved arbitrarily"—just as Turpius does.[21]
Clarinthia's sense of guilt at her father's death thus identifies her as a good
Jacobite subject of her father.

Clarinthia also expresses a rudimentary social theory that places her on
the Jacobite-Tory end of the spectrum. When a young servant maid com-
forts her by describing "the great Honour that attended patient Suffering
for the sake of Virtue" (I: 39), Clarinthia's praise of this servant leads her to
comment on the providential organization of society. She points out to her
audience that the maid's "low State" itself illustrates this order, since it demonstrates how "Human-kind becomes united, that every one having some
Quality esteemable, recommends him to the assistance of others; for none
being perfect, none can remain independant; but the mutual necessities we
have of each others assistance, causes reciprocal Obligations, which tyes the
knot of human Society" (I: 40). The mere presence of such a statement is
itself political, since it expresses a view of social relations that implies and
includes ideas about the right way to govern that society. The particular view
put forward—the idea that society is ordered into a hierarchy through mutual obligations—is conservative and linked to Tory and Jacobite political
beliefs.[22] Moreover, this reciprocal structure of obligation also suggests a gift
economy and recalls the structure of the framed-novelle itself as an exchange
of tales, suggesting that *Exilius*'s very form images the kind of political society it seeks to recreate. Like Clelia, Clarinthia comments on her own story in
such a way as to indicate her political allegiance, and she even manages to
implicate the form of the text with that political ideology.

This pattern continues throughout the book, with nearly all the narrators
discussing the need for patient suffering in exile or other trials. Scipiana,
who is initially abducted by the libertine Clodius and ends up in exile in

Egypt, cautiously attributes her moral courage to an interesting source: her learning. She explains,

> I made the Study of Philosophy, the *Greek* and Oriental Tongues, my Business and Diversion. How far this is suitable to our Sex I dare not pretend to determine, the Men having taken Learning for their Province, we must not touch upon its Borders without being suppos'd Usurpers; however, since it did not displease my Father, I regret not those Moments I bestow'd in its Service, but think 'em still my own, and not slip'd with the rest of my Life's Actions into the Abyss of Time past, which returns no more, but are always present, or at least the Product of those Moments, to wit, the good Morals I learn'd, they are always at my Command. (I: 76)

This passage employs at least two strategies in defense of female learning: it first denies any threat to male prerogative and then asserts a moral benefit to women. Scipiana carefully denies that her case is applicable to all women and suggests the seriousness of the threat by calling learned women "Usurpers," a charge that would seem particularly damning from a Jacobite perspective. Yet she immediately proceeds to defuse this apparent threat by pointing out that her studies were approved by her father, the representative of male prerogative for her. If her father permitted her to study, she cannot, therefore, be considered a usurper of the privilege. The second stage of the defense opens out from this point; once her learning has been authorized, she is free to appreciate its advantages. And given the Jacobite context, her claim that learning inculcates "good Morals" resonates with the preface's linking of morals and Jacobitism. Because Scipiana's "Morals" identify her, in the novel's terms, as a good and faithful Jacobite, her learning is further authorized as part of what leads her to that political position. The framed-novelle form, then, enables the assertion of otherwise marginalized voices, and the Jacobite and woman-centered perspectives help to reinforce each other.

Two other characters in *Exilius* present similar defenses. Jemella, part of whose story is told within Scipiana's, explains her reluctance to marry much as Scipiana explained the value of her learning: "I had no Mind to ingage myself so soon in a married State, always counting this time of Virginity more distinctly my own, as if snatch'd from the round Ring of Eternity" (I: 82). While Jemella does not claim any particular interest in education, she argues for a life that would be seen as unusual for women, and she suggests a kind of right for women to have some part of life that is their own.[23] Similarly, Galecia, the daughter of the Queen of Numidia in Asiaticus's narrative, exhibits Scipiana's learning and Jemella's inclination for the single life. Although Galecia does not narrate in this novel, Barker uses the same name for her self-representations in other works,[24] and she plays an important role in *Exilius*. As Asiaticus describes her, "She was a Lady of a masculine

Spirit, and undervalu'd the little Delicacies of her Sex, making the Study of Philosophy, and the Laws of her Country, her chief Business; in which she was pleased to entertain me very learnedly. . . . But this heroick Temper of hers . . . made her scorn to be a Subject of *Cupid*'s Empire, or to comply with feminine Formalities" (II: 32–33). Significantly, Asiaticus had earlier derided his sister Scipiana's learning. Galecia's appearance in his narrative, then, suggests his need for reeducation. And in fact, Asiaticus depicts Galecia not only as noble under pressure but also as wise in her understanding of government. These three characters, taken together, demonstrate that for Barker political virtue is associated with independent, educated women. Asiaticus's respect for Galecia further strengthens this association, since his tale demonstrates that her response—informed by Jacobite ideology—to the crisis that develops is the proper one, and he learns to respect her for that. Because it speaks to a particular public rather than to the Habermasian bourgeois public sphere, this novel can use Jacobite ideology to argue for the importance and value of female education. It constructs a community within the novel—a community united by the stories they tell, by their shared ideology, and by the framed-novelle form which brings stories and ideology together—that mirrors the community reading the novel, and that community allows for the intersection and mutual reinforcement of these marginalized positions.

Asiaticus's narrative, in fact, is one of the most overtly political tales in Barker's novel, and it develops the novel's concern with both Jacobites' and women's voices. Asiaticus travels to Numidia in his search for Clarinthia and becomes caught up in political power struggles. His commentary on these events not only validates Galecia's role and abilities but also marks him as possessing the correct political understanding. Asiaticus identifies two main problems in the Numidian political situation: first, the Queen's difficulty controlling her passion, and second, the danger of potential usurpation by the people. Significantly, although the turmoil in Numidia is touched off by Galecia's apparent murder of her fiancé, Boccus, prince of Mauritania, Asiaticus never censures Galecia for this action and does not blame her for the events that follow. As he explains it, the Queen's passion for him creates a problem largely because it causes her to forget "her Honour, Interest, and her Peoples Happiness" (II: 42). She places personal desires above political duty. Since she is ruling only as regent for her son, "her Children . . . ought to have been her principal Care" (II: 42). In effect, because of her interest in Asiaticus, she chooses to protect him at the expense of her child, who is the rightful ruler. Using her power in this way—offering to send her children as hostages—essentially makes her a usurper. Asiaticus's commentary here focuses specifically on the Queen's duties as regent rather than as a mother; one of her excuses for sending the children away is to "make the Throne and Palace more . . . secure for her and me" (II: 42). Especially since Asiaticus has no right to the throne and the Queen's right is limited to that of a regent, her crime is specifically political and public, and its familial aspects are not emphasized. She is, therefore, presented as a political figure rather than a domestic one—something of a mixed blessing, given the novel's criticism of her, but consistent with its tendency to allow women a voice and role beyond passivity and the household.

Asiaticus also comments strongly on Galecia's response to the situation, pointing out that she acts out of "Duty to the King her Brother" in calling a council to consult about the best course of action (II: 43). Her political sense guides her to act in the best interests of the king and country. At the same time, he notes that her duty and political sense also guide her to limit the council's power. Although the members of the council argue that they should rule as regent, she refuses to allow this because of "the Danger of unhinging the Government, and instead of making Things better, perhaps worse; and in thus preserving the young King from the Hands of the King of *Mauritania*, he might be cast into the Hands of his own Subjects, whose Ambition perhaps might not be so easily bounded as their Allegiance broken; well knowing how dangerous it is for a King to part with the Reins of Government" (II: 44). Such a commentary seems to reflect on the English situation at the time of James II's departure, and the Numidian council's desire to avoid one problem of governance by creating another seems to mirror the Jacobite interpretation of the Revolution of 1688. Asiaticus's warning about the dangerous tendencies of councils fits the Jacobites' understanding of the invitation issued to William III; they saw it as a betrayal of the true king arising from the ambition and self-interest of a small group of subjects. Furthermore, the warning suggests that the greater evil is to allow subjects more power, since it unsettles the very foundations of monarchy by suggesting that the subjects' allegiance can, in fact, be broken— precisely what Jacobites believed had already happened. If subjects become aware that they can change their allegiance, then something like revolution and usurpation could follow. The language of the passage also implies that if this were to happen, the entire government (not merely a particular form of it) would be undermined. Asiaticus thus explicitly praises Galecia for following the principles that guided Stuart loyalists. Interestingly, it is a woman who exemplifies the best kind of political behavior, even when the narrator is male.

The second component of the political situation Asiaticus discusses is related to the problem of subjects' allegiance. He is concerned with how easily the main body of the people can be misled by misrepresentations. After the apparent murder of Boccus, several different accounts are given out, leading to the emergence of factions: "Thus we see how diversly Things are represented to the World . . . which shews, that Men credit what they fancy, and by Degrees think they know what they have only by

Hear-say, and then act according to this mistaken Knowledge, mistaken Information, and mistaken Fancy. By this Means the *Numidians* began to be in divers Divisions" (II: 41). Although it seemingly denounces divisions and parties, this passage contains a standard feature of early eighteenth-century party rhetoric. Tories and Whigs both accused each other of creating division, and each party, claiming to aim at unification, represented its own perspective as supposedly unbiased by such misrepresentation.[25] What makes Asiaticus's attitude toward the people a conservative, Jacobite one is clarified by a later comment. Noting that some Mauritanians, at the instigation of rivals to their ruler, Boccus, believe the recovered Boccus to be a fraud, he comments, "by which one sees, how easy it is to impose upon a Populace, who are generally ready to receive any Notion, though never so ridiculous, if it does but diminish the Power of their Superiors" (II: 56). The deception and resulting divisions are dangerous not merely in themselves but also because they threaten to take power away from its rightful holders. Creating factions, in other words, can only work to unbalance the proper system of government by weakening the monarchy and creating the danger of usurpation of authority. Moreover, the problem Asiaticus describes is one of mediation, which carries political meaning. When factions hold sway, they also control information, disseminating it as "Hearsay" and misrepresentation. Since these factions are, therefore, mediating between the ruler and his subjects, they interfere with proper political relations. Not only is such control of information a usurpation of power, but it is also a shift away from older forms of the public sphere and toward the bourgeois public sphere. In premodern forms of publicness, the monarch represented her- or himself directly to the people in a kind of performance (the progresses of Renaissance rulers serve as excellent examples).[26] The emergence of other commentators who mediate between the ruler and the people is precisely what Habermas sees as foundational to the bourgeois public sphere. Public opinion, in his model, arises from exactly this type of mediation as newspapers and individuals disseminate information and comment, allowing for representations other than the state's. For Asiaticus, as for most Jacobites, this kind of interference would have been anathema because it challenged the very nature of the king's power as displayed through his public representation.[27] Asiaticus's criticisms thus reinforce the idea that the appropriate form of government—and of publicness as well—is a monarchy of the kind favored by the Stuarts.

But the novel's most overtly political narrator is Exilius, the title character. Raised in exile (as his name indicates) and possessing great virtue, he is clearly a figure for James Francis Edward Stuart, the Old Pretender. Moreover, he becomes involved in Egypt's political upheaval and uses his commentary on events to make clear how they represent versions of earlier events in English politics. Interestingly, Exilius is also a poet and speaks of poetry as his "faithful Spouse" (I: 95), much as Barker writes of Galesia making a vow to poetry in *The Amours of Bosvil and Galesia*.[28] Subtly, then, he is linked to Barker herself and to her female voice. Because both works were composed and circulated in manuscript much earlier than their dates of print publication, readers of *Exilius* (especially those who belonged to Barker's select audience) might have known the other work and made the connection. By giving a character who stands for the rightful king features of the author, the novel ties good politics and good authorship together. Both are defined by faithfulness in the face of suffering. Authorship of the right kind—whether Exilius's poetry or the story-telling of the novel's narrators—therefore becomes part of what signifies virtue in Jacobite terms. Not incidentally, it also helps to draw its community together. The framed-novelle form, in its figuring of mutual obligation through story-telling, both creates and depicts the circle of narrators. The narrators discover the many ways their stories and their values intersect; the character of Exilius connects that community to the Old Pretender as well as to writers; and Barker's novel itself, by expressing Jacobite values, helps to strengthen bonds among a Jacobite community of readers.

Exilius's experiences in many ways mirror events and ideas significant to that Jacobite community. When the king of Egypt appoints him to a high military position, he explains the hostile reaction provoked as the result of "Murmurings amongst the People . . . fomented by the disgraced Captain and his Friends, with all the subtle insinuations possible; as if the King meant to join with the *Romans*, to overthrow the Religion and Laws of the *Ægyptians*" (I: 108). Like Asiaticus, Exilius sees popular discontent as the result of deliberate misrepresentations that intervene between the king and his people. The captain creates a public representation of the king that successfully displaces the king's own representation of himself. Again, the problem of representation brings issues of the public sphere into play. And the particular complaint is obviously reminiscent of those who argued in 1688 that James II, as a Catholic, intended to overthrow the religion and laws of the English. By casting this idea as the work of someone who has been turned out of office, Exilius makes it part of a power play, a move to undermine the power of the king. Predictably (from the Jacobite perspective), this power play results in an "open and actual Rebellion" against the king (I: 109). To further emphasize the similarities to the English situation, Exilius points out that the king's brother, who is an "excellent Prince," is despised by the people because he follows "the *Jewish* Way of Worship," which stands in for Catholicism in this narrative (I: 109). This fictional situation cobbles together elements from various moments in the 1680s: the king and his brother call to mind Charles II and James II, and the hostility to them matches fears raised throughout the decade that both rulers, especially James II, would open the way to a Catholic takeover. The fictional rebellion might be identified either with Monmouth's rebellion, which was successfully put down (as is the fictional version), or with the events of 1688–1689, which the Jacobites construed as a rebellion, one they surely wished had been put down. But specific correlation here seems less important than the resonance of the events and the values encapsulated: rebellion, especially when based on misrepresentation in the public sphere, is never justified and always illegal. Both Exilius's life and his commentary reinforce core Jacobite ideas.

Given that Exilius's interest in poetry links him to Barker and that his condition of exile links him to the Old Pretender, it is not surprising that he unites both the passive suffering and the overt political commentary we have seen in other narrators in this novel. He establishes clearly, as we have seen, that the events he narrates in Egypt provide a critique of English politics, and he goes further than almost any other narrator in making openly political judgments. Explaining why the rebel army disintegrated, he says that discipline could not be maintained, "for where there is only a precarious and not a legal Authority, Commands are ill exhibited and worse obeyed: For such a kind of an usurp'd Power being as it were a Burlesque on Justice, and a Banter on Government, which serve, rather to encrease than correct Crimes" (I: 114). This explanation neatly encapsulates a number of significant Jacobite beliefs. First, it identifies usurpation as the source of the trouble, an obviously Jacobite point. Second, it argues that such usurpation means that the power thus acquired has no legal basis—just as Jacobites believed that England's government had no legal authority after the removal of James II. Government without that authority becomes, almost literally, a joke. The phrase "ill exhibited" further hints at the problem of representation: orders that come from an illegitimate authority cannot be properly represented in the correct royal manner, with the signs and tokens of royal power, so the power such orders claim to represent is delusory. Finally, this explanation points to an idea that is central not only to the Jacobites' political message in general but also to the coding that makes this novel in particular politically Jacobite: the idea that the absence of properly constituted authority leads to moral disintegration, that when the ruling power is criminal, everyone else becomes criminal as well. Exilius's narrative provides an explicit link between the general moral message stated in the preface and the specific political meaning encoded in the stories that convey that message. Thus, when he is imprisoned for loving Scipiana (called Exilia in his narrative) and notes, "I had sufficient Occasion to exercise my passive Courage," his moralizing comment has political implications: it is his correct political allegiance that allows him to maintain his moral strength (I: 149). He is, then, central to the novel in many ways: as the title character, as a figure

for the Old Pretender, as a link to the notion of authorship and suppressed or exiled voices, and as the most overt connection between the
moral and political themes of the novel.

By extension, and by the logic of the novel, each narrator's moralizing
commentary on his or her narrative can be taken as demonstrating that
same political allegiance, since only loyalty to the Stuarts can guarantee
moral purity. As they tell their stories, the narrators constitute a community
for themselves, a community based on the commonality of their experiences in exile and of their patient endurance and good faith. The novel's
hopeful ending, in which all the couples are reunited and returned home
from exile, self-evidently uses marriage to figure the reward for this moral
and political purity as restoration—a restoration also represented in terms
of form, as the stories' closure depends on the revelation that they are all
interconnected. The political good faith that authorizes each narrator also
makes them deserving of such a reward. But such loyalty is not depicted
as simple or easy. Almost every character faces a difficult choice at some
point—not always as difficult as Clarinthia's but always highlighting the
tension between obligations to opposing ideas (such as love and duty)
and the difficulty of choosing between them. This portrayal of the pain of
loyalty itself may seem surprising in a Jacobite text. But as Toni Bowers has
shown, the "myth of Jacobite certainty, ideological clarity, and unquench-
able optimism" is precisely that: a myth. [29] Barker's own life experience
certainly bears this out; neither her fifteen-year exile with James II's court
at St. Germain nor her life after returning to England in 1704 could have
been easy. And the novel's willingness to dwell on the agonies of fidelity fits
a more limited conception of audience: an audience that does not need to
be convinced of Jacobite ideals, an audience that might welcome a sympathetic portrayal of the troubles particular to it. Understanding this novel as
belonging to manuscript culture thus helps to restore its political valence.
Rather than broadcasting a polemical message to a bourgeois public sphere,
it speaks to a limited group, a subaltern public, by presenting its ideas and
values sympathetically.

But the manuscript did come to be printed, and, as King points out, this
novel, together with *The Amours of Bosvil and Galesia*, brought Barker "such
popularity as [she] was to enjoy in her own lifetime."[30] What accounts for
this success? Why would a manuscript-oriented text that was, in effect,
coded for a specific audience do well in the public marketplace of print?
There are at least two explanations. One possibility is that Barker's political
stance—made clear by Edmund Curll's marketing of her novel as well as by
the novel's encoding—had a reasonably broad appeal.[31] Historians differ
about the extent of support for the Jacobite cause in parliamentary politics,
but Paul Monod's study shows that, around the time of the publication
of Barker's two earliest novels, popular support was approaching a high

point.[32] Moreover, King shows that despite the title page's date of 1715, *Exilius* actually "appeared in August, 1714, during the interval between the death of Queen Anne . . . and the arrival of George I," further suggesting the novel's political import.[33] So it is conceivable that Curll managed to time the novel's publication to coincide with a rise in Jacobite sentiment and a burst of Jacobite activity and that readers bought the book because it appealed to their political interests and sympathies.

It is also possible that the novel did well not because its politics were attractive to readers but because they were not obvious to readers. In other words, the novel's encoding of its Jacobite values may have been successful; readers outside the privileged coterie might not have been aware of the political meaning of the marriage trope, for instance. The events of the novel correlate only loosely to historical events, and the characters cannot be identified with specific historical figures. Rather, the novel's political import emerges through associations, moral values, and form. Early readers might have done precisely what many modern critics have done: ignore the political coding in order to read the narrative that follows as a romance with no political content—even though the form itself is political.[34] Such a reading performs precisely the operation necessary to render the work and its narrator apparently acceptable to the bourgeois public sphere. By stripping the narrative of its political ideology, this kind of reading renders it less particular and more apparently disinterested, thereby making it seem to fit the criteria for public discourse. Paradoxically, the novel's reliance on allusiveness to address a manuscript circle may have helped to obscure its political particularity and, thus, to have enabled it to be more easily assimilated into the public sphere. Barker's political allegiance is there to be discovered in the novel, in the recurring tropes and in the narrators' system of moral values, but because those values come close to constituting a code aimed at a secretive group, readers not seeking such a code may not find it. To the uninitiated, a text without the obvious political allegories of a *New Atalantis* might pass as innocuous. But to the reader alert to more subtle kinds of political reference, *Exilius*'s moral message, as delivered by a particular kind of narrative community expressed in the framed-novelle form, reflects a political message as well. In fact, the existence of a work like *Exilius* reminds us of the ways that genre, narration, the public sphere, politics, and authorship intersected in the early eighteenth century: genre and narrative form carried political meaning and, together with notions of authorship, helped indicate what kind of publicness a work aimed at. So by using its form, its narrative structure, to address a specific limited kind of public audience, Barker's novel may also have found a means for that public both to join and to challenge the demands of the developing bourgeois public sphere.

NOTES

1. Kathyrn R. King, *Jane Barker, Exile: A Literary Career, 1675–1725* (Oxford: Clarendon, 2000).

2. One exception is Eleanor Wikberg's "The Expression of the Forbidden in Romance Form: Genre as Possibility in Jane Barker's *Exilius*," *Genre* 22 (Spring 1989): 3–19. Wikberg provides one of the few studies to focus on *Exilius* specifically and to give serious consideration to the issue of genre; however, Wikberg reads Barker's use of the heroic romance as a means to express female fantasies and does not connect the work to contemporary politics.

3. See Josephine Donovan, *Women and the Rise of the Novel, 1405–1726* (New York: St. Martin's, 1999).

4. Anne E. Duggan, *Salonnières, Furies, and Fairies: The Politics of Gender and Cultural Change in Absolutist France* (Newark: University of Delaware Press, 2005), 51, 86.

5. Donovan, *Women and the Rise of the Novel*, 30.

6. Ibid., 32.

7. Ibid., 33.

8. Margaret J. M. Ezell, *Social Authorship and the Advent of Print* (Baltimore, MD: Johns Hopkins University Press, 1999), 40.

9. King, *Jane Barker*, 34, 151.

10. Leigh Eicke, "Jane Barker's Jacobite Writings," in *Women's Writing and the Circulation of Ideas: Manuscript Publication in England, 1550–1800*, ed. George Justice and Nathan Tinker (Cambridge: Cambridge University Press, 2002), 140.

11. Jürgen Habermas, *The Structural Transformation of the Public Sphere: An Inquiry into a Category of Bourgeois Society*, trans. Thomas Berger and Frederick Lawrence (Cambridge, MA: MIT Press, 1989), 54. On this point, see also Habermas's claim that the bourgeois public sphere's "parity" depended on the "power and prestige of public office" as well as "economic dependencies" being "held in suspense," 36. In other words, Habermas claims that speakers who are socially, politically, or otherwise marked or particularized would be excluded from the public sphere on that ground. For the role of social markers in other kinds of publics, see Habermas's own discussion of "representative publicness," which he sees as "inseparable from the lord's concrete existence" and as "wedded to personal attributes," 7–8. Nancy Fraser provides a useful elaboration of these ideas through her discussion of "counterpublics" which "elaborat[ed] alternative styles of political behavior and alternative norms of public speech." See "Rethinking the Public Sphere: A Contribution to the Critique of Actually Existing Democracy," in *Habermas and the Public Sphere*, ed. Craig Calhoun (Cambridge, MA: MIT Press, 1992), 116.

12. Julie Choi, "Feminine Authority? Common Sense and the Question of Voice in the Novel," *New Literary History* 27.4 (1996): 641–62.

13. Jane Barker, *Exilius; or, The Banish'd Roman* (1715; reprint, New York: Garland, 1973), A2, A2v. All further references are to this edition.

14. Lois Potter, *Secret Rites and Secret Writing: Royalist Literature, 1641–1660* (Cambridge: Cambridge University Press, 1989), 111.

15. Paul Kléber Monod, *Jacobitism and the English People 1688–1788* (Cambridge: Cambridge University Press, 1989), 27.

16. King, *Jane Barker*, 161–62.

17. In Habermas's classic description of the bourgeois public sphere, "abstract universality" is required of all participants. See *Structural Transformation*, 54.

18. For purely moralistic readings of *Exilius*, see John Richetti, *Popular Fiction Before Richardson: Narrative Patterns 1700–1739* (Oxford: Clarendon, 1992), 231–37; and Marilyn Williamson, *Raising Their Voices: British Women Writers 1650–1750* (Detroit, MI: Wayne State University Press, 1990), 247–49.

19. Monod, *Jacobitism*, 63–66.

20. The "image of rape" is another persistent feature of Jacobite rhetoric. See Howard Erskine-Hill, "Literature and the Jacobite Cause: Was There a Rhetoric of Jacobitism?" in *Ideology and Conspiracy: Aspects of Jacobitism, 1689–1759*, ed. Eveline Cruickshanks (Edinburgh: John Donald Publishers, 1982), 50. The presence of rape here reinforces the sense of the wrong done to Clarinthia.

21. Monod, *Jacobitism*, 18.

22. Delarivière Manley adduces a similar idea to explain her reasons for giving herself up as the author of *The New Atalantis*: innocent people to whom she has an obligation have been arrested, and to fulfill her obligation, she must do what she can to clear them. See Delarivière Manley, *The Adventures of Rivella*, ed. Katherine Zelinsky (Peterborough, Ontario: Broadview, 1999), 107.

23. The phrase "married State" nicely encapsulates the understanding of marriage as political that helps to construct and define this particular subaltern public.

24. In *Love Intrigues* (1713), *A Patch-Work Screen for the Ladies*, (1723), and *The Lining of the Patch Work Screen* (1726), the central character, who represents Barker, is named Galesia.

25. Frank O'Gorman provides a useful summary of common ideas about party: "Parties generated damaging divisions in the body politic . . . . They thus threatened the harmony of society and endangered the very stability of the state." See *The Long Eighteenth Century: British Political and Social History 1688–1832* (London: Arnold, 1997), 44.

26. As Habermas puts it, *"publicness . . . of representation . . . .* was something like a status attribute . . . [the] incumbent represented it publicly. He displayed himself, presented himself as an embodiment of some sort of 'higher' power." See *Structural Transformation*, 7.

27. For example, when Charles Leslie writes that kings "stand before us, in the *Person* of the Great God *himself*," his language highlights this presentational type of publicity. See *A View of the Times, Their Principles and Practices: In the First Volume of the Rehearsals. By Philalethes* (London, 1708; Eighteenth Century Collections Online. Gale Group. http://galenet.galegroup.com/servlet/ECCO), 1: 130.

28. Galesia, the character who represents Barker in *The Amours of Bosvil and Galesia*, at one point composes a poem involving a *"Vow"* to the Muses and immediately afterwards "resolv'd to espouse a Book." See Jane Barker, *The Amours of Bosvil and Galesia*, in *The Galesia Trilogy and Selected Manuscript Poems of Jane Barker*, ed. Carol Shiner Wilson (New York: Oxford University Press, 1997), 14–15.

29. Bowers, "Jacobite Difference," 868.

30. King, *Jane Barker*, 189.

31. Ibid., 170.
32. Monod, *Jacobitism*, 344.
33. King, *Jane Barker*, 150.
34. See, for instance, Richetti, *Popular Fiction*, 230–31, and Jane Spencer, "Creating the Woman Writer: The Autobiographical Works of Jane Barker," *Tulsa Studies in Women's Literature* 2 (1983): 168–73.

8

Eliza Haywood's *Love in Excess* and the Personal Politics of Collectivity

Melissa Mowry

In some ways, Jerry Beasley's most obvious contribution to eighteenth-century studies lies in his unparalleled work as an archivist and editor. At a time when the case for publishing editions of eighteenth-century women writers needed to be repeated constantly, Beasley was a tireless advocate of the enterprise, editing several critical editions himself and shepherding his students towards their own expert editions. Beasley, of course, concluded his career as general editor of the monumental *Works of Tobias Smollett* published by the University of Georgia Press. Beyond his editorial contributions, Jerry Beasley was also a shrewd and deft critic, and it is his criticism that interests me most here, particularly his important article, "Portraits of a Monster: Robert Walpole and Early English Prose Fiction."[1]

In this article, which offered readers a capacious background in early eighteenth-century English politics and a focused reading of Eliza Haywood's *The Adventures of Eovaai* (1736), Beasley joined a generation of historians and critics who understood that English literary culture of the first half of the eighteenth century was, more often than not, also political. Together, these scholars opened a conversation, the potential and breadth of which has in many ways yet to be fulfilled, about the complex relationship between the imaginative possibilities of literature and the imaginative possibilities of politics. More specifically, Beasley found Haywood embracing an unvarnished Lockean politics that defended individual political rights against the insults of "arbitrary power."[2] The few critics who, like Beasley,

145

have understood Haywood as a politically engaged novelist, have more or less hewed to this Lockean interpretation.[3]

It is in the spirit of Beasley's opening invitation that I undertake my argument here that Eliza Haywood was a political writer long before she published *The Adventures of Eovaai*.[4] More importantly, I want to suggest that while Haywood's resistance to tyranny was real and unabashed, the position from which she articulated that resistance was not one of Lockean individualism, which tends to focus on opposition between individuals and their government. Haywood's politics, I argue instead, were significantly more nuanced. She viewed the constitutive dissaggregation inherent in Locke's premise that the individual precedes various iterations of political collectivity as her period's defining political problem, rather than the tool that would usher in a new period of political equity and justice in the spirit of the 1688 Revolution Settlement. The result for Haywood was a literary career initiated and sustained at critical intervals, as I have argued elsewhere, as an intervention in the prevailing debate about the nature of both personal and political sovereignty.[5] To this debate she contributed her earliest foray into fiction and her commitment to what an earlier generation might have described as "collectivity" as the guiding principle for organizing social, political, and epistemological relations alike.

For those of us in the twentieth and twenty-first centuries, "collectivity" has a Stalinist patina, evoking gray images of life on a Soviet-style commune. Haywood herself, however, was only two generations removed from the mid-seventeenth-century context that advanced collectivity as the constituent characteristic of rights and liberties. Individuals, in contrast, functioned less as the foundation of political life and more as its bulwark, emerging as politically meaningful only when those collective rights were threatened. As the Leveller leader John Lilburne put the matter,

> Freedome and Liberty being the onely Jewels in esteem with the Commonality, as a thing most pretious unto them meriting that men should expose themselves to all danger, for the preservation and defense thereof against all tyranny and oppression of what nature and condition soever.[6]

By the time Eliza Haywood launched her literary career with the publication of the first two parts of *Love in Excess* in 1719, she had already enjoyed a good deal of notoriety as an actress. *Love in Excess* augmented that fame, "running into four editions before it was collected with her other novels to date in *The Works of Mrs. Eliza Haywood* in 1724 and the following year in her *Secret Histories, Novels and Poems*."[7] With the exceptions of Daniel Defoe's *Robinson Crusoe* (1719) and Jonathan Swift's *Gulliver's Travels* (1726), the popularity of *Love in Excess* was unrivaled until Samuel Richardson's *Pamela* appeared in 1740. For Ros Ballaster and others, *Love in Excess* marks a new, simpler period in English prose fiction when novels "abandoned the complexity of the rediscovered, translated, and reconstructed source commonly employed as a means of simultaneously concealing and signifying political intent."[8] If Haywood abandons the elaborate allegories and artifices that distinguished earlier political novels by women, she does so not in the name of forsaking political commentary but rather in order to engage its principles more candidly. Most critics dismiss the political frame Haywood gives her novel as flimsy pretext for the novel's "real" focus on romance and the amorous adventures of Count D'elmont.[9] Upon closer scrutiny, the War of the Grand Alliance (1689–1697), known in England as King William's War, is the only thing that renders intelligible D'elmont's persistent, sometimes obstinate, and usually disastrous inability to understand that social interactions and information are complex aggregations of evidence—in practice, an epistemology of collectivity wherein stable bonds are possible only when the individual understands his/her identity to be a function of his/her relationship with others.[10]

The War of the Grand Alliance was the last of three major wars of expansion waged by Louis XIV. His efforts to enlarge France's borders were blocked by a loose alliance between England, the Netherlands, and the Austrian Hapsburgs. The French king had hoped to capitalize on dynastic conflicts between England and the Netherlands and the Austrian war with the Turks to annex the Palatinate. Much to Louis XIV's chagrin, William of Orange was successful in his defense of his wife's claim to the English throne against her father and successfully drove James II from England. In 1688, he began his joint rule of England as William III, together with his wife Mary II. Shortly thereafter, England joined the United Provinces in the war against France on the European continent and the ancillary conflicts in North America, India, and Africa. The major European powers thus found themselves embroiled in a costly nine-year war. The War of the Grand Alliance seems to figure for Haywood as something like the zenith of English opposition to French tyranny, where William III and the Revolution Settlement represented the virtues of English liberty and France represented the vices of royal absolutism. In the context of this larger geopolitical conflict and tyranny's defeat at the hands of England and her parliamentary government, D'elmont's multiple misadventures offer Haywood's readers repeated occasions to contemplate the socially corrosive effects of tyranny and its epistemological modality singularity, on the abilities of her characters to form affiliations and thus move toward collectivity.

Having set the stage with the War of the Grand Alliance's conclusion, Haywood immediately presents her readers with characters who are defined by their ability to forge only affiliations that are fractured, incomplete, and superficial. Inverting the conventional romantic tableau which represents the social as the impediment to the lovers' fulfillment of their romantic desires, *Love in Excess* represents the personal libidinal greed of lovers as an obstacle to social stability. In the process, Haywood reimagines desire as an effect of the social.

Readers are first introduced to the novel's main character, who is central but not heroic. Count D'elmont is a veteran of the war, where he served with some distinction under "the great and intrepid Luxembourgh," a reference that places D'elmont in direct conflict with William III, whom Luxembourgh outmaneuvered and defeated in major battles between 1691 and 1693 (37).[11] As the end of the war has eliminated any further opportunities for D'elmont to demonstrate his "valour" against the English king, D'elmont returns to the French court of Louis XIV, where he is "received by the King and Court, after a manner that might gratifie the ambition of the proudest" (37). The scene shift from battlefield to court reflects an important shift in values from morality and principles to ambition and power. But the most important modality of that shift is D'elmont's departure from his brother, who stays behind at St. Omer to convalesce from wounds he received in the war. D'elmont's willing departure from their affiliation transforms him from a man who would die for his principles and his country's honor to a court celebrity:

> The beauty of his person, the gaity of his air, and the unequalled charms of his conversation, make him the admiration of both sexes; and whilst those of his own strove which should gain the largest share of his friendship; the other, vented fruitless wishes, and in secret, cursed that custom which forbids women to make a declaration of their thoughts. (37)

Without the common cause of the war, D'elmont becomes the focus of rivalry and desire. In D'elmont, Haywood offers her readers a character who must journey from vanity and an errant belief that he need not be held to the same standards of ethics that govern the lives of ordinary people to a man who learns that he can have love only when he takes social responsibility for his actions.

Haywood's, though, is not a Hobbesian social sensibility to the extent that D'elmont's return does not merely expose the fundamental venality of human nature. On the contrary, her point here is to demonstrate the corrosive effects of individualism. For the French court only barely functions as a social context—a scant hedge against the "time of Warre where every man is enemy to every man."[12] D'elmont himself is a fundamentally decent man, but he is also naïve and thoughtless about the relationship between his integrity and the larger society in which he moves.

At the heart of Haywood's skepticism lies her belief that people afflicted with impoverished senses of social relations like D'elmont deprive themselves of other perspectives that have the collective effect of ameliorating the distortions inherent in a single point of view. Haywood makes clear her skepticism when she introduces Alovysa, an aristocratic woman who becomes infatuated with D'elmont and through whose character Haywood makes clear that in her single-minded pursuit of his affections willingly commits horrible deceptions and devastating factual distortions. Alovysa is privileged and parentless: "The late death of her parents had left her co-heiress (with her sister,) of a vast estate" (38). Just as D'elmont is separated from his brother, so, too, is Alovysa separated from her sister. Thus isolated from meaning-ful affective relationships and the consequent mitigating effect of alternate interpretations that her parents and sister might otherwise provide, Alovysa struggles and ultimately fails to interpret D'elmont's actions accurately. When she realizes that D'elmont treats her no differently than he treats the other women at court, Alovysa is beside herself, though her outrage is articulated not as disappointment over D'elmont's response but rather as the disbelief that her perceptions could be wrong and that the world has deceived her.

> "What," said she, "have I beheld without concern a thousand lovers at my feet, and shall the only man I ever endeavoured or wished to charm regard me with indifference? Wherefore has the agreeing world joined with my deceitful glass to flatter me in to a vain belief I had invincible attractions? D'elmont sees 'em not, D'elmont is insensible." (38)

Not surprisingly, Alovysa is most perturbed at the dissonance between her desire and her perceptions in public settings as she is engaged in a struggle between the epistemology of individualism on the one hand and the epis-temology of the social on the other hand. "Many days she passed in these inquietudes, and every time she saw him (which was very frequently either at Court, at church, or publick meetings,) she found fresh matter for her troubled thoughts to work upon" (38). Alovysa believes that her privilege and wealth give her dominion over the "publick" and the kinds of knowl-edge that legitimately circulate therein. D'elmont's persistent, if unwitting, subversion of what Alovysa previously experienced as a seamless relation-ship makes it clear that her attempt to master his affections are also an at-tempt to retain what she has understood to be her mastery of public social relations.

D'elmont's ignorance of Alovysa's affections threatens to expose the constitutive distortions underlying her sense of the truth. Indeed, when Alovysa attempts to "right the ship," as it were, by undertaking a secret cor-respondence to lure D'elmont to her side, she sets in motion the ill-fated subplot with Amena. Alovysa sends D'elmont a series of letters that she mistakenly believes will reveal her identity as D'elmont's secret admirer without compromising her honor. What she does not recognize is that she has chosen a lover who, though he lacks her disdain for the social world, is similarly detached from it. Alovysa is certain that if she describes herself to D'elmont, he must conclude that she is the author and, thus, his admirer. He does not do this, of course. Instead, D'elmont attributes the professions and self-descriptions of the letters to the young Amena, who is genuinely attracted to D'elmont. Amena is predictably flattered by his attentions and allows herself to be seduced and nearly ruined by D'elmont's charms.

Clearly, Haywood intends to thus elevate Amena to the status of victim in contrast to the more predatory inclinations of D'elmont and Alovysa. But what is most interesting about the confusion of evidence upon which this subplot depends is that Amena, in important ways, is guilty of the same solipsism that drives D'elmont and Alovysa, for prior to the intrigue set in motion by Alovysa's letters, Amena had no hint that D'elmont's affections lay in her direction. On the contrary, it is Amena's desire for D'elmont that allows her to believe his attentions are not *ex nihilo* and that she simply had overlooked earlier, more subtle evidences of his love. D'elmont's actions thus serve a revealing dual purpose for Amena as they both reinforce her sense of singularity and corrode the social relations that had previously sustained her and safeguarded her reputation.

Alovysa recognizes that she must now compete with Amena, both for D'elmont's affections and for a kind of sovereign authority over both his affections and the evidence thereof. Thus, she resolves to "direct his erring search" (43) and reconstitute his actions in the "valid" context of her desire for him. At this juncture Haywood offers her readers a revealing but unsurprising glimpse of Alovysa's character through her servants' eyes as "They knew her too absolute a mistress not to be obeyed, and executed her commands, without disputing the reason" (43). Alovysa's individualism is underwritten by a sense of her own absolute authority over the world in which she moves. As she explains to Amena when the girl flies to her seeking refuge after she has narrowly escaped complete ruin at D'elmont's hands, Amena has chosen her sanctuary well because in Alovysa's words: "I have no body to whom I need to be accountable for my actions, and am above the censures of the world" (62). Through Alovysa's character, Haywood neatly folds together epistemological singularity, personal desire, and absolute authority, revealing each as a dimension of the other. Amena's failure to read accurately the multiple modalities of information with which she is presented ultimately results in her exile from the novel's world as she escapes to a convent.

It is indicative of Amena's errant judgment and her consequent inability to disrupt the solipsism of Alovysa and D'elmont with her own solipsism that before her story has concluded, Haywood begins to set the stage for the central and most important subplot: the marriages of D'elmont and his brother to Alovysa and her sister Ansellina. If the Amena-Alovysa-D'elmont triangle underscores the destructiveness of individualism to social fabric and personal relations, the evocation of the doubled romantic couples traditional to romance fiction amplifies that indictment by engaging the question of community through the reunion of D'elmont and his brother Brilliard. As the brothers relate the events that have befallen them since their last meeting, Haywood provides a revealing characterization of their responses:

Nothing could be a greater cordial to the Chevalier, than to find his brother was beloved by the sister of Ansellina, he did not doubt but that by this means there might be a possibility of seeing her sooner than else he could have hoped, and the two brothers began to enter into a serious consultation of this affair, which ended with a resolution to fix their fortunes there. (75)

Discounting the effects of true affection, D'elmont agrees to marry Alovysa in order to facilitate his brother's happiness. He reasons that "Alovysa's quality and vast possessions, promising a full gratification of that, he ne'er so much as wished to know, a farther happiness by marriage" (76). Significantly, D'elmont assesses the evidence as disaggregated, singular pieces united only by the institutional formality of marriage. Barring that institution, there is nothing to unite them, and Alovysa's "quality and vast possessions" can not work collectively toward the conclusion of marriage.

Haywood's publishers were clearly attuned to the thematic tension between individual desire and collective affiliation and signaled as much in the epigram that opens the second part of *Love in Excess*:

> Each day we break the bond of humane laws
> For love, and vindicate the common cause.
> Laws for defence of civil rights are placed,
> Love throws the fences down, and makes a general waste.
> Maids, widows, wives, without distinction fall,
> The sweeping deluge love comes on and covers all.

The epigram, which comes from Dryden's translation of Chaucer's *The Knight's Tale* in *Fables, Ancient and Modern* (1700), evokes not only the Middle Ages but also the Restoration, when questions of absolutism, both personal and political, were very much on everyone's minds.[13] But the real issue for Haywood is not, or is not only, that love can become an alibi for selfishness and arbitrary actions but rather that the opposition between love and community must be abolished and that love must be understood to be the "common cause." No relationship in the novel underscores this point more vividly than D'elmont's ill-fated pursuit of his ward Melliora.

D'elmont's path crosses Melliora's when her father, ill and dying, asks his old friend D'elmont to become Melliora's guardian. No sooner has the count agreed to this pact of honor than he is overcome by Melliora's charms.

> "Friendship! did I say?" rejoyned he softning his voice, "that term is too mean to express a zeal like mine, the care, the tenderness, the faith, the fond affection of parents,—brothers,—husbands,—lovers, all comprised in one! one great unutterable! comprehensive meaning is mine! Is mine for Melliora!" (89)

D'elmont believes he has at last found love, but he is mistaken. In fact, he has discovered a desire so megalomaniacal it rivals Alovysa's desire for him. If D'elmont's solipsism rivaled his wife's prior to Melliora's arrival and prompted lapses in the count's judgment, Melliora's appearance forces the errant count to fully inhabit the same degraded and corrupt epistemology that organizes Alovysa's desire for her husband. D'elmont willingly forsakes both his marriage vows to Alovysa and his bond of honor to Melliora's father to begin a campaign that will so distort circumstances that Melliora will be transformed from D'elmont's ward into his mistress.

From his visceral response to first meeting Melliora, D'elmont immediately learns the folly of his earlier disdain for the effects of love. For inasmuch as his ignorance to personal attraction allowed D'elmont to delude himself into believing that the material value he placed on Alovysa's fortune and her physical beauty were enough to cement their relationship, he has now learned his error as he contemplates his marriage vows:

> How often did he curse the hour in which Alovysa's fondness was discovered and how much more, his own ambition which prompted him to take advantage of it? And hurried him precipitately to a hymen, where love (the noblest guest) was wanting. It was in these racks of thought that the unfortunate Amena was remembered, and he could not forbear acknowledging the justice of that doom, which inflicted on him, these very torments he had given her. A severe repentance seized on his soul, and Alovysa for whom he never had any thing more than indifferency, now began to seem distasteful to his fancy, he looked on her, as indeed she was, the chief author of Amena's misfortunes, and abhorred her for that infidelity. (90)

D'elmont's reaction is acute and predictable insofar as it reflects his and Alovysa's mutual inability to comprehend multiple modalities of evidence. D'elmont frames things to himself, using basic propositional logic that rules out any other complicating contingencies that might lead him to a different conclusion.[14] If Melliora is to be worshipped, Alovysa must be "abhorred." If D'elmont evinces a bit of empathy for the fate to which he and Alovysa condemned Amena, he does so only insofar as he now feels pain as well. In thus articulating D'elmont's thought processes, Haywood suggests that barring such personal discomfort D'elmont might never have been brought to acknowledge his role in Amena's misfortune. D'elmont's shortcomings and the dangers of his epistemology are not lost on Melliora. Indeed, it is Melliora herself who points out the dangers of D'elmont's misprisions. When D'elmont comes upon Melliora reading Ovid's *Epistles*, he challenges her reasoning, arguing that her decision is inconsistent with her earlier condemnation of amatory writing. In the process, D'elmont reveals that he understands love only in the most narrow and narcissistic terms, focusing primarily on its singular ability to influence the lover:

> When once the fancy is fixed on a real object, there will be no need of auxiliary forces, the dear idea will spread it self thro' every faculty of the soul, and in a

moment inform us better, than all the writings of the most experienced poets, could do in an age. (108)

Melliora's response is swift and clear. She wants little to do with the obsessiveness of which D'elmont speaks. But what is most striking about her rejection is the way in which Melliora directly subverts the conventional contradiction between reason and multiplicity:

> I am utterly unambitious of any learning this way, and shall endeavour to retain in memory, more of the misfortunes that attended the passion of Sappho, than the tender, tho' never so elegant expressions that produced it. "my lord, without exception they [reason and love] are indeed sometimes united; but how often they are at variance, where may we not find proofs? History is full of them, and daily examples of the many hair-brained matches, and slips much less excusable, sufficiently evince how little reason has to do with the affairs of love; I mean," continued she, with a very serious air, "that sort of love, fore there are two, which hurries people on to an immediate gratification of their desires, tho' never so prejudicial to themselves, or the person they pretend to love." "Pray madam," said the Count a little nettled at this discourse, "What love is that which seems at least to merit the approbation of a lady so extremely nice?" "It has many branches," replied she; "in the first place that which we owe to heaven; in the next to our king, our country, parents, kindred, friends; and lastly, that which fancy inclines, and reason guides us to in a partner for life; but here every circumstance must agree, parity of age, of quality, of fortune, and of humour, consent of friends, and equal affection in each other, for if any one of these particulars fail, it renders all the rest of no effect." (109)

Melliora's words sting D'elmont, but they also prove to be prophetic, for it is precisely the social complexity of reason that he must learn before he can be rewarded with love and the lessons whose failure have caused him to fall into this predicament in the first place. As Melliora points out, their love must be deferred because reason reveals that the circumstances do not agree. Exactly how critical the ability to interpret multiple modalities of evidence is to Haywood's novel is revealed in two subsequent scenes: first, D'elmont's mistaken belief that he is bedding Melliora; and second, his ignorance of Violetta's presence on their trip out of Italy.

Part II of *Love in Excess* culminates with peculiar and, at points, comedic confusion of bodies as D'elmont tries to seduce Melliora. D'elmont has become so desperate to have his ward that he takes Melantha, the sister of his friend the Baron Espernay, into his confidence. Melantha, who is herself infatuated with D'elmont, plots to revenge D'elmont's rebuffing of her advances by appearing to be his willing accessory in his counterplot to seduce Melliora. Melantha pledges to provide D'elmont with access to Melliora's room but, on the fateful night, substitutes herself for D'elmont's real object of desire. She rightly predicts that D'elmont's judgment has been sufficiently clouded so that he will accept the ruse, thereby advancing her ends rather than his own. The episode strains D'elmont's and the readers' credulity alike. Having realized the trick that has been played upon him, D'elmont

> stood like one transfixed with thunder, he knew not what to think, or rather could not think at all, confounded with a seeming impossibility. He beheld the person, whom he thought had lain in his arms, whom he had enjoyed, whose bulk and proportion he still saw in the bed, whom he was just going to address to, and for whom he had been in all the agonies of soul imaginable, come from a distant chamber, and unconcerned, ask coolly how Alovysa came to be taken ill. (144)

Haywood's point is manifest in D'elmont's confusion. Where people allow themselves to be driven by ambition and a kind of desire that is reducible to the singularity of self-satisfaction, they will inevitably misread the evidence with which they are presented.

Haywood concludes what is otherwise a tragic ending to the second section with an ironic wink to her readers when she describes Melantha's fate. Though she has indulged in despicable behavior and deception that facilitated the deaths of both her brother and Alovysa, Haywood manages to absolve Melantha's character of any dire consequences herself:

> Melantha who was not of a humour to take any thing to heart, was married in a short time, and had the good fortune not to be suspected by her husband, though she brought him a child in seven months after her wedding. (159)

The crucial moral distinction for Haywood seems to be that Melantha's desire is capricious but not predatory. She never professes, in other words, to have a burning desire to possess D'elmont's heart, which she knows has been given to Melliora anyway. Rather, what Melantha desires is revenge against D'elmont's slighting of her advances and transient pleasure. Haywood thus detaches Melantha's actions from the rest of the subplot and particularly the tragic deaths of Alovysa and Espernay because they do pursue a kind of megolamaniacal iteration of desire. Espernay desires to expose D'elmont and thereby possess Alovysa at all costs, while Alovysa will stop at nothing to secure her husband to her side. Their obsessions prove fatal.

Responding to Alovysa's cries, D'elmont runs toward her room with his sword drawn, only to have his wife accidentally impale herself on its tip. Baron Espernay, who was in the midst of attempting to ravish Alovysa, is himself mortally wounded by D'elmont's brother, the Chevalier Brilliard. The ensuing scene functions allegorically to underscore the extent to which epistemological stability depends upon a stable social collectivity:

The Count, Melliora, and the servants, who by this time were most of them rowzed, seemed without sence or motion, only the Chevalier had spirit enough to speak, or think, so stupefied was every one with what they saw, But he ordering the servants to take up the bodies, sent one of 'em immediately for a surgeon, but they were both of them past his art to cure. (158)

The social fabric has been so torn by the solipsistic desires of D'elmont, Alovysa, and Espernay that those who populate this collective social scene are disaggregated from one another, and no one can make any sense of what has happened. Only when the "whole account" was "gathered from the mouths of those chiefly concerned" is the course of events rendered intelligible (158) and is D'elmont pardoned.

At the beginning of the third section, Haywood reveals a much-chastened D'elmont and, tellingly, a D'elmont who, as he contemplates the devastating social consequences of his misprisions, is finally beginning to be capable of the interpretive multiplicities Haywood has denied him for the novel thus far.

Melliora retires to a convent but sustains a correspondence with D'elmont, who has traveled to Rome where he lives more or less reclusively, shunning "as much as possible all conversation with the men, or correspondence with the women" (166). An act of altruism reintegrates D'elmont into a set of social relations and opens the door to love for him once again. One evening D'elmont stumbles upon a young man being assaulted and intervenes to save the victim's life. After some conversation, D'elmont discovers that the young man he has rescued is Melliora's brother Frankville, who bears the count a good deal of malice for the insult his sister has suffered at D'elmont's hands. Nonetheless, the fact that D'elmont has saved Frankville's life has made the younger man indebted to the count, and Frankville finds he must lay aside his acrimony. The two men then become confederates in Frankville's quest to win the hand of the young Italian heiress Camilla.

The ensuing subplot reiterates many of the novel's earlier themes about the distorted nature of singularity and the obsessions it breeds. As Frankville and D'elmont find themselves manipulated and deceived by Camilla's aunt Ciamara, who reprises the kind of obsession formerly represented by Alovysa, and Camilla's father so that Camilla marry someone besides Frankville. D'elmont, Camilla, and Frankville finally manage to flee Rome, so enraging Ciamara and Camilla's father that the two elder characters die, leaving Camilla conveniently free to marry Frankville. But what is most interesting about the Camilla/Frankville subplot is the role played by Violetta, Camilla's companion who also has conceived an irrepressible infatuation for D'elmont. She knows that D'elmont loves someone else, but when it becomes clear that the count plans to leave Rome with Camilla and Frankville, she plots not only to facilitate the lovers' departure but also to accompany them into France. She attends the party undetected in the guise of a page.

Haywood brings her long tale of misprision full circle when D'elmont discovers that Melliora has fled her convent only to arrive at exactly the castle where the Italian party has taken refuge. The lovers are thus all re-united, and Violetta discloses her identity only to die a noble (because unselfish) death.

In her landmark study, *Seductive Forms: Women's Amatory Fiction from 1684–1740*, Ros Ballaster characterizes the 1720s as a less politicized and more ideologically stable period in the history of English letters:

> The allegorical duplicity of scandal fiction, its complex double movement between the amatory and party political plot, is superseded by the more direct aim of representing the eternal power of the disruptive force of desire, specifically female desire.[15]

Obviously, most writers did abandon the "open secret" format that defined the *roman a clef*'s imaginative interventions. That shift, as I have suggested here, did not, however, mean that writers became less political. On the contrary, in ways that *Love in Excess* underscores, they retained a high degree of political sensitivity and investment. What changed, I think, and thus rendered the *roman a clef* irrelevant except in extreme cases like Robert Walpole's, was a deepening awareness that power is not, indeed, cannot be, personal. These shifted terms of cultural debate opened new dimensions to a wide-flung conversation about the nature of sovereignty, among which amatory fictions like those Haywood produced and of which *Love in Excess* stands as a vivid example, made important contributions. Haywood was certainly less partisan than Manley or Behn, but she was, to be sure, no less, and perhaps more, political.

NOTES

1. Jerry C. Beasley, "Robert Walpole and Early English Prose Fiction," *Eighteenth-Century Studies* 14.4 (1981): 406–31. See also, "Politics and Moral Idealism: The Achievement of some Early Women Novelists," in *Fetter'd or Free? British Women Novelists 1670–1815*, ed. Cecilia Macheskis and Mary Anne Schofield (Athens: University of Ohio Press, 1985), 216–36.

2. Beasley, "Robert Walpole and Early English Prose Fiction," 411–13.

3. See especially Jonathan Kramnick, "Lock, Haywood, and Consent," *ELH* 72 (2005): 453–70.

4. Though many critics now recognize Haywood's abiding political interests throughout most of her long career, Beasley's contention in 1981 was far from the conventional critical wisdom, which tended to view Haywood's work prior to *The Adventures of Eovaai* as concerned predominantly with questions of love and romance.

5. "Eliza Haywood's Defense of London's Body Politic," *SEL* 43.3 (2003): 645–55.

6. *London's Liberty in Chains Discover'd* (1646), 1.

7. Ros Ballaster, *Seductive Forms: Women's Amatory Fiction from 1684–1740* (Oxford: Clarendon Press, 1992), 153.

8. Ibid., 153.

9. Jonathan Kramnick, for instance, characterizes *Love in Excess* as a "long, digressive novel of romantic intrigue [that] begins with a nighttime tryst," 458.

10. David Oakleaf misidentifies Haywood's reference to the "late war" as being the War of the Spanish Succession (1701–1714). See *Love in Excess; or, The Fatal Inquiry*, ed. David Oakleaf, second ed. (Peterborough: Ontario: Broadview Press, 2000), 37, n. 1. Haywood's reference to D'elmont's service under the Duke de Luxembourgh makes it clear that she had in mind the earlier conflict, as Luxembourg had died by the time France entered the War of the Spanish Succession. References to *Love in Excess* are to the Oakleaf edition.

11. Luxembourg had a history of being embroiled in both political and military scandals. In addition to leading France's forces against the English in the War of the Grand Alliance, Luxembourg had also led French armies against William III in the earlier Dutch War before William ascended the English throne and actually defeated William at St. Denis in 1678. The victory, however, was empty as it took place four days after the peace treaty had been signed, and Luxembourg was heavily criticized for engaging in the conflict. The following year Louis XIV had Luxembourg imprisoned on charges of sorcery. He was acquitted fourteen months later but exiled from court. In 1681, Louis XIV had a change of heart and recalled the duke. Luxembourg was made commander in chief of the French armies shortly after France went to war in 1689. He died at Versailles in 1695.

12. Thomas Hobbes, *The Leviathan* (Amherst, MA: Prometheus Books, 1988), 64.

13. Oakleaf, 81, n.1.

14. For a different perspective on the logic that governs Haywood's novel, see Scott Black, "Trading Sex for Secrets in Haywood's *Love in Excess*," *Eighteenth-Century Fiction* 15.2 (2003): 207–26.

15. Ballaster, 154.

9

A Brief Note on Haywood Scholarship: or, *The Fatal Enquiry* into the *Timely Discovery* and *Fruitful Enquiry* into the *Fatal Fondness* of Contemporary Scholars for Eliza Haywood

Mary Anne Schofield

Although our productions have afforded more extensive and unaffected pleasure than those of any other literary corporation in the world, no species of composition has been so much decried . . . there seems almost a general wish of decrying the capacity and undervaluing the labour of the novelist, and of slighting the performances which have only genius, wit, and taste to recommend them.

Jane Austen, *Northanger Abbey*

Eliza Haywood's first novel, *Love in Excess; or, The Fatal Enquiry* (1719–1720), rivaled Daniel Defoe's *Robinson Crusoe* for the novel of the year in 1719, and any student of the eighteenth-century novel knows that Haywood, who published more than seventy works during her forty-year career, was the most prolific of the women novelists of the period. She was so "big" that in Book II of the *Dunciad*, Alexander Pope criticized her, almost out of all proportion, for having, ironically, nothing to say. Eliza Haywood was a force to be reckoned with, and so, too, is Haywood scholarship, then and now.

Like Haywood's own "female spectator" who, with her assistants Euphrosine, Mira, and the "Widow of Quality," constructed monthly essays blending social and moral commentary with practical advice for the growing literary marketplace, I, too, explore social, political, and moral trends by examining the Haywood criticism of the past three decades in an effort to understand the unique position of Eliza Haywood, the proto-feminist novelist, and her vital importance to the eighteenth-century novel.

In many ways, Haywood scholarship has continued to feel Alexander Pope's influence as defined first by David Erskine Baker's *Companion to the Theatre* (1764) and his later *Biographia Dramatica* (1782) and then by Clara Reeve's *Progress of Romance* (1785), which established the "before" and "after" pattern used to evaluate Haywood's life and career. Pope's condemnation of her was so vile, her reputation so ruined, that Haywood took a four-year hiatus from her writing. But "Mrs Heywood [*sic*]," Reeve writes, "had the singular good fortune to recover a lost reputation, and the yet greater honour to atone for her errors."[1] Here is first the codification of the "pre-Pope"/"post-Pope" Haywood, which has defined, one might even say plagued, much of future Haywood scholarship. So, critics ask in contemporary scholarship, was Haywood's shift a moral one because she realized the wrongs of her early amatory fiction and her scandalous heroines, or was her move a financially shrewd one because she understood the temper of the post-*Pamela* literary marketplace? The conundrum is not easily solved, and critics writing as late as 2009 are still investigating the two Haywoods.[2]

But no matter how many "Haywoods" we read now, her place in today's scholarly canon is assured; it was not always so. Alan McKillop (1956) and Ian Watt (1957), for example, though institutionalizing the study of the early novel, did not view Haywood as part of the mainstream novelists of the eighteenth century, and neither critic considered why the majority of eighteenth-century novels were written by women.[3] Subsequent early scholars, caught up in the Baker/Reeve conundrum, deny Haywood a place in the history of the novel on moral grounds, when, in fact, as Juliette Merritt observes, "the falling off of Haywood's publishing was more likely due to the decline in popularity of amatory fiction, the staple of Haywood's writing in that decade." Moreover, Merritt notes, "her prominence in *The Dunciad* and the outrageousness of the attack are now regarded as Pope's businesslike endeavors to capitalize on Haywood's influential place in the London literary milieu."[4]

Almost thirty years ago, when I wrote my dissertation under the direction of Jerry Beasley, there was little actual Haywood scholarship with which to work, and what there was viewed her corpus as written by two distinct types of authors—those two Haywoods created by Baker and Reeve—the scandalously licentious and the virtuously moral. My own critical observations helped in a small way to pioneer a non-dualistic view of Haywood and her novels as innovative experiments in eighteenth-century authorial voice, narrative structure, and point of view, and I began to place her in a direct line in the history-of-the-novel narrative.[5] Today Kathryn King claims that Haywood is now "generally accounted the most important professional woman writer in the century."[6] As Christine Blouch argues, Eliza Haywood is "a sort of Augustan gadfly" who "played a key role in the novel's evolution and defined central issues in the portrayal of eighteenth-century female subjectivity" because she was interested in everything affecting women and wrote about it all, especially "the psychological imperatives that motivate human beings to act in ways contrary to their own interests."[7] Taken together, it is Haywood's innovations in narrative form and character development that first destabilize and then restabilize her place in eighteenth-century novel theory, allowing Scott Black to remark in 2003, "we can begin to recognize a Haywood who was not only a *woman* writer but a woman *writer*, one who grappled not only with questions of identity but also with issues of form, and who belongs in our histories of the novel because her texts are self-conscious explorations of narrative."[8]

THE LONG-AGO PAST:
THE 1960s AND 1970s (AND EVEN EARLIER)

Haywood studies began with George Whicher's 1915 *The Life and Romances of Eliza Haywood*.[9] Subsequent biographical work (until the new facts discovered by Christine Blouch and Kathryn King) came from his sketchy biography: that a son, Charles, was baptized in 1711 and that her husband, the Reverend Valentine Haywood, placed an advertisement in *The Post Boy* in 1721 disclaiming all responsibility for her debts. Whicher's scholarship did not spark much interest in her works at that time; there are only brief mentions of Haywood in several important studies of early fiction.[10] Not until the decade of the 1960s did scholars begin to look at Haywood in earnest. The criticism of this time, however, continued the Baker/Reeve duality that viewed Haywood's work as either sexy and erotic or prudish and exemplary.[11] The majority of the criticism of the 1970s views Haywood peripherally as, for example, Margaret Anne Doody does in *A Natural Passion: A Study of the Novels of Samuel Richardson*. Doody recognizes the importance of Haywood and her theme of seduction and concludes that "during the twenties [and] the thirties she reigned supreme as untiring chronicler of love, passion, and the vagaries of the heart," even speculating that Richardson may have met Haywood; further, Doody notes, he draws upon the same conventions and uses styles and phrases remarkably similar to Haywood's own.[12] It is the question of "female sexuality" that reigns supreme during this decade, and Haywood clearly writes about it as she examines female lust, love, and lechery. Thus, eighteenth-century novel criticism of the 1970s treats Haywood as influential, as it does several other women writers of the period, including Jane Barker, Fanny Burney, Elizabeth Griffith, Charlotte Lennox, Delarivière Manley, Lady Mary Wortley Montagu, Susanna Rowson, Hester Thrale, and Mary Manley.[13]

The 1970s are also important because some Haywood titles became accessible with the inauguration of the Garland reprint series, which included

Memoirs of a Certain Island adjacent to the Kingdom of Utopia; The Secret History of the Present Intrigues of the Court of Caramania; The Adventures of Eovaai, Princess of Ijaveo; The Agreeable Caledonia; The Rash Resolve; or, The Untimely Discovery; The Mercenary Lover; The Fortunate Foundlings; The History of Jemmy and Jenny Jessamy; Life's Progress through the Passions; or, The Adventures of Natura; and *Anti-Pamela.* In 1972 Jerry Beasley called attention to Haywood's work in *A Check List of Prose Fiction Published in England, 1740–1749,* and in 1978 he reiterated her importance in *English Fiction, 1660–1800: A Guide to Information Sources.*[14] By 1977 there was enough scholarly interest to warrant Haywood's inclusion in Paula Backscheider, Felicity Nussbaum, and Philip B. Anderson's *Annotated Bibliography of Twentieth-Century Critical Studies of Women and Literature, 1660–1800*[15]; however, full-blown Haywood scholarship was still in a nascent stage.

THE CRITICAL CHANGE: THE 1980s

The 1980s saw scholarship of eighteenth-century literature expand to include feminist, Marxist, New Historicism, and cultural studies as critical loci. Felicity Nussbaum and Laura Brown's important work legitimized these new approaches of "the historically constructed nature of subjectivity; gender's position as both a cultural construct and an important category of interpretation; the instability of dominant ideologies of the past and scholars' attempts to write about them."[16] Brown, Nussbaum, and the scholars included in their book legitimized the movement from formalism to historicism, which continues to dominant Haywood scholarship today. Along with the Brown/Nussbaum collection, other important studies of the novel, one by Michael McKeon and the second by Nancy Armstrong, helped shape scholarly appraisals of Haywood.[17] McKeon destabilizes generic categories in order to allow the romance into the novel hierarchy, thus placing Haywood within the history of the novel tradition. Armstrong introduces the vital critical language needed to read Haywood's fiction in the novel-history mainstream, rather than on the sidelines. Women novelists, not just Haywood, according to Armstrong, "concerned solely with matters of courtship and marriage, in fact seized the authority to say what was female, and . . . they did so in order to contest the reigning notion of kinship relations that attached most power and privilege to certain family lines."[18] Most importantly, Armstrong begins a scholarly dialogue on domestic fiction, thus finally placing "woman," as subject and author, in the central novel tradition. Women, she argues, are "an economic and psychological reality" and thus provide the political leverage of the period.[19] The language of sexual relations becomes the language of power. Armstrong thus links the history of the novel to the history of sexuality, and subsequent scholars and critics have not looked back.

Earlier scholarship in the decade had begun the critical conversation that Armstrong made imperative. For example, Katharine M. Rogers finds that Haywood "shows how romance centering on love for women need have no connection with feminism," concluding that "Haywood reduces [her] subjects to mere sexual puppets."[20] Jerry Beasley takes a taxonomic approach, categorizing the "amorous bulk of narrative literature published in the 1740s" as romances, spy fictions, contemporary biographies of low life, spiritual life, and "novelistic fiction," with Haywood figuring prominently into his categorical discussion because of the sheer mass of her publications.[21] Janet Todd's *Dictionary of British and American Women Writers, 1660–1800* includes a Haywood entry, and in her later *The Sign of Angellica* Todd devotes one chapter to Haywood, which continues the Reeve/Barker dualism by considering only Haywood's later works.[22] Terry Castle briefly mentions Haywood but establishes that "eighteenth-century English fiction implicitly coded the masquerade scene as a moment of symbolic revelation."[23] Ann Messenger devotes a chapter to "Educational Spectators," comparing Haywood's periodical with that of Addison and Steele and concludes that Haywood "reveals a far deeper sense of the tragedy of the human condition than anything Addison and Steele ever expressed."[24] Jane Spencer's *The Rise of the Woman Novelists* plays to the dual vision with a study of Haywood's "seduced heroine" of *The British Recluse* and, in a later chapter of the "reformed heroine," an examination of *Betsy Thoughtless*, claiming that Haywood "inherited a tradition of belief in the woman writer as an expert on love, which she exploited to the full."[25] Dale Spender, who might be called the Haywood champion of the 1980s, presents one of the longer treatments of Haywood in these studies of eighteenth-century female novelists, devoting thirty pages to an examination of her writing career, concluding that Haywood "was one of, if not *the* most versatile, prolific and popular writers of her day."[26] My own books also helped to usher in a new interest in this versatile writer, and the publication of *Fetter'd or Free?* with my coeditor Cecilia Macheski sealed the critical importance of not only Eliza Haywood but many other heretofore neglected women writers of the eighteenth century.[27] Scholarly interest in Eliza Haywood suddenly was "in," as indicated by the number of critical books in the 1980s on eighteenth-century British fiction that include a study of her works.

THE NOT-SO-DISTANT PAST: THE 1990s

The 1990s witnessed a reassessment and realignment of novel theory and studies. With Haywood studies blossoming together with critical studies of novels by other women writers of the eighteenth century, Haywood scholarship of the 1990s witnesses, first, a reevaluation of the male canon that had been in place since McKillop and Watt and, second, a shift to a new female-experience canon. J. Paul Hunter's *Before Novels* sets the stage for the ensuing debate as he declares that at "midcentury, the new form—innovative, rebellious, surprising, and full of novelty but not yet named 'the novel'—was still searching for a clear identity, terminology, and definition."[28] In 1994 John Richetti continues this discussion in *The Columbia History of the British Novel*, as he, too, searches for what he labels the "upward revaluation of the novel."[29] Thus, in terms of the traditional, male-authored canon, for instance, Defoe's *Moll Flanders* (1722) and *Roxana* (1724) (thought to be closely aligned with Haywood's *Fantomina*) replace *Robinson Crusoe* as definitive texts, while Fielding's *Amelia* (1751) pushes aside *Joseph Andrews* (1742) and *Tom Jones* (1749); the top male-authored novel is Richardson's *Clarissa* (1747–1748). Although important eighteenth-century scholars like Ros Ballaster and William Warner place Haywood in the general history of the novel and print media, so that "Haywood is everywhere," others, particularly Paula Backsheider, note that the study of her individual works is proceeding much too slowly."[30] The work by Ballaster and Warner is important in this context because it builds on the previous decade's critical work, further legitimizing Haywood studies. For example, Ballaster moves beyond Terry Castle's earlier study to conclude that the "masquerade is more than a plot device from which to explore the pleasures and perils of female sexuality." Instead, she notes, "it stands as a metaphor for the practice of Haywood's female romance writing itself, the transformation of the mute and 'written upon' female body into the active profit-making of the female writing subject."[31] Warner's *Licensing Entertainment* builds on Jane Spencer's earlier observations to conclude that Haywood "defends novel reading as an autonomous pleasure of the private reader . . . [and] figures the general reader of her novels as one free of particular ideological and moral investments, and open to the diverse play of fantasy."[32] Warner not only examines Haywood in her eighteenth-century context but he also explores "the signal traits of formula fiction on the market recognizable from the eighteenth century to the present day," thus clarifying and solidifying Haywood's position in the continuing canon wars of the decade.[33]

The "new approaches" criticism of the 1990s reads and evaluates Haywood's fiction in terms of its cultural density and generic diversity, uncovering the multiple layers of her narratives. Haywood's works are now studied, for example, in terms of the print culture of the period, allowing Kathryn King to conclude that Haywood's fictions were not "so much a phenomenon of gender as an epiphenomenon of culture, a shaking and airing, as it were, of the cultural anxieties generated by print."[34] Studies and comparisons with architecture, politics, epistemology, and even scientific discoveries make Haywood criticism in the 1990s exhilarating. What the 1990s criticism shows us is that Haywood is no longer marginalized and is no longer considered a minor author; she is now part of the mainstream of the history of the novel, and scholarly studies of other women writers of the eighteenth century during the 1990s place her in a contemporary milieu of writers of romances, fantasies (especially oriental tales), political utopias, didactic moral tales, and conduct books.

The criticism of the 1990s concludes that Haywood uses the familiar literary tropes of the eighteenth century to great effect, especially the hegemonic power imbalance between men and women, the individual and the government. This new scrutiny of the power and gender imbalance dominates this decade's scholarship. Catherine A. Craft sets the tone when she observes, "As greater numbers of women began taking up pens and writing books, men became increasingly nervous about what women would say."[35] And oddly enough, the same sort of questions were being asked among the scholars/critics themselves.

The 1990s scholars realize that though the "exterior" of the women's fictions seemingly coalesces with male narratives, there are contradictory elements that must be recognized and examined. This is the "new" methodology of the 1990s: an examination of the parenthetical and encoded fictions of the women novelists using the earlier seminal studies by Patricia Meyer Spacks, Elaine Showalter, and Sandra M. Gilbert and Susan Gubar as its touchstone.[36] In some ways, this is not a new critical stance; for example, I had been advocating reading the parenthetical meaning of women's texts since the mid-1980s.[37] This new critical stance allows for spectacularly innovative readings. For example, Sally O'Driscoll, in her gay/lesbian reading of Haywood's *La Belle Assemblée*, concludes that the "cumulative effect of the book as a whole is to show the supposedly natural trope of heterosexual marriage as besieged by innumerable dangers."[38] O'Driscoll builds on McKeon as she notes that reading the novel in this fashion allows for "the inscription of a new social order," challenging, perhaps, the notion of the companionate marriage previously writ large on the pages of novel history theory.[39]

Amatory fiction, the supposed staple of women novelists of the eighteenth century, is also reconsidered in the 1990s. G. Gabrielle Starr offers an innovative reading of *Love in Excess*, observing that Haywood "reinterprets the metaphysical tradition of amatory poetry . . . to create her own figures of emotional excess."[40] Epistolary fiction comes in for a reassessment as well. Stephen J. Hicks goes beyond Robert Adams Day and Ruth Perry to conclude that Haywood "manipulated the technique in a manner beyond any single contemporary prose writer"; consequently, "instead of being marginalized as just another cheap romancer, Haywood needs to be recognized for her narrative acuity, ingenuity and perspective."[41]

The 1990s scholars also turn their attention to the reading public and question previous assumptions about Haywood's audience. Deidre Lynch and William B. Warner argue that there is a fundamental shift in the concept of reading in the early years of the eighteenth century.[42] Suddenly,

the critics argue, eighteenth-century readers read for pleasure, thus creating
a sense of liberation for the writers and the tropes they manipulate in their
fictions. This realization allows scholars to examine new venues, including
gossip, commerce and the marketplace, courtship, motherhood, pornography, theatricality, and patrilineage, as fresh ways to read the Haywood novel
because, they have discovered, these are the interests and concerns of her reading public. Lorna Beth Ellis's "Engendering the *Bildungsroman*: The *Bildung* of
Betsy Thoughtless" is a good example of reading Haywood's audience in order
to read her texts. Ellis explores the difference between the supposedly female
bildungsroman, in which the female protagonist "dwindles" into the role of
wife, and those *bildungs* of male development, concluding that Haywood's
Betsy Thoughtless is a new kind of female *bildungs* protagonist that challenges
the notion of female development in a novel as oxymoronic.[43] Ellis—rightly,
I think—replaces the earlier *bildungsroman* heroine, who does not mature with
marriage but remains dependent and childlike, with a heroine who "matures
by learning to understand herself and her relationship to her environment so
that she may manipulate that environment in order to maintain some form
of agency."[44] New critical directions like Ellis's are important because they
attempt to move scholars beyond the Baker/Reeve two-Haywoods approach,
which continues throughout the 1990s. For example, Deborah J. Nestor per-
petuates the Reeve/Baker duality by claiming that *"Betsy Thoughtless* is Haywood's most important novel in terms of its influence on women's literary
history" because it reflects Haywood's change of heart after the publication of
Anti-Pamela.[45] Ellis's new direction, unlike the more conventional reading by
Nestor, allows Paula Backscheider to write that the "debate continues about
whether her novels are shallow, trivial, and repetitious, whether they provide
important social commentary or are an important part of the literary history
of the novel, and whether Haywood is an erotic writer producing (knowingly
or not) arousal literature and pleasure machines or a skillful social allegorist
or an important literary innovator."[46] The new century begins to answer these
and similar questions.

THE NOW: 2000s AND THE NEW CANON

In the 1990s, *Love in Excess* and *The History of Betsy Thoughtless* were the
most-examined Haywood novels because they allowed critics to continue
to view the two Haywoods. In the 2000s, the focus shifts to *Fantomina* and
Betsy Thoughtless, with a twist that begins to undermine the two-Haywoods
theory: that is, the titular heroine, Fantomina, is now viewed as both an object to be desired but also, new to Haywood and eighteenth-century fiction,
a seeing subject who is asked to view herself from the perspective of being
objectified in someone else's eye. Haywood's narrative innovations in this

early novel thus move *Fantomina* from being only an early, licentious and ribald text to one of complex authorial artistry and moral depth. Scholars in the new century read her novels as both a cultural and an aesthetic phenomenon, what John Richetti labels "interventions in an ethical and social world."[47] Richetti goes on to observe—by way of justifying his earlier work, I think—"The current dominant critical understanding of fiction in early eighteenth-century England is that all narratives are simply part of the jostling for market share in the new world of expanding print media . . . there is in this main line of eighteenth-century fiction what I want to call a superior socio-cultural fullness and density, an engagement both explicit and implicit, with the ideas and issues of their historical moment."[48] Similarly, Juliette Merritt concludes that Haywood "studies have arrived at a point at which we can begin to take the long view of her career and recognize that she sustained a set of preoccupations and strategies over the course of nearly forty years as a professional writer. Haywood is an exceptional candidate for this kind of investigation because of her self-consciousness as a writer, her solid position within the literary marketplace, the sheer size and variety of her canon, and the length of her career."[49]

This solidification of Haywood's position in the eighteenth-century canon opens up new venues for criticism in the 2000s. For example, legal narratives form the critical touchstone of an engaging study by Miranda J. Burgess that examines the "travels" of the early Haywood heroine "between home, marketplace, and literary arena," which "encapsulate Haywood's polemical prehistory of separate private and public spheres" by examining her use of rhetoric from the court system.[50] Similarly, political rhetoric becomes a major point of examination in this decade's criticism. Melissa Mowry observes that "conventionally, there has been a good deal of resistance to interpreting Haywood's early works as political, with the exception of *The Memoirs of a Certain Island Adjacent to the Kingdom of Utopia* (1725) and *The Secret History of the Present Intrigues of the Court of Caramania* (1727)."[51] Mowry writes to change this older view by examining the psychological realism that we attribute to her novels with what has been previously thought incompatible: political commentary. By studying the history of pornographies that emerged during the English civil wars (the prostitutes were the daughters of ruined civil war veterans), Mowry concludes that "Haywood's reworking of pornography's thematics offers tantalizing insights into the discursive possibilities that confronted early novelists when they used women's bodies as an encrypted site of political commentary."[52] Marta Kvande examines the newly forged paradigm of party politics, which "constitute a specific party-political attack on the corruption and vice of those in power" in Haywood's use of Tory rhetoric.[53] Haywood's narrators are outcasts who are "denied positions of power but who still claim the right of public, political discourse because of their virtue"; thus, Kvande concludes, by studying Haywood's narrators "we can identify continuities and show the connections between her amatory, political, and domestic fictions," which would finally end the two-Haywoods syndrome.[54] The two-Haywoods conundrum is based, ultimately, on sex: the early licentious tales were sexual romps, while the later moral tales punish sexual escapades. But even though Haywood criticism in the 2000s is moving away from this dualistic view, sex and sexual language continue to be of prime interest. For example, Tiffany Potter argues that "Haywood breaks important ground in creating a cultural idiom for the expression of the prescriptively private and female in realms territorially public and male, using the derogatorily feminized genre of amatory fiction to create a multi-climatic form and content that interrogate the determinist linguistic regulation of most eighteenth-century narrative."[55] Potter asks whether or not the female experience can be transmitted at all "through standard linguistic and generic constructions, and how Haywood might manipulate regulation and cultural-linguistic expectation in order to make the private experiences of femininity into a publicly recognizable (and saleable) commodity."[56] Scott Black asks similar questions and finds "another way to situate the novel in its social context—a context defined not by a choice *between* aesthetics and the market, but by an aesthetics *of* the market that was articulated in terms of the contemporary discourse of 'novelty.'"[57] Rather than reading her work as an alternative female-centered history of the novel with an ubiquitous plot of naive, female victim versus cruel, male seducer, Black offers male figures (i.e., the Baron) both "as a figure of narrative productivity" and also a "figure for the author," allowing the Baron/Haywood to have the "mechanisms of plotting" in his/her control.[58] Thus, Black concludes, the "novel engages the reader along *two* axes of seduction . . . not only sexual desire but also epistemological desire," which places an active reader in full participation "with Haywood in constructing the pleasures of the text."[59] Hence, the Haywood novel is a "novelty" to the curious reader of the text and part of the history of "wit" and "play."

Not all of the 2000s criticism is commodity- or sex-based. For example, Helen Thompson rereads *Fantomina* in relation to the seventeenth-century natural philosopher Walter Charleton in an effort to resolve and "recover the formal and thematic resources with which Haywood's romance resolves patriarchal contradiction."[60] Shea Stuart rereads *Betsy Thoughtless* in terms of the period's conduct books, especially George Saville, Marquis of Halifax's *The Lady's New-year's Gift: or, Advice to a Daughter*, and concludes that "Haywood is in dialogue with Halifax, but she critiques his advice to his daughter Betty by illustrating its inadequacies in her character Betsy."[61] Stuart notes that "*Betsy Thoughtless* is a dialogic rendering of emergent ideology housed in didactic form, accomplishing both of Haywood's goals— message and market."[62] Kelly McGuire rereads *Betsy Thoughtless* in terms of the graveyard poets. McGuire finds in the novel "a bizarre co-mingling of the grave and the comic" and identifies "the role of mourning as a catalyst for consumption."[63] Jonathan Brody Kramnick examines the philosophical paradox of consent, which "dwells on the mind and can only be inferred in practice."[64] Consent, Karmnick argues, is central to modern democracy as touted by John Locke in his 1690 *Essay Concerning Human Understanding* and sexuality as examined by Haywood and other women writers of the period: both attempt to locate the provenance of moral virtue. Kramnick concludes that with Haywood, the "self is no longer an isolated agent acting upon the world from a position of unfettered autonomy," but rather is "placed in concert with others, a world that shapes the agency misunderstood by Locke to come from within."[65]

The study of the inner sexual self moves us back to a further evaluation of Haywood's audience and prompts Kathleen Lubey to reexamine the Wolfgang Iser reader-response viewpoint by observing that "Haywood's conception of reading as an act that stimulates the body while it edifies the mind situates her work firmly in the period's ongoing consolidation of the aesthetic as a category of affective, edifying experience. . . . Haywood conceives of her readers' imagination as a mediating force that, when employed purposefully, sustains the pleasures of body and mind but forestalls a decline into unthinking sensual gratification."[66] Basing her reading on Addison's "On the Power of the Imagination," Lubey concludes that Haywood uses her erotic themes and language for pedagogic ends by observing that Haywood's reader's imagination is "capable of performing interpretive acts of abstraction even as it is aroused by the most extreme subject matter: illicit erotic images of feminine sexuality."[67]

Reading and pedagogy go hand in hand in the 2000s scholarship. Margo Collins, for example, argues that Haywood de-genders her audience and "elides the difference between male and female readers and is thus able to address her lessons to both men and women."[68] Collins rereads *Betsy Thoughtless* for a universal audience, not strictly a female one, as has been critically understood for the majority of earlier examinations, and discovers that Haywood relates her pedagogical lessons and thematic concerns in the novel to her male readers as well as her female audience. "Ultimately, Haywood intends for all her fiction to speak to everyone," and by "inviting the male reader into the 'us' of the narrator's feminine community, Haywood masculinizes that feminine community."[69]

In the 2000s, critical attention also turns to Haywood's nonfictional works, especially *The Female Spectator* (1744–1746), her monthly periodical, which Patricia Meyer Spacks had earlier likened to miniature novels.[70] In 1978 Helene Koon had stressed that its emphasis on the "female experience" made *The Female Spectator* valuable. Critics today clearly note, but also call into question, the journal's supposed watershed quality in what can be viewed as Haywood's supposedly bifurcated career.[71] Lynn Marie Wright and Donald J.

Newman's collection, *Fair Philosopher: Eliza Haywood and The Female Specta-tor,* includes Newman's timely *"The Female Spectator:* A Bibliographic Essay," which not only does an admirable job of assessing *The Female Spectator* scholarship to date (especially tracing its critical reception in the eigh-teenth and nineteenth centuries) but also gives direction to future critical examinations.[72] As Newman notes, "knowing as much as we do about *The Female Spectator* merely shows us how much we don't know about it."[73] Wright and Newman believe that the 2000–2001 publication of the six-volume *Selected Works of Eliza Haywood* by Pickering and Chatto, which contains all of Haywood's known journalism, has led to this renewed interest in this periodical. The essays included in their collection address what they find to be the prime questions about the importance of *The Female Spectator:* "What does the periodical reveal about its author? How is *The Female Spectator* related to Haywood's other writings, especially her novels? And what place, if any, does *The Female Spectator* occupy in the history of British periodical journalism beyond its generally acknowl-edged status as the first periodical for women written by a woman?"[74] They find that these questions and their answers help current readers and scholars to understand Haywood's relationship to her emerging literary marketplace as well as give clues about the lives of early women writers. *The Female Spectator,* they conclude, addresses the expanding, new, liter-ate middle class reader and, therefore, it cannot be read in isolation to Haywood's career or her times.

There is also interest in Haywood's work for the theater. Patsy S. Fowler argues that Haywood's *The Fair Captive, The Wife to Be Lett,* and *Frederick, Duke of Brunswick-Lunenbergh* "reveal a self-reflexive confidence in her literary talents and a solid determination to define herself as a legitimate player within the literary marketplace."[75] Fowler concludes that Haywood markets herself in a variety of roles in order to get a major portion of the public market; she is "willing to confront the critics rather than sim-ply beg for their approval."[76] Haywood knows she deserves the public's respect. And that respect is given in large amount by the scholars and critics of the new millennium. Paula R. Backscheider's edited collection, *Revising Women,* presents seventy-five years of feminist scholarship with "revisionary contributions to the understanding of the eighteenth-century English novel," including new critical readings of six Haywood novels.[77] Kirsten T. Saxton and Rebecca P. Bocchicchio's collection, *The Passionate Fictions of Eliza Haywood,* is the first critical book-length study on Hay-wood to put her novels in conversation with the social, aesthetic and political discourses of her day. "Haywood's well-plotted and carefully crafted novels," Saxton and Bocchicchio note, "may well have suffered from neglect because of their frankness about female sexuality and the complicated machinations of heterosexual romance, marriage contracts, and female economic independence."[78] Alison Conway's *Private Interests* includes a penetrating analysis of *The History of Miss Betsy Thoughtless* and what Conway labels the "privatization of spectacle" as she reads the novel in the light of the Trueworth miniature as a part of the link between fiction and eighteenth-century portraiture.[79] Kevin Cope and Rudiger Ahrens's collection, *Talking Forward, Talking Back,* includes an important essay by Alexander Pettit, in which he expertly examines "victimage" and concludes that it is the result not of "the action of the patriarchy against inert young women but the consequence of wrong-headedness among young women in the first place."[80] Janine Barchas's *Graphic Design, Print Culture, and the Eighteenth-Century Novel* briefly examines four Haywood novels and their juxtaposition of text and printed page (for example, the frontispiece portrait which expands the textual meanings) and gives new directions that novel criticism can take.[81] Juliette Merritt's *Beyond Spectacle: Eliza Haywood's Female Spectators* is one of the most exciting critical studies of the millennium. Merritt examines Haywood's exploitation of "women's vulnerability within a specular social field that privileges male looking and confirms woman in her traditional place as object of sight" but notes that Haywood imbues many of her women characters with the ability to view themselves in a voyeuristic/self-reflexive way, thus creating what Merritt labels "spectorial texts," which are "an ongoing set of discursive strategies" that reveal "Haywood's preoccupation with structures of sight and seeing, especially as they relate to women's assigned place in the gendered, dichotomous structure of subject/object relations."[82] In 2004, Patrick Spedding compiled a lengthy *Bibliography of Eliza Haywood.* In a recent essay, Kathryn King focuses on Haywood's readers and debunks the long-standing myth of readership begun by Edmund Gosse. King finds that using a fictive reader to understand a Haywood text does great disservice to the novels and is a lazy form of scholarship.[83] Jeanne Moskal's and Shannon Wooden's *Teaching British Women Writers, 1750–1900* includes a chapter on Eliza Haywood and is a rich, hands-on study with pedagogical tips.[84]

This period marked by the millennium is best defined by borrowing Kevin Cope and Rudiger Ahrens's book title, *Talking Forward, Talking Back.* Contemporary critics examine the earlier scholarly field and "talk it forward" by applying new methodology and critical ideologies to earlier studies, thus "talking back." In his essay, "Our Fictions and Haywood's Fictions," Alexander Pettit, for example, asserts that we should no longer view Haywood as an author who radically changes from immoral to moral writer. Rather, she is a consistent author who "reiterates one familiar precept throughout her career: young, single, and attractive women must accept the responsibility for resisting the illicit sexual entanglements encouraged by adolescent physiology and accommodated, often insidiously, by patriarchal culture."[85]

At long last, we witness the demise of the two Haywoods—a marvelous end to the first decade of the new millennium.

THE FUTURE: CONCLUSION

To conclude about Haywood scholarship is, perhaps, to conclude that one cannot conclude. The many and varied works of Haywood remain, in the eyes of the critics, challenging, sometimes frustrating, but certainly still read and discussed. The new critical vision is toward a socio-cultural fullness and density heretofore unseen. Critics continue to "talk forward" and "talk back" and will continue to do so long into the new millennium. There is no "Fatal Secret," then, to the future of Haywood scholarship. There will be "Constancy," but it is "not in Distress," with both male and "female specta-tors" offering a "Compendium of the [scholarly] Times."

NOTES

1. Clara Reeve, *The Progress of Romance* (1785; reprint, New York: Facsimile Text Society, 1930), 120.

2. See, for example, Amy Wolfe, "Female Spectator and the New Story of Eliza Haywood," *Eighteenth-Century Life* 33.1 (2009): 74–82.

3. Alan McKillop, *The Early Masters of English Fiction* (Lawrence: University Press of Kansas, 1956); Ian Watt, *The Rise of the Novel* (Berkeley: University of California Press, 1957).

4. Juliette Merritt, *Beyond Spectacle: Eliza Haywood's Female Spectators* (Toronto: University of Toronto Press, 2004), 7.

5. See for example, Elizabeth Bergen Brophy, *Women's Lives and the Eighteenth-Century Novel* (Tampa: University of South Florida Press, 1991); Katherine Sobba Green, *The Courtship Novel, 1740–1829: A Feminized Genre* (Lexington: The University Press of Kentucky, 1991); Ruth Perry, *Women, Letters, and the Novel* (New York: AMS Press, 1980).

6. Kathyrn King and Alexander Pettit, eds. *The Female Spectator,* four vols. (London: Pickering & Chatto, 2001), 1, 2. 3.

7. Christine Blouch, "Eliza Haywood and the Romance of Obscurity," *Studies in English Literature, 1500–1900* 31.3 (1991): 536.

8. Scott Black, "Trading Sex for Secrets in Haywood's Love in Excess," *Eighteenth-Century Fiction* 15.2 (2003): 207.

9. George Whicher, *The Life and Romances of Eliza Haywood* (New York: Columbia University Press, 1915).

10. See, for example, Charlotte E. Morgan, *The Rise of the Novel of Manners: A Study of English Prose Fiction Between 1600 and 1740* (New York: Columbia University Press, 1911); Myra Reynold, *The Learned Lady in England 1650–1760* (Boston: Houghton Mifflin Co., 1920); Ernest A. Baker, *The History of the English Novel,* ten

vols. (London: H. F. & G. Witherby, 1924–1936); Joyce M. Horner, "The English Women Novelists and Their Connection with the Feminist Movement (1688–1797)," *Smith College Studies in Modern Language* 11.1–3 (1929); and Bridget G. MacCarthy, *The Female Pen*, two vols. (Cork: Cork University Press, 1944).

11. See, for example, W. H. McBurney, *A Checklist of English Prose Fiction, 1700–1739* (Cambridge, MA: Harvard University Press, 1960), and his later anthology, *Four Before Richardson: Selected English Novels, 1720–1727* (Lincoln: University of Nebraska Press, 1963); James Paul Erickson's 1962 dissertation, *The Novels of Eliza Haywood*; Robert Adams Day, *Told in Letters: Epistolary Fiction before Richardson* (Ann Arbor: The University of Michigan Press, 1966); and John J. Richetti, *Popular Fiction Before Richardson: Narrative Patterns 1700–1739* (Oxford: Clarendon Press, 1969). See especially Richetti's chapter, "Mrs. Haywood and the Novella—The Erotic and the Pathetic."

12. Margaret Anne Doody, *A Natural Passion: A Study of the Novels of Samuel Richardson* (Oxford: Clarendon Press, 1974), 138.

13. See Patricia Meyer Spacks's "Ev'ry Woman is at Heart a Rake," *Eighteenth-Century Studies* 8.1 (1974): 27–46; Jerry C. Beasley's "Romance and the 'New' Novels of Richardson, Fielding, and Smollett," *Studies in English Literature* 16.3 (1976): 437–50; Margaret Anne Doody's "Deserts, Ruins, and Troubled Waters: Female Dreams in Fiction and the Development of the Gothic Novel," *Genre* 10 (1977): 529–72.

14. Jerry C. Beasley, *A Check List of Prose Fiction Published in England, 1740–1749* (Charlottesville: University Press of Virginia, 1972); and Jerry C. Beasley, *English Fiction, 1660–1800: A Guide to Information Sources* (Detroit: Gale, 1978).

15. Paula Backscheider, Felicity Nussbaum, and Philip Anderson, eds., *An Annotated Bibliography of Twentieth-Century Critical Studies of Women and Literature, 1660–1800* (New York: Garland Publishing, Inc., 1977).

16. Laura Brown and Felicity Nussbaum, eds., *The New Eighteenth Century: Theory, Politics, English Literature* (New York: Methuen, 1987), 5.

17. Michael McKeon, *The Origins of the English Novel, 1600–1740* (Baltimore, MD: Johns Hopkins University Press, 1987); and Nancy Armstrong, *Desire and Domestic Fiction: A Political History of the Novel* (Oxford: Oxford University Press, 1987).

18. Armstrong, *Desire and Domestic Fiction*, 5.

19. Ibid., 8.

20. Katharine M. Rogers, *Feminism in Eighteenth-Century England* (Urbana: University of Illinois Press, 1982), 101–2.

21. Jerry C. Beasely, *The Novels of the 1740s* (Athens: University of Georgia Press, 1982), xii.

22. Janet Todd, ed., *A Dictionary of British and American Women Writers, 1660–1800* (Totowa, NJ: Rowman & Alanheld, 1985), and *The Sign of Angellica: Women, Writing, and Fiction, 1660–1800* (New York: Columbia University Press, 1989).

23. Terry Castle, *Masquerade and Civilization: The Carnivalesque in Eighteenth-Century English Culture and Fiction* (Stanford, CA: Stanford University Press, 1986), 161–62.

24. Ann Messenger, *His and Hers: Essays in Restoration and Eighteenth-Century Literature* (Lexington: The University Press of Kentucky, 1986), 147.

25. Jane Spencer, *The Rise of the Woman Novelist: From Aphra Behn to Jane Austen* (Oxford: Basil Blackwell, 1986), 62.

26. Dale Spender, *Mothers of the Novel* (London: Pandora, 1986), 81.

27. See *Quiet Rebellion: The Fictional Heroines of Eliza Haywood* (Washington, DC: University of America Press, 1982); *Eliza Haywood* (Boston: Twayne, 1985); *Masking and Unmasking the Female Mind: Disguising Romances in Feminine Fiction, 1713–1799* (Newark: University of Delaware Press, 1989); and *Fetter'd or Free? British Women Novelists, 1690–1815* (Athens: Ohio University Press, 1986).

28. J. Paul Hunter, *Before Novels: The Cultural Contexts of Eighteenth-Century English Fiction* (New York: W. W. Norton & Co., 1990), 22.

29. John Richetti, ed., *The Columbia History of the British Novel* (New York: Columbia University Press, 1994), 6.

30. Ros Ballaster, *Seductive Forms: Women's Amatory Fiction 1684 to 1740* (Oxford: Clarendon Press, 1992); William B. Warner, *Licensing Entertainment: The Elevation of Novel Reading in Britain, 1684–1750* (Berkeley: University of California Press, 1998); Paula Backscheider, "The Shadow of an Author: Eliza Haywood," *Eighteenth-Century Fiction* 11 (1998): 83.

31. Ballaster, *Seductive Forms*, 194.

32. Warner, *Licensing Entertainment*, 116.

33. Ibid., 112.

34. Kathryn King, "Spying Upon the Conjurer: Haywood, Curiosity, and 'The Novel' in the 1720s," *Studies in the Novel* 30.2 (1998): 190.

35. Catherine A. Craft, "Reworking Male Models: Aphra Behn's 'Fair Vow-Breaker,' Eliza Haywood's *Fantomina*, and Charlotte Lennox's *Female Quixote*," *Modern Language Review* 86.4 (1991): 821.

36. Patricia Meyer Spacks, *The Female Imagination* (London: Allen & Unwin, 1975); Elaine Showalter, *A Literature of Their Own* (Princeton, NJ: Princeton University Press, 1977); and Sandra M. Gilbert and Susan Gubar, *The Madwoman in the Attic* (New Haven, CT: Yale University Press, 1979).

37. See, for example, "'Descending Angels': Salubrious Sluts and Pretty Prostitutes in Haywood's Fiction," in *Fetter'd or Free?*, 186–200.

38. Sally O'Driscoll, "Outlaw Readings: Beyond Queer Theory," *Signs* 22.1 (1996): 39.

39. Ibid., 39.

40. G. Gabrielle Starr, "Rereading Prose Fiction: Lyric Convention in Aphra Behn and Eliza Haywood," *Eighteenth-Century Fiction* 12.1 (1999): 2.

41. Stephen J. Hicks, "Eliza Haywood's Letter Technique in Three Early Novels (1721–27)," *Papers on Language and Literature* 34.4 (1998): 421, 435.

42. Deidre Lynch and William B. Warner, *Cultural Institutions of the Novel* (Durham, NC: Duke University Press), 1996.

43. Lorna Beth Ellis's "Engendering the *Bildungsroman*: The *Bildung* of Betsy Thoughtless," *Genre* 3 (1995): 279, 280.

44. Ibid., 281.

45. Deborah J. Nestor, "Virtue Rarely Rewarded: Ideological Subversion and Narrative Form in Haywood's Later Fiction," *Studies in English Literature, 1500–1900* 34.3 (1994): 580.

46. Paula Backscheider, "The Shadow of an Author: Eliza Haywood," *Eighteenth-Century Fiction* 11.1 (1998): 80.

47. John Richetti, "An Emerging New Canon of the British Eighteenth-Century Novel: Feminist Criticism, the Means of Production, and the Question of Value," in *A Companion to the Eighteenth-Century English Novel and Culture*, ed. Paula Backscheider and Catherine Ingrassia (Oxford: Blackwell Publishing, 2005), 370.

48. Ibid.

49. Merritt, *Beyond Spectacle*, 5.

50. Miranda J. Burgess, "Bearing Witness: Law, Labor, and the Gender of Privacy in the 1720s," *Modern Philology* 98.3 (2001): 393, 394.

51. Melissa Mowry, "Eliza Haywood's Defense of London's Body Politic," *SEL* 43.3 (2003): 646.

52. Ibid., 662.

53. Marta Kvande, "The Outsider Narrator in Eliza Haywood's Political Novels," *SEL* 43.3 (2003): 625.

54. Ibid., 627, 640.

55. Tiffany Potter, "The Language of Feminised Sexuality: gendered voice in Eliza Haywood's Love in Excess and Fantomina," *Women's Writing: The Elizabethan to Victorian Period* 10 (2003): 169.

56. Ibid., 170.

57. Black, "Trading Sex for Secrets," 208.

58. Ibid., 215.

59. Ibid., 217, 219.

60. Helen Thompson, "Plotting Materialism," *Eighteenth-Century Studies* 35.2 (2002): 196.

61. Shea Stuart, "Subversive Didacticism in Eliza Haywood's *Betsy Thoughtless*," *SEL* 42.3 (2002): 560.

62. Ibid., 560.

63. Kelly McGuire, "Mourning and Material Culture in Eliza Haywood's *The History of Miss Betsy Thoughtless*," *Eighteenth-Century Fiction* 18.3 (2006): 283.

64. Jonathan Brody Kramnick, "Locke, Haywood, and Consent," *ELH* 72 (2005): 453.

65. Ibid., 468.

66. Kathleen Lubey, "Eliza Haywood's Amatory Aesthetic," *Eighteenth-Century Studies* 39.3 (2006): 310.

67. Ibid., 310, 321.

68. Margo Collins, "Eliza Haywood's Cross-Gendered Amatory Audience," *Eighteenth-Century Women: Studies in their Lives, Work, and Culture* 2 (2002): 46.

69. Ibid., 57, 58.

70. See Spacks's introduction to *Selections from The Female Spectator* (Oxford and New York: Oxford University Press), 1999.

71. Helene Koon, "Eliza Haywood and *The Female Spectator*," *Huntington Library Quarterly* 42 (1978): 42–55.

72. Lynn Marie Wright and Donald J. Newman, eds., *Fair Philosopher: Eliza Haywood and "The Female Spectator"* (Lewisburg, PA: Bucknell University Press, 2006).

73. Ibid., 241.

74. Ibid., 223.

75. Patsy S. Fowler, "Rhetorical Strategy and the 'Dangerous Woman-Poet': Eliza Haywood and the Politics of Self-Promotion," in *Prologues, Epilogues, Curtain-Raisers, and Afterpieces: The Rest of the Eighteenth-Century London Stage*, ed. Daniel J. Ennis and Judith Bailey Slagle (Newark: University of Delaware Press, 2007), 179.

76. Ibid., 182.

77. Paula R. Backschedier, ed., *Revising Women: Eighteenth-Century "Women's Fiction" and Social Engagement* (Baltimore, MD: The Johns Hopkins University Press, 2000), viii.

78. Kirsten T. Saxton and Rebecca P. Bocchicchio, eds., *The Passionate Fictions of Eliza Haywood: Essays on Her Life and Work* (Lexington: The University Press of Kentucky, 2000), 3–4.

79. Alison Conway, *Private Interests: Women, Portraiture, and the Visual Culture of the English Novel, 1709–1791* (Toronto: University of Toronto Press, 2001), 115–49.

80. Alexander Pettit, "Our Fictions and Haywood's Fictions," in *Talking Forward, Talking Backward: Critical Dialogues with the Enlightenment*, ed. Kevin L. Cope and Rudiger Ahrens (New York: AMS Press, 2002), 146.

81. Janine Barchas, *Graphic Design, Print Culture, and the Eighteenth-Century Novel* (Cambridge: Cambridge University Press, 2003).

82. Merritt, *Beyond Spectacle*, 3–8.

83. Kathryn King, "New Contexts for Early Novels by Women: The Case of Eliza Haywood, Aaron Hill, and the Hillarians, 1719–1725," in *A Companion to the Eighteenth-Century English Novel and Culture*, ed. Paula R. Backscheider and Catherine Ingrassia (London: Blackwell Publishing, 2005), 261–75.

84. Jeanne Moskal and Shannon R. Wooden, eds., *Teaching British Women Writers, 1750–1900* (Bern: Peter Lang, 2005).

85. Pettit, "Our Fictions and Haywood's Fictions," 148.

10

Revising the Scottish Plot in Tobias Smollett's *Roderick Random*

Rivka Swenson

Under the crushing weight, tho' not the Name,
Of Bondage, *Scotland* groaning did remain,
. . .
The *Scot[t]ish* Body, which, from Pole to Pole,
Did, once, make known the Active *Scot[t]ish* Soul.

"THE True Scots Genius, REVIVING"

During her pregnancy, a dream discomposed my mother. . . . She
dreamed she was delivered of a tennis-ball, which the devil (who, to her
surprise, acted the part of midwife) struck so forcibly with a racket, that
it disappeared in an instant; and she was for some time inconsolable for
the loss of her offspring; when all of a sudden, she beheld it return with
equal violence, and enter the earth beneath her feet, whence immediately
sprung up a goodly tree covered with blossoms, the scent of which operated so strongly upon her nerves, that she awoke.

Howsoever his externals might be altered, he was at bottom the same
individual.

Tobias Smollett, *The Adventures of Roderick Random*

During the second half of the British eighteenth century, the cultural presence of three generations of physically absent Stuart dynasts—James II (who
fled to Saint-Germain-en-Laye in 1688), his son James, and his grandson

177

Charles—was manifest in literary plots and characters.[1] It is commonly understood among historians that once Jacobitism (from _Jacobus_, James) ceased to be a threat to the Protestant Hanoverian succession, it was recuperated as a vehicle for nationalist nostalgia, and it is tempting to read backward from, say, Sir Walter Scott, in order to construct a master narrative of sentimental Scottish-Jacobite nationalism. But Jacobitism, sentimental or otherwise, was not always simply coterminous or symmetrical with Scottish nationalism. This was true both before and after the last major Jacobite rebellion, "the '45." Not all Scottish nationalists supported the effort to put a Stuart back on the throne in 1715, much less 1745; many were wary of absolute monarchy, and many more were hostile to the Stuart Catholicism that appealed to English Jacobites such as Jane Barker. Maintaining that "history, past and contemporary, enters all of Smollett's novels," Jerry C. Beasley argues that Smollett "did not regard history as something static" but rather appropriated "the facts of history . . . for fiction."[2] On the occasion of this Festschrift and in recognition of Beasley's assertion that Smollett's novels may be read profitably as historical reinflections, I argue that Smollett's first novel, _The Adventures of Roderick Random_ (1748), expresses a complicated patriotism that exploits but ultimately unhitches itself from the faded glamour of Jacobitism's falling star. The novel derives energy from the cultural mythology of Jacobitism that was being developed within ballads, verse, and material culture but swerves from the narrative possibilities attached to thwarted Stuart restoration. The novel's representative wandering Scot is finally restored to his "essential" identity when, inspired by the memory of his beloved Narcissa that guides him in his travels, he finds his father and they return (in a loosely appropriated version of Telemachus and Ulysses) to their loves, their friends, their birthrights, and their heritable community.[3]

In the preface to _Roderick Random_, Smollett appears to explain why he has given his disinherited, globe-trotting protagonist a Scottish nativity: "the disposition of the Scots, addicted to travelling, justifies my conduct in deriving an adventurer from that country."[4] Rather than taking this claim at face value, I focus on Smollet's ironic appropriation of a popular construct with historical basis: the traveling Scot.[5] Smollett's narrative hardly supports his claim that eighteenth-century Scots harbored either a love of traveling or a congenital bent toward it; Random, like his father, travels because he has to, and the two dispossessed characters are pleased to return home together at the end of the novel once circumstances allow them to do so in what Random calls "a creditable way" (233). Smollett's coy reference to "travelling" taps into and also revises an extant narrative of Scottish exile, diaspora, and depopulation.[6]

A signal moment at the beginning of the novel (quoted in my second epigraph) reveals how _Roderick Random_ formally revises that extant narrative. Taking a critical-revisionist approach to _Random_, one finds that the novel's elliptical aesthetic (proleptically introduced by Random's mother's dream)

formally subverts an extant historical and cultural trajectory.[7] While pregnant with Random, his mother Charlotte dreams he will be propelled from
her like a "tennis-ball," only to return, years later, to reciprocally rejuvenate
the homeland like a "goodly tree" (1), to become the genius of the place.
As I will show, the novel's formal circuit, which this dream anticipates,
alters the plot of dislocation and dispersion ubiquitously associated with
both Jacobites and Scottish subjects in eighteenth-century popular culture.
Specifically, the novel's design of (masculine) alienation and repatriation
topically and formally transforms "the Scottish Plot" by detaching it from
the Jacobite telos. My essay begins with contexts: I discuss the historical and
popular contexts of Scottish "travel" (beginning with the 1603 Union of the
Crowns) as foundational for this novel's manipulation of the Scottish-trav-
eler topos and the related Scottish-parasite topos; and I discuss the work-
ings of gender in the popular and material iconography of the Stuart saga as
foundational to this novel's conception of a masculine exile and a feminine
source. I then elucidate how the mother's dream acts as the formal force of
the novel, showing how a repeated pattern of reunion between Random
and people from his past fulfills the dream's resolution of the novel's three
key plots—familial, amatory, and communal. I argue that *Roderick Random*
is nothing less than a restoration narrative that operates under the generic
aegis of epic return to transform existing narratives of Scottish loss through
the trope of its own "random" traveling Scot; Smollett invigorates "the Scottish type" against the dissolution (historical, cultural, political) of Scottish
identity, poaching from Jacobite iconography to establish his protagonist's
essential and stable inner self within the borders of subnational typology.

TRAVELING CONTEXTS

The popular topos of the traveling Scot that Smollett reinflects had its genesis not in the aftermath of the '45 but in a series of historical events that
had been discursively assimilated into a history of loss: first, the Union of
Crowns in 1603, when James VI of Scotland was crowned James I of England and moved his court, its people and resources, to London (and did
not keep his promise to return triennially); second, the unsuccessful Darien
Scheme, Scotland's failure in 1698–1699 to maintain a trading colony at
what is today Panama; and, third, increased Scottish migration to England
and farther afield after the Act of Union of 1707 that formed Great Britain,
including but not limited to transportation of Scots after the '45 who supported or were believed to have supported the rebellion.

In the *History of the Union of Great Britain* (1709), Daniel Defoe wrote
that since the Union of Crowns, the "Scots had been very sensible of
the visible Decay of Trade, Wealth, and Inhabitants in their Country."[8]

He describes migration as the source of national enervation, citing "the constant Attendance of [Scottish] Gentry and Nobility at the English Court, where they spent their Estates, and suck'd out the Blood of their Country, to support their Luxury and Magnificence" (17). According to Defoe, the movement south became epidemic: "[they] all flocked to England, either for publick or private Employment and Depopulated, Impoverished, their Native Country" through "the continued emptying their Nation of their People" (17).

Ephemeral Scottish texts made a similar point. For example, in a pamphlet entitled *Observator or a Dialogue between a Country-Man, & a Landwart School-Master*, the Scottish Country-Man dates the problem of Scotland's depopulation to the sovereign's removal of the crown to London a century before.[9] In the "entry" dated Monday, June 11, 1705, he complains that the monarch's decision to not "Reside among our Selves . . . wasted the Body almost to a shaddow [sic]" (3, 2). He complains that "traveling south" amounts to an exportation of corporeal capital: "we have made our selves Poor and them Rich" (18). In sum, he argues, it is "a Truthdox, that the Scarcity of People in any Kingdom make it Poor, and the abounding of People make it Rich" (27). The Country-Man and the School-Master find themselves at an impasse; the Country-Man states that "the going Abroad of so many, makes the remainder live so much worse"; the School-Master agrees, and avers that this remainder shall be forced to migrate, too, since "those that yet Remain, can scarce make a Shift to Live" (19). The dialogue implies a self-perpetuating cycle that will eventually leave Scotland bereft of people.

The collapse of the Darien Scheme was a major event that augmented the sense of Scotland losing its inhabitants to travel. In 1698, Scotland, promised financial backing from England, sent its first ship to "New Caledonia" (capital: New Edinburgh) to start a trading colony. The project was a disaster. The human toll was significant: around two thousand settlers—the vast majority—perished, mainly from starvation and fever. The financial loss was equally considerable; Scotland's economic injury informed the agreement to forge a Union with England in 1707, a decision that heightened crucially the general sense of Scotland's enervation. The scheme's failure undercut national pride in "the *Scot[t]ish* Body, which, from Pole to Pole, / Did, once, make known the Active *Scot[t]ish* Soul"—and introduced a reality of economic "Bondage" to England.[10]

Post-Union, a variety of events contributed both to the reality and the perception of Scottish global dispersion. As early as the 1720s, feudal clansmen who sought to reestablish what they perceived to be a threatened way of life began immigrating to the North American continent with their gentry. Meanwhile, an early version of "the Highland Clearances," in which landlords forcibly drove crofters from their cottages in order to lease land to Lowland and English factors for sheep farms, was carried out as early as 1732 by MacLeod of Dunvegan on the Isle of Skye. And certainly the Battle of Culloden on April 16, 1746, which ended the Jacobite rebellion known as the '45, gave the diaspora topos increased currency. The rebellion's crushing was spectacular. Nearly thirty-five hundred Scots who were believed to harbor Jacobite sympathies were taken prisoner by William Augustus, the Duke (or, popularly, "Butcher") of Cumberland. Almost one hundred of them died in custody, a few were beheaded, 120-odd others were hung, drawn, and quartered, and more than a thousand were transported to the colonies; the fates of several hundred more are unknown.[11] At the same time, heritable jurisdictions in Scotland were summarily erased,[12] which contributed mightily to the clan system's disintegration and spurred Scots to travel in search of livelihood.

The "Scottish Plot" that *Roderick Random* revises had an additional source in the exilic status of the Stuart dynasts James II (James Francis Edward Stuart) and Bonnie Prince Charlie. The novel's chronology extends to 1747; Leith Davis rightly asks why it "bypasses the historical incident most crucial to Roderick's treatment as a Scot: the Rebellion" of 1745–1746.[13] In response, I suggest that the novel finds purchase in the overlap between the narrative of Scottish diaspora and the saga of royal dispossession that Lawrence Lipking calls "The Jacobite Plot."[14] Ultimately, the novel asserts the plots' differences from each other. The high incidence of migration from the north—contributed to by the Union of the Crowns, the Darien Scheme, the British Union, and the aftermath of the Jacobite rebellions—spurred a perceived affective mutuality between Scottish subjects, Jacobite or not, and the "king from over the water." I don't wish to indicate that Smollett was an unacknowledged Jacobite. As Lipking points out, both "enemies and friends of the [Stuarts] made use of The Jacobite Plot,"[15] precisely because it was so familiar that it could be transformed to fit a variety of agendas.

Random reinflects the literary construct of the traveling/exiled Scot inspired by the historical record of Scottish travel with which the Stuart saga resonated. Numerous popular ballads voiced concern, especially post-Culloden, about the dissolution of Scottish identity and culture. One exemplary ballad from the 1740s, "The Lamentation of David over Saul and Jonathan Imitated," complains that in Scotland "scarce a Scot remains."[16] Another, "O'er the Hills and Far Away," charts loss in sartorial terms that either anticipate or describe the effects of the Dress Act (another consequence of Culloden), which banned the wearing of kilts and of tartan: "Out o'er the Hills and far away, / The Wind has blawn [*sic*] my Plaid away."[17] Smollett's own 1746 poem "The Tears of Scotland," a response to Cumberland-led bloodshed at Culloden, mourns the spirit of Caledonia who now wanders far from the national body "in every clime, / Through the wide-spreading waste of Time."[18] Such ballads and poems imply that return to the source is longed for but impossible.

SMOLLETT'S RANDOM SCOTTISH PARASITE

Smollett's novel, which showcases a father and son who not only travel (and return) but also are enriched by their movement, is both historically based and semantically interventionist. Numerous examples from eighteenth-century English popular print assert a connection between Scottish parasitism and what Smollett calls "travelling"; in popular discourse, such "travelling" is usually shorthand for traveling-south-to-work. The association was not without real basis, and its long-lived satiric currency suggests that south-bound Scots provoked anxiety in the English body politic. For example, the poem "A Lenten Litany" (1716) indicts the "great Scots louse" as an evil plaguing England.[19] An anecdote in *Yorick's Jests* (1783), meanwhile, conveys that "a Scotch louse always travels southward"; instructions follow on how one can fashion a compass from a "Scotch louse" and a piece of paper.[20] *The New Universal Etymological English Dictionary* (1760) includes a related term, "Scotch Fiddle," to mean "the Itch" that ensues from cross-cultural contact with the traveling Scot.[21] With variations, the Scottish Louse was a cant commonplace that spanned the century.

The Scottish Locust, a hardy relation, made its way into the English canon via texts such as Daniel Defoe's 1701 poem *The True-Born Englishman*, ostensibly a celebration of cultural pluralism. Defoe's poem, while not overtly Scotophobic, nervously likens Scots to both the Egyptian plagues and the Israelites:

> Scots from the northern frozen banks of Tay,
> With packs and plods came whigging all away:
> Thick as the locusts which in Egypt swarmed
> With pride and hungry hopes completely arm'd;
> With native truth, diseases, and no money.
> Plundered our Canaan of the milk and honey.[22]

After the '45, the Scottish Locust experienced increased circulation. William Murray, for example, complained in a popular 1747 pamphlet that the Scots "have poured in upon us like Swarms of Locusts, into every Quarter, and every Scene of Life. The Army abounds with them, in unequal Proportions to our own Countrymen . . . and even the Law, which used to be pretty clear of them, begins to abound with their dissonant Notes. . . . Physic has them plentifully likeways. And, where there is any thing to be got, you may be sure to find a Number of *Scotchmen* conveen'd, like Hounds over a Carrion, or Flies in the Shambles."[23] The transmittal of the thistle-hardy Scottish Louse and Locust between texts mimics the very practice their images were invoked to illustrate.

Smollett, who was wont to appropriate the satiric energy of Scotophobic discourse for a variety of satiric uses elsewhere in his writing,[24] had fun with the Locust topos in *Roderick Random* by opportunistically claiming it and aggressively confirming it through the figure Murray's pamphlet derided, that of the Scottish parasite employed in the trade of "Physic." In a June 1, 1748, letter to Andrew Carlyle, Smollett wrote, "the whole [*Roderick Random*] is not so much a representation of my life as that of many other needy Scotch surgeons whom I have known either personally or by report."[25] Accordingly, when Random is interviewed for a job at Surgeons' Hall in London, his examiner observes, "we have scarce any other countrymen [than Scots] to examine here; you Scotchmen have overspread us of late as the locusts did Egypt" (101). Smollett reinflects typology by deflecting blame away from Random (and, by extension, other traveling Scots): Random agrees that he is locustlike, but maintains that his "indigence had been the crime not of [him], but of fortune" (379). Because his status as a wanderer is neither chosen nor essential to his nature, he feels no shame in his resourceful responses.[26] Here, Smollett pokes a finger in the eye of English vitriol about the parasitism of south-traveling Scots. The hero's response to contingency, his ability to appropriate English resources, carries the plot through to its resolution and reverberates beyond the borders of the novel with competing iterations of the parasite topos. The novel thus revises rather than supports what Bold calls the "Scottish tendency to dwell on misfortune."[27]

Smollett's hero is constructed vaguely so that the many may see themselves in the one; his "*Random*"-ness is key to his broad resonance within the historical and cultural milieu. Smollett says in the preface that within his novel "circumstances are altered and disguised to avoid personal satire" (xxxvi); critics have taken this to mean that his characters depict people whom he actually knew, and they have used his fictions to construct his biography.[28] I argue, in contrast, that Smollett avoided depicting "individuals" because he aimed at broad applicability.

The novel deploys what Gayatri Chakravorty Spivak has called "strategic essentialism,"[29] repeatedly stressing the applicability of Random's coping strategies—his ability to actively inhabit the plot history cuts for him and turn it to his advantage—to the lives of other traveling Scots. In this novel, Random is one among many wide-ranging redheads with brogues. He finds other Scots everywhere he goes, first on the road to London and then in London itself, where he reports, "I saw a great many young fellows, whom I formerly knew in Scotland, pass and repass." He tells an acquaintance, "my name was Random," to which the acquaintance replies, "Ay, ay, Random, Random, Random"; the hero Random is a random hero (88). The joke is repeated a second time when another acquaintance explains Random's identity to a London justice: "he told him I was a Scotchman . . . and that my name was Random" (107). The repeated invocation of the surname, in which "Random" is rendered as an adjective, suggests his broad typological characterization.

There is an equivalently random quality about the Scottish space he hails from; references to the place of nativity are many but vague, making it a metonym, if not a synecdoche, for Roderick Random himself. Here again, Smollett shows his skill at the strategic essential. We get no solid sense of geography, just of rural Scottish everycommunity. "I was born," Random tells us in the opening sentence of the first chapter, "in the northern part of this united kingdom," and it never gets more specific than that (9). He is simply "of the Randoms of the north—a very ancient house," a random hero from a random town (302). His successful return at novel's end thus not only ameliorates his own exilic experience; it counters a more general Scottish concern that migration south constituted an irreversible national hemorrhage.

HIGHLAND LADS, LOVERS, MOTHERS

The cultural interventionism of *Roderick Random* manifests not only in its adoption and mobilization of the Scottish parasite topos but also in its appropriation of Jacobite themes and iconography. The novel's theme of reciprocal longing for reunion between a masculine exile and a feminine source is intrinsic to the saga of Stuart dispossession depicted by Jacobite drinking glasses, medals, fans, ballads, and poems from the post-Culloden era well into the nineteenth century. Jacobite glasses boasted mottoes such as "*Redi*" (return), "*Redeat*" (may he return), and "*Revirescit*" (let it grow again) that were accompanied by images of budding roses and of new saplings emerging from stricken oaks (buds and saplings to indicate James's progeny).[30] Ballads and poems cast the Stuart exiles' affective relationship to loyal Britons back home as an amatory or familial drama in which a feminized citizenry awaited the return of a prince or other masculine equivalent (a lover, a husband, a son, and, occasionally, a brother); the Jacobite saga was easily conflated with "Scottish Plots" in which Scotland "herself" mourned a masculinized absent citizenry. By the time James Hogg pulled together versions of popular pieces such as "My Love He Was a Highland Lad" in *The Jacobite Relics of Scotland: Being the Songs, Airs, and Legends of the Adherents to the House of Stuart*,[31] the overlap between Scottish nationalism and sentimental Jacobitism was—like their gendered status—already a *fait accompli*.

Use of the gendered metaphor (exiled male figure; female figure, coequal with Scotland, who futilely awaits his return) was legion, especially when tied to seasonal temporality; the loss of masculine presence, its absence symbolized by endless winter season, was associated in popular Jacobitism with Stuart absence.[32] Moreover, Smollett's interest in creative refraction of the cultural narrative was longstanding. In his 1746 poem "The Tears of Scotland," he bemoans the treatment of the Scots in the bloody quashing at Culloden through the persona of a miserable exile who "bethinks him of his babes and wife" back home, while the "pious mother, doom'd to death, / Forsaken, wanders o'er the heath" to finally *become* the barren heath itself (l.11, 34–35). Her mate and protector doomed to wander "every clime," she stretches "beneath the inclement skies" (i.17, 47). The "wind whistles" while she "weeps" (l.43, 48). The consonance of weeping woman and whistling wind connects post-Culloden Scotland, trapped within a "dreary winter night," to the body of the mother/lover, who "dies" (l.28, 48).

Within the text of *Random*, Smollett participates in the verse tradition. He mines the overlap between Scottish nationalism and (sentimental) Jacobitism by capitalizing on the suggestiveness of a feminine presence who awaits the return of a masculine consort. Smollett's mother is thus characterized as a feminized source which the travelers return to and reinvigorate. Charlotte's importance to the novel's formal integrity is established in the very first chapter, in which we learn the details of her premonitory dream. Roderick is struck by the devil and flies far from her in the guise of a tennis ball, and she mourns his absence, until, "all of a sudden, she beheld it return with equal violence, and enter the earth beneath her feet, whence immediately sprung up a goodly tree covered with blossoms, the scent of which operated so strongly upon her nerves, that she awoke" (1). The phrase "she awoke" refers *literally* to Charlotte's awakening from her dream in chapter 1. Symbolically, however, the tree invokes the blasted oak of Jacobite mythology; Random will return to reinvigorate his own source (literally, his roots). But, first, Random and his father, separated for many years, reestablish their kinship during a chance meeting in Buenos Aires in which recognition takes place via the sign of "Charlotte Bowling"[33] (413). The image of Scotland as a "mother" and Scottish people as her "sons" was a metaphor of long standing,[34] as was the image of Scotland as a feminized beloved awaiting an exiled lover's return. Charlotte embodies both these figures. The mother's body stands in as metonym for the land itself, renewed figuratively by the return of the son, who, with the help of the transplanted Narcissa, springs forth from the land Charlotte's flesh has become—the genius of the place.[35] Through the conflation of mother, beloved, and heritable geography, *Random* participates in the thematic and narrative conventions attached to the overlapped Jacobite and Scottish Plots,[36] even as it marks an important pre-history to publications such as Hogg's *Jacobite Relics* that inscribe the project of recoverable selfhood within gendered terms.[37]

STRUCTURING ALIENATION AND REUNION

Random, who ranges both southward and abroad under duress, achieves a favorable resolution to the narrative line associated with both the Jacobite

Plot and the Scottish Plot when he and his father are replanted within the bounds of their hereditary estate. From the first page, with the information about Random's mother's dream, we *know* that is where the narrative is headed. A Highland seer interprets the dream for Random's parents, telling them that their son "[would] be a great traveller; that he would undergo many great dangers and difficulties, and at last return to his native land, where he would flourish in happiness and reputation" (1). Random assures us "how truly [the shape of the narrative] was foretold, will appear in the sequel," that is, in the narrative that follows (1). And so it does: propelled to the ends of the globe, relieved by occasional reunions with figures from the past, Random finally achieves his triumphant return. The fact that the end finally does fulfill the promise of the mother's dream is not *believable*; it is, instead, the stuff of epic.

I want to elucidate briefly the random but definitive pattern of alien-ation-and-restoration that suggests the larger narrative circle. In chapters 1–8, Random is orphaned, cut out of his inheritance, supported financially by his uncle Bowling until Bowling's fortune fails, betrayed by landlords and apothecaries under whom he studies, and travels to London to try to make his fortune, at which point he has an "unexpected meeting" with Strap, a friend from home, consummated by "mutual caresses": "I flew into his arms, and in the transport of my joy, gave him back one-half of the suds he had so lavishly bestowed on my countenance" (32). Through chapter 36, Random is abused as an apothecary in London, reduced to star-vation, and press-ganged into service on board the *Thunder*, but his trials are lightened by chance reunion with Thomson, another friend from home: "he clasped me in his arms, and bedewed my face with tears. It was some time ere I recovered the use of my reason, overpowered with this event, and longer still before I could speak. So that all I was capable of was to return his embraces, and to mingle the overflowings of my joy with his" (202). In chapters 37–44, he has a difficult time aboard the *Lizard*, is left destitute at Sussex, is employed as a footman, falls in love with his employer's daugh-ter Narcissa, is kidnapped, and enlists in the Regiment of Picardy. During this time, he chances upon his uncle Bowling—"the tears gushed down my cheeks. . . . I exclaimed, 'Gracious God! Mr. Bowling!'" (232)—and still later upon Strap, "who leaped upon me in a transport of joy, hung about my neck, kissed me from ear to ear, and blubbered like a great schoolboy" (252). In chapters 45–54, Random visits Bath, gambles, is debauched, and arrested; in chapter 55, he has a chance reunion with Narcissa, who by this point has begun to stand in for Random's sense of self-worth, which, in turn, becomes increasingly attached to his sense of his own origins, such that he exclaims, "the adorable Narcissa! Good heaven! what were the thrillings of my soul at that instant" (337). Blocked by Narcissa's family from marrying her, Random again gambles, is again jailed for debt (he meets the poetic Melopoyn in jail), and is saved from a subsequent slovenly condition by his uncle Bowling in chapter 64. Through to the conclusion, Random accompanies Bowling to South America, where he has a joyous chance reunion with his father, now called "Don Rodriguez," in Buenos Aires. Don Rodriguez settles £15,000 on him, Roderick marries Narcissa in London, and they all return to the scene of Random's nativity, where father and son are restored to lordly majesty in the affectionate bosom of a nigh-feudal community that they simultaneously restore to gaiety and solvency. Within this random pattern of alienation and reunion, many smaller reunions stud the narrative of loss. These touchstones of remembrance, virtually untouched by Smollett's critics, give the story unexpected shape by forming a thread that runs through scattered episodes and connects them to a larger narrative ellipsis predicated upon the final grand remembrance.[38] The recurrence of reunion and return, which is not only repetitive but also cumulative, suggests a submerged but powerful structuring force—that of Providence itself—beneath what Beasley calls the narrative's "dense, busy, active" surface.[39] The narrative form seems Humean, a random muddle of sticks bundled together; this narrative, however, is held together not by the simple glue of causality but by the chronotope of epic return.

The plot's episodic nature belies a formal integrity reliant on deep structure that inheres in the (random) recurrence of returns that culminates in the synergetic resolution of three main plotlines (amatory, familial, and communal). As my précis indicates, "fortune" drives Random hither and thither; he does not travel for travel's sake but is "like a wreck, d'ye see, at the mercy of the wind and weather," continually obliged to "steer another course," even when it does "not at all suit [his] inclination," the better to "push [his] fortune in the world" and finally gain "creditab[ility]" (21, 24, 25, 41, 233). Each reunion is seemingly more rapturous, more self-renewing, than the last. Thus, where Jerry Phillips concludes that for Smollett "the means are more important than the end,"[40] I find that a retinue of nested reunions (with Strap, Thomson, Bowling) point the way through the narrative of dislocation toward the confluent resolution of three crucial plotlines: first, the reunion of father and son (the familial restoration plot); second, the reunion of Random and Narcissa (the amatory restoration plot); and, finally, the reunion of elder and younger Random with their heritable community in Scotland (the communal restoration plot), in which father and son purchase their "Paternal Estate—Proceed to it" and find themselves "more and more happy" (477). Where Phillips finds that "the conclusion of Roderick's adventures in marriage, lineage, and inheritance [is] nothing short of a veritable anti-climax,"[41] I find that the end is nothing less than the legitimating telos anticipated by the other providential reunions that precede it. The form is circular; the plot does not "develop." Instead, it is reactionary; it looks back, ultimately fulfilling the promise of Random's mother's dream. The movement "toward" closing the narrative circle is uneven, but that is part of the point: the chronotope of epic return and the chronotope of providential return alike depend on a loose episodic quality that is quasi-distinct from the global plot. The dream's promise is fulfilled *despite* the haphazard affairs of lived experience.[42]

The antidevelopmental quality of the plot correlates with the antidevelopmental quality of Random himself; it cannot quite be said that he develops, either. His *bildung* is of a different sort; he does not "progress" into being an "individual." Instead, he discovers his own essential (inner) character percolating beneath the chaos of lived experience; this inner character, grounded in typology, is immutable despite the local disorder of fortune's ups and downs. Random's essential self is not authentic because it is unique but because it operates within the type of his "random" Scottishness. The series of reunions underscores the presence of a stable core of typological identity beneath the flux of outward appearances; repeatedly, the plot's circular threads of remembrance return him to the stable self he finally realizes he possesses. His appearance does change a great deal, and old family members and friends whom he chances to encounter do not recognize him at first glance. For instance, when Thomson happens upon him aboard the *Thunder*, Thomson finds him so "altered by the misery he had undergone" that "he could not recollect one feature of his countenance" (164). Random relives this experience of losing and regaining his identity with Strap, his uncle Bowling, even his father. Ultimately, each reunion serves as a touchstone, connecting him to his history when the other figure finally recognizes the "essential" true self that has been obscured by appearance. What Random says about an acquaintance, Squire Gawky, applies as well to his own character: "howsoever his externals might be altered, he was at bottom the same individual" (127). This is a novel about restoration, not development; Random is not simply a rogue who learns life lessons and becomes good.[43] Indeed, his greatest show of generous fellow feeling occurs during his first trip to London, where he provides succor—room, board, medicine, and a sympathetic ear—to Miss Williams, a woman who not only broke his heart a short time before but also gave him a venereal disease while doing so. He explains, her "deplorable situation filled my breast with compassion, and . . . I forgave all the injury she had designed for me; and . . . although my circumstances were extremely low, I would share my last farthing with her" (115–16); in fine, he saves Miss Williams's life. Random does not grow. He *does* become attuned to, and increasingly more proud of, the essential identity that the oblique narrative structure works to *eventually* make synchronous with his outer reality.

If Random "changes" in the course of the novel, it is in the following way: ironically, his awareness of his altered physical appearance enables him to intuit a disconnect between internal character and external charac-

teristic. This disconnect between inner and outer correlates with a disconnect between the deep (internal) structure of the plot and the (surface)
chaos of local episodes. Random learns to look beyond externals, beyond
the evidence offered by immediate reality, and so comes to understand
"the folly of judging from appearances" (276). Repeatedly, he refers to his
own fluctuating façade as a "disguise" (164, 167, 382), and he exploits
the possibilities of temporary cross-cultural performance. By the end of
the book, he changes his appearance many times: he cuts off his "car-
roty locks" and takes up a bob-wig (81, 82); goes by other names such
as "John Brown" or "Gentleman John" or "Mr. Randan" (245, 255, 280);
is mistaken for other people, such as "Patrick Gahagan" (107); alters his
Scottish accent in favor "of the English tongue" (112); and is variously
perceived as Scottish, Irish, English, and, simply, "foreign." Despite or
because of all this, Random proudly notes that no matter what befalls
him, he is still himself:

> I had endured hardships, 'tis true—my whole life had been a series of such;
> And when I looked forward, the prospect was not much bettered, but . . . if one
> scheme of life should not succeed, I could have recourse to another, and so to
> a third, veering about to a thousand different shifts, according to the emergen-
> cies of my fate, without forfeiting the dignity of my character beyond a power
> of retrieving it, or subjecting myself wholly to the caprice and barbarity of the
> world. (136–37)

In this important passage, Smollett emphasizes both Random's ability
to adapt his outer characteristics and still remain "myself" (136). Deidre
Lynch writes that we *"pity* Roderick for his difficulties in getting himself
acknowledged as somebody in particular" (Lynch's italics).[44] Lynch is right.
And, yet, it may be that our pity is misguided. We want *Roderick Random* to
champion progressive individualism, when, in fact, this novel insists that
identity inheres not in particulars but in typology. Ironically, the novel's
reactionary circularity—reactionary because it seeks to reassert the contours
of Random's Scottish "type"—engenders a dissonantly modern sense of an
essential, as opposed to labile, identity.[45]

Surprising us still further, *Random* celebrates a well-regulated vanity as
key to capitalizing on the enduring presence of immutable selfhood. Vanity is usually discussed in eighteenth-century discourse as negative because
it leads to being credulous and susceptible, which, in turn, leads to being
bilked by flatterers (and David Daiches thus writes that Random is plagued
by "weakness, vanity, inexperience, credulity").[46] In this novel, however,
it is naïvete (inexperience) rather than pride (vanity) that is under attack.
Early on, Random admits happily that "pride and resentment" are the "two
chief ingredients in [his] disposition" (116); we could write this admission
off as youthful folly, except that those qualities of pride and resentment

are not expunged later on.[47] Instead, pride goeth before a restoration; those qualities are deepened and rationalized in the final pages, when Random gets revenge against early foes (his female cousins and Mr. Potion) and his father—in the role of Odysseus expelling the suitors—saves the family estate from public auction.

Narcissa, a cipher for the hero,[48] is crucial to the full flowering of Random's heritable pride and resentment. She inspires him to fight the dictates of the "cruel fate [that] compelled [him] to wear a servile disguise so unsuitable to [his] birth, sentiments, and . . . deserts" (382). That her name alludes to the Narcissus myth seems indisputable, but Smollett uses the myth obliquely by attributing an unexpected positive value to vanity. He makes the narcissistic Random into the Narcissus figure, while Narcissa enables his self-regard within the terms of his birthright. She is the mirror by which, in Ovid, the Narcissus figure comes to *see* (or, depending on the translation, to *know*) himself. Just as Smollett makes use of and departs from the Jacobite Plot, he makes use of and departs from the Ovidian myth. In Ovid, the sage Tiresias promises on the occasion of Narcissus's birth that he will live a long life *only if* he avoids "looking at" or "knowing" himself. Narcissus, who falls in love with his reflection, perishes; his story is taken as a caution against vanity, self-regard, narcissism, pride. Smollett challenges the myth's basic premise by implying a happy consequence to the putative sin of self-knowledge that Narcissa's mirror gives Random.

Because of Narcissa, Random aspires to attain "the character of a gentleman, to which [he] thought himself entitled by birth"; the fact that he equates achieving that identity with "succeeding in love" with Narcissa implies the interdependence of the amatory and restoration plots (228). She functions as a catalyst: it is she who tells him he has "integrity," so that his "thoughts aspired to a sphere so high above" his current reality (390). He becomes inspired to achieve the state of "creditab[ility]" on which his restoration to his heritable lands and aristocratic roots depends (254). Because of her, he reconnects with his "learned[ness]," his "taste," he renews his talent at versification, and, most importantly, he begins to "despise [him]self for [his] tame resignation to [his] sordid fate" (253, 254–55, 228). Literally, she awakens him to a more transcendent sense of self—she "thrill[s]" his very "soul" (246). They exchange miniature portraits of each other, reminiscent of the miniatures, "touch-piece" coins, and medals with images of Stuart heirs that were carried by Jacobite subjects in Britain[49]; no matter where "necessity" takes Random, he maintains that Narcissa's "image . . . kept possession of [his] breast" (446, 453). The image of Narcissa herself has little to do with *her*[50]; his image of Narcissa is his image of himself being remembered by her (this is underscored by an important scene in which he watches her study his miniature). She is emblematic, a "dear idea" that "live[s] unimpaired in the midst of numberless cares, and animate[s] [him] against a thousand dangers and calamities" (382). It reminds him of the "unalterable" (466): those aspects of his own "self" that he will not "forfeit" (136). Her "idea" is a reflecting totem that restores him to himself by giving him a sense of what "eternal constancy" might mean and by enabling his "ambition [to] revive" (228).

In his overweening self-regard, Random resembles the major mid-century player in the Jacobite mythos: Bonnie Prince Charlie. In her periodical *The Parrot*, Eliza Haywood characterized him as "blown up . . . to such a height of Pride, that he imagined he might do any thing."[51] In the view of Charles Stuart's detractors, only a severe hubris could have led him to believe he would prevail in attaining the rewards of birthright in the face of so many practical factors against him (including his own inexperience with battle). Random's character, meeting the public eye in the immediate wake of the quashed rebellion of the '45, is highly allusive of the Young Pretender. Like him, he is "compelled" by "cruel fate . . . to wear a servile disguise so unsuitable to [his] birth, sentiments, and . . . deserts" (382), even if he is not so highborn as Charles Stuart, "Whase hame should have been," as the ballad goes, "a palace" ("Wae's me for Prince Charlie," 15). There are other local similarities between Random and the Stuarts. For instance, like Charlie's father James Francis Edward Stuart, Random is accused of being only a "pretended son"; he protests to the apothecary Crab that he "was descended from a better family than any [Crab] could boast an alliance with" (472, 39). The novel bluntly asserts similarities and repeatedly draws the reader's attention to them.

Despite parallels, Random's story ultimately departs from the saga of "the king[s] over the water," and its fulfillment suggests more than just a sentimental nationalism. Smollett exacts a contrived separation of the Scottish Plot from the impotent Jacobite Plot. Like Random, Charles Stuart claimed Providence was on his side, but he failed to achieve a triumphant (or even, in the main, *welcoming*) homecoming in 1745. Instead, he returned to find most of "his" people indifferent (if not hostile). Not so Random's beloved, or the larger population that shares her sentiment. On returning to Britain, he immediately asks, "how is Narcissa? is she the same that I left her?" and is gratified by the answer: "she is as much yours as ever" (465). She is possessed of "unalterable love," and "[a]fter a long absence . . . from the dear object of [his] hope," the exiled hero finds "the melting fair, as kind and constant as [his] heart could wish"—just as he does the peasants in his heritable community (466, 469). Smollett's narrative course thus differs from the Jacobite Plot it conjures (Charles, fueled by his father's attempt in the earlier rebellion of 1715 to reunite with the citizenry, failed miserably and crept from the country). Margaret Anne Doody has called the title character from Samuel Richardson's novel *Sir Charles Grandison* "much of what Charles Stuart *was* and all that Charles Stuart *should* have been . . . He is the Tory Prince who never came [back]."[52] How much more strongly does the first half of Doody's description—"much of what Charles Stuart *was* and all that Charles Stuart *should* have been"—suit Random, who *does* return and who receives, with his father, the heritable community's warm welcome? Through Narcissa's pregnancy that caps the novel, the promised fruition of the flowering tree is realized; the tree is itself suggestive at once of the white-petaled narcissus bulb, the white Stuart rose, and the budding oak. Resurrection springs from native soil, from the symbolic body of the mother.

Random's return to the motherland, like his reunion with Narcissa, is paralleled, amplified, and almost *overshadowed* by the return of his father to a heritable community that has waited faithful as Penelope and to the ground in which Charlotte is buried. Boucé aligns Smollett's hero with Ulysses, calling him "Roderick-Ulysses,"[53] but Roderick is, after all, his father's son; his father occupies the Ulyssean narrative seat, and it is his restoration that is made much of. Because the enthused greeting Random and his father receive from the peasantry extends primarily to the *elder* Random, the novel's ellipsis seems to stretch back in time to the 1715 rebellion. The tenants' vigorous devotion, related by Random, recalls the greeting the Old Pretender is said to have received, one that bears little resemblance to the reception of the Young Pretender thirty years later. Random explains,

> We proceeded to our estate . . . and when we came within half a league of the house, were met by a prodigious number of poor tenants, men, women, and children . . . . We were almost devoured by their affection. My father had always been their favourite, and now that he appeared to be their master, after having been thought dead so long, their joy broke out into a thousand extravagances . . . those who were near Don Rodriguez fell upon their knees, and kissed his hand, or the hem of his garment, praying aloud for long life and prosperity to him; others approached me in the same manner; while the rest clapped their hands at a distance, and invoked Heaven to shower its choicest blessings on our heads! (479)

Random's father responds with proper lordliness, giving forty pounds to the parish for the care of the poor and "order[ing] some bullocks to be killed, and some hogsheads of ale to be brought from the neighbouring village, to regale these honest people, who had not enjoyed such a holiday for many years before" (479). In Smollett's poem "The Tears of Scotland," the land is crushed by the absence of its landowner, without whom

> The rural pipe and merry lay
> No more shall cheer the happy day;
> No social scenes of gay delight
> Beguile the dreary winter nights.
> (l.22–25)

Don Rodriguez occupies the character of a king restored; with his restoration, the land is itself reborn as "their joy broke out" (479). The restoration of Don Rodriguez suggests how Smollett's revisionist Scottish Plot, as epic chronotope, engages with but also departs from the popular symbolic discourse of Jacobite saga and the historical fact of Scottish diaspora. On the surface, Don Rodriguez has changed even more than his son. Yet he is still "master," still the people's "favourite," and as such he represents the triumph of unalterable identity. Smollett transforms the tragedy of Jacobite history into a double triumph: *Roderick Random* is both Scotland's own "first novel" and Smollett's own "epic" intervention on the literary shape of the Scottish Plot. This novel defends the essential self in a way that turns its back on eighteenth-century climatological theories of identity. At the same time, this novel hearkens back to a classical emphasis on types over particulars, reclaiming an old *positive* image of the traveling Scot. The speaker of the 1704 poem "THE True Scots Genius, REVIVING" alludes to that older conception by remembering how "The *Scot[t]ish* Body, . . . from Pole to Pole, / Did, once, make known the Active *Scot[t]ish* Soul" (4). Smollett's random Scotsman, who travels far before bringing his genius home again, rejuvenates a topos that had been cast in increasingly negative terms.

The novel's ending does not allow "Scotland" to fade into an abstract idea of itself; in restoring the topos of the traveling Scot and in restoring his traveling Scots to their home, Smollett balances sentimentality with pragmatism. He does so by grounding the reunion with the heritable community in economic terms. This is a novel about restoration rather than development, but its resolution does not draw a specious line between a world of commerce and one of premodern Scottish ruralism.[54] Random's repatriation as the flowering tree is only possible because his father's dealings in the global economy can be used to buy the family estate, fund the parish, set up Strap and Miss Williams with a farm, buy hogsheads of ale for the peasants, and so forth. Moreover, Random reveals that he may travel to London in the near future to secure Narcissa's inheritance (her brother, who opposed the marriage, has blocked her inheritance, but a codicil allows her to inherit at nineteen). The possibility of his future travel has disturbed some critics, but the couple is solvent, Random's identity is beyond forfeiture, and with Narcissa's pregnancy, his "felicity" has been "crown[ed]" (480). His closing statement feels pragmatic, not fraught.[55] Smollett thus confirms but also challenges representations of Scotland as the physical manifestation of Britain's past; the novel suggests that Scots can operate in British and global economies, take advantage of progress, without losing their identities in the process.[56] Random is quite willing to use English gold to maintain his sources, and the novel's final lines, with references to wills, clauses, and annexed codicils, are at least as pragmatic as they are sentimental. Smollett utilizes the cultural and historical overlap between the Jacobite saga and Scottish diaspora but ultimately departs from the former; tempering sentimentalism with economic opportunism, offering an epic saga predicated not on progressive individualism but on an older concept of revolution as return, *The Adventures of Roderick Random* revises the mid-century Scottish Plot.

NOTES

1. James II abdicated the throne as his Protestant daughter Mary and her husband, the Dutch William of Orange, simultaneously assumed it. His son, James Francis Edward Stuart (the Old Pretender or Old Chevalier), failed to regain the throne in the Jacobite rebellion of 1715. Thirty years later, James Francis Edward Stuart's son, Charles Edward Louis John Casimir Silvester Maria Stuart (the Young Pretender, Young Chevalier, or Bonnie Prince Charlie to friends), made an unsuccessful bid to seize the throne in the Jacobite rebellion of 1745–1746.

2. See Jerry C. Beasley, *Tobias Smollett, Novelist* (Athens: University of Georgia Press, 1998), 195, 135, 20.

3. Tobias Smollett translated François Fénelon's *Télémaque* as *The Adventures of Telemachus, the Son of Ulysses* (posthumously published, 1776). See O M Brack's fine recent edition (Athens: University of Georgia Press, 1997). Leslie A. Chilton's useful introduction to the edition notes that Smollett was familiar since childhood with *Télémaque*, xvii–xxiii; xvii.

4. Tobias Smollett, *The Adventures of Roderick Random*, ed. Paul-Gabriel Boucé (Oxford: Oxford University Press, 1979, repr., 1999), xxxiii–xxxvi; xxxv. References are to this edition.

5. Alan Bold offers a contrasting view. Duplicating Smollett's own language, Bold writes that Random's character is "derived from . . . the general 'disposition of the Scots, addicted to traveling.'" See *Smollett: Author of the First Distinction*, ed. Alan Bold (London: Vision Press, 1982), 7.

6. For a discussion of this phenomenon in early nineteenth-century Scottish literature, see Caroline McCracken-Flesher, "You Can't Go Home Again: James Hogg and the Problem of Scottish 'Post-Colonial' Return," *Studies in Hogg and His World* 8 (1997): 24–41.

7. My thesis historicizes and builds upon Beasley's apt assertion that Joseph Frank's theories of anti-linear spatial form offer a way to locate narrative subversion within *Roderick Random*. Beasley insists that readers may profitably understand this novel as that which it would not appear to be, namely, a "whole construction" (36). Reading against the grain of received wisdom about formlessness in *Random*, Beasley argues that this episodic novel achieves eventual synchrony as the connections between discrete events "gradually . . . clarify, revealing a coherence of design." See *Tobias Smollett, Novelist*, 36, 40. My reading, compatible with Beasley's, foregounds the organizing force of Random's mother's dream. Conversely, John Barth brushes off the proleptic significance of the dream when he comments, "perhaps the less said about that clanking device the better." See Barth, afterword to *The Adventures of*

Roderick Random (New York: New American Library, 1964), 469–79; 471. Like Ian Haywood, I believe the novel's formal circuit demands an "allegorical examination," and, like Kenneth G. Simpson, I believe that this analysis should be historicized. See Haywood, "Dreams in Pregnancy: The Opening of Defoe's *Memoirs of a Cavalier* and Smollett's *Roderick Random*," *American Notes and Queries* 22.5–6 (1982): 71–72; 72; and Simpson's chapter on "Tobias Smollett: The Scot as English Novelist," in *The Protean Scot: The Crisis of Identity in Eighteenth Century Scottish Literature* (Aberdeen: University of Aberdeen Press, 1988), 14–40. For wider reading in spatial analysis and narrative form, see Joseph Frank, *The Idea of Spatial Form* (New Brunswick, NJ: Rutgers University Press, 1991).

8. Daniel Defoe, *History of the Union of Great Britain* (London, 1709), 42.

9. *Observator or a Dialogue between a Country-Man, & a Landwart School-Master* (Edinburgh, 1705).

10. William Forbes, "THE True Scots Genius, REVIVING. A POEM. Written upon occasion of the RESOLVE past in PARLIAMENT, the 17th of July 1704" (Edinburgh, 1704).

11. See Frank McLynn's chapter "The Bitter Fruit: Exile and Diaspora," in *The Jacobite* (London: Routledge & Kegan Paul, 1985), 126–41; esp. 127–28. See also Bruce Lenman's chapter "After the '45," in *The Jacobite Cause* (Glasgow: Richard Drew Publishing in association with the National Trust for Scotland, 1986), 112–20; esp. 116.

12. Incidentally, the 1747 act *(An Act for taking away and abolishing the Heritable Jurisdictions in that part of Great Britain called Scotland, and for making satisfaction to the Proprietors thereof . . . and for rendering the Union of the Two Kingdoms more complete)* violated the terms of the 1707 Act of Union. Indeed, Defoe wrote in the *History* that "all Heretable Offices and Jurisdictions" were "Reserv'd to the Owners Thereof, as Right of Property, not withstanding this Treaty," 57.

13. See Leith Davis's insightful chapter titled "Narrating the '45," in *Acts of Union: Scotland and the Literary Negotiation of the British Nation 1707–1830* (Stanford, CA: Stanford University Press, 1997), 46–73; 68.

14. See Lawrence Lipking, "The Jacobite Plot," *ELH* 64.4 (1997): 843–855.

15. Ibid., 844.

16. See "The Lamentation of David over Saul and Jonathan Imitated," in *English Jacobite Ballads, Songs and Satires from the Mss. at Townley Hall*, ed. Alexander B. Grosart (Lancashire, 1877), 27. Most of the pieces in Townley date from the 1740s (one dates to 1750; a few date from earlier in the century).

17. This ballad reworked older canonical ballads; Francis J. Child lists twelve variants of one source, "The Elfin Knight" (Child Ballad no. 2), in *Popular English and Scottish Ballads* (1882); versions of "O'er the Hills" appeared in *Pills to Purge Melancholy* (Thomas D'Urfey, 1706), *The Recruiting Officer* (George Farquhar, 1708), and *The Beggar's Opera* (John Gay, 1728).

18. See Tobias Smollett, "The Tears of Scotland," qtd. in Howard Swazey Buck, *Smollett as Poet* (New Haven, CT: Yale University Press, 1927), 1–3; l.17–18. Quoted hereafter by line number.

19. "A Lenten Litany," in *Poems on Affairs of State, from the Year 1640 to the year 1704*, three vols. (London, 1716), 3:23. The poem also appears in *A Collection of Loyal Songs Written Against the Rump Parliament, Between the Years 1639 and 1661*.

With an Historical Introduction to the Whole, two vols. (London, 1731), 1:116; in this version, "Scots Louse" becomes "Scotch Louse."

20. The full title is *Yorick's Jests: Or, Wit's Common-Place Book, arranged on a new plan. Being a Choice Collection of Humourous Jests, Happy Bons-Mots, &c. To which is added, a choice selection of toasts and sentiments* (London, 1783), 718.

21. *The New Universal Etymological English Dictionary: To Which is Added a Dictionary of Cant Words* (London, 1760), 713.

22. Daniel Defoe, *The True-Born Englishman*, in *The True-Born Englishman and Other Writings*, ed. P. N. Furbank and W. R. Owens (London: Penguin Books, 1997), 26–59; l.276–284.

23. William Murray, *The Thistle: A Dispassionate Examine of the Prejudice of English-men in General to the Scotch Nation; and particularly of a late arrogant insult offered to all Scotchmen, by a modern English journalist. In a letter to the author of Old England of Dec. 27, 1746* (London, 1747), 34. Murray's essay was republished twice more within the year.

24. See Walter H. Keithley, "Tobias Smollett, John Woodward, and the Satiric Inversion of Popular Medical Iconography in *The History and Adventures of an Atom*," in *Tobias Smollett, Scotland's First Novelist: New Essays in Memory of Paul-Gabriel Boucé*, ed. O M Brack Jr. (Newark: University of Delaware Press, 2007), 201–16.

25. See *The Letters of Tobias Smollett, M. D.*, ed. Edward S. Noyes (Cambridge, MA: Harvard University Press, 1926), no. 5.

26. Alfred Lutz emphasizes how Random is "at the mercy of external forces." See "Representing Scotland in *Roderick Random* and *Humphry Clinker*: Smollett's Devel-opment as a Novelist," *Studies in the Novel* 33.1 (2001): 1.

27. Bold, *Smollett*, 8.

28. Boucé warns against the practice of using Smollett's novels as mere life-history in his chapter on "Autobiography and the Novels," in *The Novels of Tobias Smollett*, trans. Antonia White and Paul-Gabriel Boucé (New York: Longman, 1976), 40–67.

29. See Gayatri Chakravorty Spivak, "Subaltern Studies: Deconstructing Histo-riography," in *Selected Subaltern Studies*, ed. Ranajit Guha and Gayatri Chakravorty Spivak (Oxford: Oxford University Press, 1988), 13.

30. See Robin Nicholson's exhibit catalogue, *Bonnie Prince Charlie and the House of Stuart 1688–1788: Works of Art from the Drambuie Collection* (Edinburgh: The Drambuie Liquor Company, 2005), esp. 14–25.

31. James Hogg, *The Jacobite Relics of Scotland; Being the Songs, Airs, and Legends of the Adherents to the House of Stuart* (Edinburgh, 1819), 323.

32. See my article, "Representing Modernity in Jane Barker's Galesia Trilogy: Ja-cobite Allegory and the Patch-Work Aesthetic," *Studies in Eighteenth-Century Culture* 38.1 (2005): 55–80.

33. The reunion of father and son turns on Charlotte's present absence: "Don Rodriguez, with an uncommon eagerness of voice and look, pronounced, 'Pray, captain, what is the young gentleman's name?—'His name (said my uncle) is Roderick Random.'—'Gracious Powers!' (cried the stranger, starting up)—'And his mother's'—'His mother (answered the captain, amazed) was called Charlotte Bowling.'—'O bounteous heaven! (exclaimed Don Rodriguez, springing across the table, and clasping me in his arms) my son! my son! have I found thee again? do

I hold thee in my embrace, after having lost and despaired of seeing thee so long?' So saying, he fell upon my neck, and wept aloud with joy; while the power of nature operating strongly in my breast, I was lost in rapture, and while he pressed me to his heart, let fall a shower of tears in his bosom. His utterance was choked up a good while by the agitation of his soul; at length he broke out into 'Mysterious Providence!—O my dear Charlotte, there yet remains a pledge of our love! and such a pledge!—so found!'" (413).

34. See, for example, William Wright's personification of Scotland as "Fergusia" in his play *A Comical History of the Marriage-union Betwixt Fergusia and Heptarchus* (Edinburgh, 1706); Fergusia, pressured by England ("Heptarchus") to unify with him in "marriage," gives her "sons" the final say-so. Toni Bowers discusses the play; see "Representing Resistance: British Seduction Stories, 1660–1800," in *A Companion to the Eighteenth-Century English Novel*, ed. Paula Backscheider and Catherine Ingrassia (Malden, MA: Blackwell, 2005), 140–63.

35. Son and father return together in an anti-Oedipal endeavor: "My father intending to revisit his native country, and pay the tribute of a few tears at my mother's grave, Narcissa and I resolved to accompany him" (432).

36. For discussion about how the gendering of nation and subject operates within Britain's later/Victorian imperialist project, see Anne McClintock, *Imperial Leather: Race, Gender, and Sexuality in the Colonial Context* (New York: Routledge, 1995); for analysis of how collective national fantasy in nineteenth-century America depends on a shared construction of feminine-passive bodily icons, see Lauren Berlant, *The Anatomy of National Fantasy: Hawthorne, Utopia, and Everyday Life* (Chicago: University of Chicago Press, 1991).

37. Hogg dedicates the collection "to the sons of the men that ne'er flinched from their faith," essentially joining them—"The Members of the Highland Society"—and joining *with* them via his project of gathering together the relics of a masculinized nationalism that he construes as (and endorses as) originally constructed by female sensibility, iv–v. In the note to "My Love He Was A Highland Lad," for instance, one of many pieces in which female Scottish voices mourn lost men, he posits that one "would think that . . . these Jacobite songs had been written by ladies . . . No man would think of writing such a song as this . . . strongly characteristic of the female mind, ever ardent in the cause it espouses" (223).

38. Damian Grant and Tuvia Bloch, both of whom imply the novel's formal deficiency, offer contrasting viewpoints. See Grant, "Roderick Random: Language as Projectile" in *Smollett: Author of the First Distinction*, 129–47; and Bloch, "Smollett's Quest for Form," *Modern Philology* 65 (1967): 103–13. John Richetti, on the other hand, insists that Smollett's "lack of structure" is "defiant" rather than deficient, and that it is moreover the source of a certain "narrative virtue." See "The Old Order and the New Novel of the Mid-Eighteenth Century: Narrative Authority in Fielding and Smollett," *Eighteenth-Century Fiction* 2 (1990): 187. Brian McCrea's argument about the presence of a certain "anamnestic" form is roughly consonant with Richetti's. See *Impotent Fathers: Patriarchy and Demographic Crisis in the Eighteenth-Century Novel* (Newark: University of Delaware Press, 1998), 103–19. Lance Bertelsen voices a tentative but amenable suspicion that within the bounds of "recurrence" one may locate "a controlling idea behind Smollett's work." See "The Smollettian View of Life," *NOVEL: A Forum on Fiction* (1978): 119. Boucé asserts the presence of a

"deep structure . . . beneath the apparent discontinuity" and asserts that the novel "follow[s] a geometrical pattern like a capital 'W', whose three high points, from left to right would represent Roderick's birth, his meeting with Narcissa again in Bath, and his marriage." See *The Novels of Tobias Smollett*, 45, 142. My reading is compatible with his but suggests a more involved, if unsteady, geometry.

39. Beasley, *Tobias Smollett, Novelist*, 41.

40. Jerry Phillips, "Narrative, Adventure, and Schizophrenia: from Smollett's *Roderick Random* to Melville's *Omoo*," *Journal of Narrative Technique* 12 (1995): 179.

41. Ibid., 183.

42. The concept of the chronotope comes from Mikhail M. Bakhtin's chapter on "Forms of Time and Chronotope in the Novel," in *The Dialogic Imagination*, trans. Michael Holquist (Austin: University of Texas Press, 1981), 84–258.

43. Random is usually thought of as a picaro. See, for example, Robert Giddings, *The Tradition of Smollett* (London: Methuen, 1967), 31. The novel's form may be picaresque, but my understanding of Random's character diverges from readings such as Boucé's, which asserts Random's supposed evolution "from a dowry-hunter to a generous-hearted man"; see *The Novels of Tobias Smollett*, 124.

44. See Deidre Lynch, *The Economy of Character: Novels, Market Culture, and the Business of Inner Meaning* (Chicago: University of Chicago Press, 1998), 109.

45. For the notion of essential identity in race during the 1700s, see Roxann Wheeler, *The Complexion of Race: Categories of Difference in Eighteenth-Century British Culture* (Philadelphia: University of Pennsylvania Press, 2000).

46. David Daiches, "Smollett Reconsidered," in *Smollett: Author of the First Distinction*, 24.

47. As Boucé points out, the last chapter is colored by Random's "[p]ride at regaining possession of the family property and resentment towards those who have maltreated or injured"; see *The Novels of Tobias Smollett*, 57.

48. Lynch calls her a "reflection"; see *The Economy of Character*, 116. Aileen Douglas calls her "an image of Roderick himself"; See *Uneasy Sensations: Smollett and the Body* (Chicago: University of Chicago Press, 1995), 65.

49. See Nicholson, *Bonnie Prince Charlie and the House of Stuart*, 27–32.

50. Jerry Beasley has written at length about Smollett's predilection for faintly drawn heroines whose function is mythical and rhetorical, heroines who serve to shore up contrasts and to highlight the heroes with which they are paired. In addition to his chapter on *Random* in *Tobias Smollett, Novelist*, see also his wider discussion, "Amiable Apparitions: Smollett's Fictional Heroines," in *Augustan Subjects: Essays in Honor of Martin C. Battestin*, ed. Albert J. Rivero (Newark: University of Delaware Press, 1997), 229–48.

51. Eliza Haywood, *The Parrot* (London, 1746), K5v.

52. See Margaret Anne Doody, "Richardson's Politics," *Eighteenth-Century Fiction* 2 (1990): 125.

53. Boucé, *The Novels of Tobias* Smollett, xviii.

54. A number of Smollett's critics have stressed the novel's opposition to commerce. Clive T. Probyn, for instance, finds that Random is firmly settled into "rural retirement." See *English Fiction of the Eighteenth Century, 1700–1789* (London: Longman, 1987), 110. Lutz similarly cites the novel's "withdrawal from the world of

commerce into a pre-commercial world, into a literary convention"; see "Representing Scotland in *Roderick Random* and *Humphry Clinker*," 17.

55. For a contrasting view, see James H. Bunn's "skeptical" argument that Random's closing statement indicates his eagerness to leave the domestic circle for another "vital" round of "adventuring, gaming, cheating, warring" in "Signs of Randomness in *Roderick Random*," *Eighteenth-Century Studies* 14.4 (1981): 469. See also McCrea, who faults Beasley for harboring "disabling expectations" about happy endings and insists that Random's "journey is far from over, even though he has found his father and returned 'home'"; *Impotent Fathers*, 158–59.

56. In a point well taken, Davis cites Random's marriage to Narcissa as proof of his "assimilation . . . into British society," *Acts of Union*, 69. At the same time, Robert Crawford is right to call attention to Random's "continuing Scottishness." See *Devolving English Literature* (London: Clarendon Press, 1992), 61.

11

Rescuing Narcissa: Monstrous Vision, Imagination, and Redemption in *Roderick Random*

Christopher D. Johnson

In 1726 Mary Toft, a poor woman from rural Surrey, perpetrated a bizarre deception when she claimed to have given birth to seventeen rabbits. The Toft story is remarkable for at least two reasons. First, Mrs. Toft did not die from the hoax, which she carried out over several weeks by positioning newly killed bunnies in her uterus, which was distended from a recent pregnancy and miscarriage. Second, prominent members of the medical community seemed strangely unwilling to refute Mrs. Toft's incredible claim. She eventually confessed when Sir Richard Manningham, a fellow of the Royal Society who doubted her claims from the beginning, threatened to perform exploratory surgery. Only then did doctors find the strength of skepticism. As Dennis Todd writes, "It is difficult to find anyone who was willing to deny the story before the hoax was exposed. Afterwards, of course, everyone denied that he had ever believed her at all."[1] Todd demonstrates that contemporary medical theory, especially as related to the female imagination, lent credibility to Mrs. Toft's claims and allowed her incident to pique the curiosity of learned men, including Dr. John Arbuthnot and others with ties to the Crown. More specifically, Toft's explanation of having been startled by a rabbit during her pregnancy and having subsequently dreamed of rabbits made her monstrous births seem plausible.

Readers of eighteenth-century novels, are, of course, familiar with fictional accounts of prenatal imprinting. Fielding uses a strawberry birthmark, caused by the mother's longing for out-of-season fruit, to reveal Joseph Andrews's true identity and bring about the novel's dénouement.

Charlotte Lennox, as Sue Howard discusses elsewhere in this volume, does something similar in *Euphemia*. In Sterne's great novel, Tristram Shandy explains his own fascination with time by recalling that his mother "happened to be thinking about a clock when he was conceived," and, of course, Smollett has a great fun with the whole idea of prenatal influence in the opening chapters of *Peregrine Pickle*, when Mrs. Grizzle fears that Mrs. Pickle's "pernicious appetite" during her pregnancy might cause her child to be "affected with some disagreeable mark."[2] The Mary Toft story invites us to read these details as more than simple plot devices and sources for broad comedy. Instead, these scattered references to prenatal imprinting reflect an underlying anxiety within eighteenth-century culture—the power of the imagination to transform the physical self. For a few chaotic months, Mary Toft became the embodiment of that anxiety, and her story was significant enough not only to spawn fistfights in the street but also to capture the attention of King George I.[3] As Todd skillfully demonstrates, the cultural assumptions that fueled this anxiety lingered long after her lie was discovered and continued to find scattered expression throughout the century.

Using the Toft story as a touchstone, I hope to explore the imagination as presented in Smollett's first novel, *Roderick Random*, published twenty-two years after the Toft episode and fourteen years before William Hogarth's treatment of the legend in *Credulity, Superstition, and Fanaticism* (1762). My purpose is threefold. First, I wish to examine Smollett's participation in a form of misogyny, prevalent in the eighteenth century, concerning the instability of the female body and the inherent dangers of the female mind. Modern critics often become apologetic when discussing Smollett's female characters, especially Narcissa, who appears to represent little more than a reductive feminine stereotype: beautiful, compliant, and vacuous.[4] Smollett's depiction of her, I argue, reflects a residual anxiety concerning the potential threat of her imagination. Throughout the novel, which begins and concludes with contrasting depictions of pregnancy, Smollett defines Narcissa as a potentially fit wife and mother because she is incapable of the dangerous imaginings that lead to birthmarks, miscarriages, and bunnies. Second, I hope to show that *Roderick Random* expresses Smollett's fears concerning the imagination more generally. Narcissa may be free from the dangerous influence of the imagination, but Roderick is not. His world, horrific by any measure, is made all the worse by the monsters of his own creation. At times humorous and at times terrifying, the exaggerated images, seemingly disjointed episodes, and chaotic narrative of *Roderick Random* reveal the narrator's inability to distinguish between the real and the fantastic. Confused and imbalanced, Roderick spends much of the novel blinded—ironically—by his own ability to create images. Finally, I return to Narcissa and discuss her role in Roderick's redemption. More than a repository for Roderick's excess passion and more than a mythic ideal representing Roderick's escape from the earthly, Narcissa becomes a force of transformation as she subdues Roderick's excessive imagination, nurtures his sympathy, and restores both his vision and his humanity.

The idea of prenatal imprinting is as old as Aristotle and has a complicated cultural history.[5] Although early modern British popular culture often viewed monstrous births as signs of divine displeasure and reminders of "God's constant Providential interventions in human life," they became in the final years of the seventeenth century less supernatural and more grounded in the management of passion and the regulation of the female imagination.[6] This shift from the theological to the medical reestablished the centrality of physiological explanations offered in works like Ambroise Paré's frighteningly illustrated *Des monsters; des prodiges* (1573), which were reiterated in a number of English books, including Mrs. Grizzle's favorite, Nicholas Culpeper's *Directory for Midwives* (1651).[7] In *Pharmacologia Anti-Empirica* (1683), Walter Harris offers a clear warning: "If any species be sent to the imagination of the mother, which she strongly receives, it may make an impression upon the child."[8] Two years before the Toft incident, John Maubray expressed a similar idea in *The Female Physician* (1724):

> Whence is it then that we have so many *deform'd Person's, crooked Bodies, ugly Aspects, distorted Mouths, wry Noses*, and the like, in all Countries, but from the IMAGINATION of the *Mother*; while she either conceives such shapeless *Phastasms* in her *Mind*, or while she frequently and intently fixes her *Eyes* upon such *deform'd Persons* or disagreeable OBJECTS.[9]

Examining these passages, Todd provides a summary of the process by which the imagination was thought to deform the fetus. Theorists such as Harris and Maubray posit a dualistic understanding in which the individual comprises a physical body and an incorporeal mind. The passions, or animal spirits, constitute the most refined portion of the body, while the imagination occupies the "lower threshold of the mind."[10] These two forces, the passions and the imagination, allow for communication between the body and the mind. Through the imagination, the mind creates a physical response within the body, which may become imprinted on the unborn child. The imagination, then, becomes the link between the intellectual and the physical, the incorporeal and the material. In developing their theories of prenatal influence, Culpeper, Harris, Maubray, and others provide an explanation for a phenomenon that had baffled the scientific community for centuries and seek to unravel that "knotty point" of intersection that Swift's persona so skillfully dodges through a specious manuscript hiatus in Section IX of *A Tale of a Tub*.[11] For all of their certainty, however, the medical theorists are no more reassuring than the satirist, for they remind us repeatedly that this capacity to bridge the gap between the physical and the incorporeal makes the imagination inherently dangerous. As Todd notes, the imagination forms "an ambiguous border between the earth of sensual perception and the sky of in-corporeal intellect" and, therefore, not only remains unstable and changeable but also produces "shapeless *Phantasms*."[12] Corrupt, chaotic, and uncertain, the imagination is a thing to be feared.

These ideas received renewed attention and scrutiny in the late 1720s in response to the Toft hoax, most notably in the bitter print battle between two respected physicians, Daniel Turner and James Augustus Blondel.[13] We should not, however, assume that the public's fascination with imprinting ended with Mary Toft's confession. During the 1740s, G. S. Rousseau notes, there were no fewer than ninety-two articles concerning extraordinary child-birth in *The Gentleman's Magazine*, including the remarkable story—pub-lished in 1746, just two years before the publication of *Roderick Random*—of a woman who gave birth to a monster "with nose and eyes like a lyon, no pal-ate to the mouth, hair on the shoulders, claws like a lion instead of fingers, no breast-bone, something surprising out of the navel as big as an egg and one foot longer than the other."[14] In many ways, such stories of monstrous births reflect misogynistic aspects of early modern culture. Julie Crawford, for example, explores the degree to which sixteenth- and seventeenth-century ob-servers posited a connection between desire and the physical features of the unborn child. "Monstrous births," Crawford notes, "were often interpreted as the result of the parents', particularly the mothers', sins, and were frequently employed in the early modern broadsheets and pamphlets as punishment for sexual crimes."[15] These assumptions persisted into the eighteenth century. Although it may be hard to imagine anything less erotic than the Mary Toft hoax, "almost everyone," Todd reminds us, "asserted that Mary Toft was sexu-ally profligate."[16] It all becomes a vicious cycle. The perversity of female ap-petites clouds the imagination, which in turn transforms that perversity into a misshaped child. The unregulated female, both in mind and body, becomes the source of disorder and madness.

Smollett would seem an unlikely contributor to this discourse, not because he lacks misogyny—*Roderick Random* is, of course, a deeply misogynistic text that presents sex as sport and women as trophies—but rather because he seems to have little respect for the theory of prenatal influence. In *Peregrine Pickle*, he reduces the theory to an old wives' tale, every bit as irrational as Mrs. Trunnion's later hysterical pregnancy. Many of the physicians who most strongly influenced Smollett—including William Hunter, Alexan-der Monro, *primus*, and William Smellie, whose *Treatise on the Theory and Practice of Midwifery* Smollett edited—doubted the possibility of prenatal imprinting.[17] As Rousseau concludes, after exhaustive examination, "there is every reason to believe that even the probability of mother marking her child seemed remote" to Smollett.[18] It makes for a good joke but is hardly something to worry about. In the beginning of *Roderick Random*, Smollett, in fact, appears to mock the idea of prenatal influence. Roderick's mother dreams "she was delivered of a tennis-ball, which the devil . . . struck so forcibly with a racket, that it disappeared."[19] We may be tempted to read this dream as formative of Roderick's identity (a picaroon is a bit like a bouncing tennis ball), but the early chapters of the novel indicate that it is not the mother's dream but the father's and grandfather's inherited personalities as well as his own exposure to horrific violence and cruelty that define young Roderick. If Smollett gestures toward prenatal imprinting in *Roderick Random*'s opening paragraph, he does so humorously and is careful to provide other explanations for Roderick's character. Still, as Geoffrey Sill has shown, Smollett received his medical training from physicians who, in spite of their doubts concerning prenatal imprinting, rejected mechanistic theories in favor of vitalistic theories, which is to say, physicians who posited connections between the passions of the body and the sensibilities of the mind. One of Smollett's most perceptive readers, Paul-Gabriel Boucé, has suggested that behind the obvious "satirical slapstick of grotesque eccentricities," Smollett's early fiction expresses a "latent form of ontological '*Angst*' surrounding pregnancy and childbirth" and in this way is reflective of a culture in which the "possible influence of mind over body preoccupied physicians, philosophers, poets, and theologians."[20] Equally important, Smollett seems to express the same anxiety toward the female imagination that fueled the Mary Toft hoax. Smollett, for example, shows repeatedly that psychological turmoil in women leads to death and miscarriage. Roderick's mother dies as a result of "grief and anxiety of mind" (4). Miss Jenny claims to have a miscarriage following a "fright" (55). Miss Williams, who has "more imagination than judgment," actually loses a child during her third illegitimate pregnancy when her "thoughts produced a fever, which brought on a miscarriage," an incident that reinforces the assumed connections between imagination and sexual transgression (118, 123). Smollett may not provide actual monstrous births, but he suggests that physiological and psychological instability, the products of the imagination and passions, disrupt the woman's reproductive capacity and endanger her life.

Smollett's clearest depiction of a woman dangerously out of balance is, of course, Narcissa's aunt, whose disheveled appearance Roderick describes with rich Hogarthian detail:

> She sat in her study, with one foot on the ground, and the other upon a high stool at some distance from her seat; her sandy locks hung down in a disorder I cannot call beautiful from her head, which was deprived of its coif, for the benefit of scratching with one hand, while she held the stump of a pen in the other.—Her fore-head was high and wrinkled, her eyes large, grey and prominent; her nose long, sharp and aquiline. . . . Her upper-lip contained a large quantity of plain Spanish, which by continual falling, had embroidered her neck that was not naturally very white, and the breast of her gown, that flowed loose

about her with a negligence truly poetic, discovering linen that was very far from fine and to all appearance, never *washed but in Castilian streams.* (217–18)

In her current condition, the aunt has compromised essential indicators of appropriate female behavior—modesty, beauty, cleanliness. In a passage that may offer a passing reference to the Toft incident, the reader discovers that the aunt's condition is associated with her unregulated imagination, which not only inspires her poetry but also leads to hallucination:

> I was told [Roderick proclaims] by the maid that her mistress was still in bed, and had been so affected with the notes of the hounds in the morning, that she actually believed herself a hare beset with hunters; and begged a few greens to munch for her breakfast—when I testified my surprise at this unaccountable imagination, she let me know that her lady was very much subject to whims of this nature; sometimes fancying herself an animal, sometimes a piece of furniture, during which conceited transformation, it was very dangerous to come near her, especially when she represented a beast; for that lately, in the character of a cat, she had flown at her and scratched he face in a terrible manner. (221)

Uncertain, malleable and lacking stable identity, the aunt reinforces the commonplace assumption captured in Pope's infamous claim that "most Women have no Characters at all."[21] For Smollett's character, this condition is unmistakably caused by an imbalance of mind and body. John Sena has demonstrated that the passage appears to be adapted "almost entirely from contemporary medical theories of hysteria."[22] The aunt possesses "delicate and refined animal spirits," which simultaneously endow her with creative ability and cause her fits of insanity. As indicated by the word *hysteria,* the aunt's condition is specifically connected to her physical body, most especially her reproductive organs. The aunt's celibacy—she has "contempt for the male part of creation" and is a follower of Rosicrucian philosophy—only exacerbates her already unstable condition.[23] Once again, Smollett reinforces misogynistic assumptions as he presents a woman whose body and sexuality need masculine management. Left unregulated and unprotected (as in the case of Miss Williams and Roderick's mother), the feminine self produces miscarriages and early death; left unattended (as in the case of the aunt), it produces equally disquieting surrogate offspring—the aunt's own monstrous births, her fragmented poetry:

> Thus have I sent the simple king to hell,
> Without or coffin, shroud or passing-bell:—
> To me, what are divine and human laws?
> I court no sanction but me own applause!
> Rapes, robb'ries, treasons yield my soul delight;
> And human carnage gratifies my sight:
> I drag the parent by the hoary hair,

And toss the sprawling infant on my spear,
While the fond mother's cries regale mine ear.
I fight, I vanquish, murder friends and foes;
Nor dare th'immortal gods my rage oppose.
(224–25)

Roderick notes that the aunt's poetry fails to address the usual topic of women's writing: love (221). Full instead of images of violence and death, it suggests that the aunt's excessive imagination as influenced by her body has compromised her identity as a woman, causing her to give voice to thoughts of horrific—and specifically masculine—aggression. In some ways, Smollett's depiction of the aunt recalls Canto IV of *The Rape of the Lock*, where the Queen of Spleen controls female poets. In both instances, the authors associate female creativity with unmanaged sexuality and present the resulting poetry as the product of madness.[24] Although the aunt remains a comic figure, Smollett's vision of the female imagination is considerably darker than Pope's. Unlike Belinda's irritability, the aunt's poems are, as Roderick points out, an "unnatural rhapsody" (225). The reference to infanticide, the most horrific perversion of traditional femininity, recalls Miss Williams's earlier fear that her "frenzy" following her abandonment would have caused her to "sacrifice the little innocent to my resentment of the father's infidelity" and demonstrates the horrifying potential of the female imagination (123). As an embodiment of uncontrolled female energy, the aunt not only reinforces key components of Smollett's other depictions of women but also reiterates the cultural anxieties that gave resonance to the Mary Toft incident twenty-two years before the publication of *Roderick Random*.

Smollett's emphasis on the dangers of the female imagination creates a specific rhetorical challenge for his depiction of the novel's heroine, Narcissa, who must remain restrained, lest she appear dangerously unstable. As a result, Narcissa never emerges as a fully developed or even an interesting character. Contemporary novelists often used the overt display of emotion as somatic expressions of appropriate feminine virtue. In *The Female Quixote*, for example, Charlotte Lennox establishes Arabella's suitability as a wife by recording her response to her father's illness. "While anyone was present," the narrator reports, Arabella's "looks discovered only a calm and decent Sorrow, but when she was alone or had only her dear Lucy with her, she gave free Vent to her Tears."[25] For Lennox, the tears function as they do in sentimental fiction: they are signs of her moral status and inherent benevolence. They represent what needs to be nurtured in Arabella, not what needs to be restricted.[26] Smollett's heroine, in contrast, must remain more controlled, and this is the difficulty. On the one hand, Narcissa must be human enough to inspire Roderick's attraction and capture the reader's interest. On the other hand, she must remain dispassionate enough to become a suitable wife and mother. Smollett's depiction of Narcissa reveals his efforts to meet these two competing demands. When the aunt is in the throes of hysterical delusion, Narcissa restores her reason by playing music on the harpsichord, which, of course, suggests the nurturing role Narcissa plays throughout the novel. The fact that the instrument cannot convey emotion through the modulation of volume emphasizes another key characteristic of Narcissa: her imperturbability and apparent lack of passion. Most often described as "amiable" and "affable," Narcissa clearly lacks those dangerous characteristics that define her aunt. To be sure, there are brief moments when Smollett suggests Narcissa's humanity by allowing her to be slightly overwhelmed by emotion. When, for example, she sees Roderick unexpectedly at Bath, she blushes with a "double glow," while her "enchanting bosom" heaves "with strong emotion" (337), but these expressions—communicating both her passional and erotic potential—remain the exception rather than the rule. Toward the end of the novel, when she learns that she may never be able to marry Roderick, Narcissa can barely cry. Her tears only "bedewed her lovely cheeks" (428). Smollett's use of "bedewed," which suggests both the expression and containment of emotion, is similar to his metonymic use of the harpsichord: both reveal the novelist's attempt to define Narcissa positively within the restricted space his novel allows women. Seeking to show the dangers of a faulty education on an otherwise healthy mind and body, Lennox uses Arabella's freely flowing tears to illustrate what is fundamentally best about her character. Assuming the inherently dangerous and destabilizing intersection of mind and body, Smollett must keep his heroine's emotions far more regulated.

Although *Roderick Random* reinscribes elements of eighteenth-century misogyny that link the feminine to the physical and posit in the feminine a dangerous instability, Smollett's treatment of passion and imagination simultaneously exceeds gender boundaries. The character most like Narcissa's aunt, in fact, is not a woman at all, but rather Roderick Random himself. Immediately after introducing the aunt, Smollett connects her and the novel's hero by showing that Narcissa's music affects Roderick as well as the aunt: "In a little time my ears were ravished with the effects of her skill.—She accompanied the instrument with a voice so sweet and melodious, that I did not wonder at the surprising change it produced on the spirits of my mistress, which were soon composed to peace and sober reflection" (222). That Roderick, who is "temperamentally disposed to emotional excess," suffers from a surplus of passion and imagination hardly needs demonstration.[27] The reader frequently finds him creating nightmarish scenes, as he does in chapter 13 when he and Strap are awakened unexpectedly by a madman and his pet raven. On other occasions, he seeks escape from immediate hardship by creating fantastic worlds. Having been unsuccessful in the Navy Office, for example, he considers enlisting in the Foot Guards and then imagines himself "charging the enemy at the head of my own regiment" (95). After being robbed by Balthazar, Roderick, in an imaginative gesture reminiscent of the aunt's transmogrifications, fantasizes about being a bear, "that I might retreat to woods and deserts, far from the inhospitable haunts of man" (243). More importantly, Roderick's imagination, like the aunt's, remains largely uncontrolled. While in jail, for example, Roderick awakens to a nightmare world where he finds his "imagination haunted with such dismal apparitions that . . . [he] was ready to despair" (377).

The most telling expressions of Roderick's imagination, however, are found in the novel's highly descriptive, disjointed, and episodic structure. As Jerry Beasley has argued, *Roderick Random* is an intensely visual narrative, organized like a Hogarthian progress, and should be read according to Joseph Frank's principles of spatial form.[28] The traditional elements of narrative, such as chronology and sequence, are present, Beasley asserts, but somewhat unimportant. Instead, Smollett uses space, as defined by an image, scene, or episode, as the central organizing principle of the work, and by so doing recreates life as experienced by Roderick, rather than as ordered by the controlling author. The narrative structure and imagistic sequence, then, become records of Roderick's perceptions as processed and transformed by his imagination and reveal as much about the central character as they do about the world in which he lives. As Beasley notes, Smollett "emphasizes an organic conception of *life* rather than of form."[29] There are, of course, occasions when Roderick's descriptions appear reasonably objective and accurate, as is the case when Roderick describes the sick bay of the *Thunder* in chapter 25. In other episodes, however, Roderick's descriptions exceed verisimilitude. The characters he describes, for example, sometimes become so exaggerated that they recall the grotesques of Thomas Rowlandson. These descriptions, particularly those of Mr. Crab and Captain Weazel, signal Roderick's fundamental instability and become, like the novel's structure, analogous to the aunt's fragmented poetry. The products of an unbalanced mind and body, the descriptions are Roderick's own monstrous births, and, like Mary Toft's rabbits, they suggest Smollett's underlying fear of the imagination's creative power.

By connecting his discussion of imagination to a male character, Smollett aligns himself with important trends in early modern culture. Although hysteria, as noted above, remained a specifically female ailment, physicians, such as Thomas Sydenham, recognized similar symptoms in male patients, which they characterized as hypochondriasis, a disease, Sill argues, "of the imagination, but by no means an imaginary disease."[30] Concern about the dangers of the male imagination also finds expression in a variety of eighteenth-century art, particularly the satires of Swift and the prints of Hogarth. Although Swift occasionally has fun with the idea of prenatal imprinting—in "The Mechanical Operation of the Spirit," women give birth to real Round Heads after seeing artificial ones—he appears more interested in exploring the dangers of the male intersection of mind and body.[31] In Section XI of *A Tale of A Tub*, where the narrator speculates about the connection between the physical and intellectual, Swift offers the story of a certain great prince:

> Having to no purpose used all peaceable endeavors, the collected part of the semen, raised and inflamed, became adust, converted to choler, turned head upon spinal duct, and ascended to the brain. The very same principle that influences the bully to break the windows of a whore who has jilted him, naturally stirs up a great prince to raise mighty armies and dream of nothing but sieges, battles and victories.[32]

Like Roderick, who is frequently overwhelmed by his own passions, the prince's physical self destroys his intellectual control. Unregulated and unbalanced, the prince commits himself to military actions that originate from the same biological sources as Roderick's consistent desire for revenge upon those who have wronged him. For Swift, of course, the subtle, sometimes unrecognizable interaction between the body and mind has political and theological implications, as is made clear when the satirist turns dissenter's enthusiasm into flatulence misinterpreted by the imagination.[33] Hogarth, too, explores the dangers of the male imagination. In his first print concerning the Mary Toft incident, *Cunicularii* (1726), he focuses not on the monstrous birth itself, which he reveals to be a hoax, but rather on the learned doctors, who cannot see what's actually before them and become monstrous fools. Thirty-six years later, when Hogarth returned to the Toft story in *Credulity, Superstition and Fanaticism*, he changed his target from the medical community to the dissenting clergy. Once again, however, Hogarth focuses not on women's potential to create monsters but on men's susceptibility to their own imaginations.[34] Through various genre and media, Smollett, Swift, and Hogarth each seem to be exploring a similar anxiety, an epistemological crisis grounded in their own subjectivity. Swift's dissenters cannot tell the difference between divine inspiration and gas; Hogarth's wise men of science and faith cannot see through the tricks of country bumpkins; and Smollett's Roderick Random cannot see what is actually present. Instead, Roderick's imagination creates men "five feet high and ten round the belly" and officers with sixteen-inch faces and six-inch thighs (26, 50).

Unlike Swift and Hogarth, however, Smollett provides a solution to uncontrolled passions and overactive imaginations—the women who awaken and strengthen Roderick's latent power of sympathy, a power Smollett's friend and fellow Scot, David Hume, believed to be the "chief source of moral distinctions."[35] In this way, Smollett both complicates and diminishes the misogyny of his text by creating for women a redemptive role. Smollett first suggests Roderick's eventual reformation through his encounter with the defenseless Miss Williams, who transforms Roderick's unregulated passion into productive action. Miss Williams's destitution, Roderick reports, "filled me with sympathy and compassion; I revered her qualifications, looked upon her as unfortunate, not criminal, and attended her with such care and success that, in less than two months, her health, as well as my own, was perfectly re-established" (138). Roderick's selfless actions to save Miss Williams, which are themselves reminiscent of those of the maidservant to whom Roderick owes his life, are repeated in his relationship with Narcissa (3). Through her intrinsic gentleness and vulnerability, Narcissa stirs Roderick's compassion and breaks him out of the self-indulgence that otherwise defines his character. Discovering that she is endangered by the brutal Sir Timothy, Roderick springs to action: "What were the emotions of my soul when I beheld Narcissa, almost sinking beneath the brutal force of this satyr! I flew like lightening to her rescue" (229). After heroically defeating Sir Timothy, Roderick discovers happiness in his good deed: "My soul was thrilled with tumultuous joy at feeling the object of my dearest wishes within my arms, and while she lay insensible I could not refrain from applying my cheek to hers and ravishing a kiss" (229). After his other encounters with adversaries, Roderick's thoughts turn immediately to revenge, an ultimately self-centered and destructive passion. Narcissa's presence causes Roderick to focus, at least partially, on her, and his toxic vengeance is transformed to curative joy. Just as Roderick's health is restored through the care of Miss Williams, his happiness is preserved through his protection of Narcissa. Roderick's response to Narcissa in this scene resembles the reaction Smollett hopes the reader will have toward Roderick himself, one in which the reader "espouses his cause" and "sympathizes with him in distress" (xxxiii). Like Smollett's imagined reader, Roderick's "indignation is heated against" Narcissa's attacker, and his "humane," as opposed to his selfish, "passions are inflamed" (xxxiii).

Narcissa, in this way, awakens Roderick's humanity and converts his often misdirected passion into the sort of "generous indignation" celebrated in the novel's Preface (xxxv). In spite of these initial gains, however, Roderick soon returns to his previous self. Separated from the woman he loves, Roderick is once again blinded by his own passion and imagination. His narrative, which becomes less episodic and chaotic when he is with Narcissa, resumes its former fragmented, spatial structure as he oscillates among emotional extremes and disparate identities. One minute he despairs after being cheated by Balthazar; the next he merrily revels with a band of French soldiers (243). Impetuously joining their ranks, he forfeits his identity as a Briton, only to reassume it when he returns to London to play the part of a dandy. Even the memory of Narcissa, which sometimes rescues him from his own impulses, betrays him as his image of her fluctuates between ideal and erotic. Before copulating with a French country girl, Roderick confesses, "In vain did my reason suggest the respect that I owed to my dear mistress Narcissa; the idea of that lovely charmer rather increased than allayed the ferment of my spirits" (240). These relapses suggest that Roderick's story is not the sudden rebirth one would associate with a narrative of spiritual conversion but rather the gradual accumulation of self-control.

Once Roderick is reunited with Narcissa, his education continues, as she actively teaches him to control his passions and limit his solipsism. Before his meeting with Narcissa in Bath, Roderick is overcome. "My imagination," he states, "was so much employed in anticipating the happiness I was to enjoy next day that I slept very little that night" (342). When they finally meet, Roderick is at first silenced by her presence and then offends and embarrasses her with a clumsy declaration of love. Narcissa, in spite of her attraction toward Roderick, responds stoically: "Recovering herself from the most beautiful confusion, [she] told me she thought herself very much obliged by my favorable opinion of her, and that she was very sorry to hear I have been unfortunate" (345). Roderick again responds with excessive passion, and Narcissa gently corrects him through her exquisite self-control and then urges him to think beyond himself: "She was startled at my ravings, reasoned down my transport, and by her irresistible eloquence, soothed my soul into a state of tranquil felicity, but lest I might suffer a relapse, industriously promoted other subjects to entertain my imagination" (346). The pattern of this scene is repeated throughout Roderick's interaction with Narcissa. In his first letter to Narcissa, Roderick begins with a certain measure of self-control but quickly returns to his old self: "Your beauty fills me with wonder! Your understanding with ravishment, and your goodness with adoration! I am transported with desire, distracted with doubts, and tortured with impatience!" (351). Roderick's claims of "genuine and disinterested love" notwithstanding, the letter shows the characteristically passionate hero overcome and distracted by his emotions. Narcissa's response provides Roderick's next lesson:

> Sir, To say I look upon you with indifference would be a piece of dissimulation which I think no decorum requires and no custom can justify, As my heart never felt an impression that my tongue was ashamed to declare, I will not scruple to own myself pleased with your passion, confident of your integrity, and so well convinced of my own discretion that I should not hesitate in granting you the interview you desire, were I not overawed by the prying curiosity of a malicious world, the censure of which might be fatally prejudicial to the reputation of
>
> Your Narcissa. (352)

It would be hard to imagine a more bland expression, and this letter has doubtlessly fueled critics' dismissive treatment of Narcissa. She is not, however, writing a love letter but rather an edifying response to Roderick's inappropriate declaration. Expressing no emotion stronger than *pleased*, Narcissa remains a study in reticence, stability, and propriety. Importantly, the same characteristics that define her as a suitable future mother also make her an effective teacher. Through her use of words like *decorum, custom,* and *discretion,* Narcissa moves the correspondence away from Roderick's private world—replete with first-person declarations of passion—and into a public, sociable world. In a subsequent letter, written while she is being sequestered by her brother, Narcissa becomes even more instructive: "As I am fully convinced of your honour and love, I hope I shall never hear of such desperate proofs of either for the future" (371). Through the postscript to this letter, Narcissa directs Roderick's attention toward Miss Williams, providing Roderick with another gentle reminder to awaken his sympathy and consider the feelings and needs of others. In this way, she takes on the role Sill defines as the "physician of the mind," and she becomes in some ways an unexpected precursor of Dr. Lewis, who in Smollett's final novel attends patiently to the needs of another unbalanced and unstable character, Mathew Bramble.[36]

While in Narcissa's company, Roderick begins to learn and eventually assumes those sociable characteristics that both he and Hume associate with sympathy and morality.[37] He gains, for example, sufficient control over his passions and enough altruism to consider the hardship Narcissa would undergo if she were to marry him before he could support her (354). Following his experience with Narcissa in Bath, Roderick becomes uncharacteristically reflective and remorseful at his unprovoked beating of Strap. Confined in prison and seized with a deep melancholy, he no longer wishes for isolation and solitude, as he does earlier in the narrative, but rather allows the remembrance of Narcissa to preserve his "attachment to that *society* of which she constituted a part" (397, emphasis added). Roderick later recognizes his father's grief before he knows his identity and sympathizes with him. These scenes stand in stark contrast to Roderick's earlier experiences as recorded in his exaggerated descriptions. While trapped in the instability of his own mind and body, Roderick sees only ugliness and deformity. Inspired by Narcissa's restorative instruction, he now recognizes the fundamental humanity of the people surrounding him. Once he is reunited with Narcissa, she completes his redemption through her careful regulation of his body and mind. When Roderick's erotic passion grows "turbulent and unruly" in Narcissa's presence, she, "with her usual dignity and prudence," redirects him and strengthens his engagement with the people around him by asking him to recount the details of his adventure at sea (425).[38]

At the end of the novel, Roderick for the first time knows true happiness. Narcissa is pregnant, and the reader, like Roderick, has every reason to believe she will produce a healthy child. Equally important, Roderick reports that "the impetuous transports of my passion are now settled and mellowed into endearing fondness and tranquility of love, rooted by that intimate connexion and interchange of hearts which nought but virtuous wedlock can produce" (435). In many ways, the ending of the novel, replete with Christian references, is mythological and represents Roderick's escape from the turmoil and hardship of earthly life.[39] But there is another story being told as well. Just as the Allworthy estate in *Tom Jones* represents both paradise and Tom's emergence into adult responsibility, and just as Sophia represents both the transcendent wisdom Tom has earned and his flesh-and-blood wife, so too does Smollett's Scotland serve both a mythic and a realistic function. Similarly, Narcissa is both the "amiable apparition" that draws Roderick away from the world and the real woman who teaches him to live within it. Safely back in Scotland, surrounded by friends and family, and under Narcissa's enduring care, Roderick Random has undergone his last transformation. It is not, as John McAllister has suggested, that Roderick has found in Narcissa a receptacle for his passions, nor that his marriage represents a way of productively channeling his sexual energy.[40] It is rather that he has been taught under the patient guidance of a loving partner to reconcile his body and mind, to regulate his passion and imagination, and recognize the needs and desires of others. Roderick begins life anew at the end, as Narcissa, with gentle direction, introduces the wayward hero to a world he has wandered through, but never before seen.

NOTES

1. Dennis Todd, *Imagining Monsters: Miscreations of the Self in Eighteenth-Century England* (Chicago: University of Chicago Press, 1995), 39.

2. Henry Fielding, *Joseph Andrews*, ed. Martin C. Battestin (Boston: Houghton Mifflin, 1961), 292; Charlotte Lennox, *Euphemia*, ed. Susan K. Howard (Petersborough, Ontario: Broadview Press, 2008); Laurence Sterne, *The Life and Opinions of Tristram Shandy, Gentleman*, ed. Ian Campbell Ross (Oxford: Oxford University Press, 1983), 9; Tobias Smollett, *Peregrine Pickle*, ed. Walter Allen, two vols. (London: J. M. Dent & Sons; New York: E. P. Dutton, 1962), 1:21. See Howard, "Transcultural Adoptions," above, 109–20.

3. Todd, *Imagining Monsters*, 64, 15.

4. Robert Spector states the case bluntly: "Narcissa does not exist as genuine woman in the novel." In some of the most useful discussions of Smollett's female characters, Jerry Beasley treats Narcissa more sympathetically but still downplays her humanity. Both an agent of and reward for Roderick's eventual redemption and return to edenic Scotland, Narcissa remains for Beasley an "amiable appari-

tion" and serves a largely mythological role: "lovely, virtuous, constant," Narcissa remains "everything the world is not." Without diminishing the importance and appropriateness of Beasley's reading, I hope to explore Narcissa's earthly role and suggest that she is instrumental in an aspect of the novel that has not received sufficient critical attention: the reformation of Roderick's uncontrolled passions and imagination. See Robert D. Spector, *Smollett's Women: A Study in an Eighteenth-Century Masculine Sensibility* (Westport, CT: Greenwood Press, 1994), 33; and Jerry C. Beasley, *Tobias Smollett, Novelist* (Athens: University of Georgia Press, 1998), 31.

5. In addition to Todd, see G. S. Rousseau, "Pineapples, Pregnancy, Pica, and *Peregrine Pickle*" in *Tobias Smollett: Bicentennial Essays Presented to Lewis M. Knapp*, ed. G. S. Rousseau and Paul-Gabriel Boucé (Oxford and New York: Oxford University Press, 1971), 79–109; and Paul-Gabriel Boucé, "Imagination, Pregnant Women, and Monsters in Eighteenth-Century England and France," in *Sexual Underworlds of the Enlightenment*, ed. G. S. Rousseau and Roy Porter (Manchester: Manchester University Press, 1987), 86–100.

6. Julie Crawford, *Marvelous Protestantism: Monstrous Births in Post-Reformation England* (Baltimore, MD: Johns Hopkins University Press, 2005), 18.

7. Amboise Paré, *Des monsters; des prodiges; des voyages* (Paris, 1573); Nicholas Culpeper, *A Directory for Midwives; or, a Guide for Women in their Conception, Bearing, and Suckling their Children* (London, 1651).

8. Walter Harris *Pharmacologia Anti-Empirica: or a Rational Discourse of Remedies both Chymical and Galenical* (London, 1683), 312, qtd. in Todd, *Imagining Monsters*, 45.

9. John Maubray, *The Female Physician, Containing all the Diseases Incident to that Sex* (London, 1724), 62; qtd. in Todd, *Imagining Monsters*, 46.

10. Todd, *Imagining Monsters*, 56.

11. Jonathan Swift, *A Tale of a Tub, to which is added, The Battle of the Books, and the Mechanical Operation of the Spirit*, ed. A. C. Guthkelch and D. Nichol Smith, second ed. (Oxford: Oxford University Press, 1958), 170. Many early modern thinkers seem to have given up trying to define the exact functions of the corporeal and incorporeal. Rev. Issac Watts notes that the passions arise "either from the Impressions or Commotions which the animal Powers receive by the Soul's Perception of that Object which raises the Passion, or from the Impression or Sensation which that Soul receives by this Commotion of the animal Powers, or perhaps from both of these." Alexander Monro *primus* expressed a similar uncertainty: "We have not, and perhaps cannot have any Idea of the Manner in which Mind and Body act upon each other . . . we must remain ignorant of the Manner how man Phaenomena depending on this Connexion of Mind and Body are produced." See Issac Watts, *The Doctrine of the Passions, Explain'd and Improv'd: or, a brief and comprehensive scheme of the natural affections of mankind . . . to which are subjoined, moral and divine rules for the regulation and government of them* (London: 1732; third ed. 1739), iii–iv; qtd. in Geoffrey Sill, *The Cure of the Passions and the Origin of the English Novel* (Cambridge: Cambridge University Press, 2001), 1; and Alexander Monro, *The Anatomy of the Human Bones and Nerves: with an Account of the reciprocal Motions of the Heart, and a Description of the Human Lacteal Sac and Duct*, third ed. (Edinburgh, 1741), 354; qtd. in Sill, *The Cure of the Passions*, 64.

12. Todd, *Imagining Monsters*, 58.

13. Ibid., 108–16, and Rousseau, "Pineapples, Pregnancy and Pica," 90–91.

14. Rousseau, "Pineapples, Pregnancy, and Pica," 93. See *Daily Life in Georgian England as reported in the* Gentleman's Magazine, ed. Emily Lorraine de Montluzin (Lewiston, NY: Edwin Mellen Press, 2002), 57.

15. Crawford, *Monstrous Protestantism*, 94.

16. Todd, *Imagining Monsters*, 84

17. Rousseau, "Pineapples, Pregnancy, Pica," 93.

18. Ibid., 93.

19. Tobias Smollett, *The Adventures of Roderick Random*, ed. Paul-Gabriel Boucé (Oxford: Oxford University Press, 1979). References are to this edition.

20. Sill, *The Cure of the Passions*, 63; Boucé, "Imagination, Pregnant Women, Pregnant Women and Monsters," 96.

21. Alexander Pope, "Epistle II. To a Lady," *Epistles to Several Persons*, ed. F. W. Bateson, *The Poems of Alexander Pope*, vol. 3.2 (London: Methuen; New Haven: Yale University Press, 1951), 39.

22. John F. Sena, "Smollett's Portrayal of Narcissa's Aunt: The Genesis of an 'Original,'" *English Language Notes* 14 (1977): 270.

23. "Smollett's insistence on the celibacy . . . reflects the most traditional and widely accepted medical theory of the etiology of hysteria. It was believed from the time of the ancients through the eighteenth century that hysteria was caused by a lack of—or at least infrequency of—sexual activity"; Sena, "Smollett's Protrayal of Nacissa's Aunt," 271.

24. Alexander Pope, *The Rape of the Lock and Other Poems*, ed. Geoffrey Tillotson, *The Poems of Alexander Pope*, vol. 2 (London: Methuen; New Haven, CT: Yale University Press, 1962), 183–98.

25. Charlotte Lennox, *The Female Quixote*, ed. Margaret Anne Doody (Oxford: Oxford University Press, 1989), 134.

26. See Paul Goring, *The Rhetoric of Sensibility in Eighteenth-Century Culture* Cambridge: Cambridge University Press, 2005), 142.

27. John McAllister, "Smollett's Use of Medical Theory: *Roderick Random* and *Peregrine Pickle*," *Mosaic* 22.2 (1989): 3.

28. Beasley, *Tobias Smollett, Novelist*, 36–37. See also Joseph Frank, "Spatial Form in Modern Literature," *Sewanee Review* 53 (1945): 221–40.

29. Beasley, *Tobias Smollett, Novelist*, 38.

30. Sill, *The Cure of the Passions*, 16.

31. Jonathan Swift, *A Tale of a Tub*, 268–69.

32. Ibid, 164–65.

33. See especially Section VIII of *A Tale of a Tub*: "The Learned *Aeolists*, maintain the Original Cause of all Things to be *Wind*, from which Principle this whole Universe was at first produced, and into which it must at last be resolved; that the same Breath which had kindled, and blew *up* the Flame of Nature, should one Day blow it *out*" (150).

34. My understanding of Hogarth's two Mary Toft prints owes a debt to Todd's insightful discussion in *Imagining Monsters*, 88–101.

35. David Hume, *A Treatise of Human Nature*, ed. L. A. Selby-Bigge (Oxford: Clarendon Press, 1965), 618.

36. See Sill, *The Cure of the Passions*, 13–18. Sill notes, however, that the role of physician of the mind is an exclusively masculine one: for the cure to be credible, it had to be accomplished by a "doctor, and the doctor had to be gendered male" (22).

37. This idea is central to Hume's understanding of humanity and finds frequent expression throughout *A Treatise of Human Nature*: "Thus it appears *that* sympathy is a very powerful principle in human nature, *that* it has great influence on our taste of beauty, and *that* it produces our sentiment of morals in all artificial virtues. From thence we may presume, that it also gives rise to many of the other virtues; and that qualities acquire our approbation, because of their tendency to the good of mankind" (577–78); and "Now we have not such extensive concern for society but from sympathy; and consequently 'tis that principle, which takes us so far out of ourselves, as to give us the same pleasure or uneasiness in the characters of others, as if they had a tendency to our advantage or loss" (579).

38. Roderick's transformation is similar to those of other eighteenth-century heroes, including Tom Jones and Sir Charles Grandison, who, as Tita Chico argues, eventually enter into "affective communities." Chico's analysis provides a much-needed challenge to the critical assumptions that have privileged "progressive individualism" and blinded readers "to the ideologies of community formation promulgated by the mid-century novel." See "Details and Frankness: Affective Relations in *Sir Charles Grandison*," *Studies in Eighteenth-Century Culture* 38 (2009): 63.

39. See Beasley, *Tobias Smollett, Novelist*, 66–74; and "'Amiable Apparitions': Smollett's Fictional Heroines," in *Augustan Subjects: Essays in Honor of Martin C. Battestin*, ed. Albert J. Rivero (Newark: University of Delaware Press, 1997), 229–49.

40. McAllister, "Smollett's Use of Medical Theory," 129.

12

Smollett, the Picaresque, and Two Medical Satires

Leslie A. Chilton

Literature, produced by individual intelligence, imagination, and passion, is idiosyncratic, and it is a truism that good literature is not written by rules. Yet the temptation to organize literature and the reader's response to it around genres, definitions, and classifications has proven irresistible. By the early twentieth century the paradigm of science had extended to all areas of human behavior, and by mid-century, literary critics—perhaps because science, at least to the amateur, seems to have the stability and self-definition that literature lacks—had adopted this paradigm. Numerous studies appeared classifying texts by themes, imagery, plot, structure, and character type. In the course of this extensive classification and reclassification, it was inevitable that the searchlight would eventually fall on the picaresque, a development that would have far-reaching effects for the study of Smollett's novels.

The two seminal works in this particular examination of Smollett and the picaresque were Robert Alter's *The Rogue's Progress* and Stuart Miller's *The Picaresque Novel*. Well written and carefully argued, these works had an immediate and widespread influence. Within the emerging field of Smollett studies, Robert Giddings claimed Smollett for the picaresque tradition, and by 1968 Robert Spector declared that "Smollett maintained the picaresque throughout his five novels, [and] that *Humphry Clinker*, no less than *Roderick Random*, belongs to that genre." Spector's table of contents for his popular Twayne book on Smollett clarifies his position: "Roderick Random: The Rogue Sets Forth"; "Peregrine Pickle: The Rogue in High Society"; "Lancelot

Greaves: Quixotic Picaresque"; and "Humphry Clinker: The Picaresque Me-
nage."[1]

It was not long before Spector received a sharp rebuttal. George S. Rousseau argued that "Smollett never has been the best understood writer of
English prose . . . and in . . . relation of his imaginative prose works to the
so-called picaresque tradition, he has been patently misunderstood."[2] Rousseau dismisses critics like Spector, who consider the novels to be picaresque,
on the principle that picaresque works are not defined by their superficial
qualities but rather by their content. Why make the picaresque quality the
determining factor of Smollett's novels, Rousseau asks, unless it is demonstrated that this attribute and no other somehow is more intrinsic than all
others? In 1972 Paul-Gabriel Boucé refined and extended Rousseau's argument against loose applications of the term picaresque.[3] In his influential
The Novels of Tobias Smollett, Boucé argued that the term picaresque cannot
be used to say anything meaningful about the novels.[4] Although Boucé's
compelling and forceful argument appears to have brought the controversy
to a close, the presence of picaresque features in Smollett's works cannot be
denied. Smollett's employment of certain picaresque elements in his first
novel, *Roderick Random* (1748), is well documented, beginning with his
own admission in the Preface that he has taken his inspiration from *Gil Blas
de Santillane* (1715–1735) and that his work is "modeled on his [Le Sage's]
plan."[5] In the same year that he published *Roderick Random,* Smollett also
published his fresh, excellent translation of all four volumes of *Gil Blas,* and
his future novels feature characters and adventures drawn, often loosely,
from the picaresque tradition. [6]

    With that said, it must now be said that the purpose of this essay is not to
reopen the controversy surrounding Smollett and the picaresque but rather
to examine the controversy in the context of two early, almost forgotten,
medical pamphlets. Because these works addressed medical men and medical squabbles, it is understandable how these works have been overlooked
for their contributions to Smollett's use of the picaresque. These works
evidence Smollett's emerging understanding of the function of picaresque
characters and narrative and demonstrate that Smollett understood the
picaresque tradition not as a model to be copied but as a set of rhetorical
tools that could be used for a variety purposes, especially satirical purposes.
These two pamphlets, then, shed light on Smollett's early understanding
of texts that he later imitated and translated. They also provide a modest
amount of insight into Smollett's development as a writer in the turbulent
and ruthless publishing industry of the 1740s and 1750s.

    These two overlooked pamphlets are Smollett's first-known printed prose
works, *Thomsonus Redivivus* (1746), and *Don Ricardo Honeywater Vindicated*
(1748).[7] Described as "medical polemics," both were written in Smollett's
early London medical career and have been largely ignored by Smollett

historians and critics, yet the works are far from insignificant. Of particular interest is the fact that they reveal Smollett's engagement with the picaresque tradition, albeit in a limited capacity, several years before he turned to writing novels. The first pamphlet, *Thomsonus Redivivus*, makes references to Alain René Le Sage's well-known picaresque adventure-romance *Gil Blas de Santillane* and predates the *Gil Blas*–inspired *Roderick Random* and Smollett's translation of the work by two years. The later *Don Ricardo Honeywater Vindicated* reveals Smollett drawing more heavily on the picaresque tradition, even to the extent of using several superficial Spanish elements of the picaresque.

When Smollett published *Thomsonus Redivivus* in 1746, he was a novice writer experimenting in a variety of genres and without a clear artistic identity. Working tirelessly to get his tragedy *The Regicide* on stage, he simultaneously wrote two Alexander Pope–inspired satires, *Advice* and *Reproof*. *Thomsonus Redivivus* marks two new directions for the emerging man of letters: his participation in the rough world of eighteenth-century medical literature and his use of the picaresque. By mid-century, medical literature had been stirred up and sharpened by an exciting era of discovery and innovation as well as by an urban medical profession racked by class and party affiliation. *Thomsonus Redivivus* was one title in a lively medical print war engendered by Dr. Thomas Thompson's unsuccessful treatment of a high governmental figure. Thompson's subsequent defense of his treatment, *The Case of the Right Honourable Thomas Winnington*, provoked, as Robert Adams Day discusses, a "savage medical squabble."[8] Dr. Thompson, a Scotsman, was a physician practicing in London who moved in the world of politics and important names. He had successfully treated the asthma of Sir John Eyles and joined the attack on Pope in his last illness. At this time, Thompson was "Physician in Ordinary" to the Prince of Wales's household and grandly, if curiously, described himself as "Prosyndic of Padua." His treatment of the Honorable Thomas Winnington, paymaster general of His Majesty's forces, and the entrusted of George II, however, was thoroughly unsuccessful. After a regimen of thin diet, exercise, frequent bleedings, and purgings, the patient died, provoking criticism which, in turn, provoked Thompson's defense.

One of the first attacks on Thompson was made by another Scots physician, William Douglas, in *A Letter to Dr. Thompson*, published in June 1746.[9] Joining the squabble with *Thomsonus Redivivus*, Smollett defended Thompson's methods and arraigned Douglas for the virulence of his attack: "But was there, Sir, any particular challenge to you? What could possibly provoke you to take up Cudgels, with that bitterness and animosity?"[10] Smollett emerges as a man learned in both medicine and literature as he reveals knowledge of pharmacy and surgery, and ancient and modern authorities. He also identifies rhetorical constructions, including exordium and peroration, and evokes mythology when appropriate. Smollett concludes by protesting, "We have no Design to impeach your Knowledge in Chymistry,

Pharmacy and Anatomy, but we cannot allow your Skill in Criticism" (23). Although Smollett would eventually express regret for his participation in medical pamphlet wars, his contribution to the Thompson case reveals him as a professional in medicine and suggests his future in criticism.[11]

For *Thomsonus Redivivus*, Smollett did not identify himself as the author, preferring to style himself as "Doctor Sangrado Physician to Gilblas [*sic*] de Santillane."[12] Smollett's use of this persona comprises his most conspicuous debt to the picaresque tradition. Two reasons exist for Smollett's reinventing himself as this fictional character, a smug, deadly, though well-meaning physician, in Book 2 of *Gil Blas*. Douglas had started the allusion in *A Letter to Dr. Thomas Thompson* by comparing Thompson to Sangrado: "And that you know nothing of Symptoms, Diseases, or Cures . . . differ very little from Dr *Sangrado* in *Gil-Blas*" (25). Second, and more speculatively, is that Smollett, a born narrator, found that using a character like Sangrado to enunciate his response not only concealed his identity as a would-be playwright but perhaps offered him an opportunity for a great deal of fun. Certainly it strengthened Smollett's voice, allowing him to be more plain-spoken, as in such statements as "as you have taken the Liberty to mention my Name, without any Respect to my Character, you must not resent my taking Arms in vindication of myself" (3).

Nevertheless, Smollett's use of Sangrado is erratic, at times clumsy, and in error. For example, Smollett declares "Dr. Sangrado takes up the gauntlet and accepts your doughty challenge" (11), but he later seems to forget he is speaking as the Spanish doctor: "You draw a parallel between Sangrado's hot water and Thomson's cooling purges" (22). In his ending words, "till we meet again at *Batson's* [a coffeehouse patronized by surgeons]," Smollett, not Sangrado, seems to be speaking. Moreover, Smollett misrepresents Sangrado: on the title page, he is misidentified as "physician to Gilblas [*sic*]." Sangrado is actually Gil Blas's master and, later, his mentor. Smollett's mistakes in spelling and relationships suggest that he was recalling Sangrado and Gil Blas from memory and that he had little more than a passing familiarity with Le Sage's work at the time he wrote the pamphlet. Indeed, *Thomsonus Redivivus's* timing is intriguing for those interested in Smollett's biography and his development as a writer. In 1748, Smollett openly deferred to Le Sage and *Gil Blas* in *Roderick Random's* Preface. Nine months later, he published his new and delightful translation of *Gil Blas*. At the time Smollett was writing *Thomsonus Redivivus*, however, Douglas's references to Dr. Sangrado seem to have stirred nothing more than memories of a book read long ago, one which he apparently did not take the time to reexamine. After the publication of the pamphlet, the references to *Gil Blas* may have piqued his interest sufficiently for him to reread the work and may have subsequently helped shape his first novel. The evidence of *Thomsonus Redivivus* suggests that whatever debt *Roderick Random* owes to the picaresque in general and *Gil Blas* in particular seems to be the product of only a few months, not a lifetime, of reading. Equally important, from *Thomsonus Redivivus* we can clearly see that Smollett's association of *Gil Blas* and the picaresque tradition with the "generous indignation" celebrated in the Preface to *Roderick Random* has its origins in the author's first foray into medical literature (xxxv).

The ambitious Smollett seems to have been always seeking new literary avenues, and his timing was propitious. In 1747, the year after *Thomsonus Redivivus* appeared, Le Sage's last edition of *Gil Blas de Santillane* was published in Paris, bearing his final corrections. Not only would a new translation bring Le Sage's final changes to an English audience but it would also correct the persistent errors of the only available English version of *Gil Blas*, accomplished by an unknown translator (or translators) between 1715 and 1735.[13] Smollett, with a wife and new daughter to support, would not have balked at doing such work, even though he remained wary about taking on the rather maligned work of professional translation.[14]

In 1748, the same year *Roderick Random* and *Gil Blas de Santillane* appeared, Smollett published his second medical polemic, *Don Ricardo Honeywater Vindicated*, once more in response to William Douglas. Earlier in that same year, Douglas, perhaps for political reasons, attacked the venerable Richard Mead (1673–1754), physician and collector of books and art, in a nasty satire, *The Cornutor of Seventy-Five: Being a Genuine Narrative of the Life, Adventures, and Amours of Don Ricardo Honeywater*. Douglas's new target was quite different from the irascible Thompson. Mead was renowned for his learning, benevolence, and kindness. Though a descendant from a dissenting household and educated abroad, Mead was elected a member of the Royal College of Physicians, and he published widely in both medicine and religion. If not a particularly brilliant physician, he was nevertheless capable, hardworking, and dedicated to public service. His book and art collections, second only to those of Hans Sloane, were open to the public. He assisted young physicians and attended coffeehouses to write prescriptions for apothecaries. Mead's timely work, *A Short Discourse Concerning Pestilential Contagion* (1720) allayed fears over outbreaks of plague and suggested better handling of the sick. Although fashionable people consulted him, including Sir Robert Walpole and Isaac Newton, Mead also treated the poor and refused fees. For his many good works, Mead earned praise from no less than Samuel Johnson, who declared the physician "lived more in the broad sunshine of life than any other man."[15]

Beyond the sheer size of his target, what attracted Douglas's wrath? Mead had a few peccadilloes, including a degree of pomposity. Also, Mead was a Tory and Douglas a committed Whig for the Prince of Wales. Finally, the origins of the attack may have been within Douglas himself; this attack and other erratic behavior suggest he was subsiding into insanity. Notably, in 1747, Douglas had stolen a poem titled "The Resurrection," written by Hugh Blair (1718–1800) and his cousin George Bannatyne. Douglas published it in a pompous folio under his own name, dedicating it to the Princess of Wales. This incident, as we shall see, disgusted Smollett as much as, if not more than, his attack on Mead.

Showing some sense of aesthetics, which seems at odds with his headlong attacks, Douglas avoided exposition in his *Cornutor of Seventy-Five*. He chose, instead, to be satiric, styling his attack as a picaresque narration of the life, adventures, and loves of the "Don Ricardo Honeywater," who is a pedantic phony, trading on reputation rather than skill. Described as being written by the "author of Don Quixote"[16] and translated by a "*Graduate of the College of Mecca* in Arabia," the work features an introduction that shows a degree of humor about its literary type (a romance or a real portrait of a person), professes not to take sides, and concludes with a claim that seventeen versions of the work were collated and compared against the original Latin version.[17]

Though not a particularly skillful work, *The Cornutor of Seventy-Five* is made interesting and fairly readable by superficial qualities of the picaresque, which include a nominally Spanish setting and a rogue hero. While his parents are only "some Degrees remov'd from the vulgar," Ricardo himself not only is witty and resourceful but also maintains a gravity of aspect that "his Parents mistook for Solidity of Judgement" (7–8). Although not an ideal medical student, he is well served by a tenacious memory and performs so well in public exercises that his professor "never dared contradict him, lest he should be put to the painful Labour of searching into these mouldy Records to refute his crude conceptions" (8). After leaving school, Honeywater journeys to Madrid. Along the way he tends to a sick traveler, and, though he practically kills him, the young man recovers and is foolish enough to think this is due to Honeywater. He introduces Don Ricardo to his master, the king's physician, and Don Ricardo so overwhelms the ignorant physician with his Greek that he makes him his associate "to the great Misfortune of many Thousands in the City of *Madrid*" (9). And so the narrative progresses, with Don Ricardo, by sheer gall, fooling everybody, writing nonsense, setting himself up as a conjuror, becoming the world's authority on "kyb'd heels," buying old manuscripts and curious antiquities, and finally becoming completely intolerable and ridiculous. The story concludes with his acquaintance with Dona Maria W—— of Via Vinculosa. Their relationship becomes a disgusting romance in which the seventy-five-year-old Honeywater's sexual attempts are thwarted by his age. Dona Maria, to oblige him and with her husband's approval, flogs him.[18]

Was Smollett inspired by Douglas's use of the picaresque in *Cornutor?*— whatever the case, Smollett responded in kind with *Don Ricardo Honeywater Vindicated in a Letter to Doctor Salguod* (Douglas spelled backward). Priced at one shilling, it was more elaborate than *Thomsonus Redivivus*, boasting three sections: "Translator's Advertisement," "A Letter to Dr. Salguod," and "A Genuine Narrative of the Life, Adventures and Writings of the Famous Doctor Salguod, Physician &c," all of which was reported to have been "Translated by A.M. a Graduate in Physic," from the work "Written Originally in Spanish, and Published in Madrid by the Celebrated Author of Gil Blas." Perhaps Smollett's first original prose work after *Roderick Random*, *Don Ricardo* radiates with new confidence in himself as a writer. Provoked by Douglas and having recently studied *Gil Blas*, Smollett draws heavily on the picaresque tradition. In some ways, this second medical pamphlet is the closest Smollett came to writing a genuine picaresque.

Smollett sets out not to defend Mead, but to assail Douglas. By 1748, Smollett had three reasons for attacking the overbearing Douglas; the first, and perhaps least important, is his disgusting attack on Mead. It cannot be established that Smollett and Mead ever met; perhaps Smollett used Mead's famous library or met him in London medical circles. There is, however, an interesting connection between Smollett's interests and the famous physician's. Mead promoted the use of ventilating equipment on naval ships, an innovation that Smollett, a former naval surgeon second mate who witnessed appalling conditions during his service on HMS *Chichester*, would have appreciated. The second reason is much plainer: Douglas's separate attack on one of Smollett's professional associates and fellow Scot, Dr. William Smellie (1697–1763), a man-midwife to whom Smollett had sent obstetrical observations and for whom he would later edit *Treatise on the Theory and Practice of Midwifery* (1751).[19] Earlier in 1748, Douglas had published *A Letter to Dr. Smelle [sic] Shewing the Impropriety of his New-Invented Wooden Forceps*, in which he declares Smellie's teaching methods "absurd." Smollett, in *Don Ricardo*, openly scolds Douglas for his attack, and the theme of man-midwifery is particularly strong. The third reason has already been noted: Douglas claiming as his own works written by others. Smollett directly confronts Douglas's theft in the prefatory "Letter" and in his narrative alludes to confused paternity and bastardry. Indeed, this plagiarism, or outright theft, emerges as the work's most consistent theme.

Before Smollett commences his picaresque narrative, he sounds the theme of literary theft in his two prefaces: the "Translator's Advertisement" narrates a complicated story about the translator attempting to ascertain the author of *The Cornutor of Seventy-Five*, an allusion to Douglas's theft of Blair's poem. The translator searches for copies in the Cotton Library, finally learning that Cervantes was not the real author. Rather, Dr. Salguod employed a young student at the university to "new model" an old manuscript into a personal satire on *Don Ricardo Honeywater*. In the following "Letter to Dr. Salguod," Smollett's narrator hints at Douglas's psychotic behavior: "As your Imagination, naturally warm may . . . deceive you, and represent your extraordinary Person and Character in a Light not absolutely just" (14). The narrator then declares, "I am not about to dispute your fatherly title to that satyrical Brat, or enquire if it was legitimately begot, in your own Brain . . . tho' I shrewdly suspect it owns its original Matter to some other Artist" (15). After denying the story about Dona Maria and her husband, he "hastens to entertain you with a picture of your dear self in much such a dress as that which you have presented the Cornutor. I shall endeavour to keep up the Manner and Stile, and preserve, as much may be, a sameness between this Child of mine and your adopted Brat" (24).

Following this elaborate opening is the "Genuine Narrative," which, as Smollett promises, is in "much such a [picaresque] Dress" (24). The narrative's spirited tone suggests Smollett enjoyed creating a low-class picaresque atmosphere and suitable characters. Appropriate for both the picaresque and for Smollett's theme of plagiarism, the hero is of confused parentage. Born in Catalonia, Salguod is the son of Cyndaraxa, a kitchen servant. She is admired by her master, who "being possessed of so inestimable a jewel, and eat [sic] his Olios with the higher Relish, as he knew that his Plates and Dishes were wash'd by the delicate Hands of his charming Skullion." Smollett's wit glows and, in a style reminiscent of Henry Fielding, describes the don's seduction of the girl: "Cupid was propitious to him, and pour'd a Philter into her ear, which banish'd Maiden Fears . . . and with a willing Coyness she trembling fell upon the Couch, over which I shall draw a Curtain and close the Scene" (29). The enamored don then composes a love sonnet, through which Smollett jabs at Douglas's theft: "this sonnet has been universally admired . . . and was long ago translated into English by one of our first-rate Poets, who however had the assurance to give it to the World as his own Original" (30). The poem is deliberately awful: "When Venus leaves her Vulcan's cell / Which all but I a Coal-hall call, / Fly, Fly, Ye that above Stairs dwell, / Her Face is wash'd, ye vanish all" (30). Clumsy and irregular, the sonnet recalls the equally dreadful poetry of Narcissa's aunt in chapter 40 of *Roderick Random*. In each case, the artistic failure suggests both inappropriate romantic longings and psychological instability.

Not surprisingly, young Salguod seems to inherit these qualities, but his parentage is disputed: the don's courier "was supposed to have his Finger in the Pye, and though the matter was never thoroughly settl'd, but as the Postilion's Name was Salguod as well as that of his Master," the boy is named Salguod and raised in the don's kitchens (31). Salguod finds some education and, refusing to be treated like a servant, leaves in quest of fortune. On the road, he meets a physician who is so humble "as to be his own apothecary" and who prescribes for pigs, cattle, and horses, as well as people (33). Salguod becomes his apprentice and, seeing so much money can be made in so little time, becomes a corn cutter and a sow gelder. Salguod later becomes a surgeon on a ship and is forced to become midwife to African slaves being transported to Spanish plantations. Back in Spain, "finding the [midwifery] business to be very lucrative," he determines to pursue it, though "his want of skill, experience, or abilities were difficulties that never entered his noodle" (27).

Coming to Madrid, he cures a tailor and marries the grateful man's daughter. Experiencing prosperity at last, he determines to launch into politics. He does so by noise and show, and his faction-leaders nominate him to Physician of the Household of his Royal Highness. After attaining the post, "he left no Artifice untry'd to push himself into Business and Reputation" (44). He seeks to see his name in print and so turns author, for which "dealers among the College [of Physicians] afforded him excellent opportunity" (45). Here Smollett, through an allusion to the Thomas Thompson affair, again strikes at Douglas's claiming the works of others: "He had an Itch to write and say Something in Answer to this Case . . . but . . . his own Abilities were not sufficient for either Matter or Stile. However, he got over this Difficulty, by employing a certain Person . . . to work they went, and hammer'd out a very elaborate treatise" (47). Smollett next addresses the Hugh Blair theft: "At last he takes it into his head to turn Poet . . . but was not oblig'd to trade on his own Stock. Resolving to have a poetical reputation, when a Youth of about fifteen presented him with a copy of Verses of no lower a Subject than the Resurrection, the Doctor lik'd them so hugely from that Minute on adopted the poetical Orphan and call'd it by his own name" (47). Still, the doctor's fame does not grow. So he resolves once more to "have a Brush with one of his Neighbours to see if he could scold himself into the Practice of Mid-wifery" (11). Not surprisingly, Salguod hires a hackney writer to abuse his adversary.

At this point, Smollett abandons the picaresque to openly mock Douglas's criticism of Smellie and his methods. Speaking in his own voice instead of that of his picaresque persona, Smollett declares, "It was the Doctor's intention to have shewn the impropriety of his wooden Instrument [forceps], but whether the Author forgot it, or the Doctor was lame in his Instructions, the impropriety happens to be demonstrated in no other place than the Title Page" (51). Smollett then concludes, "But I am weary of the Doctor's Writing, since No-body reads them, and he can prevail on any-body to answer, then it's in vain for me to give any further Account of them" (51). Thus bluntly ends Smollett's response. Douglas, interestingly, never published again. In 1752, two years after Smollett was granted his MD from Marischal College, Aberdeen, Douglas resigned as physician at Middlesex Hospital, and returned to Scotland. According to William Smellie, he died mad.[20]

The picaresque tradition within *Thomsonus Redivivus* and *Don Ricardo* can be identified in a variety of ways: historically, as Smollett's pre-novel work; professionally, as his engaging in "medical dialogues"; personally, as an expression of real anger at William Douglas; and literarily, as a set of new wings as his skills and interests developed as a result of translating and novel writing. What should we make of these works with respect to, as Boucé terms it, the "vexed problem of Smollettian pseudo-picaresque"?[21] The consensus now is that Smollett did not write picaresque novels but drew on the tradition as needed for his own purposes, an idea particularly reinforced by an examination of these two early medical pamphlets. Smollett seems to have gained interest in the picaresque quickly. In 1746 he appears to have no more than a slight understanding of the tradition. By 1748, Smollett seems to be fully aware of the picaresque, but he certainly never follows the tradition slavishly. Instead, he moves in and out of the picaresque freely, as we see in *Don Ricardo* when he drops the picaresque device to speak plainly to his target. The picaresque elements were a tool to Smollett, much like a surgical instrument to pick up and then lay down when the job was done, or a handy weapon to wield in satire, and finally, of course, a source of ideas for plots and characters. Elsewhere in this volume, O M Brack Jr. discusses the challenges facing a biographer of Smollett and the degree to which "a knowledge of the complete canon of Smollett's writing in the context of the history of the book can illuminate Smollett's life."[22] Smollett's contributions to medical literature, especially these early pamphlets with their gestures toward the picaresque, seem to have much to offer. Through them we can gain fleeting glimpses of Smollett as an emerging writer in a bitterly competitive and vicious market. We can also begin to recognize more fully how Smollett understood his own works in relations to others, which in some measure helps us identify how he understood himself as a writer and, eventually, a novelist.

NOTES

1. Robert Alter, *The Rogue's Progress: Studies in the Picaresque Novel* (Cambridge, MA: Harvard University Press, 1964); Stuart Miller, *The Picaresque Novel* (Cleveland, OH: Case Western Reserve University Press, 1967); Robert Giddings, *The Tradition of Smollett* (London: Methuen & Co., 1967); Robert Spector, *Tobias Smollett* (New York: Twayne, 1968), i, 46.

2. George S. Rousseau, "Smollett and the Picaresque: Some Questions about a Label," *Studies in Burke and his Time* 12 (1971): 56.

3. See Paul-Gabriel Boucé, "Smollett's Pseudo-picaresque: A Response to Rousseau's Smollett and the Picaresque," *Studies in Burke and his Time* 14 (1972): 73–79.

4. Paul-Gabriel Boucé's *The Novels of Tobias Smollett* (New York: Longman, 1976), see especially 72, 73, 80–87, 69–91.

5. Tobias Smollett, *The History of Roderick Random*, ed. Paul Gabriel Boucé (Oxford: Oxford University Press, 1979), xliv.

6. *The Adventures of Gil Blas de Santillane: A New Translation from the Best French Edition*, four vols. (London: 1748). A corrected second edition was published in 1750. Smollett's translation was published numerous times in the eighteenth and nineteenth centuries. Smollett's name was so connected with the work that Henry B. Malkin's 1803 translation was mistakenly published under Smollett's name in 1861. See Alain René Le Sage, *The Adventures of Gil Blas de Santillane, translated Tobias Smollett*, ed. O M Brack Jr. and Leslie A. Chilton, *The Works of Tobias Smollett* (Athens: University of Georgia Press, 2011).

7. Robert Adams Day formally attributes *Thomsonus Redivivus* to Smollett in his "When Doctors Disagree," *Etudes anglaises* 32:4 (1979): 312–26. Day bases his attribution largely on Smollett's frequent references to Dr. Thompson, who appears in seven of Smollett's works, from *Advice* and *Reproof* to his *History*. Day attributed *Don Ricardo Honeywater Vindicated* to Smollett when he prepared a facsimile production of the document for the Augustan Reprint Series. See *[William Douglas] The Cornutor of Seventy-Five [1748] and [Tobias Smollett?] Don Ricardo Honeywater Vindicated [1748]*, introduction by Robert Adams Day (Los Angeles: William Andrews Clark Memorial Library, 1987). Neither title is mentioned in Lewis M. Knapp's biography, *Tobias Smollett: Doctor of Men and Manners* (Princeton, NJ: Princeton University Press, 1949). Mary Wagoner's increasingly dated Smollett bibliography, *Tobias Smollett: A Checklist of Editions of his Works and an Annotated Secondary Bibliography* (New York: Garland, 1984), does not identify the works. Smollett, in his 1763 letter to Richard Smith of New Jersey, did not include the titles in his listing of works except, possibly, by the statement "some small detached performances that have been published occasionally in Papers and Magazines." See *Letters of Tobias Smollett*, ed. Lewis M. Knapp (Oxford: Clarendon Press, 1970), 113. All references to *The Cornutor of Seventy-Five* and *Don Ricardo Honeywater Vindicated* are from the Day edition.

8. According to Day, a brisk pamphlet war started at once, with nine combatants. Following Thompson's opening work, there came *Letter from J. Campbell, M.D.*, William Douglas's *A Letter to Dr. Thomson*; and *The Genuine Tryall of Dr. Nosmoth*, both of which appeared in June 1746. G. Dowman's *Dr. Thompson's Case* and the anonymous *Physick in Danger* appeared in July. In October, Smollett published *Thomsonus Redivivus*, followed by the anonymous *Dr. Thompson Vindicated*. Finally, in December appeared the anonymous *A Letter to Dr. Sangrado*, a direct reply to Smollett. See "When Doctors Disagree," 312ff.

9. William Douglas, *A Letter to Dr. Thompson In Answer to the Case of the Right Honourable Thomas Winnington* (London, 1746). References are to this edition.

10. Tobias Smollett, *Thomsonus Redivivus: or, a reply to W——m D——g——s* (London, 1746), 6. References are to this edition.

11. See, for example, *Critical Review*, March 1758, where Smollett laments his participation in "medical quarrels, little perhaps to the honour or emolument of the faculty," 224.

12. The unknown author of *Letter to Dr. Sangrado* points out the character mix-up: "How can you expect to have any Respect shewn to your Character, when you have none for it yourself? Is it not ridiculous to style yourself Physician to your own Servant?" (3).

13. An anonymous translator prepared an English edition of the first two volumes of *Gil Blas de Santillane* by 1716; the third and fourth volumes were translated

in 1724 and 1735, respectively. Though the translation was done with reasonable care and skill, names were misspelled, and there were spurious additions, suggesting the translator(s) used unauthorized copies of the French original. Internal evidence clearly shows Smollett consulted this flawed version when preparing his own, a common practice in commercial translation.

14. Smollett's first two novels feature portraits of professional translators. In *Roderick Random*, the character of Melopoyn, whose experiences parallel Smollett's, turns in desperation to translation, the income of which can't support him. See chapters 61–63. In *Peregrine Pickle*, Peregrine attends a "Congress of Authors," which ridicules a translator, declaring he did not understand one word of the language he pretended to translate. See chapter 101. Smollett's June 7, 1748, letter to Alexander Carlyle declares, "Gil Blas was actually translated by me, tho' it was a bookseller's job, done in a hurry, I did not choose to put my name on it." See *The Letters of Tobias Smollett*, 8. Smollett, however, goes on to boast of the work's excellent sales. Notably, Smollett's fictional translators are victims of unscrupulous booksellers and high-toned caucuses, rather than being untalented fools.

15. James Boswell, *Life of Johnson*, ed. G. Birkbeck Hill, revised and enlarged by L. F. Powell, six vols. (Oxford: Clarendon Press, 1934–1950), 3:335.

16. Douglas may have been mocking a tract Mead wrote, *The Life and Adventures of Don Bilioso de l'Estomac* (1719). Clever, though not particularly witty, this work mixes *Don Quixote* with allegory, with the latter device more a parody than used in earnest; however, the real interest of the work is the prefatory "To The College of Physicians in London," which attacks John Woodward (1665–1718), a professional foe of Mead and author of *The state of physick and diseases; with an inquiry into the cause of the late increase of them, but more particularly of the small-pox*. In this preface, Mead writes, "At last, by pure accident, I found an old French manuscript, translated from the Spanish, the Title is Les Aventures de Don Bilioso de l'Estomac" (7). Smollett's "Translator's Preface" of *Don Ricardo* parallels this, as he describes his own search for the original of *The Cornutor of Seventy-Five* in the Cotton Library.

17. This probably refers to Richard Mead's *A Discourse of the small-pox and measles* (1747). Subjoined to this work is "The Commentary of Rhazes, a most celebrated Arabian physician, on the same disease."

18. Mead's principal biographers avoid this aspect. Day, in his Introduction to the Augustan Reprint, found that Douglas's accusations were probably true, notably citing Laurence Sterne's references in his *Letters*. See also Anita Guerrini, "Richard Mead," in *The Dictionary of National Biography*.

19. See Claude Jones, "Tobias Smollett on 'The Separation of the Pubic Joint in Pregnancy,'" *Medical Life* 41 (1934): 302–5.

20. James Sambrook, "William Douglas," *Dictionary of National Biography*.

21. Boucé, "Smollett's Pseudo-Picaresque," 78.

22. See above, O M Brack Jr., "Tobias Smollett: The Life of an Author," 17–34.

13

The Publication and Revision of Smollett's *Continuation of the Complete History of England*, 1760–1771

James E. May

Tobias Smollett's *Continuation of the Complete History of England*, in its first four volumes, is a nearly seamless extension of the *Complete History* (1757–1758; revised 1758–1760), both as a historical narrative and as a publication project.[1] It was printed by Archibald Hamilton, the printer of Smollett's *Critical Review* and *British Magazine*, and published by Richard Baldwin at the Rose in Paternoster-Row, who with Volume 11 of the *Complete History* had taken over that title formerly copublished with the bankrupt James Rivington and James Fletcher. Reversing the more orthodox scheme of quarto then octavo sale employed for the *Complete History*, Smollett and Baldwin sold the *Continuation* first in three-sheet octavo numbers and only much later as two quarto volumes. As had the eleven volumes of the *Complete History*, each volume of the *Continuation* contains ten numbers, sold serially, of the original settings or reprintings or a mix of the two. The numbers forming the first four volumes of the *Continuation* appeared between May 17, 1760, and July 24, 1762. Proposed as a single publication, they have a coherent development concluding in Volume 4 with an index and directions to binders on the placement of copper plates. With the publication of No. 40, the work appeared complete, but Smollett added a fifth volume in 1765, covering 1762 through May 1765. Perhaps adding "to the Declaration of the War with Spain, 1762" to the advertised title prepared for a future extension.[2] Given the potential for additions, one might conjecture that, though he mocked Reverend Nicolas Tindal as "the rev. continuator,"[3] Smollett, had he lived longer, might have added a Volume 6, although Volume 5, printed but once, was not the success that Volumes 1–4 were.

The main rival for Smollett's illustrated, complete history of England was not David Hume's history but Paul Rapin de Thoyras's *History of England* (twelve vols.) and its *Continuation* (eight, later nine, vols.) by Rev. Nicolas Tindal (1687–1774), then rector of Alverstoke in Hampshire. Tindal had translated Rapin for the Knaptons in 1725 and in 1744 began publishing his continuation. Proposals for the *Continuation of Mr. Rapin de Thoyras's History of England, from the Revolution in 1688, to the Accession of King George II* (printed for J. and P. Knapton) appeared in the *Daily Post* (*DP*) by 3 April 1744, with the first number published 5 May. The volumes were completed in 1747 (ESTC N8358). The Knaptons initially sold the volumes serially as three- and four-sheet sixpenny weekly numbers with copperplates, issued on Saturdays (No. 2 was announced in *DP*, 17 May 1744). In 1758, Smollett imitated this publishing strategy with his *Complete History of England*, offering weekly numbers illustrated with copperplates and heavily advertised. At the same time, the Knaptons, who had published the Rapin and Tindal volumes as second and third folio editions in 1751, advertised for a new octavo edition in sixpenny numbers. Thus, the competition began. Advertisements for Tindal's series listed about five dozen plates, about half as many as Smollett offered, and with comparatively more monuments and places and fewer portraits (*Whitehall Evening Post* [*WEP*] of 11–14 February 1758). Both the competing numbers began sale on Saturday, 25 February 1758. Concurrently, John Knapton for Thomas Osborne and over a dozen publishers ("by whom Proposals are delivered and Subscriptions taken in") offered the sewn octavo volumes of this fourth edition.[4] Then on 14 June 1760 began weekly numbers of an expanded Tindal series bringing the history "to January 1760," in weekly numbers sold "by Assignment from Mr. Knapton, for" George Kearsley, on 14 June (*WEP, Public Advertiser* [*PA*], *London Evening Post* [*LEP*]). This and future weekly advertisements announced the new issue and its engraving (No. 1 had the head of the Earl of Chesterfield) and boasted as "a strong Proof of the uncommon Approbation it has met with from the Publick . . . the Sale . . . of Thirteen Thousand."[5] Advertisements for Tindal's *Continuation* ran as frequently and in the same newspapers as Baldwin's for Smollett's, with similar layouts and points of emphasis, often side by side, as occurs in *PA* of 27 September 1760, where Tindal's No. 16 includes a "Head of the Earl of Hardwicke" and Smollett's No. 15, one of Sir Piercy Brett. Not waiting for the series to reach the new volume covering events to January 1760, Tindal's "Volume IX and last," priced like Smollett's at five shillings, was brought out 20 August. Smollett reviewed it in the September 1760 *Critical Review* (*CR*, 10:186–94). Knapp and Brack have stressed the role played in Smollett's success by a massive marketing campaign, but these methods had been intensively used for Tindal's history and were contemporaneously in use for Hume's and others'.[6] Smollett's success should first be attributed to the merits of his history, with a patriotic public appetite for British history and engravings being other important considerations.

Since Volumes 1–4 cover events in 1748 through 1762, Smollett was generally "researching" the project while editing and writing other publications, as when reviewing historical works in the *CR* and selecting newspaper extracts for the "History of the Present War" and "Domestic Intelligence" (usually of foreign affairs also) in the *British Magazine* (*BM*). Volume 4 of the *Continuation* draws information from many items Smollett edited for Volume 3 (1762) of *BM*, such as "Extracts from the Papers relative to the Rupture with Spain," "Letters from Major General Monckton . . . [on] the Taking of Martinico," and the "Account of the Surrender of St. Peter's" (3 [1762], 135–40, 142–49, and 204–7). Surely the public turned to the *Continuation* in part because Smollett's *BM* testified to his mastery of the news, as the *CR* did his mastery of current scholarship. Smollett wrote at least the final third of Volumes 1–4 after serialization began and surely wished, or even needed, to make the same efforts pay twice—and there are textual complexities caused by his working on both concurrently. Phrasing as well as details are shared by the *Continuation* with the following accounts in the *BM*: Admiral Hawke's victory over a French admiral at 3:114–15 from Hawke's transcribed letter of 24 November 1759 (from the *London Gazette*) in the *BM* of January 1760 (1:50–52); two military engagements in December 1759 at 4:32 and General Breidenbach's actions near Göttingen in November 1760 at 4:57 from "History of the Present War" in *BM* of February and December 1760 (1:101, 1:719); troop movements in Germany by General Luckner and Prince Ferdinand on 4:266–67 from "Domestic Intelligence" in the *BM* of January 1761 (2:50); and the pathetic battlefield account of Capt. Ochterlony and Mr. Peyton wounded by Indians in a long footnote on 3:M8^v/192-"180" from an unsigned article in the *BM* of January 1760 (1:19–22).[7] The article "An Account of the Surrender of Pondicherry," transcribing Colonel Eyre Coote's letter of 3 February 1761 (*BM*, July 1761, 2:373–78), contains such phrasing as "On the 25th, admiral Steevens, with four ships of the line, arrived off Pondicherry, having parted . . ." (373); in the *Continuation*, this becomes "On the twenty-fifth day of December rear-admiral Steevens arrived with four ships of the line, having parted . . ." (4:110.4–7).[8] Smollett may be accused of plagiarism in his transposition of a first-person account in the September 1760 *BM*'s "History of the Present War." The original report from "Prince Ferdinand's Head-Quarters at Buhne, September 9" appeared first in the *London Gazette* of 16 September 1760 and then was reprinted in the *LCh* and *WEP* of 16–18 September, before it was reprinted in the *BM* for September. Early in the article we read, "On the morning of that day, likewise, the Hereditary Prince (upon intelligence that the volunteers of Clermont and Dauphiné, consisting each, when complete, of 600 horse and 600 foot, were cantoned at Zierenberg" (*BM*, 1 [1760], 554, as in *WEP*). The *Continuation* reads, "On the same morning, the hereditary prince set out on an expedition to beat up the quarters of a French detachment. Being informed that the volunteers of Clermont and Dauphine, to the number of one thousand, horse and foot, were cantoned at Zierenberg" (4:48.3–8). Smollett's paraphrase integrates adjacent sentences: for instance, "[the forces were] to be ready to march at eight at night. They left their tents standing, and passed the Dymel near Warbourg" (*BM*, as in *WEP*) becomes "Leaving their tents standing, they began their march at eight in the evening, and passed the Dymel near Warbourg" (48.18–20). Smollett's version is most indebted in the account of fighting: "The noise of our trampling over gardens gave them the alarm, and they began to fire; upon which our grenadiers, who had marched with unloaded firelocks . . . pushed the piquets, and, having killed the guard at the gate, rushed into the town, and drove every thing before them" (*BM*, as in *WEP*) becomes "the noise of their feet alarmed the French, who began to fire; then the grenadiers proceeded . . . with unloaded firelocks, pushed the piquets, slew the guard at the gate, and rushing into the town, drove every thing before them" (4:48.30–49.2).

This overlap with magazine articles is not surprising given that Volume 3's sheet Z (in No. 28, published 16 May 1761) covers events after the proposals for *Continuation* were published: on Z5/345 we read of legislation proposed 29 April 1760, by which point the first issue was probably in the press. Volume 4 begins with events in May 1760 and proceeds through the declaration of war with Spain to events in February 1762 (the month that No. 36 was published)—the *Continuation*, despite Smollett's own criticism of such in history writing,[9] inevitably veers into journalism and commentary on contemporary events. Thus, quarto publication of the whole work prior to weekly serialization was not possible. Periodic accounts of tabloid news function like filler in the *Continuation*, adding humor, suspense, and outrage. Among these are the story of the Cock-Lane ghost hoax (5:19–24) and the pathetic story of John Calas, a French Protestant merchant (5:69–76), presented to exemplify the prevalence of superstition among the vulgar in England and "cruelty and fanaticism" in France.[10] Magazine editing had perhaps encouraged Smollett to vary his materials (and to insert lengthy transcripts), but, clearly, he was not anxious to conserve space for only major domestic and foreign affairs.

Ironically, if Smollett had maintained the original publishing schedule, he would not have filled four volumes, for the serialization would have been completed in early 1761, more than a year before his chronology ended. As historical time caught up with the period covered in *Continuation*, Smollett fell behind, with a fortnightly schedule in the numbers of Volume 2 replacing the "weekly" one promised in proposals, and a monthly one for some issues of Volume 3 and that or longer for all those of Volume 4. The shift to a fortnightly schedule was attributed to a "Multiplicity of Materials" sent in by helpful readers.[11] But, surely, an increasing number of publication projects and personal problems prevented Smollett, disabled from illnesses, from maintaining the production he had promised, the numbers taking increasingly longer periods to complete.

Nonetheless, historical events also influenced the delay, for Smollett, who had concluded the *Complete History* with the treaty of Aix-la-Chapelle, hoped for a conclusion to the war that had been his principal focus in *Continuation*. Early advertisements had characterized the work as containing the history "from the Treaty of Aix-la-Chapelle, to the End of the Present War" (*LEP*, 6–8 May 1760). A calendar year or the completion of a fortieth number would not supply a satisfactory terminus. These considerations are genuinely stated in his excuse for further delay on 16 February 1762, accompanying announcements of No. 36's publication: "The Author of the complete History of England begs Leave to observe, that the Publication of the latter Numbers of his Continuation has been purposefully protracted, in the Hope that a general Pacification would afford a proper Period for the Conclusion of the Work. But this Prospect having lately vanished, he now proposes to bring down the History to the Declaration of the War with Spain; and to publish the remaining Numbers with the utmost Expedition" (*LEP* of 13–16 February—note how Smollett's reference to himself implies the unity of both histories). No. 37, at least partially written when No. 36 was submitted to the press (covering the war in Europe through November 1761), concerns promising negotiations between France and England through mid-September. A treaty signed the previous month between Spain and France led to England's rupture with Spain by year's end and the declaration of war with Spain on 4 January 1762 (Z2/355, in No. 38). These developments, though ensuring that no peace with France was in the offing, supplied a historical demarcation fit for closure. The decision to end the quarto edition at the conclusion of the Treaty of Paris in 1763 also underscores Smollett's concern that his history provide a structure to events.

As weekly advertisements reiterated, customers could buy the work in several different forms. They could buy three-sheet numbers at booksellers' shops or have them delivered to their house, not only during a well-advertised series but also anytime over the next decade. Or they could buy whole volumes sewn in boards for five shillings, available several weeks or more after the first numbers forming a volume were published. First-edition volumes bear title-page dates reflecting when the first issue containing the title-leaf as A1, not the whole volume, was sold: Volumes 1–2 were published fully in 1760 as dated, but Volumes 3–4 might be said to have misleading dates: Volume 3, dated "1760," was published between 30 December 1760 and 4 July 1761, and Volume 4, dated "1761," was published between 25 July 1761 and 24 July 1762, even containing references to events of 1762. Baldwin seems to have been in no hurry to sell the complete Volumes 1–3 but moved more quickly with Volume 4. Sale of the complete Volume 1 was announced on 13 August 1760 (*Lloyd's Eve Post* [*LlEP*] and *PA* of 16 August). On 12 September an advertisement appeared for Volumes 1–2 sewn in boards (one of many erroneous advertisements encountered for this work), but Volume 2 could not have been ready since at that time serial publication had only reached to No. 14 and would not reach No. 20 until mid-December. At the end of 1760, sewn copies of Volume 1 were again unavailable, requiring new impressions, but then on 16 January 1761 the *PA* announced that these numbers "being reprinted, any person may have the whole 20 Numbers together." Nos. 11–20 probably became available for sale as a sewn Volume 2 about this time. Certainly Volume 2 was available for sale on 9 April 1761, when offered in both the *LEP* and *WEP*. Volume 3 was available sewn on 26 September 1761 (*PA*), nearly three months after No. 30 appeared and Volume 4, three weeks after No. 40 was issued, on 14 August 1762 (*Gazetteer and London Daily Advertiser* [*GLDA*]—and in *PA* of that date but with the error "thirty Numbers" in place of "forty"). Since all the plates for even Volume 1 were not available until certain numbers of Volume 4 appeared, none of the volumes were sold bound in leather until a month or more after Volume 4 appeared.[12] Following the publication of all forty numbers, and thus of all the plates, subscribers could have them bound by whomever they wished. It is likely that many extant volumes were bought as sets of four or, with the *Complete History*, of fifteen (or, after Volume 5's publication in 1765, as five or sixteen). Many are bound in uniform sets with the eleven volumes of the *Complete History*, their spines numbered Volumes 12–15 or –16, and their labels typically reflecting the unity of the work (commonly "SMOLLETT'S | HIST: OF | ENGLAND"). Baldwin's advertisements long offered the *Continuation* as part of a total work in fifteen and then in sixteen volumes, with four guineas the price for all fifteen volumes bound and six shillings added when Volume 5 was the sixteenth. Copies of issues not sewn or bound have very largely disappeared, along with the thousands of printed proposals.[13]

Good sales for the *Continuation* required the subscribers' perception of the new work as but a continuing part of "Smollett's history of England," even if separate proposals and issue numbers were necessary. Even before serialization of final numbers for Volume 11 of the *Complete History* was completed, Smollett sought subscribers for the weekly publication of his *Continuation*. The *LEP* of 22–25 March 1760 contains a long undated proposal "To the Purchasers of Dr. Smollett's History | of England" for a "Continuation . . . brought down to the Close of the present War, in a Publication of Weekly Numbers," concluding with the notice that it "will be published the Saturday after the last Number of the History, printed and ornamented in the same Manner." Advertisements of various lengths followed, as in the *London Chronicle* (*LChr*) of 27–29 March 1760, announcing publication of *Complete History* No. 108 and in the *Salisbury Journal* of 14 April. The *Public Ledger* (*PL*) of 2 April inserted several paragraphs of the proposal into its recent news. Longer advertisements contain essentially the same text as a prospectus surviving in a unique copy, partially illustrated and transcribed by O M Brack Jr., promising for "Forty Numbers, at Sixpence each," on three octavo sheets, with "Fifty Copper-plates," "delivered . . . without any further Expence to the Subscribers."[14] The "first Number . . . is intended as a Specimen," with a money-back guarantee. These announcements are mostly taken up with the eight rousing patriotic paragraphs on recent British successes that, with little alteration but an added final note challenging detractors, serve as the *Continuation*'s four-page preface "To the Reader." Besides the tight narrative continuity, another link created between the *Complete History* and *Continuation* occurs in an apologetic notice about plates once intended for the *Complete History* but excluded from the 167 produced and distributed: Richard Baldwin notes that "he will do his utmost Endeavour to procure Drawing of those omitted, to be published in the Continuation; and any Subscriber to the History, not chusing the Continuation, shall have those Heads gratis, when done" (*LEP*, 19–22 April 1760). Baldwin's apology, dated 18 April, occurs within an advertisement for the final number (110) of the *Complete History*, which had to carry six engraved portraits, still owed, and so must have been a publisher's nightmare. Baldwin announces that "No. CX . . . will be publish'd on Saturday the 3d of May," but he could not pull it off. The *LEP* of 6–8 May advertised that No. 110 would appear "on Saturday next," and it was published 10 May 1760. Another round of proposals for the *Continuation* occurred at this time, with one dated "May 3" (*LEP* of 6–8 May), and another "May 10" (*PA* and *WEP*)—others followed publication (*PA* of 20 and 31 May).

As promised, the first number of the *Continuation* appeared a week after No. 110, on Saturday, 17 May ("this day" in *LEP* of 15–17 May 1760, and "Saturday last" in *PA* of 20 and 23 May). Surely the continued Saturday publication, without any gap, was important for competing with the Tindal's *Continuation* of Rapin's history of England and for leading subscribers to the *Complete History* into the *Continuation*—enough that it was better to have a gap prior to No. 110 than to No. 1 of the new series. But it appears that Smollett and Baldwin were ready for the new title's first volume: newspaper advertisements record an unbroken weekly succession of Nos. 1–9: 24 May (*PA* of 23 May notes "tomorrow"), 31 May (*WEP* of 29–31 May); 7 June (*PA*), 14 June (*LEP* of 14–17 June), [#6] 21 June (*LEP* of 19–21 June), 28 June (*LEP* of 26–28 June, listing topics of Nos. 1–5), 5 July (*PA*), and 12 July (*PA*); however, two weeks were required for No. 10 ("This Day" in *LEP* of 24–26 July). Advertisements for No. 6 contain a list of "particulars," or topics, in "the Five Numbers already published" that resembles those in advertisements for monthlies, suggesting the influence of magazine format on the varietal organization of the *Continuation*: "Character of the Ministry in 1748. Progress of the Bill relating to Seamen. . . . Severities exercised upon some Students at Oxford. Scheme for a Settlement in Nova Scotia. Scheme for reducing the Interest of the National Debt. Account of the Westminster Election," and on through "Elizabeth Canning" and "Execution of Dr. Cameron" to "General Shirley's Expedition against Niagara" (*PA* of 27 June).

Volume 2 covers events from April 1757 through December 1758, with its final number containing on all but one page an appendix of justifications by the courts in Berlin and Vienna, thus capable of earlier compilation. On July 19, in place of No. 10, came the announcement "Saturday next No. X" but with the sweetener "Saturday the 2d of August will be published, No. XI," with two plates, of "Henly" and "Lionel Sackville" (*LEP* of 17–19 July). Typically, issues beginning a new volume include an especially attractive plate or multiple plates. After the publication of No. 11 as promised on 2 August (*PA* and "Saturday last" in *LEP* of 7–9 August 1760), Baldwin began publishing issues in fortnightly installments, a schedule met for Volume 2's numbers except for a week's delay with No. 19 or 20. In the *LEP* of 7–9 August appears the first of many announcements that, due to a "Multiplicity of Materials [that have] poured in," future publication would be by "fortnight."[15] The *WEP* of 12–14 August and *LEP* of 13–15 August, carrying the explanation of the new schedule, misleadingly note that No. 11 appeared "Saturday last." The *PA* of 13 August, noting No. 11 was published 2 August, carried the same explanation for the new scheme. The shift to biweekly publication was also recorded in the *PL*, *LChr*, and *WEP* of 23–26 August, the last two noting the publication "this day" of No. 12; however, as the *LEP* of 14–16 August and the *PA* of 16 August announced, No. 12 was published on Saturday, 16 August, a date that fits into a sequence with Nos. 1–11 and 14. Number 13 appeared a fortnight later (*LEP* of 28–30 August). Issues 14–18 appeared over the course of the next five fortnights: Nos. 14–15: 13 and 27 September (*PA*); No. 16: 11 October (*PA*); No. 17: 25 October (*LEP* of 23–25 October); and No. 18: 8 November (*LEP* of 6–8 November). Here follows a gap in the newspaper advertisements, during which period, on 28 November, Smollett began his three-month sentence in prison for the libel of Vice-Admiral Sir Charles Knowles in the *CR* of May 1758.[16] No. 19 seems not to have been advertised in the usual London papers (nor was No. 23 while Smollett was still incarcerated). Either No. 19 or 20 was delayed one week, for on 13 December, five weeks after No. 18 was published, No. 20 appeared (*LEP* of 11–13 December 1760). We might thus surmise that Smollett's imprisonment slowed down completion of the issues and perhaps also reduced the publishers' posting of advertisements. Perhaps it encouraged Smollett to fill in the end of Volume 2 with material that would be cut from the quartos. Priority was probably given to the monthly *BM*, with its serialization of *The Life and Adventures of Launcelot Greaves*—always available at the start of the month.[17] At the end of his imprisonment, Smollett issued proposals for the twenty-five-volume *Works* of Voltaire (*PA* of 26 February 1761), the first volume of which was published by John Newbery and others on 2 March (26–28 February, *WEP*). To glance at advertisements in this period is to realize that Smollett was his own main competitor, leaving one to wonder how anyone had time to read all his concurrent publications.

The ten numbers of Volume 3, which, if on schedule, would have taken under five months, took seven months. Its first issue, No. 21, was announced a fortnight after the twentieth number in the *LEP* of (Saturday) 27–30 December 1760. But No. 22 required three weeks, not appearing until 17 January 1761 (*PA* of 16 January notes "tomorrow," though the *LEP* of 22–24 January notes "this day"). No advertisements are located for No. 23, but its accompanying plate of General Kingsley (between "Comyns" and "Downe") appears in a plate list in the *St. James's Chronicle* (*StJC*) of 26–28 May 1761. The *PA* and *PL* of 19 February, along with apologies for delays, note No. 24 will appear "Saturday next," that is, 21 February; however, the *WEP* of 26–28 February notes the publication "this day" of No. 24. So, an eight- or nine-week period occurred between No. 21 on 27 December and No. 24 on 21 or 28 February, at least two issues of the three requiring extra weeks. The *PA* of 13 March notes publication the following day for No. 25, thus after no more than a three-week interval. No. 26 followed a month later on 4 or 11 April, assuming publication occurred on a Saturday (both *LEP* and *WEP* of [Tuesday] 7–9 April note "this day" for No. 26, though *LChr* of 16–18 April notes the same). The *LEP* of 23–25 April announced No. 27 after a fortnight, confirmed in *General Evening Post* (*GEP*) of 30 April–2 May, which notes "last Saturday." The *LEP* of 7–9 May erroneously repeats No. 27 as "this day," but its (Thursday) 14–16 May issue notes No. 28 as "This Day" published after a three-week interval (as do *GEP* of 14–16 May and *PA* of 16 May); three weeks later, in the (Thursday) 4–6 June *GEP*, appears the announcement for "this day" of No. 29 with head of George III. The 4–6 June *LEP* announces "Next Saturday" No. 30 will be published (incorrectly, as that would only be a week after No. 29), and the issue was delayed. The *LEP* and *GEP* of 30 June–2 July 1761 announced "Saturday next [No. 30] will be publish'd," and the *PA* of 4 July and the *StJC* of 7–9 July confirm that No. 30 appeared Saturday, 4 July, after a month's interval. On 2 July the *LEP* advertised that in No. 31, "which begins the Fourth Volume, will be given a large whole Sheet, new and correct Map of all North America." Nos. 21–30 became available for sale as Volume 3 by 26 September 1761 (*LEP*).

Volume 4, which surveys events in 1760–1762, contains less historical writing than the earlier volumes. After sheet D, most pages have but thirty-three lines, one less than those of earlier volumes, and its footnotes have more leading than do most in others.[18] Smollett's historical account ends on Aa1^v/370; then, after a page of introduction, come remarks by Major-General Barrington on the expedition to Martinique, and the conquest of Guadalupe, commenting on Commodore Moore's remarks appended to Volume 3, with Moore's repeated in a parallel column (Aa2^v/372–Bb2^v/388). The index and directions to binder occupy the rest of the volume. Issues 31–40 were published monthly on average, between Saturday 25 July 1761 and Saturday 24 July 1762, with lengthy delays before the final issues. The delays can be explained by Smollett's difficulties completing the text and his hope that peace would unfold, as noted above, and should not be attributed to Hamilton's printshop, which brought out weekly, without fail, reissues of Nos. 1–20 of Smollett's *Complete History*. The period between issues is always a month or more, with publication frequently delayed past dates advertised, and never are more copies promised after further printing for any issues running short.

The issues of Volume 4, like those of Volume 3, were less often advertized than those of the first two volumes, but the schedule of publication apparently was as follows: No. 31, whose map of North America had been exploited for weeks to maintain interest, on 25 July ("next Saturday" in *GEP* of 16–19 July; prematurely "this day" in *StJC* of 21–23 July); No. 32 with map of Caribbee Islands on 22 August ("Saturday next" in *LEP* of 13–15 August); No. 33 with (the head of) Bishop Sherlock delayed until 3 or 17 October ("next Saturday" in the *LEP* and *PA* on 26 September; yet not noted as "this day" until 15 October in the *WEP*); No. 34 with Northumberland probably on 14 November ("This day" *GEP* of 12–14 November and *LEP* of 14–17 November); No. 35 with Queen Charlotte probably on 26 December ("Saturday next" in *LEP* of 17–19 December and "this day" in *LEP* of 29–31 December); No. 36 with Halifax after six weeks on 13 February (*PA*; also *LEP* of 13–16 February, both with the explanation that delay was intended with hope "that a general Pacification would afford a proper Period for the Conclusion"); No. 37 with Louisa of Denmark on 11 March (*LEP* of 11–13 March); No. 38 with map of East Indies probably on April 24 ("To-morrow" in 23 April *PA*, though "this day" in *LChr* of 27–29 April); No. 39 with Lockhart and Coram, delayed nearly two months, on 19 June 1762 ("this day" in *StJC* of 19–22 June, and "Saturday last" in *LEP* of 22–24 June); and No. 40, short a half-sheet of three full sheets but with frontispiece and two maps in compensation, on 24 July ("this day" in *LEP* of 22–24 July). Advertisements beginning with the last noted indicate that "Any Person may have forty Numbers together, making four Volumes, Price 5s. each, sewed, or begin with Number I. and go on Weekly." But presumably sewn copies of Volume 4 became available around 14 August 1762 when many advertisements offer all four volumes (e.g., *GLDA* and *PA*). On 7 October 1762 the *PA* advertized the four octavos of *Continuation* at "Price

1l. 4s. bound and lettered" and renewed the offer that "Any Person may begin with Number I. and go on Weekly."

Most sheets in the first four volumes were reprinted, without revision, twice, but sheets H–P and T–Ff of Volume 1 and A–Aa of Volume 2 were reprinted three times. Reprinted title-pages (part of the first gatherings) are dated in Volume 1: 1762 and 1771; 2: 1760, 1763, and 1767; 3: 1762 and 1765; and 4: 1764 and 1768. Smollett's decision as early as 1762 to produce a revised two-volume quarto edition removed the necessity of revising the octavo reprints—nor was Smollett in England when many sheets were first reprinted. Even if Smollett had wished to add, cut, or alter, the weekly number scheme prevented much revision in resettings, for each individual sheet had to begin and end as it had in its first setting. Baldwin's distribution scheme involving delivery boys, mercuries, and other booksellers prevented him from ensuring that all sheets in even the same number were from the same setting, as the diversity within issues of copies examined shows (e.g., four copies of Volume 3 with a 1765 title-page have the first setting of sheet O, but only one has the first sheet of N and none that of P).

New impressions came from new settings of type, there being no cases of variant states caused by the reimpression of standing type as occur in some early numbers of the *Complete History*. Yet reprinting, particularly of sheets in Volumes 1–2, was required early on. Evidently the pressruns for sheets A–G, Q–S, and Gg of Volume 1 and Bb–Gg of Volume 2 were greater than those for others needing to be reprinted in 1760 (those reprinted have sigla "1760/63" and "1760+" in the appendix). At the end of 1760, Baldwin's advertisements acknowledged that "Numbers 7, 8, 9, and 10 are reprinting and will be ready in a few days" for those who wanted to buy Volumes 1–2.[19] This information dates second settings of sheets T–Ff in Volume 1 ("1760+"). Resetting was required as sheets sold off when the *Continuation* was serialized again, which occurred immediately according to notices for No. 40 in July but also following the series of *Complete History* whose first number was republished 30 January 1762 ("this day" in *LEP*; another series was advertised as having begun "Saturday last" in the *PA* of 12 January 1764). Weekly serialization continued through the end of the decade as indicated by a *Prospectus Saturday July 1, 1769* announcing that No. 1 of the *Complete History* "July 1, 1769, will be published, Price 6d. (To be continued Weekly)."[20] Although offering the *Continuation* in weekly numbers, Baldwin's advertisements pushed for its purchase in complete volumes (weekly numbers made more sense for the lengthier *Complete History*). For instance, the *LEP* of 21–24 April 1764 advertised as forthcoming 1 May (acknowledged published in *LEP* of 1–3 May) "A New Edition, corrected of A Continuation of the Complete History of England" in "Four Large Volumes . . . Illustrated with Fifty Copper-plates," priced one pound four shillings bound. Presumably the second settings of Volume 4 with "1764" title-pages were printed to be a part of this four-volume unit. Comparable advertisements for the four volumes were run again in January 1765 (e.g., *StJC* of 19–22 January), presumably the occasion for the 1765 reprinting of Volume 3. The stress on volume sales resulted in reprint volumes tending to have uniformly second, third, or fourth settings of the sheets. One can expect that copies with the earliest dated title-pages will not include many later settings, and those with reprinted title-pages will rarely have any first settings. Indeed, as the appendix shows, copies of Volumes 3–4 with later dates have sufficiently predictable stability to treat them as editions. Nonetheless, one cannot be certain from the title-pages which settings will follow in the volume. Different press figures usually signal different settings, but not always, for there are quite a few sheets without figures and a few different settings that coincidentally share the same figures. But, as demonstrated in the appendix, from variant readings one can determine the chronology for the multiple settings, without relying on the presence of other evidence for dating (as from plates and other physical and paratextual evidence). Usually the text of a sheet was transmitted lineally from the first through the last reprinting. Non-lineal descent is relatively rare, occurring in sheets H–K, L, Z–Aa of Volume 1; H, K–R, T–U, Y and possibly G and I of Volume 2; E and H–I of Volume 3; and I and possibly U and Aa of Volume 4. The most common variation from one setting forming the text for that immediately next involves the first setting's providing copy for more than one to follow (all noted in Volumes 1, 3, and 4 and all in Volume 2 but U). This tendency to take the first setting as copy for the third as well as second settings reflects the absence of corrections and revisions.

Smollett did not revise his text for resettings in octavo. The appendix records 122 substantive variants found in comparing the original octavos settings on 700 pages of Volumes 1–4 against lifetime reprintings.[21] Less than ten percent of these changes could be considered corrections, including those made by the third and fourth reprintings. In Volume 1, with thirty substantive variants, only nine are introduced in the first reprinting, none of which appears to be a necessary correction. The only apparent correction in Volume 1 is "commission" as modifier corrected to "commissioned" in fourth setting (1771) at Ee1ᵛ/434.B.29. Most corrections could be easily made by compositors, like the alteration of "word" to "world" in Volume 3 (357.A.18). Only some corrections to the spelling of foreign place names might have come from Smollett or an educated friend of the press (e.g., "Stoltznau" to "Soltznau" at 3:229.27). The most common classes of variants are changes from singular to plural or vice versa, reversals in the order of two words, addition and removal of definite articles, changes of demonstrative pronouns and verb forms ("run" for "ran"), and alteration of prepositions (as "of" for "from"). The most substantial alterations involve the omission of two marginal glosses from No. 24. About a third of the accidental variants identified have been recorded in the appendix, though as many as half in the most correctly composed sheets. The amount of compositorial error can be gauged from the appendix's inclusion of all variants for Volume 1's sheet F (inaccurate work), Volume 2's Bb–Cc (accurate), and Volume 3's G and O–P. Few accidental changes are likely corrections, but these include some spelling corrections, such as "Greenville" to "Grenville" (1:455.9, though the quarto repeats the misspelling). The final reprintings tend to be the least accurate, as Volume 2's sheets R–S in 1767.

Volume 5 is composed of ten weekly issues of three sheets, numbered in sequence with the preceding four volumes (as Nos. 41–50), but it comes as something of an afterthought or second start. Volume 4, with its index, completed the original scheme in July 1762. Presumably the fifth volume was easy money for Smollett. He was habituated to writing history, had at hand the materials needed to cover 1762–1765, and had an interest in the success of government leaders and their initiatives and an animus against those who had vilified John Earl of Bute and stirred up anti-Scottish bigotry in an effort to topple Bute (5:115–17). One rationale for the fifth continuation volume is implicit in the claim for completeness made in advertisements late in 1763: "This is the only Complete History of England extant" (*LEP* of 1–3 and 13–15 December 1763), presumably glancing at recently advertised histories by Hume, Tindal, John Barrow, Catherine Macauley, William Ryder, Thomas Mortimer, Bishop Burnet, and others.

Advertisements represented the fifth volume as bringing the work down to "the End of the year 1764" (*PA* of 12 June 1766, in an advertisement for the sixteen-volume octavo following announcement of the quartos); however, it reaches from 1762 through the Treaty of Paris (whose text is on pp. 162–85) to May 1765 and has a marginal date of 1 July 1765 beside Smollett's concluding assessment that he finds nothing earlier written to require alteration (Ee8/449). The final two sheets are occupied by the index (Ff1–Gg8^v).

During the interim between composition of Volumes 1–4 and 5, many difficulties and sorrows befell Smollett. His mother-in-law, Mrs. Elizabeth Leaver of Jamaica, died at his house in Chelsea in early December 1762 (*PA* of 9 December). He lost his daughter on 2 April 1763.[22] After the daughter's death, from mid-June through July 1765 Smollett was in France and Italy.[23] The *LChr* of 30 June 1763 reported that on "the 16th of June Dr. Smollett set out for the South of France with his lady and family." The *GLDA* of 2 July adds, "Dr. Smollet has left his house at Chelsea, sold off all his furniture, &c. and retired into France." Presumably he began writing material that would end up in Volume 5 in 1763 while adding coverage of the Treaty of Paris for the revised quarto. Robert Adams Day thought Smollett wrote "most of volume 5" in 1764 at his home in Nice.[24] Smollett admits to having begun Volume 5 before leaving for France in a complaint to Dr. William Hunter on 11 June 1763 about the confiscation of his books at

James E. May

the Boulogne Custom House: "I can neither write the Preface to the modern Universal History, nor finish the Continuation of my own History of England, without having the Books before me."[25] Half of the volume had to be written in France, given the events covered (on page 244 he describes "the state of affairs on the 24 of June" 1763 in India). It is noteworthy that publication was not delayed so that he could read copy or oversee the press: he did not leave Nice to return to England until about 24 April and reached Boulogne in June, where he remained at least several weeks, probably reaching England in July about the time the last number was published.[26] His failure to read proof for Volume 5 suggests that Smollett may not have been directly involved in correcting proof for the earlier *Continuation* issues. Not surprisingly, I have located no variant states for Nos. 41–50 except those involving press figures and other mechanical features.

Advertisements for Volumes 1–4 of *Continuation* in late January do not mention the fifth volume as forthcoming (e.g., *StJC* 24 January 1765), and no single-leaf prospectus is known describing the work, as by detailing its plates (Smollett and Baldwin apparently had learned not to promise a specific number of plates). Brack notes that as early "as 4 March 1765, the *Salisbury Journal* announced the first number" of Volume 5 of the *Continuation* would be published "on Saturday, 30 March."[27] The earliest advertisement for Volume 5 that I have seen appears on 16 March in *LEP*: "Saturday, the 30th Instant, will be published, Price 6d. Embellished with the Heads of the Right Hon. John Earl of Bute and John Wilkes, Esq; both finely engrav'd by Miller and Hall. Number I of The Fifth and Last Volume of the Continuation of the Complete History of England. By T. Smollett, M.D. Containing the History of the late Spanish War, and an impartial Account of our Political Dispute. This Volume will make Ten Numbers, printed and ornamented in the same Manner as the former Volumes, and will be publish'd weekly, without Interruption." The advertisement was rerun on 21–23 March, and much the same advertisement appeared in *PA* of 23 and 28 March and *LChr* of 23–26 and 26–28 March, noting publication "Saturday next" and adding that "Any Person inclined to have the above work . . . [in] Weekly Numbers, may begin with No. 1 . . . by giving Notice to their Bookseller or News Carriers." Publication was announced in *LlEP* of 27–29 March, *LEP* and *LChr* of 28–30 March, and *PA* and *Gazetteer and New Daily Advertiser* (*GNDA*) of 30 March. With a second plate to induce buyers to begin, No. 1 was able to yoke the heads of the Earl of Bute and John Wilkes, presented at times as antagonists in the text. Those plates remind us of what was implied by advertisements noting that the history contains an "impartial Account of our Political Dispute." As for the first volume but not the second through fourth, the numbers of Volume 5 usually kept to the announced weekly schedule. No. 2, with head of Lord Clive by Taylor, was apparently published on 6 April (*LChr* of 6–9 April and *GNDA* of 6 April, *PA* of 8

April). No. 3 appeared 13 April ("last Saturday" in *GNDA* of 18 April). Although no "this day" advertisements for No. 4 have been located, it must have appeared 20 April, for the *StJC* announced on 27 April that No. 5 was delayed due to "an unforeseen accident at the press" and would appear 4 May. No. 5 was published 4 May as promised (*PA*; following "tomorrow" in *LlEP* of 1–3 May). Although no announcement has been found for No. 6, it could have been delayed no more than a week, for on 25 May the *PA* advertised the "7th Number . . . this Day published." On 8 and 22 June the *PA* announced publication "this day" of Nos. 8–9, noting maps of the Philippines and of Florida issued with the two. The tenth and final number, dated 1 July 1765 on Ee8/449, was published 13 July (*PA* of 6 July noting "Saturday next"), about the time of Smollett's return to London. Its many advertisements typically included a list of all the volume's plates (*GNDA* of 13–15 July, *StJC* of 13 July, *LlEP* on 15 July, *LEP* of 25–27 July, *LChr* of 27 July). On the whole, the numbers of Volume 5 were not well advertised and did not sell sufficiently to require any resetting. Moreover, this sequel did not tell a story with enough popular appeal. Before long, the sixteen volumes with 228 plates were offered bound for four pounds and ten shillings—binding Volume 5 added a shilling to the price in boards (*PA* of 6 and 16 September 1765).

Volumes 1–4 contain fifty copperplates including six maps (two each in Volumes 1–3); the forty-four portraits are decreasingly divided between the four volumes: fourteen, twelve, eight, and ten. All these plates but perhaps one portrait (York) and most of the maps had to be recut to meet demand. Volume 5 added seven portraits and four maps, none of which were recut. The plates are listed in directions to the binder at the ends of Volumes 4 and 5 and are fully described in the appendix. Although the plates in Smollett's *Complete History* were more plentiful and valuable, including some superb fold-out historical scenes unlike any engraving in *Continuation*,[28] the portraits and especially maps distributed with the *Continuation* were still important for selling the issues as testified by advertisements. Engravings were relatively expensive and so their presence greatly enhanced the value of the sixpenny numbers. Some of the plates were probably included not so much as illustrations of persons in the text but rather as inducements to purchase the text. That seems true, for instance, of Charles Churchill, whose name is never mentioned in Volume 5 but whose plate faces a page denouncing "writers in the opposition" for retailing "with peculiar virulence, all the calumnies" ever uttered against "the Scottish nation; some of them so gross and absurd, that they could not possibly obtain credit but among the very dregs of the people" (118). Although Churchill, whose *Apology Addressed to the Critical Review* had attacked Smollett and Archibald Hamilton (the printer of the *CR* and the *Continuation*), had died 4 November 1764 in Boulogne, his portrait was still topical when it appeared with No. 47, published 25 May (*PA*). That same month the *Universal Magazine* carried a biographical account, and numerous editions of his works were published in 1765. Volume 5's portraits of Churchill and his friend the politician John Wilkes, the principal author of the *North Briton* to which Churchill also contributed, were engraved by Miller. Miller makes Churchill appear angry and cruel relative to the original he adapted: J. S. C. Schaak's oil portrait (1763–1764). Similarly, he portrays the cross-eyed Wilkes as somewhat crazed.[29] These plates have a satirical thrust—the Wilkes portrait faces a page noting that the *North Briton* "was insolent and attrocious beyond the example of all former oppositions" (5:211).[30] Advertisements stressing the combined plates of the Earl of Bute and Wilkes in No. 41 surely caught the public's interest.

One measure of the importance and cost of plates can be found in 1748 advertisements for plates supplementing Tindal's translation and continuation of Rapin's *History of England*: "One Hundred Heads of Illustrious Persons, engrav'd by Mr. Houbraken, &c., proper to be bound with Mr. Rapin's History, and Mr. Tindal's Continuation, Price 6d. each Head, any of which may be had singly" (20–23 February 1748, *LEP*).[31] Now for the former price of an engraving one received three sheets of history with an engraving! Even a competitor underpricing both the Tindal and Smollett histories, William Ryder's *A New History of England*, sold in fourteen pocket volumes (priced one shilling sixpence sewn and two shillings bound and published monthly beginning May 1761 by S. Crowder and J. Wilkie), boasted eight copperplates per volume (*GEP*, 25 April 1761). The portraits in Smollett's work strike me as distinctly more elegant than those in Tindal's and Rider's histories, typically being mounted in a more refined yet adorned oval frame without any pedestal base.

As had Smollett's proposals for the *Complete History*, those for the *Continuation* made much of plates from the beginning: "May 3, 1760. Proposals for Printing in Weekly Numbers, A Continuation . . . Conditions . . . [following the stipulation of forty weekly three-sheet numbers] upwards of Fifty Copper-plate Heads of eminent and illustrious Persons, . . . Plans of Battles, Maps, &c. engraved by Strange, Grignion, Ravenet, Miller, &c. and delivered in the Course of the Work, without any farther Expence to the Subscribers" (6–8 May 1760, *LEP*). When a shortened version of the proposal appears in the *PA* of 20 May, Aliamet, a fifth engraver, is added. Besides offering more plates than Tindal's history, Smollett's boasted more prominent engravers, with advertisements usually naming artists after the subjects of plates (something not regularly seen in advertisements for Tindal's). The engravers for plates in Smollett's characteristically signed all their work (no plate is unsigned in all cuts except Miller's of author Charles Churchill in Volume 5, identified as "the late Mr. Churchill . . . by Miller" in *PA* of 25 May 1765). The forty-four portrait plates in Volumes 1–4 were cut

by eight engravers: twelve by Aliamet, six by Alexander Bannerman (sign-
ing "Benerman" for two of Devonshire and for Kingsley and "Bennarman"
for Lionel Sackville), four by William Philip Benoist, one by Fouquet (that
of Forrest in two cuts, but not a third cut signed "—B—," very probably by
Benoist, who cut this same drawing for John Entick's *The General History
of the late War* [London: Dilly, 1765]), one by Charles Grignion, fourteen
by Johann Sebastian Miller (sometimes, as in one of two cuts of General
Townshend and both of Saunders, signed with his German-born name,
"Müller"), two by Simon François Ravenet, and four by William Sherlock.
Three engravers signed the seven portraits in Volume 5: Miller cut two, and
John Hall and Isaac Taylor, who did not contribute engravings to Volumes
1–4, cut three and two respectively (Miller alone of those engraving for
Volumes 1–4 was commissioned to cut plates for Volume 5). Of artists contributing to *Continuation*, Benoist, Grignion, Miller, Ravenet, and Sherlock
cut plates for the octavo *Complete History*; and Grignion cut the frontispiece
for the quarto of Volume 1 (drawn, as was Volume 2's, by Francis Hayman),
and Miller cut that for Volume 2 and designed and cut those for Volumes
3–4. Also, Aliamet, Bannerman, Benoist, and Miller cut plates for early issues of the *BM*. As for the maps, the celebrated mapmaker Thomas Kitchin
signed his maps of Germany, Newfoundland, and the Philippines (adding
"Geog^r"); Thomas Jefferys signed his of France (one state is unsigned) but
did not that of the West Indies attributed to him in advertisements; John
Spilbury signed that of North America 1761 (presumably another recut the
design, for a second engraving dated 1763 is unsigned); and "J. Prockter"
signed that of Florida. I have not identified the engravers of unsigned maps
of the East Indies, the Caribbe Islands, and Havanna. Advertisements attributed the Newfoundland and Philippines maps to Kitchin, who had cut the
superb map of Great Britain in the *Complete History*, and the maps of France
and the West Indies to Thomas Jefferys, styling him "Geographer to his
Majesty." Most of the engravers have sufficient reputations to be included
in Thomas Mortimer's 1763 guide to artists.[32]
      Baldwin's advertisements always plug artists with the best reputations.
All but one of Aliamet's twelve plates are advertised with notice that he cut
them, and most or all by Miller and Ravenet are advertized with reference
to them. But Bannerman, who cut six plates (and even more for Smollett's
BM during 1760–1763), is not mentioned in any advertisements seen. To
puff sales, the *LEP*'s advertisement 7–9 April 1761 for No. 26 again states
that the engravers include "Strange, Grignion, Ravenet, Aliamet, Miller,
&c.," but Sir Robert Strange cut none, Grignion only one (George III), and
Ravenet but two. Strange is mentioned among the engravers as late as 9
April 1761 (*LEP*) but is dropped from such catalogues of artists as early as
29 January 1762 (*LEP*, noting only "Grignion, Ravenet, Aliamet, &c."). Presumably, Strange was supposed to cut a plate, and another, perhaps one of

his former apprentices, took over the work. Some of the plates are said to be cut from drawings or paintings by the artists, and, when these are of current heroes or royals, they were executed by the more celebrated engravers, particularly Aliamet. For instance, the plate of Colonel Coote is from Aliamet's "original drawing" (*LEP* of 7–9 April 1761), and those of Halifax, Louisa (late queen of Denmark), and Queen Charlotte are from a "painting" by him. But Miller too is so credited, as for that of Thomas Cumming, "drawn from the Life, and engrav'd by John Miller" (*LEP* of 24 January). Smollett's regard for Aliamet is indicated by his choice of him to cut his own portrait for the frontispiece. Smollett had arranged for Aliamet's engraving of Queen Charlotte (from his painting) to appear in the November 1761 issue of his *BM*, a month before it or a similar engraving was issued with No. 35. Attention to this plate of Charlotte dominates advertisements for the issue (she had arrived in England only in September): "Proprietors of the British Magazine hope" the plate—worth at least "Three Shillings" but given gratis—will "convince the Public of their Endeavours to oblige their Subscribers." The most frequent advertisement notes, "The abovementioned Print was engraved by Aliamet, who engraved Mr. Pine's Prize Picture, voted to him by the Society for the Encouragement of Arts and Sciences" (*LEP* of 28 November). Baldwin made double use of some engravings for his *London Magazine*, such as John Spilsbury's "new map of North America" in its 1763 volume (the second, 1763 cutting of this map, found in some copies of *Continuation*). Partly in response to public recognition that the same plates were being sold in multiple publications, a few plates are publication-specific: that of Cumming has below the caption "See Vol II. p. 271" (the page it faces), and Volume 3's "A New Map of the Caribbee Islands . . . 1761" has centered over the frame: "Engraved for Smollet's Continuation of the History of England." Since generally the same plate could not produce enough impressions to serve the needs of both the *BM* and *Continuation*, drawings, not plates, were doubly used. For instance, the same profile portrait in reverse and in different frames occurs of Field Marshall Keith unsigned in the *BM* of February 1760 (facing 1:81) and signed by Miller in *Continuation* (facing 2:357, issued in March 1761 with #25); and the same drawing of Marquis of Granby with different frames is cut by "I. Hall" in April 1760 *BM* and by Aliamet in the *Continuation* (4:44, issued with #1 in May 1760). This coordination did not always occur: different drawings were cut for portraits of Halifax in the *BM* (by Bannerman, August 1761) and *Continuation* (by Aliamet, facing 1:39) and Edward Duke of Yorke (by Walker in *BM* of April 1760 and by Ravenet in *Continuation*, 2:252).

As occurred also for the serialized *Complete History of England*, the engravings, distributed one, sometimes two, to an issue, did not accompany the issue numbers they illustrated. Presumably the time when the plates were printed largely determined in which issues they were distributed. No doubt intentional, this system encouraged consumers to continue subscribing to the entire multivolume work so that they could obtain the illustrations for texts already bought and the text for illustrations already bought. It also allowed the publisher to offer the plate of someone then currently in the news while they were in the spotlight rather than a year later when the relevant text would appear. For instance, a portrait of the Marquis of Granby, designed to illustrate issue No. 31 (not published until July 1761), was issued in May 1760 with No. 1 when his leadership of troops in the European war was in the papers. Also, with fifty plates in Volumes 1–4, the disjunction allowed a plate to accompany each issue (with margin enough to overcome gaps caused by delays), a distribution impossible if plates appeared with issues they illustrated. For instance, the last plate in Volume 4 appears on page 254 (in sheet Q), there being no plates in the volume's last third. This disjunction of engravings and text prevented delays resulting from the failure of engravers to provide the plates for specific issues, though eventually it delayed the publication of the final numbers of Volume 4 and the last number of Volume 5. The maps were more often delayed than the portraits: No. 38 (24 April 1762) contained the map of the East Indies, though it was to be bound in No. 3; No. 40 contained those of France and the West Indies, intended to illustrate Nos. 16 and 23; and Nos. 48 and 49 contained maps of the Philippines and Florida intended to illustrate Nos. 43 and 46.

The bibliographical appendix first describes the plates at their ideal positions stipulated by the directions to the binder, but it also lists the plates accompanying each issue. That second listing by issue is possible because newspaper advertisements for numbers consistently noted the plate sold with an issue (and periodically ran summaries of plates published to date). Corroborative evidence for when and with what issue the plates were published comes from copies, such as May4, May5, and Bibliothèque Nationale (PN), wherein the plates are bound with issues with which they were sold, without regard to the directions to binders. PN Volume 1 has all thirteen portrait plates issued with Nos. 1–10 (it lacks the map of Germany issued with No. 4); similarly, PN Volume 2 has all twelve plates issued with Nos. 11–20. May 4 Volume 1 contains thirteen plates, twelve issued with Nos. 1–10, all of which are also in PN—only the adjacent No. 11 of Henley is out of place, and the map of Germany and plate of Yorke Earl of Hartwicke are missing. May 5 Volume 1 has fourteen plates, nine issued with Nos. 1–10 and five others that accompanied Nos. 11–12, 17, and 19–20. These three copies of Volume 1 all have General Townsend, Marquis of Granby, Saunders, Woolfe, and Edward Duke of York, though the cuts were intended for other volumes (respectively, Volumes 3, 4, 3, 3, and 2). May 4 Volume 2 (with all first settings of the text) has eleven plates for diverse volumes, all issued with Nos. 11–20 but Amherst, issued with No. 21; of the eleven, all but Amherst are found in PN Volume 2 (with all first settings but for second in sheets A–I), which has all twelve plates issued with Nos. 11–20 and only those, bound between pages 16/17 in the order they were issued. PN's Volume 3 has all the plates issued with Nos. 21–30 except General Amherst, presumably issued with No. 21.[33]

As references to the newspapers demonstrate, advertisements contain information supplementing that offered by the plates themselves, in rare cases indicating the artist for an unsigned plate. The advertisements do not duplicate the captions on the plates; for instance, "Edward" and "Augusta" precede "Duke of York" and "Princess Dowager of Wales" on the plates but never in advertisements for their issues. The plate captioned "Thomas Cumming" is always named "Thomas Comyns" in advertisements that provide additional information on him (e.g., 24 January 1761, *LEP*)—the directions spell the surname "Cumming." (The directions sometimes contain variants from the caption on the plates, as using "Wolfe" for the General when the plate reads "Woolfe.") Encomiastic comments and language are sometimes added to the newspapers' listings of subjects, as "late brave" before "General Wolfe" (3 June 1761, *LEP*), the addition to Cumming: "Comyns, who plan'd the Success and Expedition [*sic*] against Senegal; drawn from the Life, and engrav'd by John Miller" (24 January 1761, *LEP*); or "Colonel Coote, who bravely distinguished himself this Wai [*sic*] in the East-Indies" (9 April 1761, *LEP*). These additions underscore the use of patriotic enthusiasm to sell the *Continuation*. Claims in advertisements about the maps often contain additions. No. 4, for example, contains an "accurate whole Sheet Map of Germany, from the Berlin Atlas," a source that would otherwise be unrecorded (7 June 1760, *PA*). Some advertisements contain lists of plates that add information, as the description of the last map as "a new and correct whole Sheet Map of the Seat of War in the Empire of Germany, as also in the Kingdom of Prussia, with the adjacent Countries" (2 August, *LEP*). Here and with advertisements for other maps, the size of the maps is misrepresented: the map of Germany is on a *half*, not a whole, sheet—examination of the paper for tranchefiles and watermarks confirms what the size indicates. There are no whole-sheet maps in this work though several are called such.[34] The maps are usually printed on unmarked paper like that employed for printed sheets; whereas, the portraits are nearly always printed on a heavier stock typical of plates (most on a paper stock with a Strasbourg lily watermark).

Advertisements were often frequent and lengthy at the start of the series and whenever disruptions occurred and volumes were begun and finished. Only four issues appear not to have been announced; these occur in periods when advertisements are few for issues announced and when Smollett is in prison (Nos. 19 and 23) or in France (Nos. 44 and 46). Widespread advertisement of No. 45, announcing a delay caused by an "unforeseen accident at the press" (*PA, GNDA, LEP, LlEP,* at least from 4 to 10 May 1765) helped make up for the failure to promote Nos. 44 with a chart of Havanna and 46 with Newfoundland map (issues with maps were normally heavily advertised). Beginning in early 1762, advertisements for the reserialization of *Complete History* numbers note the publication of *Continuation* numbers. Usually the same newspaper issue will carry advertisements for one or the other work, though there are issues with advertisements for both (*LEP* of 13–16 February 1762 has lengthy advertisements for *Complete History* No. 3 and *Continuation* No. 36). Baldwin sensibly staggered advertisements over a two- to four-week interval for each issue, with forward- and backward-facing and this-day announcements. For instance, No. 26 is "This Day" in 7–9 April 1761 issues of the *LEP* and *WEP* (rerun 9–11 April), and then "This Day" in *LChr* of 16–18 April; No. 27 is "this day" in 23–25 April *LEP* (rerun as this day in 7–9 May), and 25 April *PA* (rerun 9 May); but "last Saturday" in 30 April–2 May *GEP*; No. 28 is "Saturday next" in 12–14 May *LEP* and *StJC*; "This day" in 14–16 May *LEP* and *GEP* and 16 May *PA*; then "Last Saturday" in 26–28 May *StJC*. For Volumes 1–4, the most common "this day" announcements occur in the *LEP* and *PA*, and initial issues of Volume 5 are announced in *LEP* and final in *PA*, but great use is also made of the *GNDA*. (Baldwin did run some advertisements in the *PL, LlEP,* and some other papers, but those noted for Nos. 26–28 seem to be his principal venues for London advertisements.)

The revised edition in two quarto volumes, intended to carry forward Smollett's reputation as a historian, reaches only to the Treaty of Paris, excluding the second half of Volume 5's text, but including relevant entries from its index.[35] Newspaper advertisements record the progress of the edition. In the *LEP* of 25–27 April 1765, about a month after the fifth volume is announced as forthcoming, in an advertisement for No. 3 of the *Complete History*, the public is advised that "An Edition of Dr. Smollett's Continuation complete, in two Volumes in Quarto, with the Author's last Corrections, is in the Press and will be published about November next." That due date was immediately pushed back to "the Beginning of next winter, to accommodate Gentlemen, who have desired to purchase the work in that Size" (*GNDA* of 30 April, *LChr* of 30 April–2 May, *LlEP* of 1–3 May, *LEP* of 4–7 May). In late January, the public was told that the quartos, with "a full and accurate Index to the whole Work in that Size," would "be published next Month" (*PA* of 29 January 1766, repeated in *GNDA* the next day, with the boast that "Since its first appearance in 1758, near twenty thousand copies have been sold: a circumstance unknown in any age or country"). These advertisements imply that the quarto *Continuation* was being printed; however, it does not appear until early summer, after a delay greater than might be expected. In early June advertisements rebuilt expectation: "Thursday, June 12, will be published, Elegantly printed in Two Volumes Quarto,

With the Author's last Corrections, and copious Indexes to the whole Work in that Size, The Continuation . . . from the Treaty of Aix la Chapelle, to the End of the Year 1764, including, A Complete History of the Late War . . . Gentleman who purchased the former Volumes in Quarto, to which a full and accurate Index is given . . . are desired to complete their Setts as soon as possible" (*LlEP*, 2 June 1766). Baldwin often pointed out to owners of the *Complete History* in quarto (1757–1758) that these volumes contained no index. The urgency added at the end is sales rhetoric thought to be effective. Note that the advertisement misleadingly indicates the history reaches to 1764, the date to which Volume 5 is said to reach (repeated in the *PA*'s "this day" advertisements of 12 and 22 June). Baldwin's advertisements for Smollett's *Travels through France and Italy* mention the volumes (e.g., *GEP* of 8–10 July 1766). The price in boards held firm: "30 shillings" in the *LChr* on 3 June 1769. Baldwin never announced a price for bound volumes (gentlemen were expected to bind them to match their sets of the *Complete History* in quarto).

The delay in publishing the quarto might have been due to the production of the indices for the *Complete History* and the *Continuation*, that is, the adaptation of indices already published, but Smollett is unlikely to have performed that task or to have read proof. As will be noted, he did not revise the section of Volume 5 reproduced in the quarto. Baldwin's publication of Smollett's two-volume *Travels* on 9 May (*PA*) might have encouraged further delay, for bringing both works out the same month might have impacted sales, and Baldwin might have hoped that a good reception of the *Travels* would increase sales of the quarto *Continuation*; however, he probably expected modest sales for the quartos, which seem to have had a small press run and lacked a fine-paper issue, of which Hume's history could boast.[36] They were mainly advertised in notes within advertisements for other editions. As noted in the appendix, copies—held by fewer than a dozen institutional libraries—were diversely bound, most at considerable expense, with labels numbering them Volumes 5 and 6.

We do not know what Smollett was paid for the revision, but he had finer motivations than money, wishing to leave posterity a text that would stand comparison to the great histories of contemporaries like David Hume. Smollett, in a letter to Richard Smith of May 8, 1763, after speaking of the time spent writing the "four first volumes of the History of England," wrote, "I spent the best part of a year in revising, correcting, and improving the Quarto Edition which is now going to Press and will be continued in the same Size to the late Peace. Whatever Reputation I may have got by this work has been dearly bought by the Loss of Health."[37] Note that from spring 1763 he intended to reprint only the material through the Treaty of Paris. Even allowing for exaggeration (I suspect that Smollett included in "the best part of a year" time spent completing the first four volumes), his claim to have spent much time in revision sounds genuine, as does the motivating satisfaction with the reputation the work had earned him. He had revised the *Complete History*, and he surely wanted to correct his historical record, some of it written before all the historical dust had settled, and purge portions of the text no longer felt to deserve space in the record. Moreover, there were stylistic problems, such as wordy expressions that surely irritated him. In editorial terms, the quartos contain his final authorial intentions. The quartos contain the fourth or fifth edition of the material in most volumes, though only the second edition of that material reprinted from Volume 5. Unlike the quartos of the *Complete History*, these new volumes contain no frontispieces or maps, fittingly underscoring, as does the quarto format, serious scholarly pretensions. Basker notes that Hume instructed his publisher Andrew Millar that his history was not to include even frontispieces, that his would not be "the better for them," though they had helped sell Smollett's *Complete History*.[38] Probably Smollett appreciated the convenience of the quarto format, of having but four volumes of the *Complete History* in place of eleven or seven and but two of the *Continuation*—his own reference to the *Complete History* within the text is to the quartos (e.g., 3:441–42), the edition that he took with him to France.[39] Smollett marked his revisions on octavo copies of Volume 1 with first settings in sheets A–H and second thereafter, of Volume 2 with second settings in A–Dd and possibly thereafter, and with first settings of Volumes 3–4 (indicative variants are noted in the appendix). Many compositorial errors introduced by second settings of Volumes 1–2, overlooked by Smollett, entered the quarto text.

Besides Volume 5's pages 193–450, Smollett also cut the volume's six-page preface and a paragraph on peace initiatives between Berlin and Vienna, outside the closing focus (5:191–92). Some sections in Volumes 1–4 were cut wholesale, including the patriotic preface (1:iii–vi) and supplementary material at the end of Volumes 2 and 3, which might well be seen as filler: "Justifying Proofs, Published by Authority at Berlin" as well as its introductory paragraph (Volume 2's Ee1^v/434–Gg7^v/478), and a vindicating correction of what is said at the end of the *Complete History* about Alderman Heathcote as well as the inclusion of Commodore Moore's comments to the historical narrative within Nos. 23–24 of the *Continuation* (Volume 3's Ff5/441.11–Gg8/463). Some deleted passages had added variety and a degree of entertainment but were more suited to the *British Magazine* than this history. These include the account of "A Lady murdered by her coachman," as the marginal gloss characterizes it (3:386.13–387.5), the "Remarkable story of miss Bell," a murdered prostitute (4:16.17–19.5), and the "remarkable will" of Lieutenant-General Henry Hawley, with its lengthy transcript in the footnotes (3:88.26–95.2). While such sensational news items were understandably cut from the version Smollett wished handed to posterity, other omissions involve transcripts offered as documentation. These include many footnotes, such as the following: *"Abstract of an Act for better supplying the Cities of* London *and* Westminster *with Fish,"* a transcript taking up most of 3:327.A–330.B; *"Abstract of the Act lately passed for preventing the excessive Use of* Spirituous Liquors," another taking up most of 3:308–12; the "Treaty of Peace" with the Cherokee, "Dec. 26, 1759," on 3:399.A.1–401.B.34 (ult. l.); *"Copy of a Letter from Mr. Secretary* Pitt, *to the several Governors . . . in North-America,"* 23 August 1760, transcription on bottom halves of 4:4–5 (Smollett was probably inclined to give less attention to Pitt's actions); two pages of "orders" to soldiers issued by Sir John Mordaunt on 2:12–14; "An account of the barbarous manner, in which the Russian, Austrian, and Saxon troops, laid waste the marche of Brandeburgh" in October 1760, "Published at Berlin by Authority," taking up over half an octavo sheet, on 4:79.A.1–90; and the capitulation agreement for Belleisle signed by Keppel on 7 June 1761 (on 4:260.A–264). Smollett cut from the quarto much transcribed material supplementing his own account of the history. He also condensed and increased its narrative flow by placing text in footnotes. Along with examples of horrendous crimes moved to footnotes (e.g., 1:108.14–109.12), much of the text reduced to footnotes involves parliamentary acts, especially related to economics, such as the paragraph glossed as "Additional clause to the money bill" in 1755 (1:242.14–30) made into a footnote on I:113 and the gloss cut.[40] In the light of his deletions, we should suppose Smollett thought valuable for arguments on foreign policy those lists and transcriptions left in the text, such as of "forces and fleets of Great Britain," including English and French men-of-war at the end of the reign of George II, showing Britain "is more than a match for all the maritime powers of Europe" (4:132–43). More text than was reprinted in the quartos could have been, for there are several blanks (172 and 366), a final advertisement leaf, lines lost to starting anew second entries for Volume 5 in the index, and a decrease in the total number of lines per page in the latter half of Volume II: Volume I has forty-seven or forty-eight lines per page (the *Complete History* quarto volumes have forty-eight usually), but Volume II by gathering Aa typically has forty-six lines per page. Perhaps cuts were encouraged to keep the price of the two volumes equivalent to competing histories.[41]

Besides the deletions, Smollett made extensive revisions and some additions, particularly to foreign affairs. The biggest substantive changes (adding the most value to the revision) involve new information on affairs in the East Indies, particularly military campaigns in India and its geography (e.g., the expansion of 1:205–11 in I:93–98 quarto, including the addition of I.93.31–94.26).[42] One of the lengthiest additions concerns Colonel Ford's ("Forde's" in quarto, though "Ford" is the surname in its index) campaign against the French on a plain near Golapool and then his siege of Masulipatam, detailed on II:3.3–5.7, which replaces a single sentence in the octavo (3:205.1–5). Further expansion follows on Captain Richard Maitland's expedition and its aftermath (as new sentences in II.6.1–7). Other changes are short corrections of fact, as that nabobs were appointed under the authority of the tributary princes, rather than the khan's (1:200.6–7 versus I:91.11). Footnotes are added on geography and on the movements of ships and men (I:94.A–B and I.96). The spellings of names are corrected as "Anawerde" at 1:205.18 and 205.28 to "Anaverdy" on I:94, and "Gingen" to "de Gingins" (206.25, 209.27 vs. I:95.10 and 96.34); "Sundah Saheb" is regularly changed to "Chunda Saib" (e.g., 1:209.33 vs. I:96.38—thrice on 210–11). Some North American names are similarly corrected: "Frontignac" in 1:271–75, for instance, is changed thrice to "Frontenac" on I:127–28.

Some alterations suggest the pressures put upon the historian by contemporaries and may call into question the impartiality claimed by or for Smollett in prefaces, advertisements, and reviews in the *CR*. Among these are significant changes in the account of Major-General Edward Braddock's disastrous march on Fort Duquesne (1:258–60). Smollett's original account severely criticizes not only Braddock's carelessly inept advance but also the valor of the regular troops when ambushed by the French and Indians. For instance, the phrase "particularly of the regulars" following "confusion" in the octavo (1:258.22) was cut in the quarto (I.120.45). Also, the octavo's remark that Braddock "himself . . . discovered at once the greatest intrepidity, and the highest imprudence; for, instead of ordering a retreat till he could scour" the thickets (1:258.26–29) is reduced by the quarto to "himself, instead of scouring" (I.120.47–121.1). From the description of the rout, Smollett cut the lengthy detailing of how "the provincial militia, so much despised by the general, that he made them march always in the rear . . . alone bravely formed, and advanced against the Indians: to which gallantry it was owing that the regulars were not all cut off" (1.259.21–35; missing at I:121.18). Perhaps for the same reasons he cut a remark crediting the French and Indians "who had cunningly given the whole army time to enter the defile before they began to fire" (1:258.18–20, omitted at I.120.43). Remarks critical of military leaders were deleted from other volumes as well, such as contradictory orders at 2:10.24–11.8. One cut from the North American theater sheds light both on a potential rationale for omitting some ignoble details and on Smollett's sense of the content and method proper to history: "Of these horrid ravages [by Indians] many dismal accounts have been published in our news-papers . . . but as a particular recital of them would lead us into detail too minute for a general history, we shall pass over those private calamities, and return to the public affairs of Europe" (1:275.23–30, later cut on I:128).

However, some corrections and added details must have resulted from further information, such as "four days after" (1:259.10) to "in a few hours"

(I:121.11) and "flight" to "flight, across a river which they had just passed" (I.121.13–14). Slight corrections of fact are scattered throughout the text, such as the changes of "Five days" (3:130.11) to "Ten days" (I:468.30) and of the Prussian army's size from 150,000 to 140,000 by changing "fifty" to "forty" (1:49.33, I.21.25). Some changes may result from new information on individuals that was gained in conversation or correspondence: "soldiers fell" (1:211.7) becomes "soldiers, under the command of Mr. Law nephew to the famous Law who schemed the Mississippi company, fell" (I:97.19–21), and, in praising the Spanish minister Don Ricardo Wall, Smollett added to the noun "gentleman" the ancestry note "of Irish extract" (1:86.28; I.33.5–6). Smollett often made a passionate effort to celebrate virtuous actions and individuals.

All changes that involve the major political powers deserve special scrutiny, offering potential insights into how Smollett's opinions changed in 1762–1766. There seems, for instance, to be greater allowance for the grounds offered by Maria Theresa, the "Empress Queen" of Hungary and Bohemia, in refusing England's request for troops to protect the Lowlands against France (I.133.25–34)—fear of Frederick of Prussia, whom Smollett had come to believe a formidable villain. This addition begins "a reason for her alliance with France," which alters "a pretence for her unnatural alliance" (1:286.8–9). Frederick is said to be "very free with the lives of his subjects" in an account of the Battle of Cunersdorf, 1759 (3:254.27–28), which leads Smollett to lament, "At no time, since the days of ignorance and barbarity, have the lives of men been squandered away with such profusion as in the course of this German war" (254.28–31). In *Continuation* Smollett was often passionate about the horrors that men do, and much of the history reads like an anti-war tract. New forthright assessments also deserve attention, such as the addition "Thus the late treaty with Russia, was virtually renounced" (I:141.14–15, added to 1:302.22) and the footnote conjecturing that the elector of Hanover was "more afraid of the P——n monarch than" of the French king (I:132, added to 1:284).

Revision to the octavos decreases throughout the work, mirroring the progression of corrections within the first volume. If we count as equal all substantive changes, whether a single word that may be non-authorial or a lengthy addition, we can graph the number of substantive changes through Volume 1 as follows: twenty-two substantive changes to page 50 of the octavo, twenty-one in pages 51–100, ten in 101–50, eleven in 151–200, fifty-two in 201–50, and seventy-one in 251–300; seven in 301–50, eight in 351–400 (but including substantial additions to 370–73), five in 400–50 (including four shifts of text into footnotes), and two in 451–80 (one authorial, a movement of text into footnote). Smollett's involvement in the middle of Volume 1 is evident from all the marginal glosses added between pages 229 and 245 (I:107–14—and the rephrasing of other glosses on 208 and 210). To Volume 1's last eighty pages, Smollett made no more than half a dozen substantive changes, but his attention to the section is suggested by at least nineteen new paragraph indentations. The insertion of new paragraphing to divide the longer paragraphs of the octavo occurs sporadically through stretches of Volumes 3–4 where few other authorial changes are suggested.[43] Although I have not collated all the work, it would appear that Smollett's revisions to later volumes involve progressively rarer passages thoroughly revised with new information and also very few stylistic changes of the sort common in Volumes 1 and occasional in Volume 2 (for instance, there are no stylistic revisions at all to 3:314–38 and 4:260–70 on II.53–64 and II:227–30). Other than to delete the preface and one paragraph on peace initiatives between Berlin and Vienna, outside the closing focus (191–92), Smollett appears not to have revised Volume 5. Only a few isolated corrections could be attributed to Smollett, most to the spelling of geographical locations.[44] Almost no substantive variants occur, and only a few accidental variants occur on each page, usually involving hyphenation, comma pointing, and case (occasionally the quarto places words like "protestant" in upper case).

The majority of verbal changes involve only one or two words, often nearly synonymous, like "ships of war" (I:130.26) for "men of war" (1:280.7), "march" (I:131.12) for "go" (1:281.19), and "persuaded" (I.133.8) for "misled" (1:285.16). Some changes remove the overuse of a word. Smollett must have cringed on noticing how often he had originally written "importing" (deleted from Volume 1 at 10.26, 12.16, 85.14, and altered to "implying" at 28.7, 34.22, 135.14 to "representing" at 19.20, and to "signifying" at 62.13). Revisions also hacked at unnecessary words, such as the following: "Finally" cut from sentences at 1:117.32 and 1:127.27 (I:52.30 and 57.14 quarto) and changed to "therefore" at 1:50.15 and "At length" at 1:55.31 (I.21.35 and 24.16); "While this was doing" at 1:259.1 changed to "Meanwhile" (I:121.5); "flatly refused" at 1:285.25 changed to "refused" (I:133.14); and "It must, however, be confessed, that" at 1:283.17, cut from I:132.8. Other common adjustments improve pronoun reference ("he" at 1:158.8 and 1:261.4 changed to "he, the doctor" at I:71.19 and to "their commander" at I.121.46, and "he" at 4.271.29 changed to "the prince" at II.231.4) or they insert qualifications (some hedging does occur, such as "seemingly" added at I:79.35 after "were" in "directions given were the very reverse of these professions" at 1:176.6–7). The absence of single-word variants from the quarto's unrevised reprinting of Volume 5 indicates that these verbal changes, occurring between more substantial changes and in the vicinity of authorial changes in paragraphing, should usually be accepted as authorial. These include changes in the tense of verbs throughout a passage (e.g., "may" to "might" at 1:241.27, 241.30, and 1:242.5, connected to "will" to "would" at 1:241.34, 1:242.6—all on I:113 quarto).

Authority ought also to be given to certain accidental changes never made by compositors, like the new paragraph divisions and, also, the insertion of periods to break up long sentences. In many instances, the creation of a new sentence is accompanied by clipping "and" between the independent clauses in the octavo (e.g., at 1:56.18, 155.28, 157.34, 254.21, 261.10, and 265.8). Also, there may be classes of consistently altered accidentals that lend a formal dignity to the text and are probably authorial, such as the regular change of "tho'" to "though"; however, changes involving commas, colons, and semicolons, hyphenation, and upper- and lowercase are more often compositorial errors than authorial interventions. There are dozens of compositorial blunders in the reprinting of Volume 1 octavo alone (e.g., "put" for "but" in the quarto's addition at I:133.31), the volume most carefully revised—proof that the quartos were not carefully read (thus arise such errors as "the the" at II.230.8). The quartos should never be used as a copy-text.

In conclusion, the *Continuation* was a popular success, written sometimes in haste with materials later removed or reduced to footnotes. But it was also a serious account of domestic and foreign affairs whose quarto, revised with some care and stripped of illustrations, was intended to be shelved by the distinguished and the learned alongside other great historical works. The bibliographical complexity of the octavo numbers has here been clarified by the identification of the first edition and succeeding octavo reprints (see the Appendix). The substantive revisions in the rare quarto edition have been shown to merit a critical edition of this important historical record and political commentary. From the variants recorded in that edition and from adapted source materials, scholars might gain much insight into Smollett's evolving response to English politics and policy, allowing insight into his intellectual and emotional development and into such subsequent works as *The History and Adventures of an Atom*. The satire in the *Atom* encourages a close examination of the degree to which Smollett in the *Continuation*, eager at times to support the Earl of Bute, maintained the impartiality that he and advertisements for the work claimed (*PA* of 6 September 1765)—his strongest attacks on the Duke of Newcastle, John Wilkes, and others accused of fomenting hate and practicing blind Whiggism occur just beyond the material reprinted from Volume 5 in the quarto. A new edition could produce a more thorough index than those in the originals, which overlook many parliamentary acts, locations, and battlefield leaders (as General Breidenbach noted above). But in any edition, the *Continuation* is a fascinating fusion of history and journalism, in part a chronicle but more valuable for an analytical and moral response to individual, social, and governmental actions by one of the most well-informed and enlightened men witnessing those events.

NOTES

1. This study and its appended descriptive bibliography are modeled on and sometimes supported by my "The Authoritative Editions of Smollett's *Complete History of England*" in *Tobias Smollett, Scotland's First Novelist: New Essays in Memory of Paul-Gabriel Boucé*, ed. O M Brack Jr. (Newark: University of Delaware Press, 2007), 240–305. Its account of the publication history benefits from O M Brack Jr.'s "Tobias Smollett Puffs His Histories" in *Writers, Books, and Trade: An Eighteenth-Century English Miscellany for William B. Todd*, ed. O M Brack Jr. (New York: AMS Press, 1994), 267–88, which records and transcribes proposals and advertisements for the first edition of the *Continuation*, particularly in the *Salisbury Journal*. As Brack has done, I correct certain errors and fill in omissions in Lewis M. Knapp's "The Publication of Smollett's *Complete History* . . . and *Continuation*," *Library*, fourth series, 16 (1935): 295–306. Knapp assumes that Volume 5 of the *Continuation* was not issued in numbers. In *Tobias Smollett: Doctor of Men and Manners* (Princeton, NJ: Princeton University Press, 1949), Knapp wrongly remarks that in summer 1765 Smollett was "completing the fifth and final volume of his *Continuation* . . . published in October 1765," 259–60. With characteristic indebtedness, Jeremy Lewis parrots this: Smollett, back in London in July, "busied himself completing the fifth and final volume of his *Continuation*." See *Tobias Smollett* (London: Pimlico, 2004), 249. Donald Greene's "Smollett the Historian: A Reappraisal" in *Tobias Smollett: Bicentennial Essays Presented to Lewis M. Knapp*, ed. G. S. Rousseau and Paul-Gabriel Boucé (New York: Oxford University Press, 1971), 25–56, is often called the best study of Smollett as a historian, though its main achievements were to show that Smollett was not a Tory partisan and wrote history better than David Hume. Greene shows no understanding of or regard for the textual history of the *Complete History* and *Continuation*, failing even to cite and quote from an authoritative edition (note the blunders in notes 1 and 8). Robert Adams Day's introduction and notes to his and Brack's edition of *The History and Adventures of an Atom* (Athens: University of Georgia Press, 1989) provide a more detailed and accurate account of Smollett's historical and political positions than any earlier essay treating the histories, though Day is not all-knowing, remarking, for instance, that Volumes 1–4 of the *Continuation* have "thirty-nine numbers." For the sorely needed edition or study relating *Continuation* to Smollett's other writings, James Basker's *Tobias Smollett: Critic and Journalist* (Newark: University of Delaware Press, 1988) is the most essential point of departure.

2. The phrasing "From the Treaty of Aix-la-Chapelle, 1748, to the Declaration of the War with Spain, 1762" is regularly added, as if a subtitle, beginning with advertisements for No. 40 (e.g., *London Evening Post* [*LEP*] of 22–24 July 1762 and 27–29 January 1763). Previous to this, advertisements defined the *Continuation* with other supplementary phrases: "Including a Complete History of the Present War" (*LEP* of 22–24 January 1761, 13–16 February 1762) and "from the Peace of Aix-la-Chapelle" (*Public Advertiser* [*PA*] of 21 February 1761). After Volume 5 was published with its account of the Treaty of Paris, Baldwin could honestly employ the title "Smollet's Continuation of his History of England, including a complete History of the late War" (*PA* of 22 June 1765). Given the publication of a "continuation" making it no longer "complete," the *Complete History* was sometimes referred to without

that adjective, as in a notice to "Purchasers of Dr. Smollett's History of England to the Peace of Aix la-Chapelle, in Seven Volumes Octavo" (*PA* of 19 November 1760).

3. Review of *Continuation of Mr. Rapin's History of England*, vol. 20, by Rev. Nicolas Tindal, in *Critical Review* (*CR*), 8 (July 1759), 44.

4. Volume 2 and 3 appeared in January and February 1758; the eighth in 1759; the multivolume set is recorded as ESTC T144217.

5. Six volumes based on most of these issues would be published in 1761 as the "fifth edition." The set is recorded as ESTC T140787.

6. Brack's treatment in "Tobias Smollett Puffs His Histories" is the most thorough. While Knapp attributes the "unprecedented sale" to "quite modern methods of advertising the *History* in the newspapers on a much larger scale than was customary at that period," he also recognizes that Smollett's "unerring sense of organization and . . . lively style, outdid contemporaneous historians in making history interesting and readable for the layman." See "The Publication," 299.

7. A much shorter account of Ochterlony and Peyton appeared in *PA* of 2 November 1759.

8. All quotations from the octavos are from first settings. I use Arabic numerals for volume numbers of the octavos and roman for those of the quarto. See the appendix for title and publication information.

9. Basker notes Smollett's reservations in his review of Hume's history about "reflecting" and "dogmatizing," which break the narrative flow; even some of Hume's "reflections" are found "superfluous." See Basker, *Tobias Smollett: Critic and Journalist*, 106–8, on this review in the *CR*, 2 ([December] 1756): 385–404. And Smollett's sneering at mere reporting of events, as "annals," is voiced in his review of the ninth volume of Tindal's *Continuation* of Paul Rapin de Thoyras's *History of England* (*CR*, 10 [{September} 1760]: 194).

10. Voltaire's protest of the case is excerpted in *BM* of November 1762, 3:589–90.

11. *LEP* of 7–9 August, *PA* of 13 August, and many other newspaper issues. Brack reprints the text of this advertisement as printed in the *LChr* of 23–26 August. See "Tobias Smollett Puffs His History," 277–78.

12. Some extant copies in incomplete sets have bound in them the plates issued with the numbers, ignoring the "Directions to the Binder," indicating some purchasers probably chose not to await completion of the work.

13. Aside from a single copy of No. 36 in the original blue wrappers in which they were presumably all sold, which Brack located at the Bodleian, none have been located. See Brack, "Tobias Smollett Puffs His History," 278–79; 285–86 n. 31.

14. Brack, "Tobias Smollett Puffs His History," 274–77. The prospectus, whose recto Brack reproduces in facsimile, is in the John Johnson Collection at the Bodleian Library. Brack notes the proposal was printed "on the wrappers of the *British, Gentleman's, London*, and other magazines," none of which have been traced, 274.

15. Brack reprints the text of this advertisement from the *LChr* of 23–26 August. "Tobias Smollett Puffs His History," 277–78.

16. Knapp gives the sentence as "three-months" and notes Smollett was in prison for eleven weeks. See *Tobias Smollett*, 191–96; see also Knapp's "Rex *versus* Smollett: More Data on the Smollett-Knowles Libel Case," *Modern Philology* 41 (1944): 221–27; and *Tobias Smollett*, 214–19 and 230–36, which notes Smollett was released from prison by 25 February 1761, perhaps on 23 February.

17. With no evidence that the novel was begun "much before the first number (January 1760) of the *British Magazine*," Robert Folkenflik and Barbara L. Fitzpatrick infer that "Probably a few chapters, perhaps more, were completed during Smollett's months in the King's Bench Prison." See *The Life and Adventures of Sir Launcelot Greaves*, in *The Works of Tobias Smollett* (Athens: University of Georgia Press, 2002), xix, 257, 265 n. 11.

18. See the remarks on typography within the appendix's description of Volume 1.A.

19. *LEP* of 11–13 December 1760. On 30 December the *LEP*, in advertising publication of No. 21, announced "Numbers 7, 8, 9, and 10, [had been] reprinted"; however, that claim may have been premature, for the notice is given two weeks later. See 17 January in *PA*, and 24 January in *LEP*.

20. An octavo slip at Cambridge University Library, 7850.c.54[7], in a box with thirteen printing proposals from the 1760 to the 1770s. The verso lists the "217 Copper-plates" for both titles in the sixteen-volume octavo set. The prospectus and advertisements accompanying it (*LChr* of 3 and 10 June and *Jackson's Oxford Journal* of 24 June) also offer the "Work complete, in Sixteen Volumes, Price 4 l. 16s. bound" and the *Continuation* in two quartos for thirty shillings.

21. I collated no more than a sample of the index. The altered substantives include tense changes and some word changes that might more loosely be considered simply spelling changes, as "whither" to "whether" and "route" to "rout."

22. The *LEP* of 5–7 April 1763 reported, "On Sunday died at her father's house at Chelsea, aged 15, Miss Elizabeth Smollet, daughter of Dr. Smollet."

23. Knapp, *Tobias Smollett*, 248–58.

24. Day, *The History and Adventures of an Atom*, l.

25. *The Letters of Tobias Smollett*, ed. Lewis M. Knapp (Oxford: Clarendon, 1970), 116; see also Knapp, *Tobias Smollett*, 249, noting the books were returned in six weeks and included the histories, twelve volumes of *CR*, and four of the *BM*.

26. Knapp uses Smollett's 15 July letter to Dr. Moore as evidence that he had returned to London. This evidence does not, however, preclude Smollett's arrival in late June, the time offered in Knapp's earlier essay. See *Tobias Smollett*, 258, and "The Publication," 306–7.

27. "Tobias Smollett Puffs His History," 279–80.

28. See my "Authoritative Editions," 244–45, and notes on the octavo edition's plates in its appendix, such as 275–76 on Volume 1's whole-sheet map of Great Britain by Kitchin and folding plates of the "Landing of Julius Caesar" by A. Walker and L. P. Boitard, Caractacus by F. Hayman and C. Grignion, and the conversion of the Druids by Hayman and Walker. These plates and others led Robert Dodsley to remark to John Scott Hylton on 29 February 1758: "I have seen some of the Cutts of Dr Smollet's History, & think as you say that . . . they alone will be worth the money [sixpence per issue]." See *The Correspondence of Robert Dodsley*, ed. James E. Tierney (Cambridge: Cambridge University Press, 1988), 343–44.

29. Schaak's portrait (at the National Portrait Gallery) is attached to the *Oxford Dictionary of National Biography* entry, along with two engravings dated 1763–1764 and 1765, by Mary Morris and Thomas Burford. The clothing and position of the head are identical in all three engravings to those of Schaak's, but Miller alters the expression more than the others did. Miller's plates of Churchill and of Wilkes are

not among those early portraits attached to the *Oxford DNB* webpages on the two men, and Miller's very early copy of Schaak's painting is not among those noted by James Sambrook in his entry on the poet, though other later engravings are noted. The attached images from the National Portrait Gallery for Wilkes include a full torso print by Miller that is even less flattering than the *Continuation*'s portrait.

30. Churchill is not cited in indices to the *Continuation*. Wilkes is not noted in the indices of Volume 4 or the quarto, for he is principally treated in Volume 5 after the point where the quarto stops reprinting the text. Volume 5's index notes him as the subject of pages 211–31.

31. Presumably these are for the octavo edition mentioned in the advertisement's previous paragraph; the Knaptons had offered illustrations with octavos of Rapin's *History of England* from their first volume in 1725.

32. Thomas Mortimer's *The Universal Director; or, the Nobleman and Gentleman's True Guide to the Masters and Professors of the Liberal and Polite Arts and Sciences* (London: J. Coote, 1763) identifies the following (by trade and with addresses): Francis Aliamet, "History and Portrait Engraver" in Soho, 3; Alexander Bannerman, "History and Architecture Engraver" in Leicester-Fields, 4; John Hall, "History and Portrait Engraver" in the Strand, 12; Thomas Jefferys, "Engraver, and Geographer to his Majesty" in the Strand, 15; Thomas Kitchen, "Geographer and Engraver to his Royal Highness the Duke of York" in Holborn, 17; [Johann] Sebastian Miller, "History and Portrait Designer and Engraver, Maiden-lane, Covent-garden," 18; Simon Ravenet, "History and Portrait Engraver" in Soho, 23; William Sherlock, "Miniature Painter and Engraver" in Soho, 25; and John Spilsbury, "Engraver and Map Dissector in Wood" in Drury-Lane, 27. Mortimer does not list the other artists employed on *Continuation*, but, aside from Fouquet and Prockter, they are identified in Michael Bryan's *Dictionary of Painters and Engravers: Biographical and Critical*, revised and edited by Walter Armstrong and Robert E. Graves, two vols. (London: George Bell, 1889): William Philip Benoist or "Benoit," born Normandy 1725, resided during the later half of his life in London, portrait engraver (portraits include Pope and Newton), died in 1780 (1:70); Charles Grignon ("Grignion" as spelled by his younger kinsman and in plates for *Complete History*), born London 1716, died 1810, helped found the Academy in 1750s, cut engravings for Bell's *British Poets* (1:602); and Isaac Taylor [senior], born Worcester 1730, died 1807, English engraver and book illustrator, whose "best work" is for Richardson's *Sir Charles Grandison* (2:555). This *Dictionary* adds the following about the other artists: Francis Aliamet, born 1734 in Abbeville, France, an engraver like his more famous older brother Jacques (born 1728), came to London after studying in Paris and worked for a time under Sir Robert Strange (1:12–13); Alexander Bannerman, born Cambridge 1730, living in Cambridge in 1770 (death date unknown), engraved for Horace Walpole's *Anecdotes of Painting* and Alderman Boydell's collection (1:76); Johann Sebastian Müller ("known in this country under the name of Miller" [though the National Portrait Gallery uses "Müller"]), born Nuremberg 1720, emigrated to England with his brother in 1744, engraved for Newton's edition of Milton and the Boydell Collection (2:185); Simon François Ravenet, born Paris 1706, settled in London c. 1750, died 1774; worked for Hogarth and Alderman Boydell and engraved portraits of Hume, Alexander Pope, and James Thomson (2:349); William Sherlock, painter and engraver, born Dublin 1738,

studied at St. Martin's Lane Academy and later under J. P. Le Bas in Paris (plates for Smollett's histories noted in the article, 2:493).

33. PN vol. 2 has Lionel Sackville and Henley-#11, Charles Townshend-#12, Grafton-#13, Devonshire and Tyrrel-#14, Brett-#15, Pocock-#16, Monckton-#17, Grenville-#18, Blakeney-#19, and Carolina-#20. PN vol. 3 has Cumming-#22, Kingsley-#23, Downe-#24, Keith-#25, Coote-#26, Loudoun-#27, Ferdinand-#28, George III-#29, and Lawrence and Forrest-#30.

34. I caution those who grab at the first advertisement located that my review of notices for *Continuation* in London papers located many containing erroneous information. For instance, on 24 January 1765, the *StJC*, after listing the *Complete History* in eleven volumes, offered "Another edition of the same Work, in Twelve Volumes Octavo, brought down to the End of the Year 1763," which cannot exist. Another in the *PA* of 12 June 1766 wrongly notes for the sixteen-volume edition "217 Copper-plates, by Strange, Grignion, &c." Strange did not cut a plate for the edition, and "217" is the number of plates in the fifteen-volume edition. A number of conflicting dates for issue publication can only be resolved by supposing the reprinting of old or erroneous information, as when the *LEP* of 25–27 April 1765 notes No. 3 appeared 20 April, a week after it had.

35. The first quarto volume reprints the octavo text through Volume 3's O4^v/200 (final paragraph of Volume I quarto begins "The City of Quebec being reduced"); the second reprints text from the next paragraph through 5:193.6. The octavo text of Volume 1 is in the quarto on I:3–225.10 (through the first paragraph); Volume 2's pp. 3–434, on I:225–414.14; Volume 3's pp. 3–441.10, on I:414–II:109.38; Volume 4's 3–370, on II:109–277 (through the second paragraph); Volume 5's pp. 9–193, on II:277–365 (followed by two lengthy indices, the first for the *Complete History* in quarto, adapted from that in the eleventh octavo volume). Also, the index to Volumes 1–4 in Volume 4 (Bb3/389–Mm3^v/470) and that to Volume 5 (Ff1^{v}451/–Gg8^v) are fused, though not fully integrated, to produce the quarto's index (II:465–514, i.e., 3O1–3U1^v)—references for pp. 9–193 of Volume 5 are inserted into the longer index for Volumes 1–4. Entries from both indices tend to be copied verbatim but for alteration to page numbers. When Volume 5's index adds to an entry in the other, the new information is stacked as a succeeding entry for the same reference (thus, a second paragraph is given to Albemarle on II:465 to present Volume 5's additions verbatim). Of course, reference to pages after 5:193 are eliminated.

36. Two volumes of Hume's *History of England* priced at 1-8-0 in boards and 1-12-0 bound were also offered in a superfine quartos for 2-2-0 in boards and 2-10-0 bound. See *LEP*, 21–23 April 1757.

37. Knapp, *Letters*, 112–13.

38. Basker, *Tobias Smollett: Critic and Journalist*, 109.

39. The inventory of books that Smollett took to France includes "Complete History of England 8 vols.," which number equals the four quartos of *Complete History* added to four octavos of *Continuation*. See Knapp, *Tobias Smollett*, 249.

40. Ten other examples of parliamentary and economic news reduced to notes are 1:62.11–63.21 (bill setting interest for national debt bonds) to [quarto] I:27; 1:68.21–70.27 (petitions debating bill to remove duties on American pig iron) to I:29–30; 1:121.12–27 (new duties and taxes) to I:54; 1:137.23–29 (new duties) to I:61; 1:301.19–34 (appropriations for improving rivers in Ireland, etc.) to

I:140.A–B; 1:418.10–422.20 (on "Funds provided") to I:196–97; 1:440.1–28 (impressment commission rules) to I:205–6; 1:442.6–34 (laws on pawnbroking) to I:206.B.17–46; 1:443.21–442.2 (more details of laws controlling weavers' wages) to I:207; 3:295.22–302.15 (ways and means legislation) to II:47–50.

41. Hume's *History of England from the Invasion of Julius Caesar to . . . Henry VII* in two vols. 4to sold for 1-10-0 sewn in boards (*LEP*, 15–17 October 1761); Hume's six vols. 4to sold for 3-19-0 in boards and 4-10-0 bound (*LEP*, 16–18 February 1762).

42. Expanded treatments of India occur at 1:286 in I:133.25–34; 1:364.6–16 in I:170.17–32; 1:370.20/21 in I:173.24–27; 1:370.25–371.25 in I:173.32–174.24; and 1.373.8 in I:175.9–14.

43. The sporadic attention to paragraph divisions during the revision is evident in paragraphs still many pages long in the quarto (e.g., II:44–46, II:240–48) while others of less length are repeatedly broken up: for instance, II.23–24 have new paragraph indentations for the octavo text at 3:242.35, 243.12, 245.2, and 245.27; and II:53, for text at 3:312.11, 312.24, and 313.1.

44. I closely collated 5:1–38 and 92–193 (versus II:277–91 and II:317–65), but only skimmed the text and marginalia in between. The few corrections are "Zieremberg" on 5:103 corrected to "Zierenberg" in the quarto on II:322.11; "Kerchayn" twice on 5:112 corrected to "Kirchayn" at II:326.26–27 and 326.45—spelled "Kirchhain" today; and the marginalia "Surrender of Schweidnitz" moved properly one paragraph later on II:319.

Appendix

A Descriptive Bibliography with Collation of Variant Readings for the Lifetime Editions of Smollett's *Continuation*

James E. May

This abbreviated descriptive bibliography with sample lists of variant readings identifies all the settings, issues, and multiple impressions of the octavo editions printed from 1760 to 1771. It concludes with a description of the ideal copy of the two-volume revised quarto edition (1766). The account of the octavos is organized by volume and therein by issue and sheet. The initial serial publication of the five octavos required that all resetting to meet demand occurred in new sheets that replicated the earlier printed sheets in order to fit them in between others already printed. On occasion the resetting is not line by line within sheets (on rare occasions, not page by page), but all settings for each sheet, as required, begin and end on the same word. Also, the contents, collational formulae including signatures and pagination, and running-titles (RTs) in the first settings for a volume were repeated in the resettings. Thus, for instance, since the first printing of sheet N of vol. 3 regressed sixteen places (from 193 to 177), shortening the count in all later sheets, that error needed to be repeated. One cannot tell from a title-page in sheet A what other sheets or even issues will lie ahead in the volume. In particular, the first and second octavo volumes, largely reset three times, are too unpredictable to focus description on the volumes as wholes. Only for vols. 3 and 4, with sheets reprinted only twice (and apparently with reprintings at greater temporal remove from one another), and for vol. 5, never reprinted, can one fruitfully focus on the volume. Since there are instances, as nos. 3 and 10 of vol. 1, where one sheet of an issue was twice reprinted but two others were three times reprinted, even the issue is not the fundamental printed unit. So, for uniformity, the description of vols. 1–4 focuses on their sheets, alone having the sort of edition status that allows one to speak of "ideal copy." General information on the volume and its issues (title-pages, collational formula, plates, paper, etc.) precedes an analysis of sheets designed for their identification as well as the registers of copies examined. The full account of irregularities in pagination, signatures, RTs, catchwords (CWs), and the like occurs in descriptions of sheet-settings. In describing sheets, to save space and avoid redundancy, I have truncated physical details conventional in descriptive bibliography. Physical features are not described again later when what is true of vol. 1 or of the first setting of a sheet is true of others. On the other hand, unless indicated, an error or variant reading noted to distinguish a setting should be understood as not occurring in alternate settings.

The settings of sheets have sigla usually with the date on the title-page found on most copies with that sheet. However, this system cannot be employed for all settings of vols. 1–2, for there are four settings of most sheets (four for sheets H–P and T–Ff of vol. 1 and four for A–Aa of vol. 2), but only three dates on title-pages (two "1760" title-settings of vol. 2 cannot be readily distinguished, and the second 1760 settings of vol. 1, called "1760/63" and 1760+ do not include a sheet A). Designations of settings that cannot be simply linked to a title-page date are given the sigla "1760+" when known to be a second printing in 1760 (those in nos. 7–10) or a sigla conflating the dates of two volume dates behind which the settings frequently appear (e.g., "1760/63"). Although these are sigla, akin to "O2," they often offer a chronological range for when the sheet was printed. The settings are principally distinguished by press figures, but sometimes other details (often errors) in the head- and directional-lines serve for identifying features; sometimes, when multiple settings lack press figures, the positions of the signatures serve to identify editions. Also, aside from the gatherings late in vol. 4 containing the index (not regularly collated), textual variants serve to distinguish settings. Press figures are often absent in the later reprintings, such as of sheets in vols. 1–2 for which very few copies exist. In particular, the rare fourth settings of issues 14–18, sheets K–Aa of vol. 2, contain no figures, as do some other settings of these sheets, like O–S of the second settings. In some cases, as in vol. 1's sheet Ee, the same figures on the same pages occur in multiple settings. Pressed for time, I have had sometimes to conjecture what settings are in particular copies, indicating these conjectured locations with italic font.

After describing all type-settings for a gathering, I indicate the copies collated, the extent of collating done, the transmission of text through the settings, and variants supporting the claims for transmission. These lists of variant readings record *all* substantive variants on pages collated, but they only provide enough accidental variants (many times more common than substantive variants) to justify decisions about the order of the settings and the transmission of the text through them. To give a sense of how many variants occurred in the reprintings, I record all variants found on collated leaves of some gatherings: specifically, the relatively inaccurate sheet F of vol. 1 and G of vol. 3, and the relatively accurate Bb of vol. 2 and O–P of vol. 3. Some comparative readings in the quartos (Q) are given to indicate what settings Smollett marked up for the revised quarto (the first settings of vol. 1's A–H and the second settings of its I–Gg; the second settings of vol. 2; and the first of vols. 3–4). In the initial reference to the location of variants, "marg" abbreviates "marginalia" and "A" or "B" stands for the footnote column (left or right).

Many variant states were created as type pieces were lost, such as a hyphen from a CW, a CW, or one digit in a page number. These are not treated here as separate states; rather, I classify as states with a capital letter suffix only those variants suggesting multiple impressions of stored type, particularly altered or missing press figures. Figures missing from only one or two copies, such as T5^v/282-4 of vol. 3 1760 absent from EU and PPT, are recorded, and may reflect multiple impressions, which apparently occurred in the 1760-B, -Q, and -S settings of this volume, but I suppose that they more likely indicate type lost during the run.

Introductory remarks applicable to the treatment of all volumes precede vol. 1's lists of plates and then of copies examined. All measurements are in millimeters. The recto of the leaf is indicated without superscript "r." All titles and half-titles have blank versos. All paper stocks with fleur-de-lys or Strasbourg lily watermarks (WMs) have "IV" countermarks. And in the lists of variants "lowercase" and "uppercase" are abbreviated "*l.c.*" and "*u.c.*"

VOLUME 1.A–D: NUMBERS 1–10: THREE SETTINGS IN SHEETS A–G, Q–S, AND GG; FOUR IN H–P AND T–FF

(VOLUME 1.A: RICHARD BALDWIN, 1760)

Title-page [tp]

CONTINUATION | OF THE COMPLETE | HISTORY | OF | ENGLAND. | By T. SMOLLETT, M.D. | VOLUME THE FIRST. | Non tamen pigebit vel incondita ac rudi voce memoriam prioris servitutis, ac | testimonium præsentium bonorum composuisse. Tacit. Agricola. | [design of cast printer's flowers and other devices, also found in vols. 2–5, 11 x 15] | LONDON: | Printed for Richard Baldwin, at the Rose in Paternoster-row. | MDCCLX. [Letterpress, 163; this setting was reused for first editions of vol. 2–3.]

Coll[ation] and Contents

8° (uncut, AWn, 225 x 150): (frontispiece [frt] +) A–Gg^8 [1/2 $ signed; $1 with issue signature]; pp. [2, frt] *i–iii* iv–vi 7 8–480 [pp. iv and 296 are correct, unlike later settings. Here and in vols. 2–5, the number signature on the first of the three sheets in an issue typically has "Numb." in large and small capitals followed by a roman numeral; the second two sheets in an issue typically are signed with "Numb." followed by an arabic numeral ("1" routinely appears for "1" in signatures, as in press figures). Irregularities in this pattern, including the absence of periods, will be noted (none occur in first settings). Contents: frt: Smollett's portrait [see notes on plates]; A1: title-page [tp]; A2–A3ᵛ: preface, "TO THE | PUBLIC."; A4/7–Gg8ᵛ/480: text; on Gg8ᵛ/480: "End of the First Volume."

Introduction to the Plate Listings for All Volumes

Initial page references refer to the pages facing the plates as prescribed by "Directions to the Book-Binder for Placing the Copper-Plates" (4:471–72; 5:[480]). Unless specified, all portraits are understood as being in oval frames, most of which have ribbon work atop the frame; names, typically given in capitals with slightly raised initial letters, are transcribed in full capitals, although the raised initial makes the subsequent capitals appear to be small capitals; this variation in size and also italic slant have been ignored. The first measurement or a sole measurement is the vertical measure; references to right or left are to reader's right and left. Final punctuation is moved to the end of all abbreviated words with superscript letters. Unless stated to the contrary, variant states or alternate cuts of an illustration are assumed to have the features of the first version described. Following the main descriptions of plates with their ideal placement in bound copies, I provide lists of issue numbers with which they were published serially. Since most volumes contain sheets bought serially, this information is needed to determine which is the first (or second) engraving or state of engraving for each plate. (For instance, a plate like [that of] Sir Piercy Brett bound in No. 35 of the May1 copy of vol. 4 dated 1768 might be taken for the second engraving of that illustration, but in fact it appeared in a number with first settings of the sheets in No. 15 within a vol. 2 dated 1760.)

Plates as Bound in Vol. 1.A–D (14 Portraits, Each in Two Engravings, and 2 Maps, One in Two Engravings and One in Two States)

Frt: "T. SMOLLETT, M.D." signed "Aliamet sculp."; earliest [version] with "Aliamet" beginning 3–4 to right from below the bottom button [e.g., BL4 CtHT CtY1-2 InMB InU KU LU2 May2 MBat1-2 MoJ NBuU PPiT PSt TnJoS ViLGH]; another, later cut with "Aliamet" beginning directly under the button [BL1-2 Brack CaAEU CtHi CtY2 CU-B DN DT EU InTU LU1 May3 MB1 MWA NNS Oa Oc May3 MGNA PCD PPL2 TnVN Vi ViU1-2—the second occurs in most 1763 reprints and all 1771 issues]; C4/39 "LORD HALLIFAX." signed

"Aliamet sculp."; one with "Aliamet" beginning over left side of "F" in "HAL-LIFAX" (BL1-2 May2 IU NNS), another over the right side (CtHT May1 PSt); F8/95: "AUGUSTA Princess Dowager of WALES." signed "Miller sculp."; one with knob just left of "D" and "Miller" beginning over "r" of "Dowager" (BL1 DGW PPL1); another, later, with knob below frame over "D" in "Dowager" and "Miller" beginning over "f" of "of" (CtHT May1-2 PSt); G7/109: "LOU-ISA Late QUEEN of DENMARK."; one signed "Aliamet sculp." with a period (LU1 May1 PSt) and signature beginning under right side of fur-border of cloak, another without period and beginning on left edge of the fur (BL1-2 MnGA NNS); K1ᵛ/146: "YORKE Earl of HARDWICKE." signed "Ravenet sculp."; one with the fourth line upward in circular frame running clockwise (to the left) from over "A" in "HARDWICKE" (BL1-2 May2), another with the fourth in running clockwise from over the "ar" in "Earl" (Brack May1); M2ᵛ/180: "GENERAL LAWRENCE." signed "Sherlock sculp."; one with "Sher-lock" beginning over right side of "N" in "LAWRENCE" (BL1-2 CtHT PSt), another over the "EN" (MdU May2); N2/195: "LIONEL SACKVILLE Duke of DORSET, | born Jan: 18, 1687–8." signed "Bennarman sculp."; one with "Bennarman" beginning over "e" of "Duke" (BL1-2 May1,3 IU NNS), an-other over the "D" of "Dorset" (BL3 CtHT May2 PSt); N4/199: folded map, "A GENERAL MAP OF THE EAST INDIES, FROM THE LATEST SURVEYS. 1762."; frame, 296 x 421; block, 307 x 431; unsigned; in two states, one with heavy horizontal shading around islands printed with horizontal chain-lines (BL1 May3 MoJ), and another with less shading printed with vertical chain-lines (May1-2 CtHT MnGA PPL1 PSt); O3/213 "A | NEW MAP | OF | NORTH AMERICA | FROM THE | LATEST DISCOVERIES, | 1761."; note urn present to left of title; signed "J Spilsbury sculp."; frame, 274 x 380; block, 282 x 387 (CtHT EU May2 PSt); another engraving with same caption but dated "1763" and without urn by title; unsigned: frame, 276 x 380; block, 284 x 388 (May1 and most late reprints, as BL1 DT ICarb MB2)—the lat-ter was issued in a colored state as a supplement to the *London Magazine* of February 1763 (also printed for R. Baldwin); Q4/247: "CHARLES FITZ-ROY Duke of GRAFTON." signed "Benoist sculp." (two engravings, most as BL1,3 May2 PSt, yet another at IU and PPiT); T1ᵛ/290: "The Right Honᵇˡᵉ. HENRY FOX Esqʳ. | Secretary of State." signed "Benoist sculp."; two engravings, each in two states: 1A) two-line caption above with "Benoist" beginning at end of "HENRY" (May PSt); 1B) first line only of caption and signature position of 1A (BL1,3 InU NNS); 2A) two-line caption with "Benoist" beginning over "F" of "Fox" (PPiT May2); 2B) first line only of the caption and signature posi-tion of 2A (May3); T8/303: "The Honourable CHARLES TOWNSHEND." signed "Miller sculp."; one with a knob flank by leaves at base of frame (BL1-3 May1,3 NNS PSt), another without elaboration below frame (InU May2,4-6); X3/325: "LORD BLAKENEY." signed "Sherlock sculp."; one with two leaves formed by framing lines reaching toward "k" in "Sherlock" as at

5:00 (May1,2,6 PSt), another with two combining to form one blade (BL1-3 CtHT May4 NNS); Z3/357: "LORD LOUDOUN." signed "Miller sculp."; one with scrollwork flourish below the frame reaching to left of "D" in "LORD" (BL1,3 PPL2), another with it stopping over the "D" (CtHT May1,2 PSt); Cc8^v/416: "Captain CORAM, Projector | of the Foundling Hospital."; one signed "Bannerman, Sculp." (BL1,3 CtHT May2 NNS PSt), another [earlier] signed "A. Bannerman sculp" (May1 PPL1); Gg7/477: "ADMIRAL BYNG." signed "Benoist sculp." beginning 11 mm. above "YN" of "BYNG" (BL1,3 CtHT DGW May1-3,5 PPiT PPL1-2 PSt), a second cut with signature placed further up the right side (e.g., EU IU MdU). Copies known to have all plates in proper places (as prescribed in "Directions" on 4:471–72) include BL1 BmU Brack CtHT InMB InTU LU1-2 MB1 MnGA PPL Vi ViLGH ViW; with all plates but frt: EU May1; with all but Byng: DT Oc PSt.

Plates as Issued with Nos. 1–10 (13 Portraits and 1 Map)

[with issue] #1: Granby and General Townshend [for #31 & #25]; #2: Saunders [for #24]; #3: "late brave General Wolfe" "engraved from Mr. Isaac Gossel's Model by Mr. Miller"; and Yorke, Lord Hardwicke [for #25; 31 May–3 June, *London Evening Post* (*LEP*)]; #4: "accurate whole Sheet Map of Germany, from the Berlin Atlas" [for #13, 7 June, *Public Advertiser* (*PA*)]; #5: Willes [for #35]; #6: Duke of York and Augusta, "Princess Dowager of Wales" [for #16 & #2]; #7: "late unfortunate Admiral Byng" [for #10; 26–28 June, *LEP*]; #8: Charles Duke of Marlborough and Lord George Sackville [for #11 & #28]; #9: Keppel [for #36]; #10: Fox [for #7].

RTs and CWs

A2-A3^v: "TO THE PUBLIC." A4^v–Gg8^v: "HISTORY of ENGLAND | GEORGE II." *CW*: H6/123: [in-]stead ["in" skipped in text of 1760 and 1760+; 1763 corrects to "instead"]; T2/291: master [other editions include "master" in text on T2 (thus with CW "of") and are a word ahead]; X5/329: two [others include "two" on X5 (thus with CW "of") and are a word ahead; at times 1760 is ahead of the other settings, as at P6/235, where it ends "put-", the syllable first on P6^v of others].

Paper in Vols. 1–3.A

Good quality (relatively thin but hard), creamy paper stock with crisp chain-lines, 102-106/4; no tranchefiles; no WM. The same or comparable paper appears in all sheets of 1.B and A–I of 2.B. Frt and portrait plates have one stock: fairly distinct 80-82/3; tranchefiles, 16–17; Strasbourg lily WM with "L|V|G" below, typically found at the top in the inside or outside corners; maps are on diverse paper stocks.

Typ. in Vols. 1–4

[E1] 34 ll., 169 (158.5) x 99 (text-block, 83.5); 20 ll., roman, 94, with .6 for leading; 20 ll. of footnotes (as Ee1), roman, 66. Usually 34 ll. per page but in vols. 1–3 sometimes one more or less (35 ll. on vol. 3's C1); in vol. 4, 33 lines is the rule after sheet D (text-block measures 153 x 84 on E2). The index in vol. 4, typically 44 ll. per page, appears to have the same font as the footnotes, but with slight leading, thus, 20 ll. (on Cc2), 73; in vol. 4, comparable leading is added to footnotes (e.g., N6/203).

Notes on Vol. 1.A–D

Although there are four settings of most sheets, there are only three of A–G, Q–S, and Gg; their first settings were impressed in more copies than the other sheets, probably in some cases, as sheet A, in a second impression from stored type. Soon after the run of 1760 sheets H–P and T–Ff of vol. 1, another setting was called for (in December 1760 for T–Ff), and this first resetting is usually found bound in copies with the title-page dated 1760, but also in some cases (especially resettings after sheet M) with 1763; second reprintings in rare cases appear in volumes dated 1771 (e.g., Bb–Dd of BL1). Because the issues were not distributed solely from one location, volumes tend not to be unified groupings of first, second, third, and fourth impressions—one distribution agent ran out of an impression sooner or later than another. Thus, the English Short Title Catalogue's (ESTC's) conventional treatment of the work as a series of dated volumes is inadequate.

The ESTC includes vol. 1 in three records based on BL copies with 1760, 1763, and 1771 title-pages: T55304, a five-volume set with earliest dated titles; T55305, another five-volume set with the 1763, 1763, 1762 and 1764 reprintings of vols. 1–4 joined to vol. 5, based on volumes in BL's set 291.h.20-24; and T55309, vol. 1 1771 alone, based on and including only BL's 9502.e.5. ESTC T55304 wrongly notes the set was filmed for *The Eighteenth Century* by Research Publications (as reel 157, no. 12): vols. 1–3 1760 were not filmed in the series (only vols. 4–5 were) and, thus, are not reproduced on ECCO. Many copies listed in T55304 as having the 1760–1761 volumes 1–4 do not, but most do (and some located by ESTC are unexamined copies supplementing this appendix). ESTC T55305 indicates, "Issued in 50 weekly numbers, some of which occur in variant settings" (whatever ESTC intended, this should be understood to mean, not variant states within an edition, but multiple settings, all being reset more than once). The original copy of record (BL3) is a mixture of first, second, and third settings, as are many others located. The "weekly" schedule was lengthened beginning with No. 10. Moreover, T55305 describes five volumes not published consistently as a unit—only first settings (T55304) can be described in a single multi-volume entry—three quarters of the nineteen copies listed for T55305 lack the same grouping of vols. 1–4 found in the record (1763, 1763, 1762, 1764). Furthermore, vol. 5 is thus given a duplicate record. T55309 wrongly describes the 1771 copy BL1 as "a reissue of some sheets of the 1763 edition": only sheets Bb–Dd appear in earlier dated volumes. As ESTC indicates, BL3 referenced to T55305 and BL1, to T55309, were filmed for *The Eighteenth Century* (on reels 1630 and 183 [BL1's vols. 1–3 are on reel 183 and 4–5 on reel 157]) and are reproduced on ECCO. At least one and usually two settings of each sheet of vol. 1 are not reproduced on ECCO.

With regard to paper in settings of vol. 1, there is no falling off in paper quality in the sheets reprinted later. It is noteworthy that the second settings of sheets H–P ("1760/63") and T–Gg ("1760+"), have the same or much the same unmarked paper as the first settings: chain-lines, 102-06/4, with tranchefiles (rarely seen), 10–12, as do the second settings of sheets Q–S (called "1763" below), indicating continuity of printing. Most of the paper used in the reprinting lacks a WM, and so WMs rarely demonstrate continuity of printing for specific settings. One instance, however, involves the second settings of sheets D–F and the third of K–M, common in 1763 copies; these have the same fleur-de-lys paper stock (chain-lines 81-82/3; tranchefiles 16). The only other paper stock with a WM has chain-lines 103-105/4 and the WM "L|V|H" (sometimes appearing as "E|V|H" or "I|V|II"); it links the third printing of sheets O–Aa and Ee–Gg, found in about a dozen copies with 1763 and 1771 title-pages (e.g., BL2). The rare fourth printings of H–P and T–Ff occur on unmarked paper.

Tp 1763 and Notes on Related Settings

Same letter-press as vol. 1.A but for addition after the motto of "A NEW EDITION," a different design of printer's devices (13 x 23), and the date change to "MDCCLXIII." Most commonly joined behind this title-page are second settings of sheets A–G, Q–S, and Gg and the third of all other sheets. These tend to have the pagination: [2, plate] *i–iii* iv–vi 7 [=A4] 8–49 56 51–157 *158* 159–239 242 241–382 833 384–480 [pp. 7 and 158 unpaginated; D1^v/50, P8^v/240, and Aa8/383 misnumbered "56," "242," and "833." This group of settings has irregular issue signatures without period after "Numb" on O1, U1, Z1 and Ee. Copies with these features are BL2,5 BmU Brack CaAEU CaOTU CtHT CYc MB2 MBat2 MWA ViU1-2. This group of copies also has such RT errors as "HISTOYR" on N8^v/208; "HISTROY" on R1^v/258; "GEORGE. II." with an extra period on Q3/245 and R3/261. Many paper stocks occur in this group of settings: most have no watermark, but one with a fleur-de-lys between chain-lines commonly occurs in D–N (chain-lines 80-83/3 and tranchefiles 15-16) and another, chain-lines 103-05/4, with an "L|V|H" WM (or "E|V|H" or "I|V|H"), appears within O–Gg of most copies.

Tp 1771 and Notes on Related Settings

Same letter-press as vol. 1.A but for the addition after the motto of "A NEW EDITION," a different design of cast pieces, and the imprint: "LON-DON, | Printed for R. Baldwin, at the Rose in Paternoster-row. | MDC-CLXXI." Note there are too few copies with final settings to compile a brief profile of them; indeed, in Nos. 7–8, the final settings exist only in a handful of copies with 1763 title-pages (shown to be the final setting by variant readings). The final settings do not contain a noteworthy number of pagination, RT, or signature errors.

Press Figures or Other Identifying Features and Textual Variants for All Settings of Vol. 1

Note: *All* substantive variants in all pages collated are listed together with a selection of accidental variants providing evidence of the transmission.

Issue No. 1: Sheets A–C: pp. [i–iii] iv–vi [7] 8–48: Three Settings

A-1760.A–B: A5^v/10-1: AWn BL4 CtY1-2 DN EU InMB InTU InU IU KU LdU LU1-2 May1-6 MBat1 MdU MoJ MnGA NBuU NjM O Oc OCX PCD PPiT PN PPL PSt TnJoS TnNV Vi ViLGH ViWCF—hereafter abbreviated as "all with 1760 tp." Two states and impressions: state B, with A2^v and A3 both paginated "v" (probably later, as most copies with pagination error have resettings in later sheets, e.g., May3,5 PN Vi), and state A correctly paginated, found in most copies;
A-1763: A7/13-3, A8/15-2: BL2-3,5 BmU Brack CaAEU CaOTU CT CtHi CtHT CYc DGW ICarb MB1-2 MBat2 MWA Oa PPL2 ViU1-2 ViW—hereafter abbreviated as "all with 1763 tp";
A-1771: A5^v/10-2: [1771 tp:] BL1 CU-B DT NNS.
Textual variants in three settings of sheet A: cf. [texts compared] 1760 (May2), 1763 (Brack), 1771 (BL1) on A2-A5 [lineal descent {i.e., of text from first to second to third settings}]:
A3/v.28 [up 4 ll.]: applause, 1760] ~$_\wedge$ 1763, 1771
A3^v/vi.14: credit, 1760, 1763] ~$_\wedge$ 1771
A3^v.21: animadversions, 1760, 1763] ~$_\wedge$ 1771
A4^v.20: Flanders; 1760, Q] ~: 1763, 1771

B-1760: B6^v/28-2, B8/31-2: all with 1760 tp;
B-1763: B8/31-1: all with 1763 tp plus [with tp] 1771: NNS [rare variant presumably due to poor inking: p. 18 paginated as "8" and p. 23 with only top of "2" inked in CT];
B-1771: B7^v/30-6: BL1 CU-B DT.
Textual variants in three settings of sheet B: cf. 1760 (May2), 1763 (Brack), 1771 (BL1) on B1-B3^v [lineal descent]:

B1/17.1: petition, 1760, 1763, Q] ~ₐ 1771
B2ᵛ.26: from 1760, Q] of 1763, 1771
B3ᵛ.5-6: judica- | ture: 1760, Q] ~, 1763, 1771
B3ᵛ.12: arguments 1760, Q] argument, 1763] arguments, 1771
B4/23.2: trusted, 1760, Q] ~ₐ 1763, 1771

C-1760: C3ᵛ/38-5, C6ᵛ/44-6: all with 1760 tp;
C-1763: C1ᵛ/34-3, C7/45-2: all with 1763 tp plus 1771: NNS;
C-1771: C1ᵛ/34-6, C2ᵛ/36-6: BL1 CU-B DT.
Textual variants in three settings of sheet C: cf. 1760 (May2), 1763 (Brack), 1771 (BL1) on C1–C4 [lineal descent]:
C1ᵛ.2–3: in | votes 1760, 1763, Q] in the | votes 1771
C2.30: rule, 1760, Q] ~ₐ 1763, 1771
C3/37.8: cause 1760, 1763, Q] ~, 1771
C3ᵛ.2–3: open- | ing, 1760, Q] ~ₐ 1763, 1771

Issue No. 2: Sheets D–F: pp. 49–96: Three Settings

D-1760: D6/59-4, D6ᵛ/60-3: all with 1760 tp;
D-1763: D1ᵛ/50 [misnumbered "56"]-2: BL2-3,5 BmU Brack CaOTU CaAEU CtHi CtHT CYc ICarb MB1-2 MBat2 MWA ViU1-2 ViW;
D-1771: D7ᵛ/62-2: 1771: BL1 CU-B DT NNS; 1763: CaOTU CT DGW Oa PPL2.
Textual variants in three settings of sheet D: cf. 1760 (May2), 1763 (Brack), 1771 (BL1) on D1–D3ᵛ [lineal descent]:
D1/49.10: terms, 1760, Q] ~ₐ 1763, 1771
D1.23: King 1760, Q] *l.c.* [i.e., lowercase] 1763, 1771
D3/53.4: Two 1760, 1763, Q] *l.c.* 1771

E-1760: E5/73-6, E8/79-4: all with 1760 tp;
E-1763: E2ᵛ/68-2 [under "ve" of "nevertheless"], E8/79-7: BL2-3,5 BmU Brack CaAEU CaOTU CtHi CtHT (incomplete "7") CYc ICarb MB1-2 MBat2 MWA ViU1-2 ViW;
E-1771: E2ᵛ/68-2 [under "r" of "nevertheless"]; no figure on E8/79: BL1 CT CU-B DT NNS; 1763: DGW Oa PPL2.
Textual variants in three settings of sheet E: cf. 1760 (May1–2), 1763 (Brack), 1771 (BL1) on E1–E3ᵛ [lineal descent, with only one acciden-tal variant in 1763 and three in 1771]:
E1ᵛ/66.29: who, 1760, 1763, Q] ~ 1771
E2/67.15: North 1760, 1763, Q] ~- 1771
E2ᵛ/68.4: America, 1760, Q] ~ₐ 1763, 1771

F-1760: F1ᵛ/82-1, F6ᵛ/92-2 [under "o" of "of"]: all with 1760 tp plus 1763: Brack ViW;

F-1763: F7/93-1, F7^v/94-6: BL2-3,5 BmU CaAEU CaOTU CtHi CtHT CYc ICarb MB1-2 MBat2 MWA ViU1-2;

F-1771: F6^v/92-2, F8/95-8: BL1 CU-B DT NNS; 1763: CT DGW Oa PPL2.

All textual variants in three settings of sheet F1–F3^v: cf. 1760 (May1–2), 1763 (BL3), 1771 (BL1) [lineal descent, with thirteen accidental variants, all but two introduced in 1763; all thirteen follow]:

F1/81.22: himself, 1760, Q] ~$_\wedge$ 1763, 1771

F1.marg.9 [ult l.]: Sweden. 1760, 1771] ~, 1763

F1^v/82.17: Emperor 1760, Q] *l.c.* 1763, 1771

F1^v.30: payed 1760, 1763, Q] paid 1771

F1^v.33: Emperor or Empire 1760, Q] *l.c.* 1763, 1771

F2/83.30: co-estates 1760, Q, 1771] ~$_\wedge$~ 1763

F2^v.4: king; 1760, 1763, Q] ~: 1771

F2^v.10: christian 1760, Q] *u.c.* 1763, 1771

F2^v.13: Westphalia; 1760, Q] ~: 1763, 1771

F3^v: 6–7: na- | tions; 1760, Q] ~, 1763, 1771

F3^v.9: guarda costas 1760, Q] ~-~ 1763, 1771

F3^v.16: catholic 1760, Q] *u.c.* 1763, 1771

Issue No. 3: Sheets G–I: pp. 97–144: Three Settings in G and Four in H–I

G-1760: G5/105-6, G7^v/110-4: AWn BL4 CtY1-2 DN EU InMB InTU InU IU KU LdU LU1-2 May1-5 MBat1 MdU MnGA NBuU NjM O Oc OCX PCD PPiT PN PPL PSt TnJoS TnNV Vi ViLGH ViWCF; [plus with tp dated] 1763: BL3 ICarb MB1 [beginning in sheet G, sheets in copies of the second setting dated 1760 appear in copies dated 1763 and sheets common in copies dated 1763 appear in copies dated 1760];

G-1763: G8/111-5: BL2,5 BmU Brack CaAEU CaOTU CtHi CtHT CYc DGW MB2 MBat2 MWA ViU1-2 ViW; 1760: MoJ;

G-1771: G7/109-2, G7^v/110-1: BL1 CU-B DT NNS; 1763: CT Oa PPL2 [CW error on G6/107: terest} of (text omits "terest") in CT DT CU-B NNS Oa PPL2].

Textual variants in three settings of sheet G: cf. 1760 (May1–2), 1763 (Brack), 1771 (BL1) on G1–G3^v [lineal descent, with seven of twelve accidental variants introduced by 1763]:

G3/101.25: candour 1760, Q] ~, 1763, 1771

G3.28: electors, 1760, 1763, Q] ~$_\wedge$ 1771

G3.31: Leigh the high bailiff 1760, Q] Leigh, ~, 1763, 1771

G3^v/102.2: election 1760, 1763, Q] ~, 1771

G3^v.28: Lyttleton 1760, Q, 1771] Lyttelton 1763

H-1760: H5/121-2, H7^v/126-3: BL4 CtY1-2 DN EU InU IU KU LdU LU1 May1,3-4 MdU MnGA NBuU NjM O Oc OCX PPiT PPL1 TnJoS TnNV ViLGH ViWCF;

276 *James E. May*

H-1760/63: H1ᵛ/114-5: 1760: AWn InMB InTU LU2 May2,5-6 MBat1 PCD PN PSt Vi; 1763: BL3 ICarb MB1;
H-1763: H5ᵛ/122-5, H7/125-1: BL2,5 BmU Brack CaAEU CaOTU CtHi CtHT CYc DGW MB2 MBat2 MWA ViU1-2 ViW; 1760: MoJ;
H-1771: H8/127-4, H8ᵛ/128-6: BL1 CU-B DT NNS; 1763: CT Oa PPL2.
Textual variants in four settings of sheet H: cf. 1760 (May1), 1760/63 (May2), 1763 (Brack), 1771 (BL1) on H1–H3ᵛ [1760/63 and 1763 descend directly from 1760, 1771 from 1763; of eight variants, five are introduced by 1760/63, two by 1771; those five 1760/1763 variants are unique to it (1760/63 alone shares CW error with 1760)]:
H1/113.6: measure, 1760, 1760/63, 1763, Q] ∼ₐ 1771
H1/113.10: emperor 1760, 1763, 1771] *u.c.* 1760/63
H1ᵛ.25: writings, 1760, 1760/63] ∼ₐ 1763, 1771
H3/117.13 Petersburg 1760, 1763, Q, 1771] Petersbourg 1760/63
H3ᵛ.16: days 1760, 1760/63, 1763, Q] day 1771 [error]

I-1760: I1ᵛ/130-2, I2ᵛ/132-1: same copies as H-1760;
I-1760/63: I1ᵛ/130-3, I5/137-5: same copies as H-60/63 [CWs I7ᵛ: "London"];
I-1763: I4/136-1, I6/139-5: same copies as H-1763;
I-1771: I7/141-1, I8/143-2: same copies as H-1771.
Textual variants in four settings of sheet I: cf. 1760 (May1), 1760/63 (May5), 1763 (Brack), 1771 (BL1) on I1–I3ᵛ [five accidental variants unique to 1760/63 and two shared by 1763 and 1771 indicate that 1760/63 and 1763 descend from 1760 and that 1771 descends from 1763 (as do CWs unique to 1760/63 on I7ᵛ and I8ᵛ)]:
I1/129.9: by 1760, 1760/63, 1763, Q] by the 1771
I1/129.34 [ult. l.]: Friezland 1760] Friesland 1760/63, 1763, Q, 1771
I2/131.29: proceedings 1760, 1760/63, Q] ∼, 1763, 1771
I2ᵛ/132.29: that 1760, 1763, 1771] ∼, 1760/63, Q
I3/133.12: indulgence, 1760] ∼ₐ 1760/63, 1763, Q, 1771
I3ᵛ/134.5: unreasonable, 1760, 1763, 1771] ∼ₐ 1760/63, Q

Issue No. 4: Sheets K–M: pp. 145–92: Four Settings

K-1760: K6ᵛ/156-6, K8/159-1: same copies as H-1760 less MnGA;
K-1760/63: K2ᵛ/148-5, K3ᵛ/150-3: 1760: AWn InMB InTU LU2 May2,5-6 MBat1 MnGA PCD PN PSt Vi;
K-1763: K4ᵛ/152-5, K7ᵛ/158-3; K2 signed "R2": BL2-3,5 BmU Brack CaAEU CaOTU CtHi CtHT CYc DGW ICarb MB1-2 MBat2 MWA ViU1-2 ViW [p. 158 unpaginated in all or nearly all copies];
K-1771: K5/155-8: BL1 CU-B DT NNS; 1763: CT Oa PPL2.

Textual variants in four settings of sheet K: cf. 1760 (May1), 1760/63 (May5), 1763 (Brack), 1771 (BL1) on K2–K4ᵛ [as in sheet I, 1760/63 and 1763 descend directly from 1760, 1771 from 1763]:
K2ᵛ/148.22: heaven: 1760, 1760/63, Q] ∼; 1763, 1771
K2ᵛ.23: marriages, 1760, 1760/63, Q] ∼ₐ 1763, 1771
K4.19: incurred, 1760, 1760/63, 1763, Q] ∼ₐ 1771
CWs K5/153: In / metals, 1760, 1763, 1771] In/ores, 1760/63

L-1760: L3ᵛ/166-5, L7/173-6: same copies as H-1760 less MnGA;
L-1760/63: L2ᵛ/164-5: 1760: AWn InMB InTU LU2 May2,5-6 MBat1 MnGA PCD PN PSt Vi; 1763: Brack ViW;
L-1763: L5/169-5, L7ᵛ/174-2: BL2-3,5 BmU CaAEU CaOTU CtHi CtHT CYc ICarb MB1-2 MBat2 MWA ViU1-2;
L-1771: L1ᵛ/162-1, L4ᵛ/168-7: BL1 CU-B DT NNS; 1763: CT DGW Oa PPL2.
Textual variants in four settings of sheet L: cf. 1760 (May1), 1760/63 (May5), 1763 (BL3), 1771 (BL1) on L1–L3ᵛ [1763 and 1771 descend directly from 1760/63 (marginalia on L2–L2ᵛ have different line divisions in 1763 than those shared by 1760, 1760/63 and 1771); of 17 accidental variants, eight are introduced by 1760/63 and followed by others and eight are introduced by 1763, six being unique to it]:
L1ᵛ/162.30: another 1760, Q] ∼, 1760/63, 1763, Q, 1771
L2ᵛ.10: and 1760] ∼, 1760/63, 1763, Q, 1771
L2ᵛ.13: archduke 1760, 1760/63, Q, 1771] arch duke 1763
L2ᵛ.13: but 1760, 1760/63, Q, 1771] ∼, 1763
L3ᵛ/166.6: French, 1760, 1760/63, 1763, Q] ∼ₐ 1771

M-1760: M8/191-4: same copies as H-1760 less MnGA;
M-1760/63: M3ᵛ/182-2, M6ᵛ/188-4: 1760: AWn InMB InTU LU2 May2,5-6 MBat1 MnGA PCD PN PSt Vi: 1763: BL2 CaAEU;
M-1763: M7/189-1: BL3,5 BmU Brack CaOTU CtHi CtHT CYc ICarb MB1-2 MBat2 MWA ViU1-2 ViW [no CW on M7ᵛ/190];
M-1771: M2ᵛ/180-2: BL1 CU-B DT NNS; 1763: CT DGW Oa PPL2.
Textual variants in four settings of sheet M: cf. 1760 (May1), 1760/63 (May5), 1763 (Brack), 1771 (BL1) on M1–M3ᵛ [lineal descent: of nine variants (all accidentals), seven are introduced by 1760/63 and followed by others; two by 1763 followed by 1771 (as are marginal line divisions on M2–M2ᵛ distinct from those shared by 1760 and 1760/63)]:
M2/179.2: Nova Scotia 1760, 1760/63] ∼-∼ 1763, 1771
M3/181.1: men transported by sea 1760] men, ∼, 1760/63, 1763, Q, 1771
M3.4: opposition 1760] ∼, 1760/63, 1763, Q, 1771
M3ᵛ.13: north | side 1760, 1760/63] ∼-∼ 1763, 1771

Issue No. 5: Sheets N–P: pp. 193–240: Four Settings

N-1760: N5^v/202-2, N7/205-1: 1760: BL4 CtY1-2 DN EU InU IU KU LdU
LU1 May1-4 MdU MoJ NBuU NjM O Oc OCX PPiT PPL1 TnJoS TnNV
ViLGH ViWCF;

N-1760/63: N1^v/194-5: 1760: AWn InMB InTU LU2 May5-6 MBat1
MnGA PCD PN PSt Vi; 1763: BL3 CtHi ICarb MB1;

N-1763: N5^v/202-1, N7/205-3: BL2,5, BmU Brack CaAEU CaOTU CtHT
CYc DGW MB2 MBat2 MWA Oa ViU1-2 ViW [variant RT with "HIS-
TOYR" on N8^v/208];

N-1771: N5^v/202-7: BL1 CU-B DT NNS; 1763: CT PPL2.

Textual variants in four settings of sheet N: cf. 1760 (May2), 1760/63
(May5, PSt), 1763 (Brack), 1771 (BL1) on N1–N3^v [lineal descent:
four variants including substantive in N3^v.34 introduced by 1760/63
and followed by others; one variant introduced by 1763 followed by
1771; three spelling variants are unique to 1771 (N1^v.23–24, N2.15,
N2^v.7)]:

N2^v/196.30: intrusted 1760, 1760/63] entrusted 1763, 1771
N3/197.33: necessary 1760] ∼, 1760/63, 1763, 1771, Q
N3^v.34: off 1760, Q] of 1760/63, 1763, 1771

O-1760: O2^v/212-4: same as N-1760 [CW O6^v/220: at];

O-1760/63: O4^v/216-5: same as N-1760/63 plus Brack [CW variant on
O6^v: ther,} ∧∼];

O-1763: no figure; O1 signed "Numb" without period: same as N-1763
minus Brack ["Numb" without period in signatures of 1763/71-U and
-Z; CW on O6^v without variant: "other,"];

O-1771: O2^v/212-2 [under first "t" of "that"]: BL1 CU-B DT NNS; 1763:
CT PPL2 [CW O6^v/220: other,} ∼∧].

Textual variants in four settings of sheet O: cf. 1760 (May2), 1760/63
(PSt), 1763 (CaAEU), 1771 (BL1) on O1–O3^v [to judge from text distribution (n. CW O4^v), probably lineal descent, with 1763 avoiding
errors in 1760/63, but 1760/63 and 1763 both might directly descend
from 1760; 1771 descends from 1763]:

O1/209.8–9: fix- | ed, 1760] ∼; 1760/63, 1763, 1771
O1^v.8: whither 1760, 1760/63, 1763] whether 1771
O2/211.3: arisen 1760, 1763, 1771] risen 1760/63
O2/211.17: who, 1760, 1760/63] ∼∧ 1763, 1771
O2.20: stipulated, 1760, 1760/63] ∼∧ 1763, 1771
O2.23: districts, 1760, 1760/63, 1763] ∼∧ 1771
O3/213.8: French, 1760, 1763, 1771] ∼∧ 1760/63 [error]
O3.34 [ult. l.]: country, 1760, 1763, 1771] ∼∧ 1760/63, Q [error]
O4/215.4 ends "from" 1760; "which" 1760/63, 1763, 1771
CW O4^v/216: Island, 1760] Long 1760/63, 1763, 1771

P-1760 [225–40]: P2^v/228-1, P6/235-6: same as N-1760;
P-1760/63: P4^v/232-5, P6/235-2: same as N-1760/63;
P-1763: P1^v/226-3; P8^v/240 mispaginated "242": same as N-1763;
P-1771: P7^v/238-1, P8^v/240-2: BL1 CU-B DT NNS; 1763: CT PPL2.
Textual variants in four settings of sheet P: cf. 1760 (May2), 1760/63 (May5), 1763 (Brack), 1771 (BL1) on P1–P4^v [lineal descent]:
P1^v/226.19: two 1760, 1760/63, 1763] ∼, 1771
P1^v.32: defence; 1760] ∼: 1760/63, 1763, Q, 1771
P3.11: proprietaries 1760, 1760/63, Q] proprietors 1763, 1771
P4/231.4: Europe 1760, 1760/63, 1763] ∼, 1771
P4^v/232.20: consequences 1760, 1760/63, Q] consequence 1763, 1771

Issue No. 6: Sheets Q–S: pp. 241–88: Three Settings

Q-1760: Q4^v/248-6, Q5^v/250-4: AWn BL4 CtY1-2 DN EU InU InMB InTU IU KU LdU LU1-2 May1-6 MdU MnGA MoJ NBuU NjM O Oc OCX PPiT PN PPL1 PSt TnJoS TnNV Vi ViLGH ViWCF;
Q-1763: Q6^v/252-4, Q8/255-5: 1763: BL3,5 BmU CtHi CtHT CYc DGW ICarb MB1-2 MWA; 1760: MBat1 PCD;
Q-1763/71: no figures; variant RT with period after "GEORGE" on Q3/245: 1763: BL2 Brack CaAEU CaOTU CT MBat2 Oa PPL2 ViU1-2 ViW; 1771: BL1 CU-B DT NNS ["2" of Q2 under "ig" of "frigate" "3" of Q3 under "is" of "this"].
Textual variants in three settings of sheet Q: cf. 1760 (May2), 1763 (BL3), 1763/71 (BL1) on Q1–Q3^v and Q8–Q8^v [lineal descent]:
Q1/241.4: that 1760, 1763] ∼, 1763/71
Q1.5: England 1760] ∼, 1763, 1763/71
Q2^v.31: crowns 1760] ∼, 1763, 1763/71
Q3.7,10: That 1760, 1763] *l.c.* 1763/71

R-1760: R1^v/258-2, R5/265-4: all with 1760 tp except MBat1 and PCD;
R-1763: no figures: BL3,5 BmU CtHi CtHT CYc ICarb MB1-2 MWA; 1760: MBat1 PCD [R1 signed below "h" of "he"; "2" of R2 just before "off"; correct RTs on 258 and 261];
R-1763/1771: no figures; variant RTs on R1^v/258: "HISTROY" and R3/261: "GEORGE. II.": same as Q-1763/71, with *DT* conjectured.
Textual variants in three settings of sheet R: cf. 1760 (May2), 1763 (BL3), 1763/71 (BL1, Brack) on R1–R3^v [lineal descent, with 1763 and 1763/71 carelessly composed (e.g., 1763 has "ercting" in R3.27, and 1763/71 has "westeren" in R3.3)]:
R2^v/260.10: out, 1760] ∼ₐ 1763, 1763/71
R3/261.31: richness 1760, Q] riches 1763, 1763/71
R3^v/262.6: their 1760, 1763, Q] the 1763/71
R3^v.32: their 1760, 1763, Q] their own 1763/71

S-1760: S4ᵛ/280-1, S8/287-3: same as R-1760;

S-1763: no figures; no variant RT on S1ᵛ/274: same as R-1763 [S1 signed under "n" of "not"; "2" of S2 under "F" of "French"];

S-1763/71: no figures: variant RT S1ᵛ/274 with "HISTROY": same as R-1763/71 [variant RT previously on R1ᵛ; S1 under "t" of "not"; "2" of S2 under "e" of "French"].

Textual variants in three settings of sheet S: cf. 1760 (May2), 1763 (BL3), 1763/71 (BL1) on S1–S3ᵛ [lineal descent, with careless errors in 1763 and 1763/71]:

S1/273.13: ran 1760] run 1763, 1763/71 [error]
S1.33: and, 1760, 1763] ∼ₐ 1763/71
S2ᵛ/276.5: well acquainted 1760, Q] acquainted [*om.*] 1763, 1763/71
S3.27: upon 1760] on 1763, 1763/71
S3ᵛ.10: banco, 1760, 1763] ∼ₐ 1763/71

Issue No. 7: Sheets T–X: pp. 289–336: Four Settings

T-1760: T3ᵛ/294-6, T7/301-2: BL4 CtY1-2 DN EU InU IU KU LdU LU1 May1-4 MdU MoJ NBuU NjM O Oc OCX PPiT PPL1 TnJoS TnNV ViLGH ViWCF;

T-1760+: T3ᵛ/294-5; p. 296 mispaginated "396": 1760: AWn InMB InTU LU2 May5-6 MnGA PCD PN PSt Vi; 1763: BL3 CtHi ICarb MB1;

T-1763/71: T3ᵛ/294-1: 1763: BL2,5 BmU Brack CaAEU CaOTU CtHT CYc DGW MB2 MBat2 MWA Oa ViU1-2 ViW; 1771: BL1 DT NNS [punched out]; 1760: MBat1;

T-1771: T5ᵛ/298-6: 1771: CU-B; 1763: CT PPL2 [T1 under "abl" of "remarkable"; "2" of T2 under "d" of "appointed"].

Textual variants in four settings of Sheet T: cf. 1760 (May2), 1760+ (PSt), 1763/71 (Brack), 1771 (PPL2) on T1–T3ᵛ [lineal descent: eight variants introduced by 1760+ recur in 1763/71 and 1771; three unique variants and unique line divisions in 1771 indicate that it was printed last]:

T1/289.3: engagements 1760] ∼, 1760+, 1763/71, Q, 1771
T1.11: Britain," 1760, 1760+, 1763/71, Q] ∼,ₐ 1771 [correction]
T2/291.26: upon almost 1760, 1760+, Q] almost upon 1763/71 1771
T2/291 CW: master 1760] of 1760+, 1763/71, 1771
T2ᵛ/292.4: Lyttelton 1760, 1760+, 1763/71] Lyttleton 1771
T3/293.3: pounds, twelve shillings, 1760] pounds ∼ 1760+, 1763/71, Q, 1771

U-1760: U1ᵛ/306-4 [under "b" of "been"], U2ᵛ/308-1: same copies as T-1760, plus Brack (1763);

U-1760+: U7ᵛ/318-5: same as T-1760+, plus ViW (1763);

U-1763/71: U5/313-1, U7^v/318-6; signed "Numb" without period on U1: 1763: BL2,5 BmU CaAEU CaOTU CtHT CYc DGW MB2 MBat2 MWA Oa ViU1-2; 1771: BL1 DT NNS; plus 1760: MBat1;

U-1771]: U1^v/306-1 [under "we" of "were"]: 1771: CU-B; 1763: CT PPL2 [U1 under "a" of "each"; "2" of U2 under "m" of "formidable"].

Textual variants in four settings of sheet U: cf. 1760 (May2), 1760+ (PSt), 1763/71 (BL1) on U1–U3^v; 1760 (May2) and 1771 (PPL2) on U1–U2^v, with errors checked to U3^v [lineal descent]:

U1^v/306.18: on 1760, 1760+, 1763/71] one 1771 [error]

U1^v/306.28: conjecture: 1760] ~; 1760+, 1763/71, 1771] ~. Q

U2.24: France: 1760, 1760+, 1763/71, Q] ~; 1771

U3^v.34: land, 1760, 1760+, Q] ~; 1763/71, 1771

U4/311.15: troops, 1760] ~; 1760+, 1763/71, Q, 1771

X-1760: X1^v/322-2, X7/333-1 [under "i" of "sustain"]: same as T-1760;

X-1760+: X3^v/326-5: same as T-1760+ [figure not printed in AWn];

X-1763/71: X1^v/322-3, X5/329-1: same as T-1763/71;

X-1771: X5^v/330-6, X7/333-1 [under period after "sustain"]: 1771: CU-B; 1763: CT PPL2 ["3" of X3 under left of "w" in "were"; "4" of X4 under second "e" in "escape"].

Textual variants in four settings of sheet X: cf. 1760 (May2), 1760+ (PSt), 1763/71 (BL1), 1771 (PPL2) on X1–X3^v [lineal descent; five punctuation variants introduced in 1760+ repeated by later reprints; 1763/71's variants appear in 1771 but not vice versa]:

X1/321.5: but, 1760] ~$_\wedge$ 1760+, 1763/71, Q, 1771

X1.17: Defiance, 1760, 1760+, Q] ~; 1763/71, 1771

X1^v/322.7: excuseable 1760, 1760+, 1763/71] excusable 1771

X2/323.5: James's 1760, 1760+, Q] ~, 1763/71, 1771

X3/325.30: however, 1760, 1760+, 1763/71] ~$_\wedge$ 1771

X3^v.22: Philip's: 1760] ~; 1760+, 1763/71, Q, 1771

Issue No. 8: Sheets Y–Aa: pp. 337–84: Four Settings

Y-1760 [pp. 337–52]: Y4^v/344-6, Y5^v/346-2: BL4 CtY1-2 DN EU InU IU KU LdU LU1 May1-4 MBat1 MdU MoJ NBuU NjM O Oc OCX PPiT PPL1 TnJoS TnNV ViLGH ViWCF;

Y-1760+: Y5^v/346-5, Y7/349-4: 1760: AWn InMB InTU LU2 May5-6 MnGA PCD PN PSt Vi; 1763: BL3 CtHi ICarb MB1;

Y-1763/71: Y2^v/340-1, Y8/351-3: 1763: BL2,5 BmU Brack CaAEU CaOTU CtHT CYc DGW MB2 MBat2 MWA Oa ViU1-2 ViW; 1771: BL1 CU-B DT NNS;

Y-1771: Y5/345-4 [under "th" of "those"]: 1763: CT PPL2 ["2" under "c" of "considerable"; 3 under "o" of "out"].

Textual variants in four settings of sheet Y: cf. 1760 (May2), 1760+
(May5), 1763/71 (Brack), 1771 (PPL2) on Y1–Y3 [lineal descent:
many accidental variants introduced by 1760+ in Y1–Y3 and Y4 recur
in later reprints; 1763/71 and 1771 share several separative variants
(Y3.4–5 and both alone use "+" for fn. symbol on Y3^v and alone have
CW "garrison," on Y8v); 1771 reprints nearly all variants in 1763/71
and alone has unique plausible variants]:

Y1/337.8: conquests 1760, 1760+, 1763/71, Q] conquest 1771
Y2/339.6: place, 1760] ~$_\wedge$ 1760+, 1763/71, Q, 1771
Y2^v.29: were, in some respects, 1760] were $_\wedge$~$_\wedge$ 1760+, 1763/71, Q, 1771
Y3/341.4: frigates 1760, 1760+, Q] ~, 1763/71, 1771
Y3.6: issued, 1760, 1760+, 1763/71, Q] ~$_\wedge$ 1771
Y4.A.29: West Indies: 1760] ~-~; 1760+, 1763/71, Q] ~-~: 1771

Z-1760 [pp. 353–68]: Z1^v/354-1, Z2^v/356-4: same as Y-1760;
Z-1760+: Z4^v/360-5: same as Y-1760+;
Z-1763/71: Z7/365-5; uniquely signed "Numb" without period on Z1:
same as Y-1763/71;
Z-1771: Z6/363-7: 1763: CT PPL2 [Z1 under "l" in "regular"].

Textual variants in four settings of sheet Z: cf. 1760 (May2), 1760+
(PSt), 1763/71 (BL1) on Z1–Z4^v: 1760 (May2) vs. 1771 (PPL2) on
Z1–Z3 [1760+ and 1763/71 directly descend from 1760; 1771, from
1763/71; 1763/71 and 1771 lack seven accidental variants unique to
1760+ and share separative variants (including a substantive in Z3^v.7);
most variants in 1771 are unique to it, and it has line divisions differing from other settings]:

Z1/353.18 begins "to dismiss" in 1760, 1760+, and 1763/71; begins
"from" in 1771
Z1^v.7: inhabitants, 1760, 1760+, Q] ~$_\wedge$ 1763/71, 1771
Z1^v.8: not 1760, 1763/71, 1771] ~, 1760+, Q
Z1^v.9: province 1760, 1763/71, 1771] ~, 1760+, Q
Z1^v.34: explain; 1760, 1760+, 1763/71, Q] ~, 1771
Z2^v/356.7: vigour, 1760, 1760+, 1763/71] ~$_\wedge$ 1771
Z3^v/358.7: detained 1760, 1760+, Q] retained 1763/71, 1771

Aa-1760: Aa6^v/380-3, Aa8/383-2: same as Y-1760 less MBat1;
Aa-1760+: Aa6^v/380-2, Aa8/383-4: same as Y-1760+ plus MBat1;
Aa-1763/71: Aa5^v/378-7; Aa8/383 mispaginated "833": same as
Y-1763/71;
Aa-1771: Aa2^v/372-6 [under "a" in "garrison"]: 1763: CT PPL2 ["A" of
Aa1 under right of "g" in "lodged"].

Textual variants in four settings of Aa: cf. 1760 (May2), 1760+ (PSt),
1763/71 (BL1) on Aa1–Aa4^v; 1760 (May2) vs. 1771 (PPL2) on Aa1–

Aa2 and known variants checked to Aa4 [as in Z, 1760+ and 1763/71 descend directly from 1760; 1771, from 1763/71; 1763/71 and 1771 share separative variants; and 1763/71 has but one unique variant, an obvious error, while 1771 has many unique errors]:

Aa1/369.1: last, 1760, 1760+, 1763/71, Q] ~$_\wedge$ 1771
Aa2.28: seventh 1760, 1760+, 1763/71, Q] seventeenth 1771
Aa2^v/372.5–6: surren- | der 1760, 1763/71, 1771] ~, 1760+, Q
Aa3/373.19: humanity. 1760, 1760+, 1763/71] ~*. 1771 [footnote symbol on Aa3.23 of other settings is moved up]
Aa4/375.16: principals 1760, 1760+, 1771] principles 1763/71 [error]
Aa4.26: Great Britain 1760, 1760+] ~-~ 1763/71, 1771
Aa4^v.11: En____d 1760, 1763/71, 1771] E____d 1760+, Q
Aa5.27, 31: dyet 1760, 1760+] diet 1763/71, 1771

Issue No. 9: Sheets Bb–Dd: pp. 385–432: Four Settings

Bb-1760: Bb6^v/396-6, Bb7^v/398-4 [under "is" of "minister"]: BL4 CtY1-2 DN EU InU IU KU LdU LU1 May1-4 MdU MoJ NBuU NjM O Oc OCX PPiT PPL1 TnJoS TnNV ViLGH ViWCF; 1763: Brack;
Bb-1760+: Bb7/397-3, Bb7^v/398-2 [under "pr" in "presented"]: 1760: AWn InMB InTU LU2 May5-6 MBat1 MnGA PCD PN PSt Vi; 1763: BL3 ICarb MB1; 1771: BL1 [398-2 not in LU2 and PSt, yet otherwise the same setting];
Bb-1763: Bb1^v/386-2, Bb7/397-6: BL2,5 BmU CaAEU CaOTU CtHi CtHT CYc DGW MB2 MBat2 MWA ViU1-2 ViW;
Bb-1763/71: Bb8^v/400-7: 1771: CU-B DT NNS; 1763: CT Oa PPL2.
Textual variants in four settings of Bb: cf. 1760 (May2), 1760+ (PSt), 1763 (CaAEU) on Bb1–Bb4; 1760 (May2) and 1763/71 (PPL2) on Bb1–Bb2; 1760+ (BL1) and 1763/71 (Oa) on Bb1–Bb3^v [lineal descent]:

Bb1/385.2: to, 1760, 1760+, 1763] ~$_\wedge$ 1763/71, Q
Bb1.22: had not he 1760] had he not 1760+, 1763, 1763/71, Q
Bb1^v/386.19: duke 1760, 1763/71] *u.c.* 1760+, 1763
Bb2/387.9: repaired, 1760] ~$_\wedge$ 1760+, 1763, 1763/71, Q
Bb2^v.11: Buntzlau 1760, 1760+, Q] Buntzlaw 1763, 1763/71
Bb3.A.22: this 1760, 1760+, 1763, Q] the 1763/71

Cc-1760: Cc6/411-2, Cc6^v/412-3: same as Bb-1760 less 1763 Brack;
Cc-1760+: Cc1^v/402-3: same as Bb-1760+;
Cc-1763: Cc2^v/404-1, Cc6/411-5: same as Bb-1763, plus Brack;
Cc-1763/71: Cc7/413-7: 1771: CU-B DT NNS; 1763: CT Oa PPL2.
Textual variants in four settings of Cc: cf. 1760 (May2), 1760+ (PSt), 1763 (Brack) on Cc1–Cc3v; 1760 (BL1) and 1763/71 (Oa) on Cc1–3^v

[linear descent, with many accidental variants introduced by 1763 shared by 1763/71 and many others introduced by 1763/71 not shared by 1763]:

Cc1.12: Magdeburg 1760, 1763/71] Magdebourg 1760+, 1763, Q
Cc1.24: Petersburgh 1760] Petersburg 1760+, 1763, 1763/71, Q
Cc1.26: meerly 1760, 1760+, Q] merely 1763, 1763/71
Cc1^v.24: those 1760, 1760+, Q] these 1763, 1763/71
Cc2^v/404.17: Prussia: 1760] ~; 1760+, 1763, 1763/71, Q
Cc3^v/406.1: which 1760, 1760+, 1763] ~, 1763/71

Dd-1760: Dd1^v/418-6, Dd4^v/424-4: same as Bb-1760 plus 1763: ViW;
Dd-1760+: Dd2^v/420-3: same as Bb-1760+ less ViW;
Dd-1763: Dd5^v/426-5: BL2,5 BmU CaAEU CaOTU CtHi CtHT CYc DGW MB2 MBat2 MWA ViU1-2;
Dd-1763/71: Dd5^v/426-1: 1763: CT Oa PPL2; 1771: CU-B DT NNS ["D" of Dd1 under "pl" of "plicity"; "2" of Dd2 under "b" of "before"].
Textual variants in four settings of Dd: cf. 1760 (May2) and 1760+ (BL1, May5, PSt) on Dd1–Dd4^v; 1760 (May2) and 1763 (CaAEU) on Dd1–Dd4; 1760+ (BL1) and 1763/71 (Oa) on Dd1–Dd3^v [lineal descent]:

Dd1/417.1: expences 1760] expence 1760+, 1763, 1763/71] expense Q
Dd1/417.19: expence 1760, 1760+, 1763, Q] expences 1763/71
Dd1^v/418.4: acknowledged, 1760] ~$_\wedge$ 1760+, 1763, 1763/71, Q
Dd2.22: half-yearly 1760, 1760+] ~$_\wedge$~ 1763, 1763/71
Dd3^v/422.17: loans 1760, 1760+, 1763, Q] loan 1763/71

Issue No. 10: Ee–Gg: pp. 433–80: Four Settings in Ee–Ff, With Two of Ee Sharing the Same Press Figures on the Same Pages; Three Settings of Gg

Ee-1760 [pp. 433–48]: Ee7/445-3 [under hyphen of "white-herring"], Ee7^v/446-2 [under "h" in "the"]: BL4 CtY1-2 DN *EU* InU IU *KU* LdU LU1 May1-4 MBat1 MdU MoJ *NBuU* NjM O Oc OCX PPiT PPL1 PSt *TnJoS TnNV ViLGH* ViWCF [Distinguished by period after "Numb." on Ee1, this setting is found in most copies dated 1760 and presumably all copies with Ff- and Gg-1760. But, since Ee-1760+ shares the same figures Ee7/445-3 and Ee7^v/446-2 similarly placed in skeletons, without pagination and CW variants, many copies must be conjecturally placed here based the setting of conjoined sheets (discovery of the duplicated press figures occurred well along in the examination of copies). The marginalia differs on Ee7^v/446: in Ee-1760 the third and fourth lines of marginalia read "import- | ing Ame-"; in Ee-1760+, they read "importing | America." One of the two settings is found in all copies dated "1760."];

Ee-1760+: Ee7/445-3 [under "g" in "herring" and no hyphen before "herring"], Ee7^v/446-2 [under "d" in "and"]; signed on Ee1 without period after "Numb": 1760: *AWn* InMB InTU LU2 May5-6 MnGA PCD PN Vi; 1763: BL3 CtHi ICarb MB1; 1771: CU-B. [signature positions on Ee1 and Ee4 same as Ee-60, but "2" under "i" of "finally"; "3" under far right side of "o" in "to"];

Ee-1763/71: Ee3^v/438-5, Ee8^v/448-3: 1763: BL2,5 BmU Brack CaAEU CaOTU CT CtHT CYc DGW MB2 MBat2 MWA Oa PPL2 ViU1-2 ViW; 1771: BL1 NNS;

Ee-1771: Ee6/443-6; Ee4^v/440 misnumbered "448": DT [text CW Ee1/433: On} *l.c.*; 1760 and 1763/71 correctly begin 434.1 with uppercase; RT ends on Ee2^v with "]" after final period; DT has the same unmarked paper with distinct chains 98-100/4 and wires in Ee–Ff as in Bb–Dd; BL71 and DT71 share the same paper stock in T–U and Z–Gg].

Textual variants in four settings of Ee: cf. 1760 (May2), 1760+ (May5), 1763/71 (BL1), 1771 (DT) on Ee1–Ee5, Ee8^v [lineal descent]:

Ee1/433.A.18–19 any 1760, 1760+, 1763/71] any any 1771

Ee1^v.B.29: commission 1760, 1760+, 1763/71] commissioned 1771 [correction]

Ee2^v/436.11: accurate; 1760, 1760+] ~, 1763/71, 1771 [correction, as is the next]

Ee2^v.12: parts, 1760, 1760+, Q] ~; 1763/71, 1771

Ee3^v/438.2–3: accou- | trements, 1760] ~$_\wedge$ 1760+, 1763/71, Q, 1771

Ee3^v.12: should 1760, 1760+, 1763/71, Q] ~, 1771

Ff-1760: Ff8/463-5 [under "t" of "not"], Ff8^v/464-4 [under "a" of "accused"]: same as Ee-1760 but with none conjectured and less MBat1 ["f" of Ff1 under "a" of "that"; "2" under "he" of "they"; "4" under "a" of "England"];

Ff-1760+: Ff8/463-4 [under "n" of "not"], Ff8^v/464-2 [under "o" of "of"]: same as Ee-1760+ with none conjectured ["f" of Ff1 under "b" in "being"; "2" of Ff2 under "t" in "they"; "4" under "l" of "England"];

Ff-1763/71: Ff4^v/456-1, Ff7^v/462-5: same as Ee-1763/71 ["f" of Ff1 under "at" of "that"; "2" under "t" of "they"; "4" under "E" of "England"];

Ff-1771: Ff8^v/464-6: DT [Ee1 and Ff1 signed correctly].

Textual variants in four settings of sheet Ff: cf. 1760 (May2), 1760+ (May5), 1763/71 (BL1), 1771 (DT) on Ff1–Ff5 [lineal descent]:

Ff1^v/450.7: Britain, 1760] ~$_\wedge$ 1760+, 1763/71, Q, 1771

Ff2^v/452.1: exposed; 1760, 1760+, Q] ~: 1763/71, 1771

Ff3/453.2: Medway; 1760] ~, 1760+, 1763/71, Q, 1771

Ff4/455.9: Greenville 1760, 1760+, Q] Grenville 1763/71, 1771 [correction—"brother to earl Temple"]

Ff5/457.6: commons, 1760, 1760+, 1763/71, Q] ~$_\wedge$ 1771

Gg-1760: Gg7^v/478-2: same as Ee-1760 but without conjectures;
Gg-1760+: Gg3^v/470-5 [under comma after "resolutions"], Gg7/477-2: same as Ee-1760+;
Gg-1763/71: Gg2^v/468-3, Gg3^v/470-5 [under "r" of "resolutions"]: same as Ee-1763/71 plus DT.
Textual variants in three settings of sheet Gg: cf. 1760 (May2), 1760+ (May5), 1763/71 (BL1) on Gg1–Gg5^v [lineal descent]:
Gg1/465.3: power 1760] ∼$_∧$ 1760+, 1763/71, Q
Gg1.15: place, 1760, 1763/71] ∼$_∧$ 1760+, Q [error]
Gg2/467.3: council; 1760, 1760+] ∼, 1763/71, Q [correction]
Gg2^v/468.18: London 1760, 1763/71] ∼, 1760+, Q
Gg4^v.3: with 1760] in 1760+, 1763/71, Q
Gg5^v.14: court-martial; 1760, 1760+] ∼, 1763/71 [correction]

Notes on Copies Examined of Vols. 1–5

Unless otherwise noted, assume that frt and some plates but not all are present (copies known to have all plates are noted at end of entries on plates; when "-plate X" is noted in copy locations, assume all others present). Assume that a copy belongs to a set of four volumes ("4-vol"); but "5-vol. set" indicates presence of vol. 5 1765; "15-vol" and "16-vol" indicate these sets are bound with the eleven volumes of *Complete History of England* (*CH*). For sets, call number, size in millimeters (a measurement preceded by "c." indicates all vols. are within 2 mm.), and binding information are given only under vol. 1; extention of call numbers for vols. 2–5 is sometimes given in square brackets; assume "with red labels" where spine labels are quoted; abbreviations are explained in brackets from the start:

Copies Examined of Vol. 1 with Title-Page Dated 1760: Unless Otherwise Noted, Assume All Sheets Have First Settings and the Volume Occurs in a Set of Continuation with Earliest Imprints of Vols. 2–4: 1760, 1760, and 1761

AWn ([National Library of Wales] DA455.S66; first [1760] settings in A–G [and] Q–S and second [1760/63 & 1760+] in H–P T–Gg; map [of] East Indies torn out and facing p. 201; uncut 225 x 150; in 15-vol set, with second settings in vol. 2; quarter calf with marbled-paper boards); **BL4** (1608/476; 194 x 129; in 4-vol set reb[oun]d by BL); **CSt** ([Stanford U.] PR3694.C61 vols. 1–3 1760, unexamined; vol. 4 dated 1768, examined by John Mustain; cont calf with armorial bookplate of Charles Vere Dashwood); **CtY1–2** (#1: Im Sm 79 757ck; -4 plates; +plate Earl Temple intended for *CH*, vol. 11; 195 x 126; rebd in 5-vol half-calf set, c. 195 x 127; numbered XII–XVI; bookplates noting "Gift of Lewis M. Knapp"; #2:

By7.26/12; 209 x 130; in 15-vol set [By.7.26/1-15], rebd in red buckram); DN (J942 Smo; -[i.e., lacking] plate Byng and map East Indies; 213-14 x 134; bound with *CH* vol. 11 in 16-vol set in half-leather with blue buckram, binding two volumes together passim); EU (E.E10.12[–16]; all plates but frt; in 16-vol set in half-leather with marbled-paper boards; [with red labels,] "SMOLLETT'S | HISTORY | OF | ENGLAND"); InMB ([Ball State U., Muncie] DA30.S66; first [1760] settings in A–G Q–S, second [1760/63 & 1760+] settings in H–P T–Gg; in 15-vol cont-calf set, with second settings in vol. 2 and v. 3 dated 1762; "SMOLLETT'S | HIST: OF | ENGLAND"; c. 198 x 128; bookplates, "Sold by James Lambert in the Cliff | Lewes"); InTU ([Indiana State U.] first settings in A–G Q–S; second in H–P T–Gg; in 5-vol set; second settings in vol. 2; vol. 3 dated 1762; rebd in green buckram; cont autograph "Charles Grant" on tp); InU (PR3694.H69; -plates Augusta, Coram, Byng; 16-vol set; cont[emporary] suade; "SMOLLETT'S | HISTORY | CONTINUED"; bookplates of "Henry Edmund Taylor | Whickham"); IU (942.Sm7co; -frt and 8 plates, +6 plates from other vols; cont-calf set with gilt spine, "CONTINUAT | OF | SMOLLETT"); KU ([U. of Kansas] C5301; in 15-vol set, half calf with marbled-paper boards; "HISTORY | OF | ENGLAND"; bookplate of Sir Josa. Van Neck); LdU (P-0.00; in 16-vol. set); LU1-2 (5-vol sets with all plates: #1: MUA Smo; all first settings; 208 x 130; rebd by LU with its bookplate on pastedown; #2: Porteus K3; first settings in A–G Q–S; second in H–P T–Gg; 5-vol set, second settings in vol. 2, vol. 3 dated 1762; c. 208 x 130; marbled-paper boards with armorial bookplate and autographs of [Bishop] Beilby Porteus; MS on margins of pp. 9 and 11 and back pastedown, noting pages with references to Pitt and Murray); May1 (all plates but frt; 201 x 127; in 15-vol cont-calf set, *CCH* vols. 1–3 dated 1760 and 4, 1768; "SMOLLETT'S | HIST. OF | ENGLAND"; cont bookplate with motto "Mors Sola Resolvit" engraved by "M. Mordecai & I. Levy scu."); May2 (all first settings but 1760/63 in H–M; 208 x 130; -plate Coram; in 15-vol cont-calf set with bookplates of Wolverhampton Public Libraries; "SMOLLETT | HIST: OF | ENGLAND"); May3 (203 x 129; in 16-vol cont-calf set, *CCH* vol. 4 dated 1764; -map North America [torn out]; c. 202 x 129–30; rebacked with original spines; "SMOLLETT'S | HIST. OF | ENGLAND"; bookplates, "William Browne | Surry, 1768"); May4 (-frt, replaced by plate of Queen Carolina; with 14 plates for diverse vols., mostly issued with Nos. 1–10; "SMOLLETT'S | HIST: OF | ENGLAND | VOL : XII."; bought with matching vol. 2 1760 from Owl Books, Ireland); May5 (first settings in A–G Q–S; second: H–P T–Gg; -frt, replaced by plate of Granby; with 13 plates for diverse vols., most issued with Nos. 1–10; speckled calf; lost label, which had read, "SMOLLETT'S | CONTINUATION"; tp signed "Williamson"); May6 (first settings in A–G Q–S; second: H–P T–Gg; cont-calf; vol. 1 only; -frt and maps; "SMOLLETT'S |CONTINUATIO"; cont autograph "Abraham Duryee" on tp); MBat1 ([Boston Athenaeum] $8E.Sm7;

first settings in A–G, Y–Z, Ee, and Gg; second: H–P and Aa–Dd and Ff; 1763:
Q–S; 1763/71: T–X; in 16-vol set, vols. 1–2 alone examined; tp signed "Mr
C Maure" in vol. 1 and "Christ Maure" in 2); **MdU** (DA40.S51 1760; -frt,
-maps of East Indies and N. America; 208 x 129; in 16-vol set in quarter calf
with marbled-paper boards; "SMOLLETT'S | HIST. OF | ENGLAND"; MS
annotations, esp. identifications of proper names in blanks); **MeB** ([Bow-
doin College] DA.S666C76; vol. 3 only); **MnGA** ([Gustavus Adolphus College, St. Peters, MN] DA470.S6C6; first settings in A–I Q–S; second: K–P
T–Gg; in 16-vol set, with some second settings in vol. 2; cont quarter calf
with paper boards; "T SMOLLET | HISTORY | OF | ENGLAND"); **MoJ** ([Wil-
liam Jewell College, Liberty, MO]; S.C. C9; first settings in A–F K–Gg; 1763:
G–H; in 16-vol cont-calf set; "SMOLLETT'S | CONTINUATION"; bookplate
of Lady Ashburton); **NjM** ([Drew U.]; 941.S666co; -frt, -plate Coram; in
15-vol cont-calf set; bookplates of Borden Parker Browne); **NBuG** ([Buffalo
and Erie Co. Pubic] 942.S666; 16-vol cont-calf set lacking *CCH* vol. 1; c.
196 x 132); **NBuU** ([U. of Buffalo] DA30.S6 1758; in 15-vol cont-calf set;
"SMOLLETT'S | HIST: OF | ENGLAND"); **O** (8° Godw 638[–42]; 16-vol
quarter-leather set; size varying; MS annotations); **Oc** ([Christ's Church
College] uncat.; -plate Byng; in 4-vol set joined to *CH* vols. 3–11, in cont
calf, labels lost; *CCH* vols. with armorial bookplate of "Thomas Fowler |
Pendeford," with vignette of crowned hawk); **OCX** ([Xavier U.] DA30.S662
1760; -frt, plates; in rebd 16-vol set lacking *CH* v. 11); **PCD** ([Dickinson
College, Carlisle, PA] SC 942.S666; first settings in A–G; second: H–P T–Gg;
1763: Q–S; cont calf; "SMOLLETT | CONTINU- | ATION"; with vol. 2 only,
in second settings); **PN** ([Bibliothèque Nationale, Paris]: Na 137-12; first
settings in A–G and Q–S; second: H–P T–Gg; -maps; with 13 plates bound
together after p. 16, for diverse vols., mostly issued with Nos. 1–10; in a
cont-calf set with vols. 2–3 [-vol. 4], with second settings in vol. 2; "SMOL-
LETT'S | HIST. OF | ENGLAND"); **PPiT** ([Pittsburgh Theological Seminary]
DA30.S66C76 1760; in rebd 5-vol set [yet *CH* vols. 3–11 present in calf]);
PPL1 ([Library Company of Philadelphia] Am 1760 Smol. [Acc. 77906.0
Wolf]; 204 x 126; in 15-vol cont-suade set; "SMOLLETT'S | CONTINUA-
TION | VOL: I."; pastedown signed "C. Paulette Harris | Clifton"; bookplate
noting gift of Edwin Wolf II, 1989 [PPL2 with reprint settings and a third,
partial set, Upl.483.0, with *CCH* vols. 4–5 unexamined]); **PPT** ([Temple U.]
DA30.S5 1758; vols. 2–4 only in incomplete 15-vol. set); **PSt** ([Penn State
U.] DA30.S62 1760; first settings in A–G Q–S; second: H–P T–Gg; in 4-vol
cont-calf set, with some second settings in vol. 2; "SMOLLETT'S | CON-
TINUATION"); **ScF** ([Francis Marion U., Florence, SC]; DA30.S664.1760x;
cont-calf set of vols. 2–4 [-vol. 1], with second settings of vols. 2–3 dated
1763 and vol. 4 1761; "SMOLLETT's | CONTINUATION"; gift with 7-vol
CH [1758] of Mr. and Mrs. Robert Cummings Bronson; cont bookplates of
Alex'r Fothringham); **TnJoS** ([East Tennessee State U.] -3 plates, -1 map; in

15-vol set; -vol. 2 of *CCH*; "SMOLLETT'S | HIST. OF | ENGLAND | XII"); **TnNV** ([Vanderbilt U.] in cont-calf 15-vol. set, with vols. 1–2 of *CCH* rebd; leaves with three stab holes for pamphlet sale); **Vi** ([Commonwealth of Virginia Library, Richmond] DA30.S666; first settings in A–G Q–S; second: H–P T–Gg; 4-vol. set, with second settings in vol. 2; in cont calf but not uniform: vols. 1–2 c. 204 x 129 without two gilt fillets around boards of vol. 3 [204 x 131]; "SMOLLETT'S | CONTINUATIO[N]"; MS on endpapers: "Thomas Pleasants jun." and below "M M Robinson | Richmond | April 11 1821"); **ViLGH** ([Gunston Hall, Lorton, VA] DA470.S6 1758 s. 13; all plates +Earl Temple for *CH* vol. 11; in 16-vol cont suade set; "SMOLLETT'S | HIST: OF | ENGLAND"; MS inscription "Jane-Caroline Derby | 1791"); **ViWCF** ([Colonial Williamsburg Foundation] "Palace"; in 4-vol cont-calf set; "SMOLLETT'S | CONTINUATION"; with stab holes for pamphlet sale; bookplates of "John Bennet Lawes. Esq. Rothamstead").

Copies Examined Dated 1763

BL2 (G4874[–4878]; 1763 settings in A–L N–P Bb–Dd; 1763/71: Q–Aa Ee–Gg; 1760/63: M; -2 maps; 209 x 131; in 16-vol cont- or near-cont-calf set; "SMOLLETT'S | HIST: OF | ENGLAND," c. 210 x 132; armorial bookplates of "HON[BLE] THO. GRENVILLE"; tps of vols. 1 and 3–5 signed "Sophia Ziegenhist" [or "Ziegenhirt"]; bound with vols. 2–4 dated 1767, 1765, 1768; c. 209 x 134); **BL3** (291.h.20[–24]; 1763 settings in A–F K–M Q–S; 1760: G; second [1760/63 & 1760+] settings: I N–P T–Gg [same as ICarb, MB1]; in 5-vol set with stamps of Royal Library; on ECCO); **BL5** (597.g.4; all third settings: 1763 in A–S Bb–Dd; 1763/71: T–Aa Ee–Gg; 205 x 127; rebd in red cloth by BL in 1942; tp signature "Cochrane" crossed out; verso stamped "DUPLICATE | 1804"; BL catalogue incorrectly calls it vol. 5); **BmU** ([U. of Birmingham] DA30; all third settings: 1763 in A–S Bb–Dd; 1763/71: T–Aa Ee–Gg; in 15-vol cont-calf set, vols. 2–4 [of *CCH*] dated 1763, 1762, 1764; "SMOLLETT'S | HIST: OF | ENGLAND"; armorial bookplate with "TOUTZ FOITZ CHEVALIER"); **Brack** ([O M Brack Jr., Phoenix] 1763 settings in A–E G–K M–N P Cc; 1760: F U Bb Dd; 1760/63: L and O; 1763/71 in Q–T X–Aa Ee–Gg, suggesting it was made up late from remainders; 203 x 127; in 16-vol cont-calf set, vols. 2–4 dated 1767, 1765, 1768 [and late reprints of *CH* vols. 1–5 and 11]; "SMOLLETT'S | CONTIN= | = UATION"; armorial bookplate of "Forman"); **CaAEU** ([U. of Alberta] DA30.S662.1765; 1763 sheets: A–L N–P Bb–Dd; 1760: M; 1763/71: Q–Aa Ee–Gg; in 16-vol cont-calf gilt set, vols. 2–4 dated 1767, 1765, 1764; "SMOLLETT'S | HIST. OF | ENGLAND"; signed "R L 1768"; R. Harris London bookplate); **CaOTU** ([U. of Toronto] B-11 7467; 1763 settings in A–P Bb–Dd; 1763/71: Q–Aa Ee–Gg; in 16-vol cont-calf set, vols. 2–4 dated 1763, 1765, 1764; "SMOLLETT | HISTORY"; bookplates noting given to

CaOTU by David G. Esplin); **CT** (X.9.21[-24]; 1763 settings in A–C; 1771: D–P; 1763/71: Q–S; 1771: T–Aa; 1763/71: Bb–Gg; in 15-vol calf set, vols. 2–4 dated 1767, 1765, 1768; c. 205 x 127; "SMOLLETT'S | HIST: OF | ENG-LAND"); **CtHi** ([Connecticut Historical Society] Robbins, 1999[-2002]; 1763 settings in A–M Q–S Bb–Dd; second [1760/63 and 1760+]: N–P T–Aa Ee–Gg; in 15-vol cont-calf set); **CtHT** ([Wilkinson Library, Trinity College, Hartford]; DA30.S6; all third settings: 1763 in A–S Bb–Dd; 1763/71: T–Aa Ee–Gg; 204 x 131; 4-vol cont-calf set, vols. 2–4 dated 1763, 1762, 1764; tps signed "S [or "J"] L James"); **CYc** ([Canterbury Cathedral] H/E-23-12[-15]; all third settings: 1763 in A–S Bb–Dd; 1763/71: T–Aa Ee–Gg; in 15-vol cont-calf gilt set, vols. 2–4 dated 1763, 1762, 1764; "SMOLLETT'S | HIST. OF | ENGLAND"; bookplates of Matthew Harrison); **DGW** ([George Washington U.] DA30.S652; 1763 settings in A–C G–K N–Q Bb–Dd; 1763/71: D–F [assuming E], L–M R–Aa and Ee–Gg; -maps; in 5-vol cont-calf set, vols. 2–4 dated 1767, 1765, 1768; rebacked and disintegrating); **ICarb** (942 S666c; 1763 settings in A–F K–M Q–S; 1760: G; second [1760/63 and 1760+]: H–I N–P T–Gg; in a rebd set, vols. 2–4 dated 1763, 1762, 1764; all uncut, 217–228 x 137–140); **MB1-2** (#1: Adams 240.8; 1763 settings in A–F K–M Q–S; 1760: G; second [1760/63 & 1760+]: H–I N–P T–Gg; in 16-vol set, vols. 2–4 dated 1763, 1762, 1764; vol. 1 in half-calf with marbled-paper boards; later vols. rebd; endpaper signed by [President] "John Adams"; with MB's Adams Library bookplate; #2: **K.88.20; 206 x 131; all third settings: 1763 in A–S Bb–Dd; 1763/71: T–Aa Ee–Gg; -frt and most plates but with 2 maps; 206 x 131; in 16-vol. cont-calf set, vols. 2–4 dated 1763, 1765, 1764; vols. 1, 3, 5 rebd); **MBat2** ([Boston Athenaeum] 8.E.Sm.77.2; as in ViU1-2: 1763 settings in A–P Bb–Dd; 1763/1771: Q–Aa Ee–Gg; 205 x 127; in cont-calf set, vols. 2–4 dated 1763, 1765, 1764; MBat bookplate noting gift of Louisa Waterhouse, 14 Aug. 1855; endpaper signed "Lee" and "Waterhouse"); **MWA** (J430.Smollett.C763; all third settings: 1763 in A–S Bb–Dd; 1763/71: T–Aa Ee–Gg; in 5-vol cont-calf set, vols. 2–4 dated 1763, 1765, 1764; "SMOLLETT'S | HISTORY | CONTINUED"; armorial bookplates of Gardiner Chandler engraved by "P Revere sculp," crest of swan above shield with three lions in oblique line); **Oa** ([All Souls College] SR.27.c.3/1[-5]; 1763 settings in A–C N–P; 1771: D–M; 1763/71: Q–Gg; in 5-vol cont-calf set, vols. 2–4 dated 1767, 1760, 1761; gilt stamp of All Soul's on front board and its cont bookplate; lost label had read, "SMOL-LETTS | CONTINUATION"; vol. 2 collated with assistance of photographs by Librarian Gaye Morgan); **PPL2** (Am 1763 Smoll [acc. 6619.0 {Mackenzie}]; like CT, final settings in all but A–C and Ee–Ff: 1763 settings in A–C; 1771: D–S; 1763/71: T–Aa; 1763/71: Bb–Gg; 204 x 133; 5-vol. cont-calf set, vols. 2–4 dated 1767, 1765, 1768; rebacked); **ViU1-2** (both in 5-vol cont-calf set, vols. 2–4 dated 1763, 1765, 1764, with same settings in vol. 1: 1763 in A–P Bb–Dd; 1763/71 in Q–Aa and Ee–Gg: #1: DA30.S52 1763;

-9 plates; 201 x 129; bookplate of Hartwell Cabell; ViU bookplate on 1949 presentation of Cabell Library assembled by ViU-founder Joseph Cabell and his nephew Nathaniel Francis Cabell; endpapers signed by N. F. Cabell; "SMOLLETT'S | CONTINUATION"; #2: Temp. control AJ C0828; all plates but map E. Indies; c. 205 x 131; "SMOLLETT'S | CONTINUAT"; 1970 bequest of Judge Bennet J. Gordon; tps signed "John Hay"); **ViW** ([William and Mary College] DA470.S52; in 16-vol cont-calf set, with labels lost; ViW bookplate notes presented by Rebecca Yancey Williams; vols. 2–4 dated 1767, 1765, 1768 [and late reprints of *CH* vols. 1–5 and 11]);

Copies Examined Dated 1771

BL1 (9502.e.5; 1771 settings in A–P; 1763/71: Q–Aa Ee–Gg; 1760+: Bb–Dd; in 16-vol set, vols. 2–4 dated 1767, 1765, 1761; c. 210 x 132 and rebd by BL in quarter-leather with red buckram; on ECCO); **CU-B** ([Bancroft Library, U. of California–Berkeley] DA30.S623 1765; 1771 settings in A–P; 1763/71: Q–S Y–Dd; 1771: T–X; 1760+: Ee–Gg; in rebd 5-vol set, vols. 2–4 dated 1767, 1765, 1768); **DT** (OLS L 3 296[–300]; 1771 settings in A–P Ee–Ff; 1763/71: Q–Dd Gg; -plate Byng; in 16-vol cont-calf set, vols. 2–4 dated 1767, 1765, 1761; "SMOLLETT'S | ENGLAND"; bookplate of John Kellingham); **NNS** ([New York Society Library] 942.S [#185 of the 1793 catalogue]; 1771 settings in A D–P; 1763: B–C; 1763/71: Q–Gg; -plates Augusta, Loudoun, -map N. America; in 5-vol cont-calf set, vols. 2–4 dated 1767, 1765, 1768; spines taped; vols. 1–3: 201 x 127; vols. 4 and 5: 210 x 134, 208 x 132; with NNS's 1789 engraved bookplate).

VOLUME 2.A–D: NUMBERS 11–20:
FOUR SETTINGS IN ISSUES 11–18, THREE IN 19–20

(VOLUME 2.A: RICHARD BALDWIN, 1760)

Tp

Same letterpress and ornament as vol. 1.A's except for "VOLUME THE SECOND." in l. 7 (an alteration of vol. 1.A's title-setting).

Coll., Contents, RTs, and Paper

8° (uncut, 220–25 x 142 [AWn, mostly second settings]): A–Gg⁸ ($1–4 signed; $1 with issue signature [no variants]); pp. *1–3* 4–478 *479–80*. A1: tp; A2–Gg7ᵛ: text on reign of George II, Nos. 11–20, with Ee2/435-Gg2/467, "JUSTIFYING PROOFS, | Published by Authority at Berlin" (29 numbered items beginning with one on "Treaty of Eventual Partition, dated

May 18, 1745."), and then, on Gg2ᵛ–Gg7ᵛ, "ANSWERS of the COURT of
Vienna, | TO THE | Prussian Declarations, circular Re- | scripts, and Memori-
als," a discussion of incidents noted Ee2ᵛ–Gg2; on Gg7ᵛ: "End of the Second
Volume"; Gg8–Gg8ᵛ: blank. Same RTs and same paper for text and plates
as vol. 1's.

Plates as Bound in Vol. 2.A–D (14 Engravings, Including 2 Maps; Multiple Engravings of All But Maps and York)

A4/7: "LORD HENLEY. | Lord Keeper of the Great Seal" signed "Miller
sculp."; one with knob at the bottom of the frame centered over the "H"
in "HENLEY" (CtHT May1 PSt); another with knob below frame over the
left side of the "E" in "HENLEY" (BL1-2 May2); B2/19: "CHARLES Duke
of MARLBOROUGH." signed "Bannerman sculp."; one with three circles
forming a knob under the frame above "f" in "of" (May1,3 InU NNS), another with flattened off knob with reverse "J" hanging below to right of "of"
(BL1-2 May2 PSt ViW); B8/31: "Honᵇˡᵉ. JOHN LOCHART, late Commander
| of His Majesty's Ship Tartar." unsigned; ribbon atop frame forming eight
windows, two white flowers on rocks to right (CtHT NNS PSt), also in retouched state with oblique lines downward to the left in the sky (BL1-2);
another cut signed "A Bannerman sculp" and six windows atop the frame
and without flowers (May1 IU NBuU); C8/47: "COLONEL COOTE."; one
signed "Aliamet sculp" (May1 NBuU PSt), another with period after "sculp"
(InU PPL1 and most 1767 copies as BL1-2 DT); G8ᵛ/112: folded map, "An
ACCURATE MAP | of the SEAT of WAR in the | Empire | of | Germany | as
also in the | KINGDOM of PRUSSIA | with the adjacent Countries" signed at
bottom right "T. Kitchin Sculp"; frame, 305 x 425; block, 315 x 436 (apparently one cut); M3/181: "BRIGADIER GEN.ᴸ MONCKTON." signed "Miller
sculp."; one with knob over "EN" (May1-2 MB1 PSt and most later imprints
as BL1-2), another with knob over "GE" (May3-5 NBuU MnGA); N6ᵛ/204:
"The Right Hon.ᵇˡᵉ GEORGE GRENVILLE." signed "Aliamet sculp."; one
with period after "Grenville" 31 from that after "sculp" and knob centered
over "O" of "GEORGE" (May1 MB1 PSt and most 1767 as BL1-2), another
(earlier) with periods 38 apart and knob over "EO" (May2,4 NBuU PPL1);
P6ᵛ/234: "CAPTAIN ARTHUR FORREST."; three cuts: two signed "Fouquet
sculp.": 1) with top line of arm on right moving downward to period after signature and horizontal shading lines only (May1 MB1 PPL1 PSt); 2)
another with same signature but top line of arm on right above the period
(IU InU May1 NBuU), retouched with oblique shading lines added on right
(CtHT May2); 3) signed "—B—Sculp.": seen only in some 1763 and all
1767 copies (BL1-2 CYc DT PPL2 ViW); Q3ᵛ/246: folded map, "FRANCE";
frame, 180 x 222; block, 193 x 232; two states: one signed bottom left, "T
Jefferys Sculp" (May1-2 PSt), another unsigned (BL1-2 May3); Q6ᵛ/252:

"EDWARD Duke of YORK." signed "Ravenet sculp." (only one identified); R8/271: "THOMAS CUMMING. | See Vol II. p. 271." signed "Miller sculp." [surname as in "Directions," but newspaper advertisements all give surname as "Comyns" (e.g., 22–24 January 1761 *LEP*)]; one with two elaborations flanking knob at base and knob over "C" (CtHT May1-2 O), another without two balancing elaborations on right of knob and with knob over left edge of "C" (BL1-2 DT May3 NNS); T5ᵛ/298: "RICHARD TYRREL Esqʳ. | late Captain of the Buckingham." signed "Bannerman sculp."; one with less than 1 mm. between knob at the base and the "Y" in "TYRREL" (CtHT MB1 PSt), another with over 2 mm. (BL1-2 May1-2,4 ViW); Z3/357: "MARSHAL KEITH." signed "Miller sculp."; one with knob below frame over right side of "A" (InU May1-2 PSt), another with knob over "AL" (BL1-2 CYc May3 ViW); Cc6ᵛ/412: "HUGH Earl of NORTHUMBERLAND." signed "Aliamet sculp." with "Aliamet" beginning 9 above right edge of the "M" (MdU PPL1 PSt), another with signature beginning 7–8 above "B" (BL1-2 CtHT May1-2 NBuU NNS). Copies with all plates in proper places include BL1-2 BmU Brack CT DT CtHi CYc May1 MB1 MnGA NBuU NNS Vi ViW.

Plates as Issued with Nos. 11–20 (12 Portraits)

#11: Henley and Sackville Duke of Dorset [for #11 & #5]; #12: Charles Townshend [for #7]; #13: Fitzroy, Duke of Grafton [for #6]; #14: Duke of Devonshire and Tyrrel [for #35 & #17]; #15: Brett [for #35]; #16: "Admiral Pocock" [for #25]; #17: Monckton by Miller [for #14]; #18: George Grenville [for #15]; #19: Blakeney presumed [for #7; untraced but likely to judge from summary advertisements, as in 11–13 December, *LEP*]; #20: "Queen Caroline, Consort to his late Majesty King George the Second, engraved by Mr. Aliamet," with "Carolina" in Directions [for #33; 11–13 December, *LEP*];

Notes to Vol. 2.A–D

In vol. 2 (with issues 11–20), sheets A–Aa are reset three times; Bb–Gg, twice. Resetting to meet demand began presumably in 1760 and may well have continued to 1769 or later, to judge from how long serialization preceded—though sheet A with the title was printed in 1767, other sheets may have run out a year or more later (as those in rare settings at DT). As with vol. 1, the reset sheets and issues of vol. 2 are too intermingled to allow ideal second through fourth editions to be described. Copies cannot be usefully grouped into three reset editions around the new title-pages (1760, 1763, 1767), but they divide fairly well into five groupings (covering 37 of the 61 copies examined) and so are divided below under locations. Copies with the reset 1760 title-page divide into a group with first edition settings after sheet I and another with nearly all second settings; those with 1763 title-page divide up into those with third settings in A–I and second thereafter and those with all or nearly all third settings. Irregularities in pagination, signatures, and the like are given sheet by sheet as identifying features along with press figures.

Different figures usually indicate different settings; on rare occasions varying press figures probably indicate a separate impression, as in vol. 2's sheet K-1760 and S-1760/63. Copies with the 1767 title-page have few sheets from earlier settings. Every sheet of the volume seems to have been reset after 1763 (some possibly more than once). The classification of settings and impressions is difficult as many settings lack press figures: unfigured sheets occur in 1763 settings for A–B (third settings); 1760/63 in M and O–S (second settings); in 1763/1767 settings of Y–Dd (third settings), and 1767 for K–Aa (fourth settings). Also, one state of sheet S-1763/67 (third setting, as in Brack and ViW) lacks press figures. If fourth settings occurred in 1767, they could be masked in Bb–Dd by unfigured third settings. The scarcity of some unfigured sheets makes the identification and classification of settings more difficult: I located only one copy with unfigured settings of sheets T–U (Oa), and only two of unfigured R–S and X (CU-B and Oa) and unfigured K (DT and Oa). Oa is the sole copy with all fourth-settings of sheets A–Aa.

The ESTC has three records for vol. 2 based on differently dated title-pages (it fails to record that two different title-pages were dated 1760): T55304 includes the 1760 volume within a five-volume set with the earliest dated volumes, indicating incorrectly that these were filmed on reel 157, no. 12 of *The Eighteenth Century* and reproduced on ECCO. ESTC T55305 includes the 1763 volume (BL3 was the copy of record), noting it was filmed for *The Eighteenth Century* in 1986 (reel 1630, no. 2) and reproduced on ECCO, and misleadingly adding that some issues "occur in variant settings." Most locations listed for set T55305 do not have vol. 2 1762. ESTC T55307 is devoted only to vol. 2 1767: it neglects blank leaf Gg8 in its pagination and misleadingly notes "some numbers occur in variant states." The BL's 9502.e.5, the original copy of record for T55307, has principally third and fourth settings, though it has the second of sheet O; it was filmed for *The Eighteenth Century* (reel 183, no. 5) and is reproduced on ECCO. The eight copy locations in T55307 are accurate. The second settings of sheets A–I (1760+ below) and many of the fourth settings (1767) are not in any copy filmed or reproduced on ECCO.

Tps, Typ., and Paper in Vol. 2.B–D

The tp of vol. 2.B (1760+) has identical letter-press to that in vol. 2.A and may have been set with some standing type. The later reprints have titles with identical letter-press until the two final lines: 2.C, with the same ornamental design as 2.A, has: "Printed for RICHARD BALDWIN, at the Rose in Paternoster-row. | M DCC L XIII." [half spaces after "D" and first "C"]; and 2.D, with a different ornamental design, has: "Printed for R. BALDWIN, in Pater-noster-Row. | MDCCLXVII." The third settings of sheets E, K and Bb have pagination errors E6^v/76 as "68," K8/159 as "195" (correct in a few), Bb3/389 as "367" and Bb6/395 as "399." The third settings of Nos. 12 and 15–16 abandon the conventional signature scheme for the first sheet of an issue, employing lowercase letters and arabic numerals (as "Numb. 12." at D1, repeated in the fourth setting); they employ the abbreviation "Num" on Ff1. Also, the misspelling "ENGLND" appears in RT of D4^v/56 and an erroneous "III" for "II" appears in the RT of most copies (correct in CaOTU and MWA). A distinctively injured RT links the unfigured fourth settings (2.D) of sheets K–Aa (all in Oa). In the 1767 settings at Oa and ViW, A1 is glued to A2 as if a cancel, but watermark and chain-line evidence suggests these are both repairs (A1 and A4 were evidently once joined at the top in both).

Continuities and discontinuities in the paper stocks clarify the relation-ship of settings shared by volumes with differently dated title-pages. The run of settings beginning at sheet K called "1760/63" below involves copies previously with 1760 title-pages (settings A–I 1760+) and those with 1763 tp and settings. The 1760+ have an unmarked paper stock like the first setting's in A–I (103-04/4). The 1763 copies (like BL3, BmU, and MB1) have two stocks in A–I: unmarked paper with chain-lines 102-05/4 and tranchefiles 10-11: A–B D–G, and another with fleur-de-lys WM between chain-lines in C H–I (chains, 104-07/4; tranchefiles, 15-16). This fleur-de-lys paper stock continues when the streams fuse: 1760/63 copies have it through sheet Dd, when they switch to an unmarked stock 105-07/4 in Ee–Gg, possibly the stock in A–B and D–G of the 1763 sheets. There is no con-tinuous run for the second setting, which was first required through sheet I only, and those sheets of A–I were available until 1763. The other com-mon pattern in reprints beginning at sheet K involves copies with A–I 1763 that then have a third printing of most later sheets, here called "1763/67." The copies with 1767 title-pages have four stocks in A–I: 1) chain-lines, 76-77/3; tranchefiles, 15-16; fleur-de-lys between chains with head 21–23 and tail 21: A–B (BL1-2 Oa DT ViW; 2) 77-80/3; tranchefiles, 12-13; fleur-de-lys WM *on* chains: C (as BL2 CaAEU ViW); 3) 77-79/3; no WM: D–G; 4) 78-79/3; tranchefiles, 15-17; fleur-de-lys between chains, head 16–18 and tail 21: G–I BL1-2 DT ViW Oa; H–I and N of CaAEU; Q of DT). Many copies dated 1763 and others dated 1767 share the same settings beginning in K, but K has a paper stock not yet seen in either: chain-lines, 104-05/4, with "L|V|H" WM. In later sheets, two other new paper stocks dominate: L–X: chain-lines, 87-90/3; tranchefiles, 15-17: and Y–Gg: chain-lines 104/4;

tranchefiles usually never seen (but 12 in Cc of BL2; this stock may appear in S and U of ViW, etc.); this latter stock is distinctive for having molds in which chain-lines in $5-8 "wander," narrowing some chain-widths down to 12 mm. while expanding others. The rare fourth resettings ("1767") of sheets K–Aa have two unmarked stocks with wide chain-lines: one 109-12/4 in K–P, another 116-20/4 in Q–Aa (Oa and in most cases DT).

Issue No. 11: Sheets A–C: pp. 1–48: Four Settings as in Nos. 1–8

A-1760: A2^v/4-3, A6/11-4: BL4 CtY1-2 EU InU IU LdU LU1 May1-4 MdU MoJ NBuG NBuU NjM O Oc OCX PPiT PPL1 PPT TnNV ViLGH ViWCF;

A-1760+: A8^v/16-4: 1760: AWn InMB InTU LU2 MnGA PCD PN PSt ScF Vi [an accurate resetting adding no variants on A2^v–A3^v and A4^v–A5];

A-1763: no figures: BL3 BmU CaOTU CtHi CtHT CYc ICarb MB1-2 MBat1-2 MWA VIU1-2;

A-1767: A8^v/16-7: BL1-2 Brack CaAEU CT CU-B DGW DT NNS Oa PPL2 Rulon-Miller ViW.

Textual variants in four settings of sheet A: cf. 1760 (May2), 1760+ (PSt), 1763 (BL3), 1767 (Brack) on A3–A4 [lineal descent]:

A3/5.9: surrounded 1760, 1760+, Q] surround 1763, 1767

A3.17: suggestions, 1760, 1760+, Q] ~$_\wedge$ 1763, 1767

A4/7.2: half-way 1760] ~~ [i.e., "half way"] 1760+, 1763, Q, 1767

A4.24: prudent, 1760, 1760+, 1763, Q] ~$_\wedge$ 1767

A4^v/8.13: subsisted: 1760] ~; 1760+, 1763, 1767] ~. Q

B-1760: B7/29-5, B7^v/30-6: same as A-1760 [On B3, p. 21 misprinted "2" in EU, not noted elsewhere];

B-1760+: B1^v/18-1, B5/25-3: same as A-1760+;

B-1763: no figure: same as A-1763 [B1 under "am" of "clamours"; "2" under "l" in "should"];

B-1767: B4^v/24-6: same as A-1767.

Textual variants in four settings of sheet B: cf. 1760 (May2), 1760+ (PSt), 1763 (BL3), 1767 (Brack) on B2–B2^v, B7–B8^v [lineal descent]:

B2/19.2: shall 1760] should 1760+, 1763, Q, 1767

B2^v.17: or as 1760] or [om.] 1760+, 1763, 1767

B8/31.34: corporations, 1760, 1760+, 1763] ~$_\wedge$ 1767

B8^v/32.3-4: home- | ward-bound 1760, 1760+] ~$_\wedge$~ 1763, 1767

C-1760: C1^v/34-4, C2^v/36-1: same as A-1760;

C-1760+: C3^v/38-1: same as A-1760+;

C-1763: C8^v/48-2: same as A-1763;

C-1767: C5/41-1: C6/43-3: same as A-1767.
Textual variants in four settings of sheet C: cf. 1760 (May2), 1760/63 (PSt), 1763 (BL3), and 1767 (Brack) on C1–C3^v, C8–C8^v [lineal descent]:
C1^v/34.10: order, 1760] ~$_\wedge$ 1760+, 1763, Q, 1767
C1^v.13: fortifications, voted in parliament, 1760] ~$_\wedge$~$_\wedge$ 1760+, 1763, Q, 1767
C2^v/36.20: command, 1760, 1760+, 1763] ~$_\wedge$ 1767
C8/47.17: storehouses 1760] store houses 1760+] store-houses 1763, 1767
C8.30: men, 1760, 1760+, 1763] ~$_\wedge$ 1767
C8^v.16: appertaining: 1760, 1760+] ~; 1763, 1767

Issue No. 12: Sheets D–F: pp. 49–96

D-1760: D4^v/56-2, D5^v/58-3: same as A-1760 plus 1767: Rulon-Miller [error in RT on D7/61 with "GEORGE I." for "II" (corrected in a few copies)];
D-1760+ D8/63-2 [under "e" in "Bestucheff"]; D5^v/58 mispaginated "96": same as A-1760+ [in some copies D2^v/52 mispaginated " 2" (e.g., PSt) or unpaginated (e.g., InTU)];
D-1763: D5/57-3 [in right margin], D8/63-1: same as A-1763 [as in D-1767, D1 signed irregularly, "Numb. 12."; erroneous spelling "ENGLND" in RT on D4^v/56];
D-1767: D8/63-2 [under second "o" of "soon"], D8^v/64-7: same as A-1767 less Rulon-Miller [no CW on D6^v–D7].
Textual variants in four settings of sheet D: cf. 1760 (May2), 1760+ (PSt), 1763 (BL3), 1767 (Brack) on D1–D3^v, D8 [lineal descent]:
D2^v/52.26: subah 1760] suba 1760+, 1763, Q, 1767
D3.1: intirely 1760, 1760+] entirely 1763, 1767
D3^v.marg.4: assassinate | 1760, 1760+; assassi- | 1763, 1767
D8.18: forward; 1760] ~: 1760+, 1763, 1767] ~. Q

E-1760: E1^v/66-1, E7/77-5: same as D-1760;
E-1760+: E6/75-5, E8^v/80-4: same as A-1760+;
E-1763: E5^v/74-1 [after "having"], E7/77-2; E6^v/76 mispaginated "68": same as A-1763;
E-1767: E5^v/74-1 [in left margin], E8^v/80-2: same as D-1767.
Textual variants in four settings of sheet E: cf. 1760 (May2), 1760+ (PSt), 1763 (BL3), 1767 (Brack) on E1–E3 [lineal descent]:
E1/65.27: replying, 1760, 1760+, Q] ~$_\wedge$ 1763, 1767
E3/69.5: fate; 1760] ~: 1760+, 1763, Q, 1767
E3.24: Marechal 1760] Marshal 1760+, 1763, Q, 1767

F-1760: F1^v/82-5 [under "u" in "Hungarian"], F2^v/84-3: same as D-1760;
F-1760+: F7/93-1: 1760: AWn InMB InTU LU2 MnGA PCD PN PSt ScF [F1^v/82 incorrectly paginated "28" in a few copies (e.g. AWn PSt) but correct in most];
F-1763: F1^v/82-5, F8^v/96-4: BL3 BmU CaOTU CtHi CtHT CYc ICarb MB1-2 MBat1-2 MWA ViU1-2; 1760: Vi; 1771: CU-B [variant RT with "III" on F3/85 and F7/93 in most but corrected to "II" in some (e.g., CaOTU, MWA); on F4 p. 87 misprinted "8 " in CU-B];
F-1767: F2^v/84-2: BL1-2 Brack CaAEU CT DGW DT NNS Oa PPL2 ViW.
Textual variants in four settings of F: cf. 1760 (May2), 1760+ (PSt), 1763 (BL3), and 1767 (Brack) on F1–F3 [lineal descent]:
F1/81.16: way, 1760, 1760+] ~$_\wedge$ 1763, Q, 1767
F1^v/82.17: attempted 1760] attempting 1760+, 1763, Q, 1767
F3/85.8-9: Em- | press-queen 1760, 1760+, 1763] ~$_\wedge$~ 1767
F3.32: experience, 1760, 1760+, Q] ~$_\wedge$ 1763, 1767

Issue No. 13: Sheets G–I: pp. 97–144

G-1760: G1^v/98-3, G5/105-2: same as D-1760;
G-1760+: G7/109-2, G7^v/110-4: 1760: AWn InMB InTU LU2 MnGA PCD PN PSt ScF Vi; 1767: CaAEU;
G-1763: G8^v-112-1: BL3 BmU CaOTU CtHi CtHT CYc ICarb MB1-2 MBat1-2 MWA ViU1-2 [as in G-1767, with irregular volume signature on G1: "Numb. XIII." as G-1767; no figure on 112 in MBat1, yet otherwise the same setting];
G-1767: G2^v/100-4: BL1-2 Brack CT CU-B DGW DT NNS Oa PPL2 ViW [no CWs for text on G8–G8^v].
Textual variants in four settings of sheet G: cf. 1760 (May2), 1760+ (PSt), 1760/63 (BL3), 1767 (Brack) on G1–G3 [probably lineal descent, but 1767 could descend directly from 1760+]:
G2^v/100.1: vanguard 1760] van-guard 1760+, 1763, 1767
G2^v.19: Weser, 1760] ~$_\wedge$ 1760+, 1763, 1767
G2^v.22, 34: Bielefeld 1760] Bielefeldt 1760+, 1763, 1767
G3/101.26: war; 1760] ~: 1760+, 1763, Q, 1767

H-1760: H1^v/114-1, H6^v/124-5: same as D-1760;
H-1760+: H2^v/116-2: same as A-1760+ (or G-1760+ minus CaAEU);
H-1763: H8/127-5: same as G-1763 plus CaAEU;
H-1767: H8/127-4, H8^v/128-7: same as G-1767;
Textual variants in four settings of sheet H: cf. 1760 (May2), 1760+ (PSt), 1763 (BL3), 1767 (Brack) on H1–H3^v and H8^v [1763 and 1767 descend independently from 1760+]:
H1/113.A.31: and 1760, 1760+, 1767] *om.* 1763
H2/115.34 [ult. l.]: for, 1760] ~ 1760+, 1763, 1767

H3/117.9: war: and, 1760,] ~; ~ 1760+, 1763, Q, 1767
H3.marg.7: ports 1760, 1760+, 1767] port 1763, Q

I-1760: I4^v/136-3, I7^v/142-2: same as D-1760;
I-1760+: I7^v/142-4: 1760: same as A-1760+;
I-1763: I1^v/130-3: 1763: BL3 BmU CaOTU CtHi CtHT CYc ICarb MB1-2 MBat1-2 MWA ViU1-2 [figure not noted at CaOTU; as in 1767, CW error on I6/139: of} battle (not in 1760 and 1760+, which begin I6^v with "of")];
I-1767: I2^v/132-4, I6/139-2: 1767: BL1-2 Brack CaAEU CT CU-B DGW DT NNS Oa PPL2 ViW.
Textual variants in four settings of sheet I: cf. 1760 (May2), 1760+ (PSt), 1763 (BL3), 1767 (Brack) on I1–I2, I6^v–I8^v [as CW on I6 suggests, lineal descent, unless, as in gathering H, 1767 descends from 1760+ as suggested by variant at I8^v.27]:
I1/129.20: Britannic 1760, 1760+, Q] Britannick 1763, 1767
I1.29: pacquet-boats 1760, 1760+, Q] ~$_\wedge$~ 1763, 1767
I1.33, I6^v.23: farther 1760] further 1760+, 1763, Q, 1767
I2/131 marg: 18–19 detached | parties of 1760] *om.* 1760+, 1763, Q, 1767
I7^v/142.16: Kameke 1760] Kemeke 1760+, 1763, Q, 1767
I8.27: Winsteben 1760, 1760+, Q] Winstebin 1763, 1767
I8^v/144.26–27: Aus- | trians, 1760, 1760+, Q, 1767] ~$_\wedge$ 1763

Issue No. 14: Sheets K–M: pp. 145–92

K-1760.A–B: Two states both with K7/157-4 but differing in press figure on K5^v/154 on the inner forme [under "ss" in "Prussian" in both]: state A with K5^v-2: BL4 CtY1-2 EU InU IU LdU LU1 May1-4 MdU MnGA MoJ NBuG NBuU NjM O Oc OCX PPiT PPL1 PPT PSt TnNV ViLGH ViWCF; plus 1767: Rulon-Miller; state B with K5^v-4: PN plus 1767: Brack];
K-1760/63: K6^v/156-5 [under "t" of "this"]: 1760: AWn InMB InTU LU2 PCD ScF Vi; 1763: BL3 BmU CtHi CtHT ICarb MB1-2 MBat1 [CW K1/145: "lect" without comma found in others];
K-1763/67: K6^v/156-5 [5 under "m" in "time"] and K8/159-4; 1763: CaOTU CYc MBat2 MWA ViU1-2; 1767: BL1-2 CaAEU CT CU-B DGW NNS PPL2 ViW; [K8/159 misnumbered "195" in all but a few (BL2 and NNS)];
K-1767: no figure: DT Oa [p. 159 correctly paginated; RT on K5^v/154 with "O" in "HISTORY" dented at 7:00 and second "N" in "ENG-LAND" cut in middle of ligature (second) stroke, recurring $5^v from K–Aa; 2 of K2 under "e" of "their" (Oa); as in K-1760 CW on K3/149

is "ground" without the comma found in 1760/63 and 1767 and on
K3ᵛ; CW on K4: "Schweidnitz," as in 1760 and 1760/63, and unlike
1763/67 without comma].

Textual variants in four settings of sheet K: cf. 1760 (May2), 1760/63
(BL3), 1763/67 (BL1), and 1767 (Oa) on K1–K3 and K8ᵛ [1760/63
and 1767 descend independently from 1760, and 1763/67 descends
from the accurate 1760/63 (1760 and 1767 alone share the same line-
ending at K3.1, CW on K3, and variants K1ᵛ.32, K2.16; 1763/67 and
1767 each introduce many unique variants]:

K1ᵛ/146.32: city; 1760, 1767] ~: 1760/63, 1763/67, Q
K2/147.10: plains 1760, 1760/63, 1763/67, Q] plain 1767
K2.16: Meresburgh {as in K2ᵛ.27} 1760] Meresbourg [as in K2.13]
  1760/63, 1763/67, Q] Meresbourgh 1767
K2ᵛ/148.1: nearer 1760, 1760/63, 1763/67, Q] near 1767
K2ᵛ/148.27: Merseburgh {error} 1760, 1760/63, 1763/67, Q] Meres-
  burgh 1767
K3/149.24: was 1760, 1760/63, 1763/67, Q] were 1767
K8ᵛ/160.24-25: not, however, 1760, 1760/63, 1767] ~ₐ~ₐ 1763/67

L-1760: L1ᵛ/162-1, L8ᵛ/176-3: BL4 CtY1-2 EU InU IU LdU LU1 May1-4
  MdU MnGA MoJ NBuG NBuU NjM O Oc OCX PN PPiT PPL1 PPT PSt
  TnNV ViLGH ViWCF; 1767: Rulon-Miller;
L-1760/63: L8/175-4 [under "h" of "their"]: 1760: AWn InMB InTU LU2
  PCD ScF Vi; 1763 BL3 BmU CtHi CtHT ICarb MB1 MBat1;
L-1763/67: L2ᵛ/164-5 [under "re" of "refuse"]: 1763: CaOTU CYc MB2
  MBat2 MWA ViU1-2; 1767: BL2 Brack CT CaAEU DGW PPL2 ViW [CW
  L4ᵛ: trea-} ties, (leaves "trea-" out of text unlike others that end page
  with "trea-"];
L-1767: no figure: BL1 CU-B DT NNS Oa [L2 ends "pas-" with CW "sed";
  but 1763/67 "passed with his corps" with CW "from"; recurrent RT
  with "O" dented at 7:00 in "HISTORY" and "N" cut in middle of liga-
  ture stroke on L5ᵛ, as in K–Aa on $5ᵛ].

Textual variants in four settings of sheet L: cf. 1760 (May2), 1760/63
(BL3), 1763/67 (Brack), 1767 (BL1) on L1–L6, L7ᵛ–L8ᵛ [as in K and
M, 1760/63 and 1767 both descend independently from 1760, and
1763/67 descends from 1760/63 (the latter pair contain more text on
L2); both 1763/67 and 1767 introduce many variants not shared by
the other]:

L1/161.29: principal 1760, 1760/63, 1763/67, Q] principle 1767
L1ᵛ.14: and, 1760] ~ 1760/63, 1763/67, Q, 1767
L1ᵛ.18: commanding-officer 1760, 1767] ~ₐ~ 1760/63, 1763/67, Q
L2ᵛ.13: for 1760, 1767] ~, 1760/63, 1763/67, Q
L3/165.1: [re- ||] quest, 1760, 1760/63, Q, 1767] ~ₐ 1763/67

L3.34: Europe 1760, 1767] ~, 1760/63, 1763/67, Q
L3^v/166.26: courts, 1760 1760/63, Q, 1767] ~$_\wedge$ 1763/67
L3^v/166.34: in of 1760, 1760/63, 1763/67, Q] in [*om.*] 1767
L8/175.9: them, 1760, 1760/63, 1763/67] ~$_\wedge$ 1767

M-1760: M1^v/178-4 [under right side of "h" in "approach" (May3)],
M8^v/192-2: same as L-1760 plus 1767: CU-B [M1^v/178-4 is missing
from May2,4, MdU, MoJ, but usually present];
M-1760/63: no figure: 1760: AWn InMB InTU LU2 PCD ScF Vi; 1763:
BL3 BmU CtHi CtHT ICarb MB1 MBat1; plus 1767: BL2 [M1 under
"ic" of "which"; "2" of M2 under "i" of "which"];
M-1763/67: M5^v/186-4: 1763: CaOTU CYc MB2 MBat2 MWA ViU1-2;
1767: BL1 Brack CaAEU CT DGW NNS PPL2 ViW;
M-1767: no figures: DT Oa [recurrent damaged "O" and "N" in RT on
M5^v, as $5^v K–Aa in 1767; M1 under "hi" in "which"; "2" of M2 un-
der "c" of "which." Textual variants do no determine priority between
1763/67 and 1767].
Textual variants in four settings of sheet M: cf. 1760 (May2), 1760/63
(BL3), 1763/67 (Brack), 1767 (Oa) on M1–M3 and M8^v [as in L,
1760/63 and 1767 appear to descend directly from 1760, and 1763/67
from 1760/63 (1767 lacks rare variants introduced by 1760/63 as
M1^v.23); neither 1763/67 or 1767 follows the other]:
M1/177.33: resolute, 1760, 1760/63, 1763/67, Q] ~$_\wedge$ 1767
M1^v/178.12–13: Schuy- | lenbourg; and, 1760, 1760/63, Q, 1767] Schuy-
| lenbourgh; ~$_\wedge$ 1763/67
M1^v.23: officer, 1760, 1767] ~$_\wedge$ 1760/63, 1763/67, Q
M2/179.5: subject; 1760, 1760/63, Q, 1767] ~, 1763/67
M8^v/192.7: not improperly be 1760, 1760/63, 1763/67, Q] not be im-
properly 1767
M8^v.15: Indeed, 1760, Q, 1767] ~$_\wedge$ 1760/63, 1763/67
M8^v.27: she 1760, 1760/63, 1763/67] we 1767

Issue No. 15: Sheets N–P: pp. 193–240

N-1760.A–B: state A: N5/201-3, N5^v/202-4 [under first "o" in "com-
mons"]: AWn BL4 CtY1-2 EU IU InU LdU LU1 May1-4 MdU MnGA
NBuG NBuU NjM O Oc OCX PN PPiT PPL1 PPT PSt TnNV ViLGH
ViWCF; plus 1767: Rulon-Miller [N5-3 not recorded at AWn]; state B:
N5^v/202-5 [under second "o" in "commons"]: MnGA, MoJ;
N-1760/63: N6/203-1: 1760: InMB InTU LU2 PCD ScF Vi; 1763: BL3
BmU CtHi CtHT ICarb MB1 MBat1; 1767: CaAEU. [N1 irregularly
signed "Numb. 15."—the same variant signature with lowercase occurs
on D1 and Q1 (e.g., BmU)];

N-1763/67: N7/205-3: 1763: CaOTU CYc MB2 MBat2 MWA ViU1-2; 1767: BL1-2 Brack CT DGW NNS PPL2 ViW; [N1 signed under "t" of "expiration"; "2" under "n" of "bounds"; CW on N8^v: "contents" (without the comma in 1760 and 1760/63)];

N-1767: no figure: CU-B DT Oa [recurrent damaged "O" and "N" in RT on N5^v; N1 signed "Numb. XV."; N1 under right side of "x" of "expiration"; "2" under "ou" of "bounds"; no CW on N8^v. Textual variants do not determine priority between 1763/67 and 1767].

Textual variants in four settings of sheet N: cf. 1760 (May), 1760/63 (BL3), 1763/67 (Brack), and 1767 (Oa) on N1–N3 and N8^v [1760/63, 1763/67, and 1767, all with many unique variants, descend directly and independently from 1760]:

N1/193.A.6: tickets, 1760, 1760/63, 1763/67, Q] ~$_\wedge$ 1767

N1.B.12: year, 1760, 1760/63, Q, 1767] year; 1763/67

N1^v.A.11: sums 1760, 1763/67, 1767] sum 1760/63, Q

N1^v.B.12–13: pay- | ments 1760, 1760/63, Q, 1767] ~, 1763/67

N2/195.1: upwards; 1760, 1760/63, Q, 1767] ~: 1767

N2.17: drawbacks 1760, 1763/67, 1767] draw backs 1760/63

N2.20: first having 1760, 1763/67, 1767] having first 1760/63, Q

O-1760.A–B: state A: O1^v/210-1, O7/221-2: BL4 CtY1-2 EU IU InU LdU LU1 May1-4 MdU MoJ NBuG NBuU NjM O Oc OCX PPiT PPL1 PPT PSt TnNV ViLGH ViWCF; 1767: BL1 Rulon-Miller; state B: O7/221-2 [O1^v-1 missing]: MnGA, PN (both with second settings of A–I and with rare B states of 1760-K in PN and of 1760-N in MnGA)];

O-1760/63: no figures: 1760: AWn InMB InTU LU2 PCD ScF Vi; 1763: BL3 BmU CtHi CtHT ICarb MB1 MBat1; 1767: BL1 [O1 signed under "e" in "the"; "2" under "es" of "monopolies"];

O-1763/67: O3^v/214-3, O5/217-4: 1763: CaOTU CYc MB2 MBat2 MWA ViU1-2; 1767: BL2 Brack CaAEU CT DGW NNS PPL2 ViW;

O-1767: no figures; CU-B DT Oa [recurrent damaged "O" and "N" in RT on O5^v; O1 under "h" in "the"; "2" under "li" of "monopolies." Textual variants do not determine priority between 1763/67 and 1767].

Textual variants in four settings of sheet O: cf., 1760 (May2), 1760/63 (BL3), 1763/67 (Brack), 1767 (Oa) on O1–O3 and O8^v [1760/63 and 1763/67 descend directly from 1760; 1767 descends from 1760/63; as usual, 1767 has many careless errors, including foul-case errors (as O1.9), suggesting it is a late or hurried reprint]:

O1/209.2: This, however, 1760, 1760/63, Q] ~$_\wedge$~$_\wedge$ 1763/67] ~$_\wedge$~, 1767

O1.13: them 1760, 1760/63, Q, 1767] ~, 1763/67

O1^v/210.6: of, 1760, 1763/67, Q-unfigured state] ~ 1760/63, Q-figured, 1767

O1^v.8: enforcing 1760, 1763/67] inforcing 1760/63, 1767

O1^v.16–18 and O2.25–26: line endings shared by 1760 with 1763/67 and by 1760/63 with 1767

O2^v.17: been been 1760, 1760/63, Q, 1767] *om.* 1763/67 [correction]

O8^v/24.12: homeward-bound 1760, 1760/63, 1763/67] ~$_\wedge$~ 1767

P-1760: P2^v/228-4, P5^v/234-3: BL4 CtY1-2 EU InU IU LU1 LdU May1-4 MdU MnGA MoJ NBuG NBuU NjM O Oc OCX PN PPiT PPL1 PPT PSt TnNV ViLGH ViWCF; plus 1767: Rulon-Miller;

P-1760/63: no figure: 1760: AWn InMB InTU LU2 PCD ScF Vi; 1763: BL3 BmU CtHi CtHT ICarb MB1 MBat1 [P1 signed under "ol" of "soliciting"; "2" after "that"];

P-1763/67: P1^v/226-5, P8^v/240-3: 1763: CaOTU CYc MB2 MBat2 MWA ViU1-2; 1767: BL1-2 Brack CaAEU CT DGW NNS PPL2 ViW [p. 237 mispaginated "225" in some (e.g., BL1 CT DGW NNS) but correct in others (e.g., BL2 Brack ViW)];

P-1767: no figure: CU-B DT Oa [recurrent damaged "O" and "N" in RT on P5^v; P1 under "li" of "soliciting"; "2" under "h" of "have." Textual variants do not determine priority between 1763/67 and 1767].

Textual variants in four settings of sheet P: cf. 1760 (May2), 1760/63 (BL3), 1763/1767 (Brack), and 1767 (Oa) on P1–P4, P8^v [1760/63 and 1767 descend directly from 1760 and each have many unique variants; 1763/67 descends from 1760/63]:

P1^v/226.2–3: mer- | chants, 1760, 1760/63, Q, 1767] ~$_\wedge$ 1763/67

P1^v.5: advanced, 1760, 1760/63, 1763/67, Q] ~$_\wedge$ 1767

P1^v.11: of 1760, 1763/67, 1767] a 1760/63, Q

P1^v.25: the British 1760, 1763/67, Q, 1767] this British 1760/63

P1^v.32: thereafter, settle 1760, 1767] ~$_\wedge$~, 1760/63, 1763/67, Q

P3/229.4: else 1760, 1767] less 1760/63, 1763/67, Q

P3/229.23: measures 1760, 1760/63, 1763/67, Q] ~, 1767

Issue No. 16: Sheets Q–S: pp. 241–88

Q-1760: Q6^v/252-5, Q7^v/254-2: same as P-1760;

Q-1760/1763: No figure in Q: 1760: AWn InMB InTU LU2 May3 PCD ScF Vi; 1763: BL3 BmU CtHi CtHT CYc ICarb MB1 MBat1; 1767: DT [as in Q-1767, Q1 irregularly signed "Numb. 16." and Q1 under "h" of "himself"; but "2" of Q2 under comma after "Hawke"];

Q-1763/67: Q3^v/246-3, Q4^v/248-1: 1763: CaOTU CYc MB2 MBat2 MWA ViU1-2; 1767: BL1-2 Brack CaAEU CT DGW NNS PPL2 ViW [Q1 signed "Numb. XVI."];

Q-1767: no figure in Q: CU-B Oa [Q1 signed "Numb. 16."; recurrent RT on Q5^v; "2" under "k" of "Hawke." Textual variants do not determine priority between 1763/67 and 1767].

Textual variants in four settings of Q: cf. 1760 (May2), 1760/63 (BL3), 1763/67 (Brack), 1767 (Oa) on Q1–Q3 and Q8^v [1760/63 and 1763/67 descend directly from 1760; 1767 derives from 1760/63, introducing many careless errors, such as "fram" for "from " at Q2^v.4; 1763/67 and 1767 with many unique variants]:

Q1/241.5: time 1760, 1763/67] ∼, 1760/63, Q, 1767
Q2.24: overboard 1760, 1763/67] over-board 1760/63, Q, 1767
Q2^v/244.4: from 1760, 1760/63, 1763/67] fram 1767
Q2^v.15: people 1760, 1760/63, 1767] ∼, 1763/67, Q
Q2^v.30: moreover 1760, 1760/63, 1767] however 1763/67
Q3.30: frenzy 1760, 1763/67] phrenzy 1760/63, Q, 1767
Q8^v.14: of the reach 1760, 1760/67, 1763/67, Q] of reach 1767

R-1760: R1^v/258-5, R8^v/272-2: same as P-1760;
R-1760/63: no figure: 1760: AWn InMB InTU LU2 PCD ScF Vi; 1763: BL3 BmU CtHi CtHT ICarb MB1 MBat1 MWA [R1 under "he" of "whence"; "2" of R2 just after "This"; "3" under "xe" of "exercise"; R7^v/270.15 ends "dif-" in R-1760/63 and "differ-" in R-1763/67 (ViU1-2)];
R-1763/67: R3^v/262-3; "Numb" without period on R1: 1763: CaOTU CYc MB2 MBat2 ViU1-2; 1767: BL1-2 Brack CaAEU CT DGW DT NNS PPL2 ViW;
R-1767: no figure in R: CU-B Oa [recurrent damaged "O" and "N" in RT on R5^v; R1 under "om" of "from"; "2" under "s" of "This"; R3–R4 unsigned; textual variants cannot determine priority between 1763/67 and 1767. 1767's existence in so few copies and its carelessly being composed (following the revised quarto) argue it is the final octavo].
Textual variants in four settings of sheet R: cf. 1760 (May2), 1760/63 (BL3), 1763/67 (Brack), 1767 (Oa) on R1–R3 and R8^v [unlike in Q, 1760/63 and 1767 descend directly from 1760; 1763/67 descends directly from 1760/63; 1763/67 and, especially, 1767 introduce many unique variants]:

R1/257.3: Guildo 1760, 1767] ∼, 1760/63, 1763/67, Q
R1.CW: have 1760, 1767] noyed 1760/63, 1763/67
R1^v/258.15: proceeding, 1760, 1760/63, 1763/67, Q] ∼$_∧$ 1767
R1^v.20: halts 1760, 1760/63, 1763/67, Q] ∼, 1767
R2^v.18–19: as, in all probability, 1760, 1767] as ∼$_∧$ 1760/63, 1763/67, Q
R3/261.5–6: ves-|sels 1760, 1760/63, Q, 1767] ∼, 1763/67
R8^v/272.10: approved, 1760, 1760/63, 1763/67] ∼$_∧$ 1767

S-1760: S1^v/274-4, S8^v/288-1: same as P-1760;
S-1760/63: no figure: 1760: AWn InMB InTU LU2 PCD ScF Vi; 1763: BL3 BmU CtHi CtHT CYc ICarb MB1 MBat1 [S1 under "f" of "If"];
S-1763/67.A–B: state A with figure S8/287-5 [under second "r" in "Brad-street"]: 1763: CaOTU MB2 MBat2 MWA ViU1-2; 1767: BL1-2 CaAEU

CT DGW DT NNS; state B: no figure: 1767: Brack PPL2 ViW. [nearly all copies have a gap after "2" in pagination "288"];
S-1767: no figure: CU-B Oa [recurrent damaged "O" and "N" in RT on S5^v; S1 signed with comma after "Numb"; S1 under "h" of "the"; S2^v has CW "last" before footnote].
Textual variants in four settings of sheet S: cf. 1760 (May2), 1760/63 (BL3), 1763/67 (Brack), 1767 (Oa) on S1–S3 and S8^v [lineal descent]:
S1^v/274.3: Senegal: 1760, 1760/63, 1763/67, Q] ~; 1767
S2/275.24: numbers, 1760] ~$_\wedge$ 1760/63, 1763/67, Q, 1767
S3/277.13: French 1760, 1760/63, Q] ~, 1763/67, 1767
S8^v/288.6: secured 1760] ~, 1760/63, 1763/67, Q, 1767
S8^v.20: stroke 1760, 1760/63, Q] blow 1763/67, 1767
S8^v.A.2: through 1760, 1760/63, Q] thro' 1763/67, 1767

Issue No. 17: Sheets T–X: pp. 289–336

T-1760: T5^v/298-5, T8^v/304-3: BL4 CtY1-2 EU InU IU LdU LU1 May1-4 MdU MnGA MoJ NBuG NBuU NjM O Oc OCX PN PPiT PPL1 PPT PSt TnNV ViLGH ViWCF; plus 1767: CT DT Rulon-Miller;
T-1760/63: T5/297-2, T8/303-5 [under "us" of "dangerous"]: 1760: AWn InMB InTU LU2 PCD ScF Vi; 1763: BL3 BmU CtHi CtHT ICarb MB1 MBat1; plus 1767: NNS PPL2;
T-1763/67: T8/303-5 [under "n" in "number"]: 1763: CaOTU CYc MB2 MBat2 MWA ViU1-2; 1767: BL1-2 Brack CaAEU CU-B DGW ViW;
T-1767: no figure: Oa [recurrent damaged "O" and "N" in RT on T5^v; T1 under "t" of "with"; "2" of T2 under "te" of "Masters"; CW T4^v/296: "kings,"].
Textual variants in four settings of sheet T: cf. 1760 (May2), 1760/63 (BL3), 1763/67 (Brack), 1767 (Oa) on T1–T3 and T8^v [as in P and R, 1760/63 and 1767 descend directly from 1760, and 1763/67 descends from 1760/63]:
T1^v/290.14: enemy 1760, 1767] ~, 1760/63, 1763/67, Q
T1^v.17: reinforcement: 1760, 1760/63, 1763/67, Q] ~; 1767
T1^v.marg.2 reads: Fort Fron- 1760, 1760/63, 1767] Fort 1763/67
T2.15: provision 1760, 1767] provisions 1760/63, 1763/67
T2^v.marg.5: Fort 1760, 1763/67, 1767] Port 1760/63
T3/293.26–27: Misissip- | pi 1760, 1760/63, 1767] Mississip- | pi 1763/67
T8^v/304.5: islands 1760, 1767] island 1760/63, 1763/67, Q
T8^v.15–16: go-|vernor, 1760, 1760/63, 1763/67, Q] ~$_\wedge$ 1767

U-1760: U1^v/306-5, U8^v/320-4: 1760: same as P-1760 (same as T-1760 minus CT DT);
U-1760/63: U8/319-3, U8^v/320-2: 1760: AWn InMB InTU LU2 PCD ScF Vi; 1763: BL3 BmU CtHi CtHT ICarb MB1 MBat1;

U-1763/67: U8/319-6 [before "he"], U8ᵛ/320-5 [after "the"]: 1763: CaOTU CYc MB2 MBat2 MWA ViU1-2; 1767: BL1-2 Brack CaAEU CT CU-B DGW DT NNS PPL2 ViW;

U-1767: no figure: Oa [recurrent damaged "O" and "N" in RT on U5ᵛ; U1 under "ge" of "forage"; "2" of U2 under "c" of "ineffectual"].

Textual variants in four settings of sheet U: cf. 1760 (May2), 1760/63 (BL3), 1763/67 (Brack), 1767 (Oa) on U1–U3 and U8ᵛ [variant in U1ᵛ.8 suggests that 1763/67 and 1767 each descend directly from the accurate 1760/63]:

U1ᵛ/306.2: war 1760] ∼, 1760/63, 1763/67, Q, 1767
U1ᵛ.8: jealousies 1760, 1760/63, Q, 1767] enemies 1763/67
U2.8: shared in 1760, 1760/63, 1763/67, Q] shared 1767
U2ᵛ/308.32: Mecklembourg 1760] Mecklenbourg 1760/63, 1763/67, 1767
U8ᵛ/320.14–15: country, and advancing to Bremen demanded ad- | mittance, threatening 1760] ∼ₐ threatning 1760/63, 1763/67] country, threatning 1767

X-1760: X2ᵛ/324-3, X5ᵛ/330-4: same as P-1760;
X-1760/63: X7ᵛ/334-5: 1760: AWn InMB InTU LU2 PCD ScF Vi; 1763: BL3 BmU CtHi CtHT ICarb MB1 MBat1; plus 1767: CaAEU;
X-1763/67: X2ᵛ/324-6, X7ᵛ/334-4: same as U-1763/67 less CaAEU;
X-1767: no figure: CU-B Oa [recurrent damaged "O" and "N" in RT on X5ᵛ; X1 under the "s" of "hands"; "2" of X2 under right of "l" of "valour"; X3/325 and X4/327 unpaginated or nearly so (a recurrent problem: Y3/341 and Z3/357 are unpaginated in Oa)].

Textual variants in four settings of sheet X: cf. 1760 (May2), 1760/63 (BL3), 1763/67 (Brack), 1767 (Oa) on X1–X3 and X8ᵛ [lineal descent, with 1760/63 introducing five variants and 1767 twice that number; as in sheet U, 1763/67 is accurate]:

X1/321.7: Ottersburg, 1760, 1763, 1763/67, Q] ∼ 1767
X1.22–23: pre- | tend, 1760, 1763/67, Q, 1767] ∼ 1760/63
X1ᵛ.23: Clermont; 1760, 1760/63, 1763/67, Q] ∼: 1767
X1ᵛ.26: sermons 1760] Sermons 1760/63, 1763/67, Q, 1767
X2/323.18: abandoned, 1760, 1760/63, 1763/67, Q] ∼ 1767
X2ᵛ/324.24: Vechte 1760, 1760/63, Q] Vecht 1763/67, 1767

Issue No. 18: Sheets Y–Aa: pp. 337–84: Without Figures in the Third and Fourth Settings

Y-1760: Y2ᵛ/340-4, Y6/347-2: same as P-1760;
Y-1760/63: Y1ᵛ/338-4: 1760: AWn InMB InTU LU2 PCD ScF Vi; 1763: BL3 BmU CtHi CtHT CYc ICarb MB1 MBat1 [no period or but a speck after "Nᴜᴍʙ" on Y1];

Y-1763/67: no figures: 1763: CaOTU MB2 MBat2 MWA ViU1-2; 1767: BL1-2 Brack CaAEU CT CU-B DGW DT NNS PPL2 ViW ["Y" of Y2 under "an" of "and"; RT with "O" in "HISTORY" broken at 10:00 and 2:00 on Y5^v/346, recurs in 1763/67 gatherings Z–Dd];
Y-1767: no figures: Oa ["Y" of Y2 under "d" of "and"; Y3/341 unpaginated; recurrent damaged "O" and "N" in RT on Y5^v].
Textual variants in four settings of sheet Y: cf. 1760 (May2), 1760/63 (BL3), 1763/67 (Brack), 1767 (Oa) on Y1–Y3 and Y8^v [1760/63 and 1763/67 directly descend from 1760; and 1767 descends from 1763/67 (1763/67 is the most accurate)]:
Y1^v/338.3: forces 1760, 1763/67, 1767] force 1760/63, Q
Y1^v.24–25: Konings- | gratz 1760, 1760/63, Q] Konins- | gratz 1763/67, 1767
Y1^v.marg.5: of Prussia 1760, 1760/63, Q] *om.* 1763/67, 1767
Y2/339.6: made shift 1760, 1763/67, 1767] made a shift 1760/63, Q
Y2.14: Neiss 1760, 1760/63, Q] Niess 1763/67, 1767
Y2^v/340.20: Morava 1760, 1760/63, Q] Moravia 1763/67, 1767
Y2^v.26: provision 1760, 1760/63, Q] provisions 1760/63, Q
Y3/341.9: by one 1760, 1763/67, 1767] by an 1760/63, Q
Y3.21: motion 1760, 1760/63, 1763/67, Q] motions 1767

Z-1760: Z1^v/354-1, Z5/361-5: same as P-1760;
Z-1760/63: 3 figures: Z7/365-4, Z7^v/366-5, Z8^v/368-4: same as Y-1760/63 [three figures consistently present and no evidence of cancellation];
Z-1763/67: no figure: same as Y-1763/67 [Z1 under "t" in "North"; "2" of Z2 under second "s" of "possession"; RT with damaged "O" in "HISTORY" on Z6^v/364, recurring Y–Dd 1763/67];
Z-1767: no figures: Oa [Z1 under "No" of "North"; "2" under "e" of "possession"; recurrent damaged "O" and "N" in RT on Z5^v; p. 357 is unpaginated and most of "359" is not inked in Oa].
Textual variants in four settings of sheet Z: cf. 1760 (May2), 1760/63 (BL3), 1763/67 (Brack), 1767 (Oa) on Z1–Z3 and Z8^v [lineal descent]:
Z1/353.5: days, 1760] ~$_\wedge$ 1760/63, 1763/67, Q, 1767
Z1^v.12: Brandenburgh 1760, 1760/63, Q] Brandenburg 1763/67, 1767
Z2/355.1: Rittlitz 1760, 1760/63, 1763/67, Q] Rittliz 1767
Z2^v.23: upon 1760, 1760/63, 1763/67, Q] on 1767
Z2^v.25: another 1760, 1760/63, Q] no other 1763/67, 1767

Aa-1760: Aa6/379-1, Aa6^v/380-2: same as P-1760;
Aa-1760/63: Aa3^v/374-3: same as Y-1760/63;
Aa-1763/67: no figures: same as Y-1763/67 ["A" of Aa1 under "b" of "by"; recurrent cut "O" in RT on A1a^v/370];

Aa-1767: no figures: Oa [A of Aa1 under "th" of "the"; recurrent damaged "O" and "N" in RT on Aa5^v].

Textual variants in four settings of sheet Aa: cf. 1760 (May2), 1760/63 (BL3), 1763/67 (Brack), 1767 (Oa) on Aa1-Aa3 [lineal descent, with half the score of variants unique to poorly corrected 1767]:

Aa1/369.4: where 1760, 1760/63, 1763/67, Q] when 1767
Aa1^v.13: money, 1760] ~; 1760/63, 1763/67, Q, 1767
Aa1^v.31: quarters; 1760, 1760/63, Q] ~, 1763/67, 1767
Aa2/371.marg.3: P____'s 1760] Prussia's 1760/63, 1763/67, Q, 1767
Aa3/373.14: was 1760, 1760/63, Q, 1767] *om.* 1767
Aa3.29: that 1760, 1760/63, 1763/67, Q] the 1767

Issue No. 19: Sheets Bb–Dd: pp. 385–432 [Three Settings]

Bb-1760: Bb1^v/386-5, Bb5/393-4: same as P-1760;
Bb-1760/63: Bb2^v/388-6: same as Y-1760/63;
Bb-1763/67: no figure; Bb3/389 and Bb6/395 mispaginated "367" and "399": 1763: CaOTU MB2 MBat2 MWA ViU1-2; 1767: BL1-2 Brack CaAEU CT CU-B DGW DT NNS Oa PPL2 ViW [cut "O" in RT on Bb5^v/394, recurring in Y–Dd of 1763/67].

All textual variants in three settings Bb1–Bb4: cf. 1760 (May2), 1760/1763 (BL3), 1763/67 (Brack) [lineal descent]:

Bb2/3387.21: function 1760] ~, 1760/63, 1763/67, Q
Bb3/389.20: embarkation: 1760] ~; 1760/63, 1763/67, Q
Bb3^v/300.3: Scotland: 1760] ~; 1760/63, 1763/67, Q
Bb3^v.8: sugar-colonies 1760, 1760/63, Q] ~$_\wedge$~ 1763/67
Bb4/391.5: Empress- 1760, 1760/63, Q] empress- 1763/67
Bb4.14: Empire 1760, 1760/63, Q] empire 1763/67

Cc-1760: Cc7^v/414-1: same as P-1760;
Cc-1760/63: Cc2^v/404-6: same as Y-1760/63;
Cc-1763/67: no figures: same as Bb-1763/67 ["3" of Cc3 under "li" of "puplic" {*sic*}; cut "O" in recurrent RT on Cc7^v/414].

All textual variants in three settings of Cc1–Cc3 and Cc8^v: cf. 1760 (May2), 1760/63 (BL3), 1763/67 (Brack) [lineal descent]:

Cc1^v/402.12: land-forces 1760, 1763/67, Q] ~$_\wedge$~ 1760/1763
Cc2. 17: West-Friesland 1760, 1760/63, Q] ~$_\wedge$~ 1763/67
Cc3/405.10: conquest: 1760] ~; 1760/63, 1763/67, Q
Cc3.34 [ult. l.]: public 1760, 1760/63, Q] puplic 1763/67
Cc3.15: which, 1760] ~$_\wedge$ 1760/63, 1763/67, Q

Dd-1760: Dd1^v/418-4 [just after "d" in "third"], Dd4^v/424-5: same as P-1760 [stop-press corrections on Dd1/417.22, where the word "told" had been repeated in some copies (May1 PPL1 PSt—in the last two one iteration is crossed out in MS), but it was correct in others (e.g., May2); this correct state occurs with slightly shifted signature positions on only Dd2 and Dd4, suggesting a change on the inner forme as well];

Dd-1760/63: Dd1^v/418-4 [under "r" of "received"], D8^v/432-6: same as Y-1760/63;

Dd-1763/67: no figures: same as Bb-1763/67 ["D" of Dd1 under "an" of "any"; "2" of Dd2 under "w" of "Tower"; cut "O" in recurrent RT on Dd8^v/432].

Textual variants in three settings of sheet Dd: cf. 1760 (May2), 1760/63 (BL3), 1763/67 (Brack) on Dd1–Dd4 [lineal descent]:

Dd1^v/418.13: duke 1760, 1760/63, Q] ~, 1763/67
Dd2/419.8: to, 1760] ~$_\wedge$ 1760/63, 1763/67, Q
Dd2.12: These, 1760] ~$_\wedge$ 1760/63, 1763/67, Q
Dd2.29: letter: 1760, 1760/63, Q] ~; 1763/67
Dd2^v/420.16: than 1760, 1763/67, Q] then 1760/63

Issue No. 20: Sheets Ee–Gg: pp. 433–80 [Three Settings]

Ee-1760: Ee5/441-4, Ee7^v/446-2: 1760: same as P-1760 plus AWn;
Ee-1760/63: Ee4^v/440-4 1760: same as Y-1760/63 minus AWn;
Ee-1763/67: Ee3^v/438-3, Ee4^v/440-6 [under "w" in "well"]: same as Bb-1763/67.

Textual variants in three settings of sheet Ee: cf. 1760 (May2), 1760/63 (BL3), 1763/67 (Brack) on Ee1–Ee3^v [lineal descent]:

Ee1/433.33 [ult l.] concludes "the" 1760; "future" 1760/63, 1763/67 [final line in 1760/63 and 1763/67 is the first on Ee1^v in 1760]
Ee2^v/436.28: happens 1760, 1760/63] ~, 1763/67
Ee3/437.11: bourg 1760] burg 1760/63, 1763/67
Ee3^v/438.6: Prussia, 1760, 1760/63] ~$_\wedge$ 1763/67

Ff-1760: Ff2^v/452-1, Ff8/463-5: same as P-1760 plus AWn;
Ff-1760/63: Ff1^v/450-5: 1760: InMB InTU LU2 PCD ScF Vi; 1763: BL3 BmU CtHi CtHT CYc ICarb MB1 MBat1; 1767: Brack [Ff4^v/456 begins "Nnmb."];
Ff-1763/67: Ff5/457-7: 1763: CaOTU MB2 MBat2 MWA ViU1-2; 1767: BL1-2 CaAEU CT CU-B DGW DT NNS Oa PPL2 ViW [Ff1 signed with "Num."].

Textual variants in three settings of sheet Ff: cf. 1760 (May2), 1760/63 (BL3, Brack), 1763/67 (BL1) on Ff1–Ff3^v [lineal descent]:

Ff1/449.28: *Privy-Council.* 1760] ~, 1760/63, 1763/67
Ff1.36: Prussia 1760, 1760/63] ~, 1763/67
Ff2/451.33: 1756 1760, 1763/67] 1739 1760/63
Ff2.37: guaranty 1760] guarantee 1760/63, 1763/67

Gg-1760: Gg3^v/470-4, Gg4^v/472-2: same as P-1760 plus AWn;
Gg-1760/63: Gg7/477-5: 1760: same as Ff-1760/63 minus Brack;
Gg-1763/67: Gg5^v/474-1 [under "a" of "act"—blurred and sometimes appearing as "2" (e.g., Brack CU-B)], Gg6^v/476-4: same as Ff plus Brack 1763/67.
Textual variants in three settings of sheet Gg: cf. 1760 (May2), 1760/63 (BL3), and 1763/67 (Brack) on Gg1–Gg3^v [lineal descent]:
Gg1/465.29: long run 1760, 1760/63] ~-~ 1763/67
Gg1^v.32: through 1760] thro' 1760/63, 1763/67
Gg2^v/468.17: proceedings 1760, 1760/63] ~, 1763/67
Gg3/469.36: undertaken 1760] taken 1760/63, 1763/67

Copies Examined of Vol. 2 With Title-Page Dated 1760, With First Settings Throughout

BL4; CtY1-2 (#1: Im Sm79.757ck; -Gg8; -plates Monckton, Northumberland; Knapp's copy; #2: By7.26/13; +Gg8; rebd in red buckram); EU (E.E10.13); InU (+Gg8; -4 plates, -map Germany); IU (+Gg8; -maps and 6 portraits); LdU; LU1 (210 x 133, rebd); May1 (+Gg8); May2 (+Gg8; -plate Lockhart; 208 x 129-30; bookplates of Wolverhampton Public Library); May3 (+Gg8; -plate Grenville; 203-4 x 129); May4 (-Gg8; with 11 plates for diverse vols., mostly issued with Nos. 11–20 [10 of them are also in PN]; three sheets of No. 21 bound at the end); MdU (DA40.S51 1760; -maps, -plate Monckton misbound in vol. 4; MS notations); MoJ (S.C.C9; variant figure in 1760-N); NBuG (+Gg8; -portrait plates; +maps; 196 x 132); NBuU (+Gg8); NjM (+Gg8; -all plates); O (-plate Monckton; extra-illustrated copy with inserted leaves after p. 272 containing the text in Arabic and drawings of seals of a charter given to Mr. Cumming; the Arabic is above a translation by Dr. Browne, Rector of Taunton in Oxfordshire; MS in English and Arabic appears in the margin of p. 271; this material relates to the historical discussion of Cumming on 2:271-272; portrait of Legge from *CH* vol. 11 facing A2^v); Oc (+Gg8); OCX (-Gg8; -all plates); PPiT; PPL1 (Am 1760 Smoll; +Gg8; -first 3 plates); PPT (-Gg8; -all plates [torn out]; 202 x 128); TnNV (-Gg8); ViLGH (MS notations; inserted "Plan of Cherbourg" after p. 254, "Engraved for Geographical Dictionary"); ViWCF (+Gg8).

Copies Examined Dated 1760 With Second Settings (1760+) of Gatherings A–I and Then First (1760) in K–Gg (With One Exception)

MnGA (rare states of second settings M and O; +Gg8); PN (with rare states of K and O; -maps; with 12 plates bound together after p. 16, for diverse vols., mostly issued with Nos. 11–20 [10 of them are also in May4 and others in vol. 1 of May4); PSt (+Gg8; -plate Cumming; MS on tp, "Mr. Gage's Book bought at Mr. Volance's, | dublin, October 1799").

Copies Examined Dated 1760 With All Or Nearly All Second Settings (1760+ in A–I; 1760/63 in K–Gg)

AWn (DA455.S66; second settings in A–Dd [1760+ in A–I; 1760/63: K–Dd]; 1760: Ee–Gg; 225 x 142, uncut); InMB (all second settings); InTU (all second settings; tp with cont autograph "Charles Grant"); LU2 (Porteus K3; all second settings); PCD (all second settings; probably +Gg8); ScF (all second settings; +Gg8; 202 x 129); Vi (all second settings but 1763 in F).

Copies Examined Dated 1763 With Third (1763) Settings in Gatherings A–I and Second (1760/63) in K–Gg

BL3 (291.h.21; on ECCO [shelf number in MS on tp]); BmU (probably +Gg8); CtHi (+Gg8); CtHT (+Gg8; -plate Lockhart, map France); ICarb (+Gg8; -most plates; uncut, 218–24 x 137–40); MB1 (Adams 240.8; 204 x 130; part of tp at top right cut away as if for autograph); MBat1 ($8E.Sm7; -Gg8; 197 x 128; tp signed "Chris^t Maure").

Copies Examined Dated 1763 With All Or Mostly Third Settings

CaOTU (B-11 7467; all third settings: 1763 [settings] in A–I, 1763/67: K–Gg; +Gg8); CYc (H/E 23-13; 1763 in A–I; 1763/67: K–X; 1760/63: S; 1760/63: Y–Gg; -Gg8); MB2 (**K.88.20; all third settings: 1763 in A–I; 1763/67: K–Gg; -plates; 205 x 130); MBat2 (8E.Sm77.2; all third settings: 1763 in A–I; 1763/67: K–Gg); MWA (1763 in A–I; 1763/67: K–Q S–Gg; 1760/63: R); ViU1-2 (both with all third settings: 1763 in A–I; 1763/67: K–Gg: #1) DA30.S52; 201 x 127; #2) uncatalogued, 206 x 131).

Copies Examined Dated 1767

BL1 (9502.e.5; 1767 [fourth settings] in A–I; 1763/67: K M–N P–Gg; 1767: L; 1760/63: O; -Gg8; 210 x 131, leaving some outer edges untrimmed; on ECCO [octagonal "MVSEVM . . ." stamp on Gg7^v]); BL2 (G4875; 1767 in A–I; 1763/67: K–L N–Gg; 1760/63: M; +Gg8; -maps of East Indies and North America; 210 x 131); Brack (1767 in A–I; 1760: K; 1763/67: L–Ee Gg; 1760/63: Ff; -Gg8; some loss of text in Gg); CaAEU (1767 in A–F I; 1760+: G; 1763: H; 1760/63: N X; 1763/67: K–M O–U Y–Gg; +Gg8; endpaper signed "RL" 1768); CT (1767 in A–I; 1763/67: K–S U–Gg; 1760: in T); CU-B (1767 in A–E G–I L N–S X; 1763: F; 1763/67: K T–U Y–Gg; 1760: M; -Gg8); DGW (1767 in A–I; 1763/67: K–Gg); DT (OLS L 3-297;

1767 in A–P; 1760/63: Q; 1763/67 in R–S U–Gg; 1760 in T); NNS (1767 in A–I L; 1763–1767: K M–S U–Gg; 1760/63: T; +Gg8; -plate Forrest); Oa (SR.27.c.3/2; rare copy with 1767 in A–Aa; 1763/67: Bb–Gg; +Gg8; 208–10 x 129; $1–3 and 8ᵛ of K–Aa collated with photographs from Gaye Morgan); PPL2 (Am 1763 Smol [6619.0]; 1767 in A–I; 1763/67: K–S U–Gg; 1760/63: T; -Gg8; 203 x 131); Rulon-Miller (offered for sale by Robert Rulon-Miller of Minneapolis in 2009; 1767 settings in A–C; 1760: D–Gg; in 4-vol. set with vols. 1 and 3–4 dated 1760, 1760, 1761; cont-calf spines with marbled-paper boards, red labels); ViW (1767 in A–I; 1763/67: K–Gg; +Gg8).

VOLUME 3.A–C: NUMBERS 21–30: THREE SETTINGS PASSIM

(VOLUME 3.A: RICHARD BALDWIN, 1760 [–1761])

Tp

Same letter-press and ornament as in the tps of vols. 1.A and 2.A except for "THIRD" in l. 7's volume statement (an alteration of the same setting, to judge from shared broken type).

Coll., Contents, RTs, and Paper

8° (uncut, 226 x 145 [AWn]): A–Gg⁸ [$1–4 signed; $1 with issue signatures (all regular)]; pp. *1–3* 4–192 177–463 *464 blank* [=480]. The count drops back 16 places after M8ᵛ/192 and remains off until the end (this error reappears in second and third settings); numbers in the erroneous second series between 177 and 192 are placed in quotes when referenced; ignoring p. 57, unpaginated in some copies (AWn IU MnGA Oa PN PSt), the count fits all copies seen but EU, which has 429 unpaginated. Contents: A1: tp; A2–Gg8ᵛ: text of nos. 21–30 (Gg8ᵛ blank), with Ff8ᵛ–Gg8 containing observations of Commodore Moore on Smollett's remarks on pp. 130ff.; on Gg8: "PS" noting likely error in account of murder of Mrs. Clarke in vol. 2; on Gg8: "End of the Third Volume." RT: "HISTORY OF ENGLAND. | GEORGE II." without variant. Same unmarked paper as in vol. 2.

Plates as Bound in Vol. 3.A–C (8 Portraits, Each in Two Engravings, and 2 Maps)

G3ᵛ/102: folded map, "WEST INDIES"; unsigned; within single-ruled frame, 178 x 293; block, 197 x 308 (identified along with the map of France [signed by Jefferys] as by "Thomas Jefferies, Geographer to his Majesty," in the *PA* of 14 August 1762; no second engraving identified for this or next); H8/127: folded map, "A NEW MAP | of the | CARIBBEE | ISLANDS | in

| AMERICA | 1761."; centered over the frame is the statement "Engraved for Smollet's Continuation of the History of England."; unsigned; single-ruled frame, 243 x 182; block, 252 x 189; L8^v/176: "GENERAL AMHERST." signed "Aliamet sculp."; two cuts distinguishable by elaboration in oval frame at 3:00 and 9:00 and by the position of the signature; one begins 13 from "R" in "AMHERST" (BL1 May1 MdU PSt), another 12 (May2-3 MnGA NBuU); M2^v/180 ["Directions" specifying "Sheet M" due to pagination error]: "ADMIRAL SAUNDERS." signed "Müller sculp.": one with two circular shapes forming knob below frame (BL1,3 May2-3 PSt) and another with knob a small loop hooking to right—also with a smaller signature (May1,4 and MnGA); N4/"182" ["Directions" specifying "Sheet N"] "GENERAL WOOLFE." ["Wolfe" in "Directions" and advts]; signed "Engrav'd from M^r. Isaac Gosset's Model by J. Miller.": one with ornamental bud of frame touching first "l" in "Miller" (BL1 CtHT May1-2), one with bud over "i" in "Miller" (InU NBuU PSt); O1^v/194: "GENERAL TOWNSHEND."; one signed "Müller sculp." (with period) and with knob below frame over "TO" (BL1 CtHT May2-4 PSt), another signed "Miller sculp" (without period) and with knob over "T" (LU2 May1 MdU); O8^v/208: "ADMIRAL POCOCK." signed "Miller sculp."; one with period after "POCOCK" 18 from period after "sculp" and with narrower knob than other (May2 NBuU Vi), another with periods 16 apart (BL1 CtHT May1,3-4 PSt); Q3^v/230: "PRINCE FERDINAND." signed "Sherlock sculp."; one with wormy elaborations in frame at 3:00 and 9:00 (BL1 CtHT May1,3-4 PSt), another without the elaborations at 3:00 and 9:00 (May2 MdU); Y7^v/334: "GENERAL KINGSLEY." signed "Benerman sculp."; one with 23 between periods of signature and caption and two or three windows formed by ribbon at top right (BL3 CtHT May3-4 PSt); another with 25 between periods and with five windows formed by ribbon at top right (BL1 May1-2 Vi); Aa8/367: "LORD GEORGE SACKVILLE." signed "Miller sculp."; one with two leaves to left of knob below frame (May3); another with one leaf on left, three on right (BL1,3 May1-2,4 PSt—nearly all). Copies known to have all plates in proper places include BL1 BL3 (but Ferdinand faces 227), Brack CT CtHT CtY1 CYc DT EU InMB InTU InU LU2 MnGA Oc PSt Vi ViU (but Sackville faces 380), ViW.

Plates as Issued with Nos. 21–30 (11 Portraits)

#21: Amherst [for #24]; #22: "Thomas Comyns, who plan'd the Success and Expedition [*sic*] against Senegal; drawn from the Life, and engrav'd by John Miller" [for #16; 22–24 January, *LEP* ("Directions" have "Thomas Cumming")]; #23: Kingsley, presumed [for #28; between "Comyns" and "Downe" in plate list of 26–28 May, *St. James's Chronicle*) and positioned there in PN copy with plates as issued]; #24: Lord Downe [for #32]; #25:

Keith [for #18]; #26: "Colonel Coote, who bravely distinguished himself
this War in the East-Indies, . . . original drawing by Aliamet" [for #11; 7–9
April, *LEP*]; #27: "Earl of Loudon" [for #8; 25 April, *PA*]; #28: Prince Ferdinand [for #26]; #29: George III [for #34]; #30: Lawrence and Forrest [for
#4 & #15].

Notes to Vol. 3

The ESTC has three records for vol. 3: T55304 includes the 1760 vol. 3
within a set of first settings and notes that set was filmed for *The Eighteenth
Century* (reel 157, no. 12); it is not reproduced on ECCO. ESTC T55305
records the 1762 vol. 3 (3.B) as part of set with reprint editions of vols.
1–4 dated 1763, 1763, 1762, and 1764 (modeled on BL3); BL3 (with all
1762 settings) was filmed with this set (reel 1630) and digitized on ECCO.
ESTC T55306 records the 1765 vol. 3 (3.C), wrongly noting the pagination
as "463, [1]p." (overlooking the count's regressing sixteen places at N1,
when No. 25 begins) and misleadingly noting "Some of the numbers occur in variant settings." The ESTC notes 3.C was filmed for *The Eighteenth
Century* (reel 183, no. 4) and reproduced on ECCO. The ESTC copy locations for the 1760 and 1762 volumes are not especially accurate since the
record is for sets. Vol. 3 1762 is not found in twelve of the nineteen sets
listed for T55305; for instance, CaAEU, CT, CU-B, NNS, PPL, and ViW all
have the 1765 vol. 3, as T55306 accurately notes. Although there are many
exceptions, as the summary of issues in "copies examined" below indicates,
volumes dated 1760, 1762, and 1765 have, respectively, largely all first,
second, and third settings.

Tp to Vol. 3.B (1762)

Same letter-press (and ornamental design) as 3.A's tp until "Rose, in
Paternoster-Row. | MDCCLXII." (half-spaces in date; letter-press: 162–63).

Pp., Sigs., Contents, RTs, Paper in Vol. 3.B

Pp. *1–3* 4–192 177 [=N1]–394 195 [=Cc6] 396–462 468 [*1*]. The same
regression in page count begins in sheet N as in 3.A; Cc6/"395" and
Gg8/"463" mispaginated; in some copies I4^v/136 as "135" (BmU CtHT)
and M6^v/188 as "88" (BmU CtHi CtHT CYc ICarb); 244 as "44" in CU-B.
Issue signatures are regular, but L1 lacks period after "24" in all or most
copies. Variant RT on G1^v/98: " ISTORY" in many copies (e.g., CYc InMB
InTU LU) but some correct (e.g., CtHT ICarb ScF). Paper: uncut, 218–25
x 142–47 (ICarb); probably two unmarked paper stocks divided between
issues 1–5 and 6–10: crisp, distinct wire- and chain-lines, 108-11/4; no

tranchefile: sheets A–P; and chain-lines, 103-05/4; tranchefiles, 11-12: Q–Gg.

Tp to Vol. 3.C (1765)

Same as 3.B but with date, "MDCCLXV." (with half-spaces after the first four letters; letter-press: 158).

Pp., Sigs., Contents, RTs, Paper in Vol. 3.C

8° (209 x 131, DGW): A–Gg⁸ pp. *1–3* 4–192 177–463 *464* [as in 3.A–B, the page count starts over again as 177 on N1/[193]; without misprintings at 244, 395, and 463 in 3.B. Irregularities in issue signatures include: N1 lacks its final period after "Numb. XXV"; S1 lacks the period after "Numb." Contents and RT same as 3.A. RTs variants include E4ᵛ/72 with no final period in BL(2) Brack CT CU-B DT NNS ViW (with speck for final punctuation in CaAEU ViU1). Paper: (cut, 209 x 131 [DGW]): probably all one unmarked paper stock, with fairly distinct wire- and chain-lines, 103-105/4; with knotting on chain-lines; remarkable for having some wandering chain-lines within leaves $5–8 of perhaps half the sheets, causing chain-widths to narrow from 24 down to 11; tranchefiles 11-13 (e.g., B C H M–P S–U Z Bb Dd of CaAEU).

Note on the Collation and Variants Listed

There are consistently three settings of all gatherings, labeled by volume dates in which these commonly occur: 1760, 1762, 1765. Collation of the three settings employed May2 for 1760, BL3 and May4 for 1762, and Brack for all 1765 but BL1 for sheets D, F, I, and Ff, where Brack has other settings. As an abbreviation for copy locations, "all 1760 [1762, 1765] copies" refers to all copies listed under sheet A—these copies (aside from anomalous May5) are also those listed under the location entries for those dated volumes.

Issue No. 21: Sheets A–C: pp. 1–48

A-1760: A2ᵛ/4-5, A6/11-1: all 1760 copies: i.e., all dated "1760": AWn BL4 CtY1-2 EU InU IU LU1 May1-3 MdU MeB MnGA MoJ NBuG NBuU NjM O Oa Oc OCX PN PPiT PPL1 PPT PSt TnJoS TnNV ViLGH ViWCF; plus May5 [vol. 2 with no. 21 bound in extra];
A-1762: no figures: BL3 BmU CtHi CtHT CYc ICarb InMB InTU LU2 May4 MB1 ScF;
A-1765: A5ᵛ/10-7: BL1 [9502.e.5] BL2, Brack CaAEU CaOTU CT CU-B DGW DT MB2 MBat2 MWA NNS PPL2 Vi ViU1-2 ViW.

Textual variants in sheet A: cf. A2–A3^v [lineal descent]:
A2^v.19: land-service 1760] ~$_\wedge$~ 1762, 1765, Q
A3/5.5: Hesse Cassel 1760, 1762, Q] ~-~ 1765
A3.26: seven pence 1760, Q] ~-~ 1762, 1765
A3^v.30: judges; 1760, 1762] ~, 1765, Q

B-1760.A–B: Two states varying only in press figures: state A with both
B6/27-1 and B7/29-4: BL4 EU InU IU May2-3,5 MeB MnGA MoJ
NBuG NBuU Oa Oc PN PPiT PPT PSt TnJoS TnNV ViLGH ViWCF; and
state B: with only B6/27-1: CtY1-2 LU1 May1 MdU NjM OCX PPL1
[state uncertain: AWn O];
B-1762: B5/25-6: all 1762 copies;
B-1765: B2^v/20-8, B5^v/26-6: all 1765 copies.
Textual variants in sheet B: cf. B1–B3^v [lineal descent]:
B1^v/18.23: that, 1760] ~$_\wedge$ 1762, 1765, Q
B2/19.5: the lying out of 1760] the lying out 1762, Q] lying out of 1765
B2/9: intirely; 1760] ~: 1762, 1765] entirely: Q
B2.10: great, 1760, Q] ~$_\wedge$ 1762, 1765

C-1760: C7/45-4 (after "of"), C8/47-2: all 1760 copies plus May5;
C-1762: C7^v/46-2: all 1762 copies [distinctive "T" cut downward to right
cross cap-stroke and top of ascender in RT on C3^v/38 as on E1^v, F3^v,
G3^v, H4^v, I3^v];
C-1765: C7/45-4 [under "n" in "incurred"]: all 1765 copies [CW on C4
is "Great-" with hyphen unlike 1760 and 1762].
Textual variants in sheet C: cf: C1–C3^v [lineal descent]:
C1^v/34.33: intire 1760, Q] entire 1762, 1765
C2^v/36.22: famine 1760, 1762, Q] Famine 1765
C2^v.22: cold 1760, 1762, Q] Cold 1765
C3/37.5: Ireland 1760, Q] ~, 1762, 1765
C3^v.9: which 1769, Q] ~, 1762, 1765

Issue No. 22: Sheets D–F: pp. 49–96: Two of Three Settings
Without Press Figures

D-1760: D4^v/56-1, D7^v/62-5: all 1760 copies plus [with tp] 1765: Brack
DGW DT ViW [D5/57 usually paginated but unpaginated at AWn IU
MnGA Oa PN PSt];
D-1762: no figures: all 1762 copies [D1 under the "e" of "the"; 4 of D4
under "s" of "lies"];
D-1765: no figures: BL1-2 CaAEU CaOTU CT CU-B MB2 MBat2 MWA
NNS PPL2 Vi ViU1-2 [D1 in space after "the"; "4" under right side of
"in"; BL2); recurrent RT in 1765 settings D–I, with "O" in "HISTORY"

cut at 10:00 and 2:00: D2^v/52, E4^v/72, F3^v/86, G1^v/98, H1^v/114, and I4^v/136, and the "O" recurs on T7^v/286, U5^v/298, X6^v/316 (e.g., CaAEU CU-B NNS Vi ViU1-2).

Textual variants in sheet D: cf. D1–D3^v [lineal descent]:

D1/49.10: their 1760, 1762, Q] the 1765

D1^v/50.1: *quam diu* 1760, Q] *quamdiu* 1762, 1765

D2/51.24: ryder; 1760, Q] ~: 1762, 1765

D2^v/52.11: carts, 1760, Q] ~$_\wedge$ 1762, 1765

D3/53.15: bankrupts 1760, 1762, Q] ~, 1765

D3^v/54.5: with the 1760, 1762, Q] with a 1765

E-1760: E7/77-3 [at far right], E7^v/78-2: all 1760 copies plus 1765: CT [Usually no CW on E5/73];

E-1762: No figures: all 1762 copies plus 1765: DGW [E1 signed under "p" of "multiples"; "2" of E2 under "n" in "ner"; CW E5/73: "command-"];

E-1765: No figures: BL1-2 Brack CaAEU CaOTU CU-B DT MB2 MBat2 MWA NNS Vi ViU1-2 ViW; not PPL2, which has vol. 4's E-1764 sheet [E1 under "o" of "of"; "2" between footnote columns; CW E5/73: "com-"; RT with cut "O" on E4^v/72 recurring in gatherings D–I].

Textual variants in sheet E: cf. E1–E5^v [1762 and 1765 both descend directly from 1760]:

E1/65.A.9 and all 1760, 1765, Q] and that all 1762

E1^v/66: text CW "The" in 1760; no text CW in 1762, 1765

E1^v.A.26: aforesaid 1760, 1762, Q] ~, 1765

E1^v.B.10: weight, 1760, 1762, Q] ~$_\wedge$ 1765

E4/71.16 liberty: 1760, 1765, Q] ~; 1762

F-1760: F2^v/84-1: all 1760 copies;

F-1762: no figures: all 1762 copies plus 1765: BL2 Brack CT ViW [text-CW error on F4^v/88: did} died; F1 under "t" of "the" (other signature positions same as F-1765); recurrent damaged "T" in RT on F3^v/86];

F-1765: no figures: BL1 CaAEU CaOTU CU-B DGW DT MB2 MBat2 MWA NNS PPL2 Vi ViU1-2 [CW variant on F8: tled} led; F1 under "th" of "the"; in volume signature on F1 second "2" broken in "22"; recurrent RT with cut "O" on F3^v].

Textual variants in sheet F: cf. F1–F6 [lineal descent, with accurate composing (no variants on F2–F3^v)]:

F1/81.24: mariners 1760, Q] ~, 1762, 1765

F1^v/82.25: nations: 1760, Q] ~; 1762, 1765

F5/89.A.15: show, 1760, 1762] ~$_\wedge$ 1765

F5.A.26: Anne 1760, 1762] Ann 1765

F5^v/90.A.28: Birchen 1760, 1762] Birchin 1765

Issue No. 23: Sheets D–F: pp. 97–144

G-1760: G1^v/98-4, G2^v/100-2 [under comma after "damaged"]; all 1760 copies plus 1762: May4;

G-1762: G1^v/98-1 [under "ll" of "called"]: all 1762 copies minus May4 [ScF has same G1^v/98-1 plus G2^v/100-2 (under "e" of "the") but its outer forme seems otherwise regular, with usual variants on G3 and the "3" of G3 after "o" of "into" as in other G-1762 copies; some copies with "ISTORY" in RT on G1^v/98; recurrent RT with distinctive cut "T" on G3^v];

G-1765: no figures: all 1765 copies [recurrent RT with cut "O" on G1^v/98].

All textual variants in G1–G5^v: cf. G1–G5^v [lineal descent, with typical composing]:

G1^v/98.up 3: a-head 1760, 1762, Q] a head 1765

G2/99.8: sides 1760, 1762, Q] ~, 1765

G2^v/100.4: Hotham 1760, 1762, Q] Hothman 1765 [error]

G3/101.marg.7–8: India | man. 1760. Q] India- | man. 1762] In- | dia-man 1765

G3.29: Le Chasseur 1760, Q] Chasseur 1762, 1765

G4/103.10: Basse-terre 1760, 1762, Q] Basse terre 1765

G4.24: channel 1760, 1762] Channel 1765, Q

G4.25: Florissant 1760, Q] ~, 1762, 1765

G5^v/106.10: look-out 1760] look out 1762, 1765

G5^v.17: day-light 1760, 1765, Q] day light 1762

H-1760: H1^v/114-5, H2^v/116-1: all 1760 copies plus 1762: May4; 1765: BL2 [H1 under "ps" of "ships"];

H-1762: no figures: all 1762 copies minus May4, plus 1765: ViW [left ascender of H1 under ";"; "3" under "d" of "day"; recurrent RT with cut "T" on H4^v/120];

H-1765: no figures: BL1 Brack CaAEU CaOTU CT CU-B DGW DT MB2 MBat2 MWA NNS PPL2 Vi ViU1-2 [H1 centered under ";"; "3" under "a" in "day"; CW variant: frus- | trate (as 1760) due to text error on H2/115; recurrent RT with cut "O" on H1^v/114].

Textual variants in sheet H: cf. H1–H3 [both 1762 and 1765 descend directly from 1760]:

H1^v/114.3: port 1760, 1762, Q] Port 1765

H1^v.43 (ult. l.): frigates 1760, 1765] ~ 1762, Q

H2^v/116.1: trate {skipping "frus"} 1760, 1765] frustrate 1762

H3, ult. l.: squadron; 1760, 1765, Q] ~: 1762

I-1760: I1^v/130-1: all 1760 copies plus 1762: May4;
[figure missing from AWn; it is a smudge in Oa under usual position ("b" of "breadth")];

I-1762: I2ᵛ/132-1: all 1762 copies minus May4, plus 1765: BL2 Brack [I4ᵛ/136 mispaginated "135" in a few copies (e.g., BmU CtHT)];

I-1765A: no figures: BL1 CaAEU CaOTU CT CU-B DGW DT MB2 MBat2 MWA NNS PPL2 Vi ViU1-2 [not ViW, which has sheet I from vol. 2 1767; recurrent RT with cut "O" on I4ᵛ/136].

Textual variants in sheet I: cf. I1–I4ᵛ [both 1762 and 1765 descend directly from 1760]:

I1/129.28: Hughes 1760, 1765, Q] Hughs 1762

I1ᵛ/130.29: amongst 1760, 1762, Q] among 1765

I3/133.2: squadron, 1760, 1765, Q] ~ₐ 1765

I3.9: fleet, 1760, 1765, Q] ~ₐ 1762

Issue No. 24: Sheets K–M: pp. 145–76

K-1760: K2ᵛ/148-5 [under "tr" of "troops"]: all 1760 copies minus May1, plus 1762: InMB;

K-1762: K2ᵛ/148-5 [after "river,"], K3ᵛ/150-2: all 1762 copies minus InMB, plus 1765: MB2 MWA;

K-1765: K1ᵛ/146-3, K7/157-4: BL1-2 Brack CaAEU CaOTU CT CU-B DGW DT MBat2 NNS PPL2 Vi ViU1-2 ViW; 1760: May1.

Textual variants in sheet K: cf. K1–K3 [lineal descent]:

K1/145.31: island 1760, Q] islands 1762, 1765

K2/147.20: service, 1760, 1762, Q] ~ₐ 1765

K3.27: Petitbourg 1760] Petit-bourg 1762, 1765, Q

K4/151.marg.2–6: The island | surren- | dered on | capitula- | tion. 1760, 1762, Q] *om.* 1765

K6ᵛ/156.A.1: island, 1760, Q] ~ₐ 1762, 1765

K8ᵛ/160.marg.2–6: General | Barring- | ton re- | turns to | England. 1760, 1762, Q] *om.* 1765

L-1760: L4ᵛ/168-4: all 1760 copies minus May1, plus 1762: InMB LU2; 1765: MB2;

L-1762: L1ᵛ/162-4: 1762: all 1762 copies minus InMB LU, plus 1765: MWA [period lacking on L1 after "Numb. 24"];

L-1765: L2ᵛ/164-5 [tilted to right], L8/175-3: BL1-2 Brack CaAEU CaOTU CT CU-B DGW DT MBat2 NNS PPL2 Vi ViU1-2 ViW; 1760: May1.

Textual variants in sheet L: cf. L1–L3ᵛ [lineal descent, with 1765 very accurate]:

L1/161.5: established, 1760, Q] ~ₐ 1762, 1765

L1ᵛ.26: sense, 1760, Q] ~ₐ 1762, 1765

L1ᵛ.29: similes 1760, 1762] similies 1765

L3ᵛ/166.A.2–3: grie- | vances 1760, Q] grie- | vance 1762, 1765

M-1760: M8/191-5: all 1760 copies minus May1, plus 1762: InMB LU2; plus 1765: MB2 MWA;

M-1762: M1ᵛ/178-4, M5/185-6: all 1762 copies minus InMB LU2, plus 1765: Vi [M7ᵛ/188 misprinted "88" in roughly half the copies];

M-1765: M6/187-1: BL1-2 Brack CaAEU CaOTU CT CU-B DGW DT MBat2 NNS PPL2 ViU1-2 ViW; 1760: May1.

Textual variants in sheet M: cf. M1–M3ᵛ [lineal descent]:

M1/177.8: city; 1760, Q] ∼: 1762, 1765

M2ᵛ/180.11: integrity 1760, 1762, Q] ∼, 1765

M3.25: family rank 1760, Q] ∼-∼ 1762, 1765

M3ᵛ/182.4: heir apparent 1760, 1762] ∼-∼ 1765

Issue No. 25: Sheets N–P: pp. 177–224 (All Three Settings of Sheet N Paginated "177–92" as was M, Lessening the Final Page Count by 16)

N-1760: N6ᵛ/"188"-4 [under "gl" of "single"], N7ᵛ/"190"-5: all 1760 copies plus 1762: InMB LU2; 1765: Vi;

N-1762: N6/"187"-2, N6ᵛ/"188"-4 [before "which"]: BL3 BmU CtHi CtHT CYc ICarb InTU May4 MB1 ScF; 1765: BL2 MB2 MWA;

N-1765: N8/"191"-3, N8ᵛ/"192"-2: BL1 Brack CaAEU CaOTU CT CU-B DGW DT MBat2 NNS PPL2 ViU1-2 ViW [signature on N1 in 1765 lacks period after "XXV"; in rare copies N1ᵛ/178's pagination misprinted as " 8" (e.g., DT)].

Textual variants in sheet N: cf. N1–N3 [lineal descent]:

N1/"177".A.1: arm; 1760, 1762, Q] ∼: 1765

N1/"177".A.4: day: 1760, Q] ∼; 1762, 1765

N1.A.27: shot, 1760, Q] ∼ₐ 1762, 1765

N2/"179".B.7: plain 1760, 1765] plan 1762 [error]

N2ᵛ.22–23: slip- | pery, 1760, 1762] ∼ₐ 1765

O-1760: O3ᵛ/198-5: all 1760 copies plus 1762: InMB LU2; 1765: DT MWA PPL2 Vi;

O-1762: O7ᵛ/206-7: BL3 BmU CtHi CtHT CYc ICarb InTU May4 MB1 ScF; 1765: MB2;

O-1765: O8/207-3, O8ᵛ/208-7: BL1-2 Brack CaAEU CaOTU CT CU-B DGW MBat2 NNS ViU1-2 ViW.

All textual variants in O1–O2ᵛ: cf. O1–O2ᵛ [lineal descent]:

O1/193.4: considered, 1760, 1762, Q] ∼ 1765

O1.A.1: Capitulation 1760, 1765, Q] *l.c.* 1762

O1ᵛ.A.29: bona 1760, 1762, Q] bonâ 1765

O1ᵛ.B.2: 1759, 1760] ∼. 1762, 1765, Q

O2.ult l.: consternation, 1760, Q] ∼; 1762, 1765

P-1760: P6ᵛ/220-[backwards] 3, P7ᵛ/222-1: all 1760 copies plus 1762: LU2;
P-1762: P2ᵛ/212-6, P8/223-2: BL3 BmU CtHi CtHT CYc ICarb InMB InTU May4 MB1 ScF; 1765: BL2 MB2 MWA;
P-1765: P5/217-2: BL1 Brack CaAEU CaOTU CT CU-B DGW DT MBat2 NNS PPL2 Vi ViU1-2 ViW.
All textual variants in P1–P3: cf. P1–P3 [lineal descent]:
P1/209.3: centre; 1760, Q] ~: 1762 1765
P1.29: men 1760, 1762, Q] ~, 1765
P2/211.24: river, 1760] ~ₐ 1762, 1765, Q
P2ᵛ.6: prepared: 1760, 1762, Q] ~; 1765
P3/213.15, 16: were 1760, Q] was 1762, 1765

Issue No. 26: Sheets Q–S: pp. 225–72

Q-1760.A–B: Two states and probably impressions, both with Q2ᵛ/228-4, differing only in second figure: state A with Q1ᵛ/226-1 [under "y" in "by"]: BL4 CtY1-2 EU InU LU1 May1,3 MdU MnGA MoJ NBuG NBuG NBuU NjM O Oc OCX PN PPiT PPL1 PPT PSt TnJoS TnNV ViGLH ViWCF; plus 1762: May4; state B with Q1ᵛ/226-6 [after "y" in "by"]: AWn IU May2 MeB Oa PN; plus 1762: InMB InTU LU2 [presence of state B in copies with 1762 tps argues it is the second impression];
Q-1762: Q8/239-2: BL3 BmU CtHi CtHT CYc ICarb MB1 ScF; 1765: CaAEU MB2 MWA Vi [RT with second "G" cut wide at 10:00 on Q4/231, as on T1/273, Y3/325, Bb4/375, Cc1/385, Ff1/433 in MB1-2];
Q-1765: Q4ᵛ/232-3, Q7ᵛ/238-1: BL1-2 Brack CaOTU CT CU-B DGW DT MBat2 NNS PPL2 ViU1-2 ViW.
Textual variants in sheet Q: cf. Q1–Q6ᵛ [lineal descent, with a total of nine variants]:
Q2/227.13: inconveniences 1760] inconveniencies 1762, 1765, Q
Q2.22: dispersed; 1760, 1762, Q] ~: 1765
Q2.29: a dearth 1760, Q] dearth [*om.*] 1762, 1765
Q2ᵛ/228.26: troops] 1760, 1762, Q] ~, 1765
Q3.27: Stoltznau 1760, 1762] Soltznau 1765, Q [correction]

R-1760: R6/251-5 [under the "e" in "defile"], R6ᵛ/252-3: all 1760 copies plus 1762: InMB InTU LU2 May4;
R-1762: R6/251-1 [under the "s" of CW "doubts"]: BL3 BmU CtHi CtHT CYc ICarb MB1 ScF; 1765: MB2 MWA Vi [figure missed or missing in BmU];
R-1765.A–B: Two states differing only in presence (in state A) and absence (in B) of the first press figure: R7/253-6 and R7ᵛ/254-2: state A: BL2

Brack CaAEU CaOTU CT CU-B DGW DT MBat2 NNS PPL2 ViU1-2 ViW; state B (with only figure R7^v/254-2): BL1 [rare internal variant at CU-B with R2^v/244 paginated " 44"].

Textual variants in sheet R: cf. R1–R2^v [lineal descent]:

R1^v/242.13–14: Man- | teussel 1760, Q] Man- | teusel 1762, 1765

R1^v.27: considerable 1760, 1765] consideerble 1762

R2/243.2: and, 1760, Q] ~$_\wedge$ 1762, 1765

R2^v/244.1: Greifenberg 1760, 1762, Q] Greiffenberg 1765

R2^v.10: provision 1760, 1762, Q] provisions 1765

S-1760.A–B: Two states and impressions, both with S6^v/268-4, differing only in a second figure: state A with S7^v/270-1 [under "n" in "French"]: BL4 CtY1-2 EU InU LU1 May1,3 MdU MnGA NBuG NBuU NjM O Oa Oc OCX PN PPiT PPL1 PPT PSt TnJoS TnNV ViLGH ViWCF; plus 1762: May4; state B, with S7^v/270-6 [under "a" of "ambassador"]: AWn IU May2 MeB; plus 1762: InMB InTU LU2 [presence of state B in copies dated 1762 argues it is the second impression];

S-1762: S8^v/272-3: BL3 BmU CtHi CtHT CYc ICarb MB1 ScF; 1765: MB2 MWA Vi;

S-1765: S5^v/266-2, S8^v/272-1: BL1-2 Brack CaAEU CaOTU CT CU-B DGW DT MBat2 NNS PPL2 ViU1-2 ViW.

Textual variants in sheet S: cf. S1–2, S3–S3^v, and S8 [lineal descent]:

S1/257.4: September, 1760, Q] ~$_\wedge$ 1762, 1765

S1.19–20: pri- | soners; 1760, 1762, Q] ~, 1765

S1^v.16: route 1760, Q] rout 1762, 1765

S1^v.27: about 1760, Q] above 1762, 1765

S8/271.27: thro' 1760, 1762] through 1765

Issue No. 27: Sheets Q–S: pp. 273–320: With No Figures in T–X 1765

T-1760: T5^v/282-4, T8^v/288-2: all 1760 copies plus 1762: InMB InTU LU2 May4 [T5^v/282-4 missing from EU and PPT];

T-1762: T3^v/278-3, T6^v/284-7: BL3 BmU CtHi CtHT CYc ICarb MB1 ScF; 1765: CaOTU MB2 MBat2 MWA Vi ViU2;

T-1765: no figures: BL1-2 Brack CaAEU CT CU-B DGW DT NNS PPL2 ViU1, ViW. [T1 under "fu" of "funeral"; recurrent RT with "O" cut at 10:00 and 2:00 on T7^v/286, U5^v/298, and X6^v/316].

Textual variants in sheet T: cf. T1–T3^v [lineal descent]:

T1/273.19: to all 1760] to [*om.*] 1762, 1765

T1.31: queen-dowager 1760, 1762] ~$_\wedge$~ 1765

T2/275.A.1: stature, 1760] ~; 1762, 1765

T3/277.19: and, 1760] ~$_\wedge$ 1762, 1765

T3^v/278.26: Aveiro 1760, 1762, Q] Averio 1765

U-1760: U1ᵛ/290-1, U7/301-5: all 1760 copies plus 1762: InMB InTU LU2 May4; 1765: CaOTU;

U-1762: no figures: BL3 BmU CtHi CtHT CYc ICarb MB1 ScF; 1765: MBat2 MB2 MWA Vi ViU2 [U1 under "ul" of "fulfil"; "2" of U2 under first "o" of "provision"];

U-1765: no figures: BL1-2 Brack CaAEU CT CU-B DGW DT NNS PPL2 ViU1 ViW [U1 under "fil" of "fulfil"; "2" under first "s" of "provisions"; unlike 1760 and 1762, CW "year," on U2ᵛ/292, and recurrent RT with cut "O" on U5ᵛ/298].

Textual variants in sheet U: cf. U1–U3 [lineal descent]:
U1/289.1: ordnance 1760] ordinance 1762, 1765, Q
U1.28: majesty's 1760, Q] Majesty's 1762, 1765
U1ᵛ.15: through 1760, 1762] thro' 1765
U2ᵛ/292.34 (ult l.): twenty-fifth 1760, 1762, Q] ∼ₐ∼ 1765
293.1: year 1760, 1762, Q] ∼, 1765

X-1760: X4ᵛ/312-4, X8/319-2: all 1760 copies plus 1762: InMB InTU LU2 May4;

X-1762: X2ᵛ/308-2: BL3 BmU CtHi CtHT CYc ICarb MB1 ScF; 1765: CaOTU MB2 MBat2 MWA Vi ViU2;

X-1765: no figures: BL1-2 Brack CaAEU CT CU-B DGW DT NNS PPL2 ViU1 ViW [X1 under "sid" of "consideration"; "X" of X2 under "th" of "the"; recurrent RT with cut "O" on X6ᵛ/316].

Textual variants in sheet X: cf. X1ᵛ–X5ᵛ [lineal descent, with eight of eleven variants introduced by 1762]:
X1ᵛ/306.1: agreed, 1760, 1762, Q] ∼ₐ 1765
X2ᵛ/308.5: bread corn 1760] ∼-∼ 1762, 1765, Q
X2ᵛ.A.3–4: Li- | quors, 1760] ∼ₐ 1762, 1765
X3ᵛ/310.A.30: shipped 1760, 1762] ∼, 1765

Issue No. 28: Sheets Y–Aa: pp. 321–68

Y-1760: Y7/333-4, Y7ᵛ/334-5: all 1760 copies plus 1762: InMB InTU LU2 May4;

Y-1762: Y5ᵛ/330-1: BL3 BmU CtHi CtHT CYc ICarb MB1 ScF; 1765: BL1 CU-B MB2 MWA NNS Vi;

Y-1765: Y2ᵛ/324-1, Y6/331-2: BL2 Brack CaAEU CaOTU CT DGW DT MBat2 PPL2 ViU1-2 ViW.

Textual variants in sheet Y: cf. Y1–Y3 [lineal descent]:
Y1/321.9: because, 1760, Q] ∼ₐ 1762, 1765
Y1.18: commons 1760, 1762, Q] ∼, 1765
Y1.19: gentlemen, 1760, 1762, Q] ∼ₐ 1765
Y3/325.B.13: any 1760, Q] an 1762 1765

Z-1760: Z6/347-4, Z6ᵛ/348-3: all 1760 copies plus 1762: InMB InTU LU2 May4;

Z-1762: Z7/349-2: BL3 BmU CtHi CtHT CYc ICarb MB1 ScF; plus 1765: CU-B MB2 MWA Vi;

Z-1765: Z6/347-2: BL1-2 Brack CaAEU CaOTU CT DGW DT MBat2 NNS PPL2 ViU1-2 ViW.

Textual variants in sheet Z: cf. Z1–Z2 [lineal descent]:

Z1/337.A.37: share 1760 {error}] shire 1762, 1765, Q

Z1/337.B.1: ports; 1760, 1762, Q] ∼, 1765

Z1.B.39 [up 2 ll.]: oath 1760, Q] oaths 1762, 1765

Z1ᵛ/338.2: seat 1760, Q] ∼, 1762, 1765

Z2ᵛ.B.1: his, 1760, 1762, Q] ∼ₐ 1765

Aa-1760: Aa1ᵛ/354-1, Aa7/365-3: all 1760 copies plus 1762: InMB InTU LU2 May4;

Aa-1762: Aa8ᵛ/368-3: BL3 BmU CtHi CtHT CYc ICarb MB1 ScF; 1765: CaAEU MB2 MWA Vi;

Aa-1765: Aa2ᵛ/356-8 [upside down], Aa7ᵛ/366-3: BL1-2 Brack CaOTU CT CU-B DGW DT MBat2 NNS PPL2 ViU1-2 ViW.

Textual variants in sheet Aa: cf. Aa1–Aa3 [lineal descent]:

Aa1ᵛ/354.9-10: ca- | binet-maker 1760, Q] ∼ₐ∼ 1762 1765

Aa3/357.A.18: word 1760 {error}] world 1762, 1765, Q

Aa3.A.26: inconveniences 1760] inconveniencies 1762, 1765, Q

Issue No. 29: Sheets Bb–Dd: pp. 369–416

Bb-1760: Bb1ᵛ/370-1, Bb5/377-3: all 1760 copies plus 1762: InMB InTU LU2; 1765: DGW;

Bb-1762: Bb6ᵛ/380-7: BL3 BmU CtHi CtHT CYc ICarb May4 MB1 ScF; 1765: MB2 MWA;

Bb-1765: Bb2ᵛ/372-3: BL1-2 Brack CaAEU CaOTU CT CU-B DT MBat2 NNS PPL2 Vi ViU1-2 ViW.

Textual variants in sheet Bb: cf. Bb1–Bb4 [lineal descent]:

Bb1ᵛ/370.15: trial, 1760, 1762, Q] ∼ₐ 1765

Bb1ᵛ.22: truth 1760, Q] ∼ₐ 1762, 1765

Bb3ᵛ/374.18: that 1760, 1762, Q] ∼, 1765

Bb4/375.marg.4: house 1760] House 1762, 1765

Cc-1760: Cc7/397-5, Cc7ᵛ/398-6: all 1760 copies plus 1762: InMB InTU LU2;

Cc-1762.A–B: Two states, both with figure and pagination error Cc6/395 ["195"]-3: BL3 BmU CtHi CtHT CYc ICarb May4 MB1-2 MWA ScF; 1765: CU-B MB2 MWA; those with state A also have Cc2ᵛ/388-1 (e.g.,

BL3 BmU CYc MB1 ScF); others with state B, probably the second state, lack a figure on Cc2^v and have CW variant "n} an" with lost letter "a" (e.g., CtHi CtHT ICarb May4 MB2 MWA)];

Cc-1765: Cc1^v/386-1, Cc7/397-2: BL1-2 Brack CaAEU CaOTU CT DGW DT MBat2 NNS PPL2 Vi ViU1-2 ViW [397-2 missed or missing at ViU1-2; n. fn CW Cc8/399: "Art." (in Brack ViU2) missing from ViU1 (otherwise ViU1=ViU2)].

Textual variants in sheet Cc: cf. Cc1–Cc4 [lineal descent]:

Cc1^v/386.8: publicly 1760, 1762, Q] publickly 1765

Cc2/387.2: eyes, 1760] ∼$_∧$ 1762, 1765

Cc2, up 4: people 1760, 1762] ∼, 1765, Q

Cc3/389.11: East-Indies 1760, Q] ∼$_∧$∼ 1762 1765

Dd-1760: Dd2^v/404-3 [under "n" in "been"], Dd8/415-1: all 1760 copies plus 1762: InMB InTU LU2;

Dd-1762: Dd2^v/404-1 [under first "e" of "been"], Dd8/415-7: BL3 BmU CtHi CtHT CYc ICarb May4 MB1 ScF; 1765: MB2 MWA [the figure on 404 in MWA is an illegible mark where figure elsewhere occurs];

Dd-1765: Dd2^v/404-3 [under second "n" in "abandoned"], Dd7^v/414-7: BL1-2 Brack CaAEU CaOTU CT CU-B DGW DT MBat2 NNS PPL2 Vi ViU1-2 ViW.

Textual variants in sheet Dd: cf. Dd1–Dd3 [lineal descent]:

Dd1/401.30: In- 1760, 1762] in- 1765

Dd1^v.15–16: Ocunnastota 1760, Q] Ouconnostata 1762, 1765

Dd2^v/404.13: Charles-town 1760, Q] Charles-Town 1762, 1765

Dd2^v.14: River 1760, 1762, Q] river 1765

Dd2^v.15: June 1760, Q] ∼, 1762, 1765

Issue No. 30: Sheets Ee–Gg: pp. 417–64

Ee-1760: Ee5^v/426-5, Ee7/429-1: all 1760 copies plus 1762: InMB InTU LU2;

Ee-1762: Ee1^v/418-3, Ee4^v/424-1: BL3 BmU CtHi CtHT CYc ICarb May4 MB1 ScF; 1765: BL2 MB2 MWA Vi [418-3 missed or missing in MWA];

Ee-1765: Ee8/431-1, Ee8^v/432-4: BL1 Brack CaAEU CaOTU CT CU-B DGW DT MBat2 NNS PPL2 ViU1-2 ViW.

Textual variants in sheet Ee: cf. Ee1–Ee3^v [lineal descent]:

Ee1/417.27: bomb battery 1760, 1762, Q] ∼-∼ 1765

Ee3/421.A.6: Soubise, 1760] ∼$_∧$ 1762 1765, Q

Ee3.B.14: projected; 1760, Q] ∼: 1762 1765

Ee3^v.21: about 1760, Q] above 1762 1765

326   *James E. May*

Ff-1760: Ff1ᵛ/434-3, Ff5/441-1: all 1760 copies plus 1762: InMB InTU LU2;
Ff-1762: Ff5/441-3: BL3 BmU CtHi CtHT CYc ICarb May4 MB1 ScF;
    1765: Brack MB2 MWA Vi ViW;
Ff-1765: Ff6/443-6, Ff7/445-7: BL1-2 CaAEU CaOTU CT CU-B DGW DT
    MBat2 NNS PPL2 ViU1-2.
Textual variants in sheet Ff: cf. Ff1–Ff4, Ff8ᵛ [probably lineal descent,
    but both reprints are too accurate for certainty]:
Ff1ᵛ/434.B.20–21: no- | ble 1760, 1762, Q] ~, 1765
Ff3ᵛ/438.B.22: 8th 1760] eighth 1762, 1765
Ff4/439.12: time, 1760, 1762, Q] ~ₐ 1765
Ff4.14: commanders 1760, Q] ~, 1762, 1765 [error]

Gg-1760: Gg5ᵛ/458-3, Gg7/461-2 [under "o" of "ordered"]: all 1760 cop-
    ies plus 1762: InMB InTU LU2;
Gg-1762: no figures; Gg8/463 mispaginated "468": BL3 BmU CtHi CtHT
    CYc ICarb May4 MB1 ScF; 1765: CaAEU MB2 MWA Vi ["4" of Gg4
    under "ps" of "troops" (under "op" of "troops" in 1760 and under "p"
    in 1765)];
Gg-1765: Gg5ᵛ/458-6 [under right of "G" of "Guadalupe"], Gg7/461-2
    [under right of "o" in "to"]: BL1-2 Brack CaOTU CT CU-B DGW DT
    MBat2 NNS PPL2 ViU1-2 ViW].
Textual variants in sheet Gg: cf. Gg1–Gg2ᵛ [lineal descent]:
Gg1/449.8: Fort-Royal 1760] ~ₐ~ 1762, 1765
Gg1.23: should make 1760, 1762] should made 1765
Gg1ᵛ/450.1: general-officers 1760] ~ₐ~ 1762 1765
Gg1ᵛ/450.7: Pierre: 1760, 1762] ~; 1765
Gg2/451.28: an half 1760] half [*om.*] 1762 a half 1765

Copies Examined of Vol. 3 With Title-Page Dated 1760: Unless Noted, All Sheets With First Settings

AWn (uncut, 226 x 145); BL4; CtY1-2 (#1: Im.Sm79.757ck; Knapp's copy; #2: By7.26/14; MS on pp. 386, 462); EU; InU; IU (-2 maps; -plates Pocock and Sackville; +plates Lawrence and Loudon from vol. 1; +plates Coote and Keith from vol. 2); LU1 (MUA Smo.; with MS notations); May1 (200 x 127; 1765 settings in sheets K–M); May2 (Wolverhampton Library copy; -map W. Indies); May3; May5 (vol. 2 with the first three sheets [issue #21] bound in at the end); MdU (all plates but -2 maps; MS notations); MeB ([Bowdoin College] DA.S666C76; vol. 3 alone); MnGA; MoJ (-plate Townshend); NBuG; NBuU (-plates Townshend, Kingsley, and Sackville); NjM; O (+plate of Granby from vol. 4; MS identifications and correc- tions, as changing "ninety guns" to "nine guns" 6 ll. up 137); Oa; Oc; OCX (-X3/309-10); PN (-2 maps; with 11 plates issued with Nos. 21–30 intended for diverse vols. bound after A1); PPiT; PPL1 (Am 1760 Smoll [77906.0 Wolf]; cont suade); PPT (all plates torn out); PSt; TnJoS; TnNV; ViLGH (plate of Amherst bound before tp as frt; MS marginalia); ViWCF.

Copies Examined Dated 1762: Unless Noted, All Sheets With Second [c. 1762] Settings

BL3 (291.h.22; on ECCO); BmU; CaOHM (B1156; notes lost); CtHi; CtHT; CYc (sheet R may have a rare unfigured state); ICarb (-all plates but 2 maps; uncut, 218–25 x 142–47); InMB (1762 [settings] in A–I and P; 1760 in K–O Q–Gg); InTU (1762 settings in A–P; 1760: Q–Gg); LU2 (Porteus K3; 1762 in A–I; 1760: K–Gg); May4 (1762 in A–F K–P Bb–Gg; 1760 in others); MB1 (Adams 240.8; -W. Indies map; John Adams's copy; with MS comments); ScF (Caribbean map facing p. 126 partly torn out).

Copies Examined Dated 1765: Unless Noted, All Sheets With Third [c. 1765] Settings

BL1-2 (both with all plates: #1: 9502.E.5; all 1765 [settings] but 1762: Y; on ECCO [n. "19" in MS on tp]; #2: G 4876; 1765 but 1760: H; 1762: F I N P Ee); Brack (1765 but 1760: D and 1762: F I Ff); CaAEU (1765 but 1762: Q Aa Gg); CaOTU (1765 but 1762: T and X; 1760: U); CT (1765 but 1760: E and 1762: F); CU-B (1765 but 1762: Y–Z Cc); DGW (1765 but 1760: D Bb; 1762: E; -2 maps and plate Sackville; +Townshend plate at p. 180, belonging in vol. 1); DT (1765 but 1760: D and O); MB2 (**K.88.20; 1765: A–I; 1762: K N–Gg; 1760: L–M; -most plates; +Caribbean map "1761"); MBat2 (8E.Sm77.2; 1765 but 1762: T–X); MWA (1765: A–I; 1762: K–L N P–Gg; 1760: M and O; Caribbean map torn); NNS (1765 but Y: 1762; -Caribbean map and plates Saunders, Ferdinand, and Kingsley); PPL2 (Am 1763 Smol; 1765 settings but sheet E, signed "Numb. 32.," from vol. 4 1764, and 1760: O); Vi (1765: A–L P Bb–Dd; 1760: N–O; 1762: M Q–Aa Ee–Gg); ViU (2: #1: DA 30.S52 1763; all 1765; -P1; -6 plates; #2: uncat.; 1765 but 1762: T–X; tp signed "John Haye"); ViW (1765 settings but 1760: D and 1762: F H and Ff; -sheet I, replaced with I of vol. 2 1767 [figures 132-4 and 139-2]).

VOLUME 4.A–C: NUMBERS 31–40: THREE SETTINGS PASSIM

(VOLUME 4.A: RICHARD BALDWIN, 1761[–1762])

Tp

Same letterpress and ornament as in first printings of vols. 1–3 except for "FOURTH" in the volume statement (l. 7) and the date "MDCCLXI." (largely an alteration of stored type).

Coll., contents, and RTs

8° (uncut, 226 x 145 [AWn]): A–Aa⁸ Bb–Mm⁴ [1/2 $ signed; $1 with issue signature (T1 irregularly signed "Numb. 37." in place of "Nᴜᴍʙ. XXXVII."; $1 in C, Cc–Gg, and Ii–Mm signed with "No." for "Numb.")]; pp. *1–3* 4–143 *144* 145–237 239 238 240–404 054 406–72. Note: Bb–Mm⁴ were printed with half-sheet imposition: WM or countermark regularly recurs in many sheets in a row (e.g., countermark in Gg–Ll of MB2). Contents: A1: tp; A2–Bb3: text of Nos. 31–40: on reigns of George II until I8/143 (I8ᵛ blank) and George III (to Aa1ᵛ/370); Major General Barrington's remarks on General Moore's in vol. 3, with Moore's reprinted, the two in parallel columns (Aa2–Bb2ᵛ/388); Bb3ᵛ–Mm3ᵛ/470: index; Mm4–Mm4ᵛ/472: "Directions to the Book-Binder for Placing the Copper-plates" [in vols. 1–4]. Recto RTs with "GEORGE II." to I8/143, then "GEORGE III." (K2/147-Bb2/387); on rectos and versos from Bb3ᵛ/390 to Mm3ᵛ/470: "INDEX."

Plates as Bound in Vol. 4.A–C (10 Plates, In Two Engravings Each, Several With Multiple States)

C6ᵛ/44: "MARQUIS of GRANBY." signed "Aliamet Sculp."; one with knob below frame over space before "of" and budding of frame over "p" of "Sculp" (BL3 May2 O), one with knob below over the "o" of "of" and no budding by "Sculp" (BL1 May1,3 PSt); D3ᵛ/54: "LORD DOWNE." signed "Aliamet sculp."; one with two cashews flanking and touching a circle (PSt and nearly all copies), another with these shapes separated (MdU PPL1); I1ᵛ/130: "QUEEN CAROLINA." signed "Aliamet sculp."; one with second "A" in "CAROLINA" under "sc" in "sculp" (BL1,4 DT PSt), another with second "A" under "m" in "Aliamet" (May2-3 PPL1); K1/145: "GEORGE III. | King of Great Britain &c. &c." signed "Grignion sculp"; one with "Grignion" beginning over second ampersand (DT May2 O PSt), another over "c" of first "&c" (BL1-3 May1,3); K2/147: "Dʳ. THOMAS SHERLOCK | late Lord Bishop of London." signed "Benoist sculp."; one with circle at 9:00 separated from worms above and below (BL1,3 May1,3), one with these shapes touching (DT May2 PSt); N8ᵛ/208: "LORD Chief Justice WILLES." signed "Aliamet Sculp."; one with signature 14 in length, in states with "Justice" (BL1-2 May2 Vi) and "Iustice" (May1), another cut with signature 10–11, "J" in "Justice" and without period after "WILLES" (BL3 PSt); M8ᵛ/223: "DUKE of DEVONSHIRE."; one signed "Banerman sculp." with "J" hook under knob below frame (BL3 May2 PSt), another with hook opening on right (BL1-2 Vi), in states with "Banerman" in signature (Brack) and with "Benerman" (May1 May6 of vol. 1); P1/225: "Sʳ. PIERCY BRETT Kᵗ." signed "Miller sculp."; one with head within 4 of frame above (IU May1 MdU), one with over 6 between head and frame (BL3 May2 O PSt); P3ᵛ/230: "CHARLOTTE | Queen of Great Britain &c." signed "Aliamet sculp."; one with "Aliamet" beginning to the right of the fur border of cloak and over the "&" (BL3 May2-3 Vi), one with "Aliamet" at left of fur and beginning over "n" in "Britain" (BL1 May1 O PSt); Q7^v/254: "COMMODORE KEPPEL." signed "Sherlock sculp."; one common cut with leaf within frame forking by "s" of "sculp" (BL1,3 Brack May1-3 PSt), another with different elaboration in frame at 2:00 and 6:00 and more shading under left eye (EU MdU). Copies known to have all plates in proper places include BL1,3 Brack CaAEU (but Carolina and Charlotte switched), CT DGW InMB LU2 May1-2 MdU MnGA MoJ PPL1 ViU2; copies with all but Sherlock: DGW MB1 Vi.

Plates As Issued With Nos. 31–40 (8 Portraits and 5 Maps)

#31: map of North America [for #5]; #32: map of Caribbee Islands [for #23]; #33: Sherlock, Bishop of London [for #34]; #34: Northumberland [for #19]; #35: Queen Charlotte [for #35]; #36: Halifax [for #1]; #37: Louisa, late Queen of Denmark [for #3]; #38: "whole sheet map of East Indies" [for #5; "tomorrow" in 23 April, *PA* (in fact, half-sheet)]; #39: Lockhart and Coram [for #11 & #9]; #40: "Head of the AUTHOR, engraved by Aliamet; a new and accurate Quarto Map of France, and another of the West-Indies; by Jefferies, Geographer to his Majesty" [for #1, 16, & 23; 14 August 1762, *Gazetteer and London Daily Advertiser* and *PA*].

Paper in Vol. 4.A

Five paper stocks coordinated to issue numbers: 1) same and comparable paper stock as vols. 1–3.A: crisp chain-lines, 103-106/4, with much knotting; no tranchefiles; no WM: issues 1–2: A–F; 2) like #1 but thinner with more distinct and narrower chain-lines, 100-103/4: issue 3: G–I; 3) fairly distinct, 101-103/4; no tranchefiles; fleur-de-lys centered between chainlines, head 16–18 across, with wide arms and diamond tail: issues 4–5 and 7: K–P T–X (Gg also in O and PPL); 4) fairly distinct chains- and wire-lines; 103-107/4; Strasbourg lily WM, centered between chain-lines, with "L|V|G" below: issue 6: Q–S (and T of a few copies); 5) distinct wire- and chainlines, 104-107/4; tranchefiles, 17-18; no WM: issues 8-10: Y–Mm.

Notes to Vol. 4

This volume (with issues 31–40) is eight pages shorter than the others, for No. 40 has only five half sheets (40 pp., not 48). Although it has ten portrait plates, one per issue (bringing to forty-four the total for vols. 1–4), it lacks any maps. In addition, it typically has thirty-three lines per page after sheet D, one less than the other volumes, and its footnotes have more leading than do most in earlier volumes (see vol. 1.A on typography). And

Smollett wrote only the text to Aa2/371: thereafter come remarks by Major-General Barrington on the expedition to Martinique and the conquest of Guadalupe, commenting on Commodore Moore's remarks appended to vol. 3, with Moore's repeated in a parallel column (Aa2^v/372–Bb2^v/388. The index and directions to binder occupy the rest of the volume. Volumes with the first settings are dated 1761 since No. 31 was published in August 1761; No. 40 appeared around 24 July 1762. The frontispiece of Smollett found in vol. 1—placed there by the directions to the binder—was not distributed until the final issue, also loaded up with "quarto" maps of France and the West Indies.

Vol. 4's sheets were reprinted only twice for later serial distribution and sale as complete volumes, probably in 1764 and 1768, the dates on the title-pages of resettings. Although some sheets with figures found primarily in copies dated 1764 and 1768 are also found in copies with other title-pages, these volumes, like the reprints of vol. 3, have sufficiently predictable stability to treat them as editions, though, as the varying paper stocks in reprints suggest, they are best described as three-sheet issues.

The ESTC has records for 1761, 1764, and 1768 editions of vol. 4. ESTC T55304, grouping the five-volume set with earliest dated titles, indicates availability on microfilm in *The Eighteenth Century* (reel 157, no. 12) and on ECCO; however, only the vols. 4–5 of BL1, the only volumes of set BL1 with first settings and covered by T55304, were filmed on reel 157 (my copy of the Research Publications film of vol. 4 is numbered "reel 201, no. 12"). On ECCO, the BL1 copies of vols. 4–5 are listed as a two-volume set, with vol. 4 called "Vol. 1 of 2." ESTC T055305 includes vol. 4 1764 (4.B) within a five-volume set with reprints of vols. 1–4, modeled on BL3 (-Mm4; with all 1764 settings but 1761 in sheet Ff), microfilmed with this set (reel 1630) and digitized on ECCO; and T55308 indexes a single vol. 4 1768, based on BL2 (G.4877), filmed for *The Eighteenth Century* (reel 4971, no. 3) and reproduced on ECCO. T55308's list of seven locations includes all library locations but George Washington University.

Tp to Vol. 4.B (1764)

Same letter-press and ornamental design as in 1761 (4.A) but lacking punctuation after "LONDON" and reading "-Row. | M DCC LXIV."

Tp, Pp., Sigs., RTs, CWs, and Paper in Vol. 4.B

Pp. *1–3* 4–12 15 [=A7] 14–143 *144 blk.* 145–440 141–42 [=Ii1–Ii1^v] 443–72 [i.e., A7/13 and Ii1–Ii1^v/441–42 misnumbered]. As in 1768, A3 missigned "A2"; as in 1761, T1 signed "Numb. 37." Signature irregularities include, as in 1761, "No." for "Numb." on \$1 C, Cc–Gg and Ii–Mm. Same RTs as 1761;

with RT errors: "ENGLND" on G7^v/110, R3^v/262, X4^v/328; "GFORGE" on A5/9, B8/31, D6/59; "OEORGE II." on C7/45, E1/65, F6/91; "II" for "III" on K5/153, L5/169; "INEEX." on Dd2/403; and "INDEX," on Ff3/421. CW L2/163: seven] subject ("seven" omitted from text). Several paper stocks: 1) chain-lines, 79-81/3; tranchefiles, 14-18; fleur-de-lys between chain-lines, diamond-shaped head 21-22: Nos. 31–33 and 39–40: A–I and Bb–Mm; 2-3?: two or more unmarked paper stocks in K–Aa, chain-lines varying 77-83/3; one with chain-lines 77-78/3 and tranchefiles 11-12 in K–X, often with varying chain-widths in leaves $5–8 (the principal paper stock also in vol. 3.C).

Tp to Vol. 4.C (1768)

Same letter-press as on 1761 and 1764 tps through motto; then, different design of printer's devices (18 x 15), and "LONDON, | Printed for RICHARD BALDWIN, in Paternoster-Row. | MDCCLXVIII."

Pp., Sigs., RTs, CWs, and Paper in Vol. 4.C

Pp. *1–3* 4–77 76 [=E7^v] 79–143 *144* 145–96 297 198–472 [in some copies (e.g., Brack, DGW and ViW) Dd1/401 and Dd2^v/404 are unpaginated]. A3 missigned "A2" (as in 1764). In the issue signatures, the first sheets of Nos. 32–39 are signed with "NUMB." and then a roman numeral; the pattern is broken on Hh1 with "No. XL." As in 4.A–B, $1 of C, Cc–Gg, Ii–Ll are signed with "No." Mm1 is signed "No," (with comma). RTs have the errors: G7^v/110 with "ENGLND."; Dd2^v/404 with "INDEY." CW variants caused by errors in the text occur, as text CW Z3: last-] ing

Five distinct paper stocks are found in most copies: 1) waving wire- and chain-lines, 100-102/4; much knotting; no WM: A–H; 2) chain-lines 101-102/4, with "L|V|H" WM: I; 3) crisp wire- and chain-lines, 103-105/4, with width varying on one or more of $5–8, especially $5; with knotting; tranchefiles almost never seen but 12 when seen: K–Aa; 4) chain-lines, 100-03/4; tranchefiles, 14-16; fleur-de-lys WM centered between chain-lines, head 22-24 across, tail 20-21: Bb–Ff and Ii–Mm; 5) distinct chain-lines, 105-07/4; no WM: Gg–Hh.

Note on the Collation and Variants Listed

There are three settings of type for all sheets, labeled by volume dates in which these commonly occur: 1761, 1764, 1768. Sheets G–I and N–P of 1764 and N–P of 1768 lack press figures. Collation of the three settings for gatherings A–Bb employed May2 for 1761 (except May1 used for Bb), May3 for 1764 (except BL3 for K–X), and Brack for 1768 (except May1 for A–C). Gatherings Cc–Mm with index were not collated, but identifiable variants are usually noted in the descriptions of settings. Textual transmission is usually lineal.

Issue No. 31: Sheets A–C: pp. 1–48

A-1761: A7/13-3: 1761: AWn BL1,4 CtY1-2 DT EU InU InMB InTU IU LU1-2 May2 MdU1 MnGA NBuG NBuU NjM O Oa Oc OCX PPL1 PPT PSt ScF TnJoS TnNV ViLGH ViWCF [hereafter abbreviated as "all 1761 copies"];

A-1764: A5ᵛ/10-5: BL3 [291.h.23; on ECCO], BmU CaAEU CaOTU CtHi CtHT CYc ICarb May3 MB1-2 MBat2 MoJ MWA Vi ViU1-2 [RT error "GFORGE" on A5/9; A7/13 mispaginated "15"];

A-1768: A2ᵛ/4-8, A5ᵛ/10-6: BL2 [G4877; on ECCO], Brack CSt CT CU-B DGW May1 NNS PPL2 ViW [A3 missigned "A2" as is 1764].

Textual variants in sheet A: cf. A2–A4 [lineal descent]:

A3/5.1: merchants, 1761, Q] ∼ₐ 1764, 1768
A3.16: negro-slaves 1761, 1764, Q] ∼ₐ∼ 1768
A3.A.19: will 1761, 1764] ∼, 1768
A3.B.18–19: ne- | cessary 1761, 1764] ∼, 1768
A3ᵛ/6.33: insurgents: 1761, Q] ∼; 1764, 1768

B-1761.A–B [pp. 17–32]: Two states, possibly two impressions, differing only in press figures: state A with two figures: B4ᵛ/24-5, B8/31-1 [in the right margin]: AWn BL4 CtY1-2 EU LU1-2 May2 MdU1 NBuU NjM O Oc PPT PSt TnJoS TnNV ViLGH ViWCF; state B with B4ᵛ/24-5 but without B8-1 (though easily overlooked): BL1 DT InU InMB InTU IU MnGA NBuG O Oa OCX PPL1 ScF; [plus with tp] 1768: NNS;

B-1764: Two states: state A with both B1ᵛ/18-2 [under first "u" in "judicious"] and B8ᵛ/32-1: BL3 BmU CaAEU CaOTU CtHi CtHT CYc ICarb May3 MB1-2 MBat2 MoJ MWA Vi ViU1; state B without figure on B1ᵛ: MBat2 ViU2; 1768: NNS. [RT error "GFORGE" on B8/31; like B-61 and unlike B-68, lacking CWs on B6–B6ᵛ];

B-1768: B1ᵛ/18-2 [under "p" in "physician"], B7/29-8: BL2 Brack CSt CT CU-B DGW May1 PPL2 ViW.

Textual variants in sheet B: cf. B1–B3ᵛ [lineal descent]:

B1/17.3: declared, 1761] ∼ₐ 1764, 1768
B2/19.1: he, 1761, 1764] ∼ₐ 1768
B2ᵛ.4: but, 1761] ∼ₐ 1764, Q, 1768
B2ᵛ.6: women, 1761, 1764] ∼ₐ Q, 1768

C-1761.A–B: Two states (and impressions) with identically placed skeletons but differently placed figures on same pages: state A: C7/45-3 [un-

der "u" in "dukes"], C7^v/46-2 [under "r" in "ri-"]: BL4 CtY1-2 EU InU
LU1 May2 NBuG NBuU NjM O Oc OCX PPL1 PPT PSt TnJoS TnNV
ViLGH ViWCF; state B: C7/45-6 [under "g" of "forming"], C7^v/46-5
[under first "n" in "evening"]: AWn BL1 DT IU InMB InTU LU2 MdU1
MnGA Oa ScF; 1768: NNS;

C-1764: C2^v/36-2: BL3 BmU CaAEU CaOTU CtHi CtHT CYc ICarb May3
  MB1-2 MBat2 MoJ MWA Vi ViU1-2. [RT error "OEORGE" on C7/45,
  recurring in 1764 settings for E1 and F6];

C-1768: C1^v/34-6, C7/45-2: BL2 Brack CSt CT CU-B DGW May1 PPL2
  ViW [C1 signed "No. 31."].

Textual variants in sheet C: cf. C1–C3^v [lineal descent]:
C1^v/34.9: Brunswic 1761, 1764, Q] Brunswick 1768
C2^v/36.6: army 1761, 1764] ~, 1768
C2^v.7: Luckner 1761, 1764, Q] ~, 1768
C2^v.23: Geissa 1761, Q] Gissa 1764, 1768
C3^v/38.19: piquets 1761, Q] picquets 1764, 1768

Issue No. 32: Sheet D–F: pp. 49–96

D-1761: D5^v/58-3, D6^v/60-2: all 1761 copies plus [with tp] 1768: CSt
  CU-B May1;

D-1764: D5/57-2: BL3 BmU CaAEU CaOTU CtHi CtHT CYc ICarb May3
  MB1-2 MBat2 MoJ MWA Vi ViU1-2 [RT error "GFORGE" on D6/59];

D-1768: D5^v/58-2, D7/61-8: BL2 Brack CT DGW NNS PPL2 ViW.

Textual variants in sheet D: cf. D1–D3^v [lineal descent]:
D1/49.2: town, 1761, Q] ~$_\wedge$ 1764, 1768
D1.28: camp 1761, Q] ~, 1764, 1768
D1.32: Bulow, 1761] ~$_\wedge$ 1764, 1768
D2/51.8: armies, 1761] ~$_\wedge$ 1764, 1768

E-1761: E1^v/66-2, E8^v/80-3: all 1761 copies plus 1768: CSt CU-B May1
  ViW;

E-1764: E1^v/66-1: BL3 BmU CaAEU CaOTU CtHi CtHT CYc ICarb May3
  MB1-2 MBat2 MoJ MWA Vi ViU1-2. [RT error "OEORGE" on E1/65];

E-1768: E6/75-4, E6^v/76-1; and E7^v/78 as "76": BL2 Brack CT DGW NNS
  PPL2.

Textual variants in sheet E: cf. E1–E4 [lineal descent]:
E1.B.22–23: be- | leaguered; 1761, 1764, Q] ~: 1768
E1^v/66.30: route 1761, 1764, Q] rout 1768 [error]
E2/67.13: Kadetz 1761, 1764, Q] Cadetz 1768
E3/69.20: Kesseldorf 1761, Q] Xesseldorf 1764, 1768
70.13: mountains, 1761, Q] mountain 1764, 1768

F-1761: F8/95-3, F8^v/96-2 [small font]: all 1761 copies plus 1768: CU-B May1;

F-1764: F4^v/88-6, F6/91-1: BL3 BmU CaAEU CaOTU CtHi CtHT CYc ICarb May3 MB1-2 MBat2 MoJ MWA Vi ViU1-2 [RT error "OEORGE" on F6/91];

F-1768: F8/95-6: BL2 Brack CSt CT DGW NNS PPL2 ViW.

Textual variants in sheet F: cf. F1–F3 [lineal descent]:

F1/81.A.33: Francfort 1761, 1764] Frankfort 1768

F1^v.A.19: Nevertheless 1761] ~, 1764, 1768

F1^v.B.7: with 1761] by 1764, 1768

F2/83.A.4: were 1761, 1768] was 1764

F2.A.5–6: re- | proach: 1761] ~; 1764, 1768

F2.B.38: unpunished; 1761, 1764] ~: 1768

Issue No. #33: Sheets G–I: pp. 97–144

G-1761: G8/111-3, G8^v/112-5: all 1761 copies plus 1768: May1;

G-1764: no figures: BL3 BmU CaAEU CaOTU CtHi CtHT CYc ICarb May3 MB1-2 MBat2 MoJ MWA Vi ViU1-2 [all copies with 1764 tps have unfigured sheets G–I as well as F-1764; "3" of G3 before "in"; "4" under "r" of "raised"; without RT error on G7^v of 1768; with fn. CW variant on G2^v/100 shared with G-1768 but unlike G-1761: ple;} ple: and with recurrent RT with second "N" cut at center left on G3^v/102, H3^v/118, I7^v/142];

G-1768: G7/109-6; RT error "ENGLND." on G7^v/110: BL2 Brack CSt CT CU-B DGW NNS PPL2 ViW.

Textual variants in sheet G: cf. G1–G2^v [lineal descent]:

G1^v/98.8–9: ex- | tortions; 1761, 1764, Q] ~: 1768

G1^v.21: these 1761, Q] those 1764, 1768

G1^v.25: ban 1761, 1768] band 1764 [obvious error]

G2/99.10: treatment 1761, Q] ~, 1764, 1768

G2^v.B.38: its 1761, 1764, Q] the 1768

H-1761.A–B: Two states and impressions, differing only in inner forme figure on H1^v, both sharing figure H7/125-5: state A with H1^v/114-2 [under first "t" in "imputation"]: BL4, CtY1-2 EU InU LU1-2 MdU1 NBuG NBuU NjM O Oc OCX PPL1 PPT PSt TnJoS TnNV ViLGH ViWCF; plus 1768: May1; state B with H1^v/114-3 [under "t" of "imputation"]: AWn BL1 DT IU InMB InTU May2 MnGA Oa ScF. [Some type is shifted slightly in the skeleton of the inner forme; for instance the "4" of signature H4 in the IU copy (state B) is in a position different from that shared by May1 (state A) and May2 (state B); also, the RT on H4 ends over second "l" in "allies" in May2 and ScF and over "al" in "allies" in May1];

H-1764: no figures: all 1764: same as for 1764: F–G ["3" of H3 under the "t" of "the"; 4 under the "w" of "now"; CW variant: H4^v/120: ciety,} ~.];

H-1768: H5^v/122-2, H8^v/128-8: BL2 Brack CSt CT CU-B DGW NNS PPL2 ViW.

Textual variants in sheet H: cf. H1–H3^v [lineal descent]:

H1/113.1: regard 1761, Q, 1768] reguard 1764

H1.15: prince 1761, 1764] ~, Q, 1768

H1.19: passion, 1761, 1764, Q] ~$_\wedge$ 1768

H1^v.12: wavering; 1761, 1764, Q] ~: 1768

H3^v/118.9: impetuous; 1761, 1764, Q] ~: 1768

H4/119.4: pretend, 1761, Q] ~$_\wedge$ 1764, 1768

I-1761.A–B: Both states share figure I6/139-5 [under "o" in "months"]; state A in addition has I6^v/140-2 [under first "t" in "that"]: AWn BL1,4 CtY1-2 DT IU InMB InTU InU LU1-2 May2 MdU1 MnGA NBuU NjM O Oa Oc OCX PPL1 PSt ScF TnNV ViWCF; state B lacks any figure on I6^v/140: EU NBuG PPT TnJoS ViLGH; 1768: May1;

I-1764: no figures: all 1764: same as 1764: F–H ["2" of I2 under comma after "wood"; 3 under "r" in "Marquis"; CW I1^v/130: neg- (others have "ne-")];

I-1768: I6/139-1: BL2 Brack CSt CT CU-B DGW NNS PPL2 ViW [second figure was apparently lost early in the run: I7^v/142-5 occurs in ViW, 21 mm. below "l" in "line"; it appears in DGW as an illegible mark and in Brack as a faint bar or, if any number, a "2" with dirt below (no figure here in BL2 CT CU-B NNS PPL2)].

Textual variants in sheet I: cf. I1–I2^v [both 1764 and 1768 descend directly from 1761]:

I1/129.14: obtained, 1761, Q, 1768] ~$_\wedge$ 1764

I1^v/130.7: family, 1761, 1764, Q] ~$_\wedge$ 1768

I1^v.17: Musick 1761, 1768, Q] Music 1764

I1^v.B.4-5: landgra- | viate 1761, 1764, Q] landgra- | vine 1768

I1^v.marg.2: Music, 1761, 1768] ~. 1764

I2.28: Rysbach 1761, 1764] Rysbrack 1768, Q

Issue No. 34: Sheets K–M: pp. 145–92

K-1761.A–B: two states and impressions, both with K5/153-3; state A also has K7^v/158-1: BL4, CtY1-2 EU IU InU LU1 May2 MdU1 MnGA NBuG NBuU NjM O Oc OCX PPL1 PPT PSt TnJoS TnNV ViLGH ViWCF; 1764: May3; 1768: May1; state B, the second impression to judge from other sheets conjoined with it, lacks any figure on K7^v/158: AWn BL1 DT InMB InTU LU2 Oa; plus 1764: Vi;

K-1764: K8/159-4: BL3 BmU CtHi CtHT CYc ICarb MB1-2 MoJ MWA; 1761: ScF [variant RT with "II" for "III" on K5/153];

K-1764/68: K2^v/148-3 [under "s" of "consent"; dirty, appearing like an "8" in some copies]: 1764: CaAEU CaOTU MBat2 ViU1-2; 1768: BL2 Brack CSt CT CU-B DGW NNS PPL2 ViW.

Textual variants in sheet K: cf. K1–K3^v [lineal descent]:

K2/147.5: privy council 1761, 1764, Q] ~-~ 1764/68

K2^v/148.B.22: it, 1761, Q] ~$_\wedge$ 1764, 1764/68

K3/149.A.4: diction 1761, 1764, Q] action 1764/68

K3.B.16: fellow subjects 1761, 1764] ~-~ 1764/68, Q

K3.B.30: through 1761, 1764] thro' 1764/68

K3^v.A.1: new paragraph in 1761; no new paragraph 1764, 1764/68

L-1761: L7/173-5: all 1761 copies minus ScF, plus 1764: May3; 1768: May1;

L-1764: L7^v/174-3: BL3 BmU CtHi CtHT CYc ICarb MB1-2 MoJ MWA; 1761: ScF [variant RT with "II" for "III" on L5/169];

L-1764/68: L1^v/162-2, L8^v/176-1: 1764: CaAEU CaOTU MBat2 Vi ViU1-2; 1768: BL2 Brack CSt CT CU-B DGW NNS PPL2 ViW.

Textual variants in sheet L: cf. L1–L3^v [lineal descent]:

L1/161.23: intail 1761] entail 1764, 1768

L2^v/164.1: seven 1761, Q, 1768] *om.* 1764 [error—CW on p. 163 is "seven"]

L2^v.8: line ends "and" in 1761; ends "and these" in 1764, 1768

L3/165.30: but, 1761, Q] ~$_\wedge$ 1764, 1768

L3^v.18: or 1761, Q] nor 1764, 1768

M-1761.A–C: Three states varying only in press figures: state A with M6^v/188-1 [under second "g" of "belonging"], M7^v/190-3: CtY2 InU May2 MnGA NBuU O TnJoS ViLGH ViWCF; 1764: May3; state B with M6^v/188-2 [under "nd" of "and"], M7^v/190-3: CtY1 EU InTU LU1 MdU1 NBuG NjM Oc OCX PPL1 TnNV; 1768: May1; and state C with M6^v-2 as in state B but without figure on M7^v/190: BL1,4, DT IU InMB LU2 Oa PPT PSt;

M-1764: M1^v/178-1: BL3 BmU CtHi CtHT CYc ICarb MB1-2 MoJ MWA; 1761: ScF;

M-1764/68: M7^v/190-7, M8^v/192-6: 1764: CaAEU CaOTU MBat2 Vi ViU1-2; 1768: BL2 Brack CSt CT CU-B DGW NNS PPL2 ViW.

Textual variants in sheet M: cf. M1–M3^v [lineal descent]:

M1^v/178.22–23: encou- | raged, 1761] ~$_\wedge$ 1764, 1768

M3^v/182.10: continue 1761, 1764] contine 1768

M3^v.19: armies 1761, Q] arms 1764, 1768

M3^v.26: made, 1761] ~$_\wedge$ 1764, 1768

M3^v.33 [ult. l.]: dangerous 1761] ~, 1764, 1768

Issue No. 35: Sheets N–P: pp. 193–240: Two Settings Lack Press Figures

N-1761: N6^v/204-5, N7^v/206-4: all 1761 copies plus 1768: May1;

N-1764: no figures; N3/197 as "197": BL3 BmU CtHi CtHT CYc ICarb MB1-2 MoJ MWA Vi [N1 under "es" of "majesty"; "2" of N2 under period after "next"];

N-1764/68: no figures; N3/197 mispaginated "297": 1764: CaAEU CaOTU May3 MBat2 ViU1-2; 1768: BL2 Brack CSt CT CU-B DGW NNS PPL2 ViW [N1 under "sty" of "majesty"; "2" under "d" of "day"; recurrent RT with "O" in "HISTORY" cut at 10:00 and 2:00 on N4^v/200 (also on O2^v/212, and P2^v/228; this "O" also found in copies of vol. 3 dated 1765)].

Textual variants in sheet N: cf. N1–N3^v [lineal descent]:

N1/193.11: which, 1761, Q] ~$_\wedge$ 1764, 1768

N1.13-14: esti- | mates 1761, Q] esti- | mate 1764, 1768

N2/195.A.32: annuities, 1761, 1764] ~$_\wedge$ 1768

N2.B.13–14: an- | nuities. 1761] ~, 1764, 1768

N2^v/196.A.1: On 1761, 1764] One 1768 [error]

O-1761: O7/221-5, O8/223-3: all 1761 copies plus 1768: May1 [variant state with first figure only in BL4];

O-1764: no figures: BL3 CtHi CtHT ICarb MB1-2 MoJ MWA Vi, and, to judge from other settings joined with it: *BmU CYc* [O1 under "je" of "majesty", "2" of O2 under "i" of "will"];

O-1764/68: no figures: 1764: CaAEU CaOTU May3 MBat2 ViU1-2; 1768: BL2 Brack CSt CT CU-B DGW NNS PPL2 ViW [O1 under "st" of "majesty"; "2" under first "l" in "will"; recurrent RT on O2^v with cut "O" in "HISTORY" (also on N4^v and P2^v)].

Textual variants in sheet O: cf. O1–O3^v [both 1764 and 1768 descend directly from 1761]:

O1^v/210.14: conjuncture 1761, 1768] ~, 1764

O1^v.22: sixty-one 1761] ~$_\wedge$~ 1764, 1768

O2.A.4: present— 1761, 1764] present.— 1768

O2.A.30: which, 1761, 1768] ~$_\wedge$ 1764

O8/223.23: solicitation: 1761, 1764] ~; 1768

P-1761: P7^v/238 ["239"]-3, P8^v/240-2; 238-239 mispaginated "239" and "238": all 1761 copies plus 1768: May1;

P-1764: no figures: BL3 CtHi CtHT ICarb MB1-2 MoJ MWA Vi; and, to judge from other settings joined with it: *BmU CYc* [P1 under "om" of "domestic"; 4 under "ye" of "enjoyed"];

P-1764/68: no figures: 1764: CaAEU CaOTU May3 ViU1-2; 1768: BL2 Brack CSt CT CU-B DGW May3 NNS PPL2 ViW, and to judge from

sheets joined with it, 1764: *MBat2* [P1 under "me" of "domestic"; "4"
of P4 under "ed" in "enjoyed"; recurrent RT on P2ᵛ with cut "O" in
"HISTORY" (also on N4ᵛ and O2ᵛ)].
Textual variants in sheet P: cf. P1–P4 [lineal descent]:
P1ᵛ/226.27: spectacle: 1761] ~; 1764, 1768
P2ᵛ.27: convoy 1761, 1768] convey 1764
P2ᵛ.28: convey 1761] convoy 1764, 1768
P3/229.19: arms: 1761, 1764] ~; 1768
P3.19–20: illumi- | nated: 1761, 1764] ~; 1768
P3ᵛ/230.13: wells, 1761] ~ 1764, 1768

Issue No. 36: Sheets Q–S: pp. 241–88

Q-1761: Q2ᵛ/244-3, Q5ᵛ/250-2: all 1761 copies plus 1768: May1;
Q-1764: Q3ᵛ/246-1, Q4ᵛ/248-3: BL3 BmU CtHi CtHT CYc ICarb MB1-2
   MoJ MWA Vi;
Q-1764/68: Q4/247-4, Q8ᵛ/256-7: 1764: CaAEU CaOTU MBat2 ViU1-2;
   1768: BL2 Brack CSt CT CU-B DGW NNS PPL2 ViW.
Textual variants in sheet Q: cf. Q1–Q3ᵛ [lineal descent]:
Q2ᵛ/244.4: death; 1761, 1764] ~: 1768
Q2ᵛ.11: their own 1761, Q] their [*om.*] 1764, 1768
Q3.5: called 1761, Q] called the 1764, 1768
Q3.20: suba 1761] subah 1764, 1768
Q3.22: suba 1761, 1764] subah 1768
Q3ᵛ/246.2: Nattal 1761, Q] Natal 1764, 1768

R-1761: R1ᵛ/258-3, R8ᵛ/272-2: all 1761 copies plus 1764: May3 MoJ;
   1768: May1;
R-1764: R8/271-1: BL3 BmU CtHi CtHT CYc ICarb MB1-2 MWA Vi [RT
   error with "ENGLND" on R3ᵛ/262];
R-1764/1768: R6/267-7, R7/269-1: 1764: CaAEU CaOTU MBat2 ViU1-2;
   1768: BL2 Brack CSt CT CU-B DGW NNS PPL2 ViW.
Textual variants in sheet R: cf. R1–R3 [lineal descent]:
R1ᵛ/258.10: aids-du-camp 1761] aids-du camp 1764, 1768
R2/259.12: island, 1761] ~ₐ 1764, 1768
R2ᵛ.B.9: made, 1761] ~ₐ 1764, 1768

S-1761: S2ᵛ/276-2, S8/287-3: all 1761 copies plus 1764: May3 MoJ;
   1768: May1 [figure on S8/287 is punched out in ScF];
S-1764: S1ᵛ/274-1: BL3 BmU CaAEU CtHi CtHT CYc ICarb MB1-2 MWA
   Vi;
S-1764/1768: S7ᵛ/286-1: 1764: CaOTU MBat2 ViU1-2; 1768: BL2 Brack
   CSt CT CU-B DGW NNS PPL2 ViW.

Textual variants in sheet S: cf. S1–S3 [lineal descent]:
S1/273.10–11: Shaum- | bourg-Lippe 1761 | ~ | ~ ~ 1764, 1768
S1.25: -Vilinghausen 1761, 1764] -Villinghausen 1768
S1^v.33: colours 1761] ~, 1764, 1768
S2: Five lines of marg. in 1761; four lines in 1764 and 1768
S2^v/276.10: Dassel 1761, Q] Cassell 1764, 1768 [correct]

Issue No. 37: Sheets T–X: pp. 289–336

T-1761.A–B: Both states share figure T5/297-4; state A also has T8/303-3: BL4 CtY1 EU InTU InU LU1 May2 MdU1 NBuG NBuU NjM O Oc OCX PPL1 PPT PSt ScF TnJoS TnNV ViLGH ViWCF; 1764: May3 MBat2; 1768: May1; instead, state B has T8/303-2: AWn BL1 CtY2 DT InMB IU LU2 MnGA Oa; 1764: CaOTU ViU2;
T-1764: T7/301-1 and T7^v/302-5: BL1,3 BmU CtHi CtHT CYc ICarb MB1-2 MoJ MWA ViU1;
T-1768: T2^v/292-6, T7^v/302-2: BL2 Brack CSt CT CU-B DGW NNS PPL2 ViW; 1764: CaAEU [T1 signed "Numb. XXXVII." (unlike 1761 and 1764 signed with "Numb. 37.")].
All textual variants in T1–T4: [lineal descent, with accurate reprinting]:
T1/289.20: compel even 1761, 1764, Q] even compel 1768
T1^v.3: head-quar- 1761] ~ ~ 1764, 1768
T2/231.19: acted, 1761] ~ 1764, 1768
T2.marg.10 [ult. l.]: Versailles 1761] ~; 1764] Ver- | sailles. 1768

U-1761: U2^v/308-5, U6/315-2: all 1761 copies plus 1764: May3 ViU1; 1768: May1;
U-1764.A–B: two states: state A with both figures U4^v/312-6 [under "a" in "and"] and U8/319-3: BL3 CtHi CYc ICarb MB1-2 MBat2 MWA Vi; state B with only U8/319-3: BmU CaOTU CtHT MoJ ViU2;
U-1768: U8^v/320-3: BL2 Brack CSt CT CU-B DGW NNS PPL2 ViW; 1764: CaAEU.
Textual variants in sheet U: cf. U1–U4 [possibly 1764 and 1768 directly descend from 1761, but the evidence is weak and most adjacent sheets descend linearly; 1768 introduces many accidental variants]:
U1/305.B.19: reason, 1761, 1764] ~ 1768
U1.B.24: tranquillity 1761, 1764] tranquility 1768
U1^v.6, 33: intire 1761] entire 1764, 1768
U3/309.3: made, 1761, Q, 1768] ~ 1764
U3.5: harbour 1761, 1764, Q] shelter 1768 [used below at 309.9]
U3.8: subject, 1761, 1764] ~ Q, 1768
U3.16: all the 1761, 1764, Q] the [*om.*] 1768

X-1761.A–C. States A and B have figure X8/335-4 [under "en" in "lessen"]: state A also has X7/333-2 (e.g., BL1 CtY2 DT IU InMB InTU LU2 MBat2 MnGA Oa); state B has X7/333-3 [under "t" of "the"] (e.g., AWn BL4 CtY1 EU InU LU1 May2 MdU1 NBuG NBuU NjM O Oc PPL1 PPT ScF TnJoS TnNV ViLGH ViWCF; 1764: CaOTU May3 MBat2 ViU1-2); state C has only X7/333-3: OCX PSt; 1768: May1;

X-1764: X1ᵛ/322-5: BL3 BmU CtHi CtHT CYc ICarb MB1-2 MoJ MWA Vi [RT error with "ENGLND" on X4ᵛ/328];

X-1768: X2ᵛ/324-3, X7ᵛ/334-2: BL2 Brack CSt CT CU-B DGW NNS PPL2 ViW; 1764: CaAEU.

Textual variants in sheet X: cf. X1–X3ᵛ [lineal descent]:

X1/321.26: traders, 1761] ~ₐ 1764, 1768

X1ᵛ.9: but, 1761] ~ₐ 1764, 1768

X2.21: that, 1761, 1764] ~ₐ 1768

X2ᵛ/324.11: Spain; 1761, 1764] ~: 1768

Issue No. 38: Sheets Y–Aa: pp. 337–84

Y-1761: Y3ᵛ/342-2, Y8ᵛ/352-4: all 1761 copies plus 1764: MBat2 ViU1; 1768: May1 NNS;

Y-1764: Y5ᵛ/346-1: BL3 BmU CaOTU CtHi CtHT CYc ICarb May3 MB1-2 MWA Vi ViU2;

Y-1768: Y5/345-2: BL2 Brack CSt CT CU-B DGW PPL2 ViW; 1764: CaAEU MoJ.

Textual variants in sheet Y: cf. Y1–Y4 [lineal descent]:

Y2/339.5: hath 1761] had 1764, 1768

Y2.22: efforts, 1761, 1764] ~ₐ 1768

Y2.27: war, 1761, 1764] ~ₐ 1768

Y4/343.18, part, 1761] ~; 1764, 1768

Z-1761: Z7/365-3, Z7ᵛ/366-5: all 1761 copies plus 1764: ViU1; 1768: May1 NNS;

Z-1764: Z8/367-6: BL3 BmU CaOTU CtHi CtHT CYc ICarb May3 MB1-2 MBat2 MoJ MWA Vi ViU2;

Z-1768: Z3/357-3: BL2 Brack CSt CT CU-B DGW PPL2 ViW; 1764: CaAEU.

Textual variants in sheet Z: cf. on Z1–Z2ᵛ [lineal descent]:

Z1/353.A.2–3: at- | tacked, 1761, 1764] ~; 1768

Z1.A.30: wherein, 1761] ~ₐ 1764, 1768

Z1.B.5–6: jus- | tice, 1761, 1764] ~ₐ 1768

Z1ᵛ.A.3: ended: 1761] ~; 1764, 1768

Aa-1761: Aa8/383-2, Aa8ᵛ/384-4: all 1761 copies plus 1764: CaOTU MBat2 ViU1-2; 1768: May1 NNS;

Aa-1764: Aa5^v/378-1: BL3 BmU CtHi CtHT CYc ICarb May3 MB1-2 MoJ MWA Vi;

Aa-1768: Aa4/375-4, Aa8^v/384-8: BL2 Brack CSt CT CU-B DGW PPL2 ViW; 1764: CaAEU [1768 alone lacks text CW "Art." on Aa4/375].

Textual variants in sheet Aa: cf. Aa1–Aa4 [both 1764 and 1768 probably descend directly from 1761]:

Aa1.15: governor-general 1761, 1768] ~$_\wedge$~ 1764

Aa1^v.13: enemy; 1761, 1764] ~, 1768

Aa2/371.18: we, 1761, 1764] ~$_\wedge$ 1768

Aa3/373.A.19: Fort 1761, 1768] ~- 1764

Issue No. 39: Half-Sheets Bb–Gg: pp. 385–432

Bb-1761: Bb4^v/392-3 [under "o" of "to"]: all 1761 copies plus 1768: CU-B May1 NNS ["b" of Bb1 under second "1" of "1761"; "2" of Bb2 under first "n" of "Barrington"; CW Bb3/389: *Albemarle,*} ~$_\wedge$];

Bb-1764: Bb4^v/392-1: BL3 BmU CaOTU CtHi CtHT CYc ICarb May3 MB1-2 MBat2 MoJ MWA Vi ViU1-2;

Bb-1768: Bb4^v/392-3 [backwards, under right side of "3" in "435"]: BL2 Brack CSt CT DGW PPL2 ViW; 1764: CaAEU ["2" under "gt" of "Barrington"; CW Bb1: "orders,} *General* ('"orders' is second line of col. B); CW Bb3: *Albemarle,*} ~].

All textual variants in sheet Bb: cf. Bb1–Bb2^v [lineal descent]:

Bb1/385.B.18: Crump 1761] ~, 1764, 1768

Bb1^v.B.4: and, 1761] ~$_\wedge$ 1764, 1768

Bb2^v/388.B.3: Petite-terre 1761, 1764] ~$_\wedge$~ 1768

Bb2^v.8: days 1761] ~, 1764, 1768

Cc-1761: Cc3^v/398-2: all 1761 copies plus 1764: BL3 ViU1; 1768: CU-B May1 NNS [Cc1^v/394.1 begins "Covelt," in 1761 but "Coveldt," in others];

Cc-1764: Cc1^v/394-4: BmU CaOTU CtHi CtHT CYc ICarb May3 MB1-2 MBat2 MWA Vi ViU2;

Cc-1768: Cc4^v/400-4: BL2 Brack CSt CT DGW PPL2 ViW; plus 1764: CaAEU [missing period in signature: "No. 39$_\wedge$"; Cc3^v/398.1 reads "war" but "~," in 1761 and 1764].

Dd-1761: Dd2^v/404-2; Dd3/405 mispaginated "054": all 1761 copies plus 1764: CtHT; 1768: CU-B May1 NNS [Dd1/401, lines 5 and 7 end "colonel" and "in" in 1761; "Clive," and "in" in 1764; and "Clive, and "prisoner" in 1768];

Dd-1764: Dd3/405-2 or 3; RT error "INEEX." on Dd2/403: BL3 BmU CaOTU CtHi CYC May3 MB1-2 MBat2 MoJ MWA ViU1-2 [under the "c" in "contributions" is a figure with a curved line at top as "2" or "3" but with ink blot obscuring lower half; probably "3", as thought at BL3 CaOTU CYC MB2 MBat2 MoJ MWA (but noted as "5" or "8" at Vi ViU1); punched out in BmU May3 MB1 MoJ];

Dd-1768: Dd2^v/404-4; RT error "INDEY." on Dd2^v/404: BL2 Brack CSt CT DGW PPL2 ViW; plus 1764: CaAEU [Dd1/401 and Dd2^v/404 unpaginated in some copies (e.g., Brack DGW ViW), but paginated in others (e.g., BL1 CaAEU CSt NNS)].

Ee-1761: Ee3^v/414-2 [under "pa" of "company's"]: all 1761 copies plus 1768: CU-B May1 NNS; [Ee1^v/410.3 begins "His" in 1761, "motions" in 1764, 1768; Ee3/413.1 ends "com-" in 1761, 1764; "commis-" in 1768];

Ee-1764: Ee3^v/414-5 [in left margin]: BL3 BmU CaOTU CtHi CtHT CYc ICarb May3 MB1-2 MBat2 MoJ MWA Vi ViU1-2;

Ee-1768: Ee3^v/414-7: BL2 Brack CSt CT DGW PPL2 ViW; 1764: CaAEU.

Ff-1761: Ff2^v/420-2: all 1761 copies plus 1764: BL3; 1768: CU-B May1 NNS;

Ff-1764: Ff4/423-1: BmU CaOTU CtHi CtHT CYc ICarb May3 MB1-2 MBat2 MoJ MWA Vi ViU1-2 [variant RT with comma: "INDEX," on Ff3/421; no CW on Ff1/417, but "Fisher," in 1761 and ~$_\wedge$ in 1768];

Ff-1768: Ff3/421-8: BL2 Brack CSt CT DGW PPL2 ViW; 1764: CaAEU [Ff1^v/418, penultimate line begins "Called" in only 1768].

Gg-1761: Gg4/431-2 [under comma after "again"]: all 1761 copies plus 1768: CU-B May1 NNS;

Gg-1764: Gg4/431-2 [under first "n" in "minions"]: BL3 BmU CaOTU CtHi CtHT CYc ICarb May3 MB1-2 MBat2 MoJ MWA Vi ViU1-2 [Gg1^v/426 begins "familp"; unique CW variant due to text error: Gg3/429: *Gottingen,} Gottengen,*];

Gg-1768: Gg1^v/426-3: BL2 Brack CSt CT DGW PPL2 ViW; 1764: CaAEU [Gg3^v/430.1 ends "Evacuated," only in 1768].

Issue No. 40: Half-Sheets Hh–Mm: pp. 433–72

Hh-1761: Hh1^v/434-3 [under "i" of "Sails"]; all 1761 copies plus 1764: MoJ; 1768: May1; [Hh4^v/440, penultimate line contains "tion, iii.95" in 1761; "95" in 1764; "iii.95" in 1768];

Hh-1764: Hh4^v/440-1: BL3 BmU CaOTU CtHi CtHT CYc ICarb May3 MB1-2 MBat2 MWA Vi ViU1-2 [signed "Numb. XL." as is 1761];

Hh-1768: Hh1^v/434-3 [under period after "241"]; signed "No. XL.": BL2 Brack CSt CT CU-B DGW NNS PPL2 ViW; 1764: CaAEU.

Ii-1761: Ii4/447-3: all 1761 copies plus 1768: May1;
Ii-1764: Ii2ᵛ/444-3; Ii1–Ii1ᵛ/441–42 misnumbered "141–142": BL3 BmU CaOTU CtHi CtHT CYc ICarb May3 MB1-2 MBat2 MWA Vi ViU1-2 [RT variant "INDEX," on Ii1ᵛ/442 as on Ff3/421];
Ii-1768: Ii1ᵛ/442-2: BL2 Brack CSt CT CU-B DGW NNS PPL2 ViW; 1764: CaAEU MoJ [at Ii3ᵛ/446.2 "North America" unhyphenated only in 1768].

Kk-1761: Kk4/455-4 [under second "e" in "amendment"]: all 1761 copies plus 1768: May1 [Kk1/449.1 has "Basse-terre" as does 1768; 1764 has "Basseterre"];
Kk-1764: Kk4ᵛ/456-4: BL3 BmU CaOTU CtHT CYc ICarb May3 MB1-2 MBat2 MWA Vi ViU1-2;
Kk-1768: Kk1ᵛ/450-2: BL2 Brack CSt CT CU-B DGW NNS PPL2 ViW; 1764: CaAEU MoJ [Kk2ᵛ/452 begins "for" unlike others with "worsted"].

Ll-1761: Ll4/463-2: all 1761; copies plus 1768: May1 NNS [Ll1/457.2 with "North Ame-" but hyphenated in others];
Ll-1764: Ll3ᵛ/462-2: BL3 BmU CaOTU CtHi CtHT CYc ICarb May3 MB1-2 MBat2 MWA Vi ViU1-2 [final line on Ll2/459 begins with misspelling "*Rochefore*"; "*Rochefort*" in 1761 and 1768];
Ll-1768: Ll4ᵛ/464-2 [under "str"]: BL2 Brack CSt CT CU-B DGW PPL2 ViW; 1764: CaAEU MoJ [Ll1/457.10: concludes "of Lon-" in 1768 but "of" in others; unique CW variants: Ll2ᵛ/460: S.} S. and Ll3ᵛ: *Sicily,*} ~.].

Mm-1761: Mm3/469-5: all 1761 copies plus 1768: CU-B May1 NNS;
Mm-1764: Mm4/471-1: BL3 BmU CaOTU CtHi CtHT CYc ICarb May3 MB1-2 MBat2 MWA Vi ViU1-2 [Mm2/467.2 ends "191" in 1764 but "191, 192" in 1761 and 1768];
Mm-1768: Mm1ᵛ/466-4: BL2 Brack CSt CT DGW PPL2 ViW; 1764: CaAEU MoJ Vi [variant signature with "No, 40."; Mm1ᵛ/466.8 begins "*Thesee*" but "*Thesée*" in 1761 and 1764].

Copies Examined of Vol. 4 With Title-Page Dated 1761: All First Settings [1761–1762] Unless Noted

AWn (uncut, 226 x 145); BL1 (9502.e.5; +Mm4; BL stamps on A1ᵛ and Mm3ᵛ; on ECCO); BL4 (1608/476; +Mm4); CtY1-2 (both +Mm4: #1: Im Sm 79 757ck; Knapp's copy; #2: By7.26/12); DT (+Mm4; -plate Charlotte); EU (+Mm4); InU (-maps); InMB; InTU (+Mm4); IU (-A1, Mm4; -plate Keppel); LU1-2 (#1: MUA Smo; +Mm4; #2: Porteus K3; -Mm4);

May1 (see 1768); May2 (bookplate of Wolverhampton Public Library; +Mm4; -Bb–Gg/385–432); MdU (-Mm4; all plates + "Monckton" facing 364 and belonging in vol. 2; MS annotations); MnGA (+Mm4); NBuG (-Mm4); NBuU (+Mm4); NjM (-Mm4; -plates); O (-Mm4; -4 plates, with Carolina misplaced in *CH* vol. 11; insert from a 1761 newspaper after p. 232); Oa (+Mm4); Oc (Gg–Mm damaged); OCX (-plates); PPL1 (Am 1760 Smoll [77906.0 Wolf]; -Mm4); PPT (-A1, +Mm4); PSt (+Mm4; Gg4 pitted, not fully legible); ScF (examined by Christopher Johnson); TnNV (-Mm4); TnJoS (+Mm4); ViLGH (-Mm4; plate Granby as frt; MS correction "Conflan's" for "De la Clue's" at 432, ult. l., etc.); ViWCF (-Mm4; -plates);

Copies Examined Dated 1764 (16 Copies): All Second Settings [c. 1763–1767] Unless Noted

BL3 (291.h.23; -Mm4; 1764 settings but 1761: Ff; on ECCO [MS shelfmark on tp]); BmU (+Mm4; -3 plates); CaAEU (+Mm4; 1764 settings in A–I S; 1768: K–R T–Gg); CaOTU (1764 settings in A–I U Y–Z Bb–Mm; 1768: K–S; 1761: T [1761.B], X [1761.B], Aa; +Mm4); CtHi (+Mm4); CtHT (1764 settings but 1761: Dd; -plate Willes); CYc (+Mm4); ICarb (-Mm4); May3 (1764 settings in A–I N–P Y–Mm; 1761: K–M Q–X); MB1-2 (both with all 1764 settings and +Mm4: 1) ++Adams 240.8; +plates; bookplate of MB's "John Adams Library"; 2)**K.88.20; +Mm4; -plates); MBat2 (8E.Sm77.2; 1764 settings in A–I, U, Z, and Bb–Mm; 1768: K–S; 1761: T [1761.A] X [1761.B] Y Aa; +Mm4); MoJ (1764 settings but 1761: R–S Hh; 1768: Y Ii–Mm; +Mm4); MWA (+Mm4); Vi (1764 settings but 1761: K; 1768: L–M; +Mm4); ViU1-2: (same settings in sheets A–S X Aa–Bb Dd–Mm; +Mm4 in both: 1) DA30.S52 1763; 1764 settings but 1768: K–S; 1761: U–Aa Cc; -many plates; #2: uncat., 1764 settings but 1768: K–S; 1761: T [1761.B], X [1761.B], Aa);

Copies Examined Dated 1768: All Third Settings Unless Noted

BL2 (G.4877; +Mm4; tp signed "Sophia Ziegenhirt"; on ECCO); Brack (+Mm4); CSt (third settings but 1761: D–E; examined by John Mustain); CT (+Mm4); CU-B (third settings but 1761: D–F Bb–Hh Mm; -Mm4); DGW (+Mm4); May1 (third settings in only A–C; 1761: D–Mm; +Mm4); NNS (third settings but 1761: B–C, Y–Gg and Ll–Mm; +Mm4; -plates); PPL2 (Am 1763 Smol [Acc. No. 6619]; -Mm4; -plate Keppel; inserted frt, from another octavo, of "George 3d King of Great Britain" engraved by D. Sizars from painting by "T. Gainesborough"); ViW (third settings but 1761: E; -Mm4; Mm3 damaged and loose).

VOLUME 5: NUMBERS 41–50:
RICHARD BALDWIN, 1765: ONE SETTING

Tp

Same letter-press (and ornamental design) as vol. 1.A's except for "FIFTH" in l. 7, and "Paternoster-Row. | M DCC LXV." in the imprint.

Coll., Contents, RTs, and CWs

8° (uncut, 226 x 145 [AWn]): A–Gg⁸ [$1–4 signed; $1 with issue signatures (regular but for Ff1 and Gg1, where signature begins with the abbreviation "No.")]; pp. *i–iii* iv–viii 9 10–188 188 [=M7] 190–300 249 [=T7] 302–36 339 [=Y1, skipping two digits]–450 [32, index]; thus, 480 pp.; p. 301 corrected after most copies were impressed ("301" in InTU LU1 MB1 MoJ NBuG); period after "vii" on A4. Contents: A1: tp; A2–A4ᵛ: unsigned preface; A5–Ee8ᵛ/450: text of the history, beginning in 1762; Ff1–Gg8ᵛ: Index; on Gg8ᵛ: "Dɪʀᴇᴄᴛɪᴏɴs for placing the Pʟᴀᴛᴇs." organized in two columns, listing 11 plates and the page numbers facing them. RTs: "PREFACE." on A2ᵛ–A4ᵛ; "HISTORY ᴏғ ENGLAND. | GEORGE III." on A5ᵛ–Ee8ᵛ (two-thirds of copies have a variant without "D" in "ENGLAND." but with terminal period on L3ᵛ/166); "INDEX." on Ff1ᵛ–Gg8ᵛ. Some variants between CW and text show omitted words: Y3ᵛ/344: had] qualified ["had" omitted from the text on p. 345]; Z7ᵛ/368: cried] out ["cried" omitted from the text on p. 369]; Aa2ᵛ/374: of] out [last word on 374 is "out"; so, text reads "out out of"]; Cc3/407, text CW: When] While (Peter Miles has called attention to one CW variant as possibly suggesting resetting: "of" for "or" on H4ᵛ/120).

Plates as Bound in Vol. 5 (7 Portraits, 1 Plan, and 3 Maps; There Are Signed and Unsigned States of the Florida Map, But Otherwise All Are From Single Engravings)

C1/33: "EARL of BUTE." signed "I. Hall sculp."; C2ᵛ/36: "EARL of AL-BEMARLE." signed "I: Hall Sculp."; H2/115: "THOˢ. HOLLES DUKE OF NEWCASTLE." signed "JHall sculpsit."; H4ᵛ/118: "Mʳ. C. CHURCHILL." unsigned; 99 (108) x 77 ["the late Mr. Churchill engraved by Mr. Miller" in *PA*, 25 May 1765]; H6ᵛ/124: map, entitled at top, "A PLAN of the CITY and HARBOUR of HAVANNA, | Capital of the Island of CUBA."; unsigned; double-ruled frame, 179 x 115; block, 188 x 124; I4ᵛ/136: folded map laid out sideways, entitled top right, "A New MAP of the | PHILIPPINE | ISLANDS, | Drawn from the best | Authorities: | By T. Kitchin Geog,ʳ"; frame, 229 x 168; block, 239 x 178; K4ᵛ/152: folded map, entitled at upper left "A New MAP, of the | MOST FREQUENTED | PART OF | NEW

FOUND | LAND. | By Tho,,ˢ Kitchin Geog,,ʳ"; frame, 178 x 248; block, 188 x 258; O2/211: "IOHN WILKES Esqʳ." signed "J. Miller Sculp."; Q6ᵛ/252: "ROBERT Lord CLIVE." signed "I. Taylor sculp."; S2/275: folded map, entitled at bottom center, "A NEW and | Accurate MAP | of | EAST and WEST | FLORIDA, | Drawn from the best | Authorities."; frame, 184 x 219; block, 195 x 231; in two states: one unsigned (DT PPiT), another—more common—signed at bottom right "J. Prockter sculp." (e.g., BmU BL2-3 DN LU2 May3 MB1-2 MnGA MoJ NBuG ViU1-2 ViW); a similar map but without coverage as far north as Savannah, Georgia, with the same caption but moved to the left corner, unsigned, and with headline "For the London Magazine," appeared in the *London Magazine* of March 1765, like the *Continuation*, published by Richard Baldwin (reproduced at http://fcit.usf. edu/florida/maps/pages/3800/f3890/f3890.htm); both these maps appears to be indebted to John Gibson's "A Map of the New Government of East & West Florida," which includes the Bahama Islands and has its caption title at the top right (220 x 350 mm.), published in the *Gentleman's Magazine* of 1763 (see http://fcit.usf.edu/florida/maps/pages/3500/f3583/f3583.htm); T4/295: "CHARLES | HEREDITARY PRINCE of BRUNSWICK &c." signed "I. Taylor sculp." Copies with all plates in proper positions include BL2 (except Charles Brunswick misplaced before 195), BL3 BmU CaAEU DN DT (except map of Florida before 174), EU LU2 May3 MB1 MoJ O PPiT PPL2 ViU2.

Plates As Issued With Nos. 41–50 (7 Portrait Plates, 1 Plan, and 3 Maps)

#41: Bute and Wilkes [for #41 & 45]; #42: Clive [for #46]; Albemarle [for #41]; #44: plan of Havanna [for #43]; #45: "Hereditary Prince of Brunswick" [for #47]; #46: map of Newfoundland [for #44]; #47: Churchill [for #43]; #48: map of Philippines [for #43]; #49: map of Florida [for #46]; #50: Newcastle [for #43].

Press Figures

Unless noted, in all copies (BL1-3 BmU CaAEU CaOTU CtY CU-B DGW DN DT EU InTU InU LU1-2 May3,7 MB1-2 MdU MnGA MoJ MWA NBuG NNS O OCX PPiT PPL ViLGH ViU1-2 ViW): [sheet] A: no figure ["A" of A2 under "a" of "peace"]; B6/27-8 C2ᵛ/36-8 C6/43-9 [under "B" of "Bourdeaux"; in all copies but not BL1 and NNS; no other differences between figured and unfigured states], D5/57-* [under "h" in "however" but not present in BL2 CtY DT InTU InU LU2 May7 MB1-2 OCX; no other differences between states]; E6/75-* F7ᵛ/94-* [No figures in G–O: G1 under "nd" of "and"; "2" of G2 before "were"; H1 under "ed" of "demolished; "2" of

H2 under "o" of "from"; I1 under "t" of "but"; "2" of I2 under "h" in "shipping"; K1 under "n" of "town"; "2" of K2 under "n" of "commanded"; L1 after "is"; "2" of L2 under "o" of "Tavistock"; M1 under "g" of "King"; "2" of M2 under "r" of "before"; N1 under "ho" of "those"; "2" of N2 under second "i" of "sinking"; "2" of O2 under "ed" of "applied"; "3" under "s" of "see"] P4^v/232-* [present under "m" in "marshals" in BL1,3 CtY DN DT InTU InU LU1-2 MB1 MoJ NNS OCX PPL ViLGH ViW; missing from BL2 BmU CaAEU CaOTU CU-B DGW EU May3,7 MB2 MdU MnGA MWA NBuG O PPiT ViU1-2; no other differences between states (figure lost in the run as was the "d" in CW "enced" on P4^v and a hyphen from CW on P8^v)] Q6/251-* R4^v/264-* S3^v/278-* T4^v/296-* U6/315-* X6/331-* Y4^v/346-* Z6/365-* Aa2^v/374-4 [missing from BmU CaOTU MnGA NBuG O, which also lack figure on Aa6; no other difference between states], Aa6/381-7 Bb3^v/392-7 Bb8^v/402-6 Cc5^v/412-3 or -7 [both under first "e" of "engaged": 3 in BL1-3 CU-B DGW DN DT InTU InU LU1-2 May7 MB1 MoJ NNS O OCX PPL ViLGH ViW; 7 in BmU CaAEU CaOTU EU May3 MB2 MdU MnGA MWA NBuG PPiT ViU1-2], Cc7/415-6 Dd3^v/424-6 Dd5/427-7 Ee4^v/442-3 [under "si" of "occasional"; missing in or overlooked at MoJ and NNS—at least NNS has same signature positions: "E" of Ee2 under "u" in "judged" and of Ee3 under first "e" in "There"], Ff5^v [unpaginated]-6 Ff6^v-6 Gg3^v-5, or -6 (both under "ia" of "Franconia") or no figure [5 in BL1 CaAEU CaOTU CtY EU May3 MB2 MdU MWA NBuG NNS OCX PPiT ViLGH ViU1-2; 6 in BmU DN InTU InU LU1-2 MB1 MoJ MnGA O; no figure in BL2-3 CU-B DGW DT May7 PPL ViW; no other differences between the states; all copies with the other figure in Gg], Gg7-7.

Paper

Most copies have four paper-stocks: 1) chain-lines, 100-03/4; no tranchefiles; no WM: A–E of all copies, F in half, and usually H–I; 2) chain-lines, 102-05/4; fleur-de-lys centered *on* chain-line, with head and tail, 16–18 and 25 across: G of all, plus F in half, plus H and/or I in a few; 3) chain-lines, 104-07/4; tranchefiles, 9-11; no WM: K–Q in all, usually S and Ee–Gg, and sometimes R, Bb, and Dd; 4) distinct wire-lines and chain-lines, 108-10/4; tranchefiles, 12-14: T–Dd in almost all, sometimes T–Gg, usually R and sometimes S (R–Aa and Cc only of May7). In addition two other paper stocks appear in rare copies: 5) chain-lines, 107-10/4; fleur-de-lys WM *between* chain-lines; head and tail, 22 and 19–20 across: sometimes in I, Ee, and Gg (all three in DT; I in EU MB1; Gg in PPL2; Ee and Gg in May7); and 6) distinct chain-lines, 85-87/3; tranchefiles, 14; no WM: H of DN and MB1-2. In sheet Gg there is a correlation between paper-stock recorded and press figures: copies without figure on Gg3^v tend to have #5 (e.g., DT, May7, and PPL2). Portrait plates are usually printed on a heavy unmarked paper stock, with light chain-lines 80-83/3 and tranchefiles 15-16, running vertically; maps on unmarked thin paper stock with more distinct chain-lines, 105-07/4, running across the short axis of folding maps. However, PPiT's Bute, Newcastle, and three folded maps and PPL2's New Found Land map have another paper stock with faint chain-lines, 90-92/3.

Notes to Vol. 5

Though a separate publication initiative, vol. 5 has its ten numbers signed as Nos. 41–50. No variant states have been located except those involving figures and other features outside the text. Sheets C–D and P and half-sheets Aa, Cc, Ee, and Gg have varying states related to press figures, suggesting two impressions may have occurred for some sheets (there is no evidence of resetting). Note that BL1 and NNS, with late reprints for most and all vols. 1–4, have the same states in all gatherings with multiple states. MnGA has a state of Gg with an imposition error wherein Gg4 is the second recto and Gg2 the fourth, both with CWs for the ideal state and unsuited to their positions: CWs on the versos suggest Gg2^v is behind Gg4, and Gg4^v is behind Gg2.

Vol. 5 is not covered singly by any ESTC record, but it should be since it was separately conceived, written, and published. Otherwise, too, its absence from sets with vols. 1–4 misleadingly implies they are incomplete. The ESTC records vol. 5 as part of two five-volume sets: T55304, with the earliest printings of vols. 1–4 (1760–1761); and T055305, a "New Edition" of reprint volumes dated 1763, 1763, 1762, and 1764. Two copies at the BL were filmed by Research Publications for *The Eighteenth Century*, BL1 linked to ESTC T55304 (reel 157, no. 12) and BL3 linked to T055305 (reel 1631, no. 1); both are reproduced on ECCO (BL1, called "Vol. 2 of 2," has "21" in MS on its tp and lacks two maps). ESTC and OCLC locations for five-volume sets are a poor guide to libraries with vol. 5, the rarest volume; for instance, ESTC wrongly lists under T55304: IU and ViWCF, and under T55305: BL's 597.g.4; OCLC wrongly lists CaOHM, NjM, PCD, PMA, and ScFM. Peter Miles has banished the ignorant conjecture that the volume was suppressed by explaining well why it is rarer than the other four volumes and by locating twenty-three copies—five copies once owned by Boswell and others he cannot trace ("Bibliography and Insanity: Smollett and the Mad-Business," *Library*, fifth series, 31 [1976], 202–22; see 212). I examined 34 copies noted below and have seen others (Brack, LdU, MBat1, Oa, PPL3 [Upl.483.0]). When to these are added others in Miles and credibly added by OCLC (universities of Auckland, Columbia, Monash, New Brunswick, Waterloo, Wake Forest) and ESTC (National Trust copy SCO) and library catalogues (Niedersächsische Staats- und Universitätsbibliothek and Stanford), the total extant is just over fifty (half as many as can be lo-cated for vols. 1–4).

Copies Examined of Vol. 5

BL1 (9502.e.5; -maps Philippines and Florida; 209 x 130; rebd by BL in quarter leather with red buckram; octagonal BL stamp [with "MVSEVM"] on A1^v and Gg8^v under "Duke of Newcastle"; on ECCO); BL2 (G4878; 209 x 134; cont calf; with Grenville bookplate); BL3 (291.h.24; 205 x 129; BL's oval stamp on Gg8; on ECCO); BmU; CaAEU; CaOTU; CtY (Knapp's); CU-B; DGW (-A1, -Gg8); DN (J942; bound with vol. 4); DT; EU; InU; InTU; LU1-2; May3; May7 (lacking all plates but 4 from other vols.); MB1 (++Adams 240.8); MB2 (**K.88.20; -portrait plates but with 4 maps; F1 bound between F7 and F8; Aa1 bound after Aa8 and before Bb1); MdU; MnGA (sheet Gg with an imposition error misplacing Gg4 and Gg2; -plate Newcastle); MoJ; MWA; NBuG (-7 plates, with 4 maps); NNS (MS on p. 127 partly trimmed off); O (three leaves of the August 1765 *Gentlemen's Magazine*, are appended; on p. 361 in column A begins an unsigned review of "Some Account of the Late Dr. James Bradley, D.D. Royal Professor of As-tronomy in Greenwich."; with MS notations on pp. 33, 86, 232 [where "Sir W. M." has the "M" completed to read "Meredith"] etc.); OCX (-all plates before map of Florida); PPiT; PPL2 (Am 1763 Smol [6619.0]); ViLGH; ViU1 (DA 30.S52; -plates Bute, Clive, Charles Brunswick; 200 x 127); ViU2 (uncat.; 205 x 130; +all plates); ViW.

1766: REVISED TWO-VOLUMES QUARTO EDITION: R. BALDWIN, 1766

Tps

Identical letter-press as vol. 1.A's until the imprint: "[double rules, 130.5] | LONDON: | Printed for Richard Baldwin, at the Rose in Pater-noster-Row. | MDCCLXVI." [vol. 2's letter-press is the same except for "SECOND" in line 7; it has a different setting, measuring 199, 10 less than vol. 1's.]

Coll.

4° (uncut, 275–80 x 225 [CtY]): vol. 1: A^2 B-3S^4 3T^2 [1/2 $ signed; $1 (-C G–H K O R Y–Aa Ee–Ff Kk Mm Pp Rr Tt–3D) signed "Vol. I."; Dd1 signed in full capitals]; pp. [*iv*] *1* 2-508 [without error]. vol. 2: A^4 (-2, = 3U1-2) B-3T^4 3U^4 (-2, = A1–A2 [see notes on paper for evidence]) [1/2 $ signed; $1 signed "Vol. II." (without omission; no period following "Vol" on R1/121)]; pp. [*iv*] *1* 2-171 *172-73* 176-78 177[=Aa1]–365 *366–67*

368–464 *465–516* [3O1–3U2^v, with index, unpaginated; count falls two places behind at Z3^v but is corrected at Aa1; p. 162 misprinted "62" in DT].

Contents and RTs

Vol. 1: A1: half title [hft]: "CONTINUATION | OF THE COMPLETE | HISTORY | OF | ENGLAND. | VOLUME THE FIRST."; A2: tp; B1-3T2^v: text, reaching until 1759 (surrender of Quebec); on 3T2^v/508: "END of the FIRST VOLUME." Same RT text as octavos; RT error with "GEORGE H" on Z2/171 in some copies (e.g., CaOTU DN May1 PSt) corrected in others (E May2). Vol. 2: A1: hft (same as vol. 1's except "SECOND" in l. 6); A2: tp; B1-3A3/365: text of history of George II (Z2^v blank) and of George III (Z3/173-3A3, with 3A3^v blank); 3A4-3N4^v/464: "A General Index to Dr. Smollett's Complete History of England; From the Landing of Julius Caesar . . . "; 3O1-3U1^v/514: "Index to the Continuation of Smollett's History of England, From the Treaty of Aix-la-Chapelle, to that of Versailles in 1763."; On 3U1^v: "FINIS."; 3U2: advertisement for Thomas Leland's *History of the Life and Reign of Philip King of Macedon*, printed for W. Johnston, in quarto; 3U2^v: advertisement for "TRAVELS | THROUGH | FRANCE and ITALY" [. . . .] By T. SMOLLETT, M.D.," printed for R. Baldwin, "*Just Published.*" Same RT as vol. 1's until Z1^v/170 (with verso RT on recto of I1/57 and with "GEORGE III." too early on Z2/171); rectos from Z4^v-3A3/365 with "GEORGE III." (period missing after RT on Yy1^v/346).

Press Figures (In All Copies Unless Noted)

Vol. 1: B3^v/6-3 C3^v/14-3 D2^v/20-3 E2^v/28-5 E4/31-3 F1^v/34-5 G3^v/46-3 ([under "t" of "Westminster"] not in CtHT, which has G4^v-5), G4^v/48-5 H4/55-4 I1^v/58-3 K3^v/70-1 K4^v/72-4 L3^v/78-3 L4^v/80-4 M4^v/88-5 N4/95-5 N4^v/96-3 O3/101-3 O3^v/102-4 P1^v/106-3 Q3^v/118-5 Q4^v/120-4 R1^v/122-1 R4^v/128-3 S2^v/132-3 T1^v/138-1 U1^v/146-1 U3/149-3 X3/157-5 Y2^v/164-1 Z4/175-5 Z4^v/176-2 or -3 or omitted ([both under "w" of "with"] 2: DT1 May2; -3: CtY E ICU PMA WPS; omitted in CaOTU CtHT DN DT2 May1 PSt), Aa3/181-3 Bb4/191-5 Cc4/199-3 Dd2^v/204-1 Dd4/207-3 Ee3/213-1 Ff4/223-1 Gg1^v/226-5 Gg3/229-1 Hh2^v/236-4 Hh4/239-3 Ii2^v/244-5 Kk3^v/254-4 (not in ICU PMA), Kk4^v/256-3 (ditto), Ll3/261-4 Ll4/263-5 Mm2^v/268-4 Mm3/270-3 N1^v/274-4 Oo4^v/288-1 Pp3/293-4 Qq3/301-1 Rr2/307-4 Rr3/309-5 Ss3^v/318-3 (not in May1 WPS), Tt3^v/326-3 Tt4^v/328-1 Uu3^v/334-1 Xx3^v/342-4 Yy1^v/346-1 Yy4^v/352-4 Zz3^v/358-4 3A3^v/366-4 3B2^v/372-1 3C4^v/384-5 3D3/389-3 3E1^v/394-3 3F1^v/402-3 3G1^v/410-5 3H2^v/420-5 3I4/431-5 3K1^v/434-3 3K2^v/436-5 3L4^v/448-4 3M1^v/450-4 3M3/453-1 3N2^v/460-1 3N4/463-5 3O3^v/470-1 3P2^v/476-5 3P4/479-3 3Q1^v/482-3 3R4/495-1 3R4^v/496-3 3S3^v/502-4 3T2/507-5.

Vol. 2: B2^v/4-3 C1^v/10-4 D3^v/22-8 E3^v/30-8 F3/37-2 G3/45-3 G3^v/46-4 H2^v/52-4 H3^v/54-3 I4/63-6 K3/69-4 L4/79-6 L4^v/80-7 M1^v/82-6 M3/85-8 N4^v/96-4 O1^v/98-1 P3^v/110-4 P4^v/112-1 Q3^v/118-2 R1^v/122-2 R4^v/128-8 S4/135-7 T2^v/140-4 U3^v/150-8 U4^v/152-4 X2^v/156-6 X4/159-1 Y3^v/166-7 Y4^v/168-6 Z3^v/176-1 Z4^v/"178"-4 Aa1^v/178-8 Bb2^v/188-2 Bb3^v/190-4 Cc2^v/196-8 Cc4/199-6 Dd3^v/206-6 Ee3^v/214-6 Ee4^v/216-1 Ff1^v/218-7 Gg3/229-6 Hh4^v/240-6 Ii2^v/244-4 Ii4/247-1 Kk4/255-3 Kk4^v/256-1 L1^v/258-6 Ll2^v/260-8 Mm1^v/266-7 Mm4^v/272-1 Nn2^v/276-6 Nn3^v/278-2 Oo4/287-upside down 2, Pp4^v/296-8 Qq2^v/300-3 Qq3^v/302-6 Rr2^v/308-2 Rr4/311-6 Ss2^v/316-3 Tt2^v/324-6 Tt4/327-1 Uu1^v/330-8 Xx1^v/338-3 Yy2^v/348-7 Zz2^v/356-8 3A1^v/362-3 3A2^v/364-6 3B3/373-8 3C3^v/382-1 3C4^v/384-2 3D2/387-* 3E3^v/398-4 3F4/407-4 3G2^v/412-1 3H3^v/422-4 3I3^v/430-1 3K4^v/440-7 3L1^v/442-4 3L4^v/448-6 3M1^v/450-4 3M2^v/452-3 3N2^v/460-4 3N4/463-6 3O3^v-1 3P1^v-3 3Q1^v-4 3R3-6 3R3^v-4 3S1^v-3 3S3-2 3T4-6 3T4^v-7 (all sheets of vol. 2 with figures except half-sheets A and 3U).

Paper

Both volumes contain a mixture of two paper stocks of comparable weight and color: #1 with fleur-de-lys WM centered *on* chain-line (WM's head and tail, respectively, 16 and 25 across; chain-lines, 100-103/4), and #2 with fleur-de-lys *between* chain-lines (WM's head and tail, 21–24 and 19; chain-lines, 105-09/4; tranchefiles, 14-17). Nearly all copies have #2 in vol. 1: gatherings A L P S X Aa–Bb Dd Gg Ii–Mm Oo Ss Uu–Zz 3B 3D–3T (half have #2 also in T Ff Pp and Rr); #2 in all sheets of vol. 2 except B–C (#1 appears sometimes also in P [DT1 E WPS], Q [CtY E WPS] and T [CtY DN DT1 E PMA WPS]). The first and last half-sheets of vol. 2 (A^2 and 3U^2) were apparently printed together, for in each copy they routinely combine the WM and countermark of the second stock—or WM and no apparent countermark, presumably with "IV" overlooked in fold (e.g., CaOTU CtHT CtY DN DT1-2 ICU May1 PMA PSt WPS). But half-sheets A^2 and 3T^2 of vol. 1 may not have been printed together: only in five of thirteen copies examined (CaOTU E PMA PSt WPS) did I note complementary combinations of WM and countermark: some copies have the WM (or countermark) in both half-sheets (e.g., CtHT CtY DT1-2 ICU May1-2).

Typ.

[C1, vol. 1] 48 ll., 211 (199) x 128.5 without marginalia and 148 with marginalia and page number; 20 ll, roman (no italic), 83 (no leading). No cut ornaments.

Notes

This revised edition lacks the prefaces of vols. 1 and 5 and many additional pages of material, but has some additions. Vol. 1 reprints the octavo text to vol. 3's O4^v/200 (final paragraph of first quarto begins "The City of Quebec"), and vol. 2 reprints from the next paragraph through vol. 5's p. 192. The quarto constitutes the third or fourth edition for material in vols. 1–4 but only the second for text reprinted from vol. 5.

In vol. 1, half-sheets A and 3T may have been printed on a single sheet, although the two halves of individual sheets did not end up in the same copy, for they share the same paper stock. Also, in May1 the hft has offset of 3T2^v (though 3T2^v does not of the hft). Between the two half-sheets, only 3T has a press figure, which fits their being printed together. Watermark evidence noted above strongly indicates that Vol. 1's half-sheets A and 3U were printed together and that a copy received both from the same printed sheet. This is also suggested by evidence in the PSt copy: A1.A2 and 3U1.3U2 have blurred chain-lines on the left growing crisper to the right across the combined sheet (toward A2 and 3U2). Vol. 2's advertisement leaf 3U2 (with full-page advertisements for Thomas Leland's *History of the Life and Reign of Philip King of Macedon*, printed for W. Johnston, and for Smollett's *Travels through France and Italy*) remains present in all copies examined, presumably because it allowed leaf 3U1 to be sewn into the book.

Other than two gatherings, varying states appear to be limited to the presence and absence of press figures. There was a stop-press correction to Hh1^v/234 of vol. 2, with "rein" added to "forced" at the start of l. 1 to form "reinforced"; some type was altered in l. 2 (for with "rein" added, l. 1 ends "ma"—not "maga" as in the unrevised state); l. 2 ends with the same words as line-for-line printing resumes. Broken type shared by both states appears close by, as "y" in "by" of l. 1 and "d" in "deposited" in l. 2. The revised state appears in ICU May1 PMA and PSt; the unrevised in CaOTU CtHT CtY DN DT1-2 E WPS. (Both states have the same signature positions, with the "2" of signature Hh2 under the second "t" of "attack.") More noteworthy is the resetting of all sheet Ss of vol. 1 (presumably due to an accident during press work). The rarer state (in May1 WPS) is distinguished by the absence of press figure 3 on Ss3^v/318. Variants between the two settings seem merely compositorial errors, there being no evidence of revision. The only substantive variant occurs at Ss4^v/320.24: "clause" in most copies (as in octavo 2:223.13) but "cause" in the unfigured settings, suggesting it was impressed last. There are a few accidental variants on all other pages of the gathering except Ss3/317. The most common type of variant involves the present or absence of hyphenation: e.g., Ss1/313.38: "fifty seven" in unfigured and "~-~" in figured; and Ss3^v.36: "muster rolls" in unfigured but "~-~" in figured. At Ss2^v.4, "inquiry" appears in the figured state and "enquiry" in unfigured. Punctuation variants include

"Coventry" without a comma following in the figured state, but with a comma in the unfigured (Ss2^v.B.12); and "traffick" followed by a comma in the figured but not in the figured (Ss4.21). These differences suggest the amount and kind of accidental variation likely to be compositorial error.

All copies known to be at libraries have been examined except Bayerische Staatsbibliothek's (noted on OCLC). Only one complete copy has been offered for sale in the last decade, by Wessel & Lieberman of Seattle (here described as May1), combined with the quarto *Complete History* in contemporary speckled calf. Although many copies of such an expensive book may remain in private libraries, this is a rare edition. Those examined were bound at considerable expense, such as the PSt with gilt spine ornamentation and marbled endpapers and leaf-edges. Most are still bound in contemporary calf (CtHT DN DT1 ICU May1-2 PMA PSt WPS), but CaOTU has contemporary marbled-paper boards, and CtY, the original blue-paper boards with white-paper spines. Most copies have red morocco labels with "SMOLLETT | HIST: OF | ENGLAND" (CaOTU CtHT ICU May1 PMA PSt), a label suited to those bound with the quarto *Complete History* and usually numbered "5" and "6" (e.g., CtHT DN DT1-2 E ICU May1 PMA PSt WPS); May2 copy of vol. 1 alone appears to have a cont label with "SMOLLETT'S | CONTINUATIO." ESTC T167099, since 1993, has noted eight copies (CaOTU CtHT CtY DN DT E ICU WPS), missing the PMA, PSt, and DT1 copies. The E copy was microfilmed by Primary Source Media for *The Eighteenth Century* in 2004 (reel 14713, no. 1) and, though not yet indicated by the ESTC, has been reproduced on ECCO2 (2008).

Copies Examined: Unless Noted, Assume All Copies Have Vol. 2's 3U^2 and Half-Titles to Vols. 1–2

CaOTU (E10 1750; cont calf with marbled-paper boards; cont bookplate of Richard Humber); CtHT (Quick 942.S66a; 264 x 213; cont armorial bookplate of "Hon.ble Charles Phipps"); CtY (Im Sm 79 +757cm; uncut, 275–80 x 225; cont blue paper boards with white-paper spines); DN (J.942.SMO; bookplate inscribed, "Right Hon.ble Sir George FitzGerald Hill, Bart."); DT1-2 (#1: Fag Q.4.8[–9]; 275 x 211; #2: P.e.7[–8]; 255 x 200; nineteenth-century calf); E (C.9.b.15[–16]; 261 x 210; MS marginalia; rebd with leaves attached to extenders; p. 1 inscribed "Lib. Bib. Fac. Jurid. Edin."; on ECCO); ICU (DA30.S662; bookplates of "John Templer | Trin: Coll: Camb"); May1-2 (#1: 257 x 205; #2: vol. 1 only); PMA ([Allegheny College, Meadville, PA] T924.Sm79co; 272–73 x 215; catalogued in "Miscellaneous before 1823"; bequest from William Logan Fox); PSt (DA30.S66 1757 v.5–6); WPS ([Washington State U.] 942.Sm79c; 275 x 215, leaving some bottom edges untrimmed; rebacked with old spines laid back down; Hh1/234 of vol. 2 with variant state beginning "forced").

ACKNOWLEDGEMENT

For help checking details in copies, the author thanks Norma Aubertin-Potter, Charles Benson, Anthony Bliss, Kathryn J. Blue, O M Brack Jr., Stanley Cushing, Cynthia Harbeson, James N. Green, Jeannine Green, Jeff A. Jenson, Christopher Johnson, Jeffrey H. Kaimowitz, Jennifer Matko, Erich May, Gaye Morgan, John Mustain, Sandy Paul, Kellie Roach, Suzanne Singleton, Malinda Triller, and Erica Wylie.

Select Bibliography of Works by Jerry C. Beasley

BOOKS AND EDITIONS

A Check List of Prose Fiction Published in England, 1740–1749. Bibliographical Society of the University of Virginia. Charlottesville: University Press of Virginia, 1972.

Editor (with Michael Shugrue et al.), *The Novel in England, 1700–1775* (facsimile reprint series). New York: Garland, 1974–1975.

English Fiction, 1660–1800: A Guide to Information Sources. Detroit, Mich.: Gale, 1978.

Novels of the 1740s. Athens: University of Georgia Press, 1982.

Editor (with Robert Hogan), *The Plays of Frances Sheridan.* Newark: University of Delaware Press, 1984.

Editor, *The Adventures of Ferdinand Count Fathom,* by Tobias Smollett. The Works of Tobias Smollett. Athens: University of Georgia Press, 1988.

Tobias Smollett: Novelist. Athens: University of Georgia Press, 1998.

Editor, *The Injur'd Husband and Lasselia,* by Eliza Haywood. Lexington: University Press of Kentucky, 1999.

ESSAYS

"English Fiction in the 1740's: Some Glances at the Major and Minor Novels." *Studies in the Novel* 5 (1973).

"Fanny Burney and Jane Austen's *Pride and Prejudice.*" *English Miscellany* 24 (1973–1974).

"The Role of Tom Pinch in *Martin Chuzzlewit.*" *Ariel: A Review of International English Literature* 5 (1974).

"Romance and the 'New' Novels of Richardson, Fielding, and Smollett." *Studies in English Literature* 16 (1976).

Entry on "Edmund Burke." *Dictionary of Irish Literature*, revised and expanded edition, ed. Robert Hogan (Westport, CT: Greenwood Press, 1996).

"*Roderick Random*: The Picaresque Transformed." *College Literature* 6 (1979).

"Portraits of a Monster: Robert Walpole and Early English Prose Fiction." *Eighteenth-Century Studies* 14 (1981).

"Politics and Character in the Eighteenth Century: Glances at Some Rhetorical Types." In *Studies in Eighteenth-Century Culture: XIII*, ed. O M Brack Jr. (Madison: University of Wisconsin Press, 1984).

"Smollett's Novels: *Ferdinand Count Fathom* for the Defense." *Papers on Language and Literature* 20 (1984).

Entries on the following authors in *Dictionary of Literary Biography*, vol. 39: *British Novelists, 1660–1800*, ed. Martin C. Battestin (Columbia, S.C.: BC Research, 1985):

Robert Bage	Thomas Holcroft
Aphra Behn	Charlotte Lennox
Henry Brooke	Delariviére Manley
Thomas Day	Tobias Smollett
Eliza Haywood	

"Smollett's Art: The Novel as 'Picture.'" In *The First English Novelists: Essays in Understanding. Honoring the Retirement of Percy G. Adams*, ed. Jack M. Armistead (Knoxville: University of Tennessee Press, 1985).

"Politics and Moral Idealism: The Achievement of Some Early Women Novelists." In *Fetter'd or Free? Collected Essays on Eighteenth-Century Women Novelists, 1670–1815*, ed. Mary Anne Schofield and Cecilia Macheski (Athens: Ohio University Press, 1986).

"Early English Fiction: Historical Criticism, Old and New." *Studies in the Novel* 17 (1985).

"Life's Episodes: Story and Its Form in the Eighteenth Century." In *The Idea of the Novel in the Eighteenth Century*, ed. Robert W. Uphaus (East Lansing, Mich.: Colleagues Press, 1988).

"Smollett's Novels and the Wider World." In *All Before Them* (*English Literature and the Wider World*, vol. 1), ed. John McVeagh (London: Ashfield Press, 1990).

"Translation and Cultural *Translatio*." In *The Picaresque: A Symposium on the Rogue's Tale*, ed. Carmen Benito-Vessels and Michael Zappala (Newark: University of Delaware Press, 1994).

"Tobias Smollett: The Scot in England." *Studies in Scottish Literature* 29 (1997).

"Amiable Apparitions: Smollett's Fictional Heroines." In *Augustan Subjects: Essays in Honor of Martin C. Battestin*, ed. Albert J. Rivero (Newark: University of Delaware Press, 1997).

"Richardson's Girls: The Daughters of Patriarchy in *Pamela*, *Clarissa*, and *Sir Charles Grandison*." In *New Essays on Samuel Richardson*, ed. Albert J. Rivero (New York: St. Martin's Press, 1996).

"Little by Little; or, The History of the Early Novel, Now." *Studies in the Novel* 30 (1998).

"*Clarissa* and Early Female Fiction." In *Clarissa and Her Readers: New Essays for the Clarissa Project*, ed. Carol Houlihan Flynn and Edward Copeland (New York: AMS Press, 1999).

ADDITIONAL ACHIEVEMENTS

General Editor, *The Works of Tobias Smollett* (Athens: University of Georgia Press, in progress), 1986–1997.

Member, Editorial Board, *Studies in Eighteenth-Century Culture*, 1985–1987. Published annually for the American Society for Eighteenth-Century Studies (East Lansing, Mich.: Colleagues Press).

Guest Editor, "Women and Early Fiction," special issue of *Studies in the Novel* 19 (Fall 1987).

English Books Editor, *The Eighteenth Century: A Current Bibliography*, 1987–1989. General Editor, Jim Springer Borck. Published annually for the American Society for Eighteenth-Century Studies (New York: AMS Press).

Member, Advisory Board, *Early Women Writers*, 1988–2005. Series Editor, Robert W. Uphaus (East Lansing, Mich.: Colleagues Press).

Member, Board of Advisory Editors, *Studies in the Novel*, 1988–2005.

Consulting Editor, *Selected Works of Eliza Haywood*, 1999–. General Editor, Alexander Pettit (London: Chatto & Pickering, in progress).

Papers read at the University of Utrecht, Netherlands (1982), the University of Essen, West Germany (1982), the College of William and Mary (1984), Virginia Tech (1985), the University of Missouri (1989), Gettysburg College (1989), the University of Maryland (1989), Glasgow, Scotland (1990).

Papers read and seminars chaired at national and regional meetings of the American Society for Eighteenth-Century Studies: Atlanta (1979), San Francisco (1980), Houston (1982), New York (1983), Boston (1984), University of Illinois (1984), Toronto (1985), Purdue University (1985), University of Texas at El Paso (1986), Philadelphia (1986), North Texas State University (1987), Knoxville (1988), New Orleans (1989), Charleston (1994).

Index

About the Contributors

Paula R. Backscheider is Stevens Eminent Scholar at Auburn University. Her most recent book is *Eighteenth-Century Women Poets and Their Poetry: Inventing Agency, Inventing Genre* (2007), which was the co-winner of the MLA James Russell Lowell Prize. She is the author of other books, including *Daniel Defoe: His Life* (1989), which won the British Council Prize, *Spectacular Politics* (1993), and *Reflections on Biography* (1999). She has published articles in *PMLA, ELH, Theatre Journal*, and many other journals. A former president of the American Society for Eighteenth-Century Studies, she has held NEH and Guggenheim fellowships and is one of the few American members of the Institute for Advanced Studies, University of Edinburgh.

O M Brack Jr., professor emeritus of English at Arizona State University, is founding editor and textual editor for the Works of Tobias Smollett, University of Georgia Press. He recently edited a collection of essays, *Tobias Smollett, Scotland's First Novelist* (2007) and completed a critical edition of Sir John Hawkins's *Life of Samuel Johnson, LL.D* (2009).

Leslie A. Chilton has taught first-year composition and literature at Arizona State University since 1989. She was introduced to Tobias Smollett in the same year and has since worked on Smollett's translations for the University of Georgia Press.

Robert A. Erickson is professor emeritus of English at the University of California, Santa Barbara. His books include *The Language of the Heart, 1600–1750* (1997), *Mother Midnight: Birth, Sex, and Fate in Eighteenth-Century Fiction* (1986), and *The History of John Bull*, by John Arbuthnot (edited with A. W. Bower, 1976). He has recently published essays on Swift, Sterne, and Smollett.

Susan K. Howard received her PhD in English from the University of Delaware and is associate professor and graduate director in the English department at Duquesne University. She has published scholarly editions of works by Charlotte Lennox, Frances Burney, Maria Edgeworth, and Sir Walter Scott, and her essays on the eighteenth-century novel have appeared in such journals as *Eighteenth-Century Fiction, Studies in the Novel*, and the *Journal of Narrative Technique*, as well as in essay collections. She is currently at work on a study of family configurations in the novel and society of the long eighteenth century.

Christopher D. Johnson is professor of English at Francis Marion University. He has edited Sarah Fielding's *Lives of Cleopatra and Octavia* (1994) and has recently published articles on Henry Fielding, Sarah Fielding, Jonathan Swift, and John Dryden.

Marta Kvande is assistant professor of English at Texas Tech University, where she pursues the interest in eighteenth-century women novelists she developed through studying with Jerry Beasley. She has published articles on Eliza Haywood, Jane Barker, Delarivière Manley, Frances Sheridan, Frances Burney, Charlotte Lennox, and Tabitha Tenney. She is the coeditor of *Everyday Revolutions: Eighteenth Century Women Transforming Public and Private* (2008).

James E. May is associate professor of English at Penn State University's DuBois Campus. His "The Authoritative Editions of Smollett's *Complete History of England*" appears in *Tobias Smollett: Scotland's First Novelist* (2007). He edited "The Life of Young" for the Yale edition of the *Works* of Samuel Johnson and the letters of Young and Samuel Richardson for the Cambridge Richardson, compiled *The Henry Pettit Edward Young Collection at the University of Colorado* (1989), and contributed bibliographical and textual studies to *Papers of the Bibliographical Society of America, Studies in Bibliography*, and *Swift Studies*. For fifteen years he has surveyed rare books and manuscript sales for *The Scriblerian* (and more recently for *Swift Studies*), compiled Section 1 of *The Eighteenth Century: A Current Bibliography*, and edited *The Eighteenth-Century Intelligencer*. He is completing a descriptive bibliography of Young's writings of published in English to 1775.

Melissa Mowry is associate professor of English at St. John's University. She is the author of *The Bawdy Politic: Political Pornography and Prostitution in late Stuart England, 1660–1714* (2004) and the editor of *Roxana* by Daniel Defoe (2009).

Alexander Pettit is professor of English the University of North Texas. His edition of Samuel Richardson's *Early Works* is forthcoming with Cambridge University Press.

Charles E. Robinson is professor of English at the University of Delaware, where he has taught since 1965. He is the author of *Shelley and Byron: The Snake and the Eagle Wreathed in Fight* (1976) and the editor of *Mary Shelley: Collected Tales and Short Stories, with Original Engravings* (1976; reprint in paper, 1990). He is also the editor of *Lord Byron and His Contemporaries* (1982), of *William Hazlitt to His Publishers, Friends, and Creditors: Twenty-seven New Holograph Letters* (1987), and of *Mary Wollstonecraft Shelley's Mythological Dramas: Proserpine and Midas, Bodleian MS. Shelley d. 2: A Facsimile Edition with Full Transcription and Notes* (1992). He has also coedited with Betty T. Bennett *The Mary Shelley Reader* (1990), and he published a two-volume facsimile edition of *The Frankenstein Notebooks* (1996). He has most recently published a new edition of *The Original Frankenstein* (2008; 2009), and he continues to work on a study of Charles Ollier, the publisher of Shelley, Keats, and other Romantic and Victorian writers. From 1996 through 2006, he served as the executive director of the Byron Society of America and as co-chair of the Byron Society Collection at the University of Delaware.

Mary Anne Schofield is a faculty member in the Villanova Center for Liberal Education. Her scholarly interests continue to be in the history of the novel, women and war, and the long eighteenth century.

Rivka Swenson is assistant professor of English at Virginia Commonwealth University. She has published articles in the journals *The Eighteenth-Century: Theory and Interpretation*, *Studies in Eighteenth-Century Culture*, and *Journal of Narrative Theory*, and she is the coeditor of the Festschrift *Imagining Selves: Essays in Honor of Patricia Meyer Spacks* (2008). She has received grants and fellowships from the Clark Library and American Society for Eighteenth-Century Studies, the Folger Institute, the Fox Humanities Center at Emory University, and the School of English at the University of St. Andrews. She is writing a book on subnational identity and narrative form after the Act of Union.